TRB CULTURE

TO THE MEMORY OF MY FATHER

TRB CULTURE

The First Farmers of the North European Plain

Magdalena S. Midgley

EDINBURGH UNIVERSITY PRESS

© Magdalena S. Midgley, 1992

Edinburgh University Press
22 George Square, Edinburgh

Typeset in Lasercomp Plantin
by Alden Multimedia Ltd, Northampton, and
printed in Great Britain by the University Press, Cambridge

A CIP record for this title is available from the British Library.

ISBN 0 7486 0348 4

Contents

List of figures

Acknowledgements

It would not have been possible for me to conduct my research or to complete this book without the involvement of many people. I therefore acknowledge their advice, encouragement, intellectual stimulus, wisdom, help and hospitality in various combinations and assure them all of my deepest gratitude. In particular I wish to thank the following:

N.H. Andersen, J. Bąbel, J.A. Bakker, C. Bonsall, B. Burchard, A.B. Gebauer, R. Grygiel, D.W. Harding, J. Hoika, D. Jankowska, S. Jastrzębski, P. Kjærum, E. Koch Nielsen, A. Kośko, J. Kruk, Z. Krzak, F. Laux, T. Madsen, R.J. Mercer, A. Morton, P.O. Nielsen, H. Quitta, D. Ridgeway, J. Rock, A. Sherratt, J. Skaarup, G. Thomas, A. Watson, the late T. Wiślański, the staff of the Society of Antiquaries of Scotland Library. Last, but not least, I thank my husband Stephen for always being there.

I also gratefully acknowledge the financial support from the British Academy, the Carnegie Trust and the Munro Trust which enabled the necessary study abroad.

Introduction

In the study of European prehistory, perhaps more than elsewhere, scholars have grappled for decades with extensive cultural patterns – patterns that transcend modern political boundaries as well as larger geographical regions and which offer such a wealth of archaeological information that its absorption and synthesis are an awesome undertaking. This book tackles one such enormous entity: the Funnel-necked Beaker culture (TRB or *Trichterbecherkultur*) which represents the earliest Neolithic manifestation in northern Europe; and it examines whether the time-honoured concept of a culture complex over an area covering about half a million square kilometers can still be justified as a working concept.

Such an approach, concentrating upon one cultural entity in its numerous and varied manifestations, has not featured prominently in current research, as even a cursory glance at the literature of the last decade reveals. Rather, scholars working in the field of the European Neolithic have either chosen to tackle themes of broad cultural change spanning several millennia or else directed their interest towards specific issues such as changing patterns in social organisation, economy and settlement of prehistoric societies. Such studies, while exhaustive within the bounds of individual topics, are nevertheless fragmentary considerations of a larger cultural phenomenon and not always able to demonstrate the full significance of the observed process of change.

There are a number of reasons why I embarked upon this project; the reader should appreciate that I outline them from the perspective of my own research rather than in order of their significance. Although, as the bibliography clearly reveals, there has been a steady, if slow, trickle of regional studies, this cultural complex has never before been the subject of a major synthesis. When I began my earlier research on the subject of the earthen long barrows in northern Europe (Midgley 1985), I wanted to know more about the cultural context within which these monuments were to be placed. However, I could not find even one publication in English which could enlighten me beyond the most general level.

I therefore embarked on a search through the literature outside the English language, but the situation did not really improve. Although I now faced a bewildering amount of publications in several languages and my bibliography had suddenly swelled with hundreds of entries, I was still unable to find that *one* work which dealt with this whole culture within two covers. I soon realized that the literature was so vast that it was beyond the scope of the project I was working on at the time, and the study of the earthen long barrows took precedence, for the time being, over the culture itself.

This book therefore assembles the evidence from the whole of the North European Plain, offering the English-speaking student, as well as the professional archaeologist, an up-to-date synthesis of the TRB culture. For this very reason I did not wish to discuss just one or two better-researched areas or, indeed, a few fashionable problems because my initial purpose was to find out about the whole cultural complex; I therefore felt I had to tackle as much of the subject as I possibly could.

When I finally came to write this book – and it was a long time in writing – I began to understand why not a single scholar had ever tackled the subject before. Quite apart from the linguistic problems, the assembling of disparate sources of evidence, the choosing from the vast body of data those elements which are significant to the overall discussion, and the combining of contrasting methodological approaches and widely differing interpretations into one coherent narrative which cuts across the artificially created boundaries, are all unenviable tasks, even when they are sweetened by the uniqueness of the undertaking. Indeed, on a number of occasions I came close to abandoning the whole project and, apart from the never-failing encouragement from a few confidants, the reason for carrying on lies in the intellectual stimulus of combining my education in the British archaeological tradition with the application of my skills to the conceptually different Germanic and Slavonic methods of research; appreciating the merits of both did not make the writing of this synthesis any easier.

The fundamental limitation of the general synthesis is that it cannot be exhaustive in the treatment of archaeological evidence in the same way as can a case-study based on a particular theme or a specific aspect. Thus a number of choices had to be made, relating chiefly to the amount of detail. A number of themes remain treated more briefly than one would ideally have wished. Moreover, since one of the aims of this book was to present the wealth of evidence in a clear fashion and not to obfuscate the already complex problem further by inventing new names or creating new boundaries, the conventional terminology and conventional divisions have been retained throughout. This applies particularly to the very complex sequences worked out for the area of southern Scandinavia which have been well popularised in the literature and have become an established norm not only in their own area but well beyond.

I have also attempted to present an interpretative account of the available evidence in so far as I know and understand it. In order to enable the reader to draw his or her own conclusions, I have, where possible, distinguished between the factual evidence, other scholars' opinions, and my own perception of particular issues; in the case of the latter two it is not always possible to determine whether one has arrived at a particular view through one's own perception, or whether what appears as an independent idea arose, ultimately, through an amalgam of the ideas of others. I thus acknowledge my debt to what may be called *Anon* scholarship and offer my apologies to any scholar whose ideas I present inadvertently as my own.

Of all the subjects treated in this volume it is the TRB pottery which perhaps presented the greatest challenge and difficulty, and a few words of explanation in advance may be helpful. Firstly, there is the sheer volume of vessels to be considered. Students of the British Neolithic may well feel a tinge of jealousy as they have to be satisfied with a few scores of complete pots – an amount that can easily be matched at just half a dozen TRB megalithic chambers.

This volume, as well as the bewildering variety of ceramics within the different TRB regions, meant that it has taken about two years to even begin to come to terms with this massive body of evidence and, even now, I should not consider my knowledge sufficient to pronounce upon the stylistic placement of individual vessels, even less so of undiagnostic sherds. And yet, as I will explain in more detail in Chapter 4, the TRB pottery was not only a significant element in various researches but more importantly, as its volume demonstrates, it was a very important element of the material culture made and used by the TRB populations. It would have been impudent not at least to try to do it justice.

Perhaps far more important than my own interest in the period under study is, however, the significance of the TRB culture in the context of European prehistory and, equally, its role in the context of archaeology in central and northern Europe; indeed, the two issues are more closely related than may be immediately apparent.

We shall explore the second issue in greater detail when we discuss the history of the development of TRB studies (Chapter 3) but it is worth noting that, in contrast to the pursuit of archaeology in Britain, the study and interpretation of Neolithic and other cultural complexes in central and northern Europe must be understood against the background of the very specific culture-historical circumstances dating from the late nineteenth century or even before. These relatively modern conditions have had a profound effect on the progress and direction of archaeology in general and, with reference to the TRB culture, gave rise to subjective nationalist tendencies. The most explicit were of course the ideological and chauvinistic approaches to Gustaf Kossinna and his followers which subsequently were so indiscriminately employed in the power struggles of Nazi Germany.

However, the true significance of the TRB culture in the context of European prehistory lies elsewhere. Being the first Neolithic culture in most of the area of its distribution it represents an important archaeological manifestation of the very fundamental changes in the area of the North European Plain. These changes, when viewed from a Braudelian long-term perspective, not only lay the foundations for the subsequent economic, cultural and social developments which could legitimately be traced right down to the present, but also comprise evidence which, presented within the appropriate interpretative framework, demonstrate the dynamic nature of this cultural complex. Prehistoric cultures tend to be viewed as static rather than dynamic entities, but much of the seemingly static character of the TRB culture can be shown to result from a specific, particularistic approach which far too often concentrates upon one isolated theme – be it pottery, flint axes or settlement pattern – and rarely goes beyond the descriptive. And yet it follows logically that if we are to understand and interpret the way in which a particular prehistoric culture developed, our observations must be based upon the totality of the available evidence.

The belief that guided the research presented in the following pages rests, therefore, upon two major premises. Firstly, that an archaeological culture represents an amalgam of all aspects of human activity as they reveal themselves in residual form through material culture, technology, economic practices, settlement patterns and rituals. It is the relationship and the interdependence of all these various cultural components that determine the character of the studied phenomenon. It is thus through a rigorous study of all the evidence, presented within an interpretative framework, that we may hope to define the dynamic quality of a cultural complex, with all the transitory and constantly shifting states of individual cultural components.

Secondly, it is important to emphasise that, as will be amply demonstrated in the following pages, this culture was not uniform but was from the very beginning a widespread and internally differentiated phenomenon. It is now my firm belief that cultural unity over such a vast area need not necessarily demonstrate itself, and thus be sought, in the uniformity of its material culture, economic practices or precise correspondence of perceived social patterns. Regional diversity of these elements within the TRB culture will be amply demonstrated; it accords well with a polythetic concept of culture and represents a direct response to the local conditions and specific requirements of individual human groups. Rather, cultural unity can more convincingly be demonstrated in the homogeneity of the processes of change that take place over a particular area during a particular period of time.

Moreover, in discussing such important cultural changes we must remember that we are concerned with a very specific historical process. Through a series of events, some of which were commonly registered in a prehistoric context while others were unique, this process led to the presence of a cultural complex whose particular combination of economic, social and material characteristics was not repeated elsewhere. It is the uniqueness of this phenomenon that I shall endeavour to show in the discussion throughout this book.

1

Geographical background

The low-lying terrain along the North Sea and the Baltic forms a continuous physiographical unit, the North European Plain, which extends
eastwards from the lower Rhine and merges imperceptibly into the vast
Plains of Russia. To the south of the North European Plain there is a
narrow zone which separates the plain from the Hercynian massif of central
Europe: the so-called Transitional Borderlands (Fig. 1; Shackleton 1958).
It is these two areas which set the stage for the cultural developments
covered by this work and some familiarity with the landscapes found here
is necessary if we are to pursue our enquiry within its proper geographical
setting.

The North European Plain comprises a complex arrangement of lowland
landscapes, created by the glacial and fluvioglacial action of the Weichselian
glaciation, that are traversed by some of the major European rivers such as
the lower Rhine, lower Elbe, Oder and Vistula. The chief landscape features of the North European Plain to the east of the Elbe are arranged in
concentric bands which run roughly parallel to the Baltic coast. Beyond the
narrow strip of the coastal plain, which is mainly Holocene in origin, the
Baltic Heights (the morainic hills of Jutland, the Mecklenburg and Pomeranian plateaux) are wedged between terminal moraines. These areas consist
of glacial deposits of sand, gravel and boulder clay; the landscape consists
of gently undulating hills on average between 100 m and 200 m in altitude,
although heights over 300 m are reached in Pomerania. The Baltic Heights
are dotted with many lakes, most commonly of ribbon and kettle form (such
as the Schweriner See, Müritzer See, Miedwie and Drawsko lakes). The
landscape is further diversified by numerous streams and rivers that drain
into the lakes.

Because the land at the southern edge of the glacier sloped upwards, the
outwash plains to the south became cut by wide, east–west running
channels which carried the waters of the melting glacier. Although the
Elbe, Oder and Vistula follow these routes for part of their courses, the
ancient river valleys (known in German as *Urstromtäler* and in Polish as
pradoliny) had much greater capacity; up to forty times more than the
present Elbe capacity has been estimated for the *Urstromtal* south of

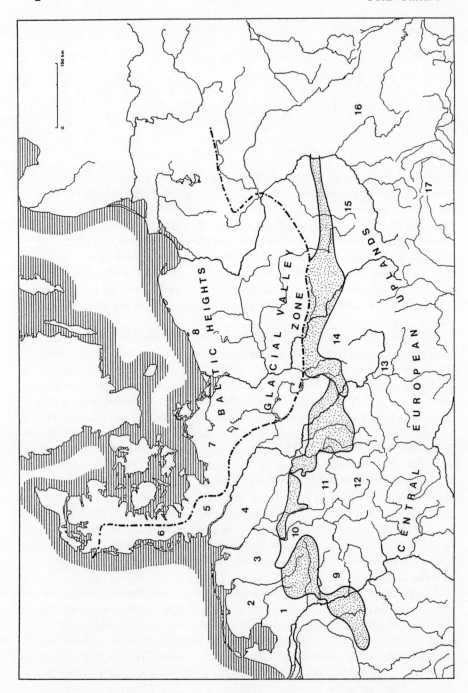

Brandenburg (Embleton 1984, 136). The very deep cutting of the rivers through the outwash plains, combined with the reduction of the ice sheet, led to the drop in the underground water level and this in turn resulted in the creation of large-scale sand dunes (some up to 20 m in height and many kilometres in length). Large parts of the *Urstromtäler* are covered with such deposits which, in the warmer climatic conditions, became suitable for settlement (Maruszczak 1983, 40).

In the areas west of the Elbe such zonal arrangements of the landscape cannot be seen, as the region lay beyond the maximum extent of the Weichselian glacier. The landscape in this part of the North European Plain is therefore the result of fluvioglacial processes and later Holocene marine transgressions, whose repercussions were felt far inland.

Beyond the coastal barriers of sandy beach ridges and dunes, such as the Frisian Islands, there is a belt of low-lying marshes which extend far inland along the major river valleys creating tidal flats and brackish lagoons (many of these lands have been reclaimed, for example the Dutch polders or north-west German koogs). Beyond the marshes, most of the lowlands consist of fluvioglacial deposits, mainly sands (known as coversands on high elevations) which were deposited to the west and south of terminal moraines. This landscape, sometimes known as *Geest*, has been divided into separate regions by the postglacial river system, and differences within it – peat and heathland – are brought about by differences in soil and drainage. In the north there are the heaths of west Jutland and Schleswig-Holstein, to the west the Drenthe and Veluwe plateaux; around western Hanover the *Geest* is interspersed with bogs; to the east, on the Lüneburger Heide where it is higher and drier, it represents a typical heath landscape.

The coast of the North European Plain is as varied in character as inland regions. The rising seal level was the chief factor affecting the development of the North Sea coast and influencing human habitation in this area. The displacement of human populations in the wake of the flooding of the North Sea Land during the Boreal is well documented on both sides of the North Sea (Louwe Kooijmans 1970–1; Newell 1973). Moreover, the last two decades of combined palaeoenvironmental and archaeological research in the Netherlands have documented that the coastal regions were subject to a continuous change due to marine transgression and regression cycles. In the Rhine/Meuse delta this resulted in the oscillation between salt marshes/

Figure 1 The geography of the North European Plain: 1-Veluwe Plateau, 2-Drenthe Plateau, 3-Geest of Hanover, 4-Lüneburger Heide, 5-Geest of Schleswig-Holstein, 6-Heath of Jutland, 7-Mecklenburg Plateau, 8-Pomeranian Plateau, 9-Sauerland, 10-Weser Hills, 11-Harz Mountains, 12-Thuringian Basin, 13-Bohemian Basin, 14-Sudety Mountains, 15-Little Poland Plateau, 16-Lublin-Wolynian Plateau, 17-Carpathian Mountains, dotted zone – Transitional Borderlands, dotted line – main stationary line during Würm-Weichsel glaciation (Source: Shackleton 1958).

estuarine creek systems and freshwater marshes which offered periodically favourable settlement conditions of the kind documented in the intermittent occupation at Swifterbant and Hazendonk (Louwe Kooijmans 1980b, 116–21).

Similar investigations along the west coast of Schleswig-Holstein have also shown considerable adjustments of the coastline. Sediments on the East Frisian Islands have revealed a pattern of alternating fossil tidal flats mixed with semi-terrestrian and lagoon environments; peat formation is documented at about 6500 BP (Behre *et al.* 1979). Although the earliest proved settlement in the marshy/clay regions of the coast dates to the Bronze Age, finds of TRB axes in Pleistocene sands suggest that the coastal barriers were also habitable during the Neolithic (Harck 1980).

The present day Baltic coastline is the result of complex eustatic/isostatic movements following the disappearance of the Weichselian ice. The final transgression of the Holocene *Ancylus* Lake took place probably not later than 7800 BP, giving rise to the *Littorina* Sea, which is named after a salt-water mollusc, *Littorina littorea*. The initial rapid rise in the water level led to a loss of up to 100 km of younger postglacial landscape along the shores. At least three major transgressions have been identified during the following three millennia, with the transgressional peaks along the southern shores averaging at about 7500 BP (L–I), 6000 BP (L–II) and 4500 BP (L–III), each followed by regression (Kliewe 1979, 191).

The coast of eastern Jutland and Schleswig-Holstein is characterised by long, deep sea inlets which represent the numerous valleys of glacial meltwater; the present Danish island configuration began to form at about 7000 BP (Krog 1979; Petersen 1985). The southern coastline, between Lübeck Bay and the Vistula estuary, is less dramatic although the profusion of coastal lakes indicates that initially the coastline was more topographically varied: it was divided by bays, sea inlets and offshore islands. At about 5800 BP the island of Rügen, for instance, consisted of several smaller islands (Gramsch 1978; Kliewe 1979). There is evidence that the silting up of bays, inlets and estuaries began at around 5600 BP (data from Rügen and Usedom) and that the formation of beach ridges and sand dunes began the long process of the straightening of the coastline (Stankowski 1981).

Wedged between the North European Plain and the Central European Uplands there is a belt of the so-called Transitional Borderlands which stretches from the Münster Bay in the west to the Lublin/Wolhynian plateaux in the east. This zone, in contrast to the North European Plain, represents an older morainic landscape shaped during the earlier, Elster and Saale glaciations. Internally this borderland is intersected by ridges and low mountain ranges which divide it into smaller landscapes. The glacial features are more abraided than in the north and they are frequently concealed beneath the cloak of wind-blown sand, the loess (Embleton 1984).

It is difficult to determine to what extent the present soil distribution reflects conditions prevailing during the 7th and 6th millennia BP. Climatic changes as well as man's continuous activities have substantially disturbed and altered the natural environment in the areas under consideration. Soil formation, moreoever, is a continuous process with differential soil distribution reflecting merely a temporary condition.

The most fertile and agriculturally advantageous soils are the czernozems and the brown earths which developed predominantly on the loess. Palaeoenvironmental studies in the region of the Elbe-Saale suggest that such soils were already developed by the early Atlantic (Mania 1973; Mania and Preuss 1975). Today, the degraded czernozems and the brown earths provide a discontinuous band in the Transitional Borderlands, from the Rhine valley to the Bohemian and Wolhynian plateaux, growing in extent eastwards and merging with the true czernozems of the Russian steppes. Initially these soils covered larger areas but they suffer from erosion, depending on the thickness of the loess. The exposing of the Tertiary parent rock in some areas of the central European loess belt has led to the development of other soils such as loamy rendzinas (Kruk 1973, 145; Gringmuth-Dallmer and Altermann 1985, 341). Under certain conditions, black earths themselves develop into the podzolic brown earths; a variety of such soils intersect the loessic belt.

An equally complex mosaic of soils covers the North European Plain. The coastal marshes to the west of the Elbe carry some fertile loam and clay soils but for the most part this area is characterised by podsolised sandy and gravel soils; peat and heath cover large areas. On the more recently glaciated deposits east of the Elbe the leaching has not progressed as far as in the west and the boulder clays offer good soils, interspersed with lighter sandy soils in the river and stream valleys. To the south of the Baltic Heights the area of the ancient river valleys (*Urstromtäler*) is composed mainly of sands and gravels covered with peat, heath and marshes but it alternates, particularly towards the east, with ground moraine where fertile brown earths have developed on clays and loams (for example in Uckermark, Pyrzyce basin, or Kujavian upland) which approximate the edaphic conditions of the Transitional Borderlands. The ancient river valleys also carry a fair amount of recent alluvial deposits (Gramsch 1973; Stankowski 1981; Bakker 1982).

The great variety of landscape relief, soils and water networks evidenced throughout the area result in a diversity of natural environment, consitituting a further difficulty in the reconstruction of the ecological conditions of northern Europe. In the climatic division of the Postglacial, the periods which are relevant to this study are the Atlantic (8000–5000 BP) and Sub-Boreal (5000–3000 BP), especially their late and early stages respectively. There is some variation in the specific climatic conditions during both these periods between northern and central Europe on account of differential air circulation (Magny 1982) but most of our area can be assessed in terms of the climate prevalent in northern Europe.

Thus the Atlantic is characterised by mean annual temperatures generally 1.5–2.5°C higher than those of today and by an increase in humidity resulting from a northward retreat of the polar air. At about 5000–4500 BP the polar air began to advance southwards and the relatively stable Atlantic environment became subject to a slow but progressive climatic deterioration. A pronounced change in climate is not observed until the later stage of the Sub-Boreal and it is unlikely that the initial drier and cooler conditions in northern Europe (and an increased dampness further south) would have had a dramatic effect on human settlement. However, a degree of climatic instability at the beginning of the Sub-Boreal has been documented through research on Dutch peat bogs, variable tree growth in central and northern Germany and an increase in podsolisation processes (Iversen 1973; Stankowski 1981).

The optimal thermal conditions during the Atlantic were conducive to the growth of warmth-loving species (the ivy and mistletoe flowered as far north as southern Norway) and a development of deciduous forest over most of northern Europe. Depending upon specific local conditions oak, hazel or lime were the dominant tree species, but alder, maple, hornbeam and ash are also regularly encountered in pollen records (Kruk 1973, 136). The sandy soils also suported substantial areas of coniferous forest (Iversen 1973, 65). While some, less fertile areas of the Transitional Borderlands doubtless supported vegetation approximating to that further north, there is evidence that the higher and drier loessic landscapes were less heavily forested; open woodland, meadow and even steppe vegetation are thought to have been typical (Mania 1973, 39–40). While there was probably little immediate change in vegetation during the early Sub-Boreal, the proportion of dominant species was changing in favour of beech and certain conifers, such as spruce (Starkel 1983). The introduction during the Atlantic of cultivated cereals and accompanying anthropogenic plants also had a considerable impact upon the natural vegetation (see Chapter 8.1).

The mixed vegetation forests supported a rich mammalian population with red and roe deer, auroch and wild boar among the larger species, while coastlines as well as inland lakes, streams and rivers supported a wide variety of waterfowl, bird, fish and shell species. Thus each area offered an environment with a wide range of natural resources. This abundance of local environments in northern Europe and their regional diversity was particularly suitable for exploitation by human groups with wide-ranging economic strategies.

2

The late hunter-gatherers of the North European Plain and the neighbouring central European farmers

The emergence of the indigenous farming populations throughout northern Europe is perceived today as a consequence of a complex process of interaction of the Mesolithic groups which, during the 6th and 5th millennia BC, continued to occupy most of the North European Plain, and the early farming groups which at that time were establishing themselves across central Europe, occasionally even venturing onto the southern limits of the Plain itself. The inevitable contact of two such diverse cultural phenomena in the broad zone where hunter-gatherers and farmers could not ultimately avoid one another must have had a profound effect upon both, and resulted in a cultural transformation leading to the appearance of a vast new cultural complex, the Funnel-necked Beaker Culture, which is the main subject of this work. In order to set the background against which this culture arose, the following discussion will briefly review some of the more salient aspects of the late Mesolithic and early farming populations in the North European Plain.

2.1 The late Mesolithic groups

The various late Mesolithic groups which, with greater or lesser precision, can be identified across the north European lowland, belong to the final phase of the Mesolithic. On the basis of cumulative evidence from different regions, this can be said to emerge during the early 8th millennium BP. While we are still a long way from presenting a uniform typo-chronological sequence for the North European Plain, a number of general observations can be made which apply to the whole area under consideration.

Firstly, the transition from the middle to late Mesolithic is marked by distinct technological changes which involve the spread of blade and trapeze industries, the appearance of new tools and the demise of certain previously popular forms of microliths (Kozłowski 1976a; 1976b). Prior to the mid-1950s these late industries were known by the name of Tardenosian but more recent studies have tended to abandon such a pan-European terminology. Secondly, we note that what previously was a fairly uniform Maglemosian tradition of the North Sea land undergoes such strong regional diversification that, by the beginning of the Atlantic period, over a dozen regional groups can be distinguished across northern Europe. The reasons for this diversification are not entirely clear but the continuing environmental change resulting from climatic amelioration may have stimulated a change in technology and the emergence of new types of industries.

Traversing the North European Plain from west to east we perceive a number of regional groups which are distinguished predominantly by the differential composition of flint assemblages (Fig. 2). At the north-western end of the Plain, in the northern Netherlands, the emergence of the so-called *De Leien-Wartena* group during the 8th millenium BP was, according to Newell (1973, 408), a result of contact between the earlier local population and the retreating post-Maglemose groups of the North Sea land. The earliest appearance of this complex is, on present evidence, dated to the beginning of the 8th millenium BP (Bergumermeer, GrN-6845: 7940 ± 75 BP; 6842 ± 152 BC) and it appears to have existed until the arrival of the early farming communities upon whose flint industry it apparently exerted a considerable influence. The De Leien-Wartena assemblages include narrow triangles, points with retouched bases and core axes; the latter are thought to reflect influences deriving from the north (Schwabedissen's *Nordwest Kreis*; 1944).

In the area between the lower Rhine and the Weser rivers Arora (1973) has identified a number of small local groups of which two, the *Hülsten* and *Nollheide* groups, are of relevance. The materials of the former group (which virtually lacks triangles) are found in the area north of the lower Rhine. The Nollheide group is characterised by the presence of small triangles, symmetric and asymmetric trapezes and short scrapers; the presence of core and flake axes relate it to the Boberg group further north in Lower Saxony. The Nollheide group sites are found in Hessen, around Münster and in the area of the Weserbergland, where large tools are particularly prominent.

In the lower Elbe region, which comprises the south-western part of Mecklenburg, the Elbe estuary and the sandy dunes of Hanover and the Altmark regions, a small number of related assemblages form the *Boberg* group. This group, which is named after a site along the eastern bank of the Elbe (Schwabedissen 1944), is best represented by finds from Boberg and Wustrow on the Jeetze river. It is characterised among other things by the presence of small triangles, a variety of blade tools (including tanged blades), burins, transverse arrowheads, and core and flake axes. The latter three types again relate the Boberg group to the northern province (Schwabedissen 1944, 163; Jacob-Friesen 1959, 60–1; Gramsch 1973, 61–2).

Further east there is a large, relatively homogeneous complex known as *Chojnice-Pieński* (Kozłowski and Kozłowski 1975). It comprises three regional groups: the *Jühnsdorf* group in Brandenburg (Gramsch 1973, 60–1), the *Chojnice* group in Pomerania and the *Pieńki* group in Greater Poland as far east as the Vistula (Kozłowski and Kozłowski 1975, 316–18). Although there are minor differences in the composition of these regional assemblages, the unifying elements comprise a high proportion of side-scrapers, microliths (long triangles being more numerous than trapezes) and a regular presence of end-scrapers; burins make an insignificant contribution. Core and flake axes are less frequent than in the north and their importance diminishes as we move from west to east. An additional diagnostic element, especially prominent in the region of the Jühnsdorf group, are the stone axes of oval cross-section called *Walzenbeile* (Gramsch 1973, 61).

The final complex in the eastern part of the North European Plain which is of relevance here is the so-called *Janisławice* culture which, according to Polish scholars, is associated with the northern technocomplex. This culture derives its name from a burial discovered at Janisławice in Poland, but it is also sometimes known as the Vistula cycle (Więckowska 1975). It evolved sometime during the second half of the 9th millennium BP and its overall distribution comprises the area east of the Vistula to the Niemen and Prypet river basins. Three regional groups have been identified: the *Wistka* in south-eastern Poland, the *Eastern* in the Niemen basin and the *Maksymonis* along the Prypet. The main diagnostic elements of the Janisławice culture are the strong presence of side-scrapers, end-scrapers and microliths; there are also specific forms such as the Janisławice points and rectangular side-scrapers. The Wistka group assemblages additionally contain characteristic triangles retouched on all sides and narrow trapezes.

Returning northwards over the North European Plain we must mention a very small group of assemblages in the vicinity of the Oder estuary on the sand dunes of the former Ahlbecker See, in the central Ückermünde Heide and in the valley of the Płonia river. While the assemblages of this group, which was named the *Ahlbecker* group by Gramsch, are not numerous, they are characterised by the strong presence of long, narrow and irregular triangles. Transverse arrowheads and small core axes are also present, although the latter are not very frequent east of the Oder (Gramsch 1973, 61; Czarnecki 1980).

The Atlantic period assemblages from western Mecklenburg reveal such close similarities with the Younger Oldesloe materials from Schleswig-Holstein that they must be considered as another homogeneous group (known as *Younger Oldesloe* in Schleswig-Holstein and as *Oldesloe-Kobrow* in Mecklenburg; Schwabedissen 1944, 153; Gramsch 1973, 60). Large flint implements up to 15 cm in length appear as distinctive core and flake axes and provide an important contrast with the materials discussed so far. Among smaller tools triangles are common in Mecklenburg but trapezes also appear and they increase in frequency northwards. The chronology of the Younger Oldesloe-Kobrow group is somewhat problematic. Strati-

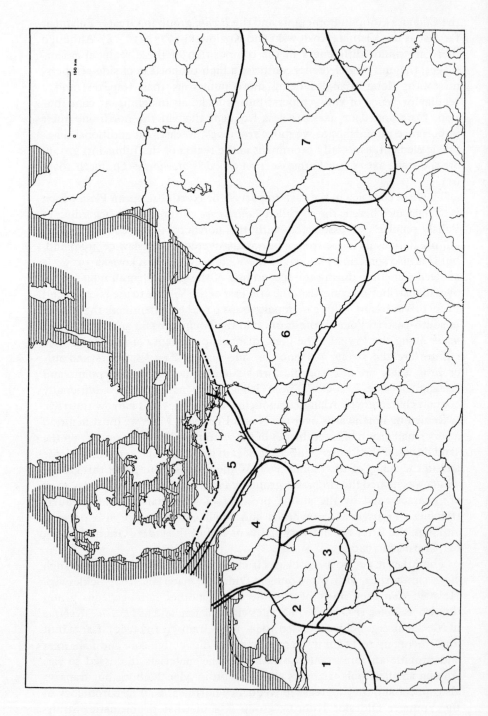

graphic evidence from Satrup Moor (Rüde 2, Förstermoor and Pöttmoor) shows that in Schleswig-Holstein the Younger Oldesloe is succeeded by the Ertebølle-Ellerbek. The available C-14 dates suggest the emergence of Ertebølle-Ellerbek by about 6000 BP (Schwabedissen 1958b; 1979a; 1979c; 1980). No stratigraphy or C-14 dates are available from inland Mecklenburg and the local variant of the Ertebølle-Ellerbek is presently known only from the coastal region where it is dated from about 5800 BP. It is possible that, in the inland regions of western Mecklenburg, the Younger Oldesloe-Kobrow continues until the onset of the Neolithic; the presence in some of the Kobrow assemblages of the typical Ellerbek flake axes would support this view.

The littoral zone of the western Baltic is an area in which, during the late Atlantic period, an independent and sophisticated development among the hunter-gatherers manifests itself in the form of the *Ertebølle-Ellerbek* culture (Fig. 3). This complex is of particular significance in the cultural development of the North European Plain, not only because over a century of research makes it the best known among the late Mesolithic hunter-gatherer groups, but also because of its unequivocal contemporaneity with the early farming populations which were settled along the southern fringes of the North European Plain.

The Ertebølle phenomenon was recognised in Denmark as early as the mid-nineteenth century when the *Køkkenmøddinge* (the shell-heaps or kitchen middens) first attracted the attention of Danish geologists and antiquarians. It is precisely one such kitchen midden, Ertebølle, along the Limfjord, that lends its name to the whole complex. Although the kitchen middens are only found along the fjords of northern and north-eastern Jutland and on northern Fyn and Zealand, the characteristic materials of the Ertebølle have been recognised on many other types of coastal and inland sites and a three-phase development of the Danish Ertebølle is now well established (Vang Petersen 1984). Similar assemblages have been identified in Schleswig-Holstein, for example at Ellerbek by Kiel, where a series of investigations between 1876 and 1903 recovered numerous deposits of comparable materials. In Schleswig-Holstein, therefore, the name Ertebølle-Ellerbek is usually applied (Schwabedissen 1958a, 42; 1962, 257). Comparable materials are also known from a number of coastal sites in Mecklenburg, where they are known under the local name of the Lietzow group (after a site on Rügen; Gramsch 1973, 62–3; 1978). Sporadic finds of Ertebølle-like pottery along the northern Polish coast suggest that

---

Figure 2 Distribution of major late Mesolithic groupings on the North European Plain: 1-De Leien Wartena, 2-Hülsten, 3-Nollheide, 4-Boberg, 5-Oldesloe-Kobrow, 6-Chojnice-Pieńki, 7-Janisławice, dotted line – southern limit of Ertebølle-Ellerbek (Source: Schwabedissen 1944; Arora 1973; Gramsch 1973; Newell 1973; Kozłowski and Kozłowski 1975).

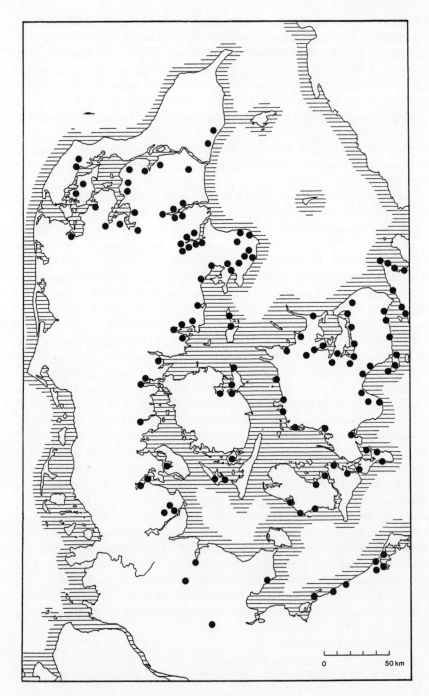

Figure 3 Distribution of Ertebølle-Ellerbek culture (Source: Gramsch 1978).

the Ertebølle-Ellerbek may have extended further east, but with the contemporary coast completely lost due to the changes in sea level, it is unlikely that any significant sites will come to light.

The chronological position of the Ertebølle-Ellerbek is now reasonably well established. In Denmark it is dated from about 6500 BP (K-1303, 6510 ± 110 BP at Vedbæk Boldbaner) to 5200 BP (K-1450, 5230 ± 100 BP at Flynderhage). The Ertebølle-Ellerbek materials in Schleswig-Holstein are dated to between 6000 BP (Y-440, 6060 ± 200 BP, Ellerbek) and 5500 BP (Rosenhof; Schwabedissen 1980, Fig. 11). The only datings from Mecklenburg are from Rügen where the Ertebølle-Ellerbek is dated between 5800 BP (Bln-561, 5815 ± 100 BP) and 5200 BP (Bln-560, 5190 ± 120 BP) at Buddelin, and a date of about 5500 BP (Bln-562, 5455 ± 100 BP) dates the layer at Augustenhof (Gramsch 1973, 63).

The most common typological features of the Ertebølle-Ellerbek assemblages are represented by a fine blade technique and the presence of end-scrapers, burins and characteristic tanged blades (Fig. 4: 4, 5); transverse arrowheads are the only significant microlithic forms (Fig. 4: 6–8). Very characteristic are the heavy implements: core axes and a variety of flake axes (Fig. 4: 2–3); on the Danish islands and in southern Sweden there are also Limhamn greenstone axes, and a few stone axes have been encountered in the Lietzow group. Excellent preservation conditions on a number of Danish and Schleswig-Holstein sites have contributed to the recovery of a variety of bone and wooden implements such as T-shaped antler axes, barbed harpoons and wooden spades (Fig. 4: 1, 9). A novel feature accompanying the later Ertebølle-Ellerbek assemblages is pottery vessels with pointed bases (Fig. 4: 10) and occasionally flat dishes (the so-called 'lamps'). In Denmark the pottery begins to appear from about 5700 BP (Vang Petersen 1984), although the finds of pointed-base pots (but not the 'lamps') from the lower levels at Rosenhof suggest that further south pottery-making may have been adopted a little earlier (Schwabedissen 1980, 132).

The presence of pottery in the north European Late Mesolithic milieu is not, however, limited to the Ertebølle-Ellerbek culture. Pointed-base vessels are known from the Mesolithic sites of the Boberg/Nollheide group in Lower Saxony, for example at Boberg (Schindler 1953), Dümmer (Deichmuller 1963), Ochsenmoor and Retlage (Jacob-Friesen 1959), and as stray finds from the moors. From the area of central Poland a number of sites of the Wistka group are known to contain pottery resembling vessels of the so-called Pit Comb Ware. The pottery and the distinctly Mesolithic flint assemblages derive on the whole from secure contexts and their association need not be questioned, but the dating of such finds remains controversial. While C-14 dates are still lacking, palynological data from some localities (for example Witów) suggest a rather broad horizon between 5500 BP and 4500 BP (Cyrek *et al.* 1983).

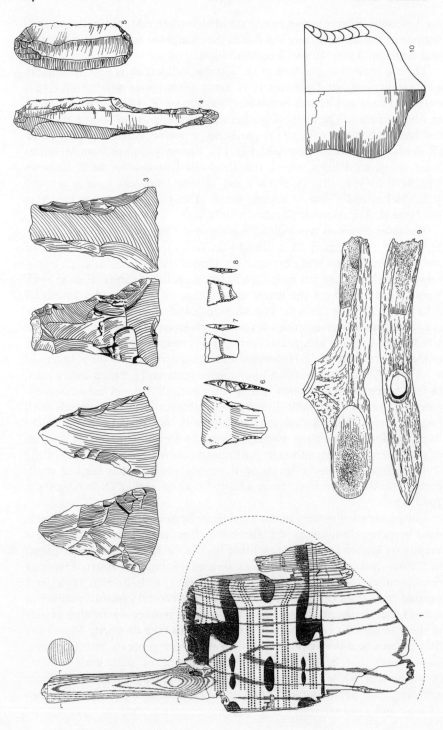

In south-western Poland (the upper Oder basin) a number of late
Mesolithic sites of the Chojnice-Pieńki group are known to have included
similar pottery. The vessels have mostly been found on sites with rich flint
assemblages or where traces of habitation structures have come to light (for
example at Dąbrowa Krępnica; Bagniewski 1979 and 1980). On present
evidence the earliest appearance of pottery in these contexts seems to be
coeval with the TRB culture here (*c.* 5200 BP). Such relatively late ceramic
horizons in the Chojnice-Pieńki complex reopen the question of the survival of some remnant Mesolithic group in a landscape largely dominated
by the farming populations. It is clear that more research is necessary to
determine the status of such late Mesolithic finds.

Finally, it should be re-emphasised that the adoption of pottery-making
by the various late Mesolithic groups is a wider phenomenon which can be
perceived much further east along the North European Plain. The area of
the eastern Baltic (Latvia, Estonia) provides ample evidence that the late
Mesolithic groups are familiar with ceramic technology as the various local
variants of Pit Comb Ware (Narva, Sarnate, Serovo) begin to make their
appearance during the first half of the 6th millennium BP (a date of
5730 ± 50 BP is available from Osa in Latvia; Okulicz 1976, 32).

Problems posed by the scanty archaeological evidence of the settlement
and economic strategies of the late Mesolithic communities, especially in
the context of multiple adaptations to the environmental conditions of the
early Atlantic period and influences deriving from contact with early Neolithic communities, form some of the key issues in the current archaeological debate. In recent years attempts have been made to formulate models
for the interpretation of late Mesolithic subsistence and settlement as well
as to provide a theoretical framework for the better understanding of the
archaeological evidence from the period in question (Price 1973 and 1980;
Jochim 1976; Clarke 1978b). Aspects pertaining to the economy of the late
Mesolithic groups on the North European Plain are discussed in Chapter
8. For the present we should only note that, with the notable exception of
the littoral zone, there is still little evidence about the nature of the late
Mesolithic economy; this lacuna is only now beginning to receive due
attention, in the form of research and theoretical discussion.

Across the whole of the North European Plain the Mesolithic sites are
found predominantly on the lighter sandy soils occupying elevations, river
terraces and dunes. The Mesolithic settlement of the sandy dunes in the
freshwater tidal area of the river IJssel at Swifterbant is very well known
(Van der Waals 1977) and similar circumstances appear to have prevailed
at Boberg on the eastern edge of the Elbe estuary (Schindler 1953). An

Figure 4 Artefacts typical of the Ertebølle-Ellerbek culture: 1, 4, 5-Tybrind Vig,
2, 3, 6–8-Rosenhof, 9-Dąbki (Source: Schwabedissen 1972 and 1980; Andersen and
Nielsen 1982; Ilkiewicz 1989).

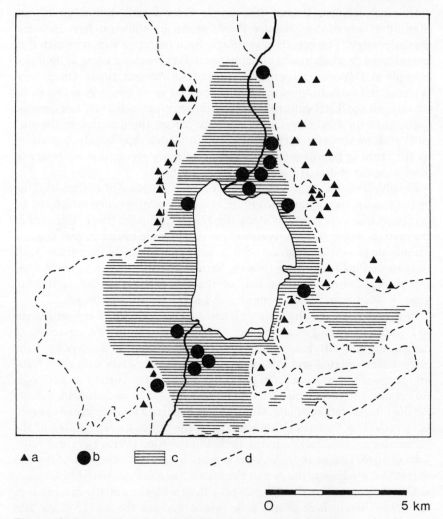

▲ a   ● b   ☰ c   ⌐ ⌐ d

O   5 km

Figure 5 Settlement pattern around the Dümmer Lake, Lower Saxony: a-
Mesolithic sites, b-Neolithic sites, c-Dümmer Lake during the Atlantic, d-boundary
between sand and peat (Source: Jacob-Friesen 1959).

excellent example is provided by the concentration of Mesolithic sites in the
vicinity of the Dümmer lake. Although the sites are a considerable distance
from the present-day lake shore, geological investigations have shown that
the lake was considerably larger in extent during the Atlantic period and the
forty-odd Mesolithic sites are seen to follow the original lake edge just
within the border between sand and peat (Fig. 5; Jacob-Friesen 1959, 58).
The same pattern has been noted to the north of the lake, along the Hunte
river.

The mapping of the Mesolithic sites in Mecklenburg and Brandenburg reveals a very clear preference for the sandy environment and location of sites along the lakes and rivers; for example, there is a heavy concentration of Jühnsdorf sites along the Havel river, especially where it flows through lakes such as Plausee or Wannsee, and there are Oldesloe-Kobrow sites along the Müritzsee and numerous smaller lakes to the east (Gramsch 1973, Maps 5, 6 and 9). Further east, in Poland, similar circumstances prevailed. Such patterns have been noted in Kujavia, where Mesolithic sites are concentrated by lakes, for example to the east of the Gopło and along the Pakość lakes, as well as along the chains of smaller lakes in the western part of the region (Cofta-Broniewska and Kośko 1982). The recent surveys along the Płonia river in western Pomerania identified over thirty Mesolithic sites clustering along the sandy river terraces (Czarnecki 1980, Fig. 2) and investigations of the Mesolithic settlement in the upper Oder basin also revealed an intensive occupation of sandy tracts along the Oder and its tributaries (Bagniewski 1979).

The environmental conditions within the Baltic littoral allowed for an even greater diversity of settlement with coastal, estuarine and inland habitats all occupied by the Ertebølle-Ellerbek culture. Consequently the sites were located directly on the coast (Rosenhof, Ertebølle or Meilgaard) or along the sea inlets (Norsminde, Vedbæk or Ellerbek) as well as further inland, by lakes and rivers (Ringkloster, Vester Ulslev, Rüde 2 or Förstermoor); offshore islands were also regularly settled (Lietzow-Buddelin, Augustenhof, Brovst or Havnø).

Apart from the traditional research in which the typo-chronological approach is still dominant, new themes, which have arisen from studies of modern hunter-gatherers, are also beginning to be addressed in the context of the European Mesolithic. Consequently much of the recent debate has shown a shift towards the investigation of the variety of human adaptations to different environments. The European littoral zone has assumed a particular significance in these new approaches; the diverse environmental conditions offered favourable circumstances for the emergence of complex hunting systems based on sedentary occupation, the sophisticated use of natural resources and a social complexity which is expressed in a relatively elaborate ritual.

The degree of complexity attained by the late Mesolithic hunter-gatherers of the North European Plain remains, however, frustratingly difficult to ascertain because of the lacunae in archaeological evidence. So far only the Danish coastal Ertebølle has been subject of broader enquiries. These studies are well known and it need only be noted that, on the basis of the high productivity potential of the north and east Jutland littoral, Rowley-Conwy (1983) has arued that the Danish Ertebølle developed a degree of sedentarism which was attained by the combined exploitation of marine, migratory and terrestrial resources. This interpretation is based partly on

Binford's (1980) model of logistic mobility, whereby a permanent base camp is served by a series of temporarily-used camp sites catering for specific activities. The difficulty of this interpretation lies in the fact that it is concerned only with the coastal settlement of north and east Jutland (it may also apply to northern Fyn and Zealand where the shell middens are also known) and it is not clear how it should be applied in relation to inland settlements, in Denmark as well as elsewhere along the North European Plain.

Rowley-Conwy (1983, 123) dismisses the suggestion of Paludan-Müller (1978) that the estuaries may also have offered conditions favourable to permanent settlement. It is perhaps worth remembering, however, that coastal regions are not the only habitats offering such conditions, as is indicated by examples of permanent settlement inland (consider, for instance, the case of Lepenski Vir; Srejović 1969; Voytek and Tringham 1989). It is possible that the lake belt of the North European Plain did in fact provide conditions allowing all-year-round settlement. Terrestrial, riverine and lacustrine resources could also have been supplemented by catching migratory birds; the latter has been suggested as a possible explanation of the Mesolithic site concentration along the Płonia river (Czarnecki 1980).

While subsistence data from the greater part of the North European Plain are gravely lacking and it is difficult to determine in what way the various late Mesolithic groups obtained their livelihood, some of the sites display not only a considerable size but also dense concentrations of flint assemblages and other materials. Moreover, while not numerous, traces of substantial domestic structures on a number of sites, for example at Jühnsdorf, Linden-Berg (Gramsch 1973, 13), Bergumermeer (Newell 1980, 256–64) and Dąbrowa-Krępnica 5 (Bagniewski 1979; 1980), suggest permanent settlement in at least some localities.

A degree of social sophistication, possibly expressing status differentiation, can be glimpsed from burial evidence. The Janisławice burial in Poland is quite extraordinary for its grave goods: forty-one chocolate flint implements, shell fragments, forty-three bone and antler objects and a necklace of twenty perforated deer teeth (Więckowska 1975, 383, Fig. CXXX). A number of burials are known from the Ertebølle culture, with the Vedbæk cemetery being particularly informative as to the treatment of various community members (Albrethsen and Brinch Petersen 1975 and 1976). Mesolithic graves were also found at Swifterbant (Van der Waals 1977) and Gramsch (1973, 16–19) quotes a number of possible Mesolithic burials from Mecklenburg.

Although the foregoing brief summary of the late Mesolithic communities of the North European Plain only touched upon some of the vital issues of the period in question, the picture that emerges shows different communities well adapted to the varying environments of this vast area, responding successfully to the constraints and advantages of individual habitats. It would be simplistic to expect that, over such a wide area, the hunter-gatherers should respond in one particular way in their encounter with the farmers. Examples from a few areas which currently offer good evidence and which are discussed in more detail in Chapter 8 show that the relationship may have taken many different forms.

2.2 The early farming groups

The earliest farming groups of the central European loessic landscape, orginally termed 'Danubian' by Childe (1925) and most recently renamed somewhat pragmatically as 'Primary Neolithic' (Bogucki 1988), comprise a cultural sequence which begins with the *Linearbandkeramik* (LBK). Of the subsequent, roughly coeval regional cultural groupings, the *Stichbandkeramik*, Lengyel and Rössen are the most relevant. Although the presence of these farmers, bordering in an enormous arc the entire southern edge of the North European Plain, clearly had an influence upon the human populations in the wider neighbourhood, our primary interest is in those groups which were in direct contact with the north European hunter-gatherers rather than those which influenced them from afar. For this reason we shall concern ourselves only with those groups of early farmers that ventured beyond the loess landscape.

While the north European lowland was clearly explored by early farmers, and there are numerous stray finds whose cultural provenance is not difficult to identify, the evidence for the permanent establishment of early farming groups in the North European Plain is presently limited to a few areas (Fig. 6). The only substantial enclaves of the LBK are known from central Poland – especially in Kujavia, although settlement further north along the Vistula near the towns of Toruń and Chełmno is now also being recognised (Kirkowski 1987) – and from the lower Oder region. In the latter area the fertile landscapes of the Pyrzyce basin and the Uckermünde Heide provided some of the most northerly foci for the LBK communities (Wiślański 1969; Gramsch 1971a). In Lower Saxony, the early settlement is documented in the south, just within the northernmost stretch of the loess between Hanover and Braunschweig (Schwarz-Mackensen 1982), but otherwise only sporadic finds are made, such as the LBK bowl dredged out of the river Weser (Nelson 1988).

The later, post-LBK settlement in the North European Plain is more difficult to correlate with the specific groupings of the *Stichbandkeramik*, Lengyel or Rössen identified in central Europe, and it appears that influences from the south were more dissipated since clear cultural groups cannot always be established. Thus, in Kujavia, pottery with typical stroke decoration does not appear to form a distinct chronological horizon and such materials are classed as marking either the end of the LBK or the beginning of the subsequent Lengyel culture (Czerniak 1980; Grygiel 1986). *Stich-*

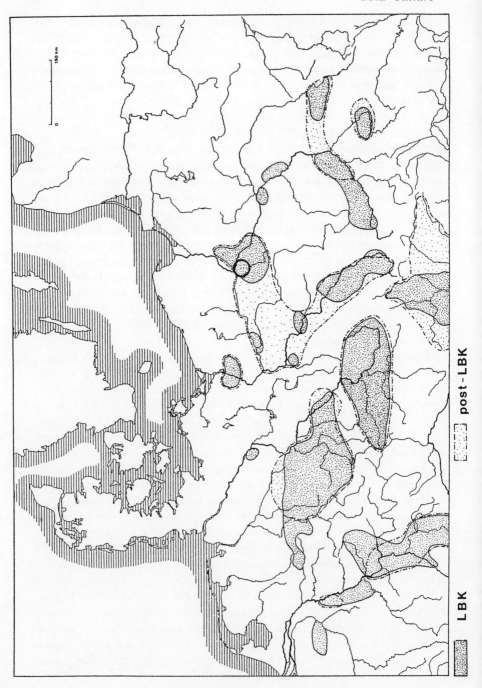

LBK

post - LBK

bandkeramik pottery is known in the lower Oder region where apparently also Rössen and the so-called *Guhrauer* ceramics have been identified (Raddatz 1956; Siuchniński 1972), but there is little to suggest internal chronology. *Stichbandkeramik* vessels are known from a few findspots in Mecklenburg and, as already noted, in the local Ertebølle-Ellerbek context on Rügen where they are accompanied by bone ornaments which are of typically Lengyel provenance and known in some numbers from the Brześć Kujawski burials (Jażdżewski 1938; Czerniak 1980). Rössen-like vessels are also known from Rügen (for example at Möhringen; Raddatz 1956, 28) and a number of isolated finds have been interpreted as Rössen burials: at Grünow, distr. Prenzlau, for example, a pot and marble armbands are thought by some scholars to have influenced the Lengyel jewellery (Czerniak 1979). The paucity of finds and their doubtful provenance therefore suggest that strict comparisons with the south in the sphere of material culture cannot be made.

Precisely the same applies to the Rössen-like material in Lower Saxony. If the finds at Hüde (Deichmüller 1965) are thought to represent an extension of Rössen settlement onto the North European Plain, they reveal interesting differences not only with the classic Rössen further south, but also with the other early farming groups that ventured outside the loess. The status of other typical Rössen finds, for example at Boberg (Schindler 1961), cannot be determined beyond the recognition that the vessels are not imitations but were made by Rössen potters; a few late Rössen (Gatersleben) finds appear in Altmark but again it is difficult to determine whether or not they represent an extension of Rössen settlement.

The numerous typical stone implements which define such an extensive area in the north are equally difficult to interpret. The unperforated LBK *Schuhleistenkeile* and the later, rectangular perforated forms – the so-called *hohle durchlochte Schuhleistenkeile* and the axe-hammers with triangular cross-section known as the *durchlochte Breitkeile* (Brandt 1967; Schwabedissen 1967) – spread well beyond the limits of the early farmers. Save for the examples encountered in undisputed Ertebølle-Ellerbek contexts (A. Fischer 1982), however, they are stray finds. They may reflect either an exploration northwards by farmers or represent a form of gift exchange with the hunter-gatherers; probably they reflect both activities (see Chapter 8).

Although generally speaking the study of the enclaves of early farmers in the North European Plain remains in its infancy, it is becoming obvious that the regularly mentioned 'ephemeral' nature of this settlement outwith the loess zone, even if it was limited only to a few suitable environments,

Figure 6 Distribution of central European farming groups: a-*Linearbandkeramik*, b-post-LBK (Rössen, Lengyel, *Stichbandkeramik*), circle denotes the position of the Brześć Kujawski group (Source: Kulczycka-Leciejewiczowa 1979).

must by and large be the result of poor investigation. This is best illustrated by the widely disparate evidence from two ecologically similar regions: the lower Oder and Kujavia. In the former, no significant research has taken place since before World War II. An analysis of LBK settlement from east of the Oder (the Pyrzyce district), published in 1972, quoted only thirteen possible settlements, most of which were identified by Dorka in 1939 (Siuchniński 1972). This contrasts dramatically with well over 130 LBK sites (excluding stray implement finds) from Kujavia (Czerniak 1980, Catalogue I). Many of these sites have come to light during the last two decades of intensive investigations.

Consequently, Kujavia is virtually the only reasonably documented centre of early farming settlement on the North European Plain. The following discussion therefore of necessity rests primarily upon the results of research carried out there and should not necessarily be taken as indicative of developments throughout the entire European lowland. Indeed, evidence from the area of Lower Saxony suggests other possibilites.

While details of chronology of early farming groups in Kujavia still remain to be worked out, and especially the internal phasing of settlement stages, the main chronological framework is now well established on the basis of more than twenty radiocarbon dates (Czerniak 1980; Grygiel 1986). The LBK culture is dated to about 6250–5959 BP, with a later stage of 5850/5750–5650 BP, during which the various influences of *Stichbandkeramik* and early Lengyel were making themselves felt. The full Lengyel settlement, previously known in the literature as the Brześć Kujawski group (Gabałówna 1966), is dated to 5650/5550–5250/5150 BP.

The domestic inventory of the populations in Kujavia comprises all the major elements typical of material culture further south, but it also displays local features. Fewer ceramic forms and the less profuse ornamentation (especially during the Lengyel culture) are clearly a result of the peripheral position of the Kujavian communities. Stone implements include all the typical southern forms but the flint industry is impoverished, being dependent by and large upon imported 'chocolate' flint and the Jurassic raw materials so expertly mined in the south (Czerniak 1980; Lech 1981a and 1981b). The availability of imported raw flint diminishes with time.

Very characteristic for the area of Kujavia is the presence, during the Lengyel culture, of personal jewellery which is found accompanying the dead buried on most settlements. Most of the jewellery appears to have been made locally (Grygiel 1986) and certain forms are limited to this area. The most common are the profusely decorated armbands, shell beads combined into necklaces and hip belts, amulets of perforated animal teeth and diadems sometimes incorporating copper elements such as cylindrical beads or spectacle spirals (Fig. 7). All these different elements combine to give style and character to the Brześć Kujawski Lengyel culture, distinguishing it from the contemporary populations to the south.

Figure 7 Jewellery of the Brześć Kujawski group: 1–3-copper, 4,5-dog and woolf teeth, coral and amber, 6,7-copper and calcite, 8,9-animal rib bones; 1–7-Brześć Kujawski, 8,9-Krusza Zamkowa (Source: Czerniak 1980).

From the point of view of landscape topography the lowland communities to an extent follow settlement patterns typical of the loessic zone, although there was less vertical differentiation of topographical features. Thus in Kujavia over 90 per cent of LBK sites were located on the lower river terraces, along lakes or below the upper valley reaches; the interfluves were not settled, but may nevertheless have been explored for grazing. The importance of the lower river terraces in particular appears to have increased significantly from 53 per cent (LBK) to 75 per cent (Lengyel; Wiślański 1969, Table II).

The degree of adaptation of the early farmers to the varied natural environment of their chosen landscapes in the North European Plain is clearly seen from Wiślański's settlement studies of north-western Poland. Thus, while 65.6 per cent of LBK settlements were located directly on black and brown soils, this figure decreased to 42.9 per cent during the Lengyel period. This pattern is well exemplified in Kujavia, where LBK settlement was initially concentrated within a limited black and brown earth area around the Gopło and Pakość lakes and the Bachorza river (Czerniak 1989, Map 2). It subsequently expanded outwith this narrow zone to take in the less fertile soils as well (ibid., Map 3).

There can be little doubt now as to the fully agricultural character of central European early farming groups. Studies of faunal and floral remains from sites where such evidence has survived demonstrate clearly that the economy was based on cultivated cereals and domesticated animals. Emmer, einkorn and barley were the main crops although legumes, flax and millet are also occasionally encountered (Willerding 1970). Among the animals cattle constituted the principal stock, variously augmented by sheep and goats (Bogucki 1988). There is little evidence to suggest that wild plants and animals contributed substantially towards food consumption, but there are occasionally sites attesting to hunting; wild plants, even if not contributing greatly, may have been a welcome variation in the diet.

How does the evidence from the North European Plain compare with the models in the south? The primary obstacle in the assessment of economic adaptations outwith the loess zone is, of course, the paucity of floral and faunal remains. There has also been a general lack of interest in subsistence studies of lowland communities, an imbalance which is only now being redressed (Bogucki 1982 and 1988).

Much has been made of the data from Brześć Kujawski, although the distinction between the LBK and the later Lengyel evidence is not always clearly drawn. However, this is not the only site with faunal evidence from Kujavia and data from other sites may be added to the evidence. Czerniak (1980) has published the data from the assemblages known in 1980, excluding Brześć Kujawski fauna. Although the assemblages were small and the bones were not studied in detail, the following picture emerges: while cattle bones are always predominant on the LBK and Lengyel sites (66 per cent and 41 per cent respectively), the quantity on individual sites varies from 100 per cent to as little as 5.4 per cent. Small ruminants are present in Kujavia from the very beginning and their contribution towards meat consumption increases from 26 per cent (LBK) to 31 per cent (Lengyel), varying from as little as 1.5 per cent to 73.3 per cent. While it is true that pigs make a negligible contribution ranging from 4 per cent (LBK) to 15.1 per cent (Lengyel), against the expectation of their suitability in forested lowland regions, we shall see latter on that the same seems to be the case in the early lowland TRB (Chapter 8). Wild animals are encountered only in small numbers, but it is important to note that they appear in about half of the assemblages. At one site with, sadly, a very small number of bones, deer bones constituted 40 per cent. Another site of the late LBK (Poznań Dębiec in Greater Poland) contained an assemblage in which cattle accounted for 20.4 per cent and sheep 12.5 per cent, while wild animals accounted for 66 per cent (Wiślański 1969, 114); so occasionally wild animals must have contributed towards the protein intake (cf. comments in Chapter 8).

The general pattern does not differ in principle, therefore, from that observed on the loess, for example in the area of Little Poland where Kruk (1973 and 1980) carried out substantial research. The drop in the percentage of cattle bones reveals the changing role of herds in the overall economy, with diversification to dairying (Bogucki 1984) and reliance upon other animals to make up for the reduction in beef consumption. On the other hand, since sheep and goats would have made a wider contribution to the economy than merely providing food and would thus have been slaughtered less frequently, their relatively strong presence, even in the LBK assemblages, indicates that sheep/goat flocks may have been quite sizeable.

Evidence of plant cultivation is very scanty, and is represented mostly by impressions of wheat, barley and rye on pottery (Kośko 1982a, 25). Some indication of cultivation may possibly derive from the fact that many sites are located just above the food plain, a pattern which further south has been interpreted as indicative of an intensive garden system (Kruk 1973). Such a system may well have proved suitable here too.

There have been suggestions that the LBK settlement in the European lowland was based on a network of impermanent camp sites used by cattle herders who seasonally brought the animals for grazing from the permanent loessland villages, and that a full farming economy was not established until the later Lengyel culture period (Bogucki 1988). This argument was based principally on the faunal data from Brześć Kujawski and on the apparent lack of traces of permanent settlement, especially the lack of long houses. However, Kruk's research in the uplands of southern Poland has not revealed any circumstances which would have induced farmers there to undertake long northward treks in search of grazing.

Moreover, there is now evidence of permanent LBK settlement in Kujavia together with traces of the ubiquitous long houses (see below, p. 28). The data from other LBK sites also suggest that herds were mixed from the beginning, and comprised substantial numbers of sheep and goats. While there are hardly any LBK plant remains, their absence from the archaeological record, which is also typical of many settlements on loess, should not necessarily be regarded as indicating an absence of cultivation altogether; as already suggested, garden cultivation was a feasible option. It is equally possible that the LBK economic strategy was, initially, deliberately based on livestock. As yet little is known about the evolution of early cereals and their initial suitability to soils other than loess. It is not inconceivable that the early farmers in Kujavia experimented with developing suitable cereal strains, meanwhile relying upon animal husbandry as a basis for their economy.

Before we can discuss other aspects of early farming groups in Kujavia, by way of contrast we should consider briefly the evidence of the Rössen-like occupation on the Dümmer lake, which was chronologically coeval with the Lengyel culture of Kujavia. Perhaps an investigation of other Neolithic sites around the lake is necessary before it can be established whether the settlement traces dated to 5650–5150 BP, which are mostly intermixed with the later TRB occupation here, should be regarded as evidence for a northward expansion of the Rössen culture or whether they represent a Rössen-acculturated local hunting-gathering group.

Here the environment is totally different from that in Kujavia: it comprises an extensive peaty basin which is surrounded by the morainic hills of the Wiehengebirge and Teutoburger Wald, an area mostly of clay and sands. The study of floral and faunal remains is beset with the same stratigraphic problems that face the study of the material culture, and it cannot be determined whether they belong to Rössen or to the subsequent TRB settlement or, indeed, both. In one sense it is perhaps irrelevant to which group the assemblage belongs, since it does not alter the interpretation of the finds, merely the cultural attribution. Whichever group claims it, the emphasis on the exploitation of wild species is apparent even now, before the final analysis has been published, since cattle account for only 36.8 per cent (or 17.1 per cent taking into account the number of individuals); the pig bones (21.5 per cent or 16.7 per cent) are thought to have come from wild pig, and the range of other wild species is enormous (Kampffmeyer 1983). Cereal plants are present in the form of carbonised grain and impressions, but the overall analysis of the find suggests a seasonal (late summer/early autumn) hunting station. Thus, whether we ascribe a Rössen or mainly TRB provenance to the assemblages, it is clear that the Hüde site was still fulfilling the function that it appears to have had since the Mesolithic.

The two areas contrast rather well, with Kujavia being a relatively close approximation of conditions typical of a southern loessic environment, while the Dümmer basin presents an environment of a totally different kind. It would therefore be incorrect to use either one or the other as wholly representative of the way in which early farming adapted itself to the north European lowlands. Rather the two examples are likely to represent the two most extreme circumstances, with many early farming populations most probably fitting somewhere in between the two.

The evidence for the actual settlements is also confined largely to Kujavia, although even here the sites tend to be only partially excavated. Thus, at Brześć Kujawski (site 4), Jażdżewski's excavations covered 10,950 m² but this very clearly did not represent the extent of the settlement complex, as was indeed intitially perceived by Jażdżewski himself and well established by Grygiel in his excavation of site 3 about 80 m to the northeast (Grygiel 1986, 239). Similarly, at Krusza Zamkowa, the settlement traces were encountered in an area of about 200 × 300 m, but less than 5 per cent of the area appears to have been excavated (Czerniak 1980, Fig. 47). However, the presence of such sites with find concentrations, domestic and industrial pits, ground plans of houses and neighbouring graves, clearly indicates that these were relatively large permanent settlements of the type witnessed throughout central Europe.

Small sites may possibly be regarded as equivalent to individual farmsteads such as have been postulated for the area of the Aldenhoven Plateau, but these are not as yet numerous. At Konary, the settlement traces covered an area of about 20 m in diameter and were associated with a relatively small (under 9 m long) trapezoidal house. Sites such as Dobre (two houses) or Biskupin (one long house accompanied by a complex of outside pits) may also belong to this category, although in each case the investigated area was small (Czerniak 1980, 112–18).

The case of the Brześć Kujawski site – the famous household cluster in the vicinity of the main settlement – is, however, somewhat different. The full publication of this site (Grygiel 1986) makes it very clear that this household did not function on its own. Over a period of time it housed a family (or families) of craftsmen who provided for the needs of the rest of the Brześć Kujawski inhabitants. These craftsmen specialised in the manufacture of T-shaped antler axes and shell-beads and, possibly, in hide processing too. The household cannot be interpreted, therefore, as a self-supporting farmstead. On the contrary, it was inextricably connected with the main settlement. Its physical separation from the main site and certain associated rituals, as well as the apparent secrecy of the industrial activities, indicate that there was a need to preserve the exclusivity of the skills involved in the manufacture of these commodities.

Investigations of the landscape in the vicinity of Brześć Kujawski identified a whole range of auxiliary sites. One of these, at Kuczyna, revealed traces of a hut and a tool assemblage clearly indicative of wood-working (ibid, 220–22); a number of other functionally different sites within a 4 km radius identify the wider catchment area of the Brześć Kujawski complex.

The history of the domestic architecture of early farmers in Kujavia, long believed to have been a relatively late, Lengyel, occurrence, can now be traced from the earliest LBK culture in the area. Recent excavations of an LBK settlement at Łojewo revealed traces of classic rectangular long houses of the type known all the way from Bylany to Elsloo. The structures were over 30 m long and 6 m wide, with outer walls based on a framework of individual posts and an arragement of three parallel rows of posts in the interior (Kośko 1982c, Fig. 3). In the later period, in accordance with principles in evidence on the loess, the ground plan changes from rectangular to trapezoidal (Fig. 8). The small house from Konary (Fig. 8: 4), based on a framework of widely spaced outer posts and a freer interior arrangement, appears to predate the emergence of the typical Lengyel houses. The latter are by now well known, showing a chronological evolution from forms with intermittent bedding trenches and a central three-post row (Fig. 8: 2), to structures with a complete bedding trench, and apparently, no need of interior roof supports (Fig. 8: 1, 3). The excavations at Brześć Kujawski have shown very clearly that such houses were built as sturdy structures, intended for prolonged use.

With the presence of large central settlements made up of households with various functions and a sophisticated range of auxiliary supporting sites within the larger settlement region, there can be little doubt that early farming settlement in this area of the North European Plain was of a permanent nature. This appears now to apply as much to the LBK, even when the stronger emphasis on animal husbandry is taken into account, as to the later, Lengyel, culture. Initially, archaeologically and economically based arguments in favour of the permanence of settlement of the LBK and subsequent communities in central Europe were put forward by Modderman (1971). Since then they have been developed by others and need no reiteration here (see Kruk 1973, 1980; Lüning 1980; Rowley-Conwy 1981; Bogucki 1988). It is of interest to note, however, that the shifting cultivation models adhered to by some researchers concerned with the area just dicussed are based purely upon hypothetical demographic considerations, taking no account of the size, the functional differentiation of sites or the economic potential of the settled landscape (Czerniak and Piontek 1980). The studies from around the Brześć Kujawski site have shown much evidence to the contrary and offer a more meaningful interpretation of the settlement system within the area.

The above brief discussion shows that, in contrast to central Europe, our knowledge and understanding of the early farming groups that ventured outside the loess zone is still inadequate. This is particularly clearly seen in our poor perception of the LBK groups. Their apparently gradual adaptation to the ecological conditions of the lowland is viewed as a tactical

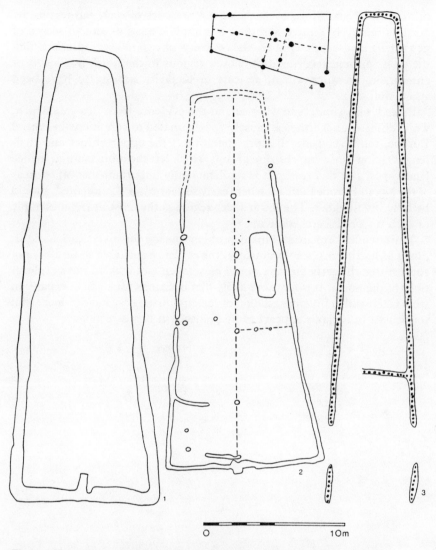

Figure 8 House plans of the Brześć Kujawski group: 1-Brześć Kujawski, 2-Krusza Zamkowa, 3-Biskupin, 4-Konary (Source: Czerniak 1980).

strategy of exploitation of a new environment in pursuit of specific economic goals.

   The primary question, concerning the reasons for or causes of the north-ward expansion of the early farmers, is yet to be answered, although it would appear to be a starting point for any investigation and interpretation of systems outside the loess zone. So far there is no evidence to suggest that demographic pressure or land shortage in the area of central Europe were primary catalysts. Moreoever, the actual presence of early farmers in the north is relatively limited and does not imply a mass exodus in search of new fertile landscapes. Quite to the contrary, one gains the impression that the early farming settlement of chosen regions in the north was a sort of enterprising venture which, at least in Kujavia, appears to have been successful.

Indeed, one wonders to what extend the evidence from this area which, while different, nevertheless closely approximated to conditions in central Europe, can be considered represenatative of the opportunities and challenges facing those enterprising groups which left the more familiar loessic landscapes. For this reason it is fundamentally important that other areas of the North European Plain, where early settlement is documented, should be fully investigated. The lower Oder region is the most obvious example of such under-researched areas.

Thus, while there are still many problems facing the investigation of this phase of north European prehistory, the evidence available so far does not suggest that the early farmers would have taken 'pot luck' in their explorations of the north. It is far more likely that decisions for such an expansion were taken with a full appreciation of the circumstances, and the successful settlement in Kujavia appears to be pointing in this direction.

3

The TRB culture: the historical background

The previous chapter was devoted to a brief discussion of cultural development during the 7th and 6th millennia BP. We saw that a variety of hunter-gatherer groups continued to inhabit the greater part of the North European Plain and that early farming communities, in their territorial expansion from the south, were establishing themselves along the region's southern limits.

While these two major complexes occupied mutually exclusive environments (the LBK and its derivatives settled on the southern loess and only venturing slightly onto the northern black earths, while the hunter-gatherers roamed in the sandy and forested habitats to the north), these populations did not live in isolation. The specific forms of contact between them will be reviewed in due course; suffice it to say that through the stimulus of mutual influences and a long period of contact between these two contrasting lifestyles a new complex emerged – the Funnel-necked Beaker culture.

This cultural complex was named 'not at all euphoniously', as Childe (1925) observed, after the most distinctive vessel from the North European Plain. The original German word for the pot – *Trichterrandbecher* (literally funnel-rimmed beaker) – appears to have been too long even for Gustaf Kossinna (1921, 29 n. 1), who advocated the shorter version of *Trichterbecher*. The German name *Trichterbecherkultur* (TRB) was translated literally into other languages: the *Funnel-necked Beaker culture, Tragtbægerkultur* (TBK), *Kultura pucharów lejkowatych* (KPL), *Trechterbekercultuur, Kultura nálevkovitých pohárů, Kul'tura voronkovidnyh kubkov* etc. Until the late 1930s the term 'megalithic culture' was also applied to the TRB culture by some Scandinavian and German scholars (Nordman 1935; Sprockhoff 1938), although others (Jażdżewski 1936) argued that this name, the application of which varied greatly throughout Europe, should be abandoned as too confusing.

I use here throughout the abbreviated form TRB culture, which is a time-honoured term in the English literature; it is consistent with my earlier usage of the term (Midgley 1985) and it still accords well with other tradition-sanctioned names such as Globular Amphora culture and Corded

Ware culture, to name but two. While not ideal, it is by no means worse than 'First Northern' (Childe 1925) or the most recently suggested 'Consequent Neolithic' (Bogucki 1988). It will be amply demonstrated in the following pages that the search for a new name is not among the most pressing issues facing the study of this cultural complex.

That the TRB was of particular significance in the subsequent cultural shaping of the North European Plain is seen from its duration, widespread distribution and considerable influence within its own area and beyond. In its distribution it covered most of the area from the present-day Netherlands in the west to central and eastern Poland in the east, and from southern Scandinavia in the north to Bohemia and Moravia in the south.

Because of the geographical vastness, the immensely varied scholarly interests and the sheer quantity of material, the TRB culture has rarely been studied as one entity. Quite to the contrary, regional studies have always been its hallmark and frequently individual themes such as the megaliths, pottery and lithic implements were further chosen as specific research subjects. Each of these topics has virtually its own history of research.

While the historical perspective of these various studies is an important prerequisite for the understanding of different issues, the various research attitudes, changing theoretical approaches and resulting interpretations are best appreciated in the context of the discussion of individual themes. Thus each chapter dealing with a specific TRB culture issue incorporates a brief summary of the history of research on the relevant theme, allowing the reader to observe the changing trends and developments in the interpretation of the various themes involved.

There is one theme, however, which recurs with a persistent regularity and has been of prime importance to many scholars engaged in the study of this culture: the question of the TRB's origins. This could be seen in the heated polemics each time a different theory was advanced; in recent years the theme has become camouflaged beneath the conceptually expanded question of the Mesolithic/Neolithic transition in the North European Plain, but the fundamental issue has remained the same. Although each and every study contributes something fresh to our understanding of the TRB culture, there are still as many theories as there are scholars working in this field. The intention here is to look at the problem in the light of the influences which, it has been claimed, contributed towards the TRB culture's main character.

Although the investigation of the TRB culture is deeply rooted in nineteenth-century antiquarian pursuits, it is perhaps surprising to find that the recognition of the TRB as a major cultural entity did not occur until the early part of the twentieth century. It is Gustaf Kossinna who must be credited with the first general synthesis of the TRB culture which involved a broad geographical approach. Kossinna (1909, 1910 and 1921) considered three main ceramic forms – funnel-necked beakers, collared flasks and amphorae. He plotted the known finds and divided the material thus compiled into four main geographical groups: Northern, Western, Eastern and Southern (Kossinna 1921, 143–51; Fig. 9). These groups, subsequently modified by Jażdżewski (1936, 227–30), who divided the Eastern group further into Eastern and South-Eastern components, form the basis of the regional division of the TRB culture which is applied to this day (Fig. 10). Kossinna (1921, 143) derived the Northern TRB group from the background of the local Ertebølle and, on the basis of the decreasing similarities to the east and west, argued for a gradual expansion of the TRB from the north (i.e. Jutland and Schleswig-Holstein) across the rest of the North European Plain and beyond.

The concern with the origins of the TRB in the work of Kossinna and, indeed, many other scholars must be perceived in a wider historical perspective. The idea of a diffusion of civilisation into Europe from the south-east found favour within the intellectual climate of late nineteenth-century Scandinavia, with Sophus Müller and Oscar Montelius among the most eloquent advocates of this view. However, this model of *Ex Oriente Lux* was not popular with the German scholarship of that period. By the time Kossinna turned his attention to archaeology, the nationalist climate in Germany was sufficently ripe to support an opposing view that the source of European civilisation was to be found in northern Europe (Sklenář 1983). Thus Kossinna, who argued that only the study of national German prehistory was worthy of scholarly interest, found little difficulty in identifying the TRB folk – the funnel-necked beaker makers and megalith builders – with Indo-Germans. The presence of culturally similar material outwith Germany was clear proof of the spread of Indo-Germans and their superior, civilising influence on their more primitive neighbours. Although Kossinna died in 1931, his ethnic views found more than verbal expression in the development and subsequent pursuit of Nazi ideology.

Jażdżewski, while critical of Kossinna's 'tendentious and, as usual, premature synthesis' (1936, 2), nevertheless shared his belief in the northern origin of the TRB culture and always strongly expounded this view (Jażdżewski 1961, 1965 and 1970). While post-war research tended against such a view, in the early years of his research Jażdżewski argued that the TRB originated in the Jutland peninsula (1936, 222). His was, in fact, a very difficult position. His scholarly integrity did not allow him to move away from the contentious 'northern origins' and he resolved the difficulty by emphasising that the cultural material of the TRB may represent one of the northern Indo-European populations, but that the correlation between archaeological cultures and ethnic identities should not be made until the material has been sufficiently studied and interpreted. Although in later years Jażdżewski often changed his opinion as to the precise location and size of the TRB's 'cradle', his thoughts inevitably turned in the same

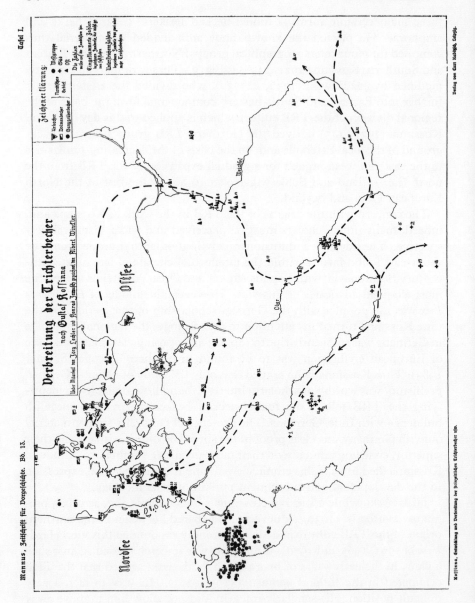

direction – always away from the south, towards the north. He regarded any suggestion even vaguely pointing southwards as 'ludicrous' and frequently listed all the features of the TRB which could not possibly have been derived from the south and therefore must have belonged to the north. The key argument in his theory of the importance of northern influences was the predominant use of flint as the raw material for the production of small and large tools (Jażdżewski 1961, 81; 1970, 56). Further support for this he saw in different hafting methods: cutting edge parallel to the handle in the TRB (cf. Brøndsted 1957, 156 Fig.) and cutting edge perpendicular to the handle among the central European farming cultures.

Influences reaching the North European Plain from the south were, on the other hand, of particular importance in the research of Behrens (1959, 1960 and 1973). Behrens sought the origins of the central German Baalberge group, which he considered the oldest in the TRB, in Bohemia and Moravia (1960, 579). The diagnostic ceramic forms of the Baalberge, such as amphorae, handled jugs and beakers, were argued by him to have had prototypes in the unpainted wares of the Moravian Lengyel culture.

On the basis of detailed but strongly selective comparisons of the middle German Baalberge group with the Danish A-phase ceramics (which were then thought to represent the earliest Danish TRB), Behrens suggested a 'modified middle European theory' (1959, 180). He noted substantial similarities between the northern (especially the Store Valby – see Chapter 4) and Baalberge materials, such as flat bases, beakers with elongated profiles and little or no ornamentation (ibid., 170, Fig. 1). The process responsible for such similarities was, according to Behrens, as follows: the Baalberge group originated in Bohemia and Moravia and spread along the Elbe to the area of its confluence with the Saale, where the group came into contact with the middle German Rössen culture. One branch of the Baalberge subsequently continued down the Elbe to Schleswig-Holstein and southern Scandinavia.

A similar trend was recognised by Schwabedissen (1958b, 26, Fig. 18: c and d; 1967, Fig. 10). He compared funnel-necked beakers from the area east of the Elbe (Becker's A/B ceramics, which are mainly undecorated, flat-based vessels) with the Danish A-phase beakers from Store Valby, and further extended such comparisons to other pottery forms (bowls and lugged jugs), all of which had their counterparts among the material classified by Becker (1947) as belonging to the northern A-phase (Schwabedissen 1967, 428). According to Schwabedissen, this A-phase pottery would ultimately have had prototypes in the Lengyel culture material and, having been modified on the way through middle and north-eastern Germany, it reached southern Scandinavia (ibid., 429, Fig. 11).

Figure 9 Kossinna's original division of the TRB culture based on the distribution of funnel-necked beakers (Source: Kossinna 1921).

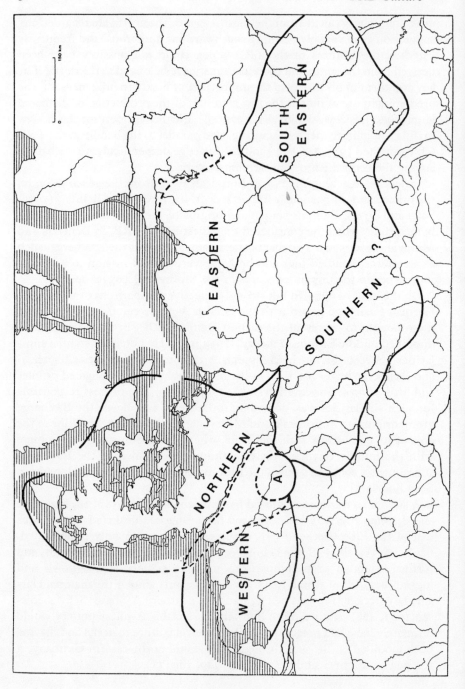

Moreover, both scholars continued such ceramic comparisons, indicating yet another (western) trend. Among the ceramic forms of the Baalberge and Danish B-phase Behrens found little correspondence, but he pointed to similarities between the latter and various Rössen pottery forms (1959, 173, Fig. 2). He suggested that Rössen pottery could have inspired the ornament as well as the shape of the B-phase pots. In addition he noted numerous Rössen axes (*Breitkeile*), which had been found in the north, well beyond the limits of the Rössen culture settlement, and interpreted such finds as influences reaching the north together with the Baalberge group (ibid., 177). In the area of middle Germany, the Baalberge group acquired some Rössen elements which accompanied its movement northwards (ibid., 180–1).

Schwabedissen (1967, 418, Fig. 3) expanded upon this idea of Rössen influences. Firstly, he pointed out that the distribution of the Rössen culture proper extended further north. Many Rössen finds were by then known both from the Ertebølle-Ellerbek and from the TRB culture areas, especially in the southern part of the Jutland peninsula (Lomborg 1962; Brandt 1967). Concerning the ceramic developments in the north-west German plain Schwabedissen pointed to the appearance of the so-called 'wobble-base' (*Wackelboden*) beakers (1967, 416, Fig. 5: a, c), which he saw as having prototypes in the Rössen globular vessels although he did not rule out their typological connections with the Ertebølle-Ellerbek pointed-base pots (ibid., 420).

Rössen elements have been pointed out in various assemblages: wobble-bases and round bases at Hüde and Rosenhof (Deichmüller 1965; Schwabedissen 1979a and 1979c); indented rims and 'stroke' ornament under the rim at Boberg, here with a typical Rössen vessel (Schindler 1961). Moreover, Michelsberg-like traits, such as pointed bases, rim decoration and tall beakers, have all been found in the north German material. The latter have also been noted as influential in the Danish B-phase as well as A-phase pottery. Some vessels, such as tall beaker from Store Valby (Becker 1954b, Fig. 19), have on various occasions been compared with western, that is, Michelsberg (Schwabedissen 1958b, 23, Fig. 18) or eastern forms (Schwabedissen 1967, 428, Fig. 10). The claim of Rössen influence was strengthened by the subsequent development of the *Tiefstich* pottery, where Rössen elements seemed to be developed in the rich ornament of the Haaßel-Fuchsberg style (ibid., 421–2, Fig. 7: a and 8: a, c).

As we review these early theories of the TRB's origins it becomes clear that their main drawbacks stem firstly from the fact that they were confined to one element of material culture, be it pottery or flint tools, and secondly from what today appears to be a simplistic theoretical approach. Two

Figure 10 Regional groups of the TRB culture: A-Altmark region (Source: Bakker *et al.* 1969).

general concepts of culture origin can nevertheless be recognised: diffusion
and acculturation. The former was based on the assumption that a fundamental TRB group had formed in a geographically limited and culturally
defined area, and from there it had spread out over the whole area of the
TRB's known distribution. Three stages of such a process were assumed:
a uniform development in a specific area, territorial expansion associated
with differentiation, and finally the appearance of different cultures. In
practice only the latter two hypothetical stages were observed in the archaeological record.

Thus Behrens (1959 and 1960) considered the origins of the Baalberge
group to be outside the area of its main distribution (the confluence of the
Elbe and Saale), in Moravia and Bohemia, where the TRB material was
scarce and rather poorly understood and where it most probably does not
represent a horizon comparable with that of the early developments further
north. Although he distinguished two different trends reaching the north
(epi-Lengyel and Rössen), he suggested that they came together in one
region (the Elbe-Saale) and then moved northwards (retaining their own
identity?), rather than allowing each its own spatial and temporal position.

Working on the Danish ceramics Becker (1947), similarly, was unwilling
to look into the TRB itself for explanations of its origins which, he wrote
'must lie more southeast than the Danubian cultures, for we must quite
ignore independent developments in Northern Europe on the background
of Mesolithic hunter cultures' (ibid., XVI). This suggestion took him as far
as the Ukraine, an area with which he was not familiar and from where no
cultural material akin to the TRB culture is known. Moreover, although
Becker insisted upon the chronological priority of the A-phase material
over the B-phase for Denmark, at the same time he assumed that the
material from the remainder of the North European Plain (which was
similar to both) represented a single A/B phase (see Chapter 4 for a detailed
discussion). Becker, who moreover argued for an invasion of southern
Scandinavia by farming groups, was strongly opposed by Troels-Smith
(1953), who viewed the final Ertebølle culture as semi-agrarian and
developing into the TRB, although he also believed in some invasion from
outside Denmark but only at a later stage.

Although after World War II the previously dominant ethnic themes
understandably receded into the background, one wonders to what extent
the new theories carried the burden of the earlier views of Kossinna and his
followers and how much conscious or subconscious effort went into re-
dressing the balance. Becker appears to have opted for what was then an
archaeologically untestable but politically poignant (Slavonic?) source.
Troels-Smith's insistence on the local (i.e. Danish) origins of the TRB
culture could plausibly be seen as the other side of the same coin. It is also
clear that both Behrens and Schwabedissen were looking for inspiration

and influence outwith the controversial north German region, to the earlier central European Neolithic farming groups.

Even in this mid-research stage, however, the examination of the known early cultural material showed quite clearly that it was not possible to explain the origins of the TRB culture in terms of diffusion from a single source. How else could this problem be approached? U. Fischer (1961, 425) argued that cultures have ancestors in older complexes (and descendants in younger) and that one should therefore not attempt to search for the origins of any culture outside the area of its distribution. The main exponents of this approach to the problem of the TRB's origins were in his later years Jażdżewski and, more recently, Wiślański and Kośko.

According to Jażdżewski (1965, 79) the TRB culture appeared in the area 'lying to the north of the northern periphery of the older Danubian cultures, alongside the southern and western coasts of the Baltic, in northern Germany and in Denmark, and perhaps in north-west Poland as well'. Such an area does not coincide precisely with the distribution of the earliest TRB material as we know it at present but, more significantly, Jażdżewski saw the process of such a development as a transformation in one direction from Mesolithic to the TRB and did not specify it beyond a very general influence of farming groups further south. Jażdżewski's approach in his later research still smacked of concealing the 'single source' theory, admittedly in a geographically expanded version, under the cloak of acculturation.

The clearly unsatisfactory theories of the origins of the TRB culture expounded in the 1950s and 1960s, together with the renewed research in the various regions of the North European Plain in the early 1970s, have resulted in a temporary shift from broader geographical considerations towards a concentration of intellectual thought upon the smaller, regional problems. This has been especially pronounced in German research where, with the exception of Schwabedissen's continued interest in the semi-agrarian nature of the German Ertebølle-Ellerbek culture, the question of the origins of the TRB has receded into the background. The relatively substantial German research into the TRB, reflected in the prolific literature, remains to this day concerned predominantly with the traditional pursuit of small-scale regional studies geared towards a typo-chronological analysis of megaliths, ceramics and other elements of material culture.

This state of affairs needs once more to be understood in the wider historical perspective. Quite apart from the problems caused by the post-war division of Germany, the earlier political exploitation of the ethnic paradigm had a profound impact on archaeology in the two Germanies (Härke 1989). In East Germany archaeology was served by a relatively small number of professionals and the evolutionary models were not conducive to extensive interpretations of the past.

Archaeology in West Germany, which has been regarded by many as the inheritor of earlier German research, has suffered from what Smolla (1980) referred to as the Kossinna syndrome. Additionally, the lack of interest in archaeology among the German public and a relatively comfortable financial basis of German research created a climate which did not demand synthesis, explanation or interpretation. It was simpler, and doubtless less controversial, to gear research objectives towards a highly disciplined approach to material culture, which could be viewed from an abstract point of view not laden with the burden of meaning and symbolism characteristic of the Anglo-Saxon traditions, towards the elaborate classification of sources and towards the excellence of excavation technology. These very positive elements of the post-war German tradition reveal themselves mostly in the context of TRB pottery, large implements and above all megalithic tombs. It will be very interesting to observe the course that German archaeology follows now that the two countries are again united, and British and American archaeological traditions are slowly permeating into the lower echelons of German scholarship.

In southern Scandinavia, especially in Denmark, the difficulties inherent in the interpretation of early TRB material have caused scholars temporarily to abandon material culture based explanations and to concentrate their efforts on the recovery of new data. It is of further significance that, in contrast to Germany, public awareness and interest in archaeology in Denmark has a very long tradition dating back well into the last century. Today this is exemplified by an active amateur involvement as well as by the extraordinary popularity of archaeological literature (in 1975 there were 50,000 subscribers to *Skalk*). Within the context of the period under study, the Danish Ertebølle culture has always inspired research interest equal to that of the TRB and the question of the emergence of farming populations there has always been inextricably bound up with the fate of the Danish hunter-gatherers.

Throughout the 1970s the increased research into both cultural complexes and the new chronological data have opened the way for new discussion. Indeed, in recent years the only serious debate on the emergence of the TRB culture has been taking place in southern Scandinavia, where the influence of New Archaeology has had a profound impact upon the whole concept of the transition from hunting-gathering to farming. Unfortunately, this debate has been geared singularly towards the interpretation of the Mesolithic/Neolithic transition in Denmark; the presence of the TRB culture to the south of the Jutland peninsula appears to be taken more or less for granted.

There is currently a general agreement among the south Scandinavian scholars that this transition should be viewed as a continuous process, although there are considerable differences as to the causes and the speed with which this process took place. Broadly speaking two main approaches can be identified: ecological and social. Supporters of the former consider such factors as population pressure, sedentarism of hunter-gatherers and depletion of natural resources, in various combinations, as leading to circumstances of which the only posssible outcome was the adoption of agriculture (Paludan-Müller 1978; Rowley-Conwy 1983, 1984 and 1985b; Zvelebil and Rowley-Conwy 1984). The exponents of the social theory argue for connections between the Danish Ertebølle and the Neolithic farming groups of central Europe which, through the exchange of prestigious and highly desirable items (pottery, domesticated animals), the acquisition of knowledge and the increased social complexity of the Ertebølle communities, resulted in a transition from a hunting-gathering to a farming way of life (A. Fischer 1982 and 1983; Jennbert 1984 and 1985; T. Madsen 1987). There are serious disagreements as to the speed with which this transition took place, with a number of scholars favouring an almost dramatically swift changeover (T. Madsen 1987) while others see it as a slower, more gradual process (A. Fisher 1982 and 1983; Jennbert 1984 and 1985).

In Poland, as in Denmark, a new generation of scholars has tried to break with the traditional explanations for the origin of the TRB culture and to move away from the 'single source' theory. Among the prime movers of this trend we must place T. Wiślański. His work on the socio-economic aspects of Neolithic populations in north-central Europe (1969) which, sadly, has never been so widely read as that of his follower J. Kruk, gave Wiślański a breadth of vision not encountered among his contemporaries. His knowledge and understanding of the TRB evidence enabled him to perceive that analogous development processes were taking place over the whole of the European lowland. On the basis of a general perception of cultural material he proposed a mimimum of five potential genetic centres which, by and large, correspond to the earlier-mentioned regional groups (see Fig. 10). The *Western centre* included the Netherlands and the area around Hanover; it was the source of *Tiefstich* pottery and is generally believed to have been the last to emerge. The *Northern centre* comprised southern Scandinavia and Mecklenburg and it arose through the mixing of cultural elements from east and west. The *Eastern centre* consisted of the areas of Kujavia, the lower Oder and Silesia. The *South-eastern centre* (Little Poland) had close connections with the Eastern. The *Southern Centre* included areas around the middle and upper Elbe, while the region south of the upper Oder was connected with the Eastern, Southern and South-eastern groups but may also have had its own sources.

Scholars working in the area of the Polish lowland have recently made attempts at a comparative study of pottery belonging to the various Neolithic groups, with a view to providing the basis for a relative chronology based on ceramic technology rather than on the traditional study of ceramic styles (Kośko and Prinke 1977; Czerniak and Kośko 1980a and 1980b; Kośko 1980 and 1981).

On the basis of these macro- and microscopic analyses of the technology of ceramic industries, the various Neolithic complexes in the area of the Polish lowland have been divided into technological sequences, comparison of which has revealed strong correspondences between the post-LBK and TRB materials. Radiocarbon dating of the Lengyel Brześć Kujawski group (see Chapter 5) suggests that the two were at least partly contemporary, and stylistic similarities in material culture tend to support this view. Some scholars, however, still find it difficult to reconcile themselves to a contemporary multi-cultural presence in certain regions of the Polish lowland.

Two main models have been current in Poland over the last decade. With regard to the Polish lowland, Kośko (1982a) has argued for a close relationship between the LBK and hunter-gatherer communities which, each in their turn, gave rise to post-LBK (chiefly Lengyel) and TRB groups. This model is based predominantly upon an intellectual perception of the cultural scene of 5th millennium BC northern Europe although, as will be seen later (Chapter 4.2), it finds a reflection in the currently available evidence. A series of parallel developments are envisaged along the broad lowland front, with the LBK/Rössen in the west and LBK/Lengyel participation in the east, an idea which expands upon the earlier interpretations of Wiślański.

A different approach characterises Kruk's (1973 and 1980) well-known studies of the economy and settlement patterns of Neolithic populations in southern Poland, where the TRB culture features as one of the links in the chain of complex socio-economic changes taking place throughout the entire Neolithic. Kruk has proposed a dynamic model of economic evolution on the loess uplands, initiated by the intensive agriculture of the LBK groups, and ultimately characterised by the transhumant, pastoral economies of the late Neolithic Globular Amphora and Corded Ware cultures.

In this model the TRB culture emerges as a result of the strong influence of the Lengyel-Polgar groups upon the local, non-loess populations of hunter-gatherers; in the context of the evolution of the Neolithic economy it is seen as a fusion of the *intensive* LBK and the incipient *extensive* Lengyel-Polgar agricultural practices.

Both of these models will be reviewed in greater detail later (Chapters 4.2 and 8), but it is important to emphasise at this point that they derive from two wholly separate schools of thought and, perhaps more significantly, reflect the very different availability and preservation of archaeological evidence in their respective regions.

The most recently published work on the subject of the origins of the TRB culture, from the pen of the American scholar Bogucki (1988), is also based on economic considerations. Its importance lies in the fact that it represents a first serious attempt to analyse the emergence of agriculture across the broad area of the North European Plain. There is no argument here as to the general premise that the TRB culture derives by and large from the indigenous hunter-gatherer populations, although Bogucki has little doubt that the reasons behind this process are more difficult to explain. Broadly speaking he offers a theoretical model in which a symbiotic relationship between the hunter-gatherers and early farmers, co-existing along the southern periphery of the North European Plain, ultimately leads to the adoption of agricultural practices throughout the entire lowland.

This brief review of various theories advanced for the explanation of the origins of the TRB culture, illustrates how our perception of cultural change has moved away from the material culture oriented approach of the 1950s and 1960s and towards interpretations based upon economic change, although these ideas have not been applied with equal zeal in all regions of northern Europe.

This change in scholarly pursuits is a natural reflection of a broader development in archaeology in general. On the one hand, the decline in dominance of the culture-historical approach has allowed scholars to move away from the concerns with 'where' and 'when' towards 'why' and 'under what circumstances'. An increased familiarity with modern non-industrial economies has refuted the naive view that hunter-gatherers would become farmers at the first opportunity and that a farming economy automatically reflected a people in natural progress. On the other hand, these changes in attitude and scholarly objectives reflect a more general interest in theoretical, explanatory models which have a wider application in a variety of prehistoric contexts.

In concluding this discussion on the history of research into the TRB culture, it is important to emphasise that what may appear as an excessive preoccupation with the subject of its origins was very deeply rooted in the specific historical circumstances of the last hundred years or so. These circumstances, moreover, were responsible not only for particular scholarly attitudes, but also for governing the relative wealth or poverty of material available for analysis.

Another factor of particular significance was the culture-historical paradigm, which for so long placed specific demands as well as constraints upon the study of these phenomena. It is very important that any discussion of the TRB culture addresses more than the specific theme of its origins. Indeed, one may go further and suggest that we cannot interpret the beginning unless we also investigate the directions in which it continued to develop and, ultimately, reached its demise.

This review of the historical background of the TRB also demonstrates most emphatically that a current milieu, with all its historical, social and theoretical burdens, weighs heavily upon any study and interpretation of prehistoric cultural complexes. This is being realised by many scholars today and makes one aware that one's own 'scientific objectivity' is forever tinted with the subjectivity of the background against which one pursues one's own intellectual development.

To understand and to interpret the TRB culture one must understand not only its role in the context of north European prehistory, but also its place in the context of the development of north European archaeology. It is thus hoped that this chapter will contribute to the understanding of some of the issues which follow.

4

Regional ceramic sequences of the TRB culture

Any discussion of such a vast body of material evidence as is now available on the TRB culture requires, of necessity, some sort of framework within which similarities and differences can be outlined and meaningful conclusions drawn. In the previous chapter the conventional division of the TRB culture into five regional groups was outlined (Fig. 10). Because of the regional nature of the history of research into the TRB, the regional groups still offer the reader, as well as the writer, the best available framework within which to conduct a discussion; this traditional division will therefore be used throughout this chapter. It will be apparent, however, that the regional groups do not make a synchronous appearance; nor is it always possible to discuss the evidence rigidly within such a framework: the earliest TRB, for instance, cannot be described in such terms. Moreover, the boundaries between the regional groups should at no time be conceived of as rigid and immovable lines but, to the contrary, must be seen as fluid and broad zones in which elements typical of two or more regions combine to create transitional phenomena. Wherever possible the discussion will transcend the artificial divisions and, at the end of the chapter, conclusions are designed to give the reader an overall understanding of developments within the broad area of the European lowland covered by this vast cultural complex.

The pottery of the TRB has always been the most-studied aspect of its material culture. The rarity of stratigraphic contexts, the initial lack of dating evidence and, above all, the strongly decorative character of the TRB ceramics have encouraged scholars to become involved in typological studies. From the beginning of this century the pottery has been the source and the back-bone of many elaborate typo-chronologies. That this approach has not yet entirely lost its appeal can be seen from the fact that the latest typo-chronological sequence was published as late as 1986 (Brindley 1986b).

Because of its significance in past and present research, the pottery of the TRB culture is discussed in considerable detail in the present work. One of the main aims of the discussion has been to provide the reader with an understanding of the various sequences which, at different times, have been worked out for each of the regional groups. Before we embark upon a detailed analysis, however, a few general comments may help the reader to appreciate the magnitude of the task and the seeming inconsistencies of TRB pottery research.

Firstly, the stylistically early TRB pottery is found over a much larger area than has generally been appreciated (Fig. 67). The concentration of research on the establishment of regional sequences is one of the reasons why this widely distributed early horizon has not always been recognised (but see Becker 1947, 200–16). Moreover, most of this early pottery is known from uncontexted finds, often recovered from bogs, and its placement within the early horizon is dependent upon comparison with the all too scarce assemblages from settlements.

Secondly, the reader must be warned that the quantity and quality of ceramic evidence varies considerably from one region to the next and this has an important influence on the direction of the discussion. Thus, the 'simplicity' of ceramic development in the Eastern and South-eastern TRB groups, for example, must in large measure reflect the poor database rather than the quality and amount of pottery produced in those regions: most of the pottery of the Eastern group survives as largely undiagnostic sherds, making stylistic interpretation very difficult. On the other hand, when one turns to the Danish or to the Dutch TRB ceramics the contrast is clearly apparent: the vast amount of available ceramics, the wide range of contexts within which they are encountered, and the distinguished history of ceramic studies all combine to give the impression of richness and of particularly advanced ceramic development. It goes without saying that, to the outsider, finding one's way through the plethora of ceramic styles is a daunting task. The writer has found it particularly hard first of all to understand the relationship between the various ceramic sequences and then to present them in such a manner that the uninitiated reader may still derive a modicum of comprehension.

It should also be realised that until recently the Danish ceramic sequence held a particular significance within the chronological ordering of the TRB culture. Because of the markedly more advanced research in Denmark, the Danish typo-chronologgy has served as a 'measure' for typo-chronological interpretation of the TRB culture outwith Denmark, a feature which in a number of instances has led to an 'unhealthy' reliance on the Danish scheme and to the continuing insistence of some scholars on matching it stage by stage in other areas.

Finally, although an attempt has been made to keep the discussion within the context of regional groups, there are a number of instances where a different procedure had to be followed. While Mecklenburg, for example, is generally considered as a region belonging to the Northern TRB group, clearly the ceramic development here took a course different from that observed in Denmark; therefore pottery from Mecklenburg is discussed separately. Similarly, the pottery known in the area of the Altmark, which has its own long history of research, shows similarities to the ceramics of Northern, Western and Southern groups and yet the specific geographical position of the Altmark at the crossroads of a number of geographical regions suggests that an individual ceramic style may have developed here precisely as a response to influences from a variety of sources. On the one hand, such an additional fragmentation of the already complex mosaic does tend to make an overall appreciation more difficult; on the other hand it reflects precisely the complexity of the material under consideration and the problems involved in researching into such a vast cultural complex.

4.1 The earliest TRB pottery on the North European Plain

Prehistoric culture is generally better documented, and thus offers greater opportunities for understanding the way in which it developed, in its fully crystallised form than in its initial phase. Yet it is the early stage that invariably holds the key information for discovering the original impulses and influences which, in a specific set of circumstances, came together to form a coherent cultural unit. Thus our discussion of the ceramic development of the TRB culture must begin with the evidence belonging to the earliest horizon. Such materials are scarce and widely distributed between the Vistula and the Elbe rivers: pottery of the so-called Rosenhof phase from north-western Germany (Holstein) and of the Sarnowo phase in central Poland (Kujavia) currently appear to identify the earliest ceramic horizon of the TRB.

In the valleys of the Vistula and Oder rivers, scholars recognise the earliest development of the TRB culture in the material of the *Sarnowo phase* (Chmielewski 1952; Gabałówna 1969a; 1971; Jażdżewski 1961 and 1965; Wiślański 1973 and 1979). The criteria for identifying this early stage are based upon stratigraphy (cultural layers underneath the Sarnowo earthen long barrows; Chmielewski 1952, 63 and 68; Gabałówna 1968, n. 2; 1969b, 45–7) as well as upon typological development of the ceramic forms (Fig. 11: 1–4; Gabałówna 1969a, 51; 1970a, 81; Kośko 1982a, 44). Material belonging to this phase has been found mainly in Kujavia, at a few settlement sites – Sarnowo 1A (Gabałówna 1969a, 54; 1969b, 51), Łącko (Kośko 1982a; 41; Domańska and Kośko 1983) – and in surface finds as well as in the votive bog deposits (Jażdżewski 1936, 194, Fig. 190).

Pottery constitutes the main diagnostic element of material culture; forms include funnel-necked beakers, two- and four-handled amphorae, flasks, bowls and flat clay discs (Fig. 11: 1–4). The funnel-necked beakers are rather low, squat, wide-mouthed vessels with relatively short necks and slightly everted rims; they display a gently curving profile and are entirely flat-based (Fig. 11: 1, 2). The amphorae from the above assemblages are known only in fragmentary form, but comparison with a number of more or less complete, typologically early vessels recovered from votive finds

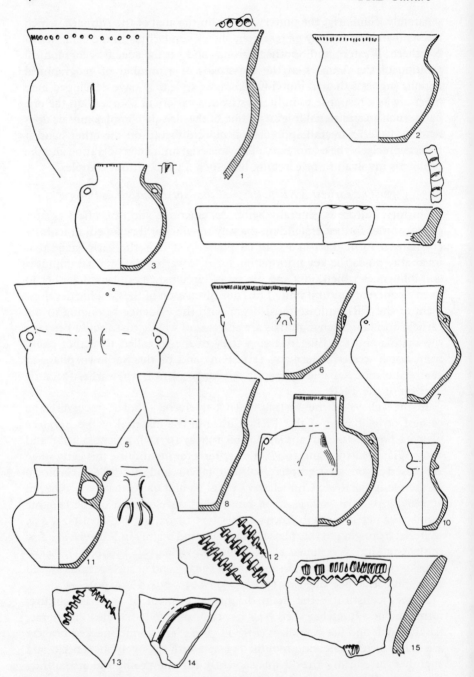

Figure 11 Eastern TRB group pottery of the Sarnowo (1–4) and Pikutkowo (5–15) phases: 1-Łącko, 2,4-Sarnowo, 3-Sadłużek, 5–9-Pitkutkowo, 10, 11-Obałki, 12–14-Gaj, 15-Wietrzychowice (Source: Chmielewski 1952; Wiślański 1979; Wiklak 1982; Domańska and Kośko 1983).

(Fig. 11: 3) suggests that some may have had a short cylindrical neck and a rounded body while others were egg-shaped with long, slightly everted rims; two or possibly four handles may have been attached to the upper belly or neck or both. Among bowls there are examples with curved or straight profiles, and the Sarnowo assemblages also contain sherds belonging to large storage vessels, some with strengthened rims and seemingly thicker walls. Flat clay discs (Fig. 11: 4) are a highly diagnostic element of the earliest Kujavian ceramic material and are found in two forms: either completely flat or displaying slightly raised rims.

Decoration of this early pottery is generally scarce (only 2 per cent at Łącko and 2.5 per cent at Sarnowo) and appears in the main to have been applied to beakers, although amphorae and clay disc sherds also bear decoration. The range of ornamentation is limited to a number of impressions made with a stick or similar implement; these take the form of stabs (the so-called 'stamp' impressions), or triangular, circular or comma-like impressions, usually forming an irregular, horizontal row below the vessel's rim. Large storage vessels have finger impressions on the thickened rim which could serve a decorative as well as a practical purpose, and finger impressions are commonly found on the rims of clay discs. Occasionally there are simple lugs (on amphorae) or knobs (on beakers). Applied decoration in the form of a clay ribbon is exceedingly rare and some beaker examples have single, vertical grooves on the upper part of the belly (Fig. 11: 1).

This early pottery is built with a coil technique, with joints between individual coils clearly visible along the broken sections. The clay itself shows various admixtures such as quartz, feldspar, granite, crushed shell, chamotte or mica. With the exception of clay discs, most of the pottery appears to be thin-walled and this is observed particularly at Łącko. These early assemblages, being the earliest TRB ceramics in Kujavia, show considerable uniformity of the Sarnowo phase. Materials from Łącko and barrow 8 at Sarnowo are particularly close in form, decoration and technology. They further underline the strong uniformity of the early material.

At Rosenhof, east Holstein, a Neolithic layer dated to between 4270 and 4000 BC and containing a mixed ceramic assemblage was found, separated from an earlier Ertebølle-Ellerbek layer by a gyttja deposit (Schwabedissen 1979a, Fig. 1). The pottery included such vessels as small, funnel-necked beakers with flat or rounded bases, which carried a simple decoration of rounded or irregular impressions under and/or on the rim (Fig. 12: 1, 3). Other forms included an undecorated, four-handled amphora, which showed traces of repair with birch resin and which Schwabedissen compared with an eastern (i.e. Baalberge) type (Fig. 12: 2); another version of the amphora may be represented by a short, funnel neck and some body sherds with the trace of a handle on the widest part of the pot. There were also large storage vessels with thickened rim and fingertip impressions

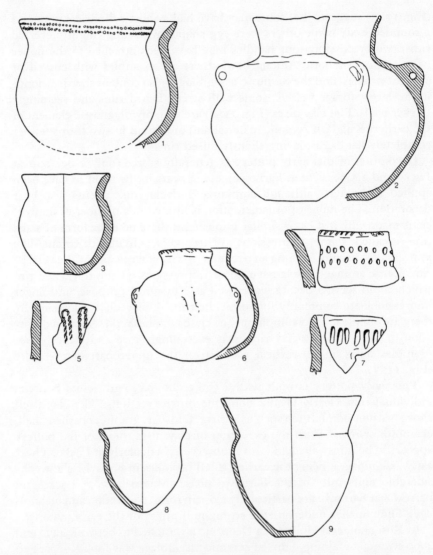

Figure 12 Early TRB pottery from north-west Germany: 1–3-Rosenhof, 5–7-Hüde,
8,9-Boberg (Source: Schindler 1953; Schwabedissen 1979c).

(considered by Schwabedissen as similar to Michelsberg forms; ibid., 168,
Fig. 2: 8); conical bowls and lugged vessels were also represented. Quite
remarkable were shallow, oval bowls (the so-called 'lamps') of a type
usually found within Ertebølle-Ellerbek contexts.

This mixed assemblage has been compared by Schwabedissen with a
number of other finds in northern Germany which likewise appear to be of
mixed character. In Lower Saxony, at the Hüde settlement on the Dümmer

Lake, there came to light a large ceramic assemblage which, at least in part, belongs to the TRB culture (Deichmüller 1963, 1965 and 1969; Kampffmeyer 1983). Unfortunately, the stratigraphy at Hüde is not reliable – the various levels were too compressed and the C-14 determinations, as well as pollen analysis, revealed a more or less uninterrupted occupation over a period of one and a half millennia. Hence the different pottery forms cannot be placed with confidence in any one of the levels.

On the basis of the frequency of appearance of various pottery types within the layers it was possible, however, to indicate different occupation stages. In the lowest level there were found mainly vessels with pointed bases and crudely manufactured large storage pots. Above this was the so-called *Dümmer Keramik* (Fig. 12: 6), which is of particular interest here for, while the pottery reveals connections with the Bischheim group forms (for instance round-based beakers with knob handles, various bowls and round-based storage vessels), it also shows elements which would not be out of place within an early TRB context. For example, there are notched rims, oblong or irregular stamp impressions (Fig. 12: 4, 5, 7) and even occasionally a simple cord decoration. These elements are comparable with some of the traits at Rosenhof; indeed some of the so-called *Dümmer Keramik* may represent an early TRB horizon comparable with that at Rosenhof. Above the *Dümmer Keramik* level there was pottery of the TRB proper, with beakers which by virtue of form as well as decoration belong to the more advanced TRB development in northern Germany (see below, Chapter 4.5).

Boberg, near Hamburg, produced pottery which, likewise, can be compared with the above-mentioned material (Fig. 12: 8, 9; point-based beakers, simple decoration) here also in close association with Rössen material (Schindler 1961). Stray finds from the north German moors are more difficult to classify. Typological and stylistic comparisons would allow us to include here finds from Alsensund, Deilmissen, Engern-Brinkhof or Eime (Schwabedissen 1958b), yet their interpretive value is subtantially reduced by their lack of context.

4.2 The ceramic sequence of the Eastern TRB group

The traditional typological sequence of the Eastern TRB group comprises four phases: the already discussed Sarnowo phase, Pikutkowo (or Early Wiórek), Wiórek and Luboń (Wiślański 1979, 175–97). The distinction between the Sarnowo and Pikutkowo phases is based upon the ceramic simplicity of the former and the stratigraphic evidence from the earthen long barrow cemetery at Sarnowo (Gabałówna 1968, 1969a and 1969b; Midgley 1985). The division between the Pikutkowo and Wiórek phases, however, is dependent upon the stylistic criteria alone, in particular the development of ornamental motifs (Chmielewski 1952; Gabałówna 1970a; 1971; Wiślański 1979).

Ceramic assemblages attributable to the *Pikutkowo phase* are known from settlement sites, for example Sierakowo and Pikutkowo (Niesiołowska 1967; Kośko and Prinke 1977) and it seems likely that a considerable number of earthen long barrows were built at this time, for example Sarnowo 1 (Chmielewski 1952), Leśniczówka (Jażdżewski 1936), Obałki, Wietrzychowice (see Midgley 1985 for detailed discussion). Some uncontexted finds, such as bog deposits from Malankowo and Bartoszewice may also be attributed to this phase. Intermediate forms between the early (Sarnowo) and later (Wiórek) phases have been noted by Chmielewski (1952, 22, for example the amphora from barrow No. 2, Fig. 3), and the publication of the pre-war excavations at a settlement site at Pikutkowo (Niesiołowska 1967; Gabałówna 1971) further drew attention to some forms revealing typological connections with both Sarnowo and Wiórek. The excavations at Sierakowo (Kośko and Prinke 1977) additionally confirmed the existence of an intermediate phase. In the sphere of ceramic development in Kujavia, the assemblages of the Pikutkowo phase thus bridge the gap between the simple pottery of the preceding Sarnowo and the more elaborate Wiórek phases.

Reviewing the pottery of the Pikutkowo phase we note the continuity of older forms, but the vessels show sharper profiles than those of Sarnowo and there is a clear distinction between the various parts of the pot (neck, belly and shoulder; Fig. 11: 5–9). Among the funnel-necked beakers we can distinguish two types: bowl-like beakers whose width is greater than their height (Fig. 11: 6) and tall slender forms where the height is equal to or frequently exceeds the width (Fig. 11: 5, 8); the contemporaneity of both forms is confirmed by their inclusion in the votive deposit from pit 25 at Pikutkowo (Niesiołowska 1967; Fig. 11: 5–9). The small beakers have distinct necks and bellies, the rims are everted and frequently pierced and there are horizontally pierced lugs on the neck/belly transition. The profiles of the tall beakers are clearly defined, necks may be slightly or considerably funnel-shaped, the widest part of the belly is above the middle of the vessel and the lower part narrows conically towards a flat base. They may or may not have pierced lugs under the rim or on the shoulder.

As in the previous phase, amphorae show either cylindrical or splayed necks with a more distinctively shaped belly, which is either biconical, egg-shaped or rounded (Fig. 11: 7, 9). The handles, two or four in number, are placed at the neck/belly transition or on the upper part of the belly. Some examples, such as at Pikutkowo, may have slightly concave bases. A vessel very similar to a Nordic lugged flask has been found at Pikutkowo, but such examples do not appear commonly in published illustrations and their frequency is unknown. Its relationship to the typical amphora is not certain and some vessels could be classed as either.

The diversity of the Pikutkowo ceramics is further seen in the wide range of bowls. A study of bowl profiles from Pikutkowo, Sierakowo and various earthern long barrows reveals forms ranging from concave, through straight-walled, everted, S-profiled, to strongly carinated forms. The bowls vary in size: examples from Sierakowo settlement range from 9 cm to 24 cm in diameter and some have knobs and protrusions. A new ceramic form is represented in the appearance of a collared flask (Fig. 11: 10; Chmielewski 1952; Gabałówna 1971). Earlier forms such as storage vessels or clay discs continue although the latter are not included in the Pikutkowo assemblage or in some of the barrows.

Ornamentation is more varied than in the preceding phase. There is an increase in the number of decorative elements as well as in the complexity of motifs. Under-rim decoration is predominant and involves a wide range of impressions: pits, rectangles, triangles, crescents etc. are vertically or obliquely impressed in a single, more rarely double, continuous row (Fig. 11: 6, 9) or arranged in groups. Fingertip impressions continue on rims of storage vessels and fingernail decoration may be found on the edges of collared flasks. Sometimes we encounter a simple zig-zag line made of individual impressions (Fig. 11: 15), a motif which heralds the rich rim decoration of the subsequent Wiórek phase.

Body decoration is less frequent; at Sierakowo this comprises only 0.3 per cent of all decoration. Mostly there are stamp impressions which may be arranged in vertical or horizontal motifs. Vertical grooves, either in groups or spread all over, also begin to appear, as does the so-called 'ladder' ornamentation (Fig. 11: 12, 13), which reaches its apogee in the Wiórek style. Amphorae in particular display 'ladder' ornamentation, which appears on the neck and upper part of the belly and may be simple, executed in a *tvaerstik* manner (Fig. 12: 12, 13) or more complex, involving vertical grooves filled in with horizontally impressed stamps. Sometimes the cavities in the ornamentation are filled with white paste. Applied decoration, in the form of thin clay strips, also makes an appearance, either as 'ribs' splaying from the amphorae and jug handles (Fig. 11: 11), or as horizontally placed crescents or M-shaped patterns (Fig. 11: 14).

In the *Wiórek phase*, which likewise is known from a number of settlement sites (such as Radziejów Kujawski and Zarębowo in Kujavia), all previous ceramic forms continue in use. Beakers and amphorae still remain dominant; beakers are either tall with long necks or small and bowl-like in form (Fig. 13: 1, 2). Several types of amphorae have been distinguished (Fig. 13: 3) and other forms include a variety of bowls, some wide-mouthed, others with a sharp carination (Fig. 13: 4, 8). There are also jugs (Fig. 13: 6) and collared flasks; new forms are represented by *ansa lunata* pots and collander-bottomed vessels (Fig. 13: 9). Clay discs are now becoming less common.

The main diagnostic element in the definition of the Wiórek phase, however, is ornamentation, which comprises a richer version of earlier motifs in both the variety of techniques and the profusion of different

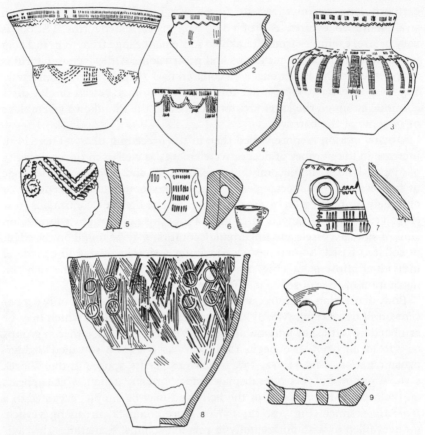

Figure 13 Eastern TRB group pottery of the Wiórek phase: 1-Modliborzyce, 2,4-Szlachcin, 3-Chełmża, 5-Zgierz, 6-Rusocin, 7,9-Zakrzew, 8-Inowrocław-Mątwy, (Source: Jażdżewski 1936; Wiślański 1979; Kośko 1981).

designs. It should be observed, however, that local differences are strong, with certain designs common in some areas and others typical elsewhere. The decorative techniques are varied and include impressed stamp, strokes, incision, grooves, *tvaerstik*, stab-and-drag and two-strand cord. Frequently a number of techniques are used in the execution of a pattern, highlighting even further the complexity of motifs. Decoration of fingertip or fingernail impressions continues along the rim of large storage vessels, but on beakers and amphorae ornamentation may cover a substantial part of the surface, being present on the rim (inside and out), on the neck and on the upper part of the belly, and occasionally extending right down to the base (Fig. 13: 1, 3). The commonest pattern below the rim involves a horizontal band of vertically impressed, longish stamps underlined below by one to three horizontal lines of zig-zags (Fig. 13: 1, 2, 3, 7), crosses, chequered patterns

(Fig. 13: 7) or lines of two-strand cord (Fig. 13: 4). In a number of vessels such a pattern is as rich on the inside of the rim as on the outside. On the neck, mostly in the case of amphorae, the same pattern may be repeated just above the shoulder. Belly decoration is commonly found on beakers and amphorae, and to a lesser degree it also appears on bowls and other forms.

Among the most diagnostic motifs we may note complex 'ladder' patterns (Fig. 13: 3), designs involving hanging triangles (Fig. 13: 1, 5), festoons (Fig. 13: 4) or semi-circles; occasionally a large part of the surface may be covered with an elaborate combination of motifs, as can be seen on some of the amphorae found within a ritual context (for example at Radziejów Kujawski; Fig. 14). Handles may also carry designs of grooves or various impressions (Fig. 13: 6). Among the more ambitious patterns we must include possible stylistic representations of the sun (Fig. 13: 5, 7), animals, wagons (Fig. 13: 8) and human figures. Zoomorphic vessels and animal figures are also encountered, although they appear to be more common in the south-eastern TRB group (see below, Chapter 4.3).

In 1936 Jażdżewski identified a 'younger' phase of the TRB culture, which he called *Luboń* (after a settlement site in central Poland; Jażdżewski 1936, 232). This now defines the final phase, a concept which to some degree still holds for the areas of Kujavia and Greater Poland. The connections with the remaining regions are now tenuous, and there are only individual manifestations in other areas (such as western Pomerania). Moreover, new cultural complexes such as the Globular Amphora and Radial Ware make a strong imprint, significantly influencing the style of various assemblages.

Substantial ceramic changes are apparent in the Luboń phase. Some forms disappear (collared flasks and flat clay discs) and the ratio of different forms also alters in relation to the preceding phase. The funnel-necked beakers now seem to be less common than bowls and amphorae; jugs and mugs increase in importance. Storage vessels still continue in use and a new ceramic form, the drum, also makes an appearance (Fig. 15: 2). Among the amphorae there are large forms, with a tall neck narrowing towards the rim and a rounded belly (Fig. 15: 4, 6), and smaller forms with a slightly flattened body. Handles are now less common than before and applied crescentic bands seem to take over their function (Fig. 15: 5, 6). Bowls are usually deep, conical and wide-mouthed, often with a conical body. The profiles of all the forms are smooth and the transition between the neck and belly is not clearly defined (Fig. 15: 1). Jugs are equipped with handles that protrude above the rim, a feature also commonly associated with round-bellied mugs (Fig. 15: 3). Since many vessels are wide-mouthed, decoration frequently appears in the interior (especially on bowls and beakers; Fig. 15: 1) and the commonest motifs include two- and three-strand cord impressions with zig-zags, festoons or chequerboard patterns below (Fig. 15: 1). Body ornamentation involves predominantly vertical or oblique bands of

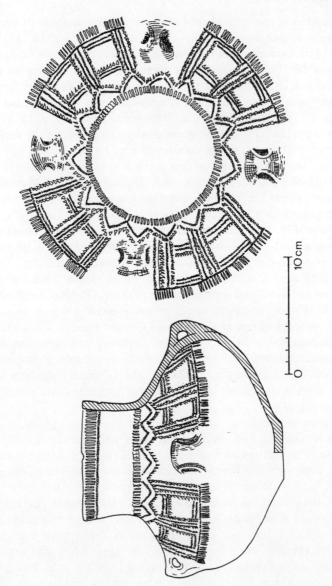

Figure 14 A richly decorated amphora from Radziejów Kujawski (Source: Kośko 1982a).

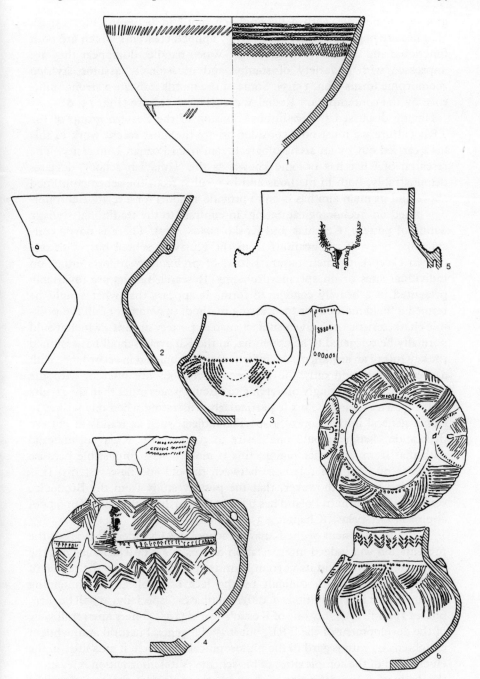

Figure 15 Eastern TRB group pottery of the Luboń phase: 1-Luboń, 2,3,5-
Mrowino, 4-Łojewo, 6-Kruszwica (Source: Jażdżewski 1936; Wiślański 1979;
Tetzlaff 1981; Kośko, 1983).

grooves, sometimes with a herringbone motif in between (Fig. 15: 4). Handles are now frequently replaced by applied crescents which are both functional and decorative (Fig. 15: 6). When handles do appear they are impressed with a variety of stamps and occasionally assume stylised zoomorphic forms (Fig. 15: 5). Some of the motifs indicate a strong influence by the contemporary Radial Ware (Baden) culture (Fig. 15: 6).

Having discussed the traditional division of the Eastern group of the TRB culture we must now consider briefly the most recent work in this field carried out by an archaeological team from Poznań University. The research of what has become known as the 'Kujavian school' deviates demonstrably, both in methods and in results, from the scheme outlined above and its main aim has been to provide a model for a relative chronology based on 'technological dating' in contrast to the traditional stylistic dating of pottery (Czerniak and Kośko 1980a, 247). There is now a considerable body of publications from the Kujavian school but, with one or two exceptions, their nature is that of preliminary reports either on individual sites or on specific problems. Research results are invariably presented in a heavily condensed form. It appears that what should be termed a 'field method' or 'processing method' (a notation of all the possible characteristics of a given subject such as pottery or flint), which would normally be relegated to an appendix, in the Kujavian school has assumed the key role of an argument. All information is tabulated in accordance with a specific code and only the briefest conclusions are offered, with the various authors seemingly preferring to discuss issues other than the results of their own research. This is particularly frustrating when one wishes to gain a general impression of a specific subject, such as trends in pottery decoration change; should one desire to compare the Kujavian material with that from any other region, this is more or less impossible because there are no points of reference between the old and new systems. It is interesting to note, however, that the pottery study from the Bronocice settlement in southern Poland has been based partly on the Kujavian school approach (see below, Chapter 4.3).

The chief exponent of the Kujavian school is Alexander Kośko, but the presentation and indeed interpretation of Kośko's typo-chronology of the TRB culture, which in its current form is applicable only to the region of Kujavia, is made very difficult by the lack of publications containing arguments for and definitions of different phases (especially, as will be seen, phases II and III). Only one of Kośko's works (1981) offers an overall view of the development of the TRB, but it is of a general natural and, while it enlightens us with regard to the philosophical approach, it aids little in the elucidation of the complexities of his scheme. Vital information relevant to the distinction and definition of the typo-chronological phases can only be secured through detailed study of the available articles dealing with individual sites (Kośko and Prinke 1977; Czerniak and Kośko 1980b; Kośko

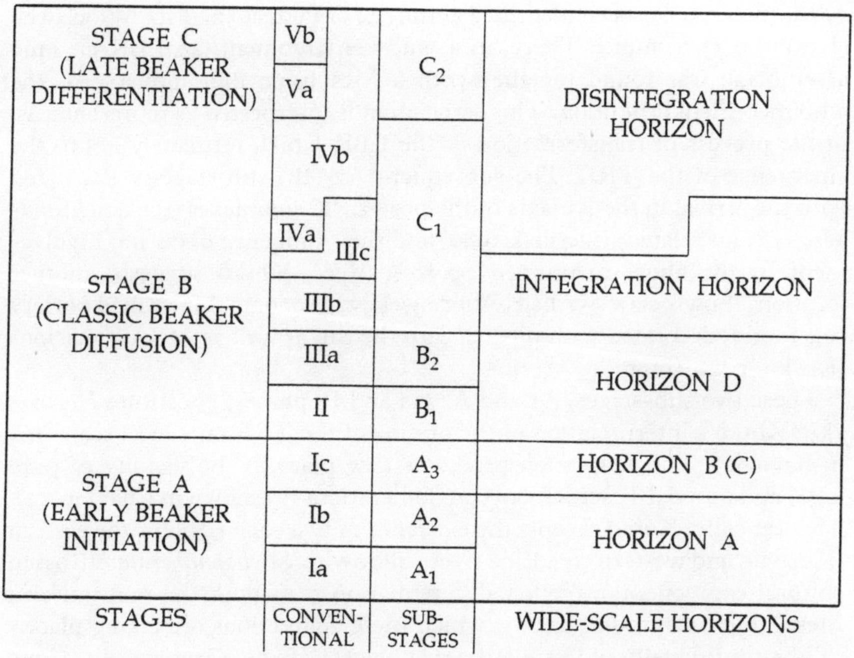

STAGES	CONVENTIONAL	SUB-STAGES	WIDE-SCALE HORIZONS
STAGE C (LATE BEAKER DIFFERENTIATION)	Vb / Va	C_2	DISINTEGRATION HORIZON
	IVb	C_1	
STAGE B (CLASSIC BEAKER DIFFUSION)	IVa IIIc	C_1	INTEGRATION HORIZON
	IIIb		
	IIIa	B_2	HORIZON D
	II	B_1	
STAGE A (EARLY BEAKER INITIATION)	Ic	A_3	HORIZON B (C)
	Ib	A_2	HORIZON A
	Ia	A_1	

Figure 16 Simplified version of Kośko's scheme for the development of the TRB culture in the European lowland region (Source: Kośko 1981).

1981, 1983 and 1988; Prinke and Weber 1983), from footnotes accompanying works of a more general character (Bednarczyk and Kośko 1974; Domańska and Kośko 1974 and 1983; Czerniak and Kośko 1980a; Kośko 1980, 1981, 1982a, 1982b and 1985) and from discussions with colleagues in Poland.

Kośko identifies three main development stages: A – *Proto-and Early Beaker* (also known as the *Initiation* stage), B – *Classic Beaker* (*Diffusion* stage) and C – *Late Beaker* (*Differentiation* stage). Each of these three stages is further subdivided (A: A1–3, B: B1–2, C: C1–2). Parallel with this is the so-called 'conventional' division of the TRB into five phases (I–V), which in their turn are broken into sub-phases giving a total of eleven typo-chronological units. Into this already complex scheme there is interwoven the additional theme of the development of the TRB (A–D, Integration and Disintegration Horizons), which outlines general tendencies in the spatial expansion of this complex in Kujavia and in the neighbouring regions of the European lowland (Fig. 16).

Stage A (*Early Beaker* or *Initiation*) includes the earliest phase of the TRB development (phase I); its three sub-stages A1–3 correspond to the three sub-phases Ia–c. The A1 (Ia) is seen as a period of adaptation of the already present LBK communities to the lowland environment, and diagnostic material has been identified at the site of Podgaj 32, distr. Włocławek (Kośko, pers. comm.). There, in a sandy environment, an LBK ceramic assemblage was found together with a Mesolithic flint industry of the Chojnice-Pieńki tradition. This association is interpreted as representative of the process of transformation of the LBK which ultimately led to the emergence of the TRB. The subsequent A2 (Ib) sub-stage is associated with the arrival in the Kujavia of the post-LBK complexes (the *Stichbandkeramik* and related; Czerniak 1980) and their influence upon and involvement in the above-mentioned process. Here, Kośko suggests another location, Inowrocław 95, distr. Włocławek, where some thin-walled pottery was found, decorated with pits beneath the rim as well as various incisions (Kośko, pers. comm.).

These two sub-stages, A1 and A2 (Ia and Ib phases) constitute *Horizon A* in Kośko's interpretation of the origins of the TRB on a local scale (i.e. in Kujavia). The adaptation processes take place in the vicinity of pure LBK and post-LBK settlement conglomerations (as shown in Chapter 2.2). Theoretically, Kośko accepts the existence of two such regions: the eastern (Kujavia) and western (the Elbe river valley with *Stichbandkeramik*/Rössen cultural components); further differentiation rests with the non-uniform Mesolithic background against which these adaptations are taking place.

The traditionally oldest TRB assemblages (of the Sarnowo phase) are assigned to the A3 sub-stage (Ic phase). In his discussion of the Łącko material Kośko suggested that assemblages from sites such as Łącko, Sarnowo 1 and Sarnowo A1 'reveal characteristics of a developed 'AB' style and should be placed in phase Ic or even at the Ic/II transition' (Domańska and Kośko 1983, 31). Incidentally, a similar opinion as to the typo-chronological position of the Sarnowo assemblage has been expressed by Gabałówna (1969b, 47). In terms of the spatial expansion of the TRB, phase Ic corresponds to the *B (C) Horizon* (the B horizon reflects developments within the great valley zone, while the C horizon refers to the larger part of the European lowland) and it is here that the earliest archaeologically visible differences in the TRB ceramics are noted, for example in Kośko's opposition of the Sarnowo/Łącko and Berlin-Britz materials (Kośko 1981, Fig. 14).

The next stage in Kośko's typo-chronological scheme is the *Stage B* (*Classic Beaker* or *Diffusion*), which involves the 'conventional' phases II and III. Phase II (sub-stage B1) is sometimes referred to as early Wiórek (this should not be confused with the same term used in the traditional division of the TRB, where it normally refers to the Pikutkowo phase). It includes such sites as Sierakowo, Leśniczówka and possibly Sarnowo 1. In the sphere of vessel technology, phase II pottery is distinguished from phase I by thicker walls (Kośko and Prinke 1977, Fig. 13) and by the appearance of non-vessel forms such as clay spoons and spindle whorls. In the vessel morphology Kośko argues for a parallel and mutually influential development of the TRB and post-LBK amphorae forms (Czerniak and Kośko 1980b, 47–50, Fig. 12). The main diagnostic elements for the definition of phase II, however, are in the pottery decoration and include the following: 1) ornamental motifs constructed from two or more decorative elements, 2) the appearance of regular stamp impressions and 3) shallow grooves on the belly of vessels, especially amphorae (ibid., n. 73). Other elements which may also be noted as indicative of phase II (but not necessarily of phase-defining quality) are features such as a relatively high proportion of decorated rims, a lack of interior rim decoration and a notable lack of any decoration involving cord impressions. At Sierakowo, moreover, Kośko still identifies LBK elements, such as applied knobs.

Phase II corresponds to the B1 sub-stage of the Classic Beaker stage, which is assumed to involve both internal (within Kujavia) and external (outwith Kujavia) expansion of the TRB, although this seems to be largely an intuitive assumption based on the evidence from the succeeding phase III. The internal expansion in Kujavia involves the establishment of peripheral settlement zones in areas not previously settled by farming communities, especially in the lake/maritime zone, where, however, some time-lag must be taken into consideration. By analogy an identical situation is assumed to be taking place in the area of Greater Poland and central Germany, although Kośko is not concerned with details of development there. The expansion of the TRB outwith the lowland environment into the upland regions (such as Little Poland or the Wolhynian Upland or Silesia) is assumed to be taking place simultaneously with the internal expansion. Again, the earliest archaeologically determined materials from the upland regions correspond in the main to phase III in Kujavia (for example Bronocice I; Kruk and Milisauskas 1983, 267), although some indications exist to suggest that this process may indeed have begun in Kośko's phase II (cf. Turkowice or Wrocław-Pracze; Wiślański 1979, 184).

Phase III of the TRB culture in Kośko's scheme is divided into three sub-phases (IIIa–c) which assume a sequential significance. Yet it is here that one encounters the greatest difficulty in appreciating the difference between individual sub-phases. With regard to this phase in particular there appears to be a notable lack of publications, not only of characteristic ceramic assemblages but also, more significantly, of the criteria employed by the 'Kujavian school' to distinguish between various assemblages and to account for their placement within one of the sub-phases. This paucity makes it very difficult for an outsider to determine which sites, previously defined simply as of Wiórek phase, should represent which sub-phase.

In a most general sense it is perhaps permissible to synchronise IIIa with the old Pikutkowo phase, while IIIb and IIIc appear to include the traditional Wiórek assemblages. This synchronisation is far from satisfactory, however, and the complexity of the problem is perhaps best reflected in Kośko's comment that only a few criteria for defining individual sub-phases are accepted by general scholarly opinion (Kośko, pers. comm.). Among the general characteristics which assume sequential significance are an increase in the overall number of decorated vessels, an expansion of the decoration over the vessel surface and a greater variety of decorative techniques. Prinke and Weber (1983, 40, Table 9), in their analysis of ceramic assemblages from phases III and IV, place a particular emphasis on decorative elements (for example complexity, intensity and variety of ornament, proportions of rim/belly decoration, percentage of specific decorative motifs etc.), to which they ascribe chronological values as a means of stylistic dating. Among the specific, phase-defining criteria the appearance of a zig-zag motif and the extension of decoration onto pottery handles mark the beginning of phase IIIa. The zig-zag motif in its simplest form of a stamp impression is found on pottery from Pikutkowo and Wietrzychowice (Jadczykowa 1970; Fig. 11: 15) as well as in a more complex arrangement at Gaj (Chmielewski 1952; Fig. 11: 12, 13).

Returning for a moment to the theme of spatial development within the TRB culture, the above-discussed phases II and IIIa constitute the *D Horizon* of a broadly understood central European area (Kośko 1981, 15 and 64–6, n. 36). The key factors involve a progressive deepening of differences between the western (Elbe valley) and eastern (Oder–Vistula valleys) regions. Simultaneously, the eastern region begins to undergo a development into lowland and upland phenomena, such as can be identified in Kujavia and Little Poland (with the resultant emergence of the South-eastern TRB group).

Among the diagnostic elements indicative of the beginning of phase IIIb, Kośko includes the appearance of interior rim decoration as well as ornamentation executed in two-strand cord (pottery from Zarębowo and Radziejów). At this stage within the Kujavian ceramic assemblages there appears what Kośko terms 'foreign' elements. In fact, the remainder of his 'conventional' scheme (IIIb–Vb) is defined predominantly by decoration for which sources are sought outside Kujavia (ibid., Fig. 7). It is within phase IIIb that we are faced with the so-called Mątwy phenomenon – the appearance within the TRB assemblages of a variable amount of pottery sherds which are technologically different and ornamented with bands executed with a multiple tooth-comb (Fig. 13: 8; Jażdżewski 1936, 323; Kośko 1981; 74–91, Plates XV–XXV; 1988, 44–67). Pottery of this type has been traced directly to the Tripolye culture and, if the attribution is correct, then it is chronologically and chronologically important.

The IIIc phase is also defined on the basis of 'foreign' stylistic elements, this time derived from the geographically nearer region of Greater Poland. Prinke and Weber (1983; Prinke, pers. comm.) argue for renewed contacts between Kujavia and Greater Poland, pointing to complex 'ladder' motifs (which they call ornamental Baroque) as originating in the latter region and being transferred into Kujavia. While there is no *a priori* reason for doubting contacts and influences between Kujavia and Greater Poland, the difficulty lies in verifying this process. The TRB culture material from Greater Poland is only superficially known and classified according to traditional terms; as such it simply cannot be used as a chronological indicator in support of narrowly defined ceramic horizons.

Phases IIIb and IIIc constitute the *Integration Horizon* within the TRB culture spatial development theme (Kośko 1981, 66–70). This horizon represents the most dynamic stage of the TRB: the expansion from the central zones and the establishment of permanent settlement in the peripheral areas which had remained unoccupied by the LBK and post-LBK communities. This involves the crossing of ecological barriers and confirms the leading role now assumed by the TRB communities in the cultural shaping of the European lowland. It is within this horizon that Kośko introduces the concept of the 'Eastern TRB group' with four centres that differ in their internal dynamics as well as in their colonising potential. A key role is still attributed to the Kujavian communities, but groups in the areas of northern Greater Poland and the lower Oder were now beginning to express their individuality and separate identity, a process that ultimately led to the formation of the new cultural complexes of the Globular Amphora and Corded Ware cultures.

Assemblages ascribed to phases IV and V form the final *C (Late Beaker)* or *Differentiation* stage and represent a period of profound change within the TRB, resulting in a complete disintegration of this cultural cycle. In terms of the traditional nomenclature most of the Kujavian assemblages correspond to the Luboń phase. Phases IV and V seem to be at least partly contemporary (towards the end of IV) and are geographically discrete, with V (the Radziejów group) apparently confined to the black earth zone of central Kujavia. Amongst the criteria initiating this Late Beaker stage is the introduction of three-strand cord impressions, which are most commonly used to decorate the interior of wide bowls and beakers (Fig. 15: 1). At the earliest that is seen in the early Luboń style (IVa) with no traces of Baden culture. Throughout the two phases, differing external influences are ascribed chronological values. For example, the early Baden elements, initiating renewed contacts with the south, appear at the end of phase IV (IVb at Papros; Kośko 1981) and this trend continues into phase V. In phase Va they are evidenced in the vertically grooved and star-shaped motifs (Fig. 15: 6); the same assemblages apparently also reveal some western (Walternienburg II/Bernburg I) elements, for example in ceramic types (drums) or decoration (herringbone and leaf motifs; Fig. 15: 14). In phase Vb the latter lapse into insignificance and give way to the developed Baden culture patterns such as may be noted on the ceramic assemblages of Radziejów and Opatów.

These two final, 'conventional' phases of the TRB represent the last horizon within the culture's development, that of the *Disintegration*

Horizon (Kośko 1981, 70–1). The chronology and chorology of the breaking up of the TRB are variable and the precise nature of the processes
involved is still poorly understood. An important role is played, however,
by the southern, that is Baden, influence as well as by the impact of the
growing and potentially expansive Globular Amphora culture.

The above scheme, so complex and so elegant in its design, has been
described here as a classic example of the traditional belief that, once one
knows the ceramic sequence, one is bound to understand the way in which
a culture developed; this of course is not the case. It is quite clear that this
ceramic sequence has been developed partly in response to the dissatisfac-
tion with the traditional typo-chronology of the Eastern group, which lacks
a mechanism for identifying subtle differences in the way in which ceramic
styles may have developed throughout the different areas of the Eastern
group. Moreover, one has little doubt that the scheme has been conceived
through an extensive background knowledge of the TRB culture within
and outwith Kujavia; hence we encounter the 'Horizon' themes which are
meant to signify the expansion of the TRB culture on a local as well as a
wider scale. But these processes, so cogently perceived, are not in any way
illuminated by reference to the mere ceramic development in Kujavia; the
recognition of yet another decorative motif or yet another ceramic sub-
phase tells us very little about the way the TRB culture developed. This is
an important point because, as will become clear in the later part of this
book, many of the themes raised by Kośko are immensely valid, and the
ceramic scheme has been designed not merely to allow the slotting in of new
assemblages, but also to provide a dynamic framework for the development
of the culture. This is a task that still remains to be accomplished, and neat
typo-chronological ceramic schemes are not very likely to play a key role in
this process.

4.2.1 Western Pomerania

Because of the specific nature of Pomeranian assemblages, their peripheral
geographical position, and the rather uneven distribution of finds, the
ordering of Pomeranian material has been based on typo-chronologies
worked out for the Eastern and Northern groups (Siuchniński 1972;
Jankowska 1980). While perhaps inevitable in the light of present knowledge, such an approach is far from satisfactory because it tends to synchronise events in two (or more) areas on the basis of a single criterion – in
this case stylistic similarities in the pottery. As such it rarely takes into
account the time difference involved in contacts between the central and
peripheral zones or, indeed, the innovatory or conserving nature of the
communities involved. It appears that not only more research but a fundamental change in approach are necessary before the Pomeranian material
can be assessed independently.

So far Pomeranian ceramic assemblages have not revealed materials comparable with the earliest TRB in the Eastern group. Siuchniński (1972, 65–6), in his typo-chronological analysis, was unable to indicate any assemblage or individual finds which could be included in Becker's pan-European A/B horizon (the Sarnowo-Rosenhof horizon). He did accept the existence of a hypothetical early phase for Pomerania, however, with the proviso that the obvious lack of such finds was a reflection of poor research rather than of a different development of the TRB in this region.

The question of such an early horizon in Pomerania is naturally linked to our understanding of the development of the TRB in each of the formative centres and its subsequent expansion over the whole of the lowland zone. Arguments pertaining to this problem are outlined in the chapter dealing with the origins of the TRB (Chapter 8.5). In the present context we should merely note that the typologically earliest material is so far represented by one ceramic assemblage, that from Kosin (Wiślański and Czarnecki 1970). The pottery forms (funnel-necked beakers, two- and four-handled amphorae and flat clay discs), as well as the scanty decoration (rows of stamp impressions below the rim), suggest that this assemblage should be placed somewhere towards the early horizon, when the TRB is already established in Kujavia and the process of lowland expansion has begun.

The next development stage of the TRB culture in Pomerania, especially around the lower Oder, is rather better known and includes a whole range of assemblages, which are generally similar to those of the Wiórek phase of the Eastern group (Siuchniński 1972; Wiślański 1979; Jankowska 1980 and 1983). The situation is far from simple, however, because as already mentioned, some of the assemblages containing typical Wiórek elements (especially ornamental motifs) also reveal traits alien to the Eastern group, for which parallels can be found in the northern milieu (Scandinavia or Mecklenburg). To complicate matters even further, a number of finds also include pottery decorated with three-strand cord. This element, which is diagnostic of the Luboń phase in the Eastern group, is in Pomerania found in assemblages with clear Wiórek affinities, as well as with the materials of the so-called Ustowo group, which represents the final stage of the TRB culture in the lower Oder region.

Technologically the Pomeranian pottery is different from that of the Eastern group. Clay used in the production of vessels always contains a deliberate admixture of temper – most commonly medium- to coarse-grained sand or crushed rocks (Jankowska 1980, 31). Most of the vessel forms correspond to the types present in the Eastern group, but among the funnel-necked beakers we may note a number of examples with different proportions, such as vessels characterised by a small base, strongly conical body and widely splayed neck (Fig. 17: 4, 6, 7), and beakers with a weak profile and poorly defined segments. From the point of view of decoration

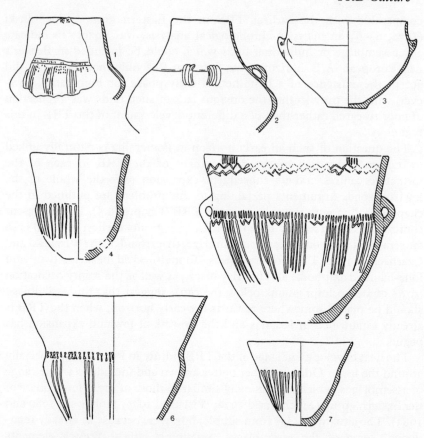

Figure 17 TRB pottery from western Pomerania: 1–3-Ustowo, 4–7-Łupawa
(Source: Siuchniński 1969; Jankowska 1980; Weber 1983).

the most diagnostic features are the technique and certain ornamental
motifs.

Good examples of such mixed character assemblages come from earthen
long barrows such as Wartin (Siuchniński 1969, 200–3, Plate XXVI) or
Krępcewo (Wiślański, pers. comm.), but especially from settlement sites
such as Miedwiecko, Kisielice and Wolin, the latter being the westernmost
site in which Wiórek traits are dominant (Jankowska 1983, Fig. 4). A study
of these and other, less well-documented assemblages shows that stamp
impressions, while reasonably common, are not as overwhelmingly dominant as in the Eastern group. On the other hand grooves and channels,
rarely encountered in the Eastern group material but common in the north,
are regularly found in Pomerania (Fig. 17: 1, 4–7), as indeed is the stab-
and-drag technique.

Among the motifs one may regularly observe northern elemens such as
vertical grooves (in continuous or interrupted bands around the body of

beakers; Fig. 17: 4, 6, 7); occasionally they may be combined with an Eastern group motif such as a 'ladder'. Belly decoration which, with the exception of amphorae, plays a lesser role in the Eastern group, is commonly found in Pomerania and on occasions is reminiscent of the rich 'carpet' designs of northern vessels. Typical Wiórek designs are particularly clearly seen at Wolin; they include horizontal bands of stamps bordered by a single or multiple zig-zag lines, 'ladders', oblique checks, festoons and such elements as handles (Siuchniński 1969, 189–90, Plates XXII–XXIII). A relatively large proportion of these ornaments are executed by a combination of grooves and stab-and-drag, however, further underlining the mixing of influences derived from various sources. A purely local, Pomeranian feature seems to be the placement of decoration along the neck/shoulder transition, especially on the beakers (Fig. 17: 6), a trait only sporadically encountered in either the Eastern or the Northern groups.

The precise interpretation of cord decoration, especially the three-strand variety, is difficult to determine. As already noted, no finds which correspond fully to the Eastern Luboń phase are known from Pomerania. However, a number of Wiórek-affiliated finds do contain sherds with unmistakably Luboń designs, for example some from Wielawino and Kisielice, (Siuchniński 1969, 50 and 55, Plates III and V; Jankowska 1983, 155). All these finds come from old excavations and in some instances the materials have been lost and our information is derived from old sketches; it is thus difficult to determine whether we are dealing with one or several settlement phases. On analogy with the Łupawa complex (see below, pp. 69–71) one may suggest, however, that the Pomeranian finds represent a horizon in which the Luboń style was already well developed in the Eastern group but only one or two of its elements were accepted in Pomerania.

Apart from the Wiórek-related ceramics, cord decoration is also found in association with yet another group of assemblages, which seem to belong to the final stage of the Pomeranian TRB (or, more precisely, of the lower Oder area). The idea of such a later horizon dates back to the 1930s when Umbreit (1937), on the basis of a different pottery style from the Brandenburg settlement at Berlin-Britz, postulated the youngest development phase of the TRB in this area. However, this suggestion was soon forgotten and only re-emerged in response to assemblages that were recovered during the excavations at Cedynia, distr. Chojna (Siuchniński 1969, 100–2) and Ustowo, distr. Szczecin (ibid., 158–60), since the pottery recovered seemed to be stylistically similar to that from Berlin-Britz (the German material is now lost). Thus Siuchniński (1972, 72–5) signalled the existence, in the lower Oder region, of a later TRB horizon which he provisionally named the Ustowo-Britz phase. Subsequently, it entered the literature as the Ustowo group, chronologically connected with the late Luboń phase and located in the lower Oder and adjacent Mecklenburg-Brandenburg region (Wiślański 1979, 195).

The Ustowo group is represented to date at four large settlement sites (Ustowo, Berlin-Britz, Cedynia and Gorzów Wielkopolski) with only sporadic single finds. The criteria for the distinction of this phase remain, to a large degree, in the sphere of ceramics. Technologically, the pottery represents a late TRB stage, mainly through the dominance of vessels made from coarsely tempered clay (Siuchniński 1981, 141; Szczurek 1981, 162). In comparison with both the earlier local phase and the Luboń stage of the Eastern group there is an impoverished assortment of forms, comprising mainly wide-mouthed bowls, buckets, forms transitional between beakers and bowls, some amphorae and flat clay discs (Fig. 17: 1–3). A slightly wider range was found at Gorzów Wielkopolski (Szczurek 1981, 167, Figs 1 and 2), where we also encounter a variety of conical bowls, jugs and mugs with protruding handles, all examples apparently having good parallels at the Berlin-Britz settlement.

Decorative techniques include grooving, stab-and-drag, cord impressions and the frequent use of applied decoration. Cord impressions are predominantly found decorating the interior of wide-mouthed bowls, and some amphorae display belly decoration of bands of vertical grooves broken up by the vertical zones of stroked forming angular motifs. Applied decoration is very common and appears in the form of handles, knobs and protrusions which are often placed singly in pairs or in small groups at the neck/belly transition (Fig. 17: 2). A highly diagnostic element is provided by crescentic hand-grips, which regularly appear on bowls and buckets (Fig. 17: 3).

The status of these assemblages as a separate, late TRB group, still remains to be verified. So far, the concept of this group has been based on similarities in ceramic assemblages, and the dangers involved in using this one criterion have already been discussed. The identification of the Ustowo-Britz phenomenon requires a wider research basis, considering not only pottery but also aspects such as settlement and economy. It is of course possible that we are beginning to observe here a phenomenon similar to that of the Radziejów group in Kujavia, a highly localised late formation. There are, clear differences, however, for example in the geographically wider range of the Ustowo-Britz finds (a distance of about 150 km separates Berlin-Britz from Gorzów Wielkopolski) and in the very scattered distribution of sites. On the other hand, it is equally possible that at this late stage of the TRB culture certain developments, even in geographically distant areas, were following a particular, as yet not clearly visible norm, which gives them the appearance of unity. In this context it may be more feasible to think about the lower Oder river not so much as a boundary separating groups, but as an artery that played a crucial role in the dissemination of elements and ideas over a large area.

A discussion of the Pomeranian TRB cannot be complete without reference to a rather isolated complex in the central part of the region. This has

recently been identified through a series of excavations in the vicinity of the
Łupawa river, and has therefore become known in literature as the Łupawa
group (Jankowska 1980, 4). This group, which occupies an area of 250 km^2
and to date numbers about twenty sites, is of special importance because the
excavations included not only a permanent settlement site but also contemporary cemeteries, thus offering an unusual insight into the settlement
strategy of the TRB. The idiosyncratic nature of the Łupawa group is
revealed not only in its relative geographical isolation, but also and primarily
in the recovered material culture (pottery, flint etc.). While undoubtedly an
integral part of the TRB culture complex, the Łupawa group none the less
reveals features which give it a very specific character and underline the
diversity of adjustment and adaptation of which the lowland communities
were capable.

For the present we may concern ourselves briefly with the ceramic
assemblages of the Łupawa group. Technologically, the pottery conforms
to the Pomeranian standard, containing large amounts of admixture (sand,
crushed pottery or rocks) and on occasion giving the impression of rock
pieces cemented together with clay (ibid., 106). Ceramic forms include the
usual assortment of vessels typical of other regions: beakers, amphorae,
bowls, buckets, collared flasks and clay discs; as elsewhere, funnel-necked
beakers are dominant (up to 74.7 per cent; ibid., 109). Many beakers reveal
similarities with Nordic rather than Eastern types (Fig. 17: 4, 6, 7), but
some are obviously local variants, such as the wide-mouthed examples
where the neck/belly transition can hardly be seen in profile and is often
merely marked by decoration (Fig. 17: 7). Another typical local feature is
the narrow base and there are a few examples of vessels with bases that are
either round or pointed. According to Jankowska (1980, 121), the beakers
of Łupawa are related to the northern tradition, indicating the mixed nature
of elements that make up this complex, but they also highlight the problem
of frequently illusory connections with distant regions (do the pointed
bases really relate to the Michelsberg tradition, as the excavator would
argue?).

The most salient feature of the Łupawa pottery is its decoration, which
underlines the mixed provenance of individual elements that give this
assemblage its unusual character. First and foremost among the decorative
techniques are various forms of grooving, deep, shallow, stab-and-drag,
which account for 53.3 per cent of decoration in the Poganice settlement
material, while 33.8 per cent of decoration is made by various stamp
impressions. Other techniques, for example strokes, stabs and applied
decoration, are also known, but they appear to be of considerably lesser
importance (ibid., 124). The richest decoration appears on the belly of
beakers and amphorae, while rim decoration tends to be confined to beakers
and bowls; the latter can be decorated on the interior as well as exterior
surfaces. It is interesting to note that, unlike in the Eastern group, the

motifs executed under the rim are rarely repeated on the belly of the same vessel. While the beakers form the largest group of decorated pots, it is the amphorae that are ornamented with all the usual motifs such as circles, geometric figures and schematic representations (ibid., Fig. 17: 11).

Jankowska identified twenty-one different ornamental motifs (1980, 133–4), of which the commonest are the northern motif of either segmented or continuous vertical grooves found predominantly on the lower parts of beakers (Fig. 17: 4, 6, 7), and the eastern motif of an impressed stamp. Both motifs are found either singly, or in combination where they form more complex designs (Fig. 17: 6). Another eastern motif is the zig-zag; it appears as a single, double or multiple line which may be continuous or segmented (Fig. 17: 5). Among the less common but interesting motifs we should note the 'ladder', which may be single, double, straight or oblique.

In the ceramic material available from the cemeteries, Jankowska (1983, 157) distinguished three separate styles of pottery which need not, however, indicate chronological differences. One style is formed by wide-mouthed beakers with weak profiles, whose neck/belly transition is often marked by a row of stamps supplemented by a segmented pattern of vertical grooves (Fig. 17: 4, 6, 7). She compared such vessels with what was termed by Jażdżewski (1932, 90–1) the Moltzow style, a style found predominantly in eastern Mecklenburg. The second style includes vessels that have strong parallels in the north and east of the TRB and whose local character is expressed, for example in an eastern-style decoration imposed on a northern-form vessel (Fig. 17: 5). The third style includes slender beakers with clearly defined necks, small bases and grooved belly decoration. An additional component of this group is bowls, richly decorated inside and/or outside the rim (Jankowska 1932, Fig. 6).

The pottery from the cemeteries has clear parallels in the settlement material, but all the styles are commonly encountered. This makes it difficult to determine their chronological relationship. The chronological position of the Łupawa group is generally synchronised with the fully developed Wiórek style of the Eastern group of the TRB and the old sequence of EN-C and MN I of the Northern TRB group (Jankowska 1980, 154–6; Weber 1983, 46–53). The internal chronology of the Łupawa group is far from clear, but it is nevertheless possible to see an interesting criterion in the appearance of cord decoration. This appears on some of the pottery from the Poganice settlement as well as some from the adjacent cemeteries, and is found predominantly on bowls. It forms multiple horizontal lines or festoons, or it may fill triangular spaces. The chronological difference between assemblages with and without cord decoration seems to be documented at the long barrow cemetery near Łupawa, where the two groups of ceramics have been identified (Wierzbicki, pers. comm.). The first group, indisputably associated with the construction of the cemetery, consists of beakers with vertical grooves and sherds with stamp and zig-zag decoration. The second, chronologically later assemblage, located only in the vicinity of the barrows, is represented mainly by bowls with two-strand cord decoration. While the situation at the Poganice settlement is less clear, possibly because of long occupation and more complex stratigraphy, a similar pattern comprising a phase without cord decoration followed by a phase with cord decoration, is also indicated (Jankowska 1980, 132–3; 1983, 159). Unfortunately the precise chronological position of the Łupawa group is still difficult to define, mainly in view of the scarcity and inconsistency of the available C-14 dates.

4.3 The ceramic sequence of the South-eastern TRB group

The ceramic material from the South-eastern TRB group, while abundantly present in the large, permanent upland settlements such as Ćmielów (Podkowińska 1950, 1952 and 1961) and Gródek Nadbużny (Kowalczyk 1956, 1957 and 1958) as well as at smaller settlement sites such as Zawarża (Burchard 1981), still remains to be studied adequately; one hopes that prompt presentations of the Bronocice settlement material (Kruk and Milisauskas 1977, 1979, 1982, 1983 and 1985) will set a precedent for the future. Apart from this obvious lack of publication of the basic source material, other factors also make it difficult to present the South-eastern TRB pottery. Firstly, we encounter here a rather peculiar distribution of the TRB sites: they form dense concentrations on the loess uplands (the Lublin-Wolhynian upland, Sandomierz upland) separated by virtually empty (unresearched?) areas (Kruk 1980, 48–53, Maps 3 and 4), giving an impression of seemingly unrelated groupings. Secondly, particularly striking is the fact that, while scholars regularly indulge in comparison and synchronisation of the South-eastern materials with those from distant areas and other regional groupings (Wojciechowski 1970 and 1981; Bukowska-Gedigowa 1975; Burchard 1981; Kruk and Milisauskas 1983), no attempt has yet been made to present a coherent sequence of pottery development for the South-eastern group as a whole. Thus it is very difficult to offer a detailed discussion of the South-eastern ceramics and the comments which follow must be regarded as of a general nature.

It must be said straight away that even a perfunctory glance at the available material reveals that the early South-eastern pottery is not early in the same sense, for instance, as the assemblages of the Eastern TRB such as Łącko or Sarnowo. The earliest dated materials (Gródek Nadbużny, Bronocice I; see Chapter 5.2) are typologically well developed and do not compare with early forms elsewhere. While such assemblages may, of course, be the earliest in their respective locations, they need not automatically represent the earliest horizon in the South-eastern TRB group. This problem is inextricably related to our understanding of the appearance of the TRB culture in the south-east and is discussed in more detail in

Chapter 8. We may note, however, that the assemblages dated to around 5000 BP derive from the well-established settlements on the loess upland and are therefore likely to represent the TRB in its developed and mature form. Little research has yet been directed at the non-loess environment, which reflects conditions similar to those of the European lowlands, and it is precisely these areas which may hold the key information pertaining to the process of initial colonisation of the south-east.

In each of the denser individual concentrations of the TRB finds, there are assemblages which may pre-date the large settlement horizon. Thus, in Silesia, two rather primitive-looking amphorae have been found at Wrocław-Pracze (Fig. 18: 1; Wiślański 1979, Fig. 90: 9) and these are generally ascribed to the earliest (in the traditional A/B sense) horizon of the TRB and paralleled with the Sarnowo-type material from the Eastern group. While there are no *a priori* objections to the early presence of the TRB in Silesia, we should remember that this is the only find of its kind in the region and it requires verification. We should also bear in mind the possible votive nature of this find (a Neolithic well?) and, in such a context, the obviously archaic form of the vessels may be indicative of their function rather than their chronology.

In the western part of the Little Poland area there is evidence of short-lived settlement episodes (surface scatters or groups of five to ten pits) at sites such as Kraków-Nowa Huta or Brzezie (Burchard 1981, 224–5). A common feature of these ceramics is the use of relatively poorly tempered clay and scanty decoration involving simply rows of horizontal stamps. To the east, on the Lublin-Wolhynian plateau, some finds have also been claimed as belonging to the very early phase. We may mention a large, rough-surfaced funnel-necked beaker from Turkowice (Fig. 18: 2; Wiślański 1979, 184), which differs stylistically and technologically from the rest of the material recovered on this site (Jastrzębski, pers. comm.) or pottery from Sobiecin (Sulimirski 1968, Table 7), which shows some resemblance to the early forms of the Eastern TRB group. Moreover, at Gródek Nadbużny pottery recovered during recent excavations has also revealed early (i.e. pre-classic phase) TRB features (Jastrzębski, pers. comm.). On the whole, however, these are sporadic examples which need to be verified by further investigation.

The greater proportion of ceramic material of the South-eastern TRB group may, however, be attributed to the so-called classic phase and it is here that most of the pottery from the large, upland settlements belongs. The classic phase currently appears as a relatively broad horizon, spanning a period from about 5000 BP to 4500 BP. While the basic vessel inventory does not differ significantly from that in other areas, in that we commonly encounter amphorae, storage vessels, mugs, jugs and collared flasks, although funnel-necked beakers are perhaps less frequently found, the characteristic feature is the wide range of variants within each category

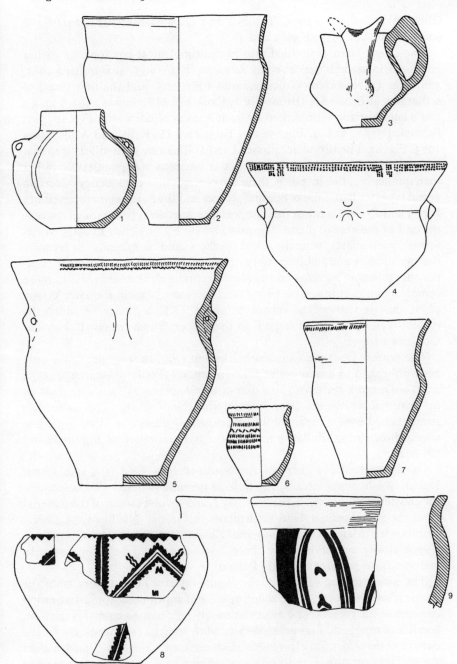

Figure 18 Pottery from the South-Eastern group: 1-Wrocław Pracze, 2-Turkowice, 3,4-Zawarża, 5-7-Niedźwiedź, 8,9-Gródek Nadbużny (Source: Wiślański 1979; Burchard 1981; Jastrzębski 1985).

(Bukowska-Gedigowa 1975, Tables I and II; Wiślański 1979, 241; Kruk and Milisauskas 1983, Figs 3 and 4).

The *classic phase* is divided into two chronological horizons: an earlier one, seen in assemblages such as Zawarża (Fig. 18: 3, 4; Burchard 1981, 226, Fig. 3), Nosocice (Wojciechowski 1981, 208) and the first phase of settlement at Bronocice (Bronocice I; Kruk and Milisauskas 1983, Fig. 3); and a later horizon represented by such finds as Niedźwiedź (Fig. 18: 5–7; Burchard 1981, 228–9, Fig. 5) and Bronocice II (Kruk and Milisauskas 1983, Fig. 4). The Bronocice phases I and II illustrate particularly well that differences between the earlier and later horizons are quantitative rather than qualitative. For instance, there are changes in the frequency of certain vessel types: collared flasks become scarcer and the *ansa lunata* mugs (ibid., Figs 3 and 4) yield some of their importance to other types of mugs towards the end of the classic phase. We may also note a tendency in some vessel forms, particularly funnel-necked beakers and amphorae, to acquire sharper profiles and, while pottery ornamentation involves the same components (stamps, zig-zags and applied decoration), they are used in more complex motifs during the later stage. It is also during the later classic phase that we witness the expansion of the TRB in Silesia, of which the earliest well-documented stage is in the Upper Silesia region (Bukowska-Gedigowa 1975).

The pottery from the Ćmielów settlement (Fig. 19: 1–4) has so far only been published in a number of interim reports (Podkowińska 1950, 1952 and 1961), but a series of C-14 dates (see Chapter 5.2) places the bulk of the material within the later stage of the classic phase. This is further strengthened by a comparison of Ćmielów and Bronocice II assemblages, which show strong similarity in the form and decoration of amphorae and tall beakers.

On the eastern periphery of the South-eastern TRB (the area of the Lublin-Wolhynian plateau), the bulk of ceramic material also belongs to the classic phase, known here as *Gródek I*, and involves some of the material from the permanent upland settlements at Gródek Nadbużny, Leżnica, Grzybowice Małe, Szychowice and Zimne (Jastrzębski, pers. comm.). Typologically and stylistically these assemblages can be compared with material from the area of Little Poland.

The most striking feature of the South-eastern TRB pottery from the classic phase, however, is the zoomorphic and anthropomorphic decoration on some of the vessels. The most commonly represented animal is the ram; handles of mugs and jugs are decorated with stylised ram heads. By far the richest collection of such vessels derives from Ćmielów (Podkowińska 1961). Here, in one of the grain storage pits (no. 180), which contained thirty-three pots, were found four mugs each with a single ram's head, two jugs each with a double ram handle (Fig. 19: 3), and a broken handle fragment; many other fragments were found throughout the site. Apart

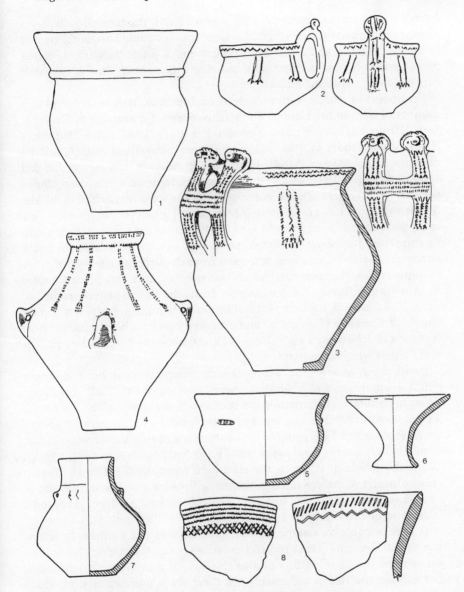

Figure 19 Classic and late phase pottery from the South-Eastern group: 1–4-Ćmielów, 5–7-Pietrowice Wielkie, 8-Janówek (Source: Wiślański 1979).

from having handles decorated with a ram's head, the pots also display a similar decoration of their respective segments (a double horizontal zig-zag line under the rim and a vertical arrangement of single 'ladder' or related motif) and it is possible that all these elements combine in the symbolic expression of a specific concept.

Fragments of vessels with ram-decorated handles have been found at a number of sites on the Lublin-Wolhynian upland, for example at Krężnica Jara, Klementowice, Nałęczów Kolonia, Las Stocki and Gródek Nadbużny (Podkowińska 1961, 53; Plate XIX: 1). Recent excavations at the latter site unearthed a double ram-handled jug (Jastrzębski, pers. comm.), which had apparently been placed as a votive deposit underneath a clay oven. Since ram-handled vessels appear commonly in the eastern periphery of the South-eastern TRB group it is interesting to observe that, with a few exceptions such as a jug from Mogiła 62 (Burchard 1981, Fig. 2: i) or a ram figurine from Jordanów (Wiślański 1979, Fig. 137: 5), such finds are rarely encountered elsewhere. None has come from the Bronocice settlement, for example, although representative art was not unknown there (see Chapter 8). Among the forms of decoration found in the South-eastern group we should also note a stylised representation of a human figure on a mug handle at Ćmielów (Fig. 19: 2) and a broken handle with a female representation (Podkowińska 1961, Plate XIX: 2); some vessels had the symbols highlighted with white paste.

From about 4500 BP the South-eastern group comes under a different cultural influence, and profound changes affecting the TRB ultimately result in its total transformation. In the eastern periphery of the region the Tripolye culture makes a certain impression, but by far the greatest area of the South-eastern TRB group is influenced by a new cultural complex, that of the Baden culture (Godłowska 1981; Kruk and Milisauskas 1983, 271–4). While the whole question of the transition from the TRB to the Baden culture needs to be considered against a broader background of socio-economic conditions at that time, the available ceramic evidence gives some indication of the strength of this process.

It is reasonable to assume that in some regions the traditional, classic trends still continue (many researchers stress not only the long chronological span of the later TRB, but also the lack of a uniform, synchronised horizon for the Baden influence), but there are a number of sites which clearly reveal a mixed character. At Niedźwiedź, pottery from two pits (nos 29 and 39) may still be classified technologically as TRB, but the form of some vessels, for example beaker-like bowls, or high-handled mugs, points towards the early Baden milieu (Burchard 1981, 231), an association further supported by radial decoration.

Correspondingly, mixed assemblages are known from Książnice Wielkie, Kraków Mogiła, Kraków Pleszów (Godłowska 1981) and from Bronocice (Kruk and Milisauskas 1983, Fig. 5). The latter site is particularly representative of this mixed, transitional stage during its phase III. Some of the pottery of this phase still displays features of the classic style but there are also a number of new elements. Salzmünde style drums indicate relatively extensive connections to the west, but mugs with high handles and a variety of bowl forms clearly derive from the early Baden cultural environment (ibid., 286–92). While the continuity of settlement to the subsequent phase (Bronocice IV) is clear, the diagnostic TRB ceramic forms are greatly reduced, so much so in fact that phase IV is confidently placed in the Boleraz horizon (ibid., 274).

A number of late TRB settlements in Silesia also reveal clear early Baden (Boleraz) impulses. Good examples of such influence come from both Lower and upper Silesia, for example from Janówek (Wojciechowski 1973, 55–6) or Pietrowice Wielkie (Bukowska-Gedigowa 1975, 137–8). Some contacts are nevertheless retained with the Eastern TRB group; this is demonstrated at Janówek where in four instances imported Luboń pottery has been encountered (Fig. 19: 8) with sherds bearing Boleraz decoration (Wojciechowski 1973, Fig. 24 and 31: d–m). Unlike in the area of Little Poland, however, we cannot point to the direct succession of the Baden culture in Silesia, and so the process which led to the demise of the TRB in this part of the South-eastern TRB province remains to be investigated further.

Finally, we must turn our attention once again to the Tripolye culture. Tripolye influences within the South-eastern group do not appear to have reached a geographical extent comparable with that of the Baden culture and, with sporadic exceptions, they are confined to the Lublin-Wolhynian upland. However, perhaps precisely because the range of influence is concentrated, its impact appears to have been so strong that some scholars refer to the Tripolyean acculturation in this area (Jastrzębski 1985). The earliest Tripolye influence is observed during the Gródek I phase but this involves sporadic finds, such as a painted vessel at Zimne or bowls with thickened rims at Rudniki (Jastrzębski, pers. comm.). Much closer contacts between the Tripolye and TRB are evident in the later, Gródek II phase and these involve a wide range of features such as domestic architecture (some influences of the ploshchadka type), the flint industry (see Chapter 6.3.1), some copper objects, anthropomorphic figurines, and above all ceramic wares. The chronological horizon for these contacts is a relatively broad span of C/I–C/II as well as C-II of the Tripolye culture (Jastrzębski 1985, 81–7, Table 1).

Technologically superior Tripolye painted pottery (the so-called table ware) has been found on thirteen upland TRB sites, most of all at Gródek Nadbużny, Zimne and Leżnica, with typical forms involving a broad range of bowls, small amphorae or lids decorated with painted motifs (Fig. 18: 8, 9; Jastrzębski 1985, 72–4). In addition, at the settlement of Gródek Nadbużny has been found some pottery of the Horodsk type (the kitchen ware of Tripolye C/II stage), which is characterised predominantly by shallow bowls with rich cord decoration. Moreover, at Gródek Nadbużny and Zimne, Tripolye pottery was imitated by local craftsmen, since painted decoration is found on sherds which are technologically inferior to Tripolyean imports.

But, however strong the Tripolyean influences may have been, there is no evidence of this culture succeeding the TRB; nor can we indicate the cultural change which resulted from the relationship between these two complexes. Towards the end of the TRB we may note some Baden elements as well as those typical of the Eastern TRB group Luboń phase, which point to a wide network of contacts for this peripheral area but none apparently having any significant bearing upon the transformation and, finally, the demise of the TRB. The sources of this may have to be sought in the more general processes which resulted in new socio-economic complexes towards the later part of the 5th millennium BP.

4.4 The ceramic sequence of the Northern TRB group

The Northern TRB group traditionally covers the area of southern Scandinavia and the adjacent parts of northern Germany: Schleswig-Holstein and Mecklenburg. Yet the research in these three sub-regions has followed a different course and, more importantly, the ceramic development was not synchronous over this whole province. Once the TRB culture is well established in the Northern group there is a considerable degree of similarity between Denmark and Schleswig-Holstein, but the same does not apply to Mecklenburg. Although the Danish sequence has regularly formed the basis for the discusion of Mecklenburg pottery, it is clear that a direct superimposition of a sequence from one area to the next is not applicable. Thus, in order to avoid confusion and oversimplification, the pottery material from the three sub-regions of the Northern group will be discussed separately although, where possible, comparisons will be made in an attempt to bridge the gaps. It must also be stressed that, because of its geographical position, the Mecklenburg area is of crucial importance to our understanding of contacts and relationships between the Eastern, Southern, Northern and Western groups; it is particularly frustrating that the paucity of evidence from Mecklenburg inhibits insight into many of the problems.

4.4.1 Schleswig-Holstein

In his interpretation of the north German early material Schwabedissen (1967 and 1968), following on from earlier ideas of Schwantes (1958), originally distinguished two phases: FN I (*Frühneolithikum* I), the Satrup phase, based on material from the moor finds at Satrup Pöttmoor and Südensee Damm; and FN II (*Frühneolithikum* II), the Fuchsberg phase, based on material from a closed moor find at Fuchsberg and a number of related sites. With the subsequent discovery and excavation of two east

SCHWABEDISSEN 1967/1968	MEURERS-BALKE 1979	SCHWABEDISSEN 1979	HOIKA 1987
MN		TROLDEBJERG	MN Ia TROLDEBJERG
FN II (FUCHSBERG)	SATRUP GROUP	FUCHSBERG	FN II FUCHSBERG
FN I (SATRUP)		SATRUP	FN Ic SATRUP
	FN A/B SIGGENEBEN-SÜD	ROSENHOF b	FN Ib SIGGENEBEN
ELLERBEK	ROSENHOF GROUP	ROSENHOF a	FN Ia ROSENHOF
	ERTEBØLLE– ELLERBEK CULTURE	ERTEBØLLE– ELLERBEK	ERTEBØLLE– ELLERBEK

Figure 20 Chronological schemes for the early TRB (FN) in Schleswig-Holstein.

Holstein sites, Rosenhof and Siggeneben-Süd, this chronology was extended by the addition to FN I of the so-called Rosenhof phase, which itself became subdivided into Rosenhof a (represented by Rosenhof) and Rosenhof b (in Hoika's 1987 scheme called Siggeneben-Süd, represented by this site; Schwabedissen 1979a, 1979b and 1979c). Thus, at present, the north German early TRB culture appears to be divided into four phases: FN Ia (Rosenhof), FN Ib (Siggeneben-Süd), FN Ic (Satrup) and FN II (Fuchsberg; Fig. 20).

We have already looked at the material from the earliest phase and may now continue the discussion of the rest of the early TRB in this area. The next stage within the German typo-chronology is the Rosenhof b (or Siggeneben-Süd) phase. Although some material from the Bistoft settlement (Johansson 1979 and 1981) can be included here (for instance a few short-necked beakers and the so-called lamps), the only representative find so far appears to be the settlement of Siggeneben-Süd, which is dated to 5200–4900 BP (Meurers-Balke 1983). The pottery inventory, while related to that from Rosenhof, contains a wider range of forms in addition to the already existing types, including lugged flasks and small flasks (but apparently not collared flasks) and clay discs, forms not witnessed at Rosenhof (ibid., 50–6).

The funnel-necked beakers constitute 90 per cent of all vessels and come in a variety of sizes from 6 cm to 40 cm in diameter; Meurers-Balke distinguishes eight profiles, from very smooth to strongly curved with a distinct shoulder (ibid., 50–2, Fig. 23). The bases of the beakers are predominantly flat but there are at least a few examples with rounded bases (ibid., Plate 27: 3). The decoration appears to be confined only to the beakers and is principally concerned with the rim area; some of the rims are notched, while others have circular, enlongated or irregular stamp impressions. A new feature appears to be horizontal shoulder decoration and a few beakers also display vertically arranged decoration. The latter involves groups of grooves on the belly (*Bauchfransen*; Fig. 21: 2), cord impressions and applied vertical ridges. Of particular note is the richly decorated lugged beaker (Fig. 21: 1) with hanging multiple crescents executed in whipped cord under the rim and whipped cord lines separated by vertical rows of impressed stamps on the belly.

According to Meurers-Balke (1983, 91–2), the greater proportion of the Siggeneben-Süd pottery has its closest parallels in the assemblage from Stengade II on Langeland (Skaarup 1975; similarities include a comparable proportion of decorated vessels, details of ornamentation and the appearance of forward-looking elements), and should be placed in the same chronological horizon, whilst appreciating that Becker's sequential A, B, C scheme is no longer acceptable (see section on Danish typo-chronology, Chapter 4.4, 3.1). While some of the Siggeneben-Süd pottery (beakers with *Bauchfransen* and the decorated lugged beaker, Fig. 21: 1) is closely related to the subsequent Satrup phase pottery, Meurers-Balke (1983, 91) considers this to be a forward-looking feature rather than evidence of multi-phase settlement, as the latter is apparently borne out neither by stratigraphy of the site nor by vessel technology. In terms of local development, Siggeneben-Süd is interpreted as a development and direct continuation of Rosenhof (this may indeed be one reason why some of the Siggeneben-Süd pottery has been classed as A-type by P.O. Nielsen 1985, 120). However, the occupation apparently lasted long enough to allow internal pottery development and modification through external influence. Hence the shoulder decoration is attributed to Rössen (or Rössen-related) influence, while the stroke decoration under the rim and the *Bauchfransen* pattern on the beakers reveal connections with the east (Mecklenburg, cf. the so-called Moltzow style of Jażdżewski).

While Siggeneben-Süd clearly represents a well-developed and varied assemblage which Meurers-Balke (1983, 90–6) compared with a wide range of early TRB finds from various regions of the North European Plain, its status as a phase-defining site should not be accepted as axiomatic. While the connections with the pottery from Rosenhof on the one hand, and with

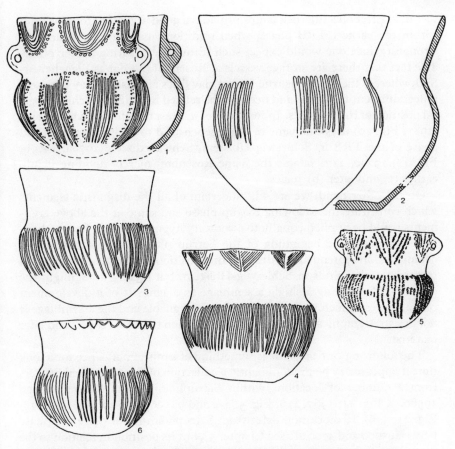

Figure 21 Early TRB pottery from Schleswig-Holstein: 1,2-Siggeneben-Süd, 3,6-Südensee-Damm, 4-Südensee Pöttmoor, 5-Rüde 31 (Source: Schwabedissen 1968; Meurers-Balke 1983).

that of the Satrup phase on the other, logically place it between the two phases, Siggeneben-Süd is presently the only sizeable assemblage of its kind in Schleswig-Holstein. Thus it is not possible to determine which of the elements observed here are of local and which are of universal, that is phase-defining, character. Moreover, differences between Siggeneben-Süd and one of the 'earlier' or 'later' sites may be as much functional as chronological. While in absolute terms later than the site of Rosenhof, Siggeneben-Süd could feasibly be included within the Rosenhof phase, possibly representing its final stage (see chapter 5.3.1). The long duration of an early phase need not be surprising, especially when viewed as a dynamic rather than static phenomenon, and in it we may well see reflected some of the changes taking place during the process of crystallisation of the TRB culture. The presence in the Siggeneben-Süd assemblage of the so-called Ertebølle-Ellerbek lamps provides a good argument for placing it within the earliest TRB phase, when traditions may have been at their strongest, since one would expect such features less during a later phase. The fact that there are storage vessels at Rosenhof but not as Siggeneben-Süd, whereas the reverse is true for flat clay discs and flasks, may precisely reflect different functions and need not be related to a different chronological position of the two sites. Indeed, it is of interest to note that while Hoika (1987; Fig. 20) uses the name of Siggeneben-Süd to designate the second phase of the TRB in Schleswig-Holstein, Schwabedissen (1979a; 1979b, Fig. 12; 1979c, 217) retains the name Rosenhof, merely dividing it into earlier (a) and later (b) stages.

On the other hand, we are still uncertain of all the diagnostic elements which constitute the following Satrup phase and some of the above arguments could be applied equally to a contrary hypothesis, that Siggeneben-Süd represents the beginning of the Satrup phase. None of the above comments are intended to dispute the position of Siggeneben-Süd in relation to other finds in Schleswig-Holstein, but merely to highlight the difficulty of choosing a single assemblage as diagnostic of a development phase, if no satisfactory local comparison is available and the assemblage is not in a stratigraphically clear position in relation to known earlier and later materials.

The following *Satrup phase* is something of a misnomer, since for a long time it appeared to be predominantly a collection of funnel-necked beakers from a number of locations within Satrupholm Moor (Schwabedissen 1958b, 7, Fig. 11; 1967, 416; Fig. 5: a–c and 9; 1968, 17–20, Fig. on p. 18; Fig. 21: 3–6). Radiocarbon dates from Satrupholm Moor place the phase between 5000 and 4700 BP (see Chapter 5), but its position in relation to the preceding and subsequent TRB phases is difficult to determine since its material is not found in any reliably stratified context. At the site of Rosenhof a sherd of the Satrup style has been found stratified above the earliest TRB material (in a *Muschelbank*; Schwabedissen 1979a, 167–8). But at Satrupholm Moor the earliest TRB phase has not been found, although there seems to be a gap between the Ertebølle-Ellerbek and Satrup levels at Pöttmoor and Südensee-Damm (Schwabedissen 1958b, 7 and 11, Fig. 2). On the other hand the presence of Satrup-like elements within the Siggeneben-Süd assemblage, which according to Meurers-Balke (1983, 96) belong to the end of the settlement period, may indicate that it is partly contemporary with the preceding development phase.

The Satrup phase, therefore, appears to be characterised by wide beakers which have flat or rounded (*Wackelboden*) bases. The vessels are most commonly decorated on the belly with a pattern of vertical lines (*Bauch-fransen*) which may be either grooved (Fig. 21: 3, 4, 6) or executed in whipped cord (Fig. 21: 5) and which either run continuously round the body or are arranged in groups. The neck also carries decoration, and published examples show small semi-circles under the rim (Fig. 21: 6), hanging triangles (Fig. 21: 4), and if a Siggeneben-Süd lugged beaker can be related to the Satrup style on the basis of its similarity to a lugged beaker from Rude 31 (Schwabedissen 1968; Fig. 21: 1, 5), also hanging multiple crescents. It is possible to add to the above collection of vessels some settlement material; at Bistoft (Johansson 1981, Figs 13 and 14) there are typical Satrup-style beakers associated with collared and lugged flasks, and the assemblage from two pits at Gremersdorf-Neuratjensdorf contains sherds decorated with vertical lines, either grooved or impressed in whipped cord, as well as a beaker-like bowl with a Satrup-style pattern of grouped vertical lines in whipped cord interspersed with vertically placed irregular stamps (Hoika, pers. comm.).

In spite of the evidence mentioned above, the definition of the Satrup phase is still unsatisfactory. Apart from the richly decorated beakers, other material is still too scanty and lacks reasonable context. More finds, especially in settlement locations, are necessary before the range of ceramic forms typical of the Satrup phase can be discussed fully.

What in northern Germany and Denmark is today known as Fuchsberg pottery (and hence Fuchsberg phase or style) was originally identified as an individual ceramic style within the *Norddeutsche Alttiefstichtonware* (North German Old Tiefstich pottery) on the basis of ceramic assemblages from the earthen long barrows at Haaßel and Tosterglope and was named *Langgrabtonware im Haaßeler Stil* by Dehnke (1940, 147–53, Plates III: 8–41, IV: 1–28, XII: 8, XIII: 2, 4, 5). In a number of excavations in the early 1950s similar assemblages came to light in Schleswig-Holstein and Lower Saxony. Thus Sprockhoff (1952a, 54) drew attention to the similarity between the pottery from Haaßel and that from the Sachsenwald earthen long barrows, noting in particular a strong tendency for zonal decoration in impressed stamp (Fig. 22: 1), which he called *Gittermuster*, and the non-megalithic context in which the pottery was found. At the same time Schwabedissen (1955a, 256; 1958a; 1958b) was noting similarities with pottery from a settlement at Oldesloe-Wolkenwehe as well as from barrows at Sachsenwald, and referred to a joint horizon with Haaßel; later material from Sachsenwaldau, a settlement near the long barrows at Sachsenwald, was also compared. Moreover, excavations in Satrupholm Moor from a locality named Fuchsberg revealed pottery comparable with that from the above-mentioned sites. The Haaßel-style pottery became known as Fuchsberg pottery or Fuchsberg group (Schwabedissen 1963, 204), and soon became the basis of the *Fuchsberg phase* (FN II; Schwabedissen 1967, Fig. 4; 1968, 22, Fig. on p. 19). In 1979 Schwabedissen provided a list of Fuchsberg sites for northern Germany and Denmark (Schwabedissen 1979b, Fig. 5).

The key site of Fuchsberg is only known from short interim reports (Schwabedissen 1963) and this is the case with some other sites containing

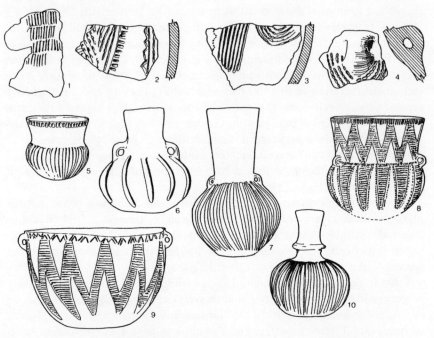

Figure 22 Fuchsberg-style pottery from Schleswig-Holstein: 1-Sachsenwald, 2–4-Sachsenwaldau, 5-Stursbüll, 6-Gjenner, 7-Hörst, 8-Wolkenwehe, 9-Flensburg, 10-Loit (Source: Schwabedissen 1968 and 1979b).

this type of pottery such as Sachsenwald (Sprockhoff 1952a; 1954), Sachsenwaldau (Schwabedissen 1955b; 1958c) and Oldesloe-Wolkenwehe (Schwabedissen 1953a; 1958c). Thus a complete inventory of ceramic forms within the Fuchsberg group in Germany is difficult to determine, but a study of the published reports does give some indication of the leading types. Before we discuss the Fuchsberg pottery, however, it is worthwhile noting that in the Danish literature the Fuchsberg assemblages tend to be defined on the basis of a specific form of decoration which appears only on beakers and bowls – the broad, infilled chevrons (Fig. 22: 8, 9; N. Andersen and Madsen 1978), a feature that is always thought to be diagnostic of the Fuchsberg pottery. While this is also the case with some German material, it should be noted that certainly in Schleswig-Holstein and Lower Saxony there is a greater number of diagnostic features; indeed it was primarily the so-called *Gittermuster* pattern that attracted comparisons with Haaßel and Tosterglope (Fig. 22: 1).

On the basis of ceramic assemblages from settlements (for example Oldesloe-Wolkenwehe, Sachsenwaldau, Kiel-Meinersdorfer Weg) and earthen long barrows (Sachsenwald, Haaßel, Tosterglope), the inventory of the Fuchsberg phase includes all the usual forms – funnel-necked beakers and lugged beakers, collared and lugged flasks, flat clay discs – while jugs and bowls are beginning to acquire greater prominence. Nevertheless, the dominant ceramic form appears to be the funnel-necked beaker, of which apparently at least 254 were found at Fuchsberg itself (Schwabedissen 1963, 203). The beakers, which are variable in size, generally have a flat or flattish base and a tall, straight or slightly splayed neck (Fig. 22: 5, 8). While some of the beakers are completely undecorated (Schwabedissen 1970, Fig. 2: 7), the ornamental motifs on others most commonly involve a horizontal band of longish vertical stamps under the rim or several such bands, on occasions interspersed with a zig-zag line in whipped cord (ibid., Fig. 2: 13 and 16; Sprockhoff 1954, Fig. 10: 1 and 2). On the belly there is frequently a pattern of continuous vertical grooves, which are sometimes so deep as to give the impression of fluting (Fig. 22: 5). Other body patterns associated with Fuchsberg pottery involve narrow bands of vertical grooves, sometimes in whipped cord, bordered on either side by circular impressions (Fig. 22: 2); this pattern has been noted on beakers from Fuchsberg and on beakers and lugged flasks at Oldesloe-Wolkenwehe. The so-called *Gittermuster* of Sprockhoff (1952a, Fig. 5: 5–8, 11–13; 1954, Fig. 9 and 11: 4), which is executed in a chisel stamp, or 'screwdriver' stamp (Bakker 1979, 179), is a motif of rectangular rows of impressions placed parallel to each other and represents another common decorative element. It is known from all the Fuchsberg group sites and it may, on occasion, form either a chess-board pattern or an arrangement similar to the 'ladder' motif known in the assemblages of the Eastern group. Hanging triangles and crescents executed in whipped cord, two-strand cord or stab-and-drag are also a regular feature of the Fuchsberg inventories, known for example from Haaßel (Dehnke 1940, Plate III: 30), Tosterglope (ibid., Plate III: 15, 19, 20) or Sachsenwaldau (Schwabedissen 1979b; Fig. 22: 3, 4).

The Fuchsberg pottery provides a starting point for the subsequent development of a new ceramic phenomenon commonly known as *Tiefstich* pottery (see section on the Western TRB group, Chapter 4.5, for discussion of the term). The areas of southern Schleswig-Holstein and Lower Saxony appear to stimulate this new development, which very quickly becomes widespread over a large area of the north German plain, the Netherlands and deep into Middle Germany. Fuchsberg-style pottery in Denmark is one of the key sources of that complex ceramic phenomenon, the south Scandinavian Middle Neolithic, and while not as yet found in Mecklenburg as such, it also seems to have had some impact in this area. The leading Fuchsberg pottery forms (funnel-necked beakers, richly ornamented lugged beakers and steep-walled bowls) continue uninterrupted, and decorative motifs such as triangles below the rim, chevron designs on bowls and lugged beakers, all clearly indicate the parentage of the ceramic forms and decoration which are diagnostic of *Tiefstich* pottery.

The reasons behind such a dramatic, widespread and seemingly swift adoption of Fuchsberg-derived ceramics are difficult to determine, especially since the existence of the early TRB west of the known Fuchsberg province still remains to be satisfactorily demonstrated. It is amply documented, however, that the arrival of *Tiefstich* pottery in the entire area of its distribution represents a full-scale settlement. It is most poignantly expressed in the tradition of monumental burial within stone-built chambers: across the North European Plain this tradition expands simultaneously with the *Tiefstich* pottery and, in the areas of the early TRB settlement, it complements, without wholly replacing, the hitherto existing earthen long barrow tradition (see Chapter 9.2).

It is also important to note that precisely at this point there is some shift in regional boundaries. The unity of the area where Fuchsberg-style pottery was used is now, apparently, breaking down. This was clearly noted by Schwabedissen (1953b, 45) when he pointed out that the pottery of the southern part of Schleswig-Holstein, which is best represented by the material from a settlement at Groß Flottbek near Hamburg where stab-and-drag technique was dominant, was much closer in style to the so-called *Alttiefstich* of the north-west German lowland. The pottery from northern and north-eastern Schleswig-Holstein is virtually identical to that from Denmark. Whether this difference reflects changes in the population of the area, different economic development, social change or a combination of these factors is not clear since too little material is known from the area of Schleswig-Holstein. However, with regard to the Northern TRB group (of which northern Schleswig-Holstein must be considered a part), this is a period of profound change, witnessed for example in the increase of ritual activities, the use of causewayed enclosures and the diversity of burial rituals to name but the most obvious phenomena. Such a boundary across Schleswig-Holstein may well imply different social patterns in the Northern and Western TRB groups.

Turning now to the later TRB pottery from Schleswig-Holstein (Fig. 23), we should note among the more significant research the work of Langenheim (1935), Schwabedissen (1953b; 1979b), Schwantes (1939; 1958) and, most recently, Hoika (1971; 1973; 1981; 1983; 1987). Langenheim's (1935) investigation of pottery was based on the stylistic development of funnel-necked beakers from chambered tombs, amongst which the key finds were those from Denghoog near Wenningstedt and Ober Jersdal. Langenheim divided the beakers into five groups which were classified on the basis of the then-current Scandinavian sequence of Dolmen Period (two groups) and Passage Grave Period (three groups); it was in the latter period that the famous Denghoog type (a beaker with a zig-zag band decoration on the neck) was placed. Schwantes' division of the ceramic material followed partly that of Langenheim and partly the Danish chronology of MN I–V, and gave rise to the Early Denghoog (I), Middle Denghoog (II and III) and Late Denghoog periods (IV and V; Schwantes 1958, Fig. 112).

SCHWANTES 1958	BECKER 1957	HOIKA 1987
LATE DENGHOOG	MN V	MN V
	GLOBULAR AMPHORA CULTURE	STORE VALBY
(MN IV & V)	MN III/IV	MN IV
		LINDØ
	DANNAU (III)	
	SÜSSAU (IV)	MN III
	(BUNDSØ/LINDØ)	
MIDDLE DENGHOOG		BUNDSØ
(MN II & III)	MN II	MN II
	SÜTEL	BLANDEBJERG
	(BLANDEBJERG)	
EARLY DENGHOOG	MN I	MN Ib
	HEILIGENHAFEN	KLINTEBAKKE
(MN I)	(KLINTEBAKKE TROLDEBJERG)	TROLDEBJERG
		MN Ia

Figure 23 Chronological schemes for the later TRB (MN) in Schleswig-Holstein set against Becker's scheme for Denmark.

Schwabedissen's 1953 publication was devoted mainly to the study of pedestal bowls from Schleswig-Holstein, for which the starting point was the finds from a group of passage graves near Schwesig, and the then-current Danish settlement chronology was applied directly to this material. On the basis of decoration technique (curved stamp, *Cardium* and tooth-comb impressions) and dominant decorative motifs (single/multiple zig-zags and vertical infilled band patterns) Schwabedissen synchronised the so-called 'pedestal bowl horizon' with the Klintebakke (MN Ib) material from Denmark. Only a few finds, such as vessels from the destroyed tomb at Viöl (Schwabedissen 1953b, Plate 1: d, e), showed any resemblance to the Danish style known from the Troldebjerg (MN Ia) settlement, and later Schwabedissen also included pottery from the extended dolmen at Birken-moor (Schwabedissen 1979b, 156, Fig. 8: 4 and 11).

As already stated, Schwabedissen (1953b, 30 and 51, Figs 14 and 15) suggested that the pedestal bowls and the accompanying ceramics from Groß Flottbek and a few other finds from southern Schleswig-Holstein as far as Dithmarschen should be classified with the German *Alttiefstchtonware*, especially with Dehnke's (1940) phase II which is better represented by material from Haldensleben. More recent research by Hoika (1987) in the area of eastern Holstein has confirmed the correspondence between the later TRB pottery there and in Denmark. Hoika identified four ceramic groups: I Heiligenhafen, II Neukirchen-Sütel, III Oldenburg-Dannau and IV Heringsdorf-Süssau, which in vessel form and decoration correspond to the Danish MN I–IV ceramic styles (ibid., 95–99). In distinguishing these groups, however, he warned against fine chronological division of pottery; his ceramic groups III and IV, for example, are so similar that they must be regarded as contemporaneous, displaying the range of vessels in contem-porary use rather than reflecting sequential stages. Hoika has also pointed out that by the time the late TRB Store Valby (MN V) style develops in Denmark, the area of Schleswig-Holstein belongs to a new cultural region where the Globular Amphora culture is displacing the TRB. The cultural boundary appears to have shifted once again.

4.4.2 Mecklenburg

A comprehensive study of the TRB pottery from Mecklenburg was pub-lished by Nilius in 1971(a). In view of the scarcity of closed assemblages and of any clear stratigraphy either in settlements or in tombs, Nilius of necessity relied upon the chronological framework from southern Scandinavia: the tripartite division of the early TRB (Scandinavian EN) and five-part division of the later TRB (Scandinavian MN). However, she was unable to identify the final phase known in southern Scandinavia (the Store Valby) among the Mecklenburg ceramics. The early TRB material was not easily classifiable according to Becker's (1947) scheme and, although Nilius argued that the later TRB pottery developed along lines similar to that in the north, she also perceived that there were no precise correspondences. The Mecklenburg material was seen by Nilius as poorer, both in its variety of ceramic forms and in its range of decorative motifs. Some typical Danish forms such as the so-called Troldebjerg or Hage-brogård bowls were lacking, and other types such as pedestalled bowls or clay ladles were relatively scarce.

Using the pottery recovered during his investigations of the megalithic chambers, Schuldt (1972b) presented a brief outline of the TRB pottery concentrating primarily upon the regional areas identified through the distribution of different tomb types. He argued that the Mecklenburg ceramics were neither sufficiently well known nor sufficiently numerous to allow a distinction of clear chronological phases along the Scandinavian lines, and consequently he applied a simple division of older (*ältere*) and younger (*jüngere*) phases to the early (*Frühneolithikum*) and later (*Mittel-neolithikum*) TRB pottery (although with reference to the MN period this division does approximate to the MN I/II and MN III/IV styles of Denmark).

A brief attempt at identification of the Danish MN styles in Mecklenburg was also undertaken by Ebbesen (1975, 133–46; 1979a, 84–6), who argued that all the Danish styles from MN Ia (which he equated with the Gingst style) through to MN V could be found here. He even provided a list of select vessels from Mecklenburg megaliths which were in direct corre-spondence with those from Denmark (Ebbesen 1975, n. 534b–q). However, these are only individual examples and not complete assemblages, and no settlement material (where such direct comparisons do not really apply) was considered. A good example of how difficult, and most clearly unsatis-factory, it is to attempt to transfer the Danish typo-chronology to Mecklen-burg is illustrated by the fact that vessels used by Ebbesen as indicative of a particular style were interpreted quite differently by Hoika (1987, 107–8).

And yet the problem of interpretation of Mecklenburg ceramic develop-ment surely cannot be solved by the identification of Danish styles. As early as 1947 Becker had to concede that the north German early TRB material defied any division into A- and B-types (Becker 1947, 200–16) and conse-quently he labelled it A/B pottery. The search for equivalents during the later TRB period tends to be based on the assumption that not only was the development identical (which it clearly was not), but also Mecklenburg was influenced directly from southern Scandinavia. Although close contacts between these two regions are perceivable, it is by no means certain that the contacts were one-sided; indeed the opposite could apply equally well.

The main problem in Mecklenburg lies in the almost complete lack of settlement assemblages (only a few quite poorly represented sites are known) and reliable close finds. This paucity is the main obstacle to determining which vessels and which decorative motifs were in contem-porary use, and thus to establishing an independent ceramic sequence

90   *TRB Culture*

against which uncontexted finds can be compared. Secondly, while in southern Scandinavia the 'unreliability' of the settlement material is offset by the sheer mass of pottery from megalithic graves, this is not the case in Mecklenburg, and the tomb investigations of Schuldt begun in 1964 resulted in only a slight increase in pottery (Schuldt 1972b). Thirdly, the few settlement assemblages which have been published reveal that, apart from connections with southern Scandinavia, this area was also in close association with regions to the west, Altmark and Lower Saxony, since typical early *Tiefstich* pottery is found side by side with ceramics similar to northern MN I/II styles (for example at Lindenbeck; Nagel 1986). This is a connection which appears to have been established during the Fuchsberg-Haaßel phase and which is subsequently expressed most emphatically in the so-called *Prachtbecher*, the ceremonial beaker, which clearly indicates contacts towards the west rather than the north. Moreover, during the later TRB period there are also clear connections with areas to the south.

For the moment, therefore, it is only possible to suggest a very broad outline of the ceramic development of the TRB in this area. The typologically earliest funnel-necked beakers and amphorae are known from stray finds, for example at Moltzow or Bernitt (Schuldt 1972b, Plates 1 and 2) and from graves such as Dargun (Fig. 24: 1, 2), Niendorf or Kläden (Just 1963; Fig. 24: 3, 4). To these can be added the rather scanty material from settlements such as Basedow (Schuldt 1974a), Pinnow (Raddatz 1952) and Berlin-Britz in Brandenburg (Dorka 1961), where apart from the sherds of funnel-necked beakers and amphorae, funnel-necked bowls, clay discs and possibly Rosenhof-like lamps supplement the range of early vessels.

Although this early material is still very scanty, the small, squat beakers with rounded body and round- or egg-bellied amphorae are virtually identical in form and decoration (they have rows of irregular stamp impressions below the rim) to the ceramics diagnostic of the Sarnowo and Rosenhof phase materials (Figs 11 and 12). The Mecklenburg finds, whose general distribution throughout this area shows that this was not a development confined to one or two localities (Bastian 1954, Map 1; Nilius 1971a, Map 3), fill in the gap between the two early areas, central Poland and Schleswig-Holstein, and while they cannot as yet be dated independently, they can be ascribed without any doubt to the same early horizon.

There are very few closed finds of the later phase of the Mecklenburg *Frühneolithikum* which would identify the range of ceramic forms in use during this time. Most of the examples derive from stray finds (for example Neuendorf, Zapel; Schuldt 1972b, Plate 7) and occasionally from graves (for example Altensien, Fig. 24: 7, 8, or Zarrenthin, Fig. 24: 5, 6). However, the largely unpublished finds from a settlement at Schönermark (Geisler 1965) indicate the presence of funnel-necked beakers and bowls, amphorae, storage vessels, collared flasks and baking plates, an inventory which in

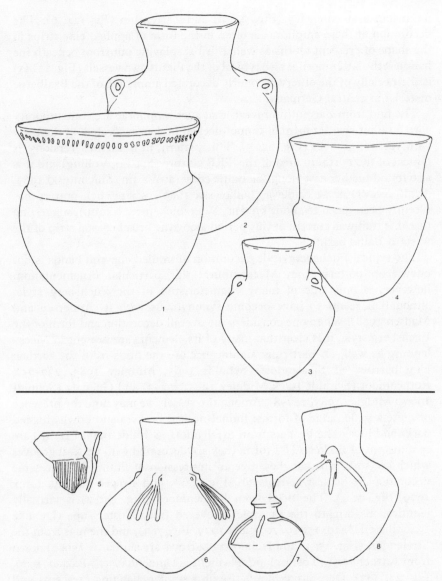

Figure 24 Early TRB pottery from Mecklenburg: 1, 2-Dargun, 3, 4-Kläden, 5, 6-Zarrenthin, 7, 9-Altensien (Source Nilius 1971; Schuldt 1972b).

general corresponds well with and is coeval with the Pikutkowo phase of the Eastern TRB group.

According to Nilius (1971a) and Schuldt (1972b), the younger FN amphorae are characterised by a greater angularity of form; examples are present at the settlement of Lindenbeck (Nagel 1986, Fig. 3) and in graves, for instance at Altensien (Fig. 24: 8) and Zarrenthin (Fig. 24: 6). The decoration of these amphorae is often in the form of applied clay strips in the shape of crescent motifs as well as 'ribs' splaying out from beneath the handles; the latter motif is also typical of the Pikutkowo vessels (Fig. 11: 11) and especially of the otherwise poorly decorated amphorae of the Baalberge material in central Germany.

The find from Zarrenthin reveals that such amphorae are contemporary with a rather slender form of funnel-necked beaker decorated on the belly with vertical grooves (Fig. 24: 5). This pattern, in numerous versions, is typical of the northern area of the TRB culture (Satrup, Volling) and it is also found further east along the Baltic coast (at Wartin (Siuchniński 1969, Table XXVI) or at Łupawa (Jankowska 1980), where such pottery has recently been dated to about 5100 BP; Wierzbicki pers. comm.), suggesting that this trait was current at this period along the broad coastal strip of the western Baltic basin.

The typical Fuchsberg-style decoration of infilled chevron bands is not known on pottery from Mecklenburg; this particular ornamentation, however, is only one of many characteristics of the Fuchsberg style, although it seems to have become synonymous with it (Andersen and Madsen 1978). When one considers the overall decoration and form of the Fuchsberg style, it is clear that many of its elements are present in Mecklenburg as well. Of particular significance are the finds from the earthen long barrows at Stralendorf (Schuldt 1965; Midgley 1985, 237–75), Rothenmoor (Schuldt 1967; Midgley 1985, 272–3) and Gnewitz (Schuldt 1966c; Midgley 1985, 267–8). Among the vessels we may note the presence of quite a wide range of forms: funnel-necked beakers and bowls, lugged flasks and jugs. The beakers from Stralendorf (Schuldt 1965, Fig. 11) are reminiscent of Becker's D-I form; they are decorated with vertical grooves which are so broad that they give an impression of fluting (cf. the same decoration in Schleswig-Holstein, Fig. 22: 5 and Lower Saxony, Laux 1979, Fig. 7: 4). The bowl from Rothenmoor (Fig. 25: 2) is virtually identical in form to the example recovered from Tosterglope (Dehnke 1940, Plate III: 10, 15, 19, 20; Laux 1979, Fig. 7: 3), and the jugs from the Stralendorf (Fig. 25: 1) and Helm long barrows are similar to those known from further west (Tosterglope, Haaßel or Tannenhausen; Bakker 1979, Fig. 28: 5–7). Decorative motifs are also similar: hanging crescents and vertical deeply incised lines. All this material is remarkably similar to the A-type pottery identified by Laux in Lower Saxony (1971, 76–7, Fig. 7), and the eastern distribution of the Fuchsberg-like finds as well as their earthen long barrow context appear to indicate a widespread horizon either side of the Elbe.

It is possible that in the same general horizon we should place the pottery of the so-called *Moltzow style* from eastern Mecklenburg. This style was identified by Jażdżewski in 1932 on the basis of pottery from a group of

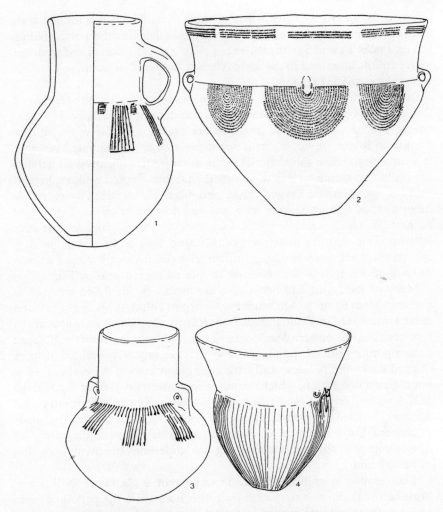

Figure 25 Fuchsberg-influenced and Moltzow-style pottery from Mecklenburg: 1-Stralendorf, 2-Rothenmoor, 3,4-Moltzow (Source: Schuldt 1972b).

graves at Moltzow ('stone cists' and flat graves). It is characterised by a very distinct decoration of alternating short and long grooves on the belly of vessels (Jażdżewski 1932, 90–1; Fig. 25: 3). Such pottery is also known from further east in western Pomerania and in Brandenburg, and may well represent an eastern version of the same phenomenon.

The earliest *Mittelneolithikum* TRB pottery in Mecklenburg is very clearly rooted in the previous ceramic tradition. This is seen in the presence of forms such as funnel-necked beakers, lugged beakers, funnel-necked bowls, lugged flasks and amphorae (Nilius 1971a, 38–43; Schuldt 1972b). The vessels tend to be bi-partite with a rounded profile and their decoration displays a largely vertical arrangement of parallel bands infilled with contrasting motifs, some of which can be paralleled in the north (Nilius 1971a, Plates 13 and 14; 1971b, 122–4, Fig. 1), while others are identical with patterns identified in the early Altmark horizon (for example Lindenbeck; Nagel 1986, Fig. 1).

In the north-eastern part of Mecklenburg we may note the presence of the so-called *Gingst style*. This style was also defined by Jażdżewski (1932, 89–90; Fig. 26), but because of the rather exclusive nature of the find at Gingst on Rügen (it was a votive bog deposit of richly decorated vessels), it is difficult to relate this material to the other pottery. Jażdżewski defined the diagnostic forms such as wide-mouthed funnel-necked beakers, lugged beakers, two-handled lugged flasks and jugs, all of which were richly decorated, as well as beakers with grooved decoration on the belly. The decoration, which is mainly vertical, consists of vertical bands infilled with horizontal or slanting lines, vertically placed zig-zag lines and 'ladder' motifs; there are often hanging, infilled triangles below the rim. The *tour de force* of this style is the profusely decorated lugged beaker (Fig. 27).

Many of the forms and decorative motifs can be identified among the pottery sherds from the settlement at Gristow (Nilius 1975, Fig. 1) as well as on a number of individual finds from Rügen; the Gingst style appears to represent a north-eastern Mecklenburg regional variant within the broader contemporary horizon. Some of the vessels are relatively archaic in form (lugged flasks and beakers) and have clear prototypes in the earlier forms, but the rich decoration, which draws upon elements typical of the Danish MN I styles (vertical bands), eastern Wiórek style ('ladder' motifs) and Altmark (infilled triangles), places the Gingst style firmly in the post-Fuchsberg horizon. Once again the mixture of elements diagnostic of developments in the neighbouring regions underlines the pivotal position of Mecklenburg.

The ceramic assemblage from the settlement at Ralswiek (Nilius and Warnke 1984) shows a transition from this horizon to the period of more angular, frequently tri-partite vessels. Among the sherds found here it is possible to identify funnel-necked bowls, vessels with cylindrical necks and a marked shoulder, forms which the excavators compared with those of Blandebjerg style (ibid., Fig. 6: m, 7 and 8: a). Similar pottery, with clear angular profiles and decoration which acquires a strong horizontal component (for example bands of horizontally placed zig-zags or criss-crossed fields separated by vertical stab-and-drag lines) is also known from megalithic tombs throughout Mecklenburg (Nilius 1971a, 43–8; Fig. 28: 3–5) and reflects a general horizon comparable with MN II style in the north and the C-type pottery from Lower Saxony (Laux 1979, 77, Fig. 9).

One settlement with an assemblage diagnostic of the late TRB development is Glasow (Nagel 1980, Figs 4, 6–10, 15–16). Although the pottery is very heavily fragmented, it is nevertheless possible to identify a whole

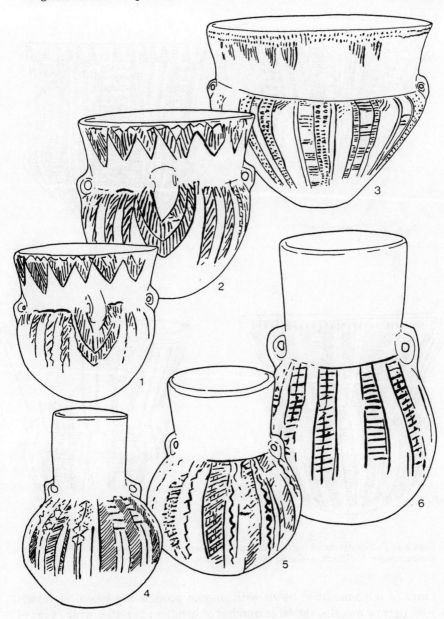

Figure 26 Votive deposit from Gingst on Rügen (Source: Schuldt 1972b).

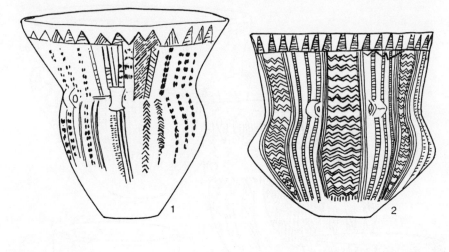

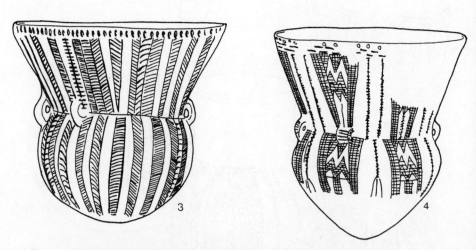

Figure 27 Richly decorated lugged beakers from north Germany: 1-Venz, 2-Flötz, 3-Neumünster Gadeland, 4-Gingst (Source: Rech 1971).

range of wide-mouthed bowls with smooth profiles and biconical vessels with narrow mouths; the large number of handles suggests a wide range of cups, mugs and bowls of the type commonly encountered in megalithic graves. Apart from the finer ceramics, at Glasow there are also coarser sherds with pits and dents below the rim (ibid., Figs 7: c–m, s–x and 14: d–g), revealing the presence of storage vessels; flat clay discs apparently still continue in use. In grave inventories of this final period the most common vessels are large bowls with or without handles, large cups with straight or

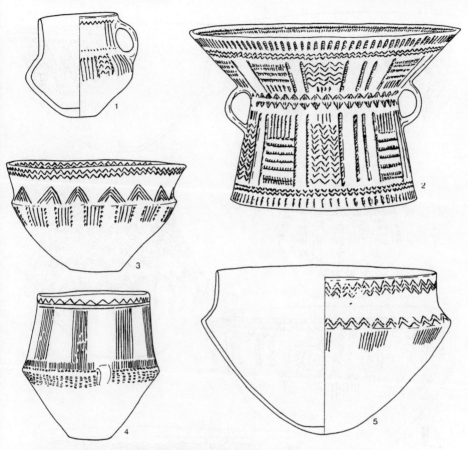

Figure 28 TRB pottery from the Mecklenburg megaliths: 1, 2-Forst Everstorf, 3, 4-Gnewitz, 5-Liepen (Source: Schuldt 1968; 1972b).

slightly flaring necks and hanging vessels with rounded bellies and conical necks (Nilius 1971a, 48–52; Fig. 29). Decoration carried out in stab-and-drag or by means of plain incising is most common, although prick-stick, chisel stamp, tooth-comb and cord techniques are also used. The designs are by and large horizontal, with broad bands of zig-zag lines covering the neck (Fig. 29: 4, 6), and bands of infilled rhomboids or broad zig-zag bands with tooth-comb impressions (Fig. 29: 1, 2) only occasionally broken up by vertical designs. Pots with 'faces' also belong to this late horizon (Fig. 29: 3, 5).

Sometime towards the end of the TRB culture a style of decoration which is closely associated with hanging vessels can be identified as a distinct stylistic entity on the island of Rügen (Fig. 30). It is known as the *Nadelitz style* after one of the great dolmens on the island, and clearly

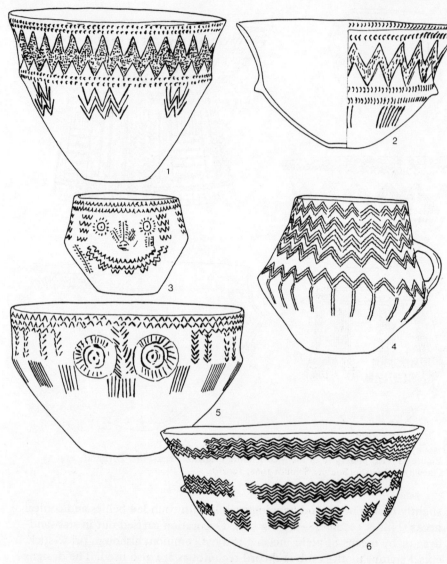

Figure 29 TRB pottery from the Mecklenburg megaliths: 1-Nadelitz, 2-Lancken-Granitz, 4-Poggendorfer Forst, 5-Ziesendorf, 6-Qualitz (Source: Schuldt 1972b).

relates to a similar development identified on the southern Danish islands by Ebbesen (the MN IVB style; Ebbesen 1975; see section dealing with the Danish pottery, Chapter 4.4, 3–2). Nadelitz decoration is very distinct: vertical, regularly spaced bands are infilled with horizontal tooth-comb impressions; sometimes a feather motif (very common in Denmark) fills in the spaces between the bands (Fig. 30: 4). While Nadelitz-style decoration

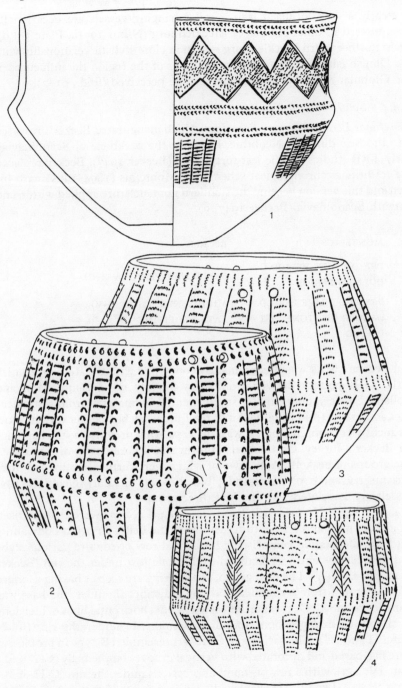

Figure 30 Late TRB pottery from Mecklenburg: 1,2,4-Nadelitz, 3-Lancken-Granitz, (Source: Schuldt 1972b).

is clearly a very localised trait, similar hanging vessels are occasionally encountered in other regions of Mecklenburg (Nilius 1971a, Plate 38: d); again north-eastern Mecklenburg is seen in close stylistic relationship with the Danish islands, although in other parts of the region the influences of the Globular Amphora culture can also be perceived (ibid., 61–2).

4.4.3 Southern Scandinavia

Mosefunde Lerkar fra yngre Stenalder, which inaugurated Becker's research into the Scandinavian Neolithic, has been the backbone of Scandinavian early TRB studies for the last forty years (Becker 1947). Becker replaced the traditional chronological schemes of Montelius (1894–1905) with his own and this version became the standard nomenclature applied within and outwith Scandinavia (Becker 1947, 9).

MONTELIUS		BECKER
I	PRE-DOLMEN PERIOD	EARLY NEOLITHIC (A–B–C)
II	DOLMEN PERIOD	
III	PASSAGE GRAVE PERIOD	MIDDLE NEOLITHIC (I–V)
IV	DAGGER OR STONE CIST PERIOD	LATE NEOLITHIC

But Becker's work was predominantly concerned with the study of Danish early TRB pottery derived from bogs (mainly on Zealand, Møn and Lolland-Falster), only slightly supplemented by material from settlement sites and graves (ibid., Fig. 1). Since the funnel-necked beaker was the most frequently encountered pot, it was this vessel that provided a starting point for Becker's survey. On the basis of form and decoration he distinguished five groups of beakers (A–E), two of which were further subdivided (four variants in C and two variants in D; ibid., 68–74). The Early Neolithic (EN) vessels are associated with the first three groups.

4.4.3.1 Early Neolithic TRB ceramics. The *A beakers* were characterised by a short neck and a smooth transition to the belly, an ovoid body and a flat base. Decoration comprised a horizontal row or rows of various stabs and impressions and was confined to the zone just under the rim (Becker 1947, Plate I: 1–4). The next group, *B beakers*, were seen as having a longer neck separated from a rounded body by a distinct shoulder; the base was round or rounded. Decoration consisted of pits, horizontal lines of incisions or simple cord impressions found predominantly under the rim (ibid., Plates II and III). The variants of *C beakers* resembled B-type in profile but were flat-based and decorated with vertical grooves on the belly (C-I, ibid., Plate IV: 2–3), with a row of stamp impressions under the rim (C-II, ibid., Plate VI: 2). Type C-III displayed rich decoration of the neck (whipped cord and stab-and-drag) and the belly had vertical grooves (ibid., Plates V:

1–2 and VI: 1), where C-IV was really a lugged beaker. The latter two types were known only from north and middle Jutland.

Lugged beakers were treated by Becker separately and were classed into four groups (A–D, ibid., 92–8). Other pottery forms such as funnel-necked and simple bowls, collared and lugged flasks and lugged jars were given a more perfunctory treatment (ibid., 98–111).

This purely typological division of the early TRB pottery was then developed by Becker into a typo-chronological framework in which the three groups were given sequential chronological order: A–B–C. Since there were no stratigraphically secure finds, the placement of the A vessels in the earliest phase (A phase, also known as the EN A or TRB A) was based on typological criteria. The whole A group collection consisted of a small number of vessels from the bog finds and two beakers from layer II at the shell midden of Sølager (ibid., 126–31). It is of interest to note here the Sølager stratigraphy: layer III (which contained C beakers) overlay layer II with the two A beakers. Becker did not feel that these pots were 'in the natural milieu of the A-beakers' (ibid., VIII) since he classified the rest of the material with the B group (see also Skaarup 1973 for a different classification). Nevertheless this stratigraphy proved for him the chrono-logical priority of the A vessels over those of the C group. Apart from the funnel-necked beakers, lugged flasks and lugged beakers were also included in the A phase inventory (Becker 1947, Fig. 24).

The assemblage representing the subsequent B phase appeared richer in diagnostic forms, including B beakers and lugged beakers, funnel-necked bowls, collared and lugged flasks and lugged jars (ibid., 131–41, Fig. 27; Fig. 31). While the settlement of Havnelev on Zealand and an earth grave from Forum were given particular importance as being representative of closed B-type finds, the main criterion nevertheless remained vessel typo-logy and decoration, which Becker considered more developed than those of the A phase. While B-phase finds apeared more numerous, the main concentration in both instances was on the Danish islands (Becker 1947, Figs 26 and 29).

For the following C phase, the pottery from the bogs was further sup-plemented by a reasonable number of finds from settlements and graves that enabled Becker to work out a general inventory of types (ibid., Figs 30 and 34). While he felt that the C vessels had 'their prototypes without exception' in the B forms, on the basis of pottery decoration as well as a recurring association of types he nevertheless distinguished three clearly defined regional groups and suggested the possible existence of a fourth.

The *north Jutland C group*, with a distribution clearly confined to the northern part of the Jutland peninsula, was known to Becker from thirty-three locations which, apart from the bog finds, included settlements (such as Lendrup or Dyrholmen) and flat graves (such as Volling; ibid., 141–51, Fig. 32). The inventory of this group included beakers of C-III and C-IV

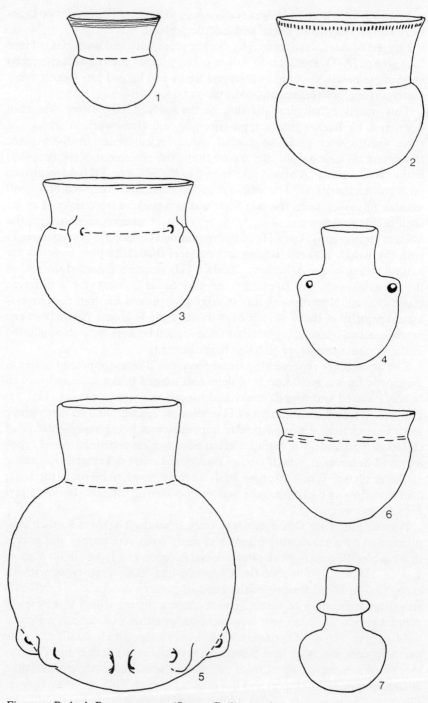

Figure 31 Becker's B-group pottery (Source: Becker 1947).

type, as well as lugged beakers of C-II. In addition there were collared flasks with a biconical belly and lugged jars. A diagnostic feature of the north Jutland group was decoration: strictly patterned designs were executed in stab-and-drag or deep stamp impressions, and more rarely in whipped cord (ibid., Fig. 30).

This was complemented in the south by an even larger group of about 100 finds, which constituted Becker's *south Danish C group* (or *Megalithic group*), found predominantly on the Danish islands and in middle and southern Jutland reaching as far south as the east coast of Schleswig (ibid., 151–60, Fig. 32). Leading pottery types included beakers of C-I types and lugged beakers of C-III type, as well as collared flasks with rounded bellies and lugged jars (ibid., Fig. 34). Decoration was also striking, and consisted most commonly of vertical grooves on the belly of beakers, and richly decorated necks on lugged forms; the predominant decorative technique was the use of whipped cord, with stab-and-drag or twisted cord appearing only rarely. More than half of the finds came from graves, the majority from the dolmens (the islands' dolmens being the earliest), thus giving this group a 'megalithic' character. Contemporaneity of the north and south groups was argued by Becker on the basis of some transitional finds (for example vessels from Tindbæk) which revealed a blending of the northern and southern styles.

Yet another C group, the *Bornholm and south Swedish group* (ten sites on Bornholm and in Skåne and Blekinge), was identified on the basis of a small number of finds, the diagnostic site being the Siretop settlement. Characteristic features included decoration of beakers in twisted or whipped cord and a repetition of the same pattern on the neck and belly of beakers (ibid., 161–69). Three vessels from Zealand (two lugged beakers and one ornamented funnel-necked beaker) remained outside the above groupings but, on typological grounds as well as on ornamentation, appeared to be of the same age as the south Danish C group and were provisionally assigned to yet another *south Danish (non-Megalithic) C group* (ibid., 169–72, Plates XIV and XIX: 1). In 1949 Becker was able to comment on three more vessels from Ulkestrup, Sønderød and Mern on Zealand (Becker 1949, 240–8, Figs 8, 11 and 12), which typologically belonged to the C group and bore a close resemblance to the three vessels originally assigned to the non-Megalithic C group. Moreover, Becker now included in this group the Zealand settlement of Havnelev (Mathiassen 1940, Figs 4: 3, 15–18 and 22–4) and Strandegård, where non-Megalithic C sherds were stratified above three Megalithic C beakers, suggesting either the contemporaneity or later existence of non-Megalithic C on Zealand.

According to Becker, then, in period C there were several contemporary cultural groups in southern Scandinavia, each with their own assemblage as witnessed in pottery, followed by their gradual displacement by 'the powerful and expansive Megalithic group' as early as the beginning of the Middle Neolithic (Becker 1949, 248).

The non-Megalithic C group of northern and central Jutland has now been re-named the *Volling group* after the grave of Volling, which contained twelve vessels characteristic of the Volling style (Thorvildsen 1940, 42–55). With minor adjustments, this group encompasses all the finds classified therein by Becker in 1947 and by other scholars since then (Becker 1947, 141–51; Ebbesen and Mahler 1980, 40–2; T. Madsen and Petersen 1985). Geographically, the Volling group is clearly defined; sites of all categories (settlements, graves, bog and other votive deposits) appear principally in Jutland, north of the line between Vejle and Ringkøbing (Fig. 32; Becker 1947, 147; Ebbesen and Mahler 1980, 42; T. Madsen and Petersen 1985, 114). The early dating of the Volling group on the basis of C-14 from the Rustrup grave (C. Fischer 1976, 40 and 61) has now been confirmed by the equally early dates from the earthen long barrow at Mosegården, which overlay a Volling settlement (T. Madsen 1982; T. Madsen and Jensen 1982; T. Madsen and Petersen 1985), so the early status of the Volling group, contemporary with the other early TRB regional groupings, is quite clear.

Pottery associated with the Volling group is very distinct; this is seen not only in the vessel forms but also in the decoration, both in the motifs and the techniques used in their execution. The ceramic inventory of the group includes all the forms characteristic of other Danish early TRB groups (Fig. 33). Among the diagnostic types we may note funnel-necked beakers (Becker's C-III and C-IV type) and lugged beakers (C-II; Fig. 33: 5). Collared flasks (Fig. 32: 2) are also a typical vessel form and these are represented by two basic variants: with a biconical and with a globular body. Lugged flasks, lugged jars (Fig. 33: 6) and clay discs are likewise present on Volling sites. The various beakers are among the most frequently decorated vessels and display the richest ornamentation, but decoration can also appear, sometimes in quite unexpected sophistication, on other forms.

Typical decorative techniques involve a predominant use of two-strand cord and stab-and-drag impressions. To a lesser degree we encounter various impressions: oblong stabs (T. Madsen 1975, Fig. 11: 1, 3–5; C. Fischer 1976, Fig. 26; T. Madsen 1977, Fig. 8: c, d; B. Madsen and Nielsen 1977, Fig. 8: B; T. Madsen and Petersen 1985, Fig. 20: a), curved stabs (T. Madsen 1975, Fig. 13: 17; 1977, Fig. 8: 1; B. Madsen and Nielsen 1977, Fig. 8: A) or round stabs (T. Madsen 1975, Fig. 13: 13, 18; 1977, Fig. 8: j) and multiple-tooth comb impressions (C. Fischer 1976, Fig. 29; T. Madsen and Petersen 1985, Figs 19 and 20: e). Very occasionally we encounter vertical grooves on the belly (Becker 1947, Fig. 33; T. Madsen 1972, Figs 7: 1–4 and 10: 1; 1975, Fig. 6: 1, 2; C. Fischer 1976, Fig. 19), applied short ridges on the belly (Becker 1947, Plate VI: 1; T. Madsen 1975, Fig. 5: 1; Ebbesen and Mahler 1980, Fig. 27); quite exceptional is the use of *Cardium* (T. Madsen 1975, Fig. 13: 1).

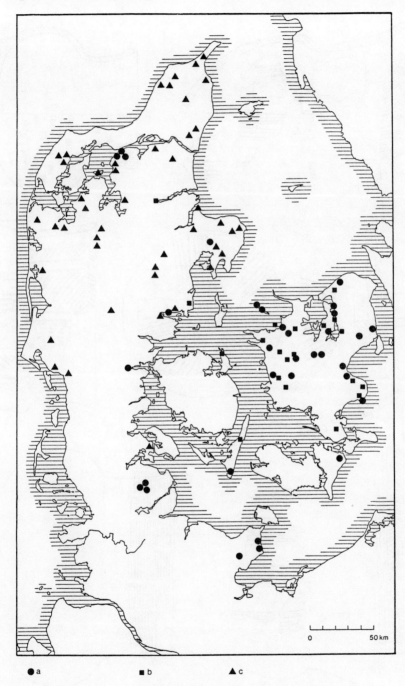

Figure 32 Distribution of the Oxie [a], Volling [b] and Svaleklint [c] pottery groups in Denmark (Source: Becker 1947; Ebbesen and Mahler 1980; P.O. Nielsen 1985).

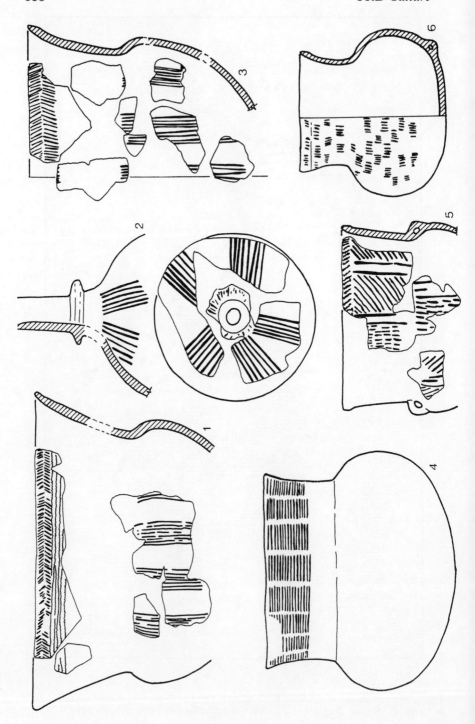

The Volling-style motifs are equally characteristic. Apparently there is no decoration on the rim (the obvious exception are of course the flat clay discs with fingertip impressions along the rim), but under-rim decoration is common. When designs are present on the neck and body, the same pattern is generally used to cover the whole surface of the vessel (Fig. 33: 3, 5, 6). Under the rim we encounter continuous or broken horizontal lines in cord or stab-and-drag (T. Madsen 1975, Fig. 10: 1; 1977, Fig. 8: a, b; T. Madsen and Petersen 1985, Figs 17: b, c, d, f and 18: b). Sometimes these may be associated with short vertical lines (individual or in groups) carried out in the same techniques (T. Madsen 1975, Figs 5 and 10: 2, 5–8, 13; C. Fischer 1976, Figs 13, 20: a and 40). Herringbone design is also quite common. Below the rim, on the neck and on the belly there may also be found vertical arrangements of short, horizontal rows which may be placed either regularly (B. Madsen and Nielsen 1977, Figs 4 and 5; T. Madsen and Petersen 1985, Fig. 17: j, k), or alternating with blank zones, creating a chess-board effect (Fig. 33: 6; C. Fischer 1976, Fig. 30; B. Madsen and Nielsen 1977; T. Madsen and Petersen 1985, Figs 18: a and 19: b). The ultimate example of the Volling style is the lugged beaker, whose surface is totally divided into strict zones by means of vertical lines of cord or stab-and-drag. The spaces in between are filled with various impressions which may be identical or may differ from one panel to the next (Fig. 33: 5; Thorvildsen 1940, Figs 1–10).

In view of the longevity of the Volling group (see Chapter 5), there has recently been a renewed interest in the changes and development in the Volling pottery style. Becker (1954a, 54) had already noted certain similarities between Volling and MN I pottery, as well as votive finds of mixed character, and argued for some MN I influence during the final stage of this group. Similarly, T. Madsen has argued for connections between the Fuchsberg style and materials of the type recognised at Tolstrup III (Andersen and Madsen 1978, 148). Elements from Tolstrup III such as herringbone decoration and horizontal or oblique rim stamps in two-strand cord are typical of Fuchsberg vessels at Toftum (T. Madsen 1978a, Fig. 5) and thus the Tolstrup III structure should be placed towards the end of the Volling group, when the MN I styles are beginning to develop. The decoration of vertical grooves on the belly of some of the Tolstrup III beakers further strengthens the connection with areas to the south.

One of the difficulties in defining Volling pottery development lies in the fact that ceramic assemblages from the Volling settlements are relatively small, such as Mosegården (T. Madsen and Petersen 1985) and Hørret Skov (T. Madsen 1977); the rich assemblage from the site at Barkær still

Figure 33 Pottery characteristic of the Danish Volling group: 1,3,5-Tolstrup III, 2-Årslev, 4-Skivum, 6-Rimsø (Source: T. Madsen 1972 and 1975; B. Madsen and Nielsen 1977).

awaits full publication. Thus in view of the lack of groups of comparative material, it is difficult to demonstrate a pattern of stylistic change. However, in their survey of early TRB rim decoration, T. Madsen and Petersen (1985, 99, Fig. 30: a) have argued for some stylistic differentiation among the ten Volling sites chosen for analysis. Among the stylistically earliest sites they include Mosegården and Rustrup (both of which have early C-14 dates), where the predominant decorative technique is two-strand cord impressions. This differs from assemblages such as Østergård and Bønnerup, where the dominant rim decoration is carried out in a stab-and-drag technique and where there is a different frequency of chisel-stamp impressions. The youngest sites, located highest in their diagram, were characterised by, among other things, very broad stab-and-drag impressions. On the basis of Tolstrup II associations one could also argue for vessels with vertical grooves on the belly being late within the Volling style although in contrast to the opinion of Ebbesen and Mahler (1980), T. Madsen and Petersen (1985, 99) consider this feature to be intrusive rather than a local trait.

The *Oxie group*, named after the Swedish early TRB site of Oxie in south-west Skåne, essentially represents just a new name for Becker's original A group (T. Madsen and Petersen 1985, 97–8) and some researchers still prefer to retain the traditional name of the TRB A group (P.O. Nielsen 1985). While the inventory of the main diagnostic elements recurrent in the Oxie group has grown since Becker's initial description, and a considerable amount of material is now known, we are still in need of a satisfactory definition of the group as a complete phenomenon and not merely as a series of ceramic forms. Recent discussion of Sigersted III by Nielsen (ibid.) goes only some way towards this goal.

The principal distribution of the Oxie group, which according to Nielsen numbers forty sites (settlements, graves, bog finds etc.; ibid., 119–20), includes Zealand, Bornholm and some of the smaller islands; a few sites are found along the eastern coast of Jutland. Swedish sites concentrate mainly in south-western Skåne and Nielsen includes in this group a few sites from Schleswig-Holstein (ibid., 120; Fig. 32). Among the Danish sites, the pits from the settlements at Sigersted III and Store Valby (Becker 1954b; P.O. Nielsen 1985) and graves at Tolstrup (T. Madsen 1975) and Dragsholm (Brinch Petersen 1974) represent the only securely contexted finds. Other assemblages derive mainly from bogs or from less secure contexts, for example Muldbjerg (Troels-Smith 1960a); occasionally, perhaps only individual pots are involved, for example at Havnelev (P.O. Nielsen 1985, 119), found with other early TRB material.

The pottery forms of the Oxie group show a wide range of vessels, with all the early types present except the collared flask. The leading vessels are of course funnel-necked beakers, variable in size but with relatively short necks. At Sigersted III pit A, classic A beakers (as defined by Becker 1947;

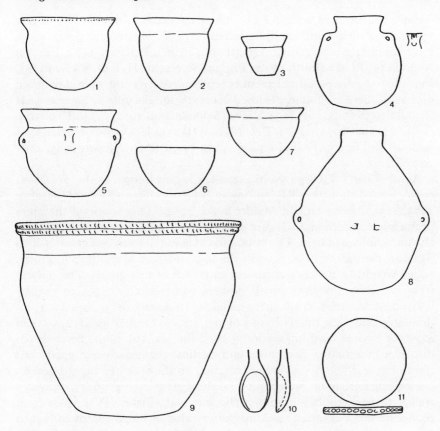

Figure 34 Pottery types characteristic of the Danish Oxie group (Source: P.O. Nielsen 1985).

P.O. Nielsen 1985, Fig. 5: 1, 2) are found together with pots revealing sharper profiles and a hint of a shoulder (P.O. Nielsen 1985, Fig. 5: 3, 5, 7, 8). Differences in profile were used by Becker to distinguish chronologically between NB and BR pits at Store Valby (1954). The multiple profiles from Sigersted III would suggest that such a distinction is no longer justified and a definition of Oxie beakers should involve more variants. The Oxie beakers are either unornamented or with horizontal row(s) of simple impressions such as irregular stamps, strokes or pits found on or under the rims (Fig. 34: 1). The large beakers (more appropriately called storage vessels) have reinforced rims with fingertip impressions (Fig. 34: 9). Short-necked lugged flasks are known from Muldbjerg I and Sigersted III and lugged jars also form a part of the regular inventory. Other forms include lugged beakers, various bowls and clay spoons.

The flint inventory of the Oxie group does, to a degree, continue the Ertebølle tradition. Among these features we may include the use of a blade technique as well as some forms such as flake axes (Store Valby, Becker 1954a, Figs 17: a–c and 22: b; Sigersted III, P.O. Nielsen 1985, Fig. 10: 1, 2) or transverse arrowheads (Dragsholm, Brinch Petersen 1974, Fig. 14; Muldbjerg, Troels-Smith 1960a, Fig. 12; Sigersted III, P.O. Nielsen 1985, Fig. 12: 1–4). A new flint element is represented by point-butted polished flint axes; these are found in closed contexts, for example at Sigersted III (P.O. Nielsen 1985, Fig. 8: 3), Värby (Salomonsson 1970, 71) and Tolstrup II (T. Madsen 1975, 143–4, Fig. 18) as well as at less well-contexted sites such as Muldbjerg, Kolind and Kolding Fjord (P.O. Nielsen 1985, 119–20).

Another early TRB group in Denmark is now known as the *Svaleklint group*, named after the TRB hunting site of Svaleklint on Zealand (Skaarup 1973, 121–7; Ebbesen and Mahler 1980, 42–4). This is one of the more problematic groups and scholars differ in their opinion as to what material should be included here. The evaluation of material from Svaleklint, which Skaarup classed as belonging to the Zealand non-Megalithic C group, added weight to Becker's argument in favour of this group. The pottery from Svaleklint included small beakers with short, straight or slightly splayed necks and a fairly sharp shoulder (Skaarup 1973, Fig. 43: 1, 2), decorated under the rim with rows of pits, strokes (ibid., Figs 41: 2, 5–7 and 42: 9) or twisted cord impressions (ibid., Fig. 42: 10). Some body sherds displayed alternating horizontal and vertical patterns in whipped cord (ibid., Fig. 42: 18). A very rich decoration on the neck of a lugged beaker, comprising horizontal rows of pits and short grooves (Fig. 36: 1), compares well with Becker's bog examples (Becker 1947, Plate XIV). Apart from funnel-necked beakers, Svaleklint pottery also included sherds of lugged jars and collared flasks but no flat clay discs.

In their discussion of the early TRB pottery, Ebbesen and Mahler (1980, 35 and 42–4) uphold Becker's distinction between the non-Megalithic C pottery of Jutland and Zealand and re-name the latter the Svaleklint group. They identify sixteen locations at which comparable material can be found (ibid., 49; Fig. 32), although some of the sites are still to be published, while elsewhere diagnostic pottery may be represented by no more than a single stray sherd as, for example, at Store Valby (Becker 1954a, Fig. 25; Ebbesen and Mahler 1980, 49, no. 10). They illustrate a selection of sherds from bog find at Sigerslev, from which the neck of a funnel beaker, decorated with an alternating pattern of pits and short grooves, is remarkably similar to that from Svaleklint (ibid., Fig. 29: 10).

Another study concerned with regional variation in Danish early pottery by T. Madsen and Petersen (1985) has already been mentioned. They analysed rim decoration from thirty-four sites in Jutland and the Danish islands and the results reveal that in the main, while no longer of chronological value, Becker's original groupings still hold good. The A group (now Oxie), Jutland non-Megalithic C (Volling) and south Danish

Megalithic C (Virum) can be clearly separated from one another (ibid., Fig. 29). In the Oxie group, the predominant decoration involves finger impressions and applied rim-thickening bands; in the Volling group two-strand cord, stab-and-drag and, to a lesser degree, oblong impressions are used; in the Virum group grooves and whipped cord appear to be dominant (ibid., 110). The difficulty appears to arise in connection with the Zealand non-Megalithic C group and B group materials, since with one exception, they also stand apart from other groups but not from each other. This underlines once again the difficult status of B pottery in the Danish TRB context. Madsen and Petersen argue that differences between the B group and Svaleklint material are not significant and, since they cannot be proved to be chronological, the sites should be considered together, that is, as the Svaleklint group. The exception is Stengade II on Langeland, where fingertip impressions and thickened rims align it with the A group (ibid., Fig. 29). Accordingly, Stengade II is regarded as a somewhat isolated phenomenon, possibly reflecting some local development.

It may be of interest to digress for a moment and comment on a few problems associated with the B material. Madsen and Petersen have arued that the traditional definition of a B-beaker, as provided by Becker in 1947 on the basis of single finds, has been rendered obsolete by the find complexes described as 'typical B', such as Havnelev or Lindebjerg, and, if we were to adhere to the old definition too rigidly, we should be obliged to include in this category finds which clearly are not of type B, such as Mosegården or Rustrup (ibid., 110–11).

This problem, although not yet overcome, has already been tackled by other scholars. Becker himself felt that a number of features at Havnelev, for instance the occasional appearance of pit impressions in shoulder ornament or the use of stab-and-drag technique, were too advanced for the B phase, and he argued for the inclusion of such traits in the C phase on stylistic grounds (Becker 1947, 245), consequently placing Havnelev in the category of 'mixed' finds.

Another assemblage assigned to the B phase was from Sølager II. In attributing this material to the B phase, Skaarup (1973, 113 n. 204), in contrast to Becker, commented on a certain similarity with Havnelev. However, for Havnelev he pointed to forty-nine flat and only three rounded bases (out of 4731 sherds) and felt that, since the round base is one of the most important characteristics of B pottery, there was a need either for a change in Havnelev's date or for an alteration to the definition of B pottery. He preferred the latter. Consequently he dated Sølager II to the B phase, with the proviso that certain elements, such as the appearance of belly decoration in twisted cord, heralded the younger C phase (ibid., 114).

Skaarup's wish for a re-interpretation of B pottery assemblages came true with the publication of Stengade II material (Skaarup 1975). Here again the Havnelev material was introduced for comparison purposes. The pit decoration under the rim and the vertical grooves on the belly observed at Stengade II were absent from Havnelev, but instead some of the rim/belly decoration typical of Havnelev was not found at Stengade II. Thus, Stengade II was thought to precede Havnelev. Skaarup felt that Stengade II material was purer and more representative of the B phase. He still accepted Becker's definition of B vessels, again with the proviso that the based were mainly flat. However, if we compare Skaarup's types for the B phase (all of which appear somewhat conjectural reconstructions), and if we ignore the collared flasks, we see little difference between this and the A-phase pottery!

Another assemblage has been claimed as 'typical B', that of Lindebjerg (Liversage 1981). We shall not concern ourselves here with the possible differences between the two separate Lindebjerg assemblages (T. Madsen and Petersen 1985), but need only comment on some general aspects. It becomes arguable, yet again, how much importance should be attached to the flat/round base dichotomy. Not many of the Lindebjerg bases are flat, but none (at least from the published drawings) are what could be called round; perhaps the German term *Wackelboden* (Wobble-base) is a more suitable description. In general, pottery from Lindebjerg compares well with that at Havnelev, and examples which Becker felt to be too early are not out of place at Lindebjerg. Moreover, some traits, for example regular bands of dots, areas of short grooves, and decoration of entire surfaces, do fit well with Zealand non-Megalithic C material (stab-and-drag, predominance of various stabs).

Of all the assemblages mentioned above, Stengade II stands furthest apart in its modest decoration as well as in some specific features. It may be of interest to note again the position of Stengade II in Madsen and Petersen's analysis as well as the fact that Skaarup himself pointed to some resemblance between Stengade II and Vårby, especially in relation to shoulder ornament, while Steinmetz (1982) has plainly argued for the inclusion of Stengade II within the A (Oxie) group.

Even the few examples quoted above give a good indication of the ambivalent status of the B pottery within the early Danish TRB; sites assigned to the B phase by one researcher have, on occasion, been given a different attribution by another, underlining the fact that the subjective interpretation of what constitutes a particular phase plays a significant role. For our present discussion two aspects are worthy of note. Firstly, the large, so-called 'typical B' assemblages, such as Havnelev and Lindebjerg, display a much wider range of both beaker type and decoration than was envisaged in Becker's original definition of B beakers. We have already noted earlier that some scholars have argued that Becker's definition of B pots, based on uncontexted vessels from bog finds, now appears too rigid (for example the flat/round base dichotomy) and requires elaboration (Skaarup 1973 and 1975; T. Madsen and Petersen 1985). Secondly, it is of note that large assemblages of the B phase, such as those of Havnelev, Lindebjerg and Sølager II, all appear to contain elements of either form or decoration interpreted as typical of the non-Megalithic C phase. Are we to think of these finds as mixed in character, or is it possible that there are no chronological differences involved and therefore, as Madsen and Petersen argue, B pottery and non-Megalithic C pottery from the islands belong to one and the same complex – the Svaleklint group?

It seems pertinent at this point to mention briefly the results of yet another survey of the funnel-necked beakers, that undertaken by E. Koch Nielsen (pers. comm.). Since Becker's original work on the typology of the early TRB vessels in 1947, the number of funnel-necked beakers in eastern Denmark has increased more than two-fold, especially from contexted sites such as settlements and graves, and it is this newly expanded source of material which forms the basis of the above-mentioned research. Koch Nielsen's criteria differ from those used by Becker, and her division of beakers into types is based upon the association of the vessel's outline (this being based on four profiles, each of which rests upon a relationship between nine key points of reference from the rim to the base of a pot) with the vessel's ornamentation (the latter being divided into a series of simple and complex patterns). It is interesting to note that the shape of the base (round, flat or any variant in between) appears to be a feature of no consequence.

While it would be premature to discuss Koch Nielsen's work in too great a detail prior to its full publication, we may note some of the results of her analysis which are startlingly different from those obtained by Becker. Koch Nielsen distinguishes five types of funnel-necked beaker (I–V; the first three are of interest here). Her type I vessel, whose main diagnostic features include a short, splayed neck, a small and slightly curved shoulder and a generally open V-profile, are found at all the key Oxie sites, such as Sigersted III, Store Valby and Muldbjerg. The same applies to the Jutland site of Tolstrup II and to the Swedish finds from Vårby. This type has also been identified by her at Stengade II.

Koch Nielsen's types II and III, while different in profile (type II: short neck, widest point of the vessel near the middle of the belly, barrel-shaped profile; type III: tall neck, barrel- or globular-shaped body, curved shoulder) are related to each other by the homogeneity of decoration which, following Ebbesen and Mahler's (1980) classification, associated the two types with the Svaleklint group. Type II includes some of Becker's A beakers from the bog finds (for example Jordløse X and Øgaarde) and some of the non-Megalithic C pots (Ulkestrup, Sønderød and Mern). To her type III belong Becker's B-beakers (Jordløse Mose XV) and non-Megalithic C vessels (Jordløse XX).

What is of particular interest to our discussion is the fact that, while type I beakers can be demonstrated to form a separate group with their own association (such as point-butted axes) and clearly correspond to the Oxie group, the beakers of types II and III cannot be separated from one another. Indeed, in a number of finds, such as at Sølager II, Svaleklint and Havnelev, both types are found together, although unfortunately none of these finds can be regarded as of absolutely secure, closed context. Moreover, at a number of other sites there are vessels which could represent either type II or type III, but where precise determination is difficult. As noted in the preceding paragraph, the decoration of types II and III is consistent with that outlined for the Svaleklint group by Ebbesen and Mahler (1980), while the association of the old B-type and non-Megalithic Zealand C-type vessels has been argued for, one somewhat different grounds, by T. Madsen and Petersen (1985).

In the light of the above discussion, and particularly in view of similar results arrived at through different analyses of the early TRB ceramic material, the suggestion that the old B and non-Megalithic (Zealand) C pottery belong to *one* regional group is very appealing indeed. Should the above arguments prove justifiable, it would then be possible to regard the Svaleklint group in the same light as the Volling group, that is, of long duration, with a varied ceramic assemblage, possibly involving stylistic changes over a period of time. However, if this is accepted, then the next stage within Danish research should be a definition of what precisely constitutes the Svaleklint group. Difficulties caused by the interpretation of B and C vessels show very clearly that this cannot be a mere lumping together of these two beaker types; this would doubtless cause more problems than it would solve. Indeed, as Koch Nielsen's and T. Madsen and Petersen's analyses independently show, there are certain assemblages, such as Stengade II, which appear to belong to neither of the eastern Danish groups but which seem to be in a class of their own. Additional difficulties, of the kind that often upset typological reasoning, arise naturally from our inadequate chronological data. The problem of the chronology of different groups is discussed in due course (Chapter 5), but it may be observed here that currently there are very good grounds for accepting that the various regional groups discussed so far belong to the same chronological horizon. While this circumstance solves some of the problems, it also adds new ones, which will have to be tackled in future.

A definition of the Svaleklint group, and this in fact applies to the Oxie and Volling groups, should be based on the study of complete assemblages, not only pottery but also flint and stone industries, and should take account of factors such as settlement types and their location within the environment, evidence of economic activities and ritual characteristics. Only then will it be possible to obtain a comprehensive picture of the Svaleklint group, and, perhaps, to attempt meaningful comparisons with other contemporary early TRB groupings in Denmark and beyond.

Before we can proceed to the next stage within the Danish TRB ceramic development, it is worth summarising the detailed evidence outlined above. Thus the early TRB culture in Denmark is present here in three contemporary and yet different groups. There can be hardly any doubt as to the distinctive status of the Volling group in northern and central Jutland; it is geographically discrete and assured in its chronological extent, and its pottery (as well as other aspects of material culture, see Chapter 6) reveals remarkable homogeneity.

The Danish islands, however, are a stage for much more complex developments during the early period. On the basis of the available assemblages of pottery we can distinguish two groups: Oxie and Svaleklint (or Oxie, Svaleklint and B group for sceptics), but these can be neither chronologically nor geographically separated from one another. We may note that, on present evidence, the Oxie group appears to be more numerous and to have a wider distribution than the Svaleklint group, especially when we take into account the adjacent eastern Jutland and southern Swedish regions (Larsson 1985), while the Svaleklint group appears to be earlier (see Chapter 5); neither of these factors, however, should be given too great a significance.

The relationship between these three groups is a key issue in early TRB studies. There appears to be no close relationship between the Oxie and Volling groups, at least as far as ceramic styles are concerned, although the find of Tolstrup, where Oxie and Volling assemblages are found within the confines of one ritual monument, may indicate that this separation is somewhat illusory. It is likely, however, that inspiration for these two groups came from separate sources further south on the North European Plain. On the other hand, the Svaleklint and Volling groups may have had quite a lot in common. While there are stylistic differences in the pottery from these two complexes, we may note some common elements which could indicate a closer relationship than is immediately apparent. In both groups decoration in two-strand cord, stab-and-drag and oblong impressions is present, albeit in different proportions. We also note the existence of motifs in which horizontal and vertical designs alternate and, occasionally, there are striking similarities even between individual vessels. For example, a beaker from Lindebjerg (Liversage 1981, Fig. 30: 7) carries a chess-board design of curved stabs, which bears an extraordinary resemblance to decoration on a lugged jar from the Rimsø grave (B. Madsen and Nielsen 1977, Fig. 8: a). It is perhaps also of some note that both groups were seemingly interested in decorating *some* vessels with very rich designs, although there are different patterns as well as decorative techniques involved, a factor which again points to similar concepts and perhaps similar sources of inspiration.

The subsequent development stage in Denmark, from about 4700/4600 BP, is frequently referred to as a transitional stage between the Early Neolithic and Middle Neolithic TRB. However, the evidence discussed

below shows that this period, far from being transitional, lays the foundations for the full establishment of the TRB culture in Denmark. As in the
preceding phase, we may distinguish three contemporary, geographically
discrete groups. In the north of Jutland the Volling group continues
although, as already observed earlier, influences from the south are beginning to make their mark on the style of ceramic assemblages. The other two
complexes are the Fuchsberg and Virum groups.

The Danish *Fuchsberg group* has been defined primarily on the basis of
bowls and lugged beakers decorated all over with a distinctive ornamentation of chevron bands (N. Andersen and Madsen 1978). The sites (settlements, graves and ceremonial places) whose ceramic assemblages include
such characteristic vessels apear mainly in eastern Jutland, on Fyn and on
some of the smaller islands (Fig. 35). Together with the already discussed
distribution of similar finds in Schleswig-Holstein and Lower Saxony, they
obviously form a geographically defined, local group within the Northern
TRB.

On present evidence the Danish Fuchsberg group appears sometime
around 4700/4600 BP and its status within the Northern TRB is now
emerging more clearly. In 1973 Hoika argued that it represented a non-
Megalithic C group (Hoika 1973, 405) Davidsen (1976, 45–9) placed it at
the beginning of the MN as contemporary with the Troldebjerg phase,
while N. Andersen and Madsen (1978, 142–4) suggested that Fuchsberg
pottery represented a transitional phase between the Early and Middle
Neolithic. With the current re-organisation of the Danish TRB, however,
it is now possible to regard the Fuchsberg group as one of the local groups
within the Northern TRB, on a par with the late Volling group of northern
Jutland and the Virum group of eastern Denmark.

As already mentioned, the most easily recognised and diagnostic vessels
of the Fuchsberg style are bowls and lugged beakers decorated with
chevron bands (Fig. 36: 3–5). The bowls are by far the most common. For
example, they constitute nine-tenths of the diagnostic pottery at Toftum
(N. Andersen and Madsen 1978, 132), and they appear in two basic forms:
a simple bowl with straight or convex sides (Fig. 36: 3), and a slightly
funnel-shaped form which is the less frequent of the two (Fig. 36: 5). Rims
of such vessels are decorated with horizontal rows of vertical impressions
which include whipped and two-strand cord, chisel stamp, oblique stamp,
Cardium or a chess-board pattern executed in the latter two techniques
(N. Andersen and Madsen 1978, Fig. 6). The principal decoration consists
of chevron bands, comprising a single row on bowls (Fig. 36: 3, 5) and a
double row on lugged beakers (Fig. 36: 2, 4). These are infilled with
horizontal impressions of whipped cord or two-strand cord (the latter is
especially common at Toftum; N. Andersen and Madsen 1978, Fig. 4),
Cardium, chisel stamp and occasionally stab-and-drag (Toftum, T.
Madsen 1978a; Nygård, Skaarup 1985). The edges of the bands are executed

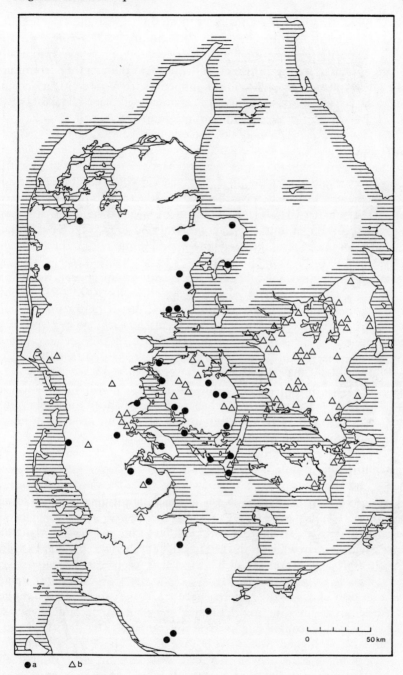

Figure 35 Distribution of the Fuchsberg [1] and Virum [b] pottery groups in
Denmark (Source: Becker 1947; N. Andersen and Madsen 1978; Schwabedissen
1979b).

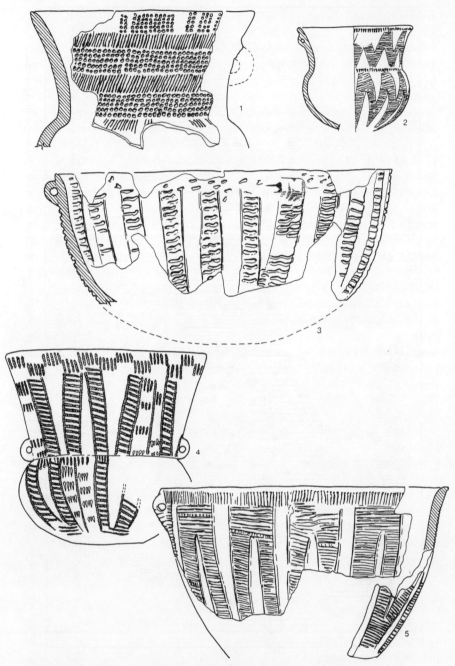

Figure 36 Pottery characteristic of the Svaleklint and Fuchsberg groups: 1-
Svaleklint, 2-Sarup, 3, 5-Toftum, 4-Rævebakken (Source: N. Andersen 1970;
Skaarup 1973; N. Andersen and Madsen 1978).

using the same techniques, although the two need not correspond on a particular vessel.

However, this specifically decorated pottery accounts on average for only 10 per cent of ceramic assemblages (N. Andersen and Madsen 1978, 139). The rest is made up predominantly of funnel-necked beakers (of Becker's C and D types; Madsen 1978a, Figs 6, 7 and 8); forms such as collared flasks, lugged jars and clay discs are less frequent. Good examples of such assemblages derive from two ceremonial sites, the already mentioned Toftum and Sarup (N. Andersen 1974a, 1974b, 1975, 1977 and 1981), but are also known from other localities (N. Andersen and Madsen 1978, 150–4).

Decoration on funnel-necked beakers is in many respects similar to that already described from the German Fuchsberg sites. Under the rim we find most commonly horizontal rows of oblique stabs, fingertip or fingernail impressions, horizontal cord lines or zig-zag lines; less frequently the more complex designs of herringbone or chess-board patterns or applied zig-zag bands appear. Similarly, the belly decoration most frequently involves grooves which are either placed in groups (Madsen 1978a, Figs 6: a, b and 7: a, c) or run in a continuous band round the whole perimeter of the vessel (ibid., Figs 7: b and 8: d). The scored grooves often lead from a deep stamp impression on the neck/belly transition; others are impressed in whipped or two-strand cord. On a number of vessels there are additional ladder patterns impressed between the vertical stripes (ibid., Fig. 8: c) or bordering the individual bands of grooves (ibid., Fig. 7: a). Sometimes the grooves are very deep, giving the impression of fluting (ibid., Fig. 7: d). Less common body patterns are also known, for example a chess-board design of multiple-tooth comb (ibid., Fig. 5: x) or infilled 'hanging' triangles (ibid., Fig. 5: q, r), all of which have counterparts in assemblages from Schleswig-Holstein and Lower Saxony.

The *Virum group*, which begins sometime around 4700 BP, principally encompasses material classed by Becker as belonging to the south Danish Megalithic C group, although its distribution is a matter of some discussion. Ebbesen and Mahler (1980, 38) state that the pottery executed in the Virum style is found on the Danish islands, in south Jutland and Schleswig-Holstein. T. Madsen and Petersen (1985, 101), however, accept the existence of the Virum group on the islands to the east of the Great Belt, but feel that the material in the west is somewhat different and therefore it is not possible to determine whether or not the Virum group precedes the appearance of the Fuchsberg group in south-western Denmark.

The ceramic inventory of the Virum group (Fig. 37) includes all the vessels present in the preceding phase (Becker 1947, Fig. 44: b; Skaarup 1975, Fig. 54: 1) and it is known from graves (for example Vedskølle, Emmelev and Løjt (Thorvildsen 1941)), settlement sites (for example Knardrup Galgebakke (Larsen 1958), Strandegård (Becker 1947), Sølager

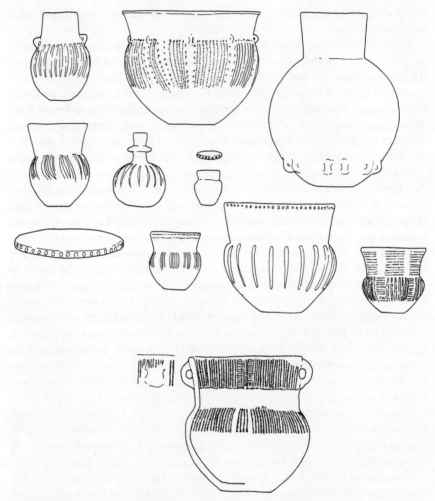

Figure 37 Pottery types of the Danish Virum group (Source: Skaarup 1975).

III (Skaarup 1973), Stengade I (Skaarup 1975), Virum and Lindsidegård (Ebbesen and Mahler 1980)) and votive bog finds (for example Lindbjerggård, Ellekærgård (Becker 1947), Skuerup Mose and Maglelyng (Ebbesen and Mahler 1980)). The leading forms include the funnel-necked beakers of type C-I and lugged beakers of C-III; however, lugged flasks or collared flasks are regularly encountered in graves (Thorvildsen 1941).

The lugged beakers carry the richest decoration (Ebbesen and Mahler 1980, Figs 11: 1 and 19: 2) but funnel-necked beakers (Fig. 38: 1), lugged jars (Fig. 38: 2) and lugged or collared flasks may also, on occasion, be profusely decorated. Most of the decoration is executed in whipped cord; this technique is now regarded as one of the diagnostic features of the

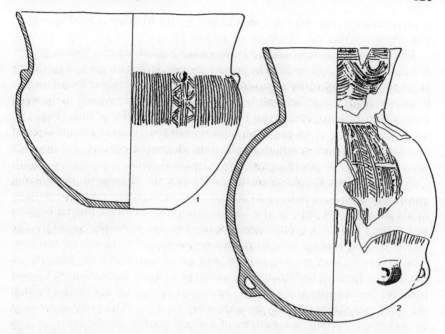

Figure 38 Virum pottery: 1-Humblemose, 2-Skuerup Mose (Source: Ebbesen and Mahler 1980).

Virum style, although two-strand cord impressions and plain grooves are also encountered. Ebbesen and Mahler (1980, 37), who included the assemblage from Stengade I within the Virum group, also added a variety of horizontal cord lines, fingertip and fingernail impressions, curved and stamp impressions and rounded pits to the inventory of the Virum style. The decoration on many vessels is characterised by a strong tendency to the regular division of the surface into zones, a feature heralding the almost mathematically strict zonal decoration of the MN I styles.

Funnel-necked beakers are often decorated on the belly with pattern of vertical lines, which are grooved or impressed in whipped cord and can be found either running continuously round the vessel (as for example on the beaker from Maglelyng; ibid., Fig. 21: 2) or arranged in groups separated by blank spaces (ibid., Fig. 12: 9, 12, 18, 20) or interspersed with other motifs. Lugged beakers represent the ultimate in Virum-style decoration: under the rim there are usually several horizontal cord lines (ibid., Fig. 19: 2), and the neck may be decorated with vertical lines, filled hanging triangles or zig-zag patterns (ibid., Fig. 11: 1, 3), sometimes interspersed with horizontal motifs (Becker 1947, Plate XIII: 1). The belly usually carries an arrangement of vertical whipped-cord lines. A very special design of the Virum style is represented by multiple hanging crescents in whipped cord or, more rarely, two-strand cord (Ebbesen and Mahler 1980, Fig. 11: 1; Fig. 38: 2).

The nature of the relationship between the Fuchsberg and Virum groups is still difficult to determine. On present evidence the two groups appear to be largely geographically separate: the Virum pottery style is found mostly to the east of the Great Belt, while the Fuchsberg's distribution is to the west, in southern Jutland, on Fyn and on some of the smaller islands (Fig. 35). There are a number of characteristics within the ceramic assemblages of both groups, however, which imply some degree of contact and possibly even a common origin of certain more unusual traits.

First of all we should note that, although the diagnostic ornamental motifs and decorative techniques are different, both groups contain especially richly decorated vessels: in the Virum group this involves lugged beakers and in the Fuchsberg group lugged beakers as well as bowls. Secondly, the funnel-necked beakers of both groups reveal a number of similar features. The C-type beakers are common in both groups, although the presence of the D-type form in the Fuchsberg group or D-type decoration on C-type beakers (for example at Sarup; N. Andersen 1977, Fig. 2: a) suggests that the Fuchsberg ceramics may be somewhat younger. The body decoration of beakers, especially the pattern of vertical stripes on the belly, is also worth noting. In the Virum group these are regularly executed in whipped cord; the Fuchsberg beakers tend to have their pattern engraved with a sharp tool, although cord decoration is by no means absent (ibid., Fig. 10: a; T. Madsen 1978a, Fig. 8: a, c). In both groups there are also examples of vessels with very deep grooving resembling fluting (Skaarup 1975, Fig. 37; T. Madsen 1978a, Fig. 7: d). With regard to neck decoration, we can point to a common use of horizontal cord impressions and zig-zag lines below the rim, as well as to the more unusual motifs of triangles and multiple crescents.

We have already noted earlier that the latter two patterns, while not excessively common, are nevertheless associated with the north German Fuchsberg assemblages, and thus are clearly an integral part of the Fuchsberg style. Indeed, similar patterns are found even further afield, for example in Mecklenburg (Nilius 1971a, Plate 16: 9), and are likely to form a regular decorative element over a large area of the Northern TRB culture. Multiple hanging crescents are found in a number of north German Fuchsberg assemblages, for example at Tosterglope (Dehnke 1940, Plate III: 9, 11, 15, 19, 20), Haaßel (ibid., Plate III: 30) and Sachsenwaldau, here associated with a handle (Schwabedissen 1970, Fig. 2: 11). As we noted earlier, the same motif has recently been identified as typical of the decorative inventory of the Virum ceramics.

The above examples show sufficiently clearly the fact that during the existence of the Fuchsberg and Virum groups there was some degree of contact between them. Whether we can argue for a common inspirational source outwith Denmark for some decorative elements, such as hanging triangles and crescents, or whether this is an instance of mutual contacts and influences between the eastern and western parts of the country, remains to be verified through future research. It will become clear in the following discussion, however, that both styles played an important role in the development of the subsequent MN I styles, since diagnostic elements of both can be perceived in the stylistic development that followed on from Fuchsberg and Virum.

4.4.3.2 Danish Middle Neolithic TRB ceramics. Before we embark upon the study of the development of the Danish Middle Neolithic (MN) pottery, a few comments of a historical nature may help to place the discussion in a broader perspective. It must be emphasised that the boundary between the Early and Middle Neolithic is a purely artificial designation and cuts across the continuous development of the TRB culture. It reflects earlier divisions of the Danish Neolithic based upon grave-form classifications by Montelius (1894–1905) which, in a version modified by Becker (1947), still remains in general use. As will be seen throughout this work, such a division cannot be sustained on archaeological grounds and appears to be retained for purely historical reasons. As a classificatory scheme, however, it has had a profound influence upon Danish research which, even today, tends to concentrate either side of this divide with little work spanning the boundary. The frequent reference to the Fuchsberg group as transitional between the EN and MN is a good example of the incongruous nature of such a division and a response to the impasse created by such a classificatory system. Additional confusion results from the complex (but not entirely clear) relationship between the TRB and Single Grave cultures during the MN, and recently an attempt has been made to designate MN TRB as the MN A period and the Single Grave culture as MN B (P.O. Nielsen 1979, 53).

One of the early attempts at a sub-division of MN pottery was the work of S. Müller (1913 and 1918). Müller consciously ignored the undecorated pottery and his typo-chronological division was based exclusively on the consideration of ornamental motifs and decorative techniques. The scheme of six chronological phases (I–VI) comprising seven decorative styles (A–F) showed a strong degenerative interpretation, clearly exemplified in the succession of names bestowed upon the ceramic styles, such as *der grosse Stil* (the Grand Style), *der schöne Stil* (the Beautiful Style), *die erste Zeit des Verfalls* (the First Declining Period), *die letzte Verzierkunst* (the Last Ornamentation) etc. This division persisted until 1936 when Forssander, on the basis of research at the passage grave of Høby, proved the contemporaneity of Müller's 'Grand' and 'Beautiful' styles and introduced a much-simplified four-period division: I – transitional from Dolmen to Rich Cord-Decorated Pottery, II – the Grand Style, III – Tooth-comb Decoration, and IV – the Degeneration Phase (Forssander 1936, 32).

The first 'settlement chronology' was indicated by Jens Winther's investigations of the three Langeland settlements of Troldebjerg, Blandebjerg and Lindø, which then appeared to span the entire Passage grave period (Winther 1926, 1928, 1935, 1938 and 1943). Winther's ideas were subsequently expanded by Mathiassen (1944, 88), who argued that 'large, systematically excavated settlement finds provide more reliable chronological criteria' than grave finds. Supplementing the results of Winther's investigations with his own from Bundsø on Als (Mathiassen 1939) and Trelleborg on Zealand (Mathiassen 1944), Mathiassen distilled from the mass of evidence what he considered to be the diagnostic elements 'of greatest significance when determining the chronological relationship between the different phases', that is, 'elements that were not in use all throughout the Passage Grave Period' (ibid., 93–5). His subsequent positioning of settlements within the chronological sequence (indicated earlier by Winther) was based on the assumption that each site represented a different settlement period, and he concluded that 'these five settlement finds cover the entire Passage Grave Period' (ibid., 96, Fig. 9).

Berg (1951) added one more settlement – that of Klintebakke on Langeland – to the above scheme, arguing for its placement between the Troldebjerg and Blandebjerg phases (ibid., 16–18). He also pointed to the existence, in the Skovtofte passage grave, of some crude and undecorated pottery which he assigned to a post-Lindø stage (ibid., 30–2). Meanwhile, Becker (1954a and 1954b) was embarking upon some fundamental research concerning the MN period, which resulted in the identification of the youngest TRB pottery stage (the Store Valby phase), an interpretation of the relationship between the TRB and other cultural complexes, and a critical revision of the Trelleborg settlement (Becker 1956), which was found to be a multi-phase site and was ultimately removed from the chronological scheme (Fig. 39). Becker's TRB chronology, modified once more in 1959, was enthusiastically accepted not only in Denmark, but also in the other areas where research on the TRB culture was lagging behind.

While with time it became apparent that the large settlement sites were far from chronologically pure and simple, and as more material became available from the research programmes of the 1960s and 1970s, the Danish MN typo-chronology came under severe criticism, especially from foreign scholars (Malmer 1962; Hoika 1971; Nilius 1971a). However, in spite of its drawbacks, the scheme still appears to provide a general working framework and few attempts have been made to change or modify it.

Most recent research into the MN TRB pottery in Denmark has been carried out by Ebbesen. Two separate monographs deal with the pottery from the Danish islands (Ebbesen 1975) and north Jutland (Ebbesen 1978); shorter accounts of pottery from votive deposits and a re-interpretation of the ceramic assemblage from Troldebjerg are also available (Ebbesen 1979a and 1979b, Ebbesen and Larsen 1980). Dissatisfied with the chronological

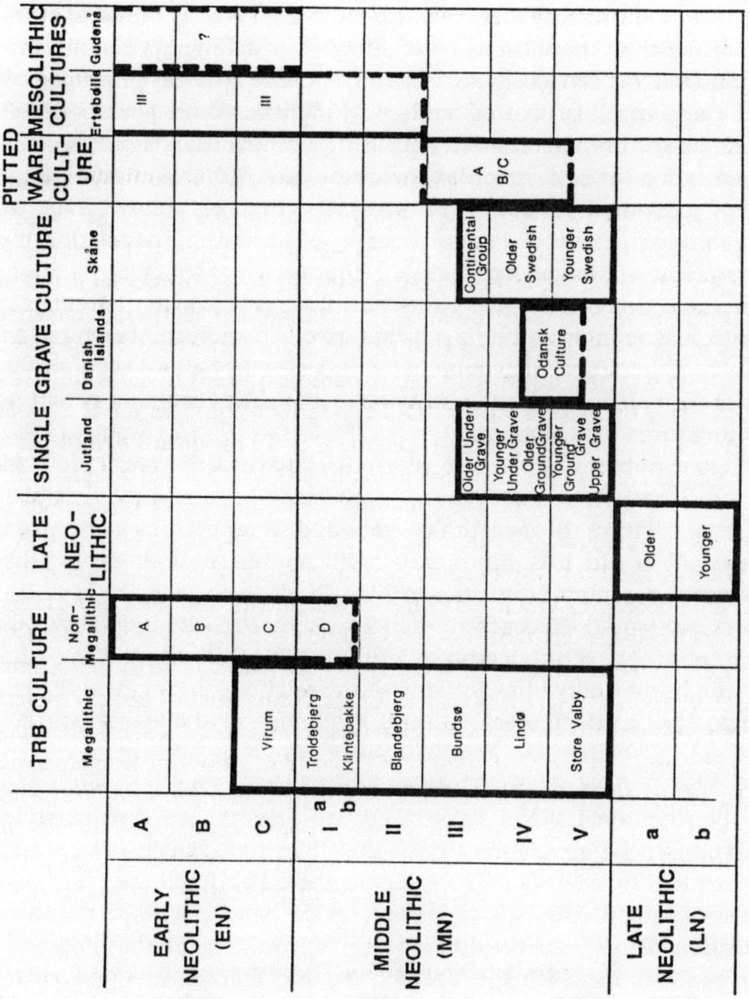

		TRB CULTURE		LATE NEO-LITHIC	SINGLE GRAVE CULTURE			PITTED WARE CULTURE	MESOLITHIC CULTURES	
		Megalithic	Non-Megalithic		Jutland	Danish Islands	Skåne		Ertebølle	Gudenå
EARLY NEOLITHIC (EN)	A		A						III	?
	B		B							
	C	Virum	C						III	
MIDDLE NEOLITHIC (MN)	I a	Troldebjerg	D							
	I b	Klintebakke								
	II	Blandebjerg							A	
	III	Bundsø			Older Under Grave		Continental Group		B/C	
	IV	Lindø			Younger Under Grave / Older GroundGrave	Odansk Culture	Older Swedish			
	V	Store Valby			Younger GroundGrave / Upper Grave		Younger Swedish			
LATE NEOLITHIC (LN)	a			Older						
	b			Younger						

Figure 39 Becker's chronological scheme for the Danish Neolithic (Source: Becker 1954a).

inadequacies of settlement materials, Ebbesen deliberately chose to study pottery derived from megalithic graves. Since Danish funerary ceramics are rarely found in stratified locations, Ebbesen chose to arrive at chronological criteria by analysis (like that of Sophus Müller) based on pottery decoration. The procedure, first carried out for the Danish islands material and subsequently for Jutland, involved the division of decoration into a large number of individual patterns (Ebbesen 1975, Figs 4–17; 1978, Fig. 50: a–e), which were then grouped into clusters on the basis of the relationship between individual designs (1975, Plate I, Fig. 19: a–d; 1978, Plate I). Eight main groups or decorative styles were thus distinguished and presented in a chronological sequence. The problems involved in such reasoning are well known, although we may note in passing that Ebbesen's typo-chronology is more reliant upon the traditional settlement chronology than he chooses to admit (1975, Fig. 30).

Apart from Ebbesen, two more researchers have been concerned with pottery – E. Jørgensen and Davidsen. Jørgensen's (1971 and 1977) publication of material from the megalithic tombs and stone-packing graves from north Jutland, in which he appears to challenge the traditional view that passage graves were not built prior to MN Ib, does not seem to have had the impact one would expect from such a contention. Davidsen (1978), on the other hand, has been concerned mainly with the final stages of the TRB culture (the Store Valby phase) and with the relationship between the late TRB and other contemporary cultural groupings in the area (1977 and 1978).

MN I: Ia Troldebjerg, Ib Klintebakke and the Jutland ceramic styles. Within the traditional MN I phase there are a number of ceramic styles which appear to be geographically distinct. On the Danish islands it is possible to identify two styles: Ia Troldebjerg and Ib Klintebakke (Fig. 40). The vessel forms of the two styles are on the whole similar; the main distinguishing features are the differences in decoration and the apparently separate contexts in which the Troldebjerg and Klintebakke pottery are found. The Klintebakke finds are more numerous and, on typological grounds at least, are generally considered to succeed rather than be contemporary with Troldebjerg (Berg 1951, 16–18; Ebbesen 1975, Fig. 21; 1978, Fig. 53).

On the Jutland peninsula the situation is more difficult to interpret. In the north, E. Jørgensen (1977) has identified the so-called Hagebrogård and Vroue I styles which tend to be synchronised with MN Ia and Ib of the islands respectively, while in the south-west the earliest MN pottery appears to show similarities with the Fuchsberg as well as the Klintebakke styles (Gebauer 1978). In 1978 Ebbesen chose to refer to the earliest MN pottery in north Jutland simply as MN I, arguing that typical Ia finds, while present, were not sufficiently numerous to allow a differentiation of material similar to that observed on the islands (Ebbesen

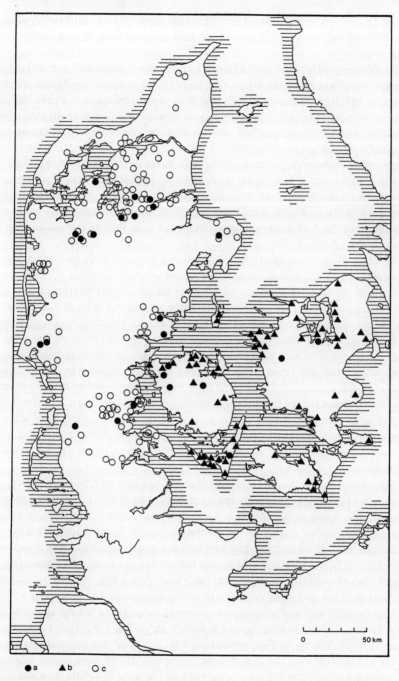

Figure 40 Distribution of MN Ia [a], MN Ib [b] and MN Ic [c] pottery styles in Denmark (Source: Ebbesen 1975 and 1978).

1978, 72). Moreover, certain decorative elements separate the north Jutland material from the rest of Denmark and thus give it a distinctly local character.

Troldebjerg MN Ia style. Material from the Langeland settlement of Troldebjerg was published by Jens Winther (1935 and 1938) and subsequently used by Therkel Mathiassen in a 'chronological valuation' of Danish settlements (Mathiassen 1944). Elements such as thin-butted axes, discoidal knives, funnel-necked beakers and cord ornamentation, connected Troldebjerg with the preceding TRB phase (the Dolmen/EN period). Mathiassen, however, pointed out new features of this assemblage, such as battle axes of the Fredsgårde type, chisels, pedestalled and Troldebjerg bowls and clay spoons as well as rich *Cardium* and stamp decoration, which placed it outwith the Dolmen period. He therefore considered the Troldebjerg find as representative of phase I within the Passage Grave period (ibid., 89, 96, Fig. 9).

In 1951 Berg compared the Troldebjerg pottery with the ceramics of another Langeland site, Klintebakke. Apart from the obvious general similarities, Berg noted a number of features which clearly distinguished the two assemblages. He observed, for instance, that decoration at Klintebakke on the whole displayed a higher quality of execution; decoration of bowls and shoulder pots was arranged more in groups, and vertical decorative panels were wider and were marked off by zig-zag bands and horizontal lines under the rim (ibid., 16). Features not encountered at Troldebjerg included the incorporation of handles into the overall design of the pot and a new ornamental tool producing a curved stamp impression. On the basis of stylistic comparisons of pottery, as well as the fact that Troldebjerg pottery was not encountered in the passage graves, Berg concluded that Troldebjerg represented an earlier stage of the first phase of the Middle Neolithic.

Pottery from the Troldebjerg settlement has recently been reviewed by Ebbesen (1979a, 48–78), who analysed ornamental motifs from vessels of identifiable form in an attempt to define the character of the so-called Troldebjerg style. The only numerous vessels at Troldebjerg are beakers (78.2 per cent of all sherds) and bowls (16.9 per cent); other forms include pedestalled bowls (3.4 per cent), clay ladles (1.3 per cent), clay discs (1 per cent) and shouldered bowls (0.2 per cent; ibid., Fig. 56). The funnel-necked beakers are most commonly decorated under the rim with a horizontal band of vertical strokes, a horizontal zig-zag or a combination of the two in a number of variations (Winther 1935, Figs 29 and 31–3; 1938, Fig. 12; Ebbesen 1979, Figs 57 and 58; Fig. 41: 3). Other decorative motifs, such a rows of pits, whipped cord impressions, applied wavy lines or designs similar to the Virum group such as hanging multiple crescents, are also illustrated in Winther's publications (Winther 1935, Figs 32 and 33) but, according to Ebbesen's (1979a, Fig. 58) statistics for decorative patterns, they are not very common. Vertical lines, grooved or scratched, appear on 98 per cent of belly sherds and may be either continuous or arranged in groups (Winther 1935, Figs 29, 31 and 33; 1938, Fig. 12; Ebbesen 1979a, Figs 59 and 60).

Eight lugged beakers have been identified at Troldebjerg. They carry a neck decoration of horizontal motifs combining zig-zag and vertical strokes, either stamped or executed in whipped cord; on the belly there is an arrangement of narrow vertical bands filled with oblique strokes and/or the so-called 'zipper' patterns (see Bakker 1979, 180 for explanation), and lugs are also decorated with individual designs (Fig. 41: 2; Winther 1938, Figs 12: 2, 5, 7, 14 and 14; Ebbesen 1979a, Fig. 59).

While there are some spherical bowls as well as miniature forms, the majority of bowls belong to the so-called Troldebjerg type. This is a somewhat unfortunate name, since the type also appears in association with other styles. The name refers to the form of the bowl which is flat-based and widest at the rim; it may have a straight, concavo-convex profile and has two opposite, horizontally pierced lugs under the rim (Ebbesen 1975, Fig. 2: a–b; Fig. 41: 1). Bowls are more profusely decorated than any other vessel form. Decoration is arranged in a horizontal band under the rim, with the rest of the body covered by vertical decorative panels that commonly reach right down to the base. Decoration under the rim involves what appears to be an infinite variety of zig-zag and short vertical stroke combinations, of which the most common is a double zig-zag separated by a row of short strokes (about 11 per cent; Winther 1935, Figs 36: 4 and 37: 6; Ebbesen 1979a, Figs 62 and 63). Among the less frequent but interesting motifs we may note criss-cross hatchings, chess-board designs and alternating zig-zags creating rhomboidal images; plain stamp is most common but the designs may also frequently be made by using *Cardium* or whipped cord (Winther 1935, Figs 36–8; 1938, Fig. 13).

The body decoration exceeds that of under-the-rim in variety, but Ebbesen observes that there are fewer dominant patterns; most common are the vertical bands filled with horizontal strokes, patterns which are strongly reminiscent of the Eastern TRB group 'ladder' motif (16 per cent of sherds; Winther 1935, Figs 36: 2 and 37: 2; Ebbesen 1979a, 57, Fig. 65: SB6) and triple 'zipper' bands with oblique or horizontal strokes filling the outer segments (13 per cent of sherds; Winther 1935, Figs 36: 10 and 37: 7, 9, 10; Ebbesen 1979a, Fig. 56: SB69–84). Other triple-band patterns include criss-cross or oblique hatchings (Winther 1935, Figs 36: 1, 10, 11 and 37: 2, 4–6, 11, 17, 18) and *Cardium* impressions either within bands (ibid., Fig. 37: 10) or placed individually (ibid., Figs 36: 9 and 38: 21). The chess-board designs under the rim are strongly reminiscent of early TRB patterns (Volling and Virum decoration) and Ebbesen (1979a, 61) comments on thirty-five pottery fragments with a pattern reminiscent of the Fuchsberg-style infilled chevrons.

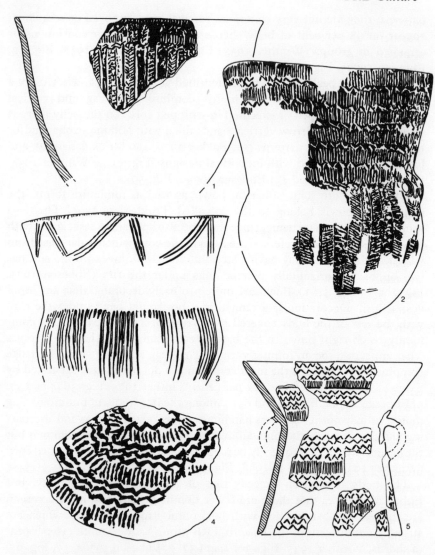

Figure 41 Pottery of the Troldebjerg (MN Ia) style: 1–3-Troldebjerg, 4-Kjølsengård, 5-Garup (Source: Winther 1935 and 1938; Ebbesen 1979a).

Pedestalled bowls and clay ladles appear to be closely associated with each other in megalithic contexts, but the Troldebjerg find is relatively poor with regard to these forms. Sherds of pedestalled bowls are not numerous and the decorative patterns are uniform, and mostly comprise alternating horizontal zig-zags and rows of vertical strokes (78 per cent of sherds), although zig-zag alternating with horizontal criss-cross bands is also known (Winther 1935, Figs 42 and 43). Clay ladles (Fig. 41: 4) may or may not carry decoration on the handle; the bowl of the spoon sometimes has an edge design and an interior filled with a different motif (Winther 1935, Fig. 44: 7); a combination of zig-zags and strokes is the most common but pits, stabs and *Cardium* impressions are also found at Troldebjerg (ibid., Fig. 44; Ebbesen 1979a, Fig. 67).

In his review of the Troldebjerg pottery, Ebbesen distinguished 356 individual decorative patterns, but many of them appear to be confined either to specific vessel types or to zones of decoration (Ebbesen 1979a, 68). He was able to distinguish thirteen patterns (illustrated here in Fig. 42), which are each found on more than 100 sherds. These patterns are considered to be diagnostic of the Troldebjerg-style finds (Ebbesen 1979a, 69, Fig. 72) which, while not numerous, appear throughout Denmark and in a wide range of contexts. They are known from settlements (such as Orelund), votive bog deposits (Rødemose), catching/hunting sites (Verup Mose), cult houses (Herrup), ritual enclosures (Såbydal) and predominantly megalithic graves of dolmen type (Præsthøj, Borre or Vedsted). The latter appear to be confined to Jutland, since so far no such finds in megalithic graves have come to light from the Danish islands (Berg 1951, 18; Ebbesen 1975, 124; 1978, 72; 1979a, Finds list 7).

Thus the Troldebjerg style appears to be widely if not densely distributed, but for the present its relationship with other MN I pottery remains ambiguous and it is not certain whether we are observing the contemporaneity of the Troldebjerg style with other local MN I ceramics or the succession of one upon the other; the available C-14 dates for the MN I contexts tend to support the former (see Chapter 5). Its position at the beginning of the Danish MN sequence does also appear to be supported by the continued importance of the earlier vessel forms (such as funnel-necked beakers or lugged beakers), but at the same time we also note the appearance of hitherto unknown types such as pedestalled bowls (Fig. 41: 5) and clay ladles, shouldered jugs and a variety of bowls.

Klintebakke MN Ib style. The Klintebakke Ib style is currently known from the Danish islands; it appears in all known contexts and is particularly well represented on the island of Langeland (Skaarup 1985) as well as on north Fyn and north Zealand (Ebbesen 1975; Fig. 21). The Ib pottery from megalithic graves has been classified by Ebbesen. On the whole, the ceramic forms known in the Troldebjerg style are also found here with the addition of shouldered cups and the so-called Hagebrogård bowls (named after the vessels discovered at the passage grave of Hagebrogård in north Jutland; Ebbesen 1975, 80–1, Figs 49: 1, 97 and 105; E. Jørgensen 1977). While a direct comparison with Jutland is not possible in view of the ambivalent relationship of all the MN I materials, we may note that the dominant Ib vessels on the islands are not the funnel-necked beakers (which account for 22 per cent), but Troldebjerg bowls (28 per cent) with pedestalled bowls in second place (24 per cent); ladles are also common (10

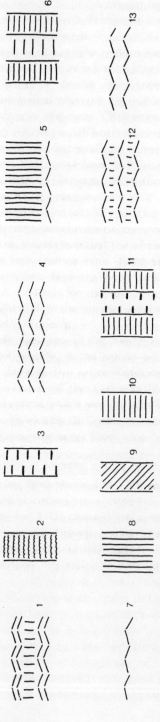

Figure 42 Major decorative patterns of the Troldebjerg style (Source: Ebbesen 1979a).

per cent; Ebbesen 1975, Figs 97 and 105). How these proportions compare with the relative importance of forms found outwith the megalithic context simply cannot be determined, since no detailed data on the settlements are available, but it is possible that we are observing the beginning of a new trend in the shift to the importance of bowls over other forms, a trend which continues right through to MN III styles.

The decoration of the Klintebakke style is very distinct and the Langeland settlement of Klintebakke itself (Berg 1951) is still the best assemblage indicative of the style's character. The Ib-style decoration, which adheres to firm rules, follows closely the shape of the vessels, and individual patterns appear only in specific zones. It is also a style of the greatest variation in patterns, with many appearing only once or twice. Decorative techniques include the use of stab-and-drag, *Cardium* impressions and a variety of stamps, of which the most notable is the curved version, used only rarely outside the Klintebakke style. Cord, both two-strand and whipped, still continues and tooth-comb impressions also begin to appear (Fig. 43: 1, 6).

The funnel-necked beakers are decorated under the rim with pits and single or multiple zig-zag lines (Berg 1951, Plate I: 1, 4), some of which are large enough to extend well onto the neck (Fig. 43: 3; Berg 1951, Plate I: 2). The pattern of the horizontal band of short vertical stokes enclosed above and below by single/multiple zig-zag lines (common in the Troldebjerg style) is also present (Ebbesen 1975, Fig. 31: 1, 5); this motif acquires a greater variety of techniques when it appears on Ib bowls. The belly of the beakers carries a decoration of vertical grooves which may be continuous (Fig. 43: 3; Ebbesen 1975, Fig. 31: 5) or grouped (Berg 1951, Plate II: 1). Thus the funnel-necked beakers on the whole appear to continue a decorative tradition noted towards the later stage of the early TRB.

The richest decoration appears on bowls and lugged beakers (Fig. 43: 1, 4, 5). Many funnel-necked bowls show a clear separation of neck and belly, which may be further accentuated by the application of decoration (Ebbesen 1975, Fig. 35: 2). The so-called Troldebjerg bowls display a clearly distinguished horizontal decoration under the rim, the rest of the body being covered with vertically arranged motifs which, at the bottom of the bowl, rest against a single or multiple zig-zag line (Fig. 43: 4). The under-rim decoration includes a variety of patterns: a combination of zig-zags impressed in chisel stamp, curved stamp or whipped cord (Berg 1951, Plates III: 1, 2, 5, 7, IV: 1, 12 and V: 12, 21; Ebbesen 1975, Fig. 44: 4, 6), zig-zag bands filled with *Cardium* or cord impressions (Berg 1951, Plates III: 3, 9 and IV: 1), criss-cross patterns (ibid., Plates III: 4 and IV: 20), horizontal bands of vertical strokes impressed with tooth-comb, chisel stamp, *Cardium* or whipped cord (ibid., Plate III: 1, 5, 12; Ebbesen 1975, Fig. 31: 1) or horizontal lines which may be grooved (Berg 1951, Plate V: 14, 22), cord impressed (ibid., Plates IV: 8, 10, 20 and V: 21; Ebbesen 1975,

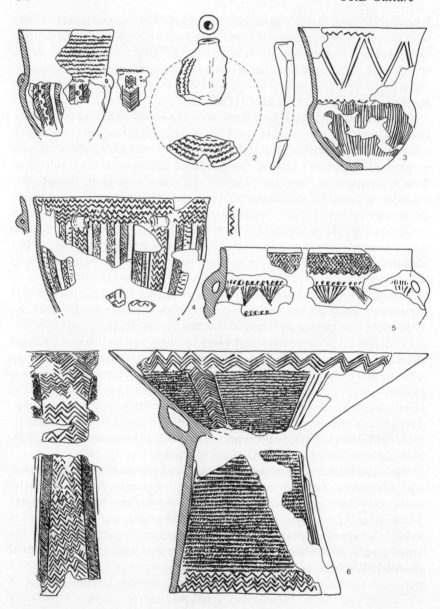

Figure 43 Pottery of the Klintebakke (MN Ib) style: 1-Rugtved, 2-Lykkeby, 3, 4, 6-Vedsted, 5-Himmelev (Source: Ebbesen 1975 and 1979a).

Fig. 83: 1) or executed in a stab-and-drag technique (Ebbesen 1975, Fig. 44: 6) or by means of curved stamp (ibid., Fig. 44: 4). Combinations of these various motifs have been illustrated by Ebbesen (1975, Figs 4–9) and the most common include patterns R4, 5, 9, 19, 22, 29, 31, 33, 56, 64 and 66.

Among the types of body decoration, the vertically placed triple-band motif constitutes a 'trade mark' of the Klintebakke style (Berg 1951, 11). This consists primarily of a 'zipper' ornament (using a curved stamp, pit or horizontal stab) in the central band, bordered on either side by a band impressed with *Cardium*, oblique stamp or criss-crossing (Berg 1951, Plates III: 1, 2, 6, 20, 21 and V: 22; Ebbesen 1975, Fig. 44: 6). This arrangement can be found repeated around the bowl, interspersed with blank spaces (Berg 1951, Plate III: 2, 4, 6) or in association with other designs firmly placed within vertical zones (ibid., Plate III: 1; Ebbesen 1975, Fig. 44: 6; Andersen 1981, Fig. 25: f). Apart from the 'zipper' pattern, the triple-band motif may be executed using other decorative elements (see Ebbesen 1975, Fig. 17, especially B5, 6, 9, 10 and 11). There is great stress on the regularity of the pattern and an almost rigid alternation between individual bands of an order not seen in the Troldebjerg style.

Another feature which distinguishes the richly decorated bowls of the Klintebakke style from those of the Troldebjerg style is the appearance of different decoration beneath the handles, which in effect divides the bowl into two halves (Fig. 43: 4). The commonest pattern of this zone is a triple band in which the central panel is filled with 'wwww' lines bordered either by blank spaces (Ebbesen 1975, Fig. 44: 4) or by bands with other impressions such as oblique stamps and criss-crossing. *Tvaerstik* decoration is also a new element and it appears quite commonly on decorated bowls (ibid., Fig. 44: 6).

The lugged beakers of the Klintebakke style display ornamentation which in technique and arrangement follows closely that of the richly decorated bowls. Berg (1951, Plate II: 4) illustrates two sherds of a lugged beaker from Klintebakke, where the decoration under the lugs differs from that of the rest of the body in precisely the manner found on the bowls; the same arrangements are illustrated by Ebbesen (1975, Fig. 34: 1) and Andersen (1981, Fig. 25: d). The decorative motifs also follow the bowl patterns closely: triple-band designs are the most common (Fig. 43: 1; Ebbesen 1975, Fig. 31: 7) and the lugged beaker from Sarup (N. Andersen 1977, Fig. 2: c) is unusual in its repetition of the same decoration on the neck and belly. The pedestalled bowls of the Klintebakke style carry predominantly horizontal designs, of which the most common is the all-over decoration with horizontal rows of uninterruped stamp impressions: for example zig-zag stamps (Berg 1951, Plate II: 10, 12, 13), curved stamps (ibid., Fig. 20: 2) or less rigidly applied *Cardium* impressions (ibid., Fig. 20: 1). While vertical arrangements on pedestalled bowls acquire greater importance only in the Blandebjerg style, we see the introduction of some vertical elements here as well. For example the handles, like on the decorated bowls and lugged beakers, provide an opportunity to introduce a different pattern above and below (Fig. 43: 6); the rim edges and lower segments of the foot carry typical Ib designs (Berg 1951, Plate II: 11, 14; 1956, Fig. 20: 2).

The Jutland MN I ceramic styles. With the recent identification by Ebbesen (1979a) of the Troldebjerg-style finds on the Jutland peninsula, one could be excused for thinking that the remainder of the MN I material in Jutland should logically correspond to the Klintebakke style as it is known on the Danish islands. Unfortunately the situation is more complex for, while some of the Jutland MN I material corresponds to that described above as Klintebakke style, there is also material which reveals differences that not only set it apart from the ceramic development on the Danish islands, but also indicate a number of local traits within Jutland itself, reflecting a somewhat different background against which the MN I styles developed in individual areas.

The general trends in the importance of ceramic forms in the north and south Jutland megalithic context appear to be similar. Ebbesen's (1978, Fig. 93) comparisons show that the most commonly encountered vessels are the funnel-necked beakers (40 per cent and 51 per cent respectively), followed by pedestalled bowls (16 per cent and 20 per cent) and Troldebjerg bowls (9 per cent and 17 per cent). In the north there are additionally considerable numbers of funnel-necked bowls (12 per cent) and clay ladles (7 per cent); other vessels appear in both regions only sporadically. However, in a paper which appeared at the same time as Ebbesen's study of the north Jutland TRB pottery, Gebauer (1978) presented the results of her work on pottery from fifteen megalithic graves in south-west Jutland. The predominant vessel there is a pedestalled bowl, followed by a shouldered vessel, a clay ladle and only then a funnel-necked beaker (ibid., Fig. 21). In view of the rather small sample, it is difficult to say whether this reflects real or illusory differences between Jutland's regions. The occurrence in the south-west of some rather unusual examples of pedestalled bowls (ibid., 136–40) may suggest, however, that this vessel form was of particular importance here. On the other hand the overall figures for Jutland and the Danish islands (Ebbesen 1975, Fig. 97; 1978, Fig. 93) do suggest that there is a real difference in the importance of funnel-necked beakers and Troldebjerg bowls in their respective areas.

From Ebbesen's (1979a, Fig. 82) distribution map of the Troldebjerg-style pottery in Denmark it is clear that this style was known in Jutland. However, when compared with the overall distribution of MN I megalithic sites (Fig. 40), we note that the former are few and far between (especially if we discount all but megalithic Troldebjerg contexts). It is therefore far from clear whether we can accept, as Ebbesen argues, the independent

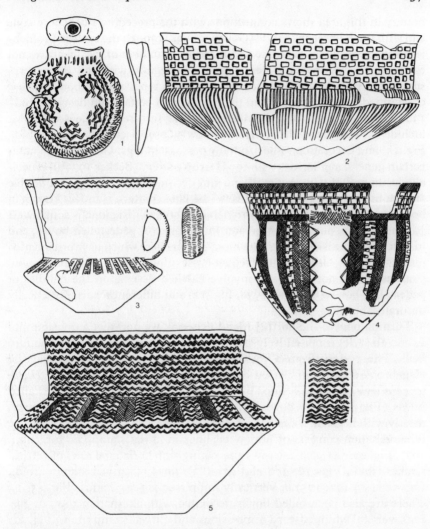

Figure 44 Pottery of the MN I style from north Jutland: 1-Tårupgård, 2–5-
Hagebrogård (Source: E. Jørgensen 1977; Ebbesen 1978).

existence of the Troldebjerg style in Jutland. The Troldebjerg settlement
still remains the only relatively large assemblage known in the literature
(Winther 1935 and 1938; Ebbesen 1979a). Of the other sites listed by
Ebbesen (1979a, Finds list 7), many appear to contain very small amounts
of typical Troldebjerg-style pottery, and with the notable exception of
Hagebrogård (E. Jørgensen 1971 and 1977), they are inadequately published. Thus the relationship between the Troldebjerg-style pottery and
the remaining material from individual sites cannot be determined.

Turning to the south-west of Jutland, we note that the earliest MN TRB pottery in this area shows connections with the preceding Fuchsberg style and with the Klintebakke style (Gebauer 1978, 130–2); the typical Troldebjerg style is hardly in evidence and there are a number of local features not encountered elsewhere in Denmark. A connection with the Fuchsberg-style pottery is seen in the continuity of certain types of open bowl, the use of whipped cord decoration and the retention of certain rim designs (ibid., 130–1, Fig. 2: 2–5). The Klintebakke-style features in the south-west include vertical band decoration on bowls, use of curved stamp (ibid., Fig. 15) and decoration of horizontally perforated lugs. Gebauer also notes certain general similarities with the Herrup pottery (Becker 1973b), especially in the use of whipped cord and rim decoration consisting of a double zig-zag interrupted by a vertical row (the latter pattern is in fact known in both the Klintebakke and Troldebjerg styles). Regional, south-west Jutland features include the greater importance of pedestalled bowls, and in contrast to the islands there are more beakers here which have ornamented necks; there is also a more frequent use of whipped-cord decoration. Contrasts with north Jutland involve hatched designs on the handles of pedestalled bowls (Gebauer 1978, Fig. 12) and different forms of vertically decorated bowls.

Turning now to the north Jutland material, we find that a division into Ia and Ib styles is not entirely satisfactory for the interpretation of pottery here. The pottery from a votive layer in front of the passage grave at Hagebrogård has been classed by E. Jørgensen (1977, 187–8) as of *Hage-brogård style*, which is defined by decorative patterns found on pedestalled bowls (Fig. 45). The bowls from Hagebrogård are decorated all over, mostly with horizontal designs which run all the way round the vessel. The ornamentation consists of horizontal lines in chisel stamp (E. Jørgensen 1977, Fig. 21: 144), zig-zag rows alternating with horizontal rows of vertical strokes (ibid., Figs 12: 170 and 22: 183), lines of curved stamps (ibid., Fig. 22: 157, 172, 175) or vertically impressed zig-zag bands (Fig. 45: 1). There are also pedestalled bowls decorated with alternating rows of zig-zags, vertical whipped-cord impressions and curved stamp (ibid., Fig. 22: 149). Three examples display vertically arranged decorative zones: vertically placed criss-cross hatched bands divide the surface into segments whose interior carries horizontally placed rows of stamps (ibid., Fig. 21: 161), simple 'zipper' ornament (ibid., Fig. 22: 172) or horizontal zig-zag with a 'ladder' motif (ibid., Fig. 22: 172). Upper and lower rims are decorated with vertical strokes or zig-zag lines and one example carries a chess-board pattern of regular stamps (ibid., Fig. 22: 183).

Jørgensen equated his Hagebrogård style with MN Ia from southern Denmark (ibid., 188). However, a number of the pedestalled bowls carry decoration which is clearly diagnostic of what was described above as the Klintebakke style, most notably the curved stamp (ibid., Fig. 22: 157, 172, 175) or infilled zig-zag bands (ibid., Fig. 22: 173). On the other hand the

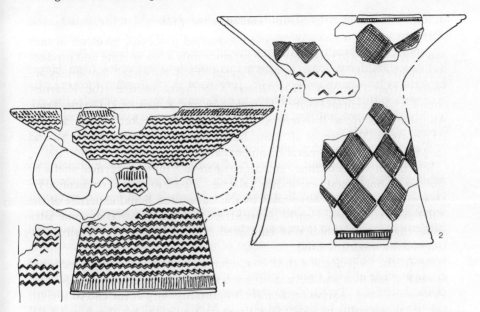

Figure 45 North Jutland MN I pedestalled bowls: 1-Hagebrogård, 2-Sødalshøj
(Source: E. Jørgensen 1977; Ebbesen 1978).

pedestalled bowls decorated in horizontal zig-zags (Fig. 45: 1) and a bowl
illustrated by Jørgensen (1977, Fig. 22: 172) are typical of the Troldebjerg
style; other bowls may also be placed here.

Various other vessels from the votive layer at Hagebrogård passage
grave could also be classified with MN Ia. We may compare some of the
Hagebrogård pottery with vessels from the cult house at Herrup, only a
short distance away. The oldest Herrup vessel (Becker 1973b, Fig. 4),
found in the foundation trench, has been classified by Becker as MN Ia.
This is a rather squat funnel-necked vessel decorated on the neck with a
chess-board pattern of rectangular stamps; vertical, possibly whipped-
cord, lines on the belly are interrupted by irregular stamps. Other pottery
from Herrup which has been assigned to the Ia style includes a pedestalled
bowl (Becker 1969, Fig. 7; Ebbesen 1979a, Finds list 7); a clay ladle (Becker
1969, Fig. 11) is identical to one from Vedsted classed by Ebbesen as MN
Ib (1979a, Plate XXIX: 11).

Returning now to the Hagebrogård assemblage, we may point to three
tri-partite bowls (Fig. 44: 2; Jørgensen 1977, Fig. 26: 144, 146, 167, 168),
where the decoration is very similar to that of the Herrup vessel; these must
surely be regarded as contemporary. The chess-board design, as we
observed earlier, was a strong decorative element of the Volling group,
especially found on the richly decorated lugged beakers. It appears that the

decoration of Hagebrogård and Herrup vessels is rooted in the earlier, local northern tradition.

Among the typically northern elements quoted by Ebbesen (1978, 137–41) are shouldered jugs. Ebbesen mentions two examples from Hagebrogård as belonging to MN Ia (E. Jørgensen 1977, Fig. 27: 150, 174); by comparison this surely would have to be extended to other vessels (Fig. 44: 3). The decorative motifs of these jugs are all known in association with the Troldebjerg style.

While the scope of this work precludes a more detailed study of MN I ceramics, interesting and controversial points emerge from the examples mentioned above. For instance, the fact that Jørgensen placed the nine Hagebrogård pedestalled bowls in MN Ia while Ebbesen, correctly it seems, split them into Ia and Ib, reveals a strong element of subjective judgement involved in these assignations and highlights the difficulties that researchers face in the interpretation of individual vessels. Moreover, the reason why Ebbesen in his 1978 publication on north Jutland ceramics chose to write of MN I pottery does not appear to be entirely related to his claim that Ia (i.e. Troldebjerg) style was very scarce there. In many instances the pottery can be desribed only as MN I in style, a fact which must surely indicate that the Troldebjerg and Klintebakke styles can account for only a part of the MN I ceramic inventory.

The identification of both Troldebjerg and Kilntebakke styles at the Hagebrogård passage grave raises a number of other issues. The fact that the Troldebjerg style is not found in the passage graves on the Danish islands has always been explained by the assertion that the Troldebjerg style preceded the Klintebakke style and that the passage graves were not built until the former went out of use. One may ask, however, whether the absence of Troldebjerg in megalithic contexts on the Danish islands should be interpreted from the point of view of chronology. Could it be explained in terms of the scarcity of the Troldebjerg style in this area, or was it simply not fashionable in this area and not used there for purposes of ceremonies at megalithic tombs?

Ebbesen has argued that there is no evidence for an overlap between the Troldebjerg and Klintebakke styles. Yet at Hagebrogård it is not possible to separate the two styles and from an archaeological point of view they have to be considered as contemporary. It therefore appears that Ebbesen's arguments in favour of defining the decorative styles by the study of pottery from megalithic contexts can no longer be sustained and that we must consider other contexts as well. Recent excavations at Hanstedgård (Eriksen and Madsen 1984) suggest that settlement inventories may contain ceramics which show features of both styles but cannot be identified specifically with one or the other. That settlement assemblages are of importance is also clear from the fact that it would be impossible to define the Troldebjerg style itself without the Troldebjerg settlement! We may thus ponder over what appears to be one of the great puzzles of the Danish TRB: how is it possible that a ceramic style which can claim 356 decorative motifs on one site, can be so poorly represented elsewhere? Is the Langeland island and its TRB settlement a unique phenomenon?

One more important theme which the above discussion reveals is the continued strength of regional groups, which is seen very clearly during the period in which the discussed styles were in use. The boundaries of earlier groupings are still visible. On the other hand we also begin to observe a certain degree of uniformity, expressed in Danish literature by the nebulous term 'only MN I'; however, the elimination of strong differences is only achieved with the development of the subsequent MN II styles.

MN II: Blandebjerg and Early Ferslev ceramic styles. The dominant ceramic style during the Danish MN II period is the so-called *Blandebjerg style*, which was originally noted at yet another large Langeland settlement, that of Blandebjerg (Winther 1943; Mathiassen 1944). On the Danish islands this style is known in a variety of contexts: settlements (Blandebjerg; Trelleborg: Mathiassen 1944, Becker 1956; Lyø: Christensen *et al.* 1979), ritual enclosures (Sarup: N. Andersen 1974a, 1974b, 1975, 1977, 1981, 1988a, 1988b), stone-packing graves (Stålmosegård: U. Hansen 1973) and numerous megalithic graves. There are eighty-eight of the latter identified by Ebbesen (1975, Figs 22 and 98) containing 218 vessels altogether; they appear to be concentrated mainly in north-west Zealand.

Dominant vessel forms encountered in the graves on the islands are shouldered bowls (55 per cent, Fig. 47: 1), shouldered cups (24 per cent, Fig. 47: 3) and hanging vessels (10 per cent, Fig. 47: 5), while other forms such as funnel-necked beakers or open bowls and pedestalled bowls are considerably less frequent (Ebbesen 1975, 119, Fig. 98). From settlement sites with MN II inventories we may add a range of vessels not found in association with graves: Troldebjerg and other bowls (Fig. 47: 4, 6; Winther 1943, Figs 24 and 25), clay discs (ibid., Fig. 39; Davidsen 1976) and clay ladles (Mathiassen 1944, Fig. 7: 10) as well as large storage vessels (Winther 1943, Figs 3, 4 and 35).

Differences in the regional importance of vessel forms are again apparent when MN II material from Jutland is considered. For while shouldered bowls also appear to be most common in megalithic contexts (40 per cent in the north, 36 per cent in the south), funnel-necked beakers are still important (13 per cent in both areas). Funnel-necked bowls are more frequent in south Jutland (20 per cent); then follow the hanging vessels (9 per cent and 6 per cent respectively), and pedestalled bowls are still relatively important (8 per cent and 5 per cent). Shouldered cups, which appear to be so popular on the islands, amount to only 6 per cent and 5 per cent in Jutland (Ebbesen 1978, 100–1, Figs 89–92). As in the preceding period the south-western corner of Jutland appears to retain its individuality, at least as far as pottery forms placed in graves are concerned. Pedestalled

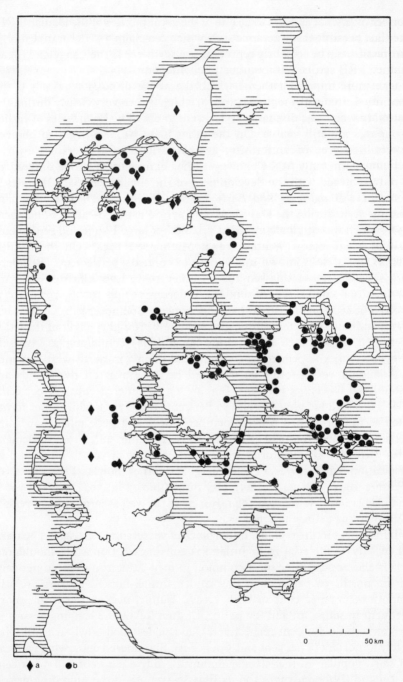

Figure 46 Distribution of the Blandebjerg [b] and Early Ferslev [a] styles in
Denmark (Source: Ebbesen 1975 and 1978).

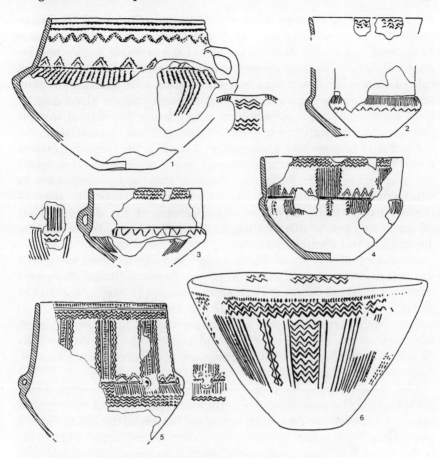

Figure 47 Pottery of the Blandebjerg (MN II) style from the Danish islands: 1-Lundbygård, 2-Sødalshøj, 3-Kyndeløse, 4-Kastrup Mark, 5-Martofte, 6-Blandebjerg (Source: Winther 1943, Ebbesen 1975).

bowls are still most important, followed by shouldered vessels and funnel-necked beakers. New ceramic forms include bi- and tri-partite shouldered vessels; funnel-necked bowls do not appear to be of importance (Gebauer 1978, 128, Figs 2: 10, 11 and 21).

With regard to the decoration of pottery we will first of all offer a few general comments which can be applied to the whole of Denmark. In her study of the stylistic variation in the Danish TRB pottery, Gebauer (1984) commented that in MN II the ornamental motifs are used more freely on various parts of the pot than was the case during MN I and that many designs are independent of the shape of the vessel. The band effect of MN I decoration is abandoned in favour of a contrast arrived at by the juxtaposition of decorated and empty zones (Fig. 47: 6). On carinated vessels the decoration begins to move below the carination (Fig. 47: 4). A smaller proportion of vessels are now decorated (18 per cent at Blandebjerg; Mathiassen 1944, 91). Motifs cover less of the available surface and are more deeply cut. Common decorative techniques include the use of denticulated stamps, stab-and-drag and occasionally also tooth-comb; plain stamp and *Cardium* impressions are less frequent than on MN I pottery. Cord impressions are becoming increasingly scarce and instead we note their imitation through the use of incised lines with short transverse strokes (barbed wire or *tvaerstik*). Contrasts in decoration are frequently accentuated by the use of different techniques on the same vessel. New motifs which appear in this period include a feather motif and circles, which are either single, concentric or with dots (Winther 1943, Fig. 31; Fig. 48: 1, 2). Highly diagnostic is the virtual disappearance of the double zig-zag separated by a row of short vertical strokes, which was so common in the Troldebjerg and Klintebakke styles.

Blandebjerg MN II style. As the name suggests, the Blandebjerg style was first identified by decoration on pottery from the Blandebjerg settlement on Langeland (Winther 1943; Mathiassen 1944). Most of the characteristics described below can be identified there. The funnel-necked beakers, which are no longer a very common vessel form, are decorated with pits or stamps under the rim and vertical incisions on the belly (Winther 1943, Fig. 23); similar beakers are also known from Sarup (N. Andersen 1981, Fig. 27: a).

The so-called Troldebjerg bowls have straight sides narrowing steeply towards the bottom and, instead of perforated lugs, they often have applied bosses. The under-rim decoration consists of horizontal lines and/or multiple zig-zag lines, often in *tvaerstik* or denticulated stamp. The body is decorated in grouped patterns of vertical grooves, stab-and-drag or *tvaerstik* lines, vertical zig-zag lines or broad panels filled with horizontal zig-zags; all these groups are separated by empty spaces (Fig. 47: 6). Decoration stops well short of the base of the pot and very often there is no horizontal border below (Winther 1943, Figs 25 and 26; Mathiassen 1944, Fig. 4: 2; Andersen 1981, Fig. 27: 2).

Shouldered cups and bowls demonstrate a variety of forms, with necks from funnel-shaped, straight to conical and variously shaped shoulders and bellies (Figs 47: 1, 3 and 48: 3, 4). The rim decoration consists of the individual or combined application of horizontal lines or multiple zig-zags which can be executed in plain, *tvaerstik* or stab-and-drag technique (Ebbesen 1975, Figs 4–9, patterns R1, 3, 8, 13–17, 35, 36, 53 and 57 for the most commonly encountered motifs). On the neck we may find upstanding triangles or groups of vertical lines sometimes bordered by a vertical zig-zag or a feather motif (Fig. 47: 4; Ebbesen 1975, Figs 10–15, especially patterns H3–5, 7, 19, 49 and 51). The shoulder may be decorated with hanging triangles (Fig. 47: 3) which are still relatively small or with patterns

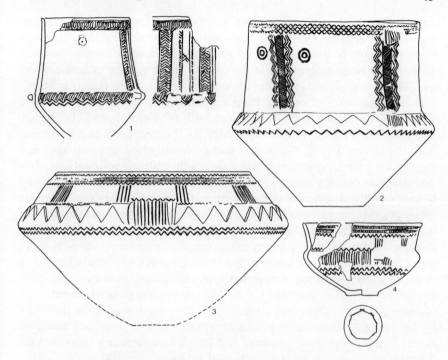

Figure 48 Pottery of the Blandebjerg (MN II) style from Jutland: 1-Næsborg, 2, 3-Trustrup, 4-Bygholm Nørremark (Source: Kjærum 1967a; Ebbesen 1978).

consisting of arrangements of vertical lines (Fig. 47: 1, 4) – in general similar to neck designs, which extend over the carination onto the belly of the bowl (Ebbesen 1975, Fig. 16, S1–3 for shoulder patterns).

The clay ladles and pedestalled bowls appear to become increasingly scarce on the islands; Ebbesen (1975, III) quotes only four MN II examples from megalithic graves. Only a few sherds have appeared at Blandebjerg (Winther 1943, Figs 37 and 38), decorated with a feather motif. However, with the demise of these two forms we note the emergence of a new form, a shouldered hanging vessel (Figs 47: 5 and 48: 2). These pots, on average between 16 cm and 20 cm in height, have conical necks of the same size as the belly. Some are richly decorated under the rim, on the neck and on the neck/belly transition. Clay discs continue in use and appear with or without perforations. From Blandebjerg we know of discs with rows of small holes and pits round the edge and in the centre, and discs scratched with radial lines (Winther 1943, Fig. 39) as well as discs decorated with parallel lines (Davidsen 1976, Fig. 11: 3, 5).

MN II and Early Ferslev in Jutland. MN II pottery in Jutland is known from a number of finds (Fig. 46). Ebbesen (1978, Chapter IV, n. 50) mentions thirty-seven megalithic graves from north Jutland and similar pottery has been recovered from settlements (Dommerby hede and Bygholm; Davidsen 1976) and cult houses (Tustrup, Ferslev; Kjærum 1955, 1957, 1967a, 1967b; Marseen 1960). While there are many similarities with the Blandebjerg style of the islands, there are also differences and it is difficult to determine whether these are chronological or merely regional.

In his discussion of pottery from cult houses at Tustrup and Ferslev, Kjærum (1967a) originally placed the bulk of Tustrup and the earlier material from Ferslev (Ferslev I) in MN Ib. The Ferslev I pottery comes from the earlier deposit of trodden sherds, found along the west wall and outside the house, which included a clay ladle and two pedestalled bowls (one decorated with a lozenge pattern impressed with a dentate tool, which Kjærum said was identical with that from Tustrup: 1967a, 329; Marseen 1960, 51). The main Ferslev deposit (Ferslev II) of thirty-six vessels was dated to MN III on the basis of its general similarity to the Bundsø style. Because of this dating, Kjærum felt there was little scope for MN II in north Jutland, in spite of the fact that there appeared to be little similarity or typological connection between the Klintebakke, Trustrup and main Ferslev pottery (Kjærum 1967a, 329). He implied a regional differentiation of pottery styles in Denmark, a feature already commented upon earlier by Becker (1954a). However, in 1969 Kjærum changed his mind and dated the earlier Ferslev (Ferslev I) material to MN II, from which it followed that Tustrup finds should also be dated to this period (Fig. 48: 2, 3).

Ebbesen (1978, 73), in his study of north Jutland material, pointed out that from the point of view of decoration there was a clear group of vessels which could be included neither with MN I nor with MN III styles; it was this material that he placed in MN II. The problem was moreover compounded by the fact that in this group there were vessels decorated with tooth-comb (Ebbesen's Ferslev style), which on the basis of form and motifs clearly belonged to MN II inventories. A somewhat similar observation was made by Kjærum (1969, 45, Figs 18 and 19) in respect of the finds from the Katbjerg-Jordhøj passage grave, where an earlier and later MN II pottery was distinguished, the four bowls in question (HAG–HAK) having a less pronounced shoulder and a decoration executed in tooth-comb. It would therefore appear, as argued by Ebbesen, that during the later part of MN II in north Jutland we see the development of the Ferslev (Early Ferslev) style, where typical MN II decoration is executed in tooth-comb.

During MN II in Jutland, funnel-necked beakers are still found in both domestic and ritual contexts. This includes beakers with relatively short and slightly splayed necks which are decorated with pit rows or horizontal zig-zags, and carry a decoration of short vertical strokes on the belly (Glob 1952, no. 147; Davidsen 1976, Fig. 4: 1). There are also beakers with a tall neck, angular belly and distinct shoulder (Fig. 47: 2). Some of the north Jutland beakers are decorated in the Early Ferslev style, but Ebbesen nevertheless thinks of them as belonging to MN II (Ebbesen 1978, Fig. 7: 2). Among the funnel-necked beakers from Jutland we must also mention examples which have chevron bands on the neck. The majority of this type belong to MN I style, but Ebbesen dates five examples to MN II and eight examples to the Ferslev style (Ebbesen 1979a, 43, Figs 50 and 51). All the MN II examples, with two exceptions (Grønhøj and Ålstrup Mark) are found in south Jutland and very clearly form an extension of what in Schleswig-Holstein are known as the 'Denghoog' beakers (see section on Schleswig-Holstein, Chapter 4.4.1).

As on the Danish islands, shouldered bowls are the most common vessels in megalithic contexts; in the north there is also a local type of a funnel bowl without a handle (Davidsen 1976, n. 39). The shoulder is often very distinct and the bowls are decorated under the rim with a variety of horizontal lines, zig-zags and cross-hatchings (Marseen 1960, Fig. 17; Davidsen 1976, Fig. 3: 9). On and over the shoulder there are vertical grooves sometimes interruped by zig-zag lines or short transversely placed strokes (Ebbesen 1978, Fig. 42: 6). Infilled triangles are also a common motif (E. Jørgensen 1977, Fig. 26: 172; Ebbesen 1978, Figs 69: 1, 3, 4).

Hanging vessels also represent a new ceramic form in Jutland, the MN II style examples having a more or less cylindrical neck and a prominent shoulder (Fig. 48: 2). There may be lugs attached under the rim or at the shoulder or just simple perforations under the rim (Kjærum 1969, Fig. 25: HBF). Decoration is fully diagnostic of MN II, with criss-cross hatchings, hanging triangles or short vertical strokes under the rim (Fig. 48: 1); the same pattern may be repeated on the shoulder or a different ornament may be placed there. The neck may be decorated with vertically placed grooves, zig-zags or narrow bands filled with horizontal zig-zag rows (Fig. 48: 2). As on the shouldered bowls, some examples have circle motifs on the neck.

Whereas on the islands the pedestalled bowls appear to have lost their importance, they are clearly still popular in Jutland. Typical decoration consists of vertical groups of lines bordered by a vertical zig-zag (Tustrup, Brøndsted 1957, 242, Fig. on far right); a vertical zig-zag also appears in combination with horizontal furrows, for example at Vroue Hede I (E. Jørgensen 1977, Fig. 39: 63) and Skibshøj (Thomsen 1971, Fig. 5). Pedestalled bowls decorated with large, infilled rhomboids which alternate with empty spaces are also known from a number of sites, for example Tustrup (found here with their appendant clay ladles; Kjærum 1967a, Fig. 3: a; Brøndsted 1957, 242, Fig.), Ferslev (Kjærum 1967a, 329) and Vroue Hede I (E. Jørgensen 1977, Fig. 39: 11). Many such examples are known from megalithic contexts in southern Sweden, where they are also dated to MN II (Bagge and Kaelas 1950). Kjærum (1967a, 331) has pointed out, moreover, that this type of pedestalled bowl appears on the whole to have a restricted distribution in northern Djursland and around the Limfjord and may indeed represent a specialised local trait characteristic of northern Jutland and the south Swedish TRB at this particular stage.

Pedestalled bowls are also common in south-west Jutland. We may return here to Gebauer's (1978, 132, Fig. 12) study of material from this area of Denmark and note that her second phase includes material typical of MN Ib as well as MN II. We have already commented on the decoration of a pedestalled bowl from Skibshøj, and Gebauer further includes here pedestalled bowls whose horizontal grooved decoration is interrupted by cross-hatched triangles which are placed vertically in the handle zone. On the whole the pottery of her second phase shows similarities with the Blandebjerg style (especially from Sarup) and the northern MN II (especially Tustrup, with neck decoration of grouped vertical lines, or vertical bands on the shoulders of bowls, as well as *tvaerstik* and vertical zig-zag bands). There is hardly any of the stab-and-drag decoration so diagnostic of the Blandebjerg style, however, and grooved-line decoration on the bellies of vessels is rare as well.

We have already noted earlier that during the MN II in north Jutland there appears a group of pottery which differs somewhat from the bulk of the material representative of this style. While by virtue of form and decorative patterns this pottery clearly falls into the MN II ceramic category, the ornamental motifs are executed in a hitherto rare technique using tooth-comb impressions. The distribution of such vessels is relatively limited, with the main concentration in West Himmerland (Ebbesen 1978; Fig. 46), and this pottery constitutes the so-called *Early Ferslev style* (Fig. 49), the developed form of which is evident, for instance, in the rich ceramic assemblage of the Ferslev cult house (Kjærum 1967a) and which seems to have spread to other parts of Denmark during the subsequent ceramic phase of MN II (Ebbesen 1975, 50–2).

Twelve megalithic contexts and one settlement with pottery exhibiting the features of the Early Ferslev style have been identified by Ebbesen (1978, Chapter 4 n. 87). This includes a number of vessels whose form is typical of MN II in north Jutland. The shouldered hanging vessel from Grønhøj (Thorvildsen 1946, Fig. 8: middle) has a tall, concave neck and in profile is very similar to the example from Ålborg-egnen (Ebbesen 1978, Fig. 74: 1). The former has typical MN II elements (decoration under the rim and vertical *tvaerstik* lines on the neck). According to Ebbesen, the rim decoration of the Ålborg-egnen vessel is typical of MN Ib (Klintebakke style) on the islands but known in north Jutland during MN II, while the rhomboids on the neck and triangles on the shoulder are infilled with tooth-comb impressions. The funnel-necked beakers from Grønhøj (Thorvildsen 1946, Fig. 5) and Sødalshøj (Fig. 49: 1) are both typical, tall-necked MN II examples with the 'Denghoog' pattern on their necks carried out in tooth-comb. Shouldered bowls from Sødalshøj (Fig. 49: 2) and Jordhøj (Kjærum 1969, Fig. 19: HAG) are placed in MN II on the

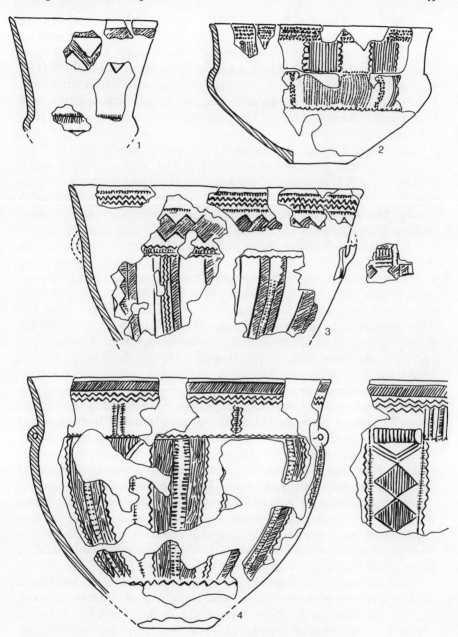

Figure 49 Pottery of the early Ferslev style from Jutland: 1, 2, 4-Sødalshøj, 3-Voldstedlund (Source: Ebbesen 1978).

basis of decoration patterns, as indeed are the Hagebrogård bowl from
Jordhøj (ibid., Fig. 18: HAF), the Troldebjerg bowl from Voldstedlund
(Fig. 49: 3) and the lugged bowls from Sødalshøj (Fig. 49: 4; Ebbesen 1978,
Fig. 7: 3). The latter two are even regarded as being early in the MN II on
the basis of decoration related closely to that typical of MN I (ibid., 76).
Kjærum (1969, 45) interpreted all the Jordhøj vessels mentioned above as
transitional in form and argued for a smooth development from MN II to
MN III in north Jutland.

According to Ebbesen (1975, 50) the above-noted examples are representative of the early phase of the new ceramic style or *Ferslev style*, which
develops in MN II in north Jutland and there is a close typological connection between MN II and the Ferslev style. Apparently no such relationship
can be observed on the islands, where the Ferslev style is said to stand
isolated among the MN III pottery.

It is perhaps appropriate at this juncture, before we move on to discuss
the MN III pottery, to digress momentarily and consider an interesting
dichotomy in definitions of the MN Danish pottery styles. As we have seen,
there is little cause to doubt that the fashion of decorating vessels with
tooth-comb impressions develops during the MN II in north Jutland and
there appears to be general agreement among Danish scholars that the
Ferslev style develops in Jutland and is foreign to the islands (Ebbesen 1975
and 1978; Davidsen 1976, n. 39). However, the definition of the Ferslev
style is far from satisfactory.

Firstly, while this may appear an insignificant point, it must be noted that
Kjærum, who proposed the name 'Ferslev style', used it merely as a sub-
stitute name for what was previously known as the Bundsø style (which was
only vaguely described earlier by Mathiassen 1944, 93), and did not
redefine the style. Kjærum felt that in the Ferslev cult house 'For the first
time we have here a reliable, closed find from this period, showing its
contents of pot shapes and further details of its style of ornament' (Kjærum
1967a, 329). In passing we may note that the Ferslev cult house pottery,
which has never been fully published, appears to be dominated by open
bowls. Even in comparison with the Bundsø settlement material it shows
that, while undoubtedly homogeneous, it can hardly be thought of as
representative (Marseen 1960, Figs 11–16).

As already outlined in detail earlier, Ebbesen (1975 and 1978) has defined
his MN styles using decoration as a typo-chronological criterion in preference to the forms of the pots. Among the leading Ferslev patterns he
includes the following: R7, 20, 25, 48, H14, 38 and B4 (Ebbesen 1975, 51,
Fig. 19). However, it is of interest to note that the ornamental motifs
employed appear either in MN II or MN III or both, although they are not
executed in tooth-comb. Indeed, Ebbesen makes it very clear that the MN
II ceramic forms and decorative patterns characterise the Early Ferslev in
north Jutland, while the Late Ferslev style is typified by MN III forms and

patterns in Jutland and on the islands (1975, 50–2; 1978, 75–6). Thus we cannot point to any decorative motifs which could be regarded as diagnostic of the Ferslev style. The only significant feature of the Early and Late Ferslev appears to be the use of tooth-comb decorative technique, although in the Early Ferslev other techniques may be found on one and the same pot.

Thus the definition of the Ferslev style appears to rest upon the use of tooth-comb decorative technique. We need only recall the elaborate and multi-feature definitions proposed for the other MN styles discussed earlier, such as the Troldebjerg or Klintebakke styles, to note the obvious inconsistency. In such a context it is surely justified to ask how we should define an independent ceramic style. Is the use of a specific ornamental technique a sufficient criterion for such a distinction? One has the impression that a fashionable technique which originated in one area and subsequently became more widespread has been used to camouflage the difficulty of redefining the criteria for distinguishing between styles. This is not to deny the existence of the Ferslev phenomenon, but such inconsistency surely underlines the need for a re-definition of MN ceramic styles in a broader context. A ceramic style need not correspond to a settlement phase (indeed, evidence outlined in Chapter 5.3.2.2 makes the distinction very clear). The Ferslev pottery is a good example of a 'ceramic style' cross-cutting the spatial and temporal boundaries of other styles, but it also needs to be re-defined with reference to other features and phenomena before it can be argued to represent an independent style.

MN III: Late Ferslev and Bundsø styles. When we come to discuss the MN III period we note a substantial difference in the available material, both in comparison with earlier periods and within different regions of Denmark (Fig. 50). Firstly, there are considerably fewer settlement materials representing period III than was the case in earlier stages, so much so that some researchers tend to combine these with the following period IV (Hoika 1987, 106, Fig. 43; Skaarup 1985, 364–5). The chief representative site remains the settlement of Bundsø on Als (Mathiassen 1939; Hoika 1987, 131–57) with smaller assemblages from Jutland (for example Signalbakken; Ebbesen 1975, 190–5, n. 110) and eastern Denmark (Trelleborg; Mathiassen 1944; Rævebakken, N. Andersen 1970).

Interestingly, period III is very poorly represented on Langeland, which provides the backbone of the Danish settlement typology and boasts a more or less uninterrupted sequence of Svaleklint to Virum to MN Ia, MN Ib, MN II and then MN IV and MN V, but appears to have no major settlement attributable to period III (small amounts of MN III pottery can however be noted at Lindø; Winther 1926 and 1928). One wonders whether this lack of MN III material reflects a real break in the settlement chronology or perhaps a degree of contemporaneity between either MN II and

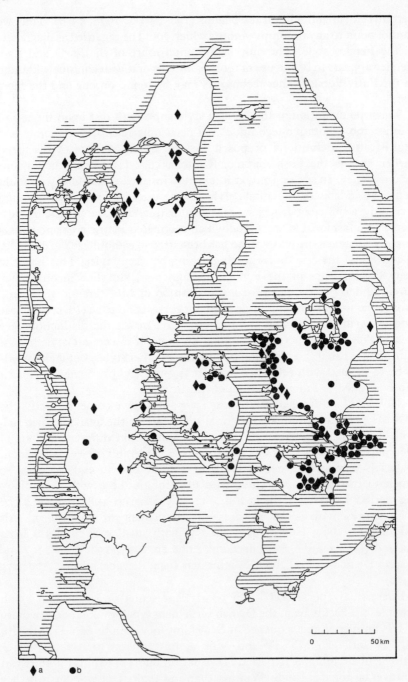

Figure 50 Distribution of the Late Ferslev [a] and Bundsø [b] pottery styles in
Denmark (Source: Ebbesen 1975 and 1978).

MN III or MN III and MN IV, with period III of relative insignificance on Langeland (see also Chapter 5).

When we move on to consider the material available from megalithic contexts the situation becomes even more difficult to interpret. In Jutland the quantity of MN pottery appears to diminish with time and by MN III pottery in north Jutland (represented mostly by the Late Ferslev style) accounts for only 12 per cent of the ceramic inventory, with south Jutland providing only 5 per cent (Ebbesen 1978, 102–3, Fig. 94). This is in direct contrast to the evidence which is available from the megalithic graves on the islands, where at 23 per cent the MN III ceramics represent the largest assemblage, equalled only by Ebbesen's IVA style (note, however that there is a clear concentration of MN III pottery in north-west and south-east Zealand; Ebbesen 1975, 119–22, Figs 23 and 103; 1978, Fig. 95). This difference between Jutland and the islands is very difficult to interpret, especially in view of the scanty contemporary settlement evidence, although the number of vessels in megalithic graves need not reflect directly the duration of a particular phase. One wonders how much stress should be placed on possible different ritual practices employed in these two regions, or whether we should perhaps seriously consider a chronological difference in the development of the TRB culture in Jutland and the islands at this stage.

The MN III potttery was therefore defined on the basis of the finds from the Bundsø settlement on Als (Mathiassen 1939), although this material formed only one section (Bundsø North) of a larger complex with a substantial assemblage of pottery from Bundsø (Bundsø Flintholm) stored in the museum at Kiel, published recently by Hoika (1987, 131–57). Of the approximately 5900 sherds recovered at Bundsø North only 221 (less than 4 per cent) were decorated; at Bundsø Flintholm the figures were similar: 4378 sherds of which 266 (c. 6 per cent) were decorated, which contrasts strongly with material from earlier periods. In 1944 Mathiassen defined the Bundsø chronological period as characterised predominantly by bowls (with or without shoulder) and shoulderless biconical pots (1944, 93). The main decorative techniques observed on the Bundsø material were plain scratches (ibid., Fig. 19, 2, 4, 8), stab-and-drag (ibid., Fig. 19: 10) and tooth-comb impressions (ibid., Fig. 19: 1, 3, 12); some *Cardium* (ibid., Fig. 18: 1) and two-strand cord impressions (ibid., Fig. 19: 14) were also noted, but these apeared sparingly. Decorative motifs identified by Mathiassen included horizontal band of zig-zag lines (in small versions, ibid., Figs 18: 1 and 19: 1, 2, 4, 6, and in larger versions Fig. 19: 3), horizontal rows of infilled rhomboids (ibid., Figs 18: 1 and 19: 3), hanging and up-standing triangles (ibid., Fig. 19: 4, 5, 7, 12) and a new design, the so-called feather motif (ibid., Figs 18: 2 and 19: 2, 10). Similar material has been identified in a number of pits at Trelleborg, where feather motif as well as the 'eye' patterns are noted on pottery (Becker 1956, Fig. 6).

While the MN III Danish ceramics have been said to reveal at least two different ceramic styles and show a variety of features, some of which reflect local traditions, there are a number of diagnostic traits through which the general character of the pottery of this period can be appreciated. Thus, in comparison with the earlier MN TRB pottery, there is a marked change in importance of certain vessel types. For instance, there appears to be a clear decline in the funnel-necked beakers, while the hanging vessel increases in popularity, and the bowl is omnipresent. The pot shapes are generally more fluid with the shoulder either much smaller or absent altogether (Fig. 51). This results in a shift of vertical decoration from the shoulder onto the lower part of the neck; where the shoulder is not present, the division between the lower and upper parts of the pot is often marked by decoration (Fig. 51: 6, 7). There are fewer decorative techniques used during this period; stab-and-drag, scoring and tooth-comb are most common, with *Cardium* and *tvaerstik* less frequent. Very occasionally cord impressions may still be found, but they disappear after MN III. Contrasting effects on individual vessels are achieved less by combining various techniques and more by an alternating pattern of densely decorated and blank spaces. Among the new diagnostic patterns we may note vertical lines bordered either by short horizontal strokes (Fig. 51: 7) or by triangles turned on their sides (the latter mainly on hanging vessels; Fig. 51: 2) and the so-called 'sun' or 'eye' motifs (Fig. 51: 6, 7), which often form part of a more complex decorative panel.

The pottery representative of the MN III period in north Jutland is referred to as the *Late Ferslev style* (Kjærum 1967a; Ebbesen 1978, 75). The general comments presented earlier in relation to the definition of the Ferslev style apply equally to its early as well as its late stages. The chief assemblages include ceramic inventories from the Ferslev cult house (Ferslev II; Marseen 1960; Kjærum 1967a), the settlement from Signalbakken (Ebbesen 1975, 190–5, n. 110) and pottery derived from north Jutland megalithic graves (Ebbesen 1978).

There were thirty-six MN III pots deposited in the Ferslev house; judging from the published illustrations, the bowl (with or without shoulder; straight, convex or funnel-shaped neck) is a predominant vessel here, but there are also a biconical vessel and a funnel-necked beaker as well as an example of a straight-sided vessel with a protruding foot (Marseen 1960, Fig. 12: topmost, 13: middle left and 16, for the latter three examples). The decoration is executed predominantly in tooth-comb, but plain grooves and *tvaerstik* can also be seen. A few vessels are without ornamentation; the decorated examples display typical MN III patterns. Under the rim of the bowls there appears either a horizontal, multiple zig-zag or a grooved band infilled with short vertical or oblique strokes; on the neck there is commonly a horizontal row of infilled rhomboids or a horizontal zig-zag band. Upstanding triangles in *tvaerstik* are noted on the biconical bowl (ibid.,

Figure 51 Pottery of Bundsø (MN III) style from the Danish islands: 1-Tjæreby, 2-Snesere Mark I, 3, 4-Munkebo, 5-Kattrup, 6-Kyndeløse, 7-Hyldehøj (Source: Ebbesen 1975).

Fig. 12: topmost). From the carination down to the belly stretch either groups of vertical lines which may rest against zig-zag bands or bands of zig-zags interrupted by vertical, infilled strips bordered by infilled triangles placed on their sides. A feather motif appears on a straight-walled vessel (ibid., Fig. 16).

Pottery from the Signalbakken settlement, originally published by Müller in 1900, has recently been published in more detail by Ebbesen (1975, 190–5, n. 110, Figs 155–9). The sherds represent funnel-necked beakers and various bowls: open forms with convex sides, funnel-, cylindrical- or concave-necked examples. Among the more interesting forms we should note sherds which may represent a lower segment of a pedestalled bowl (ibid., Fig. 156: 15) and a selection of decorated clay discs (ibid., Fig. 159). While a considerable amount of decoration is executed in tooth-comb, we should also note the use of other techniques: pits, stamps, short strokes, grooves, stab-and-drag, applied clay strips and cord impressions. Signalbakken motifs include all the typical MN III patterns; among the more unusual we should note the 'eye' motif (ibid., Fig. 155: 2) as well as crescentic cord-impressed designs along the edge of clay discs (ibid., Fig. 159: 5, 9).

Ebbesen mentions twenty-six megalithic graves in north Jutland which contain MN III pottery; on the whole these show a strong correspondence to assemblages from settlements and the Ferslev cult house. The predominant pots are various types of bowl (Fig. 52: 1, 7), followed by hanging vessels (Fig. 52: 3, 4, 5, 8) and lids; other forms appear only sporadically (Ebbesen 1978, Fig. 89). The bowls are mostly funnel-shaped, some having a very narrow shoulder (in many instances this appears only as a slight deviation in the profile) and occasionally accompanied by lugs. The Jordhøj passage grave bowls are fully representative of MN III and they compare well with the Ferslev inventory in form, decorative motifs and techniques (Kjærum 1969, Fig. 20). The most common patterns include a horizontal, obliquely impressed band under the rim (HAL) and rhomboids on the neck (HAL, HAP); the very narrow shoulder often carries vertical, tooth-comb impressed lines (HAM). The belly decoration is more varied but frequently there are vertical lines in tooth-comb which may terminate in a zig-zag line. One bowl from Jordhøj (HAN) has no parallels at Ferslev (the belly sherd appears to be divided by broad bands into triangular or rhomboidal (?) zones), but a similar example is quoted by Kjærum from Kongehøj (1969, 45). Kjærum also notes the strong general similarity with material from south Jutland, especially the Bundsø site. Ebbesen (1978) illustrates a number of bowls from other megalithic graves, some of which are presented here (Fig. 52: 1, 2, 6), which on the whole resemble the material already described. It is of interest to note that the Jordhøj MN III assemblage, like that of Signalbakken, also includes fragments of a pedestalled bowl with broad zig-zag bands impressed in tooth-comb (Kjærum 1969, Fig. 17: HAD).

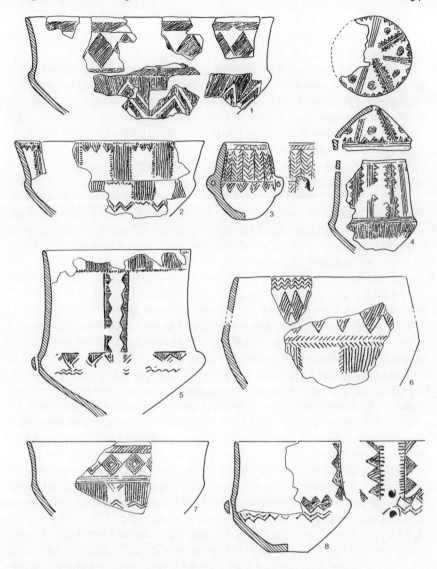

Figure 52 Danish pottery decorated in Late Ferslev style: 1, 5-Voldstedlund, 2-Himmelevgård, 3-Korshøj, 4-Snæbum, 6-Vålse, 7-Frammerslev, 8-Knud (Source: Ebbesen 1975 and 1978).

The hanging vessels generally have a neck curving slightly inward or outward, with a weakly marked shoulder which is sometimes accentuated by the placement of horizontal lines (Fig. 52: 3). On the neck there are typical MN III patterns consisting of bands of vertical lines, bordered by short, horizontal impressions, or by triangles placed on either side (Fig. 52: 5, 8); below the shoulder there are generally vertical lines. Associated lids carry similar decorative patterns.

While the predominant decoration on MN III north Jutland vessels is executed in tooth-comb, there are sufficient examples of the use of other decorative techniques to suggest that tooth-comb decoration was not employed exclusively. There are pots decorated with *Cardium*, (for example at Jordhøj; Kjærum 1969, Fig. 21: HAS) or deep grooves (ibid., Fig. 21: HAR).

During this period two ceramic styles are recognised on the Danish islands: the indigenous MN III style, and the Ferslev style, which is thought to be intrusive (Ebbesen 1975, 51). The relationship between these two styles is difficult to define; this is partly due to the inadequacies of the definition of the Ferslev style referred to earlier. The Ferslev style vessels make up just under one-fifth of the period's pottery and are found not only in the megalithic graves but also in settlements, although they are not very numerous in the latter context (Trelleborg: Becker 1956; Rævebakken: N. Andersen 1970). Comparing patterns typical of MN III and Ferslev on the islands, we note that they are mostly the same (Ebbesen 1975, Fig. 19), the only significant difference being in the use of decorative techniques. There are also examples of vessels which appear to combine tooth-comb and other techniques (for example at Splittorfs Høj; ibid., Fig. 222: 11, 13).

It seems that the MN III/Ferslev relationship on the islands will remain a problem until more settlement material from secure contexts comes to light. In fact, as already noted, the settlement material is rarer in MN III than in the earlier periods, and the comparatively strong representation in the megalithic context is equally difficult to explain. It is not certain which phenomenon is reflected in this discrepancy, although heavy representation in graves need reflect neither a short nor a long duration of the period, but may be related instead to the intensity of ritual activities or to other factors.

The megalithic graves containing MN III pottery on the Danish islands are concentrated in north-west and south-east Zealand. There are also a few graves on Lolland, Falster and Møn, but these include small assemblages numbering between one and five pots per grave (Ebbesen 1975, 53, Fig. 23). Pottery decorated in Late Ferslev style follows a similar distribution (ibid., Fig. 24). In the MN III style the most commonly encountered vessels are funnel-necked bowls (27 per cent), bowls with a weakly marked shoulder (15 per cent) and bowls with cylindrical necks (13 per cent). Shouldered cups, bowls with a concave neck and hanging vessels are also relatively frequent (8 per cent each). Among the Ferslev pottery we note funnel-necked bowls (33 per cent), bowls with a conical neck (22 per cent), shouldered cups (20 per cent) and hanging vessels (10 per cent; ibid., 122, Fig. 99).

Ebbesen comments on the great variety of decorative motifs in MN III on the islands, but it seems that only three motifs (H50, H25 and H58) are found exclusively on MN III vessels; others also appear, albeit with much less frequency, on pottery which Ebbesen assigns to MN IV (ibid., Fig. 19). This may, at least in part, be the reason for the difficulties encountered in distinguishing between these two periods and may account for the fact that some researchers do not regard III and IV as being separate (Skaarup 1985; Hoika 1987).

MN IV: Lindø, IVA and IVB styles. Assessment of the pottery from the MN IV period is beset with problems. Firstly, there appears to be a considerable discrepancy between evidence from Jutland and that from the Danish islands. While the settlement pottery on the islands is not particularly well represented, it is found abundantly in megalithic graves where it accounts for 23 per cent of all the MN island pottery (this is the so-called IVA style; Ebbesen 1975, 123, Fig. 103; Fig. 53). In Jutland, on the other hand, there is very little material attributable to this period that can be identified either from settlements or from megalithic graves (Ebbesen 1978, Fig. 89; Davidsen 1978, 113–17). It is difficult to determine whether the paucity of MN IV pottery here is a result of insufficient research or whether, in comparison with the earlier MN III and subsequent MN V periods, the MN IV represents a rather short-lived period. We may observe that the strong contrast in the quantity of ceramics between the two Danish regions would tend to support the latter argument, although it is also possible that developments in the two regions followed a different course and were chronologically separate; our perception of this problem is poor and ultimately can only be solved by future research.

The second problem of the MN IV period is the lack of pure, uncontaminated finds. The period has been defined on the basis of material recovered from the large settlement complex at Lindø on Langeland (Winther 1926 and 1928). On the basis of this material, Mathiassen defined the principal features of the *Lindø phase* as pottery with loose, blurred forms, characterised mainly by bowls with a slight belly angle, biconical pots and small suspension vessels. Ornamentation was thought to be sparse (only 4 per cent of sherds were decorated) as well as cursory, with rows of pits and infilled triangles (Winther 1926 and 1928; Mathiassen 1944, 97).

The Lindø settlement, however, is not very suitable for chronological discussion, primarily because of its mixed nature. Many ceramic periods are represented: for instance MN I (Lindø 4: Winther 1926, Figs 97 and 101), MN III (Lindø 1: Winther 1928, 33), MN IV (Lindø 2 and 7: Winther 1928; Lindø 4: Winther 1926, Figs 102–3, 108–11 and 123) and MN V (especially Lindø 4: see Davidsen 1978, 51–2, Plate 52). This mixture of material of nearly all periods, as well as the fact that MN IV here lacks diagnostic pottery which would allow comparison with ceramics from other contexts, makes it quite clear that Lindø does not serve any purpose

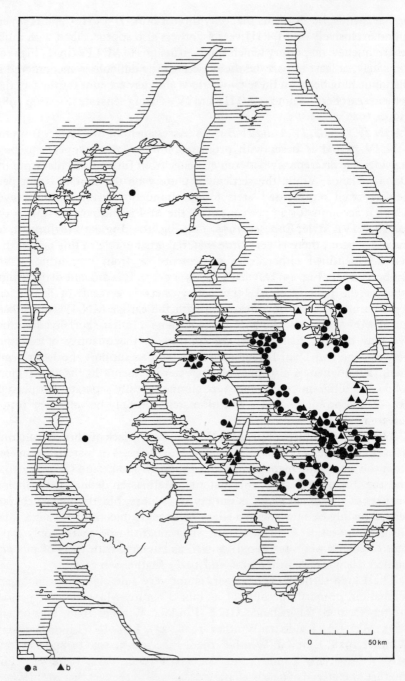

Figure 53 Distribution of MN IVA [Lindø, a] and MN IVB [b] pottery styles in Denmark (Source: Ebbesen 1975 and 1978).

in the typo-chronological division of the Danish MN and should be sub-stituted by more diagnostic assemblages.

The few examples of MN IV pottery from Jutland have been discussed recently in two separate publications. Ebbesen (1978, 11–21, Figs 4–10) has described pottery from the passage grave at Sødalshøj, Østerbølle. He discussed, among other things, fragments of six clay lids, four of which are decorated with incised designs consisting of triple triangles at the rim and motifs made up of vertical lines bordered by infilled triangles placed on their sides (ibid., Fig. 4: 1, 3, 4, 6); two examples are similarly decorated using tooth-comb impressions (ibid., Fig. 4: 7, 9). The same material has been discussed by Davidsen (1978, 114), who argued, however, that at Sødalshøj we do not have a mere collection of lids, but remains of four hanging vessels which, on the basis of their decoration, can be said to have been conceived as pairs. Indeed, Becker (1954a, Fig. 19) published two of Ebbesen's lids as an example of a hanging vessel. While we cannot become involved here in an argument as to the typological interpretation of the pottery in question, we should note that both scholars attribute it to MN IV (Ebbesen's attribution involves only four of the lids, 1978, Fig. 4: 1, 3, 4, 6, while Fig. 4: 7, 9 are classed as Late Ferslev in style). Davidsen (1978, 116) argues that the decoration appears later than is normal in MN III and that the substitution of tooth-comb by incision is a good indicator of a late date. On the other hand he believes that the tooth-comb technique con-tinued in use during MN IV and quotes examples of other hanging vessels at Voldstedlund (ibid., Fig. 57: e) and Kvosted (ibid., Fig. 57: f) and a bellyless funnel-necked beaker from Ørum (ibid., Fig. 57: g), comparing the latter with a small-bellied and tall-necked beaker from a grave at Herrup (Skov 1973, Fig. 15). We should note that, on the basis of criteria used by Ebbesen, these three vessels should be considered as representative of his Late Ferslev style and thus, presumably, belong to MN III. While Davidsen (1978, 116–17) quotes further possible Jutish examples which could belong to MN IV, he states that, on the basis of decoration, only two of the Jutland vessels can be placed without any doubt in MN IV – a feather-motif decorated sherd from Lundby Mose (ibid., Fig. 65: c) and a similarly decorated vessel from a stone-packing grave XV at Bondesgård (ibid., 116, n. 121).

The difficulties here arise from a number of circumstances. Firstly, as argued earlier, we have no diagnostic settlement set of MN IV ceramics with which to compare controversial examples. Secondly, Ebbesen is unwilling to discuss in detail the relationship between his decorative styles and the traditional chronological periods. He appears to allow considerable overlaps between styles and periods (1978, Fig. 58) but does not offer any reasonable guideline on, for instance, the continuation of the Late Ferslev style into the MN IV period.

When we turn to the Danish islands new problems of interpretation

162   *TRB Culture*

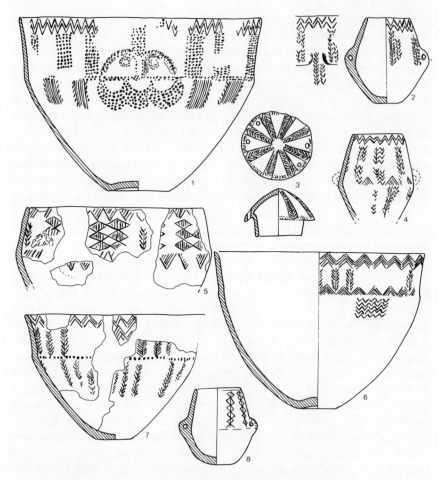

Figure 54 Danish pottery decorated in Lindø (MN IVA) style: 1,2-Kyndeløse, 3-Neble, 4,6,7-Kattrup, 5-Olstrupgård, 8-Høng (Source: Ebbesen 1975).

emerge. The megalithic period IV pottery has been divided by Ebbesen into two consecutive styles: the *IVA style* (Lindø style) which is distributed all over eastern Denmark (1975, Fig. 25) and the *IVB style* with a relatively limited distribution in the south-east of this region (ibid., Fig. 26). The IVA style pottery (Fig. 54) includes funnel-necked bowls (34 per cent), hanging vessels (30 per cent), clay lids (12 per cent) and bowls with a conical (10 per cent) and concave (7 per cent) neck; other forms are insignificantly represented (ibid., 122, Fig. 100). On the other hand the IVB style (Fig. 55), accounting for 9 per cent of megalithic MN pottery, appears to consist mainly of hanging vessels (84 per cent), although ten other types of vessels are apparently also represented, especially funnel-necked and conical-necked bowls (ibid., 122, Fig. 101).

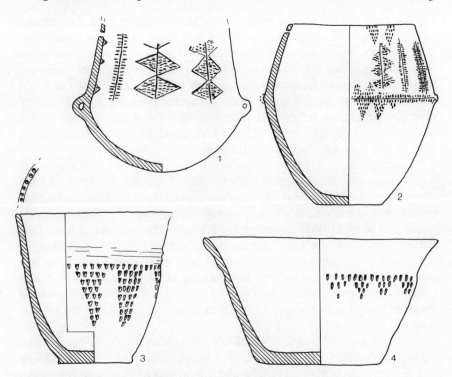

Figure 55 Danish pottery decorated in MN IVB style: 1-Kalø Mark, 2-Snesere Mark I, 3-Åkærslund, 4-Hyllehøj (Source: Ebbesen 1975).

The decoration of the IVA pottery is executed mostly through incision. Under the rim we encounter infilled hanging triangles (Fig. 54: 5) and multiple zig-zag lines (Fig. 54: 1, 6, 7). The neck may be decorated with feather-motif (Fig. 54: 6, 7), often placed individually or with upstanding triangles. Some patterns are repeated on the upper part of the belly, although often there is a chess-board alternation between the neck and belly decoration (Fig. 54: 1, 6, 7). Complex 'eye' motifs appear on funnel-necked and open bowls (Fig. 54: 1). Hanging vessels are usually biconical in form, with vertical rows of rhomboids (Fig. 54: 8) or feather-motif (Fig. 54: 2, 4) as the most common decorative patterns.

Ebbesen's hypothetical IVB style (which in settlement material can be identified only at Rævebakken and Sarup; 1975, 57, note and 184–6) causes greatest difficulty. As noted, it is represented mainly in hanging vessels; the diagnostic decorative pattern is a row of triangles consisting of stick impressions (Fig. 55: 1, 2) or obliquely impressed pits (Fig. 55: 3, 4). Diametrically opposed to this view are the ideas of Davidsen (1978, 117–19), who argues that the majority of IVb pottery represents the funerary pottery of the subsequent MN V (Store Valby) period. This argument is based mainly on the fact that hanging triangles formed by stick impressions or obliquely impressed pits are typical of MN V pottery all over Denmark, an argument apparently further strengthened by the frequent positioning of decoration in the area of the belly ridge, another typical MN V characteristic. Davidsen argues that, while hanging triangles of the type described above are known in the south-east of Denmark during MN IV, their ultimate popularity is reached only during MN V; he compares this phenomenon with the Ferslev style, which developed in north Jutland in MN II but only later became widespread (ibid., 109).

The scepticism of the outside observer is enforced by the arguments which take place among the Danish specialists and one need not feel too dismayed at the difficulties of placing any particular pot within a particular period! But the above discussion clearly emphasises the difficulties any researcher faces in trying to interpret Danish MN ceramics. These difficulties constitute the best argument for detailed study of settlement material where diagnostic features of pottery typical of individual periods can be identified, and where the relationship between them can be established with more confidence than that founded upon the study of decorative patterns associated exclusively with pottery derived from megalithic contexts.

MN V: Store Valby style. The MN V (*Store Valby style*), being the final period of the MN TRB ceramic development, was also the last to be defined. As Davidsen observed, Müller's total lack of interest in the crude, often undecorated pottery was undoubtedly an important contributory factor in the late recognition of the MN V period (Davidsen 1978, 12). While post-Lindø pottery had been familiar to a number of Danish scholars (such as Rosenberg 1929; Berg 1951), the actual period (MN V phase) was only defined properly in 1954 on the basis of the assemblage found at Store Valby on Zealand (Becker 1954a and 1954b).

Becker recognised the fact that crude, poorly decorated pottery of the kind he analysed from Store Valby (assemblage from pits AA and DV; 1954a, Figs 2 and 3; 1954b, Figs 26–31 and 33), Svanemøllevej (1954a, Fig. 4) and Kornerup (1954b, Figs 37–9) was not limited to settlement finds but has also been placed in megalithic graves (such as Skovtofte: 1954a, Fig. 5; Berg 1951, Plate VIII; and Åkærslund: Becker 1954a, Fig. 6). Such pottery, therefore, was not merely domestic ware but represented an independent group of ceramics. In 1956 Becker extended the Store Valby phase material by identifying a large assemblage at Trelleborg, where a range of vessels corresponded closely in clay fabric, shape and decoration to Store Valby and related finds (Becker 1956, 98–104, Figs 10–16). Since then there has been a tremendous increase in the amount of MN V material (Fig. 56), not only from settlements and megalithic graves but also from other contexts such as stone-packing graves (E. Jørgensen 1977) or bog

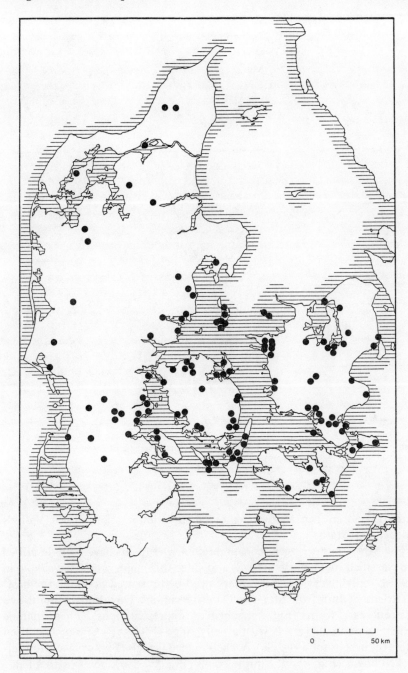

Figure 56 Distribution of Store Valby (MN V) pottery in Denmark (Source:
Ebbesen 1975 and 1978; Davidsen 1978).

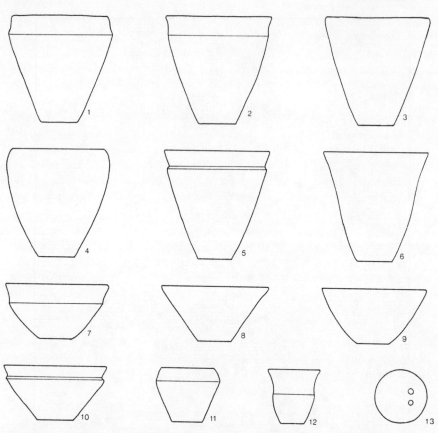

Figure 57 Schematic representation of vessel forms characteristic of Store Valby ceramics (Source: Davidsen 1978).

finds (Davidsen 1978), thus removing any doubt about Store Valby's independent status.

The MN V pottery forms encountered in settlements have been described and classified by Davidsen (1978) and since this major work is available in English, only a very short summary need be presented here. On the basis of settlement finds from fifty-two Danish locations, Davidsen distinguished thirteen vessel forms (Fig. 57: schematic representations). These include variants of storage vessels with a belly ridge (Fig. 57: 1 and 2; Davidsen refers to these as food vessels), bucket-shaped vessels (Fig. 57: 3–6), funnel-necked bowls (Fig. 57: 7), simple bowls (Fig. 57: 8–9), bowls with a ledge (Fig. 57: 10), small, biconical vessels with a raised belly ridge (Fig. 57: 11), small funnel-necked beakers with a low ridge (Fig. 57: 12) and clay discs (Fig. 57: 13; Davidsen 1978, 97–100). An important feature of this pottery

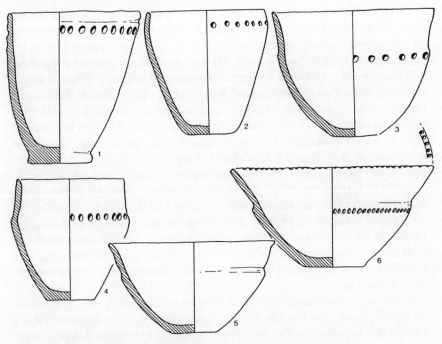

Figure 58 Danish pottery decorated in Store Valby (MN V) style: 1-Ørby Huslodder, 2,4-Tjæreby, 3-Knudshoved, 5-Besser Kirkegård, 6-Åkærslund (Source: Ebbesen 1975 and 1978).

is revealed in the clay fabric, with large-grained tempering apparently used to facilitate rapid changes in temperature (Davidsen 1978, 95).

The decoration of MN V pottery is relatively simple and scanty (Fig. 58). Most vessels are decorated with horizontal rows of evenly spaced pits (80 per cent of these are finger-pits); obliquely impressed pits, horizontally applied cordons and finger grooves are apparently typical of D-type vessels (Davidsen 1978; Fig. 57). More elaborate motifs involve hanging triangles made of pits placed below the rim; incised decoration is rare (Davidsen 1978, 100–3). A very typical MN V feature is the presence of thick clay discs, many of which have two closely spaced perforations (ibid., 103–4). Decorative patterns on discs appear to be quite varied and include concentric or radial finger grooves, fingernail impressions, rows of pits and, more rarely, triangular motifs or incised parallel lines or arcs.

MN V ceramics associated with megalithic graves are known from the Danish islands (Ebbesen 1975) as well as from Jutland (Davidsen 1978; Ebbesen 1978). According to Ebbesen's classification (which excludes the presence of hanging vessels) the MN V pottery on the islands is found mainly on eastern and southern Zealand and on Fyn (Ebbesen 1975, Fig. 27), and exhibits nine ceramic forms of which the most common are

funnel-necked bowls, barrel-shaped vessels and open bowls with convex
sides. From Jutland Davidsen catalogued thirty-two megalithic graves with
MN V pottery, which concentrate largely in the south-eastern part of the
peninsula (1978, 176–81, Fig. 59). Most of the graves contain between one
and three vessels and only in three instances (Åkærslund, Tonneshøj and
Avnevig) were there larger assemblages (ibid., 119). Like on the islands,
funnel-necked bowls and barrel-shaped vessels are dominant, with other
forms occurring only sporadically (Ebbesen 1978, Figs 89 and 90). Decoration of MN V megalithic pottery is relatively limited in range; it includes
horizontal rows of regularly spaced pits (Fig. 58: 1–4), oblique stick impressions (Fig. 58: 6), finger grooves and applied cordons (Fig. 58: 5).

In north Jutland the MN V pottery is found predominantly in association
with stone-packing graves (Davidsen 1978, 120–1, Fig. 1). Usually, the
only vessel form found in these graves is a storage vessel (a food vessel in
Davidsen's nomenclature). There also appears to be a strong correlation
with the distribution of MN V pointed-bottom storage pots (ibid., Fig. 43).
Davidsen argues that this represents a locally distinctive group of the MN
V in that region.

Some of the arguments over the inclusion of Ebbesen's MN VIb vessels
in period V on the Danish islands have already been outlined earlier.
Davidsen's argument also rests upon the assumption that a hanging vessel
represents an exclusively funerary form, and he quotes a number of other
MN V forms which are not encountered outside the funerary context (for
example barrel-shaped vessels or small, bucket-shaped pots with straight
sides; ibid., 118). While the idea of certain ceramic forms having strong
funerary associations need not be dismissed (note, for instance, the funerary
importance of pedestalled bowls and clay ladles within the earlier MN
periods), we should observe that hanging vessels are not particularly
common in Jutland MN V either, since only one megalithic grave (Tonneshøj) appears to have contained a hanging vessel asssignable to the MN
V period (Ebbesen 1975, 126, n. 483; Davidson 1978, 118, Plate 113: i).
Should a hanging vessel indeed represent a specific form associated with
funerary ritual in the later part of the MN, then its appearance in settlement
assemblages would be unlikely. On the other hand a detailed comparative
study of funerary and domestic assemblages, as well as a study of individual
megalithic assemblages in terms of their representativity of different
periods (for instance, do megalithic graves containing IVB-style hanging
vessels reveal other diagnostic forms of IV and/or V?), may contribute
towards a solution of this particular problem.

4.4.3.3 Summary. Before we embark upon the interpretation of the
development of the MN TRB pottery in Denmark, it may be pertinent to
summarise the salient points which emerge from the above discussion. In
the first instance it has to be emphasised that the division into the EN and
MN cuts across the continuous development of TRB ceramics (as well as

other elements of material culture) and it clearly represents a hangover from early attempts at ordering the Scandinavian Neolithic. It is rooted in the typo-chronological scheme of Montelius which was based on the appearance of distinct grave forms and was perpetuated by subsequent research (S. Müller 1918; Becker 1947 and 1954a).

The continuity between the EN and MN with regard to ceramic development can be seen in vessel forms as well as in decorative patterns and techniques. The many features which clearly indicate the connections between MN I and the preceding Volling/Virum/Fuchsberg ceramics have been outlined in detail earlier. By way of recapitulation, the important elements are manifest in the continued use of funnel-necked beakers with vertically striped belly (Figs 37 and 43), richly decorated lugged beakers (Figs 36 and 41) and lugged bowls (Figs 36 and 43), the latter developing from obvious Fuchsberg prototypes. The custom of infilling vertical ornamental panels, which began with Fuchsberg ceramics, undergoes further development during the MN I period (Fig. 41) and patterns clearly reminiscent of Fuchsberg designs have been identified in the Troldebjerg pottery (Ebbesen 1979a, 61). The Volling chess-board decorative patterns are plainly revealed in the ornamental features of the Hagebrogård style in north Jutland (Fig. 44), while the whipped-cord ornamental technique and a strong tendency to strict zonal decoration so characteristic of MN I were already playing a significant role in the Virum group (Figs 37 and 38).

Taking into consideration the overall MN ceramic development we may indicate the changing trends in decoration and the importance of certain ceramic forms, although it must be stressed that a large proportion of pottery is derived from megalithic contexts and that the observed changes need not therefore reflect strict chronological differences. There appears to be an overall decrease in the amount of decorated pottery; this is perhaps not so clearly seen in material recovered from funerary contexts, but becomes quite obvious when settlement assemblages are considered (for example about 37 per cent of decorated pottery at Troldebjerg, 18 per cent at Blandebjerg, 6 per cent and 4 per cent at Bundsø and Lindø; see also Ebbesen 1975, Fig. 106). Together with this we note a reduction in the amount of surface decoration on individual vessels, and a decline in the assortment of motifs and techniques used in their execution. This trend is most dramatically revealed if we consider some statistics for decorative elements: 356 were identified in the Troldebjerg style (Ebbesen 1979; 68), yet only about half a dozen motifs typical of the Store Valby style were noted (Davidsen 1978, 100–3).

Moreover, we observe changing trends in the importance of certain vessel forms. This may, to a large degree, be a result of the utilitarian-ritual demands which regulated the use of TRB pottery (for example the assumed existence of predominantly funerary forms such as hanging vessels or pedestalled bowls) and need not necessarily correspond with changes of style. While we see the disappearance of lugged jars and collared flasks towards the end of the Volling/Virum/Fuchsberg group, most of the changes appear to take place within the styles. The pedestalled bowls and clay ladles are briefly (if profusely) present at the beginning of the MN and the majority are decorated in the Klintebakke style. With their progressive loss of popularity during the Blandebjerg style, we note an increase in shouldered vessels, especially bowls and cups, which are such a striking feature of MN II styles. The funnel-necked beaker, the eponymous vessel of the TRB culture, has virtually disappeared by MN III and instead we see a rise in the imporance of hanging vessels, which appear to predomi-nante in the MN IVA (Lindø) and MN IVB styles. The range of forms in use, both funerary and domestic, also becomes narrower throughout the whole of the MN TRB ceramic sequence. One type of ceramic form, however, appears to be little influenced by all these changes: the clay disc is present throughout the duration of the TRB culture. Apart from the internal changes, TRB pottery towards the end of the MN also comes under some external influence exerted by such complexes as the Globular Amphora and, possibly, Corded Ware cultures; a discussion of this rela-tionship will be found in Chapter 11.

An important factor in the interpretation of Danish MN pottery develop-ment is the status of individual ceramic styles – their relationship with one another and correlation with the established chronological phases of the TRB. We shall consider this matter in more detail in Chapter 5. For the moment, therefore, only a few comments will be offered. First of all, we must remind ourselves once again that pottery derived from the Danish megaliths does not, on the whole, represent homogeneous, sealed contexts and therefore cannot be placed in any chronological order of its own. Noting the criticisms and reservations expressed earlier (as well as the available C-14 evidence; see Chapter 5), Ebbesen's criteria can be accepted as a means of distinguishing between individual styles (note, however, comments on the Ferslev style), but they cannot be used and are not in themselves sufficient for interpreting the styles as representing individual chronological phases, with each style ascribed to one phase. Such reasoning was used earlier by Sophus Müller (1918) and later proved wrong by Forssander (1936) and others. Davidsen correctly observes that it leads to more phases than may in reality have existed (1978, 9).

On the other hand the validity of the traditional settlement chronology has lost credence, since it became clear that large settlement assemblages can no longer be regarded as homogeneous but as representing multi-period phenomena. Moreover, the difficulties in the interpretation of pottery from multi-period settlements have caused many Danish researchers to abandon the study of ceramics and chronology in favour of more fashion-able areas of enquiry such as settlement patterns or social organisation. However, chronological difficulties will not disappear and must be solved by the meticulous analysis of settlement assemblages in conjunction with other chronological methods. That a study of multi-period sites can yield important results has been demonstrated by the research of Davidsen (1978). Indeed, in this context we may quote the example of the interpretation of chronology at the Bronocice settlement in the South-eastern group of the TRB, which yielded very rewarding results with regard to different settlement phases, not only at the site but with implications for the whole of the South-eastern TRB group (see above, Chapter 4.3; Kruk and Milisauskas 1977; 1981b; 1983).

As already noted the relationship between individual styles is directly related to the chronology of TRB pottery development. Ebbesen (1975) argues for the styles' chronological succession (indeed, we should note his heavy reliance upon otherwise criticised settlement chronology), yet there is little evidence to support this and the above discussion reveals a number of factors which could be cited in arguments to the contrary. There are clear differences between styles in terms of their spatial distribution, with some (such as the Blandebjerg and Store Valby styles) covering more or less the entire country, while others (for example the north Jutland Ferslev and islands' MN III and IVB style) are of only local significance. This varied distribution immediately raises doubts as to the sequential order of all the styles and suggest a much more complex situation, with overlaps and contemporaneity of individual styles. This complexity is further underlined by two factors. Some of the vessels apparently represent largely ceremonial, especially funerary, ceramics (this seems to be the status of most of the IV inventory) while others either do not appear within the funerary context at all or do so only rarely. This functional differentiation, which is also supported through the study of pottery from causewayed enclosures, can be a very misleading factor with regard to chronology: archaic and innovating forms may be placed side by side in the ritual context and may be related to ritual demands, or forms may change their function from domestic to ritual or *vice versa*, further complicating the relationship between the styles.

Finally, we must also bear in mind the very strong influence of the earlier local background. The early MN Troldebjerg, Hagebrogård and Klintebakke styles reveal very clearly their allegiance to the preceding ceramic development. This regionality is somewhat blurred in the Blandebjerg style but is very sharp in the Ferslev and MN III styles. The development of the so-called Early Ferslev style within the Blandebjerg *milieu* clearly underlines the problems of correspondence between ceramic styles and chronological phases.

4.5 Tiefstich Pottery and the ceramic sequence of the Western TRB group

The German word *Tiefstich* literally means 'deeply cut', and deeply executed decoration is characteristic of later TRB pottery over a large area of the culture's distribution. The most common decorative technique is the so-called *Furchenstich* (stab-and-drag) and the phrases *Tiefstich* and *Furchenstich* have, on occasion, been used synonymously. However, this is incorrect because the pottery in question is also decorated using a variety of other techniques such as *tvaerstik* (impressions made in, along, or at an angle to a guide line; Bakker 1979, 179), whipped cord, *Cardium* impressions or plain grooves. As noted earlier, the term *Tiefstich* pottery covers a vast ceramic complex and embraces the later TRB pottery of the Northern group (although this name is not used in Scandinavian literature), nearly all the pottery of the West group, and ceramics from the area of Altmark and adjacent regions. Some scholars would even include here the Walternienburg ceramics (ibid., 12). Examples of decorative motifs typical of *Tiefstich* pottery can also occasionally be found on vessels from the Eastern and South-eastern group, but on the whole this term is not appropriate for the latter areas.

Thus the name *Tiefstich* pottery covers a ceramic complex which is vast in its geographical extent and has been studied on a regional basis by many scholars, while equally many regional typo-chronologies have been proposed. Referring only to major research outside southern Scandinavia, we may note the work of Van Giffen (1925 and 1927), Knöll (1952; 1959; 1978; 1981; 1983) and Bakker (1979) covering the Netherlands and north-west Germany; in Schleswig-Holstein we note the work of Langenheim (1935), Schwantes (1939 and 1958), Schwabedissen (1953b) and Hoika (1971; 1981; 1987); Dehnke (1940) studied the ceramics of the east Hanover region and Laux (1979 and 1984) the area of Lower Saxony between the Aller and Elbe rivers; Kupka (1924; 1927; 1928; 1938) and Preuss (1980) concerned themselves with the Altmark region; Nilius (1971a) and Schuldt (1972b) worked on the pottery from Mecklenburg, and the middle German Walternienburg-Bernburg ceramics have been classified by Nikalsson (1925), with further studies by U. Fischer (1951 and 1956); Sprockhoff (1938) also attempted a general discussion of German *Tiefstich* pottery.

The studies outlined above (and the list is far from complete) indicate the difficulties encountered in the interpretation of *Tiefstich* pottery development. It is quite clear that the presence of so many local groupings with unclear boundaries and regional typo-chronologies is a result of strongly segmented research. While such an approach is perhaps inevitable in view of the large area involved, it is very difficult to combine individual sequences into a general overview of the ceramic developments which are clearly related when viewed against the broad background of events across the North European Plain.

With reference to early research, Sprockhoff (1938), following Müller (1918), classified the north German TRB, which was then commonly known as the *Megalithkultur*, into the Dolmen and Passage Grave periods. Schleswig-Holstein formed the core development area during the Dolmen period with a small, adjacent zone between the lower Elbe and lower Oder where related forms could be observed (Sprockhoff 1938, Plates 34 and 35; some of this material would today be classed as *Tiefstich* and not as early TRB pottery). During the subsequent Passage Grave period the area of the *Megalithkultur* acquired a greater geographical extent, within which Sprockhoff distinguished several culturally related provinces; the developments within his northern (Schleswig-Holstein) and north-eastern (Mecklenburg, Rügen and part of western Pomerania) provinces followed a similar pattern with pottery representing older (ibid., Plates 36, 39 and 40) and younger horizons (ibid., Plates 37, 38, 41 and 42). In the area to the west, between the Weser and Ems rivers, he distinguished the so-called Emsland style (ibid., Plates 44–9), which was thought to be contemporary with the northern province materials but which today is believed to belong mostly to a very late *tvaerstik*-decorated pottery (Bakker 1979).

In contrast to Sprockhoff who, as Bakker (1979, 34) observed, was not very successful in his study of the German *Tiefstich* pottery, other researchers concerned themselves with much smaller regions. Thus Kupka (1924; 1927; 1928; 1938) studied the ceramics of the Altmark region which he named first the *Langgrabkeramik* and later the *Langdolmenkeramik* in contrast to the *Mitteldeutsche Gangrabkeramik* (today known as the Walternienburg-Bernburg pottery). Kupka derived the Altmark *Tiefstich* from the Dolmen period pottery in Denmark and Schleswig-Holstein, arguing that it was older in Altmark than in north-west Germany.

The area east of Hanover formed the principal region of Dehnke's (1940) study, although recognising an important cultural homogeneity, he also included the Altmark region. On the basis of detailed analysis Dehnke divided the *Tiefstich* pottery into three chronological phases; as already noted, he was also responsible for the identification of the Haaßel (now Fuchsberg) pottery, which he believed to be an intrusive element within his oldest ceramic phase.

The pottery which is classed today as Western *Tiefstich* (i.e. of the Western TRB group) has been studied by, among others, Knöll (1952 and 1959) with thematic publications on specific pot types (for example collared flasks; Knöll 1981) or particular assemblages (for example the pottery from the Wechte megalith; Knöll 1983) and recently by Bakker (1979) and Brindley (1986b).

The geographical extent of the region covered by Knöll's (1959) study stretched from the Elbe in the east, along the North Sea as far west as the Zuiderzee-IJssel and Rhine and was bordered in the south by the Lippe river. With regard to the origin of the TRB culture in this area Knöll argued that *Tiefstich* pottery developed as the result of an expansion of the older TRB (Dolmen period) from the south Jutland peninsula and the Danish islands, with some Rössen culture involvement. Round-bellied jugs, funnel-necked beakers, lugged beakers and bowls derived from small passage graves represented the oldest material west of the Elbe.

In view of Bakker's (1979) extensive discussion of Knöll's work there is no need to present this elaborate ceramic sequence here. We may note, however, that since he had hardly any evidence of closed or stratified finds at his disposal, Knöll based his entire chronological sequence upon a detailed study of ceramic forms, especially shoulder vessels, bowls and steep-walled beakers (pails of Bakker) and associated decoration (Knöll 1959, 11–31). The development sequence may be described briefly as beginning with rounded forms, decorated mostly with vertically arranged patterns (Stage 1; ibid., 98); these were followed by angular and sharply profiled forms with varied, shape-related and technically varied ornamentation (Stage 1/2; ibid., 98–9); finally came more rounded and somewhat indistinct forms with progressively looser decoration (Stage 2; ibid., 99–100).

Although Knöll's chief concern was the study of Western *Tiefstich* pottery, none of his distribution maps show the precise extent of his regional group. This is because Knöll chose to map the specific ceramic forms in a much broader distribution, well beyond that of the Western TRB group itself (ibid., Maps 1–24). In a recent work dealing with the *Tiefstich* pottery of the Altmark region, Preuss (1980) referred critically to this fact, commenting that none of the German *Tiefstich* groups can be seen clearly in Knöll's distribution maps. However, it needs to be pointed out that Knöll's maps show better than any others that the division of ceramics into even smaller groupings is frequently based upon the extent of the knowledge of an individual researcher or upon some geographical consideration rather than on the available evidence. In the context of small-scale research the differences in the material tend to become over-emphasised and lead to the emergence of strict, small groupings with little understanding of transcending phenomena. In a different work, Knöll (1952) indicated that the overall distribution of specific types of vessels (or particular ornamentation) can indicate wider trends within a ceramic development, and indeed directions of contact and exchange between groups of populations. Sadly, however, this approach has not yet been pursued further. Indeed, with regard to the areas east and west of the Elbe, this situation was aggravated further by different research objectives either side of the river.

4.5.1 Altmark region

Beginning our discussion of *Tiefstich* pottery in the area between the Weser and the Elbe rivers, we should briefly consider the more recent work on the Altmark *Tiefstich* although, as will become apparent in due course, the geographical extent of this pottery is far greater than the name suggests. According to Preuss (1980, Map 1) the Altmark *Tiefstich* province stretches from the middle Elbe (north of the confluence of the Elbe and Saale) northwards to the Elbe estuary. Particularly dense concentrations (some clearly reflecting the intensive research activities of Kupka) are noticeable along the Ohre, Uhte, Biese and Jeetze rivers, and in the west, Preuss maps out the province as far as the Lüneburger Heide. The Altmark *Tiefstich* in Preuss' view clearly separates itself from the Northern TRB group by an exclusion zone in south-west Mecklenburg and Schleswig-Holstein (ibid., Map 3), although it should be pointed out that, since Preuss mapped only the distribution of pedestalled bowls for the Northern TRB group, such a gap is hardly surprising and should not be considered as necessarily significant.

Preuss (1980, 62–7) suggested a division of the *Tiefstich* pottery in the Altmark region into two chronologically distinct horizons: the older, Düsedau and the younger, Haldensleben horizons. Most of the Altmark pottery derives from contexts which offer no reliable stratigraphy and Preuss argued against a reliance upon dubious stratigraphic relationships from megalithic chambers. On the other hand, finds from large complexes, such as the Düsedau settlement, distr. Osterburg, by virtue of their ceramic homogeneity appear to represent one phase. Preuss argued further that, with reference to certain ceramic forms such as steep-walled bowls, a study of large ceramic assemblages reveals either bowls decorated with triangular motifs (Fig. 59: 2) or bowls ornamented with short, vertical stab-and-drag impressions (Fig. 60: 1); the two are apparently never mixed (ibid., 34–6). Thus the former are known for instance from Düsedau, Groß-Schwechten or Haldenslebener Forst (Bebertal grave 14; ibid., Catalogue nos 12, 40, 60) and, additionally, from the flat grave assemblage at Issendorf (Tempel 1972); the other type can be noted at the settlement of Haldensleben-Rosmarienbreite (Cat. no. 66) or Bebertal grave 33 at Haldenslebener Forst (Cat. no. 61).

Using the assemblage from Düsedau to determine the association with other ceramic forms, Preuss arrived at an identification of the Düsedau ceramic horizon. He included here the steep-walled bowls (Fig. 59: 2), which he compared with the Troldebjerg bowls of the Northern TRB, but which are also similar in some instances to the steep-walled beakers of the Western TRB (Bakker's pails). These bowls are slightly convex in profile, with two pairs of small handles just below the rim, although occasionally as many as seven handles have been encountered (Issendorf; Tempel 1972, 54, Fig. 7: c). The most common, although by no means exclusive, decorative motif under the rim is composed of standing triangles (Fig. 59: 2), which may be closely spaced or far apart and are generally infilled with vertical or oblique stab-and-drag impressions. The body decoration is arranged in strict vertical bands consisting of oblique hatching, parallel grooves, narrow zig-zag bands or leaf motifs.

The shouldered vessels of this group usually have a broad convex shoulder with one (on cups; Fig. 59: 1) or two (on amphorae) handles; the neck tends

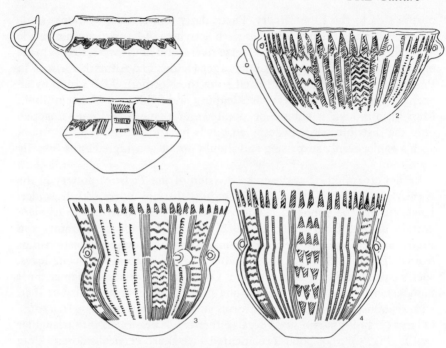

Figure 59 Pottery representative of the Düsedau horizon: 1,2-Issendorf, 3,4-
Düsedau (Source: Bakker 1979; Preuss 1980).

to be tall. Decoration consists of a horizontal pattern below the rim, a
sporadic vertical design on the neck and hanging triangles on the shoulder.
Bakker (1979, 122–6) has pointed out that one-handled, shouldered vessels
(tureens) with hatched triangles on the shoulder and vertical lines or ladders
either side of the handle (dated by him to the Drouwen C phase) represent
one of the most widespread pottery types to be found in the Western and
Northern TRB groups, clearly transcending regional boundaries.

Through further association of pottery forms at Düsedau and Issendorf,
Preuss included in this group round-bodied, funnel-necked beakers with
vertical stab-and-drag or grooved fringe decoration (Preuss 1980, Plate 8:
3) and the richly decorated lugged beakers (Fig. 59: 3, 4; the so-called
Prachtbecher). Four such vessels have been found at Düsedau and further
examples are known from the settlement at Klein-Bünstorf (Dehnke 1940,
Plate VII: 1, 2, 4), from a pit at Nenndorf (Wegewitz 1955, Fig. 8) and from
other localities (Rech 1971).

The younger phase pottery is identified in the assemblage from grave 33
at the Haldenslebener Forst (Bebertal 33) where steep-walled bowls display
a different ornamentation. They are decorated under the rim with a horizontal band of short, vertical lines executed in a broad stab-and-drag
technique (Fig. 60: 1). There is often a horizontal line dividing the upper

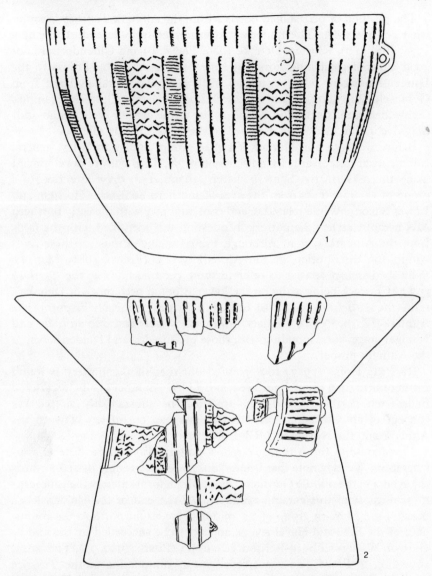

Figure 60 Pottery from Gerwisch characteristic of the Haldensleben horizon (Source: Preuss 1980).

and lower decoration and the latter is less varied than on the Düsedau-style bowls; it tends to alternate betwen the horizontal and vertical stab-and-drag patterns including lines, zig-zag bands and fir-branch motifs (Preuss 1980, Plates 55–7). The shouldered vessels associated with this horizon are more angular in profile, with a shorter neck and a reduced ledge-like shoulder; a similar angularity appears on funnel-necked beakers.

The position of pedestalled bowls within the Altmark *Tiefstich* is some-what controversial. The undecorated examples from Issendorf (Tempel 1972, Fig. 6: b), Kloster (Dehnke 1940, Fig. 5: b) and Oldendorf are not good chronological indicators but have been assigned by Preuss to the Düsedau horizon, while examples such as the pedestalled bowl from Gerwisch (Fig. 60: 2) and the well-known Groß Flottbek examples (Schwabedissen 1953b, Figs 14 and 15) by virtue of their vertical stab-and-drag decoration have been assigned to the following horizon.

Before we close our Altmark *Tiefstich* group discussion, a few general comments are necessary. In a discussion of the TRB culture development in northern Germany, Schwabedissen (1979b, 158) drew attention to a group of ceramic finds from the area of southern Schleswig-Holstein and Lower Saxony. While related to and contemporary with the early northern MN ceramic styles, the pottery in question was identified with the finds from the Altmark region. Although Preuss included most of these finds within the distribution of the Altmark group (Preuss 1980, Map 1), Schwabedissen proposed to refer to these ceramic finds as the *Curslack group* (Curslack being a site on the lower Elbe) in preference ot Dehnke's term (the *Alttiefstich Keramik*), or indeed the geographically inappropriate Altmark *Tiefstich*. The Curslack group was subdivided into an older and younger stage, corresponding with those of Düsedau and Haldensleben in the Altmark proper.

Recently Hoika (1987, 109) pointed out that similar pottery is found further north than Preuss indicated, and added a number of albeit scattered finds from north-east Holstein. In effect he substantially altered the concept of an 'exclusion zone' that Preuss had postulated between the Altmark and the Northern TRB group.

The demise of the Altmark *Tiefstich* pottery also requires further con-sideration. We may note that Preuss' discussion is strongly biased towards the events in the middle German region, which forms merely the southern-most outpost of this ceramic tradition. At the end of the Haldensleben horizon the Altmark group of the middle Elbe, as far north as the conflu-ence of the Elbe and Havel rivers, appears to be succeeded by the middle German Walternienburg-Bernburg complex (Preuss 1980, 93). The latter, according to Preuss, does not represent a continuation of the *Tiefstich* ceramic tradition, but is rooted in the middle German Baalberge/Salzmünde complex.

Leaving aside for the moment the question of the relationship between the Altmark *Tiefstich* and Walternienburg-Bernburg, it must be pointed out that the continuity of ceramic development from the Altmark *Tiefstich* has been well documented through studies in Lower Saxony. On the basis of finds from megalithic graves and settlement sites, especially on the Lüneburger Heide and along the Aller river, Laux (1979 and 1984) has established a more or less complete sequence of the *Tiefstich* pottery, a sequence which, moreover, he attempted to relate to the development of megalithic chamber forms in this region (see also Chapter 9).

The earliest group, the *Keramikgruppe A* (Laux 1979, Fig. 7), is represented by the already discussed Fuchsberg pottery. The two subsequent groups, *Keramikgruppen B* and *C* (ibid., Figs 8 and 9), correspond precisely to Preuss' Düsedau and Haldensleben horizons. The B pottery is represented by finds such as Wittenwater, distr. Uelzen (Voss 1965; Schirnig 1979e, Fig. 13), Oldendorf (Laux 1979, Fig. 8: 8–10), Rohstorf (ibid., Fig. 8: 4, 6) and Raven (ibid., Fig. 8: 7), while C pottery may be recognised at Oldendorf (ibid., Fig. 9: 3, 5), Rahmstorf (ibid., Fig. 9: 6, 7) or Barskamp (ibid., Fig. 9: 8, 9). It is during this period that Laux suggested the possibility of influences from the Altmark reaching Lower Saxony, which he identifies in the appearance of particularly long chambers. His *Keramikgruppen D* and *E* (ibid., Figs 10 and 11) continue the development of *Tiefstich* pottery in Lower Saxony along lines similar to those elsewhere within the Western TRB group, although again there are arguments for the recognition of influences from the Walternienburg-Bernburg and Globular Amphora culture ceramics.

The Altmark *Tiefstich* appears, in Preuss' reckoning, as an extremely short-lived phenomenon: the Düsedau horizon is synchronised with the MN Ia (Troldebjerg) style and the Haldensleben horizon with the MN Ib (Klintebakke) style of the Northern TRB group; both horizons, moreover, are said to correspond to the Salzmünde phase of the Southern TRB group (Preuss 1980, 93, Fig. 27). On the basis of forms and decoration diagnostic of the Düsedau horizon, one may point to a general similarity with Bakker's Drouwen A–B–C stages and Bakker himself compared pottery from Hooghalen with assemblages from Düsedau and Issendorf (1979, 122). Moreover, while vertical decoration on some of the steep-walled Altmark bowls corresponds to the Troldebjerg designs, the pendant triangle decoration is found in association with the Klintebakke as well as with the MN II Blandebjerg styles from Denmark. There may be an overlap between Bakker's Drouwen C and D and the Haldensleben horizons, but it does not allow for a synchronisation with the Klintebakke style, either on stylistic grounds or in terms of absolute chronology (see Chapter 4.4.3.2).

The so-called C-pottery of Lower Saxony, which is identical to Haldensleben pottery, cannot be associated stylistically with anything other than the Danish Blandebjerg style and, contrary to Preuss' argument, the appearance of the so-called Walternienburg drum constitutes additional support for a connection between the Haldensleben horizon and Walternienburg pottery.

4.5.2 The Netherlands and north-west Germany

Among the recent attempts at introducing some order into the vast ceramic material in the area west of the Weser river is the typo-chronological study published by Bakker (1979). His work is based upon and offers a refinement of earlier schemes, particularly those of Van Giffen (1925 and 1927) and Knöll (1959). It includes a discussion of the history of research into the Western TRB pottery as well as a detailed study of the ceramic development in the areas of the Netherlands and north-west Germany. Since Bakker's work has been published in a lucid and entertaining English version in 1979, only a brief summary is offered here; the reader is referred to the 1979 publication for a detailed account.

Van Giffen (1927) named his pottery phases after two of the Drenthe megaliths: Drouwen (D19) and Havelte (D53) and this nomenclature was retained by Bakker. The typo-chronological scheme (Fig. 61) was based on a study of shouldered vessels and bowls which were referred to as 'the pilot series' (straight-walled bowls resembling buckets were termed 'pails' by Bakker). Lugged beakers were thought to be a typologically useful form for the early stages of the scheme (A–C), while amphorae became more significant towards the younger end of the scale (E–G). The remaining pottery forms, while used in cross-regional comparisons, were regarded as unsuitable for typo-chronology on account of their rarity (for example pedestalled bowls) or their longevity of form without any noticeable change in shape or decoration (for example funnel-necked beakers or collared flasks; Bakker 1979, 54–60).

Two other important features of Bakker's scheme must also be noted. Firstly, with reference to the diagnostic pots, Bakker considered the change in ornamentation to be a more significant feature than the change in form, because the former is less affected by the potter's expertise and because ceramic analysis regularly relies upon small sherds which cannot be used for shape reconstruction (ibid., 61). Secondly, in contrast to Ebbesen's (1975 and 1978) studies of pottery from the Northern TRB group, Bakker has tried to distinguish between a 'pottery phase' and a 'chronological phase'; he defined a pottery phase as a period characterised by specific diagnostic pots during which earlier as well as later forms may also be found. In the context of his ceramic sequence Bakker stated that 'the actual development had more nuances' and a subdivision into phases is an over-simplification (1979, 61).

Let us now briefly consider Bakker's typo-chronology of the area west of the Weser river. Among the more conspicuous changes within the development of the Western TRB pottery are alterations in the shape of certain vessels and the evolution of surface ornamentation. The round-bellied and funnel-necked jugs typical of the Drouwen A phase develop into angular and wide-shouldered vessels during the Drouwen B and C phases, and subsequently into the smooth amphora-like forms of the Early Havelte E phase (Fig. 61). Lugged beakers are of short duration and are not encountered after the Drouwen C phase.

The *Drouwen A* pottery is decorated with vertically placed patterns such

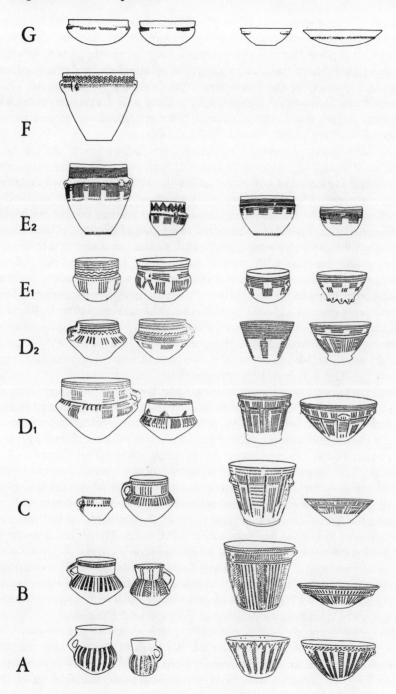

Figure 61 Bakker's scheme for the development of pottery from the Western TRB group (Source: Bakker 1979).

as 'ladders' or narrow bands with oblique impressions (Bakker 1979, Fig. 28). Lugged beakers and bowls of this phase are decorated all over their entire surface, but jugs carry patterns only on the belly. Whereas the precise origin of this pottery cannot as yet be ascertained, Bakker argued for a strong influence of the Fuchsberg style from the north and he synchronised the Drouwen A phase with the early MN I and early Altmark ceramics. In his words: 'Just as with Altmark, Drouwen began when Haaßel-Fuchsberg (ENC) finished' (ibid., 115).

The subsequent development, which may be observed during the *Drouwen B* (ibid., Fig. 29) and *Drouwen C* (ibid., Fig. 30) phases, consists of a gradual expansion of horizontal under-the-rim decoration, which from now on consists of various combinations of horizontally and vertically placed motifs such as multiple zig-zags or short vertical strokes bordered by *Tiefstich* lines. The decoration of the lower part of the body is now being broken up into separate zones; horizontal motifs (zig-zags, WWW-lines) alternate and contrast with vertical 'ladders' or straight grooves. This arrangement is particularly conspicuous on the Drouwen C pottery and has been decribed by Hodder (1982b) as 'dendritic design organisation'. The decoration is executed almost entirely using the stab-and-drag technique, and additional diagnostic features worthy of note are the appearance of decoration on the neck of shoulder pots and the presence of the hanging triangle motif, an element which, as we have already seen, was also very popular on *Tiefstich* pottery everywhere else.

With the evolution of the *Drouwen D1* and *Drouwen D2* pottery (Bakker 1979, Figs 31–2) the most conspicuous change is the appearance of the *tvaerstik* technique in D1; by Early Havelte (E), nearly all decoration is carried out in this manner. There are now fewer vertical patterns on the upper part of the pot and these are virtually absent from Drouwen D2 onwards. The vertical/horizontal arrangements still continue on the lower part of the pots, but they begin to cover smaller surfaces and the interplay between the decorated and empty zones becomes more important.

From the *Early Havelte E1–2* (ibid., Figs 33–4) onwards we also observe a merging of the upper and lower decorative zones. By *Middle Havelte F* the decoration has become so contracted that it only covers the upper part of the vessel (ibid., Fig. 35). It regularly consists of bands of vertical stamps. At the end of the ceramic sequence, *Late Havelte G*, the decoration is very scanty (ibid., Fig. 36); it involves mostly small rectangular blocks of stamps and a considerable number of pots are undecorated.

Bakker synchronises his Drouwen B/C pottery with the MN Ib and MN II period in southern Scandinavia on the basis of the pendant triangle decoration which is known in Denmark from MN Ib style onwards, but the Drouwen D phase must also be partly contemporary on account of the *tvaerstik* decoration. Furthermore, the Drouwen B/C is synchronised by Bakker with the Düsedau horizon of the Altmark *Tiefstich*, while the

Drouwen C/D pottery would then correspond to the Haldensleben horizon (which is contrary to Preuss' classification of Altmark material in relation to the Danish pottery; Preuss 1980). The late Drouwen and Early Havelte are synchronised by Bakker with MN III–IV, and the Late Havelte with MN IV–V; style F, according to Bakker (1979, 138) expresses the same 'style of the age' as the Store Valby.

4.6 The ceramic sequence of the Southern TRB group

A presentation of the typo-chronological development of pottery from the Southern group of the TRB culture is beset by a whole range of problems. Although the pottery itself is relatively easily classifiable in terms of vessel form and decoration, and although five ceramic groups have been identified (Baalberge, Salzmünde, the already discussed Altmark, Walternienburg and Bernburg), there are considerable difficulties in relating the individual ceramic groups to one another. Most of the pottery available for study derives from graves, from where there is little assistance in terms of stratigraphic evidence. Even the large central German burial mounds on the whole support only the chronological relationship between the TRB and the subsequent Corded Ware culture, and many other grave forms are simply not considered.

Very few settlements have been subjected to investigation and even these provide mostly Bernburg pottery. There is a general dearth of dating evidence and only Salzmünde and Bernburg finds are associated with C-14 dates; the German Baalberge dates are very doubtful, although some support can be derived from the peripheral development of the TRB in Czechoslovakia (see Chapter 5).

Additionally, each stylistically distinguished ceramic group has in the past been regarded as a separate cultural entity; this apears to be the case even today, and is most emphatically expressed in terms such as the Baalberge culture, or the Walternienburg/Bernburg culture. That this is not merely a matter of semantics can be judged from Behrens' comments that the Bernburg pottery cannot be included within the TRB culture because it lacks beakers (1973, 112) and that it can be regarded as a 'pure Bernburg culture' (1981a, 11). Moreover, in spite of poor chronological indicators, the division of this period in central Germany continues to be based firmly upon the stylistic differences in the pottery and little effort has been made to see how these divisions relate to other aspects of material culture, settlement patterns or the economy.

The earliest TRB horizon in the Southern group is generally believed to be represented by the *Baalberge phase* (named after a burial mound at Schneiderberg near Baalberge on the river Fuhne). Pottery typical of this phase derives mostly from burials, amongst which are the earliest burial mounds in this part of Europe, for example Pohlsberg (Latdorf), Baalberge and Preußlitz (Preuss 1966). Only a few settlements are known, such as

Diebzig and Drosa (ibid., 143–4), but they have been poorly investigated. The large burial mounds containing Baalberge pottery as well as other graves and stray finds concentrate mainly between the Elbe and Saale rivers (U. Fischer 1956, Plate 3), especially in the Köthen district (where most of the burial mounds are found), with a scattering of finds as far north as the Ohre and west along the Bode and Unstrut rivers. Small groups of Baalberge finds are also known from Bohemia and Moravia (Fig. 62).

Typical ceramic forms include beakers, amphorae, jugs, semi-conical and carinated bowls and handled cups (Preuss 1966, 11–23; Fig. 63: A); whether or not collared flasks should be associated with this phase is not certain. In contrast to the northern regions of the TRB the principal vessels, at least as far as grave goods are concerned, are amphorae and jugs. Lichardus (1976, 104) distinguished seven types of amphorae, but in general they are two- or four-handled examples, with necks that vary from splaying to conical and bellies that range from round to biconical; sometimes the strongly profiled vessels have four additional handles at the widest circumference (Preuss 1966, Plates 6: 4, 10: 3 and 11: 5). Funnel-necked beakers are always flat-based, mostly tall and slender (Fig. 63: 2; Preuss 1966, Plates 5 and 6: 3); lugged beakers are rare. Jugs and cups are common and, like amophorae, vary from smooth to angular (Fig. 63: 3, 6; Preuss 1966, Plates 6: 2, 9: 1, 2, 11: 1 and 14: 3, 4).

Only a small proportion of vessels are decorated. When ornamentation is present, it consists either of stamp impressions under the rim or of applied strips of clay which most commonly splay out in 'ribs' from beneath the amphorae or jug handles (ibid., Plates 19: 1, 26: 1 and 47: 3). This pattern has become the *leitmotif* of Baalberge pottery (Fig. 63: 4).

Typological divisions within the Baalberge pottery are difficult to establish because of the lack of large settlement assemblages that would enable us to identify contemporaneous forms. A general comparison with material from Mecklenburg and areas to the east would suggest that vessels with rounded bellies may represent an older, and those with sharper profiles a younger, horizon. Indeed, Preuss originally thought this was the case (1966, 27), but he no longer maintains this division (1980, 21). Lichardus, on the other hand, claims the existence of two horizons on the basis of horizontal stratigraphy and ceramic associations from the cemetery at Zauschwitz (1976, 143 and 195), although in Preuss' view (1980, 28) there are no grounds for such a division. Preuss has argued that a group of graves in the south of the Baalberge distribution, which show a different orientation from the majority of crouched inhumations (with the head towards the west) and which are also typical of the later (?) Salzmünde, may represent a group of late graves. These are often furnished with jugs which apparently appear late in the Baalberge.

On the basis of comparison with materials from the east and north, it would still be reasonable to regard the rounded forms as older, or more

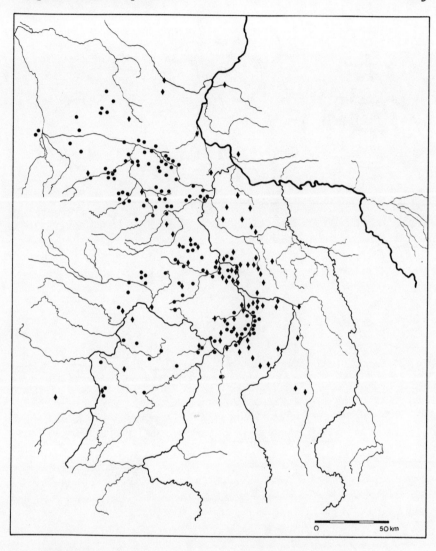

● a   ◆ b

Figure 62 Distribution of Baalberge [a] and Salzmünde [b] pottery in middle
Germany (Source: Behrens 1973).

plausibly to see Baalberge as a somewhat later development than the TRB
in the north and east – for instance after 5000 BP, by which time angular
vessels are also common. This would not be acceptable to Preuss, however,
who believes that the TRB immediately to the north of Baalberge, in other
words in Mecklenburg/Brandenburg, derives from Baalberge itself, a view

A

B

Figure 63 Pottery of the Southern TRB group: A-Baalberge style (Source: Preuss 1966), B-Salzmünde style: 7-Brachwitz, 8-Köttichau, 9,10-Salzmünde, 11-Gerstewitz (Source: Behrens 1973; Nitzschke 1986).

which is no longer reconcilable with our general understanding of the TRB's emergence.

In the south of its distribution, the Baalberge phase is followed by the *Salzmünde* phase (Fig. 62), although again this is based mainly on pottery stylistics. The range of the Salzmünde vessels is the same as previously (Fig. 63: 3), but they differ slightly in form, showing a tendency towards elongation and more pronounced handles. A new ceramic form is represented by a clay drum (Fig. 63: 11). There is a much greater emphasis on decoration, with about one-half of the known pottery ornamented. Decorative motifs commonly include single or multiple rows of dots or infilled triangles below the rim or on the shoulder; applied clay strips continue in use, often in the shape of crescents. Some vessels are decorated with radial designs (Behrens 1973, Figs 31: t and 32: o). The Salzmünde drums are generally funnel-necked, although the relative size of the upper and lower parts varies. There can be up to nine knobs on the upper half. The drums are richly decorated with bands of vertical strokes, zig-zag or plain horizontal lines and rows of dots; often there are symbols which resemble a cross, anchor, bow, sun or others (U. Fischer 1951, 100, Fig. 1: 1–8, 13; Behrens 1973, Figs 31: s, u, 32: 1 and 33: i, Plate facing p. 96; Fig. 63: 11).

Apart from the Altmark *Tiefstich* pottery, whose easternmost finds reach as far as the confluence of the Elbe and Saale rivers (Preuss 1980, Map 4), two more ceramic groups can be identified in central Germany: the *Walternienburg* and *Bernburg* ceramic groups, the former named after a large cemetery in the district of Jerichow, the latter after a burial mound at Bernburg in the district of Bernburg (Fig. 64). This pottery was initially classified by Niklasson (1925, 147–50); his sequence of Walternienburg I and II followed by Bernburg I, II and III has for long been the backbone of German Neolithic studies.

Walternienburg I (ibid., 147–8, Plate LII) comprised sharply profiled, tri-partite hanging vessels and shouldered cups as well as steep-walled bowls, whereas Walternienburg II (ibid., 148–9, Plate LIII), in addition to these types which now displayed a bi-partite form, also comprised barrel-shaped pots, large cups, twin vessels and conical bowls. The decoration was carried out in *tvaerstik*, stab-and-drag or by incision, displaying an arrangement of alternating horizontal and vertical patterns among which multiple lines, zig-zags and vertical strokes played an important role (Fig. 65).

The Bernburg pottery was divided by Niklasson into three stages. The main feature of these ceramics is the smooth profile of the vessels. Bernburg I forms identified by Niklasson (1925, 149, Plate LIV) were identical to those of Walternienburg II, so much so that it was not possible to distinguish between undecorated vessels. In the Bernburg II stage (ibid., 149–50, Plate LV) the pottery development reached its climax with rounded cups, amphorae and a wide range of bowls among the most common forms. In

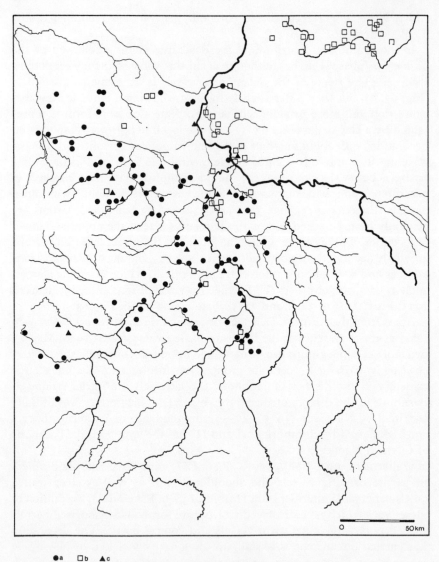

●a   □b   ▲c

Figure 64 Distribution of Walternienburg [b] and Bernburg [a] pottery [c-both] in middle Germany (Source: Behrens 1973; Kirsch 1981).

Bernburg III (ibid., 150, Plate LVI) many forms disappeared; only handled cups, bowls and rarely barrel-shaped pots remained. Decoration was mostly horizontal and, on the whole, confined to the lower part of the vessel. It comprised broad bands of zig-zags, horizontal lines and hatched lozenges alternating with blanks; hanging infilled triangles were particularly common on cups (Fig. 66).

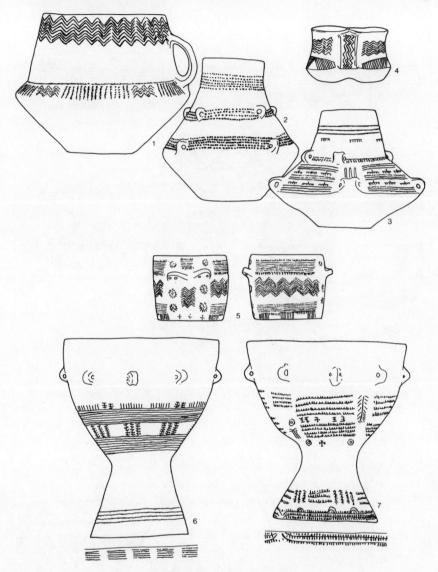

Figure 65 Pottery decorated in Walternienburg style: 1–4-Walternienburg, 5-Heiligenthal, 6-Nordhausen, 7-Hornsömmern (Source: Behrens 1973).

Both Walternienburg and Bernburg assemblages also contain drums which, in contrast to the Salzmünde forms, are heavier in appearance and often shaped like an egg-cup (U. Fischer 1951, 100). The Walternienburg drums (ibid., Fig. 2: 1–10; Fig. 65: 6, 7) are decorated with stamp- and comb-lines, bands of zig-zags, fir branches and other symbols, while the Bernburg examples (U. Fischer 1951, Fig. 2: 11–20; Fig. 66: 6–9) are most

Figure 66 Pottery decorated in Bernburg style: 1,2,4-Quenstedt, 3,5–9-Dölauer Heide (Source: Behrens 1973).

commonly ornamented with chess-board patterns, infilled lozenges, horizontal dots and fir branches. Such vessels, most frequently deliberately smashed, accompany burials, but are also known from settlements, especially of the *Höhensiedlung* type (Behrens and Schröter 1980; Starling 1988).

The relationship between these various ceramic groupings (Salzmünde, Altmark *Tiefstich*, Walternienburg and Bernburg) has always been at the heart of the problem in central German typo-chronology. The difficulties have been aggravated by the general lack of evidence (lack of stratigraphy, poor settlement investigation, insufficient dating) and primarily, it seems, by the specific philosophy whereby different ceramic groups have tended to be identified with separate cultural groups.

U. Fischer's studies (1951, 102; 1956) of the central German burials showed that Niklasson's five-stage system did not represent a straightforward chronological sequence from Walternienburg I to Bernburg III. Bernburg II and III ceramics were often encountered together (for example at Halberstadt, Latdorf and Schiepzig) and Walternienburg I and II were also occasionally found together (for example at Walternienburg itself or at Nordhausen). Fischer therefore regarded Walternienburg and Bernburg as individual ceramic styles which were partly contemporary with Bernburg I, thus providing a link between them, an idea generally endorsed by Behrens (1973).

The forms and decoration of the Walternienburg ceramics leave little doubt as to its emergence under the influence of *Tiefstich* pottery. Unfortunately, neither the Altmark *Tiefstich* nor the Walternienburg assemblages can be dated independently. Since Preuss (1980, 62–3 and 93) believed that the two Altmark horizons (the Düsedau and Haldensleben) should be synchronised with the Northern MN Ia and MN Ib styles respectively and that the Walternienburg pottery corresponds to the Northern MN II, he was unwilling to allow any chronological overlap between these two ceramic groups. Yet some of the Walternienburg decoration, especially on shouldered cups where bands of zig-zags alternate with vertical stab-and-drag strokes (Fig. 65: 1), is virtually identical with that of the Haldensleben horizon and some contemporaneity of *Tiefstich* and Walternienburg simply cannot be excluded.

The immediate source of the Bernburg pottery is more difficult to identify as various scholars have commented upon southern influences (the Řivnáč culture; Behrens 1973, 112) as well as on more westerly contacts with the Hessen ceramics (U. Fischer 1956; Schrickel 1957 and 1966). It has been suggested recently that angular Bernburg forms may have developed under the influence of the Salzmünde ceramics (Beier 1984, 51–5). The Bernburg assemblages are more numerous than those of Walternienburg pottery, and the association of Bernburg II and III has been verified by recent burial finds (for example at Barby; Behrens 1981a, Fig. 1) and, more significantly, by regular association in settlement assemblages. This is especially well

illustrated by the Bernburg finds at Dölauer-Heide and Quenstedt
(Behrens and Schröter 1980). This clear association has prompted Behrens
(1981a, 11) to argue that Bernburg II and III pottery forms a homogeneous
unit and that one can speak about a 'pure Bernburg culture'. The C-14
dates associated with the Bernburg assemblages, especially at Dölauer-
Heide, show them to be younger than Salzmünde assemblages (Behrens
1981b; see Chapter 5), but once again at least a partial overlap should not
be excluded.

The interesting suggestion of the possible synchronicity of these various
pottery groups has been put forward by Beier (1984). On the basis of his
investigations of the Walternienburg and Bernburg collective graves, Beier
was able to point to ceramic connections in pottery grave goods between
Salzmünde and Walternienburg (for example at Seeburg 2; ibid., 51,
Plate 22: 1–3) and between Salzmünde and Bernburg, with many of the
Bernburg graves containing not only the so-called *Opperschöne* jug, but also
Salzmünde-like cups (for example at Niederbösa, Nordhausen and Schönstedt; ibid., 51), as well as between Walternienburg and Bernburg (in the
graves of Friedeburg and Polleben; ibid., 52). Moreover, a number of
Bernburg assemblages also reveal a connection with the Globular Amphora
culture (for example at Pevestorf: ibid., Fig. 23: 5 and Hindenburg: ibid.,
Fig. 23: 4), suggesting that Bernburg pottery was still in use at the time of
the Globular Amphora development.

Apart from these numerous, if not entirely clear, connections between
the various central German pottery groups, one more factor is worthy of
note: their distinct geographical distribution (Fig. 64). Thus the Salzmünde
finds are noted mainly in the southern area of the earlier Baalberge distribution, along the middle Saale. This distribution is more or less exclusive
of the *Tiefstich* pottery, which is found in the northern area of Baalberge in
limited numbers, but mainly further to the north of Magdeburg outwith
the main Baalberge settlement region. The Walternienburg pottery is
found predominantly along the Havel river in Brandenburg, where it has
barely begun to be studied (Kirsch 1981), and along the Elbe from Witten-
berg to Tangermünde, with only a scattering of sites towards the eastern
Harz foreland. Walternienburg settlements are now known on the Havel,
but they remain to be investigated. The Bernburg finds come predominantly
from further south, from most of the Salzmünde area and extending west
all the way round the Harz mountains.

This distribution, noted but not considered significant by scholars
working on the central German material, is of fundamental importance.
First of all, irrespective of precise chronological position, it indicates that
all ceramic groups have their own 'core area' and that the point of contact
is in the east Harz foreland. Moreover, it also reveals that the Walternienburg pottery is found by and large outwith the so-called *Elbe-Saale-Gebiet*
and that only its southern peripheral extension has been considered in

research so far. Indeed this in itself could account for the difficulties of correlating Walternienburg with the rest of the groups.

The precise chronological relationship between these various pottery groups will not be solved merely by stylistic comparisons but requires fundamental study of settlement sites and the recovery of much-needed dating evidence. Such clear differential distribution reveals, however, that we are dealing here not with a direct succession of phases, but with a number of regional ceramic styles which developed under the influence of one another and must have been at least partly contemporary. A provisional interpretation may thus envisage the central Baalberge style developing in the south into Salzmünde, while to the north and beyond there is the contemporary Altmark *Tiefstich* with its own connections towards Lower Saxony and Mecklenburg. While these two ceramic styles are still current, the Walternienburg style begins to emerge, mostly east of the Elbe, and at the same time, or possibly a little later, the Salzmünde style is superseded by the geographically more extensive Bernburg style. The duration of the Walternienburg and Bernburg styles is difficult to determine, but it is most likely that both – not just Bernburg – come under the influence of the Globular Amphora culture.

While naturally such a staggered development of ceramic styles needs to be documented through further research, this interpretation fits the ceramic evidence better than a strict chronologically exclusive succession of one style after another. Moreover, it takes into consideration not only the transitions within popularly used pottery, but also contacts between individual groups within and outwith the original settlement areas as initially defined by the Baalberge pottery.

4.7 Summary of the TRB culture ceramic sequences

Any reader who has had the patience and perseverance to follow this lengthy and detailed discussion will surely appreciate the opening remarks of this chapter on the sway that the TRB pottery has held over generations of scholars. The various regional sequences invariably leave one with the impression that it is not possible to see the wood for the trees. And yet, in this vast body of evidence, there are broad underlying patterns. Perhaps, at long last, these can now be brought together so as to introduce some order into this seemingly disparate material.

The earliest TRB pottery, dated to the second half of the 6th millennium BP and represented by such assemblages as Sarnowo, Berlin-Britz and Rosenhof, reveals an extraordinary homogeneity of ceramic technology, form and decoration (Figs 11: 1–4 and 12). Nearly all the substantial assemblages of this horizon comprise the same set of forms (funnel-necked beakers, amphorae, flat clay discs and large storage vessels) that are virtually identical over the whole area from central Poland across Mecklenburg and Brandenburg to southern Schleswig-Holstein (Fig. 67). With

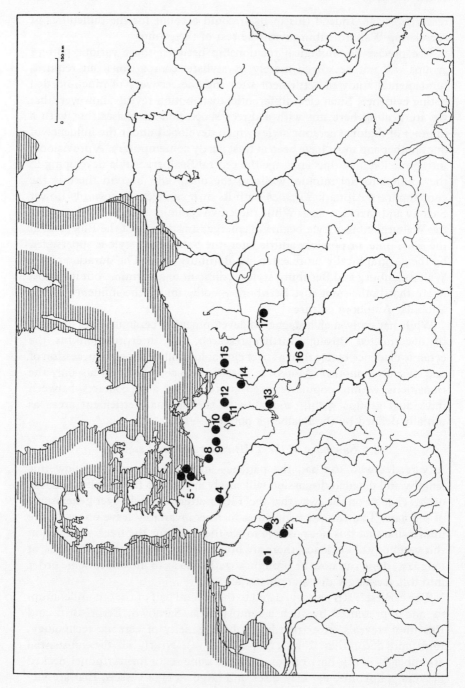

hindsight it is perhaps hardly surprising that precisely this pottery was assigned by Becker (1947, 206–16) to a general European A/B horizon. The uniformity of this pottery suggests, first and foremost, that similar processes were taking place across the central area of the North European Plain and it is here that the origins of the TRB culture, at least in geographical terms, must be sought.

With the exception of the far west of the Plain around Swifterbant and Hazendonk (Van der Waals 1977; see also extensive literature in *Helinium* 16–19; Louwe Kooijmans 1976a, 1976b and 1980a), there is currently little evidence to support the incorporation within this horizon of the area west of the Elbe. Yet there are no *a priori* reasons why similar processes should not have taken place here and future investigations around the Dümmer lake and in the Netherlands may indeed alter the picture significantly. Returning to the pottery itself, we should note that there is no difference between the domestic wares, as found on settlements, and the pottery recovered from non-domestic contexts, for example from votive bog offerings. This uniformity implies that, as yet, there is little differentiation between vessels used for everyday activities and those used in ceremonies and rituals.

During the following stage, which coincides with the geographical expansion of the TRB culture under the stimuli from the initial area, we begin to perceive the emergence of regional groups. It is not a horizon of precisely synchronised ceramic phases, but rather a horizon of a similar rhythm of ceramic development under clearly different local conditions. We may include in this broad horizon such ceramic groups as Pikutkowo, Baalberge, Oxie, Svaleklint, Volling, Satrup, Moltzow and, possibly, the *Dümmer Keramik*. It is my belief that the western part of the North European Plain was now fully participating in this process (cf. Engern-Brinkhof; Brandt 1961 and 1967), although this still needs to be documented more fully.

It is difficult to determine whether the three different pottery groups identified in southern Scandinavia are merely a reflection of a more advanced state of research (and similar groupings will in due course emerge in other regions), or whether they emphasise the geographical specificity of the area, coupled with multiple northward influences from the eastern and western parts of the North European Plain. Although on the whole there is still a considerable degree of conformity, the early Danish non-domestic

Figure 67 Distribution of the earliest TRB pottery in the North European Plain indicative of the large area over which the TRB culture origins must be sought: 1-Hüde, 2-Engern-Brinkhof, 3-Loccum, 4-Boberg, 5-Rosenhof, 6-Siggeneben-Süd, 7-Klenzau, 8-Ostorf, 9-Bernitt, 10-Kläden, 11-Moltzow, 12-Neuenkirchen, 13-Berlin-Britz, 14-Niederlandin, 15-Kosin, 16-Wrocław-Pracze, 17-Sobota; circle denotes the area of Kujavia detailed in Fig. 89 (Source: Becker 1947; Bastian 1954; Brandt 1967; Schwabedissen 1979a and 1981; Wiślański 1979 with additions).

wares, as illustrated by the collection from the north Jutland grave at Volling (Thorvildsen 1940), already foreshadow future developments in this region.

Once the TRB culture becomes well established there is a virtual explosion in pottery manufacture and use, especially, but not exclusively, in the Northern and Western groups. This is the richest horizon from the point of view of ceramic differentiation and it comprises such styles as Fuchsberg, Virum, MN I and possibly MN II, Gingst, Wiórek, Salzmünde, early *Tiefstich* (Düsedau and Haldensleben) and possibly early Walternienburg. Again it must be emphasised that precise chronological synchronicity is of lesser significance here but, rather, it is the way in which the pottery is used in a whole range of contexts that provides a common link between different regions.

As we have already seen, many new ceramic forms emerge and there is a progressive enrichment of decoration. There are differences in emphasis of the regional importance of certain forms: for example decorated 'pails' are not typical of southern Scandinavia, but are extremely common in the Netherlands. Conversely, northern forms such as pedestalled bowls with their appendant clay ladles are, on the whole, rare elsewhere. They may, however, have a close connection with ceramic drums, a form particularly common in the Southern TRB group but clearly crossing the boundary both to the east and to the west. Amphorae are a prominent form in the Eastern TRB group, but are also important along the middle Elbe. Richly decorated lugged beakers (*Prachtbecher*) are typical of the Fuchsberg style but, interestingly, later examples concentrate in the area where the various regional groups come into contact with one another.

The pottery of this horizon is characterised by a profusion of decorative patterns which are applied in accordance with strict rules. Most of the ornamental motifs are of local significance, but some, such as the 'ladder' motif, the hanging triangle, the 'zipper' pattern and above all the ubiquitous vertical grooves on beaker bellies, clearly transcend regional boundaries. The ornamentation is at its most complex in the Northern and Western groups, where the bulk of pottery derives from non-domestic contexts: causewayed enclosures, deposits in front of or within the tombs, or votive offerings. In the remaining areas the ceramics, which derive from settlements (especially in the Eastern and South-eastern groups) or where they can be fairly safely considered to represent grave goods (Southern TRB) do not display such a rich ornamentation or variety of styles. However, that differences of context are significant can be demonstrated by the fact that in these areas vessels with ritual associations (for example the amphora from a votive deposit at Radziejów or the ram-handled vessels from the South-eastern TRB group, which appear to have played a role in harvest-related rituals) also display a degree of ornamentation that would not be out of place among the northern ceramics. Indeed, there has been a suggestion that the more profusely decorated Southern TRB style of the Walternienburg may represent by and large ceremonial wares with an important function in burial rituals (Starling 1988); this cannot be assessed, however, until the Walternienburg-style pottery from settlements and graves is better known.

The final stage in the ceramic development of the TRB culture comprises the remainder of the pottery groups, which were discussed in the earlier part of this chapter. This horizon is characterised by a reduction in the variety of manufactured pots and by a dramatic decrease not only in the proportion of decorated vessels, but also in the quality and richness of ornamentation. Moreover, the pottery clearly loses its multi-functional purpose as it is now rarely found in other than domestic contexts. The previously strongly accentuated regional boundaries become blurred once again and, although it never reaches the level of homogeneity of the early TRB stage, the pottery of this horizon shows hardly any stylistic variation, becoming uniformly crude and undecorated.

In conclusion, a few comments are necessary on the subject of the interpretation of material culture, in this instance pottery, in the broader context of social relations between individual groups. The nature of TRB ceramics – their stylistic variation and frequent non-domestic associations – naturally lends itself to an investigation of its social significance, and in recent years a number of studies have attempted to interpret the pottery from the point of view of its role in the expression of ideational concepts and in the maintenance of social order within the TRB culture communities.

Thus Ian Hodder (1982b) offered an analysis of the decoration of pottery from the Western group: the development from simple to progressively more contrasting patterns with a vertical/horizontal design emphasis, which culminated in sophisticated 'dendritic' pattern, eventually breaking down the vertical/horizontal contrast leading to the general demise of decoration (ibid., Figs 3–9). This sequence of change set against a wider background of changes within the TRB in this area, was interpreted by Hodder as reflecting a series of contrasts and contradictions within the socio-economic system and reproducing, by means of decoration which was also based on opposition, the various social categories. In a later work, however, Hodder (1986, 41–2) argued that there was no *a priori* reason why there should be a direct relation between the decoration on pots and the social organisation of a community which produced and used such pots; it was necessary first of all to consider the functions of such pottery within the domestic, ritual and prestige sphere before attempting to interpret decorative patterns associated with functionally different ceramics.

Shanks and Tilley (1987, 155–7) also attempted to interpret the abstract geometricity of designs from a sample of Swedish TRB pottery as directly tied to the context of its production and use for ceremonies outside the tombs. Analysing a small percentage of vessels deposited over a long period of time in front of the Fjälkinge tomb, they noted a sequence of change in decoration over time (from simply, through elaborately, to simply decorated vessels) and a change in the deposition of pottery in relation to the entrance of the tomb at different stages of the ceramic sequence. They argued for a temporal connection between these two variations and for an emphasis on the expression of oppositions: left/right of the entrance, inner/outer space, living/dead, and so on. Moreover, in their opinion the 'lineage' type of social system was the most suitable for the interpretation of such oppositions expressed in ritual activities, since in such a system various population units are dependent upon one another and are linked in a complex network of feasting, marriage and exchange where opposing forces are constantly at work.

Gebauer (1984) offered a more general interpretation of stylistic change in the Danish TRB. She argued that stylistic variation was not present at the level of individual causewayed enclosures or megalithic tombs but lay at a higher level of social structure. Regional groups perceived during the stylistically most differentiated period reflected the competitive state among larger social units which, however, were not as clearly defined as would be expected. She argued, moreover, for a stronger internal rather than external significance of ceramic styles, a sentiment also expressed in a similar context by T. Madsen (1988, 323–4).

While such studies are of immense interest, it is becoming clear that the problems of the social interpretation of ceramic styles are more complex and that the assumptions behind the relationship between ceramic styles and social organisation in terms of dichotomous oppositions are too simplistic. The context of the pottery (and indeed any other element of material culture) is, of course, very important. At the most basic level there is a clear distinction between pottery for domestic and for ritual use; this distinction is perceived to a greater or lesser extent throughout the whole area of the TRB culture. However, there are further distinctions within the pottery employed in ceremonies (or the lack of pottery use at certain times) and these simply cannot be ignored.

Taking the Danish TRB as an example, we may distinguish between different ritual contexts which involve the use of pottery. Thus at causewayed enclosures there is ceremonial manufacture of pottery as well as its disposal (see Chapter 7.4), the latter taking place in ditches, against the palisades or in pits within the enclosed perimeter. Pottery is placed in cult houses, at entrances to megalithic tombs and within the chambers, and also in association with other grave forms. It is buried at the end of ceremonial feasts (Ellerødgård; H. Nielsen 1987) and it is placed with offerings in waterlogged places or, occasionally, in association with hoards of other objects (Bygholm; Chapter 6.7). This list could be longer still, but even now it is clear that 'ritual' vessels are employed in various ways and for many different purposes – all this within one small region, without consideration of the overall diversity of TRB ritual.

Can we therefore study, as in one of the examples above, one spatial/ temporal pattern of pottery deposition in front of one chambered tomb and hope to gain an understanding of the function that pottery and its decoration played in 'the maintenance and reproduction of the social order' (Shanks and Tilley 1987, 171)? A socio-cultural interpretation of ceramics (including decorative styles) has to consider not only whether pots are domestic or ritual, but also the kind of ritual in which they were involved. Moreover, we need to find out whether the decoration varies between pots used for the different categories of ritual activities, how these activities relate to one another, and whether they change with time and in relation to changes observed in the use of other elements of material culture, changes in the economy and so on. All these different aspects need to be taken into account and relationships on all levels need to be explored not only in one area, but in the entire cultural complex.

While further thoughts on this theme will be offered at a later stage of our discussion of the TRB culture (Chapter 10.3), we may conclude our comments on the function of the TRB pottery by affirming the need to study the totality of this material and not merely a few selected aspects which appeal to the currently popular archaeological theories.

By bringing this vast ceramic material together in the foregoing pages it was hoped to demonstrate the wealth of information contained therein and to indicate the immense potential of this evidence for the study of the TRB culture. However, having been made aware of the overall, underlying changing trends in the ways in which TRB communities made, decorated and used their pottery, as well as being in a position to compare and contrast these trends over a large geographical area, we can also see from the foregoing discussion that we must now cease considering the pottery merely as an aid to the solution of chronological issues. We must now study the TRB culture's pottery as one of its material elements, a constituent which was not made and used to while away the time, but which clearly performed a wide range of functions, from the seemingly ordinary use for storing and cooking food to their apparently wasteful, extravagant expenditure in a variety of activities which today may seem bizarre but which, without any doubt, were as important as the more mundane uses.

The chronology in this context should only be significant in so far as it can demonstrate the changing form and use of the ceramics over the particular phases of the TRB culture development. In suggesting the four broad chronological horizons, each with its own regional and temporal variations, it was hoped to divert scholarly attention away from its excessive preoccupation with typo-chronological minutiae to the more significant issues of how pottery form and function evolved throughout the TRB in relation to other aspects of the culture, issues which are to be discussed in the following chapters. It is by examining these broad geographical and chronological patterns and interrelations that we can begin a meaningful discussion of the role that material culture (which includes but does not solely consist of the pottery) may have played in the social relations of individuals and groups within the TRB.

5

The absolute chronology of the TRB culture

The absolute chronology of the TRB culture will be discussed within the context of regional groups, which will provide the basis for the overall phasing of the TRB throughout northern Europe. The radiocarbon dates for the TRB culture are presented in the Appendix.

5.1 Eastern TRB group

The beginning of the TRB culture in the Polish lowlands can now be dated to the second half of the 5th millennium BC. The earliest date in this area remains the now well-known date from Sarnowo of 5570 ± 60 BP (GrN-5035, 4417 ± 60 BC). It derives from a charcoal sample found in a pit sealed by a later barrow monument. The associated pottery belongs to the Sarnowo phase and is typical of the early TRB material such as is known in other localities throughout the European lowland. The pit also contained a shell bead for which the best parallels are found in the neighbouring group of the Lengyel culture, especially at Brześć Kujawski (Gabałówna 1970a, 77; Grygiel 1986).

In the past the Sarnowo date has been regarded as too early: Bakker et al. (1969, 7) felt it ought to have been at least 200 years younger, while Lanting and Mook (1977, 73) ignored it on the grounds of being 'unacceptably old in comparison with other dates'. Today, however, the circumstances are considerably different. Not only is it possible to indicate a closely comparable chronological horizon across a large segment of the North European Plain (notably in northern Germany), but also radicarbon dates of the subsequent TRB in Kujavia give credence to the Sarnowo date.

The chronological position of the Pikutkowo phase (which defines the clearly identified Eastern TRB group) can now be assessed on the basis of three radiocarbon dates derived from clear contextual associations. The dates range between 5170 ± 180 BP (Lod-60, 3993 ± 203 BC) and 4950 ± 60 BP (GrN-13354, 3752 ± 66 BC), suggesting a period of about 300/200 years. Thus it is possible to suggest that the Pikutkowo phase began sometime around 4000 BC and lasted until 3700 BC. This dating is further supported by evidence from the South-eastern TRB group (see below, Chapter 5.2).

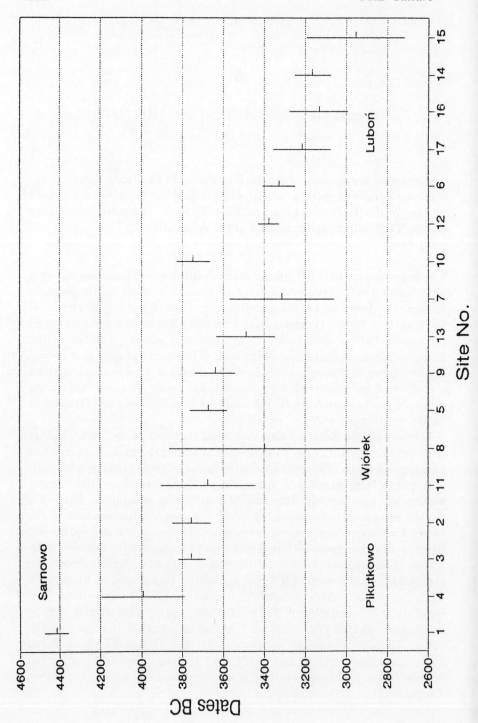

Furthermore, our better understanding of the processes which led to the emergence of farming economies across the North European Plain no longer demands chronological exclusivity between culturally different groups. Thus, in Kujavia the relationship between the early TRB (Sarnowo, Pikutkowo) and the neighbouring Brześć Kujawski group is documented not only in the similarity of certain aspects within the respective material culture, but also in C-14 dates.

The settlement at Brześć Kujawski is now confidently dated by sixteen radiocarbon dates which range between 5530 ± 220 BP (Lod-63, 4380 ± 240 BC) and 4515 ± 210 BP (Gx-6370, 3214 ± 282 BC; Grygiel 1986, Table III). One of the pits (No. 893), associated with the well-known house 56, contained deeply stratified pottery sherds which were decorated with the 'ladder' ornament typical of the Eastern TRB group from the Pikutkowo phase onwards (see Chapter 4.2). Moreover, one amphora sherd with such a pattern was considered by Grygiel (1986, Fig. 159) to have been none other than an import from the TRB. The pit is dates to 5260 ± 190 BP (Lod-195, 4093 ± 214 BC), which in spite of the large margin of error, compares well with the above-quoted C-14 dates of the Pikutkowo phase. It is also of interest to note that the female skeleton from the grave at Pikutkowo itself was adorned with a necklace of *Unio* shell beads, an ornament common not only at Brześć Kujawski, but also at other Lengyel sites. This contemporaneity and close relationship between the Brześć Kujawski group and the early TRB in Kujavia has been noted in the past by both Gabałówna (1966, 86; 1970a, 86) and Jażdżewski (1973b, 13), but it is only now that it can be confirmed by the dating of both complexes.

The absolute dating of the Wiórek phase is more difficult because so far the majority of dates are associated with fully developed and even late ceramics, the only exception being the date from Dąbrowa Biskupia (3670 ± 91 BC) quoted by Kośko (1988, 96). A timber building at Zberzyn long barrow is dated to 4720 ± 110 BP (Lod-159, 3490 ± 141 BC), with the pottery from the mound showing decorative motifs of a well-developed Wiórek style (Gorczyca 1981, 15). The C-14 dates from charred grain samples at Radziejów Kujawski and Zarębowo are associated with pottery which marks the transition between the Wiórek and Luboń ceramic styles (Gabałówna 1970c, 160; Wiślański 1979, 184). The dates are fairly consistent, ranging between 4710 ± 40 BP (GrN-5045, 3474 ± 84 BC) and 4590 ± 190 BP (M-1845, 3314 ± 225 BC), while one date from Radziejów Kujawski gave an older determination of 4860 ± 200 BP (M-1846, 3643 ± 231 BC).

Some assistance towards the dating of the emergence of the Wiórek style is forthcoming from the chronology of the South-eastern TRB group,

Figure 68 TRB radiocarbon dates: Eastern group. Dates BC by phase, ± one standard deviation. Site nos as in Appendix.

where closely comparable material is dated to about 3800/3750 BC onwards. It is therefore reasonable to suggest that the Wiórek style must have appeared in Kujavia by at least 3800 BC and was popular until 3400/3300 BC, indicating a period of about 400 years for the flourit of the TRB in this region.

The final stage of the Eastern TRB culture sees greater differentiation with Kujavia becoming a region of small distinct groups (for example the Radziejów and Mątwy groups; Kośko 1980). The Luboń ceramic style appears to have a widespread distribution, however, being witnessed in western Pomerania and at the Łupawa complex. The above-mentioned Radziejów Kujawski and Zarębowo dates suggest that the style emerged by about 3400/3300 BC. The end of the TRB culture in Kujavia is inextricably bound up with the emergence in the European lowland of two new cultural complexes: the Globular Amphora and Corded Ware cultures. On present evidence, the Globular Amphora culture emerged about 3200/3100 BC, although the TRB does appear to continue alongside for quite sometime (see Chapter 11).

5.2 South-eastern TRB group

The chronology of the South-eastern TRB group is now well founded upon a substantial series of radiocarbon dates from a number of settlements. Particularly important are the C-14 dates from the large, multi-phase upland settlement of Bronocice (Kruk and Milisauskas 1983). First of all, the Bronocice dates confirm the presence of the TRB culture on the loess upland by about 4000/3900 BC, a chronological horizon suggested by previously known but doubted C-14 dates from Gródek Nadbużny (Bakker *et al.* 1969). Secondly, the evidence from Bronocice is of particular significance because it demonstrates the value of a methodical excavation of a multi-phase (and multi-cultural) site, where a combination of stratigraphy and stylistic change of material culture in association with a large series of C-14 dates can provide evidence rarely encountered in other contexts.

The developed TRB communities are present on the loess by about 4000 BC (Bronocice I and Gródek Nadbużny). Thus, the initial formation of the South-eastern TRB off the loessic landscape, for which better evidence is now beginning to emerge, must have taken place towards the end of the 5th millennium BC, a fact entirely in agreement with the processes and chronology observed further north in the European lowland.

The three major phases identified at Bronocice (I, II and III) are confirmed by the data from other settlement sites in the region. The Bronocice phase I (paralleled with the Pikutkowo phase of the Eastern TRB) is now dated to between 5060 ± 110 BP (DIC-719, 3867 ± 122 BC) and 5010 ± 110 BP (Gd-2160, 3815 ± 122 BC), suggesting that the initial expansion onto the loess landscape was relatively swift during the period 4000/3900–3800 BC.

The subsequent, classic phase of Bronocice II (paralleled with the Wiórek phase) is dated by a series of C-14 dates from the major upland settlements. The dates range between 4940 ± 125 BP (DIC-362, 3740 ± 136 BC) and 4470 ± 190 BP (M-2321, 3150 ± 260 BC), offering a relatively long phase lasting from about 3800/3700 BC until 3400/3350 BC, which is entirely supported by archaeological evidence from the upland areas.

The final phase of the TRB culture in the South-eastern TRB, Bronocice III (paralleled with the Luboń phase) is dated to between 4610 ± 120 BP (DIC-716, 3350 ± 169 BC) and 4250 ± 180 BP (Lod-62, 2862 ± 235 BC). The C-14 dates from the Bronocice settlement suggest that the final TRB stage here may have been relatively swift and that strong influences of the Baden culture were already beginning to make their mark; a local version of the Baden culture is noted at Bronocice from about 3100 BC onwards (DIC-717, 4440 ± 80 BP). Thus the end of the TRB should be dated to about 3100/2900 BC.

5.3 The Northern TRB group

The problems of presenting a coherent absolute chronology of the Northern TRB group rest not so much with the lack of C-14 dates, but with their uneven geographical distribution. While there are now well over 100 dates from Denmark (supplemented by a few Swedish dates) and over thirty dates from Schleswig-Holstein, barely two radiocarbon dates can be associated with the TRB culture in Mecklenburg. Thus, the latter region's chronology cannot be assessed without reference to the neighbouring areas. This is particularly frustrating because archaeological evidence, as well as Mecklenburg's central position in the North European Plain, suggest very clearly its formative role in the development of the TRB.

In view of this disparity, as well as a degree of difficulty in correlating the relative chronologies worked out for the respective areas, the three geographical regions comprising the Northern group are presented separately; comments on the chronology of the whole of the Northern group follow after that.

5.3.1 Northern I group: Schleswig-Holstein

The initial division of the TRB culture into the Satrup and Denghoog phases by Schwantes (1939) was replaced by Schwabedissen's (1968, 10) scheme modelled to a large degree upon Becker's chronology for Denmark. Thus, he divided the north German material into the early Neolithic I and II (*Frühneolithikum*: FN I – Satrup, FN II – Fuchsberg) and Middle Neolithic (*Mittelneolithikum*: Ia – Troldebjerg, Ib – Klintebakke). This scheme was subsequently refined with FN I expanding to accommodate the new finds of Rosenhof and Siggeneben-Süd (Schwabedissen 1979a, Fig. 12; 1979b). Moreover, Schwabedissen (1968; 1980, 140) has always maintained that the later Ertebølle-Ellerbek culture was semi-agrarian and

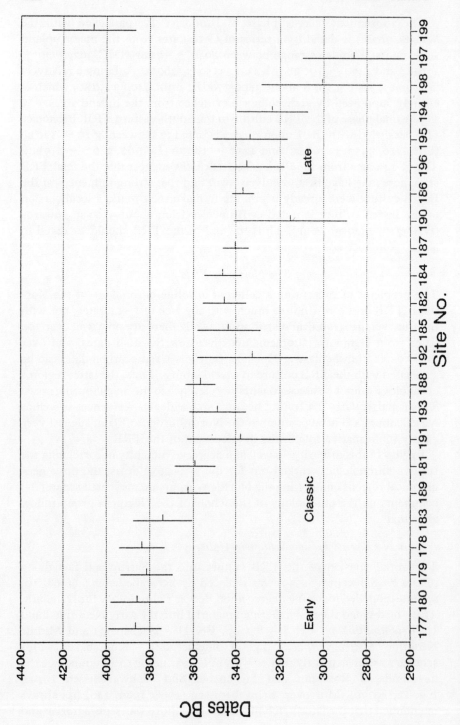

therefore remains the oldest Neolithic complex (*Altneolithikum*) in this area.

In a recent attempt to bring this chronology into line with the schemes of the TRB culture in Denmark, Hoika (1987, 104–7, Fig. 43) proposed a tri-partite division of FN I for the region of north-east Holstein where the three sites of Rosenhof, Siggeneben-Süd and Satrup form the three sub-phases of the early Neolithic I (Fig. 20). It is perhaps ironic that the German FN I phase of the TRB culture developed into a tri-partite system precisely at the moment when it was being abandoned with regard to the Danish TRB.

New discoveries of the later TRB material allowed Hoika to extend the MN section into three phases: MN I – Klintebakke/Troldebjerg/Heiligen-hafen, MN II – Blandebjerg/Sütel, and MN III/IV (which in north-east Holstein cannot be separated) – Bundsø/Lindø/Süssau/Dannau. The period during which we note the Store Valby style in Demark is not recognised in Schleswig-Holstein, where the TRB culture is apparently replaced by the Globular Amphora culture.

The Rosenhof phase, which in Schleswig-Holstein represents the earliest manifestation of the TRB culture, may according to Schwabedissen be dated to between 5460 BP and 4990 BP, with a subdivision into *Rosenhof a* (5460–5080 BP), represented by the finds from Rosenhof itself, and *Rosen-hof b* (5180–4490 BP), represented by material from Siggeneben-Süd (Schwabedissen 1979b, 157, Fig. 12). Schwabedissen has claimed twenty-eight radiocarbon dates for Rosenhof a and six dates for Rosenhof b. Unfortunately from his data table it is impossible to determine which dates have been used in the preparation of this chronological scheme. Did he, for example, rely upon the dates from Hüde which are associated with Bischheim-like pottery, or did he also use some of the Danish dates?

The cultural layer containing TRB pottery at Rosenhof is separated from the preceding Ertebølle-Ellerbek occupation of the site by a gyttja deposit and is sealed off from the subsequent activities by the so-called *Muschel-bank* of mainly natural origin. The Ertebølle-Ellerbek dates from Rosenhof are said to range between 6000 ± 45 BP (4905 ± 95 BC) and 5520 ± 75 BP (4375 ± 67 BC; Schwabedissen 1980, Fig. 11), while the dates for the *Muschelbank* span the period between 5050 BP (*c.* 3385 BC) and 4350 BP (*c.* 2970 BC; Schwabedissen 1979a, 167), thus providing a *terminus post quem* as well as a *terminus ante quem* for the chronological horizon of the TRB occupation at Rosenhof.

It is possible to identify seven C-14 dates from Rosenhof, reported piecemeal in various publications (Schwabedissen 1979a and 1979b; Preuss 1980), mostly without the necessary information about the archaeological

---

Figure 69 TRB radiocarbon dates: South-eastern group. Dates BC by phase, ± one standard deviation. Site nos as in Appendix.

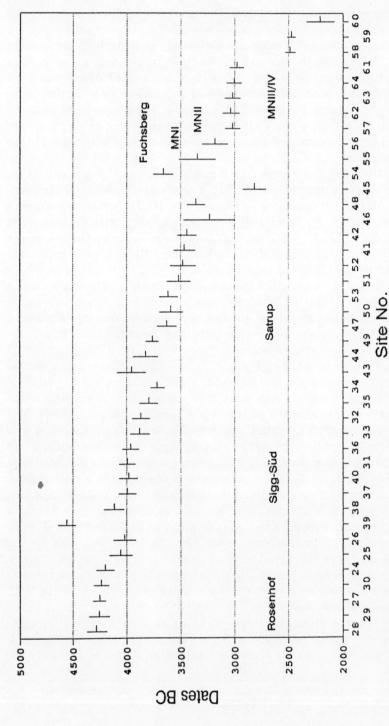

Figure 70 TRB radiocarbon dates: Northern I group – Schleswig-Holstein. Dates BC by phase, ± one standard deviation. Site nos as in Appendix.

context and often lacking a laboratory number. The dates span the range between 5410 ± 80 BP (KN?, 4274 ± 90 BC) and 5200 ± 80 BP (KN?, 4018 ± 102 BC). Three of the dates (KNI 500, KN-2135, KN-2335) are said to be associated with individual pots from the assemblage. After calibration the Rosenhof dates suggest that an occupation of this site took place during the period 4300–4000 BC, although the scanty material implies a brief rather than a prolonged episode.

The Rosenhof b (Siggeneben-Süd) material is dated primarily on the series of dates from the site of Siggeneben-Süd (Meurers-Balke 1983, 38). The two key dates, which indicate the possible duration of occupation of the site, derive from the vertical timbers used in the construction of a platform by the lake's edge. They range between 5280 ± 55 BP (KN-2425, 4115 ± 91 BC) and 4910 ± 60 BP (KN-2405, 3713 ± 65 BC). The remaining dates, obtained from various charcoal samples scattered in cultural layers, fall between these two determinations. One date is considerably earlier, however, at 5690 ± 60 BP (KN-2273, 4552 ± 82 BC). The site may therefore be said to have been occupied sometime between 4200 and 3700 BC, probably earlier rather than later during this span.

The hunting station at Bistoft also revealed a small amount of material comparable to the Siggeneben-Süd assemblage, and a contemporary C-14 date of 5180 ± 60 BP (KI-1285, 3993 ± 76 BC) suggests that some activity may have occurred here at this early stage, that is, around 4000 BC.

The chronological relationship between Rosenhof and Siggeneben-Süd sites is not clear. Although Meurers-Balke (1983, 95) and Hoika (1987, 101–3) consider the former to be older, it could equally well be argued that the Siggeneben-Süd assemblage simply represents a somewhat later facet of the same cultural phase in Schleswig-Holstein. We have noted previously the considerable similarities between the two assemblages (Chapter 4.4.1) and the existing differences may reflect a functional differentiation between the two sites. The difference in absolute dating of the two sites need not necessarily imply that they represent different cultural phases in the area.

The problem of the chronological relationship between Rosenhof and Siggeneben-Süd can be assessed only in the future, when new clearly dated assemblages in Schleswig-Hostein may come to light. Meanwhile, we should refrain from proclaiming each new site as indicative of a new chronological phase; it is necessary first of all to identify a broad range of cultural material typical of the early TRB and to observe how it subsequently evolved, before chronological phases can confidently be suggested.

For the time being, it appears that the early TRB culture is present in Schleswig-Holstein by about 4300 BC, a phase that lasts until about 3900/ 3850 BC, with Rosenhof and Siggeneben-Süd marking respectively the initial and the final manifestations rather than representing two typochronologically separate stages.

Schwabedissen (1979a, Fig. 12) has dated the Satrup phase to between 5050 BP (3850 BC) and 4720 BP (3500 BC). This dating is said to rest upon eighteen C-14 dates, but no information is offered as to the provenance of these dates. At present only thirteen dates from Schleswig-Holstein appear to be associated with the Satrup phase; most of these are derived from poorly published excavations in the various localities of Satrup Moor (Südensee Damm, Heidmoor etc.).

The Südensee-Damm dates range between 4960 ± 50 BP (Y-472, 3762 ± 58 BC) and 4610 ± 60 BP (KN-666, 3361 ± 82 BC), with the majority falling between 3650 BC and 3450 BC. At least one date (Y-472, 3762 ± 58 BC) is said to be associated with a funnel-necked beaker that was stratified above a worked wooden log which was the source of the said radiocarbon date. The remaining six dates were obtained by separate measurements of three wooden samples at Cologne and Groningen laboratories and gave results which on calibration differ by a maximum of just over 100 years.

The dates from Bistoft are closely comparable at 4700 ± 65 BP (KI-921.01, 3466 ± 96 BC) and 4610 ± 120 BP (KI-1232, 3350 ± 169 BC). The Heidmoor dates are more difficult to assess. The dates obtained from charcoal samples range between 5140 ± 115 BP (H-49/146, 3954 ± 134 BC) and 4210 ± 80 BP (Y-443h, 2818 ± 106 BC), which is rather late. One sample from wood at Heidmoor clearly dates an ancient timber to 5940 ± 100 BP (4840 ± 110 BC), and may well indicate Ertebølle-Ellerbek activities. The irregularity of the Heidmoor dates prompted Lanting and Mook (1977, 74) to dismiss them altogether. Sherds of a Satrup-style beaker were found in the *Muschelbank* at Rosenhof, which post-dates 5050 BP (*c.* 3850 BC).

As in the case of the preceding phase from Schleswig-Holstein, it is regrettable that the Satrup Moor material and the radiocarbon dates derived therefrom still remain to be published satisfactorily. At present it is only possible to estimate that the Satrup pottery was in use during the period from about 3800 BC until possibly 3400 BC.

The chronological position of the Fuchsberg-style materials in Schleswig-Holstein is currently indicated by just one date from the eponymous site, although once again its precise association is not clear. The date of 4860 ± 80 BP (KN?, 3659 ± 92 BC) precedes slightly the dating of similar materials in Denmark, but it is perfectly feasible that the Fuchsberg style developed in Schleswig-Holstein slightly earlier than further north while the Satrup style was still popular, a possibility which is not contradicted on stylistic grounds.

The chronology of the later TRB in Schleswig-Holstein is poorly documented. One C-14 date, based on charcoal from a pit at Neukirchen-Sütel of 4490 ± 60 BP (H-922, 3184 ± 122 BC), gives some indication of the chronological position of MN II ceramics which is in agreement with similarly contexted dates from Denmark. There are no grounds for the chronological division of MN III (Oldenburg-Dannau) and MN IV (Heringsdorf-Süssau) styles and this material is seen as the final manifestation of the TRB culture in this area, which was subsequently replaced by the Globular Amphora and Corded Ware cultures (Hoika 1987, 104–6).

A charcoal sample from a cultural layer at Oldenburger-Dannau (where there are mostly MN III ceramics) gave a date of 4400 ± 40 BP (KI-506, 3022 ± 74 BC). From Heringsdorf-Süssau (where mainly MN IV pottery was found) there are four acceptable C-14 dates, which range from 4410 ± 40 BP (KNI-512, 3037 ± 79 BC) to 4370 ± 45 BP (KNI-507, 2984 ± 65 BC). Taking all the available evidence into consideration, it is possible to suggest that pottery reminiscent of the Bundsø and Lindø styles was used here during the period between 3050 and 2950 BC.

5.3.2 Northern II group: Denmark

The relative chronology of the Danish TRB presented by Becker (1954a; Fig. 39) was based on a division into two main periods: the Early Neolithic (EN) and Middle Neolithic (MN). The former comprised three successive phases A, B and C, while the latter included the remaining TRB phases designated I–V; the three phases of the Single Grave culture were seen essentially as parallel with the TRB III–V phases.

When the first Danish Neolithic dates began to be published, it became obvious that a fundamental revision of this scheme was necesssary. In 1972 Tauber presented a review of Danish radiocarbon chronology suggesting that 'the Ertebølle . . . was rapidly superseded by the higher-developed Early Neolithic cultures, and that likewise the relationship between the Middle Neolithic Funnel Beaker culture in Jutland and the Single Grave culture was one of replacement rather than coexistence' (Tauber 1972, 110). Moreover, he suggested that the beginning of the TRB culture in Denmark should, upon calibration, be placed 'close to 4200 BC in calendar years' and that the EN periods of A, B and C were of 'a limited chronological validity'; the latter point subsequently found support in the work of Skaarup (1973 and 1975) and others.

A study of the typo-chronology of the Danish thick-butted axes gave P.O. Nielsen (1979, 52–3, Fig. 25) an opportunity to propose a new division of the MN period. The C-14 dates and stratigraphic evidence suggested little overlap between the final TRB and the Underground Grave period of the Single Grave culture and consequently the MN was divided into two periods: MN A comprising TRB I–V phases and MN B comprising I–III phases of the Single Grave culture. This division has been generally accepted by other scholars (Skaarup 1985, 12, Fig. 2).

Recent research, and the vastly increased number of C-14 dates from the early TRB contexts, have now fully endorsed the earlier suspicions that EN A, B and C phases were largely contemporary phenomena. Becker's terminology has now been replaced by new names designating regionally identified groups which were discussed in detail in Chapter 4.4.3.1. Their chronological relationship can now be outlined with some confidence.

There are still considerable problems in the chronological interpretation of the later TRB, however, and the detailed sequence of phases proposed by Ebbesen (1975; 1978; 1979a) still remains to be tested against regional developments in Denmark. Indeed, pedestrian though it may seem, the best solution to this problem still remains a detailed study of settlement materials in conjunction with a specific dating programme which, as the Bronocice excavation in Poland has shown, can be highly successful in determining a detailed chronological sequence.

In spite of all the difficulties and intricacies of the Danish TRB culture chronology, one thing has emerged very clearly: the traditional division into EN and MN is no longer tenable. We have already argued previously (Chapter 4.4.3.2) that this is a purely artificial division, which seems to be adhered to for traditional reasons, and can no longer be supported by either archaeological evidence or radiocarbon dates. The only recognition of this fact so far has been given expression in T. Madsen's (1982) research in east central Jutland. There, the previously cumbersome TRB chronology has been replaced by the Early, Middle and Late phases, each with its own stylistic changes which do not, however, obscure the overall development of the TRB culture in this area.

The absolute chronology of the Danish TRB culture presented below is based upon a similar phasing into the Early, Middle and Late phases. This division reflects well the general trends in the development of the TRB culture in Denmark and is borne out by archaeological evidence as well as radiocarbon dates. Moreover, it allows sufficient room for the incorporation of regional developments within a chronological framework which may be identified in future research.

5.3.2.1 The early TRB phase. The sites of the north Jutland *Volling group* curently provide some of the earliest C-14 dates in Denmark. The Mosegården long barrow palisaded enclosure is dated to between 5080 ± 90 BP (K-3463, 3887 ± 103 BC) and 4890 ± 90 BP (K-3464, 3690 ± 100 BC), providing a *terminus ante quem* for an earlier settlement here (T. Madsen and Petersen 1985, 75). An equally early date of 4970 ± 100 BP (K-2254, 3773 ± 108 BC) derives from the trench wall of a grave at Rustrup (C. Fischer 1976, 40), and a mean quoted by Troels-Smith (1982, 46, n. 15) for the Barkær complex is around 5150 BP (3960 BC). The beginning of the Volling group should therefore be placed at about 4000 BC.

Its duration appears to have been long; the latest date is that from Vroue Hede long dolmen of 4660 ± 100 BP (K-2424, 3418 ± 135 BC). From the Norsminde shell midden there is a range of dates from 4960 ± 100 BP (K-2192, 3763 ± 108 BC) to 4480 ± 85 BP (K-2665, 3480 ± 110 BC). According to T. Madsen and Petersen (1985, 99), the Volling group

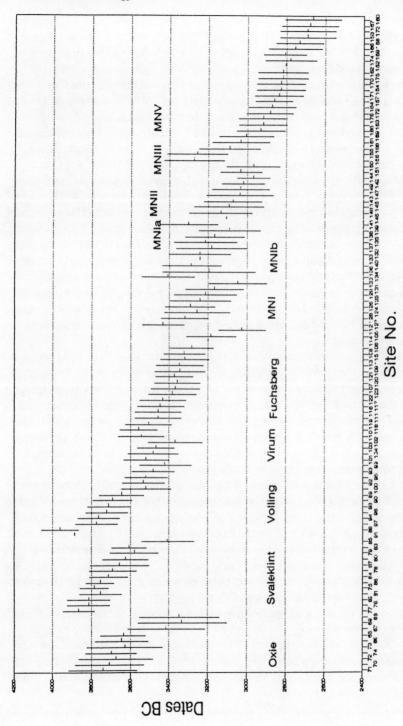

Figure 71 TRB radiocarbon dates: Northern II group – Denmark. Dates BC by phase, ± one standard deviation. Site nos as in Appendix.

apparently continued until the onset of the MN I ceramic styles *c.* 3400 BC. The late dates from Vroue Hede and Norsminde support this hypothesis. The Jutland Volling group can therefore be said to have lasted from 4000 BC until about 3400 BC at most.

The Danish islands' *Svaleklint group* is also well represented by C-14 dates. The Lindebjerg long barrow date of 5010 ± 100 BP (K-1659, 3814 ± 109 BC) is associated with the primary construction of the monument (Liversage 1981, 97). There are also four dates from food residues in funnel-necked beakers which range from 5060 ± 65 BP (Øgårde, K-4333, 3865 ± 81 BC) to 4860 ± 135 BP (Ulkestrup, K-3778, 3653 ± 154 BC).

Additionally, six dates are associated with a fireplace and a dugout canoe from Præstelyngen spanning a period from 5010 ± 100 BP (K-1473, 3814 ± 109 BC) to 4790 ± 100 BP (K-2058, 3577 ± 125 BC). The youngest C-14 date comes from a charcoal sample in a shell midden at Sølager: 4650 ± 100 BP (K-1724, 3405 ± 136 BC). It is also worth noting that the two sets of thermoluminescence dating of pottery from Stengade II average 4124 BC and 3820 BC (Skaarup 1975, 193).

On the basis of these dates it can be suggested that, as in Jutland, the TRB culture on the Danish islands also emerged at about 4000 BC and continued until 3500 BC, and possibly a little longer if the Sølager date is taken into account.

The *Oxie group* is the least well dated of the early Danish groups because the dates derive from two localities only: the Dragsholm burial is dated to 4840 ± 100 BP (K-2291, 3634 ± 117 BC), while the rest of the dates, which span the period between 4940 ± 160 BP (K-129, 3740 ± 176 BC) and 4600 ± 170 BP (K-124, 3330 ± 231 BC), come from the site of Muldbjerg on Zealand. A Swedish site at Värby dated to 4900 ± 120 BP (KN-103, 3698 ± 133 BC) confirms the overall pattern. The Oxie group is currently dated to between 3800/3750 BC and 3350 BC.

5.3.2.2 The Middle TRB phase. The subsequent stage in the development of the Danish TRB involves the emergence of the Fuchsberg and Virum and the MN I ceramic styles. The *Fuchsberg group* can now be assessed on the basis of nineteen C-14 dates from two large ceremonial centres and three burial monuments. The dates from Sarup range between 4760 ± 90 BP (K-2639, 3542 ± 118 BC) and 4580 ± 70 BP (K-2628, 3321 ± 107 BC), while those from Toftum range between 4770 ± 70 BP (K-2981, 3556 ± 99 BC) and 4500 ± 85 BP (K-2985, 3197 ± 147 BC).

The dates from the three dolmens appear to date the later part of the Fuchsberg group from 4550 ± 65 BP (K-2954, 3281 ± 112 BC) to 4390 ± 80 BP (K-3491, 3025 ± 122 BC). The Toftum dates in particular are very consistent, especially when corrections to shell dates have been carried out. The Fuchsberg group can therefore be dated to a period from about 3600/3500 BC to 3200 BC.

The *Virum group* currently offers only four radiocarbon dates. Three of these are associated with burial monuments: Bygholm Nørremark long barrow 4740 ± 90 BP (K-3473, 3517 ± 119 BC), Lohals double grave 4620 ± 100 BP (K-2277, 3367 ± 140 BC) and Ølstykke dolmen 4710 ± 65 BP (K-2356, 3480 ± 131 BC). The food residue from a bog beaker at Maglelyng gave a date of 4700 ± 65 BP (K-3779, 3466 ± 96 BC). It is interesting, however, that in spite of the few dates, the Virum group appears at roughly the same time as Fuchsberg, about 3600/3500 BC, suggesting that southern Jutland and the Danish islands were subject to the same process at least in terms of ceramic development. On present evidence, the Virum group does appear to have come to an end by about 3350 BC, but this could relate to the relatively small number of dates and need not necessarily reflect the actual demise of the Virum style.

One of the most significant results of the re-interpretation of the Danish TRB chronology is the fact that the Fuchsberg and Virum styles can be seen neither as a fleeting phenomenon nor as a purely transitional stage between the early and late TRB. We have already argued against the incongruous EN/MN division on the basis of the available evidence. The duration of the Virum and, especially, the Fuchsberg style, covering a period of about 400 years, shows that they may have lasted nearly as long as the initial TRB phase. This, coupled with a fair number of Fuchsberg sites identified not only in Jutland but also on the Danish islands, in Schleswig-Holstein and, further afield, even in Lower Saxony, makes it perfectly clear that the Fuchsberg group should be regarded as an independent and long-lived phenomenon of substantial geographical extent in northern Europe. Its longevity is clearly seen, moreover, in a considerable overlap at both ends of the chronological spectrum.

T. Madsen and Petersen (1985, 101) have argued that the Virum group may be somewhat earlier than Fuchsberg, but this is certainly not borne out by the available C-14 dates, with the two groups clearly being contemporary phenomena of relatively distinct geographical limits. So far, however, no material clearly diagnostic of either has been found in the north of Jutland, giving additional credence to the longevity of the Volling group.

At present there are seventeen radiocarbon dates associated with *MN I* (*Troldebjerg/Klintebakke*) assemblages, of which only one has been assigned to MN Ia: Vroue Hede long dolmen 4570 ± 100 BP (K-1566, 3299 ± 150 BC). Quite apart from the fact that a single determination can hardly be regarded as indicative of the chronological position of the MN Ia style, one suspects that the attribution to MN Ia is based on the fact that at the Vroue Hede complex this date precedes two other C-14 dates of 4560 ± 100 BP (K-1568, 3285 ± 152 BC) and 4430 ± 100 BP (K-1602, 3241 ± 150 BC) derived from passage graves which are assumed not to be present before MN Ib (E. Jørgensen 1977, 209). The differences in real terms are so small that they cannot be taken to represent different chronological positions for

MN Ia and MN Ib. Furthermore, we may remind ourselves that some of the deposits from the Hagebrogård passage grave have been synchronised with MN Ia, thus aborting the theory of this grave form being constructed exclusively from MN Ib onwards.

The currently known MN Ib dates all derive from non-domestic contexts. The case of the Herrup cult house is interesting in so far that here three vessels, which apparently correspond to MN Ia, were found. The sherds of a funnel-necked beaker (Becker 1973b, Fig. 4) were recovered in the foundation trench for which a date of 4650 ± 100 BP (K-1766, 3405 ± 136 BC) is available. The charcoal from the bark, lying above the house's pottery (where MN Ia and MN Ib pedestalled bowls and spoons stood), gave a date of 4530 ± 100 BP (K-1769, 3241 ± 159 BC). Taking other C-14 dates of this period, it is unlikely that the difference between these two dates reflects the different chronological position of MN Ia and MN Ib, but it may well suggest for how long the cult house was in use.

Other MN Ib dates range between 4560 ± 100 BP (K-1568, 3285 ± 153 BC) and 4430 ± 100 BP (K-1567, 3080 ± 157 BC). The grain from Sarup, which is said to be associated with late MN Ib pottery, is dated to 4480 ± 90 BP (K-2767, 3165 ± 148 BC).

Other MN Ib dates come from Jutland. At Hanstedgård the pottery is described as 'an early level of MN I with a mixture of MN Ia and MN Ib traits in individual features' (Eriksen and Madsen 1984, 63). The three dates from pit no. 11 range between 4670 ± 80 BP (K-4215, 3431 ± 109 BC) and 4560 ± 80 BP (K-4214, 3291 ± 127 BC).

Thus, material of MN I can be shown to date between 3400 and 3100/3050 BC. Ebbesen (1975 and 1979a) has argued on typological grounds that there is no overlap between MN Ia and MN Ib. This claim cannot be sustained, since not only can we indicate early assemblages which show a mixture of both styles, but also the available C-14 dates do not allow us to regard the two styles as chronologically separate. While it is possible that, within the time when MN I ceramic styles were in vogue, one style may have become more fashionable in certain regions before the other (for example Troldebjerg more in the east and Klintebakke more in the west of Denmark), we have no evidence to suggest that one definitely preceded the other. The C-14 dates suggest an even more complicated picture of a considerable overlap between the Fuchsberg, Virum and MN I styles, although the former two undoubtedly developed earlier. Indeed, we may be dealing with a situation which approximates to the circumstances of the early TRB period, with a number of contemporary styles reflecting specific groups of people except that they no longer remain geographically distinct as they were previously.

On present evidence the dating of the Blandebjerg style (MN II) appears to be highly consistent, with dates deriving from secure contexts in northern Jutland (Tustrup, Ferslev, Fannerup) and the Danish islands (Sarup on Fyn, Vindinge on Zealand). The available C-14 dates range between 4460 ± 100 BP (K-2127, 3135 ± 162 BC) at Vindinge and 4390 ± 70 BP (K-4049, 3021 ± 109 BC) at Fannerup. The attribution of the date from Lånum 4510 ± 100 BP (K-1771, 3211 ± 161 BC) is uncertain.

The two Jutland ritual houses have closely comparable dates: Ferslev 4430 ± 120 BP (K-717, 3093 ± 179 BC), and Tustrup 4440 ± 120 BP (K-727, 3108 ± 180 BC) and 4390 ± 120 BP (K-718, 3037 ± 171 BC). These dates are associated with the construction of the buildings, providing a *terminus post quem* for the bulk of the matrial from Tustrup and the nearly identical early deposits from Ferslev. This dating is closely matched by two dates from Fannerup of 4420 ± 95 BP (K-4050, 3073 ± 150 BC) and 4390 ± 70 BP (K-4049, 3021 ± 109 BC), where features of the Early Ferslev style were noted. 'Blandebjerg-like' material at Sarup is dated to 4400 ± 90 BP (K-2910, 3042 ± 138 BC). It is worthy of note that the closely comparable dates of MN II material throughout Denmark are in agreement with the previously identified presence of MN II pottery throughout the entire country. The earlier strong regionality appears to be giving way to a more uniform style, which on present evidence appears to have been in use during the period from about 3200/3150 BC until 3000/2900 BC.

5.3.2.3 The Late TRB phase. There are now three C-14 dates which help to indicate the chronological position of the MN III *Bundsø* and Late *Ferslev styles*. From Sarup we may quote two dates: 4400 ± 65 BP (K-2911, 3033 ± 107 BC) and 4340 ± 90 BP (K-2766, 2968 ± 139 BC), which are associated with what N. Andersen (1981, 92) describes as late MN II material that is stratigraphically and stylistically different from the preceding MN II and the subsequent MN V on this site. The pottery in question resembles what elsewhere is known as MN III/IV.

One of the cultural layers at Fannerup (FII, layer 3) contained twelve vessels decorated in the Late Ferslev style (which represents MN III in Jutland) and it is dated to 4350 ± 56 BP (K-4051, 2986 ± 84 BC).

There are no C-14 dates associated with the MN IV *Lindø style*. Indeed, pure MN IV assemblages are also lacking. The evidence from the Vroue Hede stone packing graves does not offer much assistance. There are four C-14 dates from three separate complexes which range between 4300 ± 100 BP (K-1571, 2919 ± 124 BC) and 4110 ± 100 BP (K-2427, 2689 ± 145 BC). One of the dates (K-1571) was obtained from charcoal found beneath the pavement of a mortuary house which contained a Store Valby axe. A similar axe was found in the vicinity of another grave, for which C-14 dates of 4200 ± 100 BP (K-2426, 2827 ± 127 BC) and 4110 ± 100 BP (K-2427, 2689 ± 145 BC) are available. On the other hand Store Valby pottery and a Lindø-type axe were found under the stone packing of another grave, dated to 4230 ± 100 BP (K-1572, 2838 ± 126 BC). Since these two types of axe were used commonly during the later TRB (Chapter

6.4.1.3) and can no longer be shown to identify with a particular ceramic style, there cannot be a specific attribution; E. Jørgensen (1977, 212) was inclined to place the structures in question with the Store Valby style.

Material of these two styles in Schleswig-Holstein (MN III/IV) is regarded as belonging to one phase and dated to about 3100–2950/2900 BC. Taking Danish C-14 dates into account a similar chronological horizon can be suggested for Bundsø, Late Ferslev and Lindø styles. This seemingly short period presents an interesting problem. While in Jutland the MN III and MN IV ceramics do not appear to be particularly numerous, together they constitute 46 per cent of all MN pottery from the Danish islands megalithic tombs. Thus, here we are faced with an apparently short horizon and vast quantities of pottery. However, as we already noted, large numbers of vessels deposited in the graves need not of course reflect a particularly long phase but can equally well signify a particularly intensive activity which in itself may be a short-lived phenomenon.

While the radiocarbon dates available for the MN V *Store Valby style* are numerous, they are not very helpful either in determining the boundary between MN III/IV and MN V styles or indeed in enlightening us about the chronological position of Store Valby itself. The chronology of this final manifestation of the Danish TRB (a phenomenon peculiar to southern Scandinavia) has been discussed by Davidsen (1975; 1977; 1978; 1982) and referred to by Becker (1954a and 1967b), Lomborg (1977) and others. In each case, however, the primary issue was the relationship between the TRB and the subsequent development of the Single Grave culture; the discussion centred upon the termination rather than the beginning of the Store Valby style.

Figure 71 and the Appendix show that there are now over twenty C-14 dates associated with Store Valby materials, altogether spanning the period from 4550 ± 100 BP (K-2432, 3271 ± 155 BC) to 4090 ± 100 BP (K-2115, 2662 ± 146 BC). Quite clearly, this is a situation both difficult to explain and wholly unsatisfactory.

The C-14 dates derive from two sources: burial monuments (stone packing graves as well as an example of a secondary TRB burial in the south-west Fyn dolmen of Klokkehøj) and settlement rubbish pits in Jutland and the Danish islands. The dates from burials, considered on their own, reveal a fairly consistent picture. They range between 4310 ± 100 BP (K-1789, 2930 ± 125 BC) and 4140 ± 80 BP (K-3014, 2732 ± 123 BC), suggesting that Store Valby ceramics were in use during the period of about 2900–2750 BC. The C-14 dates from settlements present a more difficult picture; dates from Kornerup on Zealand, Lidsø on Langeland and two pits from Dorthealund on Jutland are generally in agreement with the dating provided by the burial monuments. They range from 4390 ± 100 BP (K-2270, 3032 ± 147 BC) to 4090 ± 100 BP (K-2115, 2662 ± 146 BC), with the majority of calibrated dates falling between 2900 and 2700 BC.

However, one pit with Store Valby ceramics from Dorthealund (pit N) gave much earlier dates from charcoal samples of 4550 ± 100 BP (K-2432, 3271 ± 155 BC) and 4540 ± 100 BP (K-2430, 3256 ± 157 BC), which are far too early when compared with other dates of this style. Similarly, the Vester Årup radiocarbon dates, all of which were obtained from different organic materials found in one pit with Store Valby ceramics, are inconsistent; the charcoal and oyster samples gave older dates which calibrate to around 3100–3000 BC, while the dates from domesticated animal bones are clearly younger at 4160 ± 100 BP (K-1983, 2754 ± 138 BC) and 4100 ± 100 BP (K-1932, 2676 ± 146 BC), but are in good accord with the other Store Valby dates.

Davidsen (1975, 174–5) has argued that the excessively early dates from Dorthealund (pit N), as well as the earlier dates from the Vester Årup samples, are likely to represent older materials accidentally incorporated into the Store Valby features. Moreover, he pointed out that the C-14 dates from animal bones are consistently younger and thus in keeping with other Store Valby determinations.

While the incorporation of earlier organic material into later features on a settlement site is a perfectly feasible explanation for dates which appear too old, we have not yet arrived at a mechanism which will distinguish a charcoal sample that is too old from one that is of a correct date. With regard to Vester Årup, the charcoal and shells gave roughly comparable dates, which are clearly older than animal bone dates. The dates from Dorthealund are also aberrant and can currently only be explained as having been obtained from ancient timbers; unfortunately such assumptions cannot be proved. However, taking all the C-14 dates of Store Valby association into consideration we may conclude that, on present evidence, the Store Valby ceramics were in use during the period between 2950 BC and 2700/2650 BC.

When the Danish C-14 dates just discussed are considered in conjunction with archaeological evidence, it is possible to suggest three major phases in the development of the TRB culture in Denmark. The *Early Phase* (4000–3500 BC) comprises the three regional groups: Volling, Svaleklint and Oxie. While the actual dates for each group display certain variations, there is no reason to regard one as earlier or later than the others; this is particularly important in the context of the Oxie group, which in Denmark has been dated at only two sites. The duration of the early TRB phase (in the order of 500 years) was sufficiently long to allow the establishment of the TRB throughout Denmark. This involved not only the development of material culture, but also the emergence of a whole range of rituals and, by implication, the successful establishment of a farming economy.

The *Middle Phase*, which involved a consolidation of earlier achievements throughout the area, can be dated to between 3600/3500 and 3100/

3000 BC. It was characterised by a profusion of ceramic styles and an evolution of sophisticated and strongly differentiated forms of social ritual. These features only began to acquire a more uniform character during the final two centuries.

The *Late Phase* (3100/3000–2700/2650 BC) represents a very stable and uniform stage of the TRB in Denmark. It is characterised by ceramic styles which display a gradual decrease in the decoration and quality of wares. Important changes are observed in lithic industries and there is a fundamental transformation in the use of earlier ritual monuments, revealing a considerable shift in the social aspects of prosperous and economically stable communities.

5.3.3 Mecklenburg

It is extremely disappointing that there are still no independent chronological data for the region of Mecklenburg and, of necessity, the development of the TRB culture here has to be dated with the help of evidence from the neighbouring regions.

From the island of Rügen there is some indication of the chronological position of the final Mesolithic, where a local variant of the Ertebølle culture – the so-called Lietzow group – is dated to between 5815 ± 100 BP (Bln-561, 4708 ± 118 BC) and 5190 ± 120 BP (Bln-569, 4011 ± 144 BC). The only C-14 date associated with the TRB material derives from Schönermark, where remains of a burnt structure (house?) and pottery were found. No details of this association have been published, but the quoted date is early at 5100 ± 70 BP (?, 3913 ± 86 BC, suggesting a chronological horizon comparable with the Pikutkowo phase to the east and the final Rosenhof in the north. While not highly diagnostic, the Schönermark pottery accords well with the ceramic wares of this horizon, and the presence of collared flasks implies that this is not the earliest TRB material.

It can therefore be argued that in the inland areas of the Mecklenburg region the TRB culture is present by the early 4th millennium BC (*c.* 3950 BC) and possibly even earlier, which would be wholly in line with similar developments elsewhere across the north European lowland. The contemporary presence of late hunting-gathering communities along the Baltic littoral is fully acceptable on archaeological grounds and reflects precisely the circumstances envisaged by the cultural model of the emergence of the TRB across the North European Plain.

The subsequent development of the TRB culture in Mecklenburg cannot be dated in absolute terms. There is a series of dates based on charcoal samples from the interior of several megalithic chambers (Schuldt 1972a, 95–6), among which the Gnewitz determination is the earliest: 4250 ± 100 BP (Bln-472, 2900 ± 125 BC). This is the only date which can be accepted within a TRB context and it may reflect secondary TRB activity at the tomb. All the other C-14 dates are too late; they derive from open chambers which were used not only by the TRB, but also by communities of the Globular Amphora and Corded Ware cultures. The dates are wholly compatible with the chronological horizon suggested for these secondary users of the tombs.

5.3.4 Northern TRB group: a summary

The C-14 dates currently available from the various contexts of the Northern TRB suggest that the emergence of this group should be placed in the final centuries of the 5th millennium BC. The slight discrepancy between the earliest calibrated dates from north Germany and Denmark (in the order of 300 years) must be seen against the background of processes which resulted in the appearance of the TRB in Jutland and on the Danish islands. If our assumption that the TRB culture developed in the broad belt of the North European Plain is correct, then the slightly later emergence of this complex in southern Scandinavia and, indeed, on the northern fringes of the central European loess, fully supports this theory.

A period of about 300 years for the dissemination and adoption of novel technologies and a farming economy throughout southern Scandinavia is neither too long nor incompatible with the model proposed (see Chapter 8.5). On the other hand it should be noted that the earliest Danish C-14 dates are associated with a fully developed TRB and, moreover, derive from eastern central Jutland and Zealand, while there is a lack of early dates from southern Jutland. Further research in this area may therefore bridge the chronological gap with Schleswig-Holstein. It is worth noting that one of the sets of pottery from Stengade II (Svaleklint group), which was dated by the thermoluminescence method, gave an average date of 4124 BC (Skaarup 1975, 193, Table 30), suggesting an even earlier beginning for the Danish TRB than that implied by radiocarbon dates.

5.4 The Western TRB group

The emergence of the Western TRB group cannot be dated independently because there are currently no C-14 dates associated with early materials. On the basis of similarities between the Dutch and Northern TRB ceramics, Brindley (1986b) suggested that the beginnings of the Western group (Brindley Horizon 1, Bakker phase A) should be dated to about 3400 BC. Such a relatively late date for the appearance of the TRB in this area, however, does raise many issues. First of all, the apparent lack of stylistically early materials from Holland is very puzzling in view of the environmental disturbances and forest clearances on the Drenthe plateau which seem to have been taking place at about 3800–3700 BC (see Chapter 8.1) and we have already noted Bakker's concern over this discrepancy in the evidence. The one early date from this area, 4930 ± 120 BP (GrN-4092, 3730 ± 131 BC) from Denekamp, derived from a deep hearth, was unfortunately associated with undiagnostic finds, but it compares well with the Hüde dates from Lower Saxony.

The area of Lower Saxony, however, which forms a crucial link between the Western group and the remainder of the TRB culture area, is poorly documented in terms of dating evidence. The TRB material from the Hüde hunting station on the Dümmer lake is bracketed by C-14 dates of 4895 ± 85 BP (Hv-327, 3696 BC) and 4710 ± 90 BP (Hv-349, 3481 ± 90 BC); a cord-decorated TRB rim sherd was found stratified immediately below a charred piece of timber dated to 4840 ± 130 BP (Hv-373, 3631 ± 150 BC). The individual phases of the TRB horizon at Hüde cannot be separated due to the excessive compression of peaty layers, but the radiocarbon dates suggest a TRB presence from about 3700 BC onwards. Moreover, although a comprehensive study of different ceramic styles from Hüde is not yet available, interim reports mention not only typical *Tiefstich* pottery, but also beakers with *Wackelböden* and grooved belly decoration (Kampffmeyer 1983, 126, Figs 12 and 13) strongly reminiscent of Schwabedissen's Satrup-style pottery. A chronological horizon similar to the Satrup phase in Schleswig-Holstein is thus feasible on archaeological grounds as well as on the basis of C-14 dates.

While there is no mention of Fuchsberg-style decoration from Hüde, there is certainly no lack of Fuchsberg pottery from Lower Saxony, but none of the finds are associated with radiocarbon dates. Finally, we must mention the presence of undated but typologically early materials from this area (for example at Engern-Brinkhof; Brandt 1967), which belong to the early TRB horizon and, by comparison with materials to the north, should perhaps be dated to about 4000–3900 BC. One may further note the radio-carbon dates from sites in the west such as Swifterbant and Hazendonk, which range between 5540 ± 65 BP (GrN-5606, 4390 ± 60 BC) and 5230 ± 40 BP (GrN-6896, 4040 ± 80 BC) and which clearly show that the westernmost part of the North European Plain was equally subject to the early processes of adoption of farming elements (Louwe-Kooijmans 1974; 1976a; 1976b).

The late dating of the TRB in the area west of the Elbe is far from satisfactory; there is a clear need for more dating evidence from this region, but a comparison on archaeological grounds with neighbouring regions suggests that the TRB culture west of the Elbe may have begun to emerge as early as 4000/3900 BC and Brindley's estimate of 3400 BC may yet prove to be conservative.

The next set of C-14 dates from the Western TRB is associated with materials which constitute Brindley's Horizon 3, encompassing Bakker's phases B, C and D-1 which he himself synchronised with the Northern MN I styles. Two C-14 dates, both apparently relating to the construction of *hunebedden* in which the pottery of Horizon 3 represents the earliest finds, are Odoorn D32c 4630 ± 60 BP (GrN-13184, 3394 ± 80 BC) and Odoorn

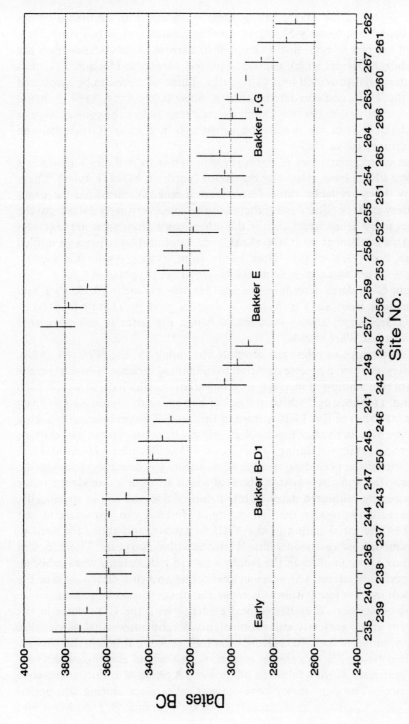

Figure 72 TRB radiocarbon dates: Western group. Dates BC by phase, ± one standard deviation. Site nos as in Appendix.

D32a 4550 ± 40 BP (GrN-12609, 3290 ± 86 BC). The calibrated values correspond well to early Northern dates associated with MN I styles. It is also of interest to note that a chamber in barrow IV at Oldendorf on the Lüneburger Heide, which contained pottery similar to Horizon 3 (Laux's C pottery) has provided four C-14 dates. Three of these can be associated with the TRB, and the date of 4625 ± 60 BP (GrN-6503, 3379 ± 80 BC) corresponds well to the two Dutch dates; it may reflect the construction of the chamber, but its precise provenance is not clear (Groenman-van Waateringe, 1979a).

The subsequent series of dates is associated with Brindley's Horizon 5 (Bakker's E-2 phase, related by him to the Northern MN III styles). There are six dates available: three derive from a recently excavated flat grave cemetery at Heek (Finke 1984; there are also some very early dates from the site regarded as incorrect), while the others come from a flat grave (GrN-12263), a settlement pit (GrN-1824C) and a cultural layer from an infilled stream bed (GrN-7746). They range from 4520 ± 35 BP (GrN-9202, 3238 ± 91 BC) to 4400 ± 60 BP (GrN-11764, 3032 ± 101 BC).

Eight C-14 dates determine the final Horizons 6 and 7 (Bakker's F and G) ranging from 4415 ± 65 BP (GrN-4200, 3056 ± 114 BC) to 4100 ± 30 BP (GrN-5070, 2690 ± 100 BC), although the latter is also associated with Corded Ware sherds.

In an attempt to refine the absolute chronology of the Western group, Brindley ascribed a precise duration to individual ceramic Horizons on the basis of the 'amount of material and the variations which occur within each horizon' (1986b, 105), which altogether add up to the assumed 550 years (3400–2850 BC) of the TRB culture in this area. The problem with such a procedure lies in the fact that it effectively divorces the ceramic associations from their calibrated dating. Thus, if we follow Brindley's Horizon durations within the period 3400–2850 BC, Horizon 3 is dated to 3300–3200 BC and Horizon 5 to 3050–2950 BC, both of which are clearly outside the range suggested by calibrated dates. While Brindley does not say so specifically, one gets the impression that her dating of Horizon 3 to 3300–3200 BC is a result of the intial dating of the TRB to 3400 BC and thus of a need to accommodate two earlier ceramic Horizons within 100 years. The difficulty in dating Horizon 5 lies in the fact that its 120 radiocarbon years calibrate to a period of about 300 years in real terms and this clearly causes the problem as to where within this range the phase should be placed.

The correlation of archaeological evidence with the C-14 dates in the Western group is clearly still problematic. We must nevertheless visualise the beginnings of the TRB culture by at least 3700 BC, although this process need not be explicit in ceramic evidence. This would encompass the very early materials (Hüde), followed by Bakker's A phase with Fuchsberg-style influences. The next major development takes place during the period 3500/3400–3200 BC, which comprises Bakker's ceramic B, C and D-1 and corresponds stylistically as well as chronologically to developments in the Northern group. The final stage of the TRB in the west can be seen to begin at around 3200 BC, with the final demise around 2850 BC. However, it is obvious that for a more detailed phasing, dates from a range of secure contexts are necessary and 'phasing' has to take into consideration more than pottery retrieved from chambered tombs. An example of how pottery-based phases expand and contract depending upon the individual viewpoint is illustrated by Brindley's Horizon 3, which comprises Bakker's three ceramic phases.

5.5 The Southern TRB group

While the number of C-14 dates associated with the Southern TRB group is not small, many of the dates derive from very ambiguous contexts where they may belong to one phase or another or, indeed, one culture or another. Combined with a relatively poor understanding of archaeological data, this can create considerable difficulty in establishing the absolute chronology of the TRB in central Germany and neighbouring areas.

Several dates are associated with the Baalberge phase. The bone sample from a grave in a long timber enclosure at Brežno in Bohemia provides the earliest date of 5090 ± 45 BP (GrN-8803, 3895 ± 70 BC) and a similarly early determination is associated with an isolated pit at Postoloprty of 4925 ± 80 BP (Bln-482, 3727 ± 87 BC). There is an additional series of dates from a settlement complex at Makotřasy which Pleslová-Štiková (1977, 66) places in the younger Baalberge phase (Salzmünde?), but the material is not diagnostic and the dates range between 4870 ± 60 BP (GrN-7102, 3672 ± 68 BC) and 4550 ± 110 BP (GrN-6928, 3269 ± 167 BC). All these dates suggest that the beginning of the Baalberge should be placed at around 3900 BC, a horizon which compares extremely well with the emergence of the South-eastern TRB group, where similar developments were observed. It needs to be stated that this view deviates considerably from the opinion of Preuss (1980, 27–8), who argues for a much earlier dating of the Baalberge on the basis of dates from the central German Gatersleben group: Kmehlen 5360 ± 60 BP (Bln-231, 4210 ± 80 BC) and Wahlitz 5300 ± 20 BP (GrN-433, 4195 ± 95 BC) and the dating of the so-called 'Baalberge' amphora from Rosenhof (KN-2334, 4196 ± 82 BC). Although Schwabedissen (1979a, 171) indeed referred to this vessel as a 'Baalberge' amphora this is a most unfortunate name, since it suggests that such pottery originated in central Germany and was then disseminated northwards. All the available evidence (discussed in Chapter 4.1) suggests, to the contrary, that such pottery developed locally in the North European Plain and that the development of the Baalberge phase in middle Germany takes place at a later stage, on present evidence not before 4000 BC. This is argued on the basis of our understanding of the way in which the TRB culture developed

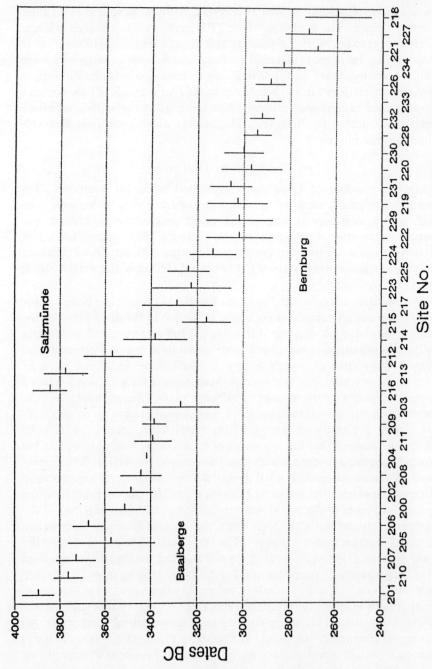

Figure 73 TRB radiocarbon dates: Southern group. Dates BC by phase, ± one standard deviation. Site nos as in Appendix.

in the central European loess region and is very clearly borne out by the available C-14 dates.

However, the above-mentioned dates contrast noticeably with two Baalberge dates from the Saale area. The Baalberge phase at Wissenfels is said to date to 4635 ± 60 BP (Bln-1253, 3380 ± 80 BC), but material of the Salzmünde and Bernburg phases was also found at this site and some mixing of assemblages may have occurred. A correspondingly late date of 4630 ± 40 BP (Bln-2005, 3384 ± 51 BC) was derived from a Baalberge grave at Quenstedt, but the bones were treated chemically prior to the dating and this may have affected the result.

The chronological position of the Salzmünde phase is suggested by the C-14 dates from three samples of carbonised wood recovered from a palisade at Dölauer Heide. These range between 4970 ± 90 BP (H209/579, 3773 ± 98 BC) and 4630 ± 90 BP (Bln-53, 3380 ± 138 BC). Again, Baalberge and Salzmünde phases cannot be separated stratigraphically at this site, although the relevant palisade segment was preserved beneath a burial mound with Salzmünde graves. The collective grave at Schönstedt is dated to 4475 ± 45 BP (GrN-8255, 3158 ± 105 BC); it contained a Bernburg-style ceramic assemblage which showed clear Salzmünde influence.

Taking into account the Bernburg dates it is possible to suggest that Salzmünde gave way to Bernburg sometime around 3200 BC, but its beginning is uncertain and the suggestion of 3500 BC is based more on an understanding of TRB developments elsewhere than on actual dating evidence from central Germany. The Bernburg phase is relatively consistently dated at both Dölauer Heide and Quenstedt. At Dölauer Heide two samples of charcoal from settlement pits on the Langberg area were dated to 4380 ± 100 BP (Bln-838a, 3019 ± 144 BC) and 4340 ± 100 BP (Bln-912, 2967 ± 132 BC). A timber chamber in mound no. 35 is dated to 4390 ± 85 BP (Bln-1856, 3027 ± 128 BC) and this close correspondence to the dates from settlement pits suggests that the grave was built during the Bernburg occupation of the site, with secondary use by the Corded Ware culture. Samples of charred grain from Quenstedt provide four C-14 dates which range from 4420 ± 45 BP (Kn-2418, 3056 ± 91 BC) to 4280 ± 50 BP (KN-2419, 2897 ± 56 BC). The dating of a Bernburg grave from Pevestorf to 4380 ± 100 BP (Hv-582, 3019 ± 144 BC) suggests the same general horizon. Only one Bernburg date from the settlement at Aspenstedt, 4560 ± 100 BP (H210/217, 3285 ± 153 BC), is considerably earlier. A general consideration of all the Bernburg dates suggests that this phase lasted from 3200/3100 BC until 2900 BC.

5.6 Summary of the TRB culture chronology

5.6.1 The emergence of the TRB 4500–4000 BC

While only a handful of the TRB assemblages are currently dated to the

second half of the 5th milennium BC, their geographical provenance demar-
cates a broad zone across the north European lowland that stretches from
the lower Elbe to the middle Vistula (Fig. 67). Our discussion of the TRB
so far has already identified this region as potentially the most effective zone
of contact between the indigenous hunter-gatherers and the early farming
communities; it is therefore hardly surprising that the earliest TRB
materials should be identified precisely in this area.

The uniform character of the early TRB assemblages from the area was
noted as early as 1947 (Becker's AB horizon), but the subsequent investigations of the more developed facets of this cultural complex have obscured
that initial uniformity. Yet throughout the area, in Kujavia, Pomerania,
Mecklenburg, and Schleswig-Holstein, the earliest TRB reveals a remarkable cultural homogeneity not encountered in its subsequent development;
at this stage it is not possible to identify any regional trends.

Thus, while it may seen anachronistic to revive the concept of a pan-
European TRB horizon, it is argued that the whole area between Schleswig-
Holstein and Kujavia represents a zone where similar and broadly coeval
processes were taking place between 4500 and 4000 BC. It is this early
horizon which formed the basis for the subsequent expansion of the TRB
through powerful influences to the north, south and west, which led to the
emergence of regional groupings.

Although for a while this area of the North European Plain appears to
loose its cultural homogeneity, it can hardly be regarded as coincidental
that the subsequent stage of the north European cultural development,
manifest in the appearance of the Globular Amphora culture, should
display a geographical extent which more or less replicates that of the early
TRB culture horizon. Evidently the cultural cohesion of this south Baltic
area was sufficiently strong to emerge more than once in the cultural record.

5.6.2 *The establishment of regional groups 4000–3600/3500 BC*

The impulses emanating from the initial TRB area, which most probably
began to affect the neighbouring areas even before 4000 BC, led to a geographical expansion of the TRB culture and resulted in the emergence of
distinct regional groups: the Eastern group (Pikutkowo phase), South-
eastern group (Bronocice I), Southern group (Baalberge) and Northern
group (which from the very beginning reveals additional differentiation in
the form of the lesser regional units of the Volling, Oxie, Svaleklint and
Moltzow groupings). While absolute dating evidence is still lacking, large
areas to the west of the Elbe should now be considered as fully participating
in the same process and it is likely that the emergence of the TRB Western
group was accomplished before rather than after 3500 BC.

It is also evident that during this phase of the TRB development a
major shift towards regional emphasis took place and that local conditions
appeared to regulate and influence the developmental trends within indi-

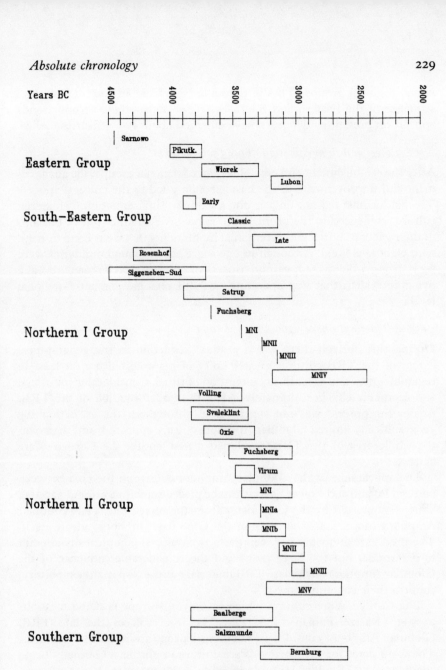

Figure 74 Absolute chronology of the TRB. C-14 dating in relation to the phases of development in individual groups.

vidual regional groups. This is particularly evident in the 'out of step' sequence of the Eastern and South-eastern groups, where certain trends appear, on present evidence, to have emerged about two centuries earlier.

5.6.3 Regional diversification 3600/3500–3200 BC

After the establishment and crystallisation of regional groups, the advancement and improvements in the basic economy led to the cultural apogee. This is documented not only in the maximum differentiation of material culture (evidenced in the profusion of successive ceramic styles), but also in the variety of burial and ceremonial monuments that went hand in hand with elaborate ritual. Although in one sense the regional boundaries were very strongly delineated, certain aspects of cultural development reveal a dynamic system that was operating on both regional and inter-regional levels.

5.6.4 The final phase 3200–2900/2650 BC

During this horizon there was a gradual reduction in the geographical extent of the TRB culture, greater unity of material culture (at least in regional terms) and a significant alteration of ritual. Considerable industrial and economic changes ultimately led to the transformation of the TRB. Again, the process was not synchronous throughout the area; first the geographically limited Globular Amphora culture appeared, and then over the whole area of the TRB developed a new entity, the Corded Ware culture.

The appearance of the Globular Amphora culture in the area between cultural Poland and Lower Saxony can be placed sometime around 3200 BC. This is supported by the C-14 dates from the mixed late TRB/Globular Amphora contexts as well as from the Globular Amphora culture itself. The precise relationship between these two cultural complexes is difficult to determine, but the C-14 dates and the considerable influence of the Globular Amphora on the late TRB material culture (especially on pottery) confirm their contemporaneity.

The Corded Ware culture, which in central Europe is dated to 3000–2800 BC (Raetzel-Fabian 1986, 221, Map 8), replaces the late TRB/Globular Amphora complex in northern Europe from 2800 BC onwards. The C-14 dates for the Corded Ware culture in northern Germany begin about 2750 BC (Etzdorf H-728/590, 4150 ± 80 BP, 2745 ± 121 BC), and similar dating is suggested for southern Scandinavia. The earliest Corded Ware culture in Denmark is dated to 4240 ± 90 BP (K-2051, 2851 ± 111 BC) with six additional dates between 4160 ± 90 BP (K-2500, 2756 ± 123 BC) and 4130 ± 100 BP (K-2441, 2715 ± 143 BC); the remainder of the Danish Corded Ware dates are younger.

Assuming that Corded Ware began in Denmark c. 2750 BC, the dates show that there is only a marginal period of overlap between the final TRB and the early Corded Ware cultures in this area. This contrasts with the cultural relationship of the late TRB elsewhere, but it is entirely in keeping with the current interpretation of the emergence of the Corded Ware culture in Denmark and does not indicate substantial co-existence between the two complexes. On the other hand, the overlap is perhaps sufficient to take into consideration the fact that cultural change does not take place overnight and that it did not in this case result from an invasion of Corded Ware groups. Indeed, many of the features of the Corded Ware culture appear to have been well rooted within the local, late TRB traditions.

6

Stone, flint and other industries of the TRB culture

6.1 Natural flint resources of northern Europe

In contrast to other areas, northern Europe is well endowed with a variety
of raw materials which were used for the production of tools prior to the
discovery and use of metals. Principal among these was flint and the TRB
communities were among the first to use it on a large scale. The two chief
sources of flint available in northern Europe were the widely encountered
surface flint and limited, deeply placed primary deposits (Fig. 75). As a
result of heavy glaciation the erratic surface flint, displaced by the ice from
its primary cretaceous deposits, is abundantly found in the North European
Plain. It stretches in a broad coastal belt from Pomerania to Schleswig-
Holstein and up the eastern Danish coast into Sweden, as well as projecting
further inland along the Oder and Elbe rivers. Such flint appears to have
been plentiful along the coasts and river valleys, where water revealed
concretions of material accumulated in moraines, gravels and fluvio-glacial
sands. Surface flint is present in many varieties which differ in colour, size
of concretions and physical properties. Some of the more commonly used
types of flint in northern Europe are as follows:

The term *Baltic flint* is sometimes used to refer to all types of surface flint
found in the North European lowland, but Balcer (1983) uses the name to
describe the good-quality flint in north Poland and it is in this sense that
the term is used here. It is known throughout the entire Polish lowland
region and appears in relatively large nodules, which frequently display
blue-grey colouring. This flint may be as good as mined varieties and only
the nodule size imposes constraints upon its use. *Pomeranian flint*, known
in central and western Pomerania, is found only in small and heavily
broken-up pieces; in Polish literature these are often referred to as
"swallows' breads". Pomeranian flint may be blue or grey and is only
suitable for the production of small implements. *Rügen flint* includes a
variety of types found along the entire length of the south-western Baltic
coast and it is usually milky or dark grey in colour. On Rügen itself (and
on the islands of Uznam and Wolin) it may still occasionally be found in
primary deposits along the sea-cliffs. Small pieces of Rügen flint are fre-

quently confused with Wolhynian or banded flint; finished implements of Rügen flint apparently develop a characteristic yellow-pink patina (ibid., 48–9). A similar type of flint is found further west, in Lower Saxony, where erratic flint is known from outcrops near Lüneburg and possibly Hemmoore; Bakker (1979, 81 and 166, Fig. 42) also mentions a possible flint source on Heligoland.

Related to the Rügen variety is *Zealand flint* (sometimes also referred to as Senonian), found for instance in the chalky cliffs along the Stevns Klint in eastern Zealand, where large quantities of rough-outs of Neolithic axes have been found (Becker 1980, 473), on Møn and in Sweden near Sallerup, Kvarnby and Tullstorp (Becker 1952b; Olausson *et al.* 1980). Becker has described this flint as clear, shining black or dark grey in colour, with an extremely thin cortex and a uniform interior. Some of this flint, for instance at Kvarnby, Scania, was extracted by a shaft technique. Of the same age is the so-called *Kristianstad flint*, known from eastern Scania and Blekinge. It is a matt grey flint with white spots, of poor quality and suitable only for the production of small implements.

The younger *Danian flint* is also easily obtainable on the surface and its sources are abundant in eastern Zealand and some areas of north Jutland in a broad belt from the Djursland peninsula towards the north-west. It is light or dark grey in colour and comes in clear or matt varieties, the latter apparently somewhat inferior but nevertheless used for production of large cutting implements. *Jutland Senonian flint*, not always easily distinguishable from the Zealand type, is found in the chalky deposits across the northern part of the Jutland peninsula. It can be found on the surface but it also occurs deeper in the morainic and littoral deposits. A variety of this flint was minded at a number of Danish flint mines: at Hov, Bjerre and later also at Aalborg (Becker 1980).

Apart from the generally abundant surface flint there are also a number of sources of primary flint which only occur in restricted locations (Fig. 75); these were either exploited by the TRB communities or at least provided raw material through exchange or other forms of acquisition. Among the latter we may include deposits of cretaceous flint from the Maastricht-Liège-Aachen area. Although the mining activities in this region did not involve the active participation of the TRB groups (most of the evidence from the explored flint mines such as Spiennes or Rijckholt is associated with the neighbouring Michelsberg culture), nevertheless this excellent-quality, black or grey flint was amply available in the Western TRB group in the form either of semi-products or of completed implements. Bakker (1979, 84) has stated that 'in all probability the large axes from Western TRB contexts in Netherlands were imported exclusively from the Aachen-Valenciennes region, which was less than 150 km away'.

There are no known TRB-exploited primary flint sources from the regions of the upper Elbe or Saale rivers, although the communities there

234   *TRB Culture*

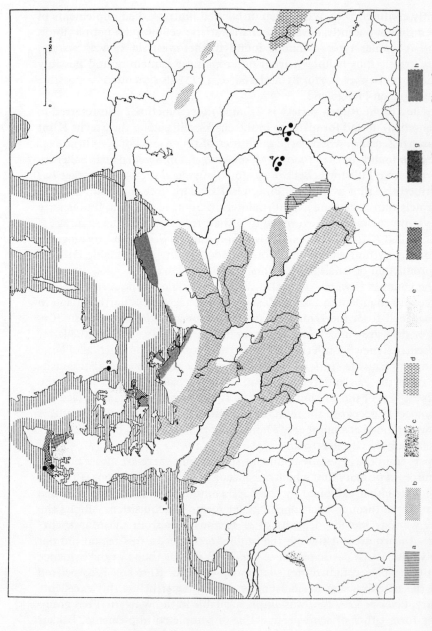

Figure 75 Distribution of flint sources in northern Europe: a-Jurassic flint, b-Baltic and other surface flint, c-Cretaceous flints from Maastricht-Liège-Aachen area, d-Wolhynian flint, e-Zealand and Danian flints, f-Senonian flint, g-Rügen flint, h-Pomeranian flint, I-Heligoland, 2-Bjerre and Hov, 3-Kvarnby, 4-sources of chocolate flint, 5-Świeciechów and banded flint (Sources: Bakker 1979; Becker 1980; Olausson *et al* 1980; Lech 1981b).

must have had their own sources for the acquisition of raw material. It is possible that the Carpathian sources of porcellanite and jasper could have provided for some of their needs (Lech 1981b, Fig. 2: VII, XX). Behrens (1973, 193) quotes Jahn on the appearance of banded flint in the TRB inventories, but more research on the middle German assemblages needs to be carried out before we can identify at least some of the sources involved.

Moving eastwards we may now consider some of the primary sources of flint available to the Eastern and South-eastern TRB groups. Among the most important flint-bearing regions we must include the Holy Cross Mountains (Góry Świętokrzyskie), in whose northern part there are deposits of the so-called 'chocolate' flint, while in the eastern sector the Świeciechów and banded flint were exploited. The *'chocolate' flint* varies in colour from grey to different browns, occurring in nodules and slabs of different sizes. Apart form deeply stratified deposits it is also found in the form of shallow layers just below the surface and it was flint from the latter that was used from the Middle Palaeolithic through to the Mesolithic. The extensive use of this flint in Kujavia (Balcer 1983, 123) shows clearly that it was available to the TRB groups there. At the recently investigated mine complex at Tomaszów (Schild *et al.* 1985), the deep extraction shafts pre-date the TRB and are associated with LBK and post-LBK activities. Two shafts may have been associated with the TRB culture, but unfortunately these still remain unexplored.

Świeciechów flint, named after the TRB mine at Świeciechów-Lasek, is encountered in the cretaceous sediments. It varies in colour from light to dark grey, and has a bluish tint and white specks about 1 mm in diameter (Balcer 1975, 46–52). The most important properties of this type of flint are its extremely good workability and the large size of the nodules; Balcer mentions a nodule ploughed up in the vicinity of the mine which measured $46 \times 26 \times 24$ cm and weighed 34 kg (ibid., 48). *Banded flint*, also known as Krzemionki flint after the main mine, is characterised by a smooth cortex and inside the nodule there are brown and grey bands, creating patterns which have given this material its name. Its technical property of splitting is variable but it does occur in relatively large nodules which facilitated the production of axes (ibid., 54–5).

Wolhynian flint was also available to the TRB communities and appears to have been highly valued. It is found in the western and southern Ukraine, particularly between the Styr and Horyń rivers and in the upper reaches of the Bug. The nodules are rounded and on average about 20 cm long. Its colour varies from black to grey with a bluish tint, and sometimes concentric bands may also be encountered. The exploitation of this flint was primarily by the Tripolye culture and it is not certain whether the TRB groups could obtain this flint directly or whether they were dependent entirely upon imports (Balcer 1983, 47–8).

6.2 Flint mining in the TRB

Our knowledge of technology and production processes involved in flint procurement is still relatively limited, since only a few mining and production centres have so far been investigated. TRB-associated flint mines are known from Denmark (Hov, Bjerre), southern Sweden (the Kvarnby complex) and central Poland (Świeciechów and Krzemionki Opatowskie). All these sites are well described in the literature (Becker 1966 and 1980; Balcer 1975; Olausson et al. 1980; Bąbel 1980b and Rudebeck 1987), and therefore only a few general comments are offered here.

Specific methods of flint extraction (open-cast mining, vertical shafts or shafts with horizontaly expanding galleries) appear to have been dictated by geological conditions rather than by the levels of skill and expertise of the TRB miners. This is clearly demonstrated by the fact that at some sites more than one method was employed, although wherever possible the simplest method was used.

Thus, the Świeciechów flint was obtained primarily through open-cast mining. This flint had been used for tool manufacture since the Middle Palaeolithic, but acquired maximum importance only at the end of the 5th and of the 4th millennium BC, with the expansion of the South-eastern TRB group (Balcer 1975). Although there are a number of localities in the eastern part of the Holy Cross Mountains from which it may have been obtained, the extent of activities in evidence at the site of Świeciechów (1,200 m × 900 m area of extraction pits, spoil heaps and primary working debris) suggests that this mine was the chief source of Świeciechów flint. The site has been badly eroded and only limited investigations have taken place (Samsonowicz 1925; Balcer 1975 and 1976). Due to the naturally sloping terrain, the deposits of flint are at variable depths. The deepest primary levels reach to about 2–2.5 m below the present-day surface; in many areas, however, the flint can be found closer to the surface. Balcer has argued that, although the probability of deep-shaft mining at Świeciechów need not be dismissed entirely, the geological nature of the site would have allowed most of the flint to be obtained by open-cast mining. This is seen in the many pits which are preserved to a depth of 55–85 cm but must originally have been deeper. Moreover, a limited range of tools (wedge-shaped and pointed pick-axes) also indicate a relatively simple method of extraction. The large quantity of debris all over the site includes blade cores, fragmented blades and blanks of quadrilateral axes, all suggesting that the primary working phase was carried out on the spot.

Exploration by the shaft method is revealed at the Scandinavian mines as well as in Poland. Simple shafts have been discovered at Hov in north Jutland and at Kvarnby in Scania. At the latter site recent excavations have revealed a complex of about thirty shafts (Olausson et al. 1980). They were between 2.5 m and 7.5 m in depth, and narrowed somewhat towards the bottom. Only very short extensions (not exceeding 1 m in length) followed the flint seams. An important discovery was in the traces of post-holes in the faces of some of the shafts. These varied between 5 and 10 cm in diameter; the posts were placed horizontally within the shaft, creating a working platform and possibly acting as a brace against the shaft's collapse. One of the shafts also revealed the impressions of a diagonally placed tree trunk with cut-off branches which has been interpreted as a ladder (ibid., 190, Fig. 181). Similar arrangements have been identified by Becker at Hov (1966; 1980, Fig. 382).

Plain shafts are also known from the largest prehistoric mine complex at Krzemionki Opatowskie, which was extensively exploited during the Neolithic and Bronze Age (Żurowski 1962; Bąbel 1980b and 1986). Because of the complexity of archaeological remains at this site (an estimated 2,500–3,000 shafts as well as workshops and camp areas), and because the investigations were limited, the precise involvement of individual cultural groupings at the Krzemionki mine is still difficult to determine. Although there is little doubt that the TRB miners began large-scale mining of banded flint, recent interpretations suggest that the fundamental role in the development of this mine should be attributed to the Globular Amphora culture (Balcer and Kowalski 1978; Bąbel 1986); The chief arguments for this are based upon the greater importance of banded flint within the latter cultural complex and some of the archaeological evidence from the site.

The entire mining area at Krzemionki is situated on the syncline; it is about 5 km long and between 30 m and 180 m wide. The depth of flint deposits is greatest towards the middle (between 9 m and 11 m) and becomes progressively shallower towards the edge, where it was easy to obtain the flint simply by digging shallow pits. It has been estimated that the shallow flint deposits along the entire length of the mine equalled in quantity half of all the raw material available at the mine of Świeciechów (Balcer 1975, 247). Observations of the change in the extraction methods from the edge of the mine towards the middle reveal a succession of shallow pits, giving way to deeper vertical shafts, which ultimately develop into an underground complex of shafts with horizontal galleries, tunnels and supporting stalls (Bąbel 1980, Fig. 603; 1986, 27). One of the recently excavated shafts of the simple vertical variety was 3.6 m deep, with a flint-bearing layer at a depth of 2.7 m, which was totally dug away creating niches along the wall. These were subsequently filled with rubble, because the shaft was deepened to reach a lower layer of flint.

On the basis of blanks of axes found within the shaft it has been suggested that it belonged to the Globular Amphora culture. However, these are not always a suitable cultural indicator and sometimes the blanks of the TRB and Globular Amphora culture are very similar and axes can be distinguished only by their different finishes. While this is not in itself an argument for assigning the shaft to the TRB culture, there is additional evidence. This shaft was closely associated with another, somewhat older shaft; charcoal discovered beneath the debris at the junction of the two shafts yielded a C-14 date of 5230 ± 170 BP (Bąbel 1986, 28), which in the light of present chronology fits appropriately within the TRB context. It is therefore possible that some of the deep shafts are the result of TRB mining activities. Additional support for such an interpretation is found in some of the large TRB banded-flint axes found at Ćmielów, whose quality of material indicates a deeply placed deposit (Balcer 1975, 248).

Miners' tools vary depending on conditions and on the degree of difficulty of flint extraction, although some of the tools made of organic materials rarely survive and we can only guess the nature of some, such as leather sacks or baskets for carrying flint nodules. At Świeciechów flint and stone tools survive: wedge-shaped and pointed pick-axes, and hammers and pick-axes made of stone. From the Krzemionki mine, in addition to the above forms, we also have antler hammers and levers. At Hov and Kvarnby red deer antler picks were left in some shafts. In one of the Kvarnby shafts there was a composite tool made of an antler point hafted into a wooden handle; an imprint of the decayed handle could be seen in the chalk (Olausson *et al.* 1980, Fig. 179); another shaft contained a poorly preserved shoulder-blade shovel. Flint tools have also been recovered: long, somewhat pointed pieces may have served as picks and more sharply pointed pieces as borers (ibid., 190–1).

There is now sufficient evidence to indicate some of the flint processing activities that were carried out in the mines. The quality of flint nodules appears to have been investigated on the spot. At the bottom of one of the Kvarnby shafts, for instance, were 300 roughly worked nodules, which were clearly tested and rejected (ibid., 191). At Krzemionki there is a striking difference in the quantity of nodules found within the shafts and in the workshops above ground, suggesting that again the quality of flint nodules was investigated here before they were brought to the surface (Bąbel 1986, 30).

There are interesting differences in the range of activities which took place at flint mines with regard to tool manufacture. Evidence outlined by Balcer (1980) suggests that only initial preparation of axe blanks and of cores for the production of blades was done there; subsequent stages of manufacture were carried out in production settlements. On the other hand the residual material recovered at Kvarnby indicates that all stages of tool manufacture, including grinding and polishing of axes as well as the making of tools, took place at the mine. The excavators argued that while most of the axes probably left the mine as blanks to be traded and finished elsewhere, at least some were finished and even hafted on the spot (Olausson *et al.* 1980, 195–9).

While we naturally require further information to explain the processes involved in the procurement of raw materials and in tool manufacture, the above examples indicate that the TRB flint industry was governed by a number of factors. Access to raw materials, supply and demand, the extent of social and economic contacts and perhaps local traditions, all created different circumstances which fundamentally affected the ways in which the basic need for working tools was satisfied among the TRB communities in different regions of the culture's distribution.

6.3 The flint industry of the TRB culture

The study of the flint industry is still one of the more neglected fields of TRB culture research; in most regions flint assemblages are studied with considerably less enthusiasm than ceramics. And yet, the studies carried out in the context of the Eastern and South-eastern TRB groups show clearly the potential contribution of lithic research to the better under-standing of economic and social relations within and between local groups, as well as providing a useful counterbalance against too fine a chronological division based upon the study of the ceramics. However, the information available to date is insufficient to allow a cross-regional discussion of the TRB flint industry. The evidence presented below is therefore of necessity based upon regional groups and on somewhat sporadic regional research.

6.3.1 Eastern and South-eastern TRB groups

The flint industry of the TRB culture in the area east of the Oder river – the Eastern and South-eastern groups – is characterised by immensely dynamic development, especially at the later stage when important tech-nological innovation takes place. Most of the research in this field has been carried out by one scholar, Balcer (1975; 1976; 1980; 1981a; 1981b; 1983), and it is largely upon the results of his work that comments in this section are based.

The oldest known flint assemblages derive from a few settlements and earthen long barrows in the region of Kujavia and it is these materials that form the basis of the so-called *Sarnowo industry* (Balcer 1981a, 60–3; 1983, 122–30 (Fig. 76: A)). They characterise the two earliest phases of the Eastern TRB. These phases have been distinguished on the basis of ceramic analysis, but such phasing is not revealed by the flint artefacts.

The imported Upper Astartian chocolate flint is of greater importance than the local Baltic surface flint. This is apparent from the total amount of flint as well as from the number of tools present in a particular assem-blage (for instance chocolate flint tools make up 84.9 per cent at Sarnowo, 58 per cent at Leśniczówka and 42.7 per cent at Sierakowo; Balcer 1983, Table 22). Balcer has identified at least thirteen types of tool, among which implements used for cutting and scraping (end scrapers, retouched blades, side scrapers, perforators and truncated blades) are the most numerous.

There are two characteristic features of the Sarnowo industry which require additional comment. First, there appear to be no flint axes (or axe-preparation waste) associated with these early assemblages. The adoption and development of the axe within the regional groups still remains to be explained satisfactorily. For the present we may observe, however, that the absence of axes is incongruous within the context of our knowledge of the economic and constructional activities of the early TRB communities in Kujavia.

The other problem presents itself in the already-noted importance of the chocolate flint, whose primary sources are over 200 km away from Kujavia. It is reasonable to assume that the use of chocolate flint in Kujavia reflects a long tradition of trading this raw material well beyond the immediate vicinity of its source (Schild *et al.* 1985). Chocolate flint had been used by various communities during the Late Mesolithic and it had also been used by the LBK and Lengyel groups in this area (Lech 1981a and 1981b; Balcer 1983, 58; Grygiel 1986; Schild 1987). The quantity of flint available to the TRB people suggests that the supply was steady and could be relied upon since the majority of tools were made of this material. But the abundance as well as the continuity of use does not explain how the Kujavian TRB people obtained their raw material. Did they have direct access to the sources, obtaining it independently by organising periodic expeditions to the Holy Cross Mountains to bring back the flint? Or did they rely upon middlemen, and if so, were they the same as those who, for example, supplied the Brześć Kujawski Lengyel group?

Neither the Brześć Kujawski nor TRB group assemblages contain much debris from the production of chocolate flint tools. It is therefore reasonable to suggest that they acquired semi-products or possibly even finished tools. Moreover, a number of scholars have argued that correpondences between the Sarnowo and LBK flint industries reveal not only a similar use of the raw material, but also a strong similarity between tool types (Lech and Młynarczyk 1981; Balcer 1981a, 72). In the context of LBK and post-LBK activities at the chocolate flint mines it is possible that all the different Kujavian communities used one and the same agency – the southern Polish LBK and then post-LBK flint prospectors – to provide them with the necessary raw material. This would correspond with the technological similarity of the LBK and TRB culture industries. On the other hand the possibility that the TRB communities were themselves engaged in the extraction of chocolate flint must not be ruled out. The supply to Kujavia of semi-products and finished tools, rather than of unworked flint nodules, would make sense with regard to the distance involved, even if the Vistula provided and excellent transport route, irrespective of cultural and trading connections.

Balcer (1983, 176) has recently advanced the idea that from about 3800 BC there were important changes which, regardless of regional distinctions within the TRB based upon other criteria, allow a division of the area east of the Oder into three regions, each identified by a specific flint industry.

Thus one region, characterised by the so-called Little Poland industry, encompasses the entire South-eastern group, as well as Kujavia which is associated through its strong reliance upon the south-eastern sources of primary flint. The second region, identified by the Pietrowice industry, includes the territories of the upper and lower Oder and a large part of the Eastern TRB group. The third identifiable area centres upon the apparently isolated Łupawa group, whose flint industry displays an individual style related primarily to the quality of the raw material.

The rich flint assemblages, sometimes numbering tens of thousands of pieces, derive primarily from large settlements of the South-eastern group (such as Ćmielów, Gródek Nadbużny, Bronocice or Niedźwiedź) and it is these materials that form the basis of the *Little Poland industry* (Balcer 1975, 57–146; 1983, 130–53; Fig. 76: 13). The major feature of this industry is its macrolithic character, seen in the production of axes and large blades for tools. This is a direct result of the large-scale exploitation of Świecie-chów and banded flint by the communities of the South-eastern TRB group, and of the acquisition of Wolhynian flint from the neighbouring Tripolye culture. The fundamental importance of these three types of flint is reflected in their extensive distribution up to 600 km from their sources.

A blade technique was dominant in the preparation of semi-products. The Świeciechów flint blades are on average 17.4 cm long, 3.2 cm wide and up to 0.8 cm thick; some examples may reach 30 cm in length. The tools were made using ordinary and pressure-flaking retouch. Seventeen types of tools have been identified, of which the most important are retouched blades (many interpreted as sickle blades), end scrapers, perforators and axes. Arrowheads are not very common; when found they are usually triangular, with flat or concave bases.

Axes of the Little Poland industry (Fig. 77) are all thick-butted, and three basic types have been distinguished (Balcer 1975, 110–23; 1983, 142–5). Type A has a wedge-shaped form, with straight sides and a relatively flat face, gradually narrowing from the cutting edge towards the butt; the cross-section is generally rectangular (Fig. 77: 1, 2). There are polished as well as unpolished examples and axes made of the Wolhynian flint mostly belong to this category. Type B represents a bulging form with both butt and cutting edge narrower than the maximum width of the axe; the latter is generally found at about one-third of the length above the cutting edge (Fig. 77: 3, 4). Sometimes the butt is poorly distinguished and in other cases is drastically thinned. Axes of this type made from Świeciechów flint are on average 16.1 cm long; and 4.8 cm and 2.5 cm wide at the cutting edge and butt respectively; the maximum thickness is 3 cm. Type C axes are small, four-sided or three-sided, flat axes (Fig. 77; 5), which on the whole appear to be related to Type A axes. Average dimensions for this form are quoted by Balcer as 9.97 cm for length, 3.94 cm and 2.12 cm for the cutting edge and butt, and 1.57 cm for thickness. Many of the axes show traces of

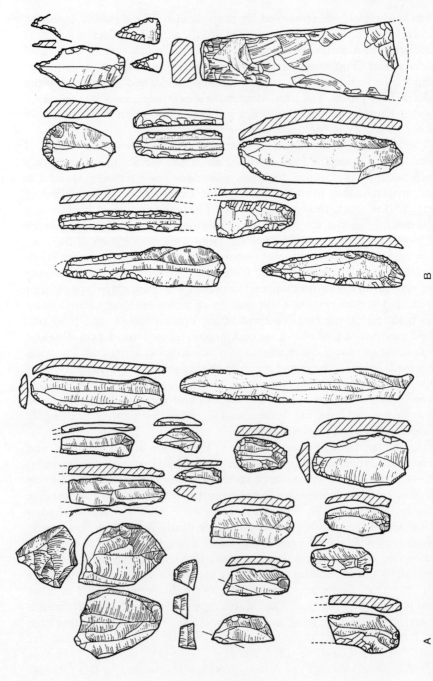

B

A

Figure 76 Flint industries of the TRB culture in Poland: A–Sarnowo industry, B–Little Poland industry (Source: Balcer 1981a).

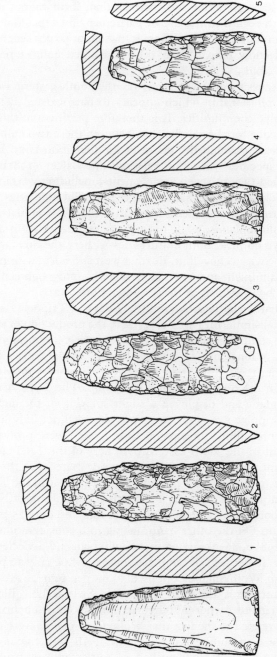

Figure 77 Axes of the Little Poland industry: 1-Zawichost, 2-Klementowice, 3.5-Kamień Łukawski, 4-Gródek Nadbużny (Source: Balcer 1975).

repeated repair and alteration and their original form cannot always be determined. With regard to the use of particular flint types Balcer, using assemblages from four key sites, estimates that about 50 per cent of axes are made of Świeciechów flint, 38 per cent of banded and 12 per cent of Wolhynian flint (ibid., 145).

The earlier discussion of the pottery from the South-eastern TRB group noted the close relationship which appears to have existed between the TRB and Tripolye communities. It is therefore pertinent at this point to discuss the evidence for the relationship between these two cultural complexes as it appears through the prism of the flint industries. In a short paper devoted specifically to this relationship, Balcer (1981b, Fig. 1, Table 1) identified twenty-seven key elements, including working techniques, types of tool etc., which characterise the two flint industries. Of these, twenty-four features can be identified within the TRB industries of the Wolhynian-Lublin uplands, while twenty-one are identified in the neighbouring Tripolye culture. Both cultures reveal here the domiance of the Wolhynian over Świeciechów flint. Further west and north within the TRB the similarities diminish, and in Kujavia there are only eighteen elements which may also be identified in the Tripolye (ibid., 82).

In the immediate neighbourhood of the TRB and Tripolye cultures the most fundamental similarities are observed in the production of maximally large blades, the common existence of axes, the nearly identical tool assortment and very rational use of blades, first as sickle knives and then, reworked, as other tools. The basic Tripolye axe is very similar to a Type A as identified in the South-eastern TRB group. The Type A axes were more carefully made and displayed a slight splaying of the cutting edge typical of the Tripolye axe. This feature is observed not only in the axes made of Wolhynian flint, but also on those which were produced from Świeciechów flint in the south-eastern periphery of the TRB culture.

Wolhynian flint was the only high-quality raw material in the Tripolye culture in its western area and it played a significant role in the TRB along its south-eastern periphery. At the TRB settlement of Gródek Nadbużny, 69 per cent of tools were made of Wolhynian flint and only 25 per cent of Świeciechów flint. On the other hand, taking into consideration only key forms, Balcer (1981b, 86–7) argued that Wolhynian and Świeciechów flint each account for 48 per cent of retouched blades, while only 36 per cent of axes are made of Wolhynian as opposed to 64 per cent of axes made of Świeciechów flint. It is therefore clear that Świeciechów flint was of importance even in areas where Wolhynian flint was easily obtainable. This may be directly related to the fact that Wolhynian sources were controlled by the Tripolye communities (none of the TRB settlements from the Wolhynian upland could be identified as settlements of primary producers). It can therefore be assumed that regular exchange took place between the neighbouring TRB and Tripolye groups. Balcer suggested that many Wolhynian flint tools, particularly axes, were simply Tripolye imports into the TRB. The distribution of the Wolhynian flint throughout the TRB culture (up to 600 km from its source), together with the lack of Świeciechów flint in the Tripolye flint assemblages, shows clearly that, as regards flint working, the Tripolye culture had more influence upon the South-eastern TRB than *vice versa*.

Returning now to Kujavia, we must note that here the flint assemblages of the later TRB culture are less numerous than those of the South-eastern group discussed above; moreover they still await the necessary analyses. However, one of the most important differences observed in comparison with the earlier period (represented by the Sarnowo industry) is the dramatic decrease in the importance of chocolate flint. Indeed, there is much greater reliance upon the local surface flint (up to 98 per cent; Balcer 1983, Table 32) although we also encounter imported southern materials such as Świeciechów and, to the lesser degree, banded and Wolhynian flint. In comparison with the use of surface flint the imported materials are relatively small in quantity, but many tools are made of the latter. The diagnostic forms include retouched blades, scrapers, semi-backed blades and, most importantly, four-sided axes of Type B (Fig. 77: 3, 4); additionally there are triangular and leaf-shaped arrowheads. Many of the tools made of Świeciechów flint are regarded as southern imports, and since there is little waste associated with foreign flint types, it is likely that this material arrived predominantly in the form of semi-products and blanks. A prime example of such imports is the 30 cm long blade found at Radziejów (Grygiel 1978, 239). With regard to the general character of the industry, Balcer (1983, 161 and 187) has argued that, apart from technological constraints imposed by the quality of local raw material, the later TRB Kujavian assemblages represent a lowland version of the Little Poland industry. The region of Kujavia, however, was also within reach of the more northern influences. This is evident from the occasional finds of thin-butted axes which, although stray finds, most probably belong within the TRB context; some are apparently even made from Świeciechów flint.

It has been suggested that the change from chocolate to Świeciechów flint was related to technology and to the need for larger tools (Balcer 1975, 210; 1983, 177 and 179; Schild 1987, 145). But this may be only a partial explanation. We know that the South-eastern TRB communities began the large-scale exploitation of Świeciechów flint, but we also see a greater importance of chocolate flint in the assemblages of the Globular Amphora and Corded Ware cultures (Balcer 1983, 207–8; Schild 1987, 145). Although the chronological aspects of these developments are not yet entirely clear, it is possible that we witness here the results of changes in ownership or in rights to the use of a particular resource (with the Globular Amphora culture in particular acquiring rights to the chocolate flint sources), which forced the TRB communities to look elsewhere for suitable flint materials.

As regards Kujavia, the tradition of north–south connections is maintained, and yet this continuity obscures the severance of old and the establishment of new contacts. The archaeological identification of the movement of communities is highly problematical, yet there is some indication that Kujavia, due to its strategic position along the Vistula, may have experienced an influx of population from the south. The expansion of settlement in Kujavia (as outlined in Chapter 7.1), coincides with the technological changes just outlined, as well as with the observed developments in ceramics (Chapter 4.2), and it may indeed demonstrate some human movement into the area. Whatever the precise explanation for these phenomena, it is evident that during the early 4th millennium BC Kujavia was not a backwater; on the contrary, its communities were familiar with and took full advantage of new developments in the neighbouring regions.

While displaying certain individual characteristics, the regions of Silesia, Greater Poland and western Pomerania may be treated together, primarily because in all these areas tool production was dependent upon the availability of surface flint, whereas imported, high-quality material is encountered only sporadically. For the area of Silesia, Balcer (1983, 161–7) identified the so-called *Pietrowice industry* (named after the TRB settlement at Pietrowice Wielkie, one of the few producer settlements in this area), which is characterised mainly by the use of a flake technique. Among the basic tools were retouched bladelets, end scrapers and side scrapers. Silesian axes are three- and two-sided, on average between 6 cm and 13 cm long, with a cutting edge 3.3–4.7 cm wide and a butt not exceeding 3 cm in width. Flake axes are also occasionally encountered. Similar axes are found in settlements in Greater Poland, for example at Mrowino; in both areas there is an apparent lack of four-sided examples.

Western Pomeranian flint assemblages are poorly known and currently there is only a little information about the flint inventory of the so-called Ustowo group. Baltic surface flint did not allow the production of tools more than 10 cm in lengh. At the Gorzów settlement (Szczurek 1981, 163) were found small, thin-butted axes of rectangular cross-section as well as rather unusual, carefully worked laurel-leaf arrowheads. An interesting aspect of flint tools from western Pomerania is represented by finds of northern, thin-butted axes, which here display their easternmost provenance. So far, 173 examples have been catalogued (sixteen are from hoards, the rest represent single finds; Siuchniński 1969; 1972, 86–9), the majority apparently made of Rügen flint. On the basis of northern parallels these are regarded as relatively early, although some Mecklenburg associations with the 'Viervitz' type (ibid., 89–90) may suggest that this kind of axe was used for longer outwith the Northern TRB group.

6.3.2 Social aspects of flint industries east of the Oder river

Concerning the later flint industry of the South-eastern TRB group, Balcer

(1980, 89) has argued that the technological processing of flint was aimed principally at: 1) the production of large core tools such as axe- or adze-blades, and 2) the production of blades for smaller tools. Within this process he distinguished four stages: I – initial preparation; II – production of blanks and semi-products; III – final shaping of tools, and IV – repairing and re-shaping of implements. These are recognisable from the archaeological material by the presence or absence of typical waste forms and of end products diagnostic of each of the stages. The identification of these stages in tool production has led to a hypothesis on the functional differentiation of sites (based on the study of flint assemblages) as well as to suggestions as to the nature of social relations and the exchange networks between communities in different regions.

Three types of functionally differentiated sites have been distinguished: *extraction sites* – the mines discussed above, such as Świeciechów or Krzemionki (stages I and II); *flint processing settlements* such as Ćmielów or Zawichost, where mass production of blanks as well as finished tools took place (stages II and III); and the *users' settlements*, where tools were generally not made but finished and repaired (mainly stage IV; ibid., 96–8). Balcer applied this model in the context of the Świeciechów, banded and Wolhynian flint, whose sources are clearly located and whose distribution pattern has been relatively well studied. While such a model does have a wider application within the entire TRB (for example in the context of north Jutland or Scanian flint sources), it refers only to imported raw materials and does not account for the production of tools from locally available surface flint. In such instances, the users of imported flint may also be identified as producers of tools from local flint, an important distinction which is not taken into account in Balcer's model.

Two settlements at the eastern edge of the Holy Cross Mountains have been identified as production centres closely associated with the flint mines in this region. Figure 78 shows the location of the settlements and mines: Zawichost lies 14 km south of the Świeciechów mine (with and easy communication route along the Vistula) and 32 km overland from the Krzeminonki mine; Ćmielów is situated 9 km south of Krzemionki and 22 km from Świeciechów.

A study of the flint assemblages from Zawichost shows that Świeciechów flint is dominant in terms of raw material (96.1 per cent) and tools (90.4 per cent). Although the investigations at this site were less extensive than at Ćmielów, the material recovered from thirty-three pits is strongly indicative of production stage II, including partially worked nodules and small pre-cores, blade cores, blanks and axe semi-products. Only very small quantities of other flint types were found, such as banded flint axes, and it is perfectly clear that the Zawichost inhabitants had direct access to the Świeciechów flint, were entirely self-sufficient in their industrial needs and

were involved in mass production of blanks and semi-products for purposes
of trade and/or exchange with other communities (Balcer 1975, 181–3).

The situation at Ćmielów is a little different. Here both types of flint,
banded and Świeciechów, were worked. In terms of raw material (by
fragments) these account for 62.1 per cent and 37.8 per cent respectively,
while for tools the situation is reversed – more tools were made of the
Świeciechów flint (69.6 per cent) than of banded (28.7 per cent ibid.,
180–1). It is clear that the inhabitants of Ćmielów had direct access to both
of the natural resources, although the practicalities involved in their procurement (as well as the relationship between Ćmielów and Zawichost in
terms of access and exploitation rights to Świeciechów sources) are not clear.

Banded flint appears to have been used mainly for the production of axes.
This can be determined from the natural properties of the flint as well
as from the debris found at Ćmielów. One of the large workshop pits
excavated there (pit no. 102) yielded a 50 cm thick layer of flint waste. This
included 122 blanks and semi-products of axes, together with 10,858 waste
pieces of banded flint, four semi-products of axes and 10,222 waste pieces
of Świeciechów flint (ibid., 180–1, Tables 1 and 19). It is obvious that the
same craftsman (or a group of craftsmen) worked with both types of
material. The total quantity of banded flint recovered from Ćmielów
accounts for 62.2 per cent and the main products made at this site were axes.

This activity reveals a fundamental difference between the Ćmielów and
Zawichost sites and we may argue that we see here a degree of specialisation, with the Zawichost craftsmen producing mainly blanks for smaller
tools, while those from Ćmielów were concentrating mainly on satisfying
the demand for axes. This situation could have been reached only in
conditions of a steady supply of raw material and a continuous demand for
tools. That such a demand existed is evident from the character of assemblages recovered at other TRB sites as well as from the distribution of the
two types of raw material within the South-eastern group and beyond.

A number of settlements within the South-eastern TRB group have been
classified by Balcer (1983, Table 30) as users' settlements, for example
Gródek Nadbużny, Kamień Łukawski or Niedźwiedź. The settlement at
Gródek is located 150 km east of the Holy Cross Mountains, but only 35 km
from the sources of Wolhynian flint. The latter is dominant altogether but,
as already noted earlier, key tools were made in roughly equal proportions
(47.8 per cent of Wolhynian and 47.5 per cent of banded and Świeciechów
flint). A fundamental difference between the settlements of users and
producers can be seen in the amount of flint waste indicative of the final
stage of the production process (repairing and secondary working of tools);

Figure 78 Location of the Krzemionki and Świeciechów mines in relation to flint-
processing settlements at Ćmielów and Zawichost: a-loess, b-deposits of flint, c-
TRB settlements, d-large processing settlements, e-mines (Source: Balcer 1975).

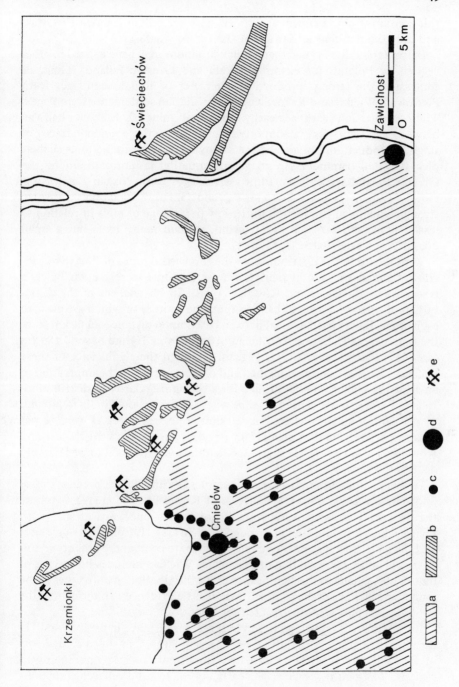

Świeciechów

Zawichost

5 km

Ćmielów

Krzemionki

a b c d e

this accounts for 31 per cent at Gródek, 20.5 per cent at Kamień Łukawski and only 0.9 per cent at Zawichost (Balcer 1975, 189).

Balcer (1977) has argued that similar situations may have existed in other regions of Poland, for example Silesia and Greater Poland. Thus, he contrasted the strong 'production' character of flint assemblages from Pietrowice Wielkie and Raków with other Silesian settlement assemblages. Their connection with a nearby open-cast mine at Maków (halfway between the two sites) is supported not only by the abundant traces of stage II production, but also by the discovery of flint mining tools such as pick-axes and hammers. An analogous situation is indicated among the Greater Poland settlements. Flint assemblages from Poznań-Lasek (previously Luboń; Jażdżewski 1936, 64) and Gorzów Wielkopolski display strong elements of production in the low percentage of tools in relation to waste, while others, such as Mrowino, contain many tools but a small quantity of waste (Balcer 1983, 183).

With regard to the distribution of the three main types of flint (Świeciechów, banded and Wolhynian), we must continue to rely upon Balcer's research (1976; Balcer and Kowalski 1978). In his analysis of the distribution of Świeciechów and banded flint, the sources of which are close to each other, Balcer used a radial pattern based upon distances of 60 km from the source (area I), between 60 km and 180 km (area II) and beyond 180 km (area III; Balcer 1976, 193–4, Fig. 9), although the significance of these distances has never been explained and one cannot avoid the impression of an arbitrary choice. He has argued for a certain regularity of distribution. In area I were 59 per cent of all sites where Świeciechów flint is found and 57 per cent of all sites where banded flint appears; in area II were 24 per cent respectively; and in area III 17 per cent and 10 per cent (Balcer and Kowalski 1978, 134–5). He suggested that the two types of flint were simply distributed together.

However, the situation is more complex. Using Balcer's catalogue of finds (Balcer 1975, 289–328; Balcer and Kowalski 1978, 141–2) we note that in area I (closest to the source) only about one-third of sites with Świeciechów flint also contain banded flint. In area II, from thirty-five sites with Świeciechów flint only five can be shown to contain the other type and in area III only one site, that of Pietrowice Wielkie, includes both types of flint. Thus, whatever the significance of the distribution of both types in the immediate vicinity of the sources, there is little evidence to indicate that the two types of flint were distributed together.

But there are interesting facts to observe; for instance in areas II and III the sites containing both flint types represent large, long-lived settlements of the TRB, which appear to have been important centres within their own regions. The two raw materials clearly appear to fulfil different functions in both use and distribution. Świeciechów flint was multi-functional (all tools could be made from it) while banded flint, but virtue of its physical properties, was used mostly for axes. It is difficult to determine to what degree the aesthetic qualities of banded flint could be considered important, bearing in mind the possible multiple function of axes (practical and non-utilitarian), this factor must not be overlooked.

The pattern of distribution of both types, while doubtless only partly reflected in and liable to change in accordance with the availability of data, not only suggests significant differences but also indicates some kind of hierarchy in the distribution of raw materials, for instance redistribution centres, by virtue of the role played by large-scale settlements within the entire system. With reference to Świeciechów flint alone, the pattern created by the three distribution areas is equally deceptive, because it depends entirely upon the presence of the material and not on its quantity. Thus in area I it accounts for between 90 per cent and 70 per cent of tools at all sites, so its fundamental importance need not be disputed. In area II, however, its importance varies between 27 per cent and 2 per cent and thus, once again, distance cannot be accepted as an important criterion, but instead social and cultural factors need to be considered. For example the River Nida appears to be an important barrier, with sites to the west of it considerably less dependent on Świeciechów flint.

The socio-cultural factors are particularly valid when we note that the area of Kujavia, well over 200 km from the sources, is an important consumer of this flint. We need to remember the earlier connections between Kujavia and the eastern Holy Cross Mountains region, exemplified in the fundamental reliance upon chocolate flint, and to bear in mind the long traditions of association which may transcend distance as well as regional boundaries. The substitution of the chocolate flint with Świeciechów variety takes place precisely at the time when important socio-economic developments take place in Kujavia and when contacts with the south-east are intensified. While this underlines the degree of continuity in long-established traditions, it also reflects an expansion of contacts between different communities.

The latter point assumes additional significance when we consider another factor, the appearance of Wolhynian flint, whose sources are found in the territory of the Tripolye culture. Balcer's distribution map of Wolhynian flint within the TRB milieu (1983, Fig. 34), where it appears most commonly in the form of axes and long blades, shows three large concentrations: on the Lublin upland, in Little Poland and in Kujavia.

The Lublin upland settlements all rely heavily upon this flint for tools and in the opinion of some scholars the overall importance of Świeciechów flint does not exceed 10 per cent (Jastrzębski, pers. comm.). But the interpretation of Wolhynian flint elsewhere is difficult. First of all, Balcer's map again shows only findspots and not the quantities of flint involved. For the Little Poland sites the quantities appear to be minimal (for example 0.18 per cent of tools at Ćmielów, 1.6 per cent at Zawichost and 0.6 per cent at

Kamień Łukawski). Only at Książnice Wielkie does Wolhynian flint
amount to 5.9 per cent of tools. A detailed analysis of the flint assemblage
from Bronocice is not yet available. We must remember that in this area
the flint supply was plentiful and there was no practical need to import
Wolhynian raw material. Its presence may be either accidental, associated
with the exchange of other commodities, or else introduced as a status
indicator. It is most clearly not present through economic demand, nor is
it large in volume. The other concentration is in Kujavia, where the local
supply of good flint was limited and imported material was valuable. Again,
there are little data available on the volume of Wolhynian flint or on its
relation to other imported types, although information collated by Balcer
(1983, Tables 32 and 33) shows a slightly lesser popularity of Wolhynian
flint in relation to other imported materials.

Balcer has argued that Wolhynian flint was distributed together with
Świeciechów and banded types. We have already seen that the latter two
types have a differential distribution pattern, and there is simply no evidence to put them together with the Wolhynian material. The Little Poland
communities had no need to obtain this flint for themselves; and that they
did not acquire it is evident from the negligible quantities found at such sites
as Ćmielów and Zawichost. Moreover, if they were involved in exchange
with Kujavia, they would have used raw materials which they could easily
obtain and not goods which they would have had to import themselves.

Thus, some of the assumptions behind Balcer's model of flint distribution within the South-eastern and Eastern TRB groups are not borne out
by the currently available evidence. The distribution of different flint types
does indicate beyond all doubts, however, the complexity of relationships
between the various communities and the multitude of economic and social
factors which must have played a significant role in establishing such an
exchange network. We see that there is no straightforward relationship
between the distance from primary source and the quantity of imported
material. The examples of Kujavia and the Lublin upland regions reveal
that it was possible to establish strong contacts to provide for industrial
needs irrespective of the distances involved and right across regional
boundaries. Moreover, cultural boundaries, as for example between
Tripolye and TRB cultures, do not appear to constrain such movements,
and cross-cultural relations appear to play a significant role during the 4th
millennium BC. Such relations are seen more closely through the prism of
the flint industry than through any other aspect of material culture.

6.3.3 North Germany and the Netherlands

With reference to the Western group of the TRB, Bakker has stated that
'The study of the small artefacts has actually not even started' (Bakker
1979, 76), and this comment applies equally well to the entire area of the
north German TRB culture. With the exception of Hoika's recent dis-

cussion of the later TRB flint industry from north-east Holstein (1987, 44–66), and a rather controversial paper by Weber (1980) comparing the Ertebølle and early TRB flint assemblages on either side of the Baltic, no general studies on this subject are available. Moreover, in many publications a discussion of small flint tools is usually confined to a few paragraphs, offering little information on the general character of assemblages, let alone individual tool types. Thus, only a superficial picture emerges from a review of publications on settlements and funerary monuments, and it is simply impossible to indicate any regional variations or chronological trends. The discussion below makes clear the imbalance between the research in the field of ceramics and that of flint industries in the region concerned.

Only a few of the early TRB sites offer information on small flint artefacts; a number of assemblages from crucial sites, such as Rosenhof and the complex from Satrup Moor, still remain unpublished. However, the available information from Siggeneben-Süd, east Holstein (Meurers-Balke 1983), Boberg (Schindler 1953) or Basedow (Schuldt 1974a) suggests, in contrast to Weber's (1980) conclusions of an insignificant Mesolithic heritage, that the early TRB flint industry was substantially influenced by the Mesolithic tradition, a fact evidenced in tool types as well as in flint-working techniques.

Flake axes, for instance are regularly encountered. At Siggeneben-Süd, fifty-three examples include triangular, trapezoidal, rectangular as well as asymmetric forms (Meurers-Balke 1983, 67–70, Plates 39–47 and 48: 1–3). They are often flaked on the upper surface and retouched along the edges. They vary in length between 4.7 cm and 10.2 cm with the majority about 7 cm long. Twelve examples of flake axes, between 7 cm and 12 cm long, come from Basedow (Schuldt 1974a). They appear to be similar to those known from Mesolithic assemblages but less carefully finished; one example was partly polished along the cutting edge. From Boberg, near Hamburg, Schindler (1953, Plate III) comments on broad-butted flake axes with a flaked surface, and on partly polished flake axes which according to him illustrate the transition from a chipped flake axe to a thin-butted polished axe (ibid., 9). Schindler also points to flake axes with a sharp, pointed or oblique butt, which can be seen in this context as forerunners of the polished point-butted examples.

Apart from the flake axes, the Mesolithic tradition of the early TRB flint industry is revealed through a relatively strong presence of good-quality blades and blade tools. At Siggeneben-Süd, 22.2 per cent of all tools and 26.4 per cent of scrapers were made on blades (Meurers-Balke 1983, 66 and 73). At Basedow (Schuldt 1974a, 25; Fig. 79), blade tools (side- and end-retouched as well as denticulated blades) are outnumbered threefold by flake tools. However, unworked blades are twice as numerous as worked blades, and Schuldt believes that the former may represent implements, since a number of them display strong gloss. At Boberg there was a substantial number of large and wide blades with careful concave retouch, as well as some denticulated examples (Schindler 1953, Plate III). It is of interest to note here that good-quality blades form an important conponent of the early TRB graves at Ostorf, distr. Schwerin, where votive deposits of blades struck from one core have been found with some burials (Bastian 1961, 93, Figs 65–7).

As in the early TRB Danish flint assemblages, the most common tool is a scraper. At Siggeneben-Süd the proportion of blade and flake scrapers is 26.4 per cent to 73.6 per cent (Meurers-Balke 1983, 73–6). The examples vary in length from 0.5 cm to 5.5 cm, most falling between 1.8 cm and 2.8 cm. Oval and irregular forms appear to be the most common, and retouch is usually found only along part of the edge. Variously shaped scrapers are the most common tool type at Basedow, where they were manufactured mainly on small, irregular flakes, but some blades with convex retouch must also be included in this category (Fig. 79). Scrapers from Boberg display a great variety of form, although large examples are relatively rare. Dominant are the small and medium forms, round or oval in shape or in some cases with a triangular base. Schindler notes that in the later stage of the early TRB (Boberg site 12), there is a noticeable decline in the importance of blades, cores are rare and scrapers are made from 'the most impossible' fragments of flakes (Schindler 1953, 10, Table V: 16).

Finally, transverse arrowheads are present throughout. At Basedow they vary greatly in form and size, most displaying concave, retouched sides (Schuldt 1974a, Fig. 26). At Siggeneben-Süd, where they appear to have been made mostly on blades, they are trapezoidal and have relatively straight edges (Meurers-Balke 1983, Plate 63: 10–20), and a wide range of forms is also present at Boberg (Schindler 1953, Plate V).

For the later TRB assemblages there are very sparse data. Judging from publications, most tools are made on flakes; blades have not disappeared altogether, but generally no data exist to evaluate the proportional relationship between the flake and blade tools beyond the preponderance of the former over the latter. Hoika (1987, 182), referring to the Heringsdorf-Süssau assemblage, quotes a figure of about 50,000 pieces of flake tools (scrapers, points, borers) and only about 500 blade tools.

Scrapers continue, therefore, to be the most common tool type, usually described as round, semi-circular or oval. They are regularly encountered in settlement assemblages, for instance at Elspeet (Bakker 1979, 76), 'Huntedorf' on Dümmer (Reinerth 1939, 236), Dohnsen (Schirnig 1979d, 242) and Wittenwater (K. Voss 1965, Fig. 5: 18–25). They are equally numerous in Mecklenburg, for example at Gristow (Nilius 1973, 259, Fig. 16: b–f), where they were made on thick, irregular flakes; at Glasow (Nagel 1980, 33) where flake as well as blade scrapers have been found; and

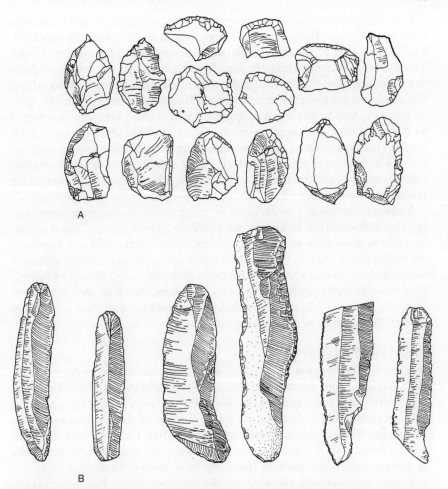

Figure 79 Flint implements from the settlement at Basedow in Mecklenburg: A-scrapers, B-blade tools (Source: Schuldt 1974a).

at Ralswiek on Rügen (Nilius and Warnke 1984, 94–7, Fig. 9), where of the seventeen tools thirteen were flake scrapers.

Blade tools are now rare, but they are still in use during the later TRB. Hoika (1987, 60–6) has distinguished a whole range of blade tools in north-east Holstein assemblages including scrapers (*Klingenkratzer*), borers and blades with concave, straight or oblique end-retouch, but they are not numerous. Small quantities of blade tools are noted at Dohnsen (Schirnig 1979d, 242) and Flögeln (Zimmermann 1979, 251), and blades are illustrated by Voss from the Wittenwater assemblage (Vos 1965, Fig. 5: 11, 17). Examples also occur in the above-mentioned assemblages from Mecklenburg.

It is important to note that throughout the area, blade tools apear in funerary contexts. Blades with gloss are found in the Dutch *hunebedden*, and blades as well as blade tools are known from megaliths in Lower Saxony, in Schleswig-Holstein and Mecklenburg. In the context of the latter, Schuldt (1972a, 83) suggests that blade manufacture (most of the blades shown no traces of use and were frequently struck from one particular core) may have played a significant role in the ceremonies associated with burial ritual. We noted earlier the inclusion of blades in the early TRB burials such as at Ostorf, and this custom appears to continue throughout the whole duration of the TRB. Moreover, it appears to be of pan-European significance, with finds of this kind known in other cultural complexes (for example, Corded Ware; Schuldt 1972a, 83–4).

Among other tools, borers, variously shaped points, hammer stones etc. are also encountered, as indeed are transverse arrowheads. These appear in various quantities in most settlement assemblages and are regularly recovered from graves. Over 100 arrowheads were discovered at Drouwenerveld and as many as 573 at Emmeln (Schlicht 1968; Bakker 1979, 77). Leaf-shaped arrowheads are relatively uncommon west of the Oder river; some are found in Mecklenburg and Lower Saxony, but their attribution to the TRB culture is not certain.

6.3.4 Southern Scandinavia

Southern Scandinavian flint research has been concerned primarily with the analysis of flint axes. Small tools have been largely neglected and the interpretation of this aspect of the TRB flint industry is very difficult. One of the immediate problems in the interpretation of the Scandinavian flint industry is the relationship between the preceding Ertebølle and the TRB culture traditions. While a number of elements, for example the continuity of certain tool types such as flake axes and transverse arrowheads, and possibly flint-working techniques (the much-reduced but nevertheless present blade technique), clearly indicate the Ertebølle culture as a source of knowledge and inspiration, the precise nature of this relationship is difficult to determine. Recent identification of clear regional styles within the Ertebølle (Vang Petersen 1984, 13–14) offers interesting possibilities for the future study of the early TRB assemblages, especially in the context of the relationship between the two complexes and in view of the TRB regional groupings apparent in the ceramic and flint axe development. Another problem in the interpretation of the TRB assemblages is the difficulty of discerning any long-term trends in the development of flint industries, trends which could be related to changes in the economy or to developing social contacts both local and distant, and which clearly exist in the context of large flint tools such as axes.

A review of the available TRB flint assemblages shows that tool manufacture was based chiefly upon flakes. This is very clearly borne out by assemblages for which published data exist. Thus, the statistics from the two assemblages at Stengade show that, with regard to production debris, flakes were forty-three times more common than blades in assemblage I (which was the later of the two), and fourteen times more numerous in assemblage II; flake tools account for 42 per cent and 55.4 per cent respectively (Skaarup 1975, 36–7). Flake-oriented production is also clearly evident in a number of other sites, for example at Sigersted III (P.O. Nielsen 1985, 114), at Havnelev where flake tools outnumber those made on blades by six to one (Mathiassen 1940, 24–5), and at Virum (Ebbesen and Mahler 1980, 16). The same situation appears to continue throughout the later TRB. While the precise data regarding waste material are lacking, the tool types most common at large settlement sites such as Troldebjerg (Winther 1935, 25–9), Blandebjerg (Winther 1943, 12–14) and Bundsø (Mathiassen 1939, 14–15), indicate beyond doubt that the flake blank was the main base for tools. A recently discussed assemblage from the MN I settlement at Penbjerg (Liversage and Singh 1985, 71) is also dominated by flake tools and Liversage comments upon the extraordinary phenomenon of producing flakes from cores to the very last, even when they were no longer suitable for tools.

The blade technique of the TRB culture is not as accomplished as that of the Ertebølle, but blank blades were produced for the manufacture of tools such as knives, denticulates and transverse arrowheads. They are more popular in the early TRB, but were made throughout the duration of the culture as is exemplified in a collection of flint blades at Trelleborg (Becker 1956, 7, Fig. 7). Following Malmer (Skaarup 1975, 35, n. 22), northern blades are classified as fragments whose width is smaller than or equal to 50 per cent of the length of a piece. Two types have been distinguished: A and B blades. The A blades are technically superior, with a regular and smooth cutting edge, and were commonly used for manufacturing knives and arrowheads; their thickness does not exceed 1 cm. The B blades are of lower quality, have irregular edges with dents and/or lateral projections, and are usually over 1 cm thick; they tend to be the more dominant blade type for tools as well as in waste material.

Among the recurrent tools from various TRB flint assemblages we can identify flake axes, knives, pointed tools (drills or borers), scrapers and transverse arrowheads as the most common tool types. The small flake axes and transverse arrowheads, the former mainly in the early TRB assemblages, represent a clear inheritance from the preceding Ertebølle culture. Among the flake axes, frequently encountered variants are symmetrical and asymmetrical axes flaked on one or both faces, and axes which are characterised only by steep retouch along the sides. With the possible exception of the Fuchsberg group, whose flint assemblages are hardly known, both types are found in all the early TRB assemblages but become less numerous later. There are, for example, only seven flake axes quoted from Troldebjerg

(Winther 1935, 26; 1938, 8), seven at Blandebjerg (Winther 1943, 12) and five at Bundsø (Mathiassen 1939, 14). In the early TRB they are found in nearly all assemblages, for example at Sigersted III (P.O. Nielsen 1985, 106–7, Fig. 10: 1, 2), Store Valby (Becker 1954b, Fig. 17: a–d, 22: b–d), Muldbjerg (Troels-Smith 1960a, Fig. 15; 1967, Fig. 6), Barkær (Glob 1949, 9), Svaleklint (Skaarup 1973, 121), Stengade I and II (Skaarup 1975, 53–4 and 115–17, Figs 49: 2–3 and 5–7, 50: 1, 17: 2–3 and 18: 1) or Lindebjerg (Liversage 1981, Figs 35: 14–16, 18–22 and 36: 28).

Another common early TRB flake axe is known as the 'Havnelev' type. This was first recognised at Havnelev (Mathiassen 1940, Fig. 1: 6–13), where it is represented by eighty-six examples (half of all the flake axes there). It is a small axe, on average between 6 cm and 8 cm long, and a distinguishing feature is the presence of the bulb of percussion at one corner of the working edge. Such axes have been identified at a number of Danish sites (for example Lindebjerg, Store Valby, Stengade) as well as among the early Swedish TRB flint assemblages at Oxie or Svenstorp (Larsson 1985, 30). According to Liversage (1981, 136), such small tools could not have been used as axes; S. Andersen and Nielsen (1982, 93) have also expressed difficulties in the interpretation of such tools from the point of view of function and possible hafting.

Transverse arrowheads form an important element within the early TRB. They are found on settlements such as Store Valby (Becker 1954b, Fig. 22: c), Sigersted III (P.O. Nielsen 1985, Fig. 12: 1–4), Havnelev (11.6 per cent of total tool assemblage; Mathiassen 1940, Fig. 1: 18–21), Lindebjerg (14 per cent of tools; Liversage 1981, Fig. 36: 1–6); on hunting stations such as Muldbjerg (Troels-Smith 1960a, Fig. 12) and Svaleklint (Skaarup 1973, 121); and in graves, for example at Dragsholm (Brinch Petersen 1974, Fig. 14). They become less numerous in settlement assemblages of the later period. At Troldebjerg, for instance, they constitute only 1.5 per cent of the assemblage and Davidsen (1978, 135) quotes an overall 1 per cent for the final TRB in Denmark. Transverse arrowheads are also occasionally encountered in megalithic graves (Ebbesen 1979a, Plate XXIV: 5–11). They are made on blades as well as on flakes, and on average are between 2 cm and 3 cm long. Among the commonly encountered forms we can distinguish regular, trapezoidal examples with a straight or pointed butt (Becker 1939, 250, type 1), straight or convex side examples (ibid., type 2) and oblique arrowheads (ibid., type 3). Although the latter appear to belong to the early TRB, Davidsen (1978, 135) does not include such examples in the late TRB contexts.

Knives represent another common tool type. At Mosegården they account for 30 per cent of tools (T. Madsen and Petersen 1985, 81) and for 11 per cent at Stengade II (Skaarup 1975, 36–7), but in a sample from Toftum they were the largest group, consisting 40.5 per cent of all tools (T. Madsen 1978a, 173). The later TRB assemblages indicate, however, that knives are becoming less numerous, ranging between 21 per cent at Hanstedgård (Eriksen and Madsen 1984, 71), 19.3 per cent at Lyø (Christensen *et al.* 1979, 85), 7 per cent at Troldebjerg, 5.7 per cent at Bundsø, and about 9 per cent for the cumulative Store Valby phase (Davidsen 1978, 132–3).

Among these specific types we can include curved knives (*Bueknive* or *Bogenmesser*), disc knives (*Skiveknive*) and possibly denticulated pieces which in the past were always thought to represent sickle knives. The curved knives have been identified by Skaarup (1975, 55, Figs 19: 5, 8–9 and 52: 1–3) at Stengade; they are easily confused with scrapers, but are distinguishable by their curved edge and a retouch steeper than that on scrapers. Apart from Stengade, these knives also come from Lindebjerg (Liversage 1981, Fig. 36: 21–4) and Virum (Ebbesen and Mahler 1980, 19, Fig. 7: 11).

An unusual form is represented by the so-called disc knives (*Skiveknive*), of which over 500 examples have been recovered at Troldebjerg (Winther 1938, Fig. 23). They can be made on flakes as well as blades, and a characteristic feature is a sharp cutting edge left deliberately between two streches of retouch. In a recent paper, Eriksen and Madsen (1984, 72) commented upon their apparent exclusiveness to all periods except MN I; are these additional examples of the ambivalent position of Troldebjerg period/style within Denmark?

Tools with a denticulated edge opposite a retouched edge are known primarily from the early TRB and become less common in time. At Mosegården they form a sizeable group (22 per cent; T. Madsen and Petersen 1985, 80), at Toftum over 9 per cent (T. Madsen 1978a, 173; however, only a small amount of the Toftum flint assemblage has been analysed so far) and count for less than 1 per cent in MN I, apparently not appearing later. Denticulated blades, many of which display a glossy edge, are regularly encountered within Neolithic assemblages. They are traditionally classified as sickle knives, and in the absence of other evidence have been used as an important indication of the growing and harvesting of cereals. It is therefore of interest to note that the microwear analysis of denticulated 'glossy' blades from Mosegården showed that they 'were used for *processing* of some kind of siliceous plant material – possibly for matting, basket making or hut building' (T. Madsen and Jensen 1982, 76).

While this analysis, carried out on a very small sample, does not mean that the function of all denticulated, glossy blades has to be revised, it does nevertheless suggest that such tools may be multi-functional, and moreover it has very important implications especially in the controversial context of the Mesolithic/Neolithic transition.

Scrapers are also a common tool throughout the entire TRB, and on many sites they form the largest group within the assemblage. This is the case in the early TRB: for example 33 per cent at Mosegården (Madsen and Petersen 1985, 79), 18.7 per cent at Havnelev (only to be equalled here by flake axes; Mathiassen 1940, 25), 31 per cent at Lindebjerg (Liversage 1981, 136), 22 per cent and 16.5 per cent at Stengade I and II (Skaarup 1975, 36–7) and 51 per cent at Virum (Ebbesen and Mahler 1980, 17). They appear to increase in importance during the later TRB for instance 62 per cent of all tools at Hanstedgård (Eriksen and Madsen 1984, 71), 68 per cent at Penbjerg (Liversage and Singh 1985, Table 1) or 73 per cent during the MN II stage at Sarup (Jeppesen 1984, 56). At the large TRB settlement sites of Troldebjerg, Blandebjerg and Bundsø they account respectively for 80 per cent, 84 per cent and 77 per cent of all tools and, for the final phase of the TRB culture, the figure is well over 70 per cent (Davidsen 1978, 132).

The scrapers do not represent a homogeneous group. They can be made on rounded, regular flakes with retouched edges known as disc scrapers; they are also made on irregular flakes as well as on blades. The dimensions also very: Stengade I scrapers, for example, measure between 3.1 cm and 8.5 cm in length and between 2.4 cm and 7.5 cm in width (Skaarup 1975, 54); Stengade II scrapers are between 2.3 cm and 7.3 cm long and between 2.2 cm and 6.5 cm wide (ibid., 117). The Virum scrapers are quoted as being between 3.1 cm and 8.2 cm in length and 3 cm and 7.4 cm wide (Ebbesen and Mahler 1980, 20, Table VI). In his study of the Lindebjerg assemblage, Liversage divided the scrapers into large roundish (1981, Fig. 36: 10–11, 14), small roundish (ibid., Fig. 36: 15–17) and longish forms (ibid., Fig. 36: 12–13, 18–20), and in recent analysis of scrapers from Penbjerg he noted a correlation between the size and weight of scrapers, which may lead to a distinction of scraper types (Liversage and Singh 1985, 71).

Interesting results were obtained from microwear analysis of scrapers from Mosegården (T. Madsen and Jensen 1982, 73–6) and scrapers from the MN II contexts at Sarup (Jeppesen 1984). In both analyses it was found that the implements were used for working wood or hide. Moreover, there appears to be no relationship between the type of scraper and its use, but the thickness of the implement's edge was related to worked material: thin-edged (on average 4.7 mm) were used on hide, while thick-edged (on average 9.4 mm) were used in activities involving working with wood. It does appear then that the typological division of scrapers (and, indeed, of any other tool) need not be indicative of the function and other factors such as the quality of raw material to be worked and an individual craftsman's skill may have played an important part.

Jeppesen has also suggested that the scrapers at Sarup were used only once and then discarded; this is seemingly the reason for such an abundance of scrapers within this assemblage. There is clearly a need for more research to establish whether the practice of discarding tools after a brief use is a universal phenomenon, although we can certainly argue against this idea in the context of axes, which were regularly reworked and broken pieces were used for making smaller implements. If the throwing away of tools can be substantiated, it would have important implications for the use of flint as a raw material. Where identification was undertaken, small tools were made from locally available surface flint which was presumably abundant. And yet, the immediate discarding of tools after use is wasteful of material even in the most prosperous economy and offers a stark contrast to the almost parsimonious use of flint noted earlier in the discussion of flint industries of the Eastern and South-eastern TRB groups.

Can such a phenomenon be identified in other assemblages, or was it perhaps somehow related to the nature of the site at Sarup and therefore confined to specific circumstances? Bearing in mind earlier comments about the nature of gloss the so-called sickles, and arguments against the traditional interpretation of such tools as harvesting implements, an interesting question arises in the context of cereal cultivation. Obviously tools were needed for the harvesting of crops; if we consider the idea of disposable tools, should we perhaps imagine the possibility that such tools were made in the field, used for harvesting and then simply throw away at the end of the day? Wood- and hide-working activities were likely to take place in most settlements, while harvesting obviously could not; should we therefore expect to find such tools within the settlement assemblages? These are problems for future research to solve.

6.3.5 Conclusions on the TRB flint industries

At the beginning of our discussion it was noted that the fragmentary knowledge and imbalanced research in the field of lithic technology hinder a cross-regional comparison of the TRB flint industries. A large component of this industry in the areas of north Germany and Denmark was geared towards the production of flint axes which we shall review shortly. This was also the case in central and south-eastern Poland, and yet there are immense contrasts in the small flint tools. The conclusion is irresistable that there was a clear trend towards the impoverishment of the tool inventory in the entire region of the TRB culture west of the Oder river. This is so much in evidence that the flint industry of Denmark has been characterised recently as 'regressive' (Liversage and Singh 1985, 78). There is clearly a great reduction in the variety of tool types, and over a period of time the scraper becomes virtually the only category of tool of any significance. What a stark contrast to the dynamic and expansive character of the Eastern and South-eastern TRB groups, where a great variety of tool types can be identified.

The extremely rich flint resources of southern Poland naturally contributed to the different character of the flint industry in this area. However, taking into consideration the extensive exchange and distribution of flint axes throughout the entire northern province of the TRB culture, one can hardly escape the impression that the availability of flint was *not* the main cause of regional differentiation in lithic equipment. While it is still difficult to point to specific factors regulating such a development, it appears that in the Eastern and South-eastern TRB groups the flint industry was diverse and apparently flourishing on all fronts, while the Northern TRB group seems to have developed a monopoly in axe production to the exclusion of all other aspects of the flint industry there. It is perhaps worth remembering that one type of tool can perform a multiplicity of functions. Indeed, it is here that future microwear analysis will assist the functional interpretation of small flint tools. The Northern TRB flint industry may yet turn out to be poor in tool types but rich in the adaptation of those types to various domestic and other tasks.

6.4 Flint axes of the TRB culture

The flint axe of the TRB culture remains the only tool form which has been extensively studied, yet even here a considerable imbalance in research may be noted, both in terms of geography and of specific approach. Doubtless the vast number of axes recovered from hoards inspired research in southern Scandinavia and Germany, where substantial analyses have been carried out from the end of the nineteenth century to the present day. The more southern provinces of the TRB culture, where flint axes are not encountered in comparable numbers, cannot provide us with detailed analyses of this tool. Here the axes are generally not singled out for specific research but are considered, if at all, together with the rest of the flint inventories. The Eastern and South-eastern TRB group flint assemblages already discussed are a good example of such an approach.

In view of this imbalance a comparative interpretation of the flint axes of the TRB cannot be undertaken. A brief description of the variety of large flint tools found within this cultural complex will suffice here, accompanied by the more detailed analysis of the northern thin-butted and thick-butted axes. These are chosen partly because they represent the most extensively studied forms, and partly because the various typological classifications serve well to illustrate the complexities in the interpretation of this seemingly simple tool form.

The earliest classification of northern flint axes rests with Montelius (1875) who, on the basis of two typological criteria – the cross-section and the relationship between the width of the butt and the cutting edge – distinguished between the two-sided point-butted and four-sided thin-butted axes, with the latter developing from the former. The thick-butted axe, which for some time had been regarded as a sort of chisel, was accorded an independent status by Sophus Müller in 1888. Soon after the new Montelian division of the Younger Stone Age into four periods based upon the forms of megalithic graves, the point-butted axe became representative of period I (Pre-Dolmen), the thin-butted axe of period II (Dolmen) and the thick-butted axe of period III (Passage Grave).

In a broader European perspective Åberg (1918) argued that in northern

Europe an independent axe development was inspired by the Mesolithic
core axes which led to point-butted, then thin-butted and finally thick-
butted axes, although Nordman (1935) was among a number of scholars
who preferred to place the point-butted axe within the kitchen midens of
the Ertebølle culture. Brøndsted (1957), Schwantes (1958) and Sprockhoff
(1938) contributed to the general discussion of the European flint axes, but
it was Becker's research which made the most significant impact upon the
typo-chronological interpretation of the TRB axes. He distinguished two
variants – the 'old' type and Blandebjerg type – among the thin-butted axes
(Becker 1957, 12–13), and three variants – Bundsø, Lindø and Valby –
among the thick-butted forms (ibid., 14–16). Further elaboration on the
subject of the thick-butted axes followed (Becker 1973a).

It is interesting to note that although Becker's axe typo-chronology, like
his studies of ceramics, was more or less universally accepted outside
Denmark, Brandt (1967) chose to develop his own typology with regard to
the north-west German material and created a scheme which not only
deviates from that of Becker, but also stands apart from the most recent
Scandinavian work carried out by P.O. Nielsen (1977 and 1979). It is this
latest Scandinavian research that opens our discussion of the northern TRB
axes.

6.4.1 Flint axes of southern Scandinavia

6.4.1.1 Point-butted axes. According to P.O. Nielsen's (1977, 65–7)
typological criteria, the point-butted axes are divided into three types, the
chief diagnostic feature being the cross-section: oval (type 1, a two-sided
axe), triangular or sub-rectangular (type 2) and rectangular (type 3, a
four-sided axe; Fig. 80: 1–3). Additionally, the curvature of the cutting
edge ranges from very strong (type 1) to gentle (type 3). Polished as well as
unpolished examples are known and differences in size suggest that, in
general, type 2 axes are shorter (average 17.3 cm) than the other two types
(18.4 cm for type 1 and 19.5 cm for type 3). The geographical distribution
of point-butted axes is clearly centred upon the eastern part of Denmark
(especially Zealand) and upon southern Sweden with only sporadic finds in
northern and eastern Jutland (Nielsen 1977, 69–72, Fig. 5).

6.4.1.2 Thin-butted axes. The thin-butted south Scandinavian axe is
thought to represent a development from the point-butted form. Using the
same set of typological criteria, P.O. Nielsen (1977, 72–82) distinguished
seven types (I–VII), all of which are known in polished as well as semi-
product versions. While individual examples may vary, his analysis indicated
specific features which allowed him to establish close correlations between
certain types. The form of the butt is one of the fundamental criteria for the
differences and similarities between types. Thus axes of types I–III are
characterised by a sharp butt (Fig. 80: 4–6), while a blunt butt is diagnostic
of types IV–VII (Fig. 81: 1–4).

Axes of type I (Fig. 80: 4) are considered transitional between the point-butted and thin-butted forms. Moreover, types I and II are closely related and differ only in the thickness of the butt (II are thicker; Fig. 80: 5) and the angle of the sides. Similarly, III and IV are distinguished from each other by their cross-section (thick-rectangular in III and thin-rectangular in VI; Figs 80: 6 and 81: 1) and by their butt shape (sharp and blunt respectively). Types VI (Fig. 81: 3) and VII (Fig. 81:4) can hardly be distinguished in their unpolished versions; the complete examples of type VII (Becker's Blandebjerg type) are unpolished on the sides. The axes vary considerably in length from 14 cm to 46.6 cm. The longest axes are of types IV (up to 46.6 cm), II (many up to 40 cm in length and 75 per cent in excess of 25 cm) and III (60 per cent exceed 25 cm in length).

Moreover, Nielsen pointed out certain regularities in the distribution as well as the use of raw materials for production of axes. Axes I–III and type 3 are made of clear or matt green Senonian flint from eastern Zealand's chalky layers. Their distribution appears to be predominantly eastern, with mid- and eastern Zealand containing the biggest hoards and longest axes. Axes of type III are particularly numerous, accounting for 24 per cent of all axes, with type I at 13 per cent and type II at 7 per cent (ibid., Fig. 7–8, 12–13). Type IV, accounting for 26 per cent, is found all over Denmark and was made of Senonian flint as well as of the dark green flint of north Jutland; a particular concentration of these axes is noted in north Jutland (ibid., Fig. 16: A–B). Types V and VI are made predominantly of the north Jutland flint and the latter has a wide distribution (ibid., Figs 18–19). Type VII is the smallest numerically (3.5 per cent) and apparently shows no particular characteristic distribution (ibid., Fig. 22).

Many of the axes are derived from hoards, and Nielsen has used the hoard material to establish spatial and chronological correlations between individual types (ibid., 90–102). Thus, hoards with axes I and II have a clear eastern distribution and appear in association with axes of type III (ibid., Figs 35 and 37). Hoards of type II are nearly twice as frequent (forty-seven hoards) and apart from their association with the above, type III is found once with an axe of type IV and once with a type VI. Since more than two-thirds of hoards come from Zealand (ibid., Fig. 37), the distribution is also predominantly eastern. Hoards of type IV are known in association with types II and VI; type V appears on its own and axes of type VI are found once with II and once with IV, with the main concentration in north Vendsyssel and northern middle Jutland (ibid., Figs 39 and 41).

Nielsen's chronological scheme of the point- and thin-butted axes,

Figure 80 Danish point-butted and thin-butted axes: 1-Pederstrup, 2-Bornholm, 3-Mørkøv, 4-Sigersdal, 5-unprovenenced, 6-Krummerup (Source: P.O. Nielsen 1977).

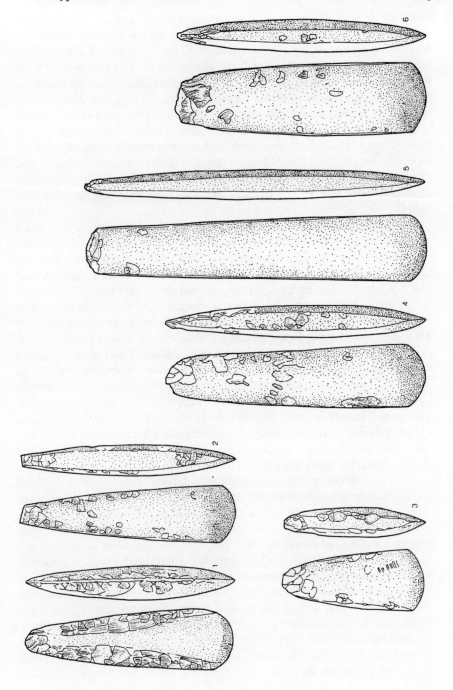

based upon associations in settlements, hoards and graves, may be summarised as follows: the point-butted axes, which develop from the
Mesolithic core axes, are characteristic of EN-A (in Becker's sense); thin-
butted axes of types I and II are diagnostic of EN-B. They are known from
settlements and hoards but are not encountered in funerary contexts;
Nielsen argued that they either precede the period of grave construction
or possibly reflect the late development in eastern Denmark of the custom
of placing an axe as one of the grave goods. Towards the end of EN-B,
axes of type III and IV appear and these dominate during the EN-C,
especially in eastern Danish hoards (type III) and Jutland's graves (type
IV). Types V and VI appear towards the end of EN-C, with IV continuing
throughout the MN I. The Blandebjerg axe (type VII) belongs mostly to
MN II.

When this typo-chronology was presented in 1977, the chronological
interpretation of the south Scandinavian early TRB culture was still largely
dependent upon the earlier tri-partite division worked out by Becker (see
Chapter 4.4.3.1 for detailed discussion). The axe typo-chronology reflected
this division by a sequential typological development from point-butted
type I through the various types to thin-butted type VII, with only minor
overlaps between consecutive types. Within the above context of the early
TRB division, the axe typo-chronology thus offered a convincing scheme
in which eastern Denmark (and especially Zealand) was seen to play a
leading and an independent role. But a fundamental reappraisal of the early
TRB from southern Scandinavia, coupled with new evidence and supported
by chronological data, have led to a new interpretation of previous theories.
The early TRB is no longer seen in terms of consecutive A, B and C stages,
but as composed of three, roughly contemporary and geographically distinct regional groups: the Oxie, Volling and Svaleklint groups (see
Chapters 4.4.3.1 and 5.3.2.1).

While the scope of this work precludes detailed analysis of early TRB
axe development, some comment may be offered in view of the above-
mentioned reinterpretations. Firstly, taking into consideration the distribution of the point-butted axes (Nielsen 1977, Fig. 5) and their contextual
associations, we may suggest that this type is diagnostic of the eastern
Danish and south Swedish Oxie group. Point-butted axes are regularly
found in settlement assemblages of this group, for example Oxie, Ebbarp,
Skabersjö and Värby (Salomonsson 1963; Larsson 1985, 30), Sigersted
III (Nielsen 1985, Fig. 8) and Muldbjerg (Troels-Smith 1960a, 597).
Moreover, it is important to note that point-butted axes can now also
be associated with funerary contexts, since a fragment of a point-butted,
bifacial axe has been found at Tolstrup II, north Jutland (T. Madsen
1975, Fig. 18; on the basis of pottery this site can be attributed to the Oxie
group).

We should note in passing that a number of Oxie sites do contain within

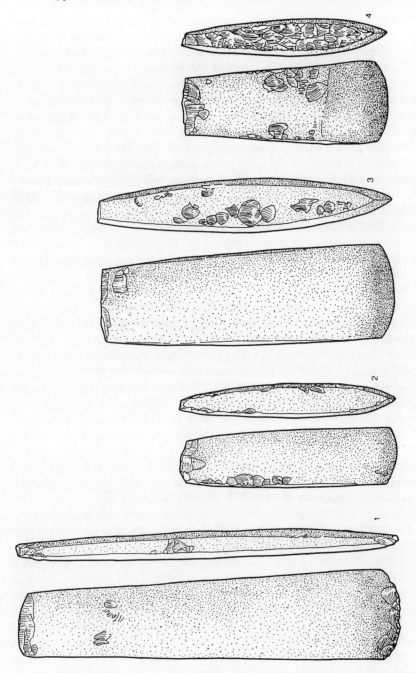

Figure 81 Danish thin-butted axes: 1-unprovenanced, 2-Tovstrup, 3-Asdal, 4-Sigerslev Mose (Source: P.O. Nielsen 1977).

their flint assemblages a number of elements of Mesolithic origin (flake axes, core axes etc.) and therefore the hypothesis of the core axe inspiring the development of the point-butted axe is not only theoretically acceptable but supported by their juxtaposition at crucial sites. On the other hand not all core axes are necessarily pointed at the butt, and examples of radially flakes adzes may have been equally suitable prototypes for thin-butted as opposed to point-butted axes. Moreover, the earlier discussed suggestion of Schindler (1953) that the flake axes provided suitable prototypes for thin-butted axes is equally appropriate; indeed, the existence of stone axes which clearly derive from the central European contexts (the so-called *hohle durchlochte Schuhleistenkeile*), while not excessively numerous, are known from the Danish Ertebølle contexts (A. Fischer 1982) and may also have provided some inspiration.

It is further interesting to observe that flint assemblages from the Svaleklint group also appear to reveal an association with axe types I and II. At Havnelev three axe fragments of type I and one fragment of types II and III have been found (Mathiassen 1940); flake axes, especially the so-called 'Havnelev' type, were also abundant, perhaps once again emphasising the connections with the earlier Mesolithic traditions. At another site belonging to the Svaleklint group, Stengade II, eight large fragments of type I have come to light (Skaarup 1975, 113). Type I axes have been identified in the flint assemblages beneath the long barrow at Lindebjerg, where 383 polished fragments (presumably derived from the reworking of polished axes) have been found (Liversage 1981, 136 and 140–2). Moreover, the presence on this site of flake axes and core axes corresponds to the situation noted at other sites, and the identification of the type IV axe (ibid., 142) throws new light upon the position of this form.

Thus, axes of types I and II may be regarded as diagnostic types of the Svaleklint group, appearing in the domestic and possibly also funerary contexts. The position of type III axes is, however, still unclear. The hoards (with one exception) are confined to this type only and therefore its relationship with other types cannot be assessed, but its existence at Havnelev may indicate that it is also related to the Svaleklint group. The association at Havnelev is not entirely satisfactory for determining whether type III should be regarded as contemporary with I and II. But we should not neglect the possibility that, within a range of contemporary forms, there may be functional as well as typological differences. It is clear that axes must have performed a variety of functions involving land clearance, preparation of timber, construction and many other tasks. Indeed, functional distinctions may be responsible to some degree for the purity of form within hoards and need not reflect chronological differences. The juxtaposition of axe types on settlement sites may be of importance in this context.

According to Nielsen's typological scheme, axes of type IV are considered later than types I and II. Axes of type IV are known all over Denmark from hoards and single finds but are particularly abundant in north Jutland around the Skive and Hjarbæk Fjords and in Vendsyssel (Nielsen 1977, Fig. 39). Moreover, it is primarily in this area that they are also known from burials – in flat graves and dolmens. Flat graves, such as Årslev, Salten, Søndergård and Skive to name but a few graves which contain type IV axes, all belong to the Volling group. A fragment of a thin-butted axe was found at Rustrup, in a context dated to 3700–3710 BC (C. Fischer 1976) and type IV axes are also known from Barkær, a Volling group long barrow complex for which a date of about 3960 BC has been quoted by Troels-Smith (1982, 46). While no actual examples have been found at the Mosegården settlement, T. Madsen and Petersen (1985) mentioned flakes with traces of grinding and polishing, which also indicate the presence of polished flint axes here.

Thus it can be suggested that, far from being a late development, the type IV axe is equally early, contemporary with point-butted axes as well as those of types I and II, representing a regional and not a chronological variant. The distribution of type IV axes in contexted finds coresponds closely to that of the Volling group. Additional support for the interpretation of the type IV as the Jutland regional axe comes from the heavy hoard concentration in the vicinity of the TRB flint mines and from the fact that locally mined Jutland flint is the predominant raw material used in the manufacture of this particular type.

The appearance of type IV axes in dolmens in Jutland as well as eastern Denmark does not preclude its early origin. The Volling group continued in existence for a long time (see Chapter 5.3.2.1); the type IV axe may have been in use over an equally long period, becoming dispersed throughout Denmark by the time dolmens were constructed. Good-quality mined flint used in the production of type IV axes may have been an important factor in creating a particular demand for this axe, not only in Denmark but beyond, and the evidence of massive-scale production at Hov and Bjerre (Becker 1980), in conjunction with the hoard concentration, further supports this idea. Moreover, if we accept that, apart from their value as tools, good-quality flint axes were also invested with symbolic value, the picture of the general distribution of type IV axes further reflects their significance within the early TRB context.

The position of types V and VI is somewhat more difficult to ascertain. Type V, manufactured from north Jutland Senonian flint, is also concentrated in the hoards and graves of north Jutland, with only a scattering of single finds over the rest of the country (Nielsen 1977, Fig. 41). Contemporaneity with type IV is confirmed by combined finds in graves but its importance, in contrast to type IV, appears to be local rather than cross-regional and its distribution argues for an interpretation in terms of a local type.

Of axes belonging to types VI and VII, Nielsen tells us that the differences are identifiable only in the finished forms. If we regard them as representatives of one type, we again note a greater concentration in Jutland (ibid., Figs 19 and 22). This axe may represent the last thin-butted form which, as in the case of type IV, acquired greater importance over the whole of Denmark. It may be a somewhat later version of the thin-butted axe, continuing well into MN II and in some Jutland regions even into MN III (Davidsen 1978, 129–30), to be replaced finally by a thick-butted axe form.

With regard to the last two types (VI and VII) the question arises whether grinding and polishing should be regarded as an important criterion affecting axe typology. Experiments in this field carried out by B. Madsen (1984, 56) appear to indicate that this process does not affect the typological characteristics of the axe, and accordingly axes in all forms of preparation should be typologically definable. On the other hand Olausson (1983) has argued that grinding and/or polishing is functionally important and it is therefore possible that specific functions did in fact require a particular method of finishing an axe, which may distinguish axes which typologically appear to belong to one and the same group. There is still insufficient evidence to determine what sort of relationship exists between the axe's function and form. One may wonder, for instance, why the later TRB axes are generally not polished along the sides; does this indicate a different function, a saving of time and effort required in their manufacture or some other fundamental change in axe production which was related to neither of these factors? Sometime during the MN II period the thin-butted axe becomes superseded by a thick-butted form; this latter version is diagnostic of the remaining part of the TRB culture.

6.4.1.3 Thick-butted axes. Becker defined the thick-butted axe types as follows: Bundsø type – an axe with a small thick butt, slightly curved face and straight sides. The greatest width is at the cutting edge, and normally only the face has been polished (Fig. 82: 1; Becker 1957, 14; 1973a, 151–4); Lindø type – an axe with a heavy rectangular butt (butt index of 50–75 per cent); practically flat face and sides and the greatest width at the cutting edge; polishing is normally confined to the face (Fig. 82: 2; Becker 1957, 14–15); Valby type – an axe with a nearly or fully square butt (butt index of 75–100 per cent), flat face and sides and the largest width at the cutting edge; as with the other types only the face appears to have been polished (Fig. 82: 3; Becker 1957, 15–16; 1973a, 157–8).

The dating of these axes was based on the study of closed contexts from settlements and as a result Becker suggested a local, Danish evolution of the thick-butted axe with each type being dominant in the relevant period: the Bundsø type in MN III, the Lindø type in MN IV and the Valby type in MN V (Becker 1957, 21–3). Bundsø was dated to MN III on the basis of

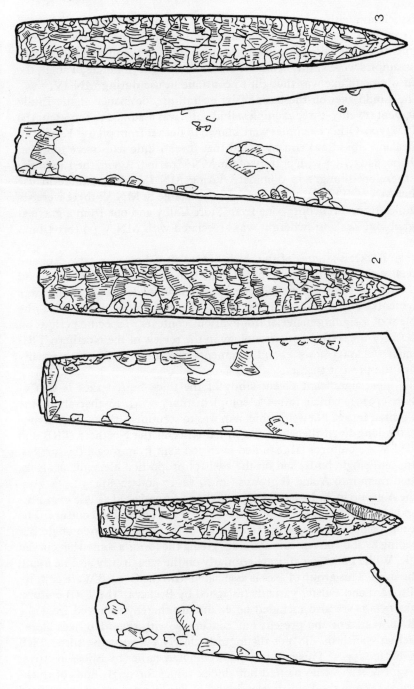

Figure 82 Danish thick-butted axes: 1–Kvoldsted (Bundsø type), 2–Gjellerup (Lindø type), 3–Gårdslev (Valby type) (Source: P.O. Nielsen 1979).

its association with that period's pottery in two pits at Trelleborg (nos 41 and 107; ibid., 21). At the Bundsø settlement itself there were fourteen fragments which were assigned to this type (ibid., 25) and since altogether five examples were known from the Lindø settlement (ibid., 26, Table), the Bundsø type of axe was thought to continue in use during MN IV.

The Lindø axe, on the basis of its overall predominance at the Lindø settlement (twenty-three examples; ibid., 26), was assumed to represent the MN IV type. Other examples were known to Becker from pit 9 at Kornerup on Zealand (ibid., 22) and he noted that three Lindø axes were found at Trelleborg together with pottery of the MN V period. Again, the Lindø axe was therefore thought to dominate during MN IV and continue in use during MN V. The Valby axe was clearly datable to MN V: there were six examples from Trelleborg, one from Store Valby and one from a grave at Ringkøbing, Zealand, where it was associated with MN V pottery (ibid., 23).

Since Becker's studies of the thick-butted axes, however, new data and especially new research – notably of Davidsen (1978), Ebbesen (1975) and P.O. Nielsen (1979) – have indicated the general inadequacies of the large settlements for chronological purposes. We have already discussed the problem of assigning material from various contexts to specific periods on the basis of the settlement chronology in the review of the Northern TRB ceramics (Chapter 4.4.3.2) and comments presented there apply equally well to the present theme.

The most significant recent study of the thick-butted axes is that of Nielsen (1979), which forms a complementary work to that about the thin-butted forms. Nielsen's chief aim was to scrutinise, through axe typology, the long-lived theory of the co-existence of the Northern TRB and Corded Ware cultures. He studied over 700 axes from megalithic graves, hoards and single finds, and on the basis of proportion elements analysis, divided them into A and B groups (ibid., 14–17 and 22–8).

The A group includes axes with straight necks and a side angle of at least 8°, and hence the Bundsø, Lindø and Valby types of the TRB culture. The B group comprises axes with straight or oblique butts, a side angle not exceeding 8° and convex/concave sides giving the forms a somewhat curved profile. While polishing appears regularly on the face, it may also be found on the sides. This group of axes is associated with the Corded Ware culture; the Brogård and Falster variants (assigned by Becker to the TRB culture; 1973a, 151–7) are also included here, and are thereby removed from the TRB context. For the present our concern is with the TRB axes alone.

Nielsen's analysis did not distinguish clearly between the three TRB thick-butted types. This has, in fact, been noted earlier by Ebbesen (1975, 147–53, Fig. 127), who plotted butt-index values for single finds of thick-butted axes from the Danish islands and noticed a clear clustering around the average value (75 per cent), which gave a distinct impression that only one type of axe, the thick-butted axe, was involved. All variations appeared to be well within the limits of statistical probability.

The Bundsø axes are not numerous; they do not appear in hoards and only twenty-eight examples are known from megalithic contexts – six in Jutland, six in southern Zealand and the rest in central and west Zealand. This type of axe, moreover, is very rare in Jutland; a few examples have been identified at the Vroue Hede funerary complex (E. Jørgensen 1977, 193–4), but in a settlement assemblage from Signalbakken, with MN III pottery and thin-butted axes of stone and flint (the latter polished on four sides), they outnumbered the Bundsø type (Davidsen 1978, 18). Davidsen has suggested that, at least in some parts of Jutland, the thin-butted axe was present during the MN I–III and that the Bundsø type may in fact represent a hybrid of the thin-butted and Lindø type axes, which appeared contemporaneously with the latter (ibid., 130).

A similar idea was hinted at by P.O. Nielsen (1979, 18). He noted, for instance, very close typological similarities between the thin-butted type VII axes and the Bundsø type, except that Bundsø axes tended to be longer. He questioned the Bundsø's independence by suggesting that it could represent a transitional form between the thin-butted Blandebjerg (VII) axe on the one hand and the thick-butted Lindø and Valby axes on the other. With reference to the Lindø and Valby axes, the crucial difference between these two types was seen previously in the different values of butt-index: 50–75 per cent for Lindø and 75–100 per cent for Valby. Neither Ebbesen's plot (1975, Fig. 127) nor Nielsen's analysis (1979, 22), however, have revealed such differences. The strong chronological significance attached to their earlier division is not so apparent in these analyses, merely a general tendency for the butt to become thicker and more square.

With regard to the TRB hoards containing both types of axes, which are dated to a general MN IV/V horizon, there are only two in which the Lindø axes outnumber the Valby type (Skaerbaek and Eggebeck; Nielsen 1979, Nos 10 and 14), interestingly both in eastern Jutland. If one excludes the east Jutland hoard at Knud (ibid., No. 13), where there were forty-eight Valby and three Lindø axes, the general proportions between the Lindø and Valby axes are 33 per cent and 66 per cent (ibid., 39). That this does reflect, to some degree, the real differences between the two types is accentuated by the very similar proportions of axes found on the Zealand settlements with the Store Valby pottery: 35 per cent of Lindø and 65 per cent of Valby axes (Davidsen 1975, 173).

What is also important is the difference in regional distribution of the Valby axes in this period, since in Jutland there are very few Lindø axes and the Valby axes account for 94 per cent of contexted finds (Davidsen 1978, Fig. 66). A similar imbalance in the Valby distribution has been noticed by Ebbesen (1975, 151, Fig. 128), who pointed out that on the Danish islands this type is numerous on Fyn, moderately represented in north Zealand and poorly represented in south Zealand, Lolland and Falster.

What conclusions can we therefore draw with regard to the subject of the Northern TRB thick-butted axes? First, we may note that the proportion analysis carried out by Nielsen does not offer such a clear division into three typologically sequential forms as had been argued by Becker. Second, the chronology of thick-butted axes cannot be fixed precisely: one can only say that the axes become thicker later in the sequence. Unless new evidence comes to light, the numerically low and chronologically insecure Bundsø type may have to be regarded as an insignificant variant inspired by the thin/thick-butted axe contact, and it will remain in a typologically ambivalent position to the Blandebjerg (type VII) and Lindø/Valby axes.

None of the researchers state this explicitly, but the typological division between the Lindø and Valby axes has become blurred, although obviously the more extreme examples of each type can be distinguished. It is now becoming questionable whether they should be distinguished as different types. If we choose to retain the division into the Lindø and Valby types, then the more numerous early associations of Lindø over Valby axes (cf. the lack of Valby type axes in Schleswig-Holstein; Hoika 1987, 41) would imply that the Lindø axe developed, or was even introduced from, outside (?) sometime during MN III, to be followed closely by the Valby type. The differential distribution of the two types during the very late TRB (Store Valby) may be a reflection of a previously existing situation, with the Lindø axes of greater importance on the Danish islands and the Valby axes in Jutland, where MN IV appears to have been of very little significance. It is possible, since there is no Valby type known in the southern end of the Jutland peninsula (Schleswig-Holstein), that the Valby axe represents a local development from Lindø and that it had assumed a leading role in Jutland.

6.4.2 Flint axes of north Germany

6.4.2.1 Thin-butted axes. The thin-butted axes of the north German plain have been studied separately in Mecklenburg (Bastian 1954) and in the area west of the Elbe (Brandt 1967). It is inconceivable that this type of axe should be substantially different either side of the Elbe, and yet a comparison between the regionally distinguished types is difficult. Different typological criteria were used by the researchers and Bastian described his types in a somewhat vague manner which precludes the recognition of similarities or differences.

There is clearly a fundamental need for a revision of views on the north German thin-butted axes. New research is necessary not only to enable correlation between Mecklenburg and north-west Germany, but also to allow a comparison with and a verification of the Danish typology outlined above. Although P.O. Nielsen (1977) indicated some correspondences between the Danish and German types, in view of the divergent set of criteria any comparison in the present circumstances is entirely superficial. Moreover, it is perhaps worth emphasising that, although new research on German axes is advocated here, we should beware of the over-typologising: complex typologies tend to accentuate the differences rather than indicate the underlying unity. Notwithstanding local differences it is perfectly clear that the thin-butted axe regional groups represent one common phenomenon within the TRB culture.

Bastian's (1954, 41–2; Fig. 84: 1, 2) a- and b-type axes apparently differ only in size, the a-type being larger, and they are characterised by a pointed butt, a flat face, a curved cutting edge and almost parallel sides. They do appear to resemble Brandt's (1967, 95; Fig. 83: 5) variant a, whose distinguishing characteristic is also revealed in the sharpness of the butt. A clear description of the Mecklenburg c-type is lacking, but Bastian indicates that the cutting edge is less curved and the polishing is often confined to the face; many are known only in a chipped state (Fig. 84: 3). This relates on the whole to Brandt's variant c (Fig. 83: 1) which has an irregular butt with somewhat curved sides. The d-type axe from Mecklenburg is the only clearly distinguished form (Fig. 84: 4), with a trapezoidal outline, a flattened butt and a maximum thickness one-third above the cutting edge. This may correspond to some of the axes included in Brandt's most numerous variant b (Fig. 83: 2). Further comparisons are not possible and it is clear that many intermediate forms cannot be classified in either of the two areas.

The chronological position of the north German thin-butted axes may be summarised as follows: in Schleswig-Holstein the thin-butted axe is associated with the TRB culture right from the beginning (Siggeneben-Süd, Boberg). Until the ambiguous finds from the Dümmer can be placed in a wider perspective, the earliest documented TRB west of the Elbe is associated with the Fuchsberg group, although this material is still relatively scantily represented. Since the association of Fuchsberg pottery and thin-butted axes is well documented in Holstein (for instance at Fuchsberg, Wolkenwehe and Sachsenwaldau), it is not unreasonable to suggest that west of the Elbe thin-butted axes were at least contemporary with Fuchsberg, although this still needs to be verified. Brandt (1967, 96–8) was able to show, through closed finds in flat graves, megalithic graves and settlements, the contemporaneity of the thin-butted axe with the early *Tiefstich* pottery and this finds support in the Netherlands (Drouwen A–C; Bakker 1979, 81). The duration of the thin-butted form is more difficult to ascertain, but it is unknown from later contexts and the sporadic associations with the Corded Ware culture are generally assumed to be secondary.

In the case of Mecklenburg we have no satisfactory evidence either to date the appearance of the thin-butted axe or to distinguish possible chronological distinctions between different types. Nilius (1971a, 56) noted that although there are very few reliable finds, thin-butted axes appear in flat graves as well as in megalithic graves; they also appear in settlements (Basedow; Schuldt 1974a, 23). Axes of Bastian's b- and d-types have been found in flat graves at the Ostorf necropolis (Bastian 1954, 47); some of the graves here clearly belong to the early TRB judging by their ceramics (two-handled amphorae, beakers etc.), but thick-butted axes as well as late TRB pottery have also been found. Bastian (1954, 45, 47) mentions a few obviously early associations (thin-butted axes and beakers in the graves at Kobrow or Wustrow), and thin-butted axes continue in use since they are known in connection with pottery which is paralleled with MN I ceramic styles in the north (Nilius 1971a, 56). It is interesting to note that the thin-butted axes from Basedow (Schuldt 1974a, 23) were assigned to the later TRB phase rather than to the early occupation of the site, although there appears to be no reason for such an assignation.

The Mecklenburg a-type is regarded as foreign and indistinguishable from the Danish axes, and it clearly incorporates several of the Danish early types; the other types, presumably, should be considered as local. The north-west German axes are more or less all considered to represent Danish exports. Indeed, the entire distribution area west of the Elbe (Brandt 1967, Map 24) is thought of as the peripheral region of the thin-butted axe province, whose centre lies in southern Scandinavia.

The above assumptions are difficult to verify. While it is likely that southern Scandinavia, and especially Jutland with its rich flint resources in the north, enjoyed a monopoly of thin-butted axe export, no petrographic analysis has so far been undertaken to examine this possibility. Bakker (1979, 80) has recently expressed doubts as to whether an investigation of the raw materials involved would identify the source of the TRB thin-butted axes, since all the north European morainic flint originally derived from Scandinavia. Yet, the study of flint raw materials from the Eastern and South-eastern TRB groups shows how successful this approach can be in tracing the extent of a particular flint type. While it would be more difficult to identify the various northern sources, an investigation of Rügen flint artefacts, for example, would provide a good starting point. Even limited identification would offer a more satisfactory interpretation than Bakker's general rule that all axes exceeding 15 cm in length should be thought of as imports from the north.

Until such investigations are carried out on any reasonable scale, our interpretation of thin-butted axes has to be based on different factors. The distribution of thin-butted axes across the North European Plain does to a

---

Figure 83 Flint axes from north-west Germany: 1-Glienitz, 2-Hamstrup, 3-Rastede, 4-Badbergen-Quakenbrück, 5-Lüneburg, 6,8-Damme, 7-Stübeckshorn (Source: Brandt 1967).

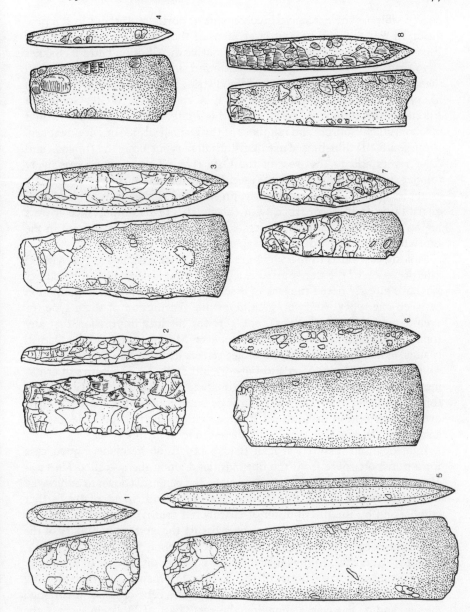

degree support the extensive involvement of northern Jutland in the provision of this tool throughout large areas of the TRB. To the west of the
Elbe the axes reveal a particularly informative distribution pattern (Bakker
1979, Fig. 43). The strongest concentration, involving one-quarter of all
the axes in this region, is noted in the district of Stade. Bakker (1979, 81)
has pointed out the significance of the Elbe crossings at Wedel-Stade and
Altona in the context of trade along this route, indicating that it would
involve Jutland sources and not those of the Danish islands or Mecklenburg.
From Stade the thin-butted axe distribution fans out along the Ilmenau and
Aller rivers and to the west of the Oste river. There is a progressively
thinner distribution along the Weser, Hunte and Hase rivers. Only a few
examples appear to have reached the present-day Netherlands. This sparser
distribution is in accordance with the much greater importance in this
region of the *Flachbeil* type, which clearly represents a local variant in the
Emsland region (Brandt 1967, Map 25).

Moving eastwards to Mecklenburg, we find that Bastian's (1954, Map 1)
interpretation of the thin-butted axe distribution is somewhat misleading.
We have already noted the lack of evidence for a chronological distinction
between axe types. And yet, looking at the distribution of the a-type (or
even a- and b-types together), one gets the distinct impression that any
traffic which took place was directly between Mecklenburg and the Danish
islands. This was doubtless possible, especially between Rügen and the
south-eastern islands (Møn and Falster), although the difficulties of crossing the Baltic should not be underestimated. However, the distribution of
thin-butted axes in Mecklenburg must be interpreted in the context of their
overall distribution in northern Europe, which clearly shows the importance of Schleswig-Holstein in the dissemination of this type.

Indeed, in an inspired article, Bakker (1976, 66–7) made a good case
for a transport route from the north Jutland along the so-called *Haervej-
Heerweg*, which follows the watershed along the peninsula down to Schleswig.
The distribution of the thin-butted axe in Jutland (incidentally further
emphasised by the distribution of chambered tombs) is clearly related to
this route; hardly any axes are known crossing the western boundary of the
clay/sand barrier of the peninsula (cf. P.O. Nielsen 1977, Figs 7, 12, 13,
16A, 18, 19 and 22). In the Holstein there is a clear divergence in this route:
1) westwards, moving north of the Treene to Husum and then skirting
along the eastern edge of Ditchmarschen to the Elbe crossing mentioned
earlier, and 2) eastwards, hugging the east coast of Holstein, across the
Trave (near Lübeck) and on to western Mecklenburg.

Because of the lack of information it is difficult to determine the relationship between the various concentrations along the Mecklenburg coast,
notably around the Wismar Bay, Recknitz Bay and Rügen with the adjacent
mainland (Bastian 1954, Maps 1, 2 and 3). It is possible that the gap
between the Wismar and Recknitz Bays may indicate a boundary between

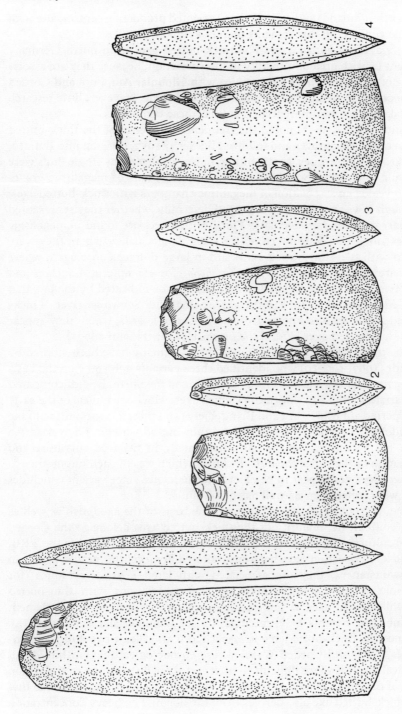

Figure 84 Thin-butted axes from Mecklenburg (Source: Bastian 1954).

the north- (Jutland) and east- (Rügen) oriented production centres, although for the time being this remains merely a hypothesis.

6.4.2.2 Thick-butted axes. The thick-butted axes from north Germany present us with greater difficulty in interpretation, because they are associated not only with the TRB but also with Globular Amphora and Corded Ware cultures. In contrast to southern Scandinavia, however, little research has taken place to differentiate between these complexes.

Nilius (1971a, 56–7) noted the frequent occurrence of the thick-butted axe in megalithic graves and followed Becker's (1957) division into Bundsø, Lindø and Valby types, commenting, however, that many single finds were difficult to classify. Schuldt's (1972a) investigations of megalithic graves also revealed an association of megalithic chambers with thick-butted axes, although it was not always possible to determine whether they represented primary or secondary deposits. Thick-butted axes are found in megalithic graves along the Warnow river (for example at Qualitz, where they were found with two thin-butted axes) and in large dolmens on Rügen, where they are regularly found with *Flachbeile* (for example at Lancken and Burtevitz). A certain regionality may perhaps be indicated by the fact that only *Flachbeile* are found in the graves along the Schwinge river. Thick-butted forms are also known from a number of hoards, where they appear with thin-butted axes, *Flachbeile* or chisels (Furthmann 1979).

The thick-butted axes from north-west Germany have been studied by Brandt (1967, 109–10) who identified three variants a, b and c on the basis of the form and two groups (1, 2) according to the finish. Brandt compared his variant a (Fig. 83: 3) with the Danish axes, which are typical of the early MN periods (Troldebjerg and Blandebjerg) and therefore, according to the Scandinavian typology, belong to the thin-butted variety. The variants b (Fig. 83: 7) and c (Fig. 83: 8) differ chiefly in the face curvature and formation of the sides; the butt thickness which was of such importance to Becker, does not appear to be of such consequence since variant c includes axes with rectangular as well as square butts.

Brandt (1967, 114) argued that, on the basis of the axe finish as well as their context, the majority of the thick-butted axes belong to the Corded Ware culture and only a small proportion should be attributed to the TRB. The axes in question have been encountered in megalithic graves where, in a few instances, they are associated with later *Tiefstich* ceramics (for example at Fahlenberg); there are also associations with thin-butted and thin-bladed axes. A few examples, moreover, derive from settlement assemblages, notably at 'Huntedorf' on the Dümmer and at Ohrsen.

Since the thick-butted axe is associated with at least two cultural complexes (TRB and Corded Ware) whose chronological relationship is still ambivalent, it is more difficult to interpret their distribution in the region west of the Elbe. As in the case of the thin-butted axe, Brandt assumed that the thick-butted axe also derives from the north. The heavy concentration in the district of Stade (ibid., Map 27) suggests not only the use of the same route, but also the continuity of contacts between the two regions. The axes are now, differently distributed, however. In some areas where the TRB culture is well represented, for example west of the Oste in the Elbe-Weser triangle, along the Ems, or in the region of Bersenbrück and Osnabrück, thick-butted axes appear sporadically. In contrast, there is a strong thick-butted axe and TRB distribution between the Hase and the Dümmer, where the Corded Ware culture is generally absent. Such a distribution may indicate that the late TRB and Corded Ware cultures used a common source, and indeed they appear to have been in competition for the northern axes. This could explain the shortage of this form in certain areas of the TRB settlement. On the other hand, the differential function of the axes (utilitarian or presige) should also be considered, although there is not sufficient evidence from the region under discussion to pursue this possibility futher at present.

6.4.3 TRB culture axe hoards

In concluding this discussion of the TRB culture flint industry, we must consider briefly the hoards of flint implements. Hoards are interpreted as collections of simultaneously deposited objects which show no apparent association either with settlement activities or with burial rituals.

Hoards of flint implements are found throughout the entire TRB culture albeit with varying frequency. They are at their densest in southern Scandinavia, with the North European Plain forming a somewhat peripheral zone. Flint hoards are not unknown from the southern TRB regions, but they are distinctly less frequent. Although by far the greatest number of hoards contain only axes, collections consisting of good-quality blades and sickle knives appear every now and then in the Eastern TRB group, for example at Radziejów (Wiślański 1969, Fig. 36). A number of hoards recovered in Mecklenburg are of mixed character, including not only axes, but also chisels or blades (Furthmann 1979).

Mixed hoards of flint and stone axes or amber beads are occasionally encountered in southern Scandinavia, but they tend to be exceptional. Most hoards comprise just axes, usually between two and four in number, but hoards with large numbers of axes are also known: the hoard of Knud contained forty-one thick-butted, twenty-three thin-bladed, four point-butted axes, three chisels and two blanks (P.O. Nielsen 1979, 38).

Over half of the axes in the thin-butted axe hoards from southern Scandinavia have been fully polished, but only a few show traces of wear; the long and medium-sized axes in particular appear to be unused. Unfinished examples reveal all the stages of production. Danish hoards on the whole reveal a strong unity of raw material, working technique and axe form. Different types of axe are rarely found in one deposit. Such a homogeneity of content, moreover, appears to be in accord with the distribution of hoards, clearly supporting the idea of a regionality of types discussed earlier.

The north German hoards generally conform to this pattern, except for the hoards which contain worked axes, in which tools of different types are found side by side. Such hoards may have had a different function.

Olausson (1983) studied the thin-butted axe hoards of southern Scandinavia in order to determine whether their composition could give any indication of the existence of prestige axes. The results of her analysis showed that, on average, axes from hoards tended to be longer than those found in settlements (25.8 cm and 15.2 cm respectively). She argued, however, that the main criterion determining the workability of an axe was not its length, but its overall proportions and weight. Moreover, there appeared to be no discernible relationship between the length of an axe and the distance from the source of raw material.

According to Olausson, different sizes of axe are associated with a multiplicity of practical functions. She argued that tools, like other objects, have practical as well as social functions within any particular cultural system; the prestigeous value of an axe was in its potential as a work tool, and as such it was not limited to any particular form.

Concerning the deposition of hoards, Rech (1979 and 1980) noted that, where find circumstances are known, the hoards can be seen to be carefully arranged deposits. Figure 85 illustrates the variety of known arrangements of axes; occasionally axe deposits were also placed under or in the vicinity of stones (for example Kalleby or Dannau, both in Holstein).

Ebbesen (1982) was able to demonstrate that, as far as the Danish evidence is concerned, there was a clear relationship between hoards, megalithic graves and the natural environment. His investigations of deposition circumstances in north Jutland near Rimsø, Skive and Højslev, showed that hoards were placed in low-lying, marshy and boggy river areas, while the megalithic tombs in the same localities were constructed on the higher, drier land overlooking the water courses. Moreover, over half of the hoards were found within a distance of 500–1500 m from the nearest megalith (although it is possible that we should regard the megaliths as being constructed in the vicinity of these deposits and not necessarily *vice versa*).

While at the simplest level the hoards of axes show the abundance of flint within the TRB culture, our knowledge and perception of this and related phenomena makes it plain that hoards cannot be interpreted in isolation and that they must be placed alongside other elements within the world of social and cultural traditions. The choice of waterlogged environments for acts of deposition which, apart from axes, involved amber beads, pottery and animal remains to name but a few, suggests that land of marginal economic value was nevertheless of great importance within the local social system. The existence of local ritual areas, exemplified in votive deposits,

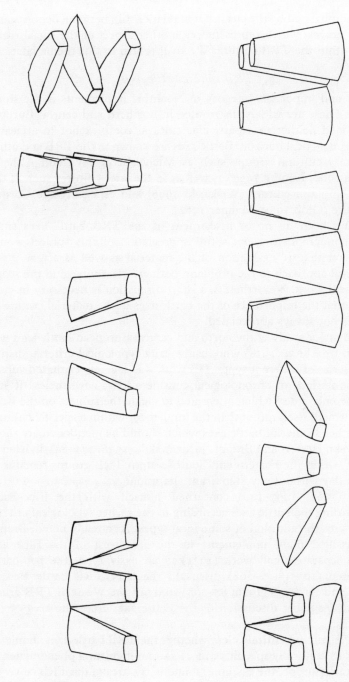

Figure 85 Arrangement of axes in hoards (Source: Rech 1980).

is further emphasised by the clear spatial relationship between deposits and megalithic graves, which represent yet another aspect of the social/ritual tradition within the TRB culture. We shall return to this theme later.

6.5 TRB culture battle axes

A separate and important category of Neolithic implements is the stone battle axe. These are widely distributed in northern and central Europe, being confined neither to a particular cultural complex nor to a clearly defined chronological horizon. Battle axes are known in the TRB and other contemporary cultural groups such as Michelsberg, Pfyn and Altheim (Driechaus 1960; Lüning 1967) as well as in the later cultures such as the Globular Amphora culture (Wiślański 1966) and especially the Corded Ware culture (Glob 1945; Malmer 1962).

There has been no major assessment of the TRB battle axes since Brandt's monograph in 1967; a full appreciation of this subject would require a complete re-evaluation of the material as well as a new typo-chronological approach to the problem: both are clearly beyond the scope of the present work. Nevertheless, a short discussion is necessary in view of the fact that the importance of the battle axes in the material culture of the TRB is not always appreciated.

The first major study of the north and central European battle axes was undertaken by Åberg (1918) who, using strict typological criteria, distinguished a series of different types. His work was severely criticised subsequently for its lack of chronological considerations; nevertheless it still remains the only study which attempted to tackle the subject on the basis of the implement itself rather than the implement within a specific cultural context. Other studies of battle axes which should be mentioned are those of Jażdżewski, Herfert and Brandt. Jażdżewski's (1936, 271–84) division of battle axes within the Eastern and South-eastern TRB groups remains in use to this day without any significant alteration.

Herfert (1962, 1097–140) concerned himself with the Elbe-Saale region, dividing the battle axes according to the earlier typological criteria of Åberg, with the addition of some local types. As already noted, Brandt (1967) classified these implements in the area west of the Elbe and devoted a separate small work (1971) to an early type, the flat battle axe. Ebbesen (1975, 172–208) discussed the later TRB battle axes in Denmark, and Bakker's (1979, 87–108) study of the Western TRB group also included a short discussion of the battle axes from the area of the Netherlands.

While it is still not entirely clear whether the TRB battle axes should be considered as culturally specific or more as a multicultural phenomenon in contemporary Europe, the examples found in the area of the TRB culture's distribution show certain important features. The primary diagnostic element, which distinguishes them from the later Corded Ware forms, is the extraordinary symmetry of the axes: the blade, seen from the side, is always straight or expands symmetrically either side of the long axis of the implement (Fig. 86). This feature was noted in 1936 by Jażdżewski and has been confirmed by other scholars.

Taking into consideration all the available studies, three major types of TRB battle axe can be distinguished: 1) flat battle axe (*Flache Hammeraxt*, Brandt 1967, 20–7; X-type, Jażdżewski 1936, 278–9); 2) knob-butted battle axe (*Knaufhammeraxt*, Brandt 1967, 27–32; *topór z guzikowatym obuchem*, Jażdżewski 1936, 273–8); 3) double battle axe (*Doppelaxt*, Brandt 1967, 34–43; also included is the Y-type of Jażdżewski 1936, 279–84). In the Danish literature the first two types are generally known by the name *mangekantøkse* (polygonal battle axes; Becker 1954b, 196), although examples with either a polygonal or an oval cross-section are known (Glob 1952, 20, Nos 93–104).

Battle axes are found even less frequently in secure contexts than flint axes, and although the double axes are clearly later than the other two types, the precise chronological position of each type still remains to be established satisfactorily.

6.5.1 Flat battle axes

On the basis of associated finds, the flat battle axe appears to belong to the early TRB culture and is found throughout most of its area. Two basic forms have been distinguished by Jażdżewski (1936a, 278) and later by Brandt (1967, 71): one with gently curving sides and a more or less oval cross-section (Fig. 86: 1–3), the other with angular (multi-faceted) sides and therefore a hexagonal cross-section (Fig. 86: 5–6). The butt end may be flat or rounded, the blade straight or splaying slightly outwards and the upper/lower face either flat or trough-shaped.

Apart from stray finds, a few flat battle axes are known from early TRB settlements such as Havnelev (Mathiassen 1940, Fig. 1: 14), Engern-Brinkhof (Brandt 1967, Fig. 40: 13), Boberg (Brandt 1961) and Hundisburg (Preuss 1966, Plate 53: 2); from graves such as Frauenmark (Beltz 1910, 106), Melzow (Preuss 1966, 91), Dragsholm (Brinch Petersen 1974, Fig. 13) and Rustrup (C. Fischer 1976, Fig. 35); and even in hoards such as Först Mützelburg (Brandt 1971, 67). On the basis of the association of multi-facetted battle axes with Fuchsberg pottery (for example at the settlement of Schöningstedt; ibid., 74, n. 5), Brandt argued that this version developed later than the axe with curved sides. He also mentioned the now-lost flat battle axe from Miedwiedzko (Madüse), whose form is not known but which was found together with typical Wiórek pottery as well as a knob-butted axe (ibid., 73; Jażdżewski 1936, 278). However, the find of a multi-facetted flat battle axe at the Rustrup grave (which, judging by the C-14 dating, is earlier than that from Dragsholm, where an axe with rounded sides was found) suggests that both forms – rounded and polygonal – were equally early and may have continued throughout the Fuchsberg-Wiórek horizon. More precise dating is not possible at present.

6.5.2 Knob-butted battle axes

The knob-butted axe (Fig. 86: 4, 7–8) is also encountered in a large area of the TRB culture's distribution as well as beyond, and this type of battle axe appears to have had a wide popularity. According to Jażdżewski (1936, 273) and Brandt (1967, 27), the diagnostic feature which distinguishes this type from others is the presence of a well-defined knob at the butt end; the cross-section, the presence or absence of a collar round the shaft-hole and the shape of the blade are all of secondary importance. It is to this type of battle axe in particular that in the north the name *mangekantøkse* (polygonal, multi-facetted) has been applied, as most examples appear to have a hexagonal cross-section (Glob 1952, Figs 93–9).

The knob-butted axes are very common in the Eastern TRB group, where examples with hexagonal, lenticular or oval cross-section are known (Jażdżewski 1936, 275–8, Figs 939–48). One of the primary graves in the earthen long barrow at Rybno (ibid., 191) contained knob-butted battle axe with a lenticular cross-section; it was associated with a collared flask which could date to the Pikutkowo phase. A miniature clay model of a similar battle axe from a contemporary settlement at Nowy Młyn supports this supposition. Moreover, this type of battle axe appears to be the only type found in the South-eastern TRB group (Wiślański 1979, 234). Finds from western Pomerania support the presence of flat battle axes as well as knob-butted axes on sites with Wiórek-phase pottery (Siuchniński 1972, 92–5), so this type also appears to be relatively long-lived.

In the Northern TRB group knob-butted axes have been found in dolmens such as Emmedsbo and Skærvad, and in flat graves such as Vedskølle and Tornby (Thorvildsen 1941, 63; Becker 1947, 157). At Emmedsbo the battle axe was accompanied by type IV thin-butted flint axes (P.O. Nielsen 1977, 133, No. 16), which are typical of the Volling group. This type of battle axe may therefore have become popular during the late Volling/Virum/Fuchsberg horizon. Becker (1947, 244) argued for a general change from the *mangekantøkse* to the double battle axe type at the beginning of MN I, but the latter may have been developed earlier, and for a while at least been contemporary with the knob-butted type in this area.

Knob-butted axes are mentioned in association with the Altmark *Tiefstich* by Behrens (1973, 96), but notably not by Preuss (1980). The examples from the Western TRB group appear to be relatively late (on the Hümmling they derive from large chambers; Brandt 1967, 29) and are distinguished by

---

Figure 86 Battle-axes of the TRB culture: 1-Schöningen, 2-Bremervörde, 3-Schauen, 4-Dobre, 5-Bevern, 6-Delbrück, 7-Fladderlohausen, 8-Westerholtsfeled (Source: Brandt 1967; Wiślański 1979).

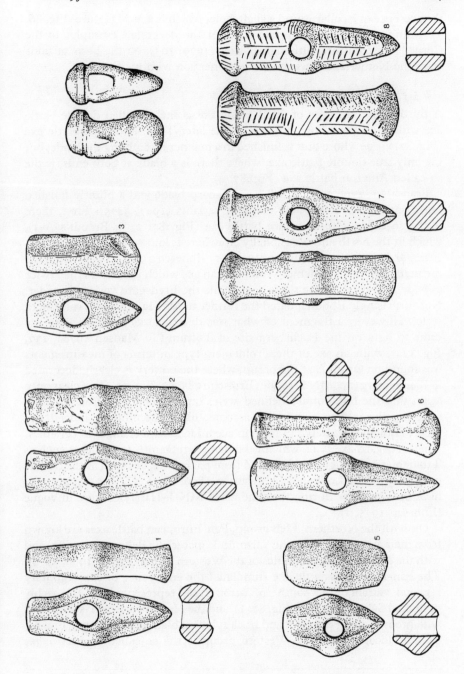

the presence of a collar round a shaft-hole, which is a local feature (Fig. 86: 7). Brandt was inclined to date some of the decorated examples to the Corded Ware culture, although Bakker (1979, 105), on the basis of finds from the Netherlands, argued for a connection with his E-phase.

6.5.3 Double battle axes

A third important type of TRB battle axe is the so-called double battle axe which, on the whole, belongs to the later TRB. A double battle axe (Fig. 87) is one whose butt is finished in a manner resembling the blade, but the only true double battle axe, where there is a blade at both ends, is the so-called Amazon battle axe (Fig. 87: 4).

Brandt's A-type axes, which have a sharp blade and a bluntly finished butt, actually cover a whole range of variants (1967, 34–5). First, there is the so-called *Pan-European* battle axe (Fig. 87: 2, 3; Brandt's A-1), which in the north and occasionally elsewhere is known as the *Troldebjerg/ Fredsgård* battle axe (Nilius 1971a, 71–2; Ebbesen 1975, 175–7). Ebbesen distinguished the Troldebjerg variant as an axe which is no more than twice as wide as it is tall at the shaft-hole, while the Fredsgård variant is wider. Not surprisingly Ebbesen dated the former to MN Ia (i.e. the Troldebjerg style). However, a fragment of what was described as a Troldebjerg axe came to light on the Fuchsberg site of Toftum (T. Madsen 1978a, 177, Fig. 12a), while an axe of the Troldebjerg type in terms of measurements was found on Ørum A at Fannerup, where the pottery is clearly decorated in Blandebjerg (i.e. MN II) style (Eriksen 1985, 54, Fig. 33). It is clear once again that the fine pottery-defined styles do not identify chronologically separate phases, nor should we assume that stone/flint, or indeed any other, implements altered in form in accordance with changes in ceramics. The Fredsgård axe type, which is known from Danish settlements such as Troldebjerg and Signalbakken, and from passage graves such as the double passage grave at Lodnehøj (A. Madsen 1896, Plate XXV: 5), appears to have been popular during the time when MN I–III styles were in vogue (Ebbesen 1975, 188).

Outwith the Northern TRB group, Pan-European battle axes are known from their association with the Salzmünde materials (Behrens 1973, 87) and with the early *Tiefstich* ceramics of the Western group (Preuss 1980, 58–9). The Pan-European battle axe stimulated the emergence of contemporary regional variants: the southern *Saxon type*, represented by the richly decorated Salzmünde axes (Fig. 87: 1), and the *Harz type*, which is decorated with grooves along the sides and has a splaying blade and butt end (Fig. 87: 6). The local type in the Western group is the so-called *Hannover axe*

Figure 87 Battle axes of the TRB culture: 1-Radwell, 2-Vehr, 3-Bruchwedel, 4-Steinbeck, 5-Buxtehude, 6-Harras, 7-Wąsewo, 8-Wallendorf (Source:Jażdżewski 1936; Brandt 1967; Bakker 1979).

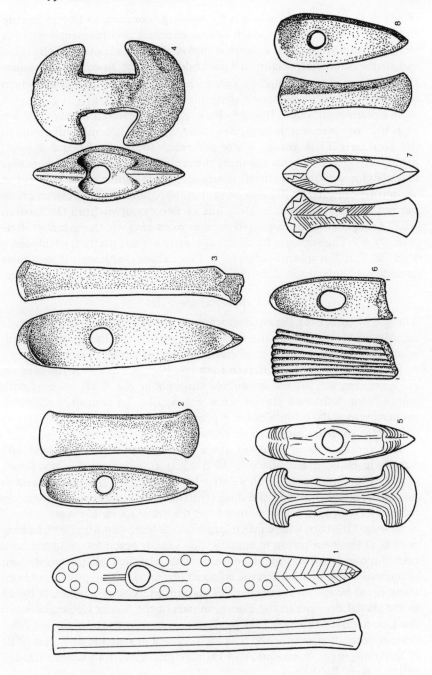

(Fig. 87: 5), whose distribution is by and large confined to Lower Saxony and the Netherlands and which is characterised by ornamental grooves along the sides and a collar round the shaft-hole. In the Eastern TRB region and to the south, especially in Czechoslovakia, the so-called *Bohemian-Polish* variant is represented by axes with a polygonal cross-section, which are occasionally also decorated along the sides (Fig. 87: 8).

As already mentioned, Brandt's B-type, the *Amazon battle axe* (Fig. 87; 4), is the only true double battle axe (1967, 35–6). It is commonly found in the Northern TRB group, where Ebbesen (1975, 177–84 and 189–98) distinguished five variants spanning the entire MN Ib to MN V sequence. It is also known from Walternienburg-Bernburg contexts (for example at Walternienburg itself; Behrens 1973, Fig. 39: c) and in the Western group but not in the Netherlands. Only one or two examples from the Eastern TRB group could be regarded as approximating to the Amazon type (Fig. 87: 7). The Amazon battle axe is clearly at least partly contemporary with the Pan-European battle axe and its variants, although it may have gained in popularity at different times throughout the distribution area.

6.6 Amber in the TRB

The use of amber for personal adornment is deeply rooted in the preceding Mesolithic tradition across the entire area of the European lowland, exemplified in the excellence of craftsmanship of amber objects fashioned by hunter-gatherers (S. Andersen 1982, 75, Fig.; S. Andersen and Nielsen 1982, 74, Fig.). This use continued throughout the TRB culture, with amber being fashioned into personal ornaments; the material's magnetic properties may have contributed especially to the use of amber objects as amulets or to their placement in graves and votive offerings.

This resinous fossil is found along the western coast of Jutland and Schleswig-Holstein and all along the Baltic coast where, to this day, lumps of amber are cast up on the shore after heavy storms. These pieces tend to be relatively small, but in the nineteenth century amber was deliberately fished out with nets a few metres from the shore along the west coast of Schleswig-Holstein, where much larger pieces were deposited by breaking waves. There is no reason to suppose that similar practices could not have been followed during the Neolithic. The so-called Baltic amber can occasionally also be found in the adjacent lowlands, where pieces had been transported by ice during the various glaciations. Amber is regularly found in the glacial deposits in the European part of the Soviet Union, between the Donetz and the lower Dniepr. Baltic amber, in contrast to that from other sources, is characterised by a high content of succinic acid. It may be either transparent or opaque, and variable in colour from white, through yellow-green, light brown, orange, red-brown to very dark red (Schuldt 1974b, 113–15).

Various beads of amber and, more rarely, amber discs, are found throughout the entire early TRB culture, and amber beads were regularly placed in graves even as far south as Little Poland (Jażdżewski 1936, 305; Wiślański 1979, 244, Fig. 141: 10, 14, 19, 20, 23). Jażdżewski mentions an enormous raw amber find from a TRB settlement near Wrocław which contained 400–500 kg of amber, giving some indication of the importance of amber as a trading commodity. Although amber objects are found everywhere in the TRB, the largest quantities are known from Denmark, and it is generally believed that the west coast of Jutland was the chief supplier of the raw material.

Brøndsted (1957, 184–5) has already noted that over 90 per cent of early TRB amber finds (mostly from graves and votive offerings) are confined to the northern part of the Jutland peninsula; particularly strong concentrations are known around the Limfjord and in Vendsyssel. Amber beads were regularly placed in graves, for example at Salten (Becker 1947, Fig. 53) and Ølstrup (ibid., 254), but usually no more than 100 beads accompanied any one burial. The votive offerings, on the other hand, contained large numbers of beads placed in vessels; the amber find from Laesten contained over 4,000 beads weighing in total 8.5 kg, while at Mollerup 13,000 beads were found in one deposit (Brøndsted 1957, 185).

Short or long tubular amber beads are the most common variety and these were made and used throughout the TRB. Other types of bead are pear-shaped, tear-shaped or conical; in addition there are spacer beads and unperforated end pieces for the fastening of necklaces, and the unusual amber rings which are known from Mecklenburg (Schuldt 1974b, 112, Fig. 14) and Little Poland (Wiślański 1979, Fig. 141: 20, 23). Very characteristic of the early TRB culture are amber discs, which have been found in graves in Denmark (Sjørup and Skibshøj; Midgley 1985, 298); similarly decorated pieces have also been found in Mecklenburg, once in a bog at Zülow (Fig. 88: 1) and with early pottery in an extended dolmen at Friedrichsruhe (Schuldt 1974b, Fig. 2), the latter with a close Danish parallel from the Boel dolmen (Randsborg 1970, Fig. 5). These are flat discs, roundish, oval or triangular in shape, often with perforations at the centre or edge; some are additionally decorated with pits all the way round the edge. Such discs are generally assumed to imitate the similarly decorated copper discs (see below).

Although amber beads, especially those of tubular form, continue in use throughout the TRB, another form of popular amber ornament is the miniature battle axe. Such amber axes, on average between 2 cm and 4 cm long, are most commonly found in passage graves and contemporary flat graves in Denmark and Mecklenburg. They are also encountered, albeit less frequently, in Lower Saxony, but only rarely in the Eastern and South-eastern TRB groups; in the latter areas, however, many miniature knob-butted axes made in clay are known.

The amber battle axes most frequently appear to imitate the Amazon type (Fig. 88: 2), although club-shaped miniatures are also known (Fig. 88: 3). Schuldt noted an interesting discrepancy between the frequency of amber battle axes in the Mecklenburg graves (over 100 examples) and the actual Amazon battle axes (only two examples), with a few stray finds here and there. All the examples of miniature battle axes have perforations, and their use in the composition of necklaces is known from the Danish passage graves, for example from Græse on north Zealand (Brøndsted 1957, Fig. facing p. 282). In Mecklenburg usually only a few miniatures are found in graves, the exception being the passage grave at Gnewitz where small and larger beads were presumably set one against the other (Schuldt 1974b, 108). The large number of amber battle axes in Denmark, with a diminishing quantity further away, suggests that Denmark was, if not the centre of production, at least the chief provider of the raw material for their manufacture.

The miniature battle axes found in Poland, mostly in the south-east but sporadically also in the territory of the Eastern group, differ from the northern examples in a number of respects. Although a few amber and bone miniatures are known (Fig. 88:5), they are made primarily of well-fired clay and represent the most popular local form, the knob-butted battle axe (Fig. 88: 7, 8). Moreover, in contrast to the Northern TRB group, they are not found in graves but occur on settlement sites such as Ćmielów, Gródek Nadbużny, Krężnica Jara and many others. The miniatures do not exceed 9 cm in length and, while generally provided with a shaft-hole, being made of clay were not suitable for wearing round the neck or being otherwise attached to garments; none show any traces of wear round the shaft-hole and it has been argued that they were hafted on sticks (Bąbel 1980a, 20).

In an interesting paper discussing the cult of the battle axe among the Neolithic communities in Poland, Bąbel (1980a), relying upon a combination of archaeological and mythological evidence, traced the origin of this cult to the earliest farming communities in the Near East and argued for its widespread practice across Neolithic Europe. He concluded that the battle axe played an important role in cult activities and became a symbol of a male deity associated with thunder, rain and water. While his arguments cannot be pursued here in any great detail, it is perhaps worth observing that, as raw material, amber appears on the shores precisely in circumstances of thunder, rain and water. This 'source of origin', as well as the already-noted magnetic properties of amber, may well have made it an extremely suitable material for the manufacture of symbolic battle axes. The different contexts

---

Figure 88 Amber and clay objects from TRB contexts: 1-Zülow, 2-Gnewitz, 3-Poggendorfer Forst, 4-Skovager, 5-vicinity of Sandomierz, 6-Forst Mönchgut, 7-Ćmielów, 8-Nowy Młyn; 1-6-amber, 7,8-clay (Source: Glob 1952; Schuldt 1974b; Bąbel 1980a).

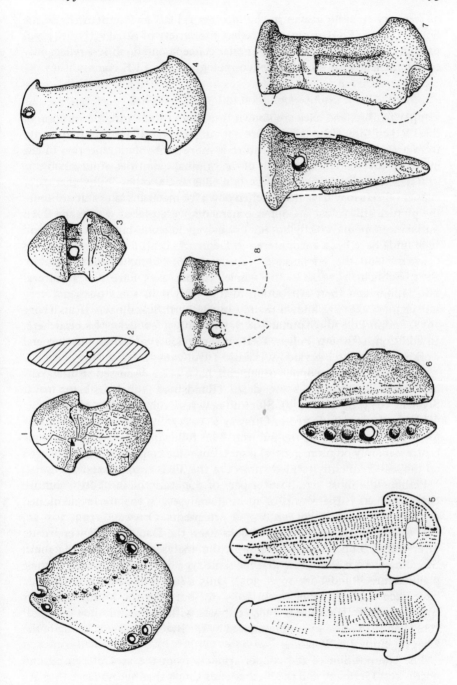

of recovery (mainly graves in the Northern TRB and settlements in the South-eastern TRB group) may reflect the variety of ritual activities practised in expressing an essentially similar concept, and doubtless reflect only one element within the complex cosmology of the TRB communities.

6.7 *Copper finds in the TRB culture*

Copper trinkets and axes are known throughout the entire distribution of the TRB culture, although they are not numerous and they vary in quantity from area to area. The latter feature is more probably a reflection of the intensity of research rather than of the original quantities of metal objects in use; the corrosive nature of certain soils and the possibility that early copper objects may have been melted down for metal at a later stage obscure the picture still further. Copper ornaments were placed within the TRB burial monuments, chiefly but not exclusively in stone-built chambers, and such finds have been encountered in Denmark, central and north-western Germany and the Netherlands (Preuss 1966; Schrickel 1968; Ottaway 1973; Schlicht 1973). On the whole, copper axes have fewer cultural associations and their attribution to the TRB is in some cases not very satisfactory; axes are known mainly in southern Scandinavia (Randsborg 1978) and in Poland (Szpunar 1987), with only a few examples elsewhere. In addition, southern Polish TRB sites provide evidence for local metal working in the later period (Wiślański 1979, 236–9).

The TRB culture copper ornaments have been discussed in the archaeological literature in some detail (Randsborg 1970; Ottaway 1973; Schlicht 1973; Bakker 1979). Since no new research has taken place in this field, the reader is referred to Ottaway's (1973) study of the TRB trinkets for a good overview of the subject. The following discussion will concentrate mainly on more general issues, but some comments will be offered on the less frequently tackled subject of the TRB copper axes.

Perhaps the most significant aspect of the study of the TRB's culture copper objects is the results of spectral analyses. In the above-mentioned work on the north European copper ornaments, Ottaway (1973, 305–10, Fig. 9) demonstrated that the trinkets from the Danish TRB were made of arsenical copper (her C-3 group); the analyses of some of the south Scandinavian flat axes show that the same type of copper was used in their manufacture (Randsborg 1978, 305). Only a few of the Polish TRB finds have been analysed (Pieczyński 1985, 6), but here too arsenical copper appears to have been used. This contrasts with the mainly non-arsenical composition of the copper objects used by the Brześć Kujawski group of the Lengyel culture in Poland.

The composition of the copper trinkets from the area of central and north-west Germany and the Netherlands shows that by and large they are made of non-arsenical coppers. This suggests that the Danish and Polish TRB groups obtained their copper probably in the form of finished articles rather than as raw material, and from a source different from that which provided the westerly regions of the TRB. Moreover, the Polish TRB copper seems to have come from a source different from that which supplied the Lengyel communities with their splendid ornaments.

Copper objects do not feature prominently in the early TRB culture in Poland. From the very early contexts we can only quote traces of copper substances which were found by Gabałówna (1970a, 82) beneath barrow No. 8 at Sarnowo and a copper ring recovered by Jażdżewski (1936, 177) from the cultural layer at the base of barrow No. 1 at Leśniczówka.

Flat copper axes, very similar to those from Denmark, are known from stray finds along the Oder and to a lesser extent the Vistula rivers, and a few examples are found scattered throughout the country (Szpunar 1987, Table 34). They are mostly the so-called Bytyń type (named after the famous hoard from Greater Poland) which appears in two variants: slightly trapezoidal or rectangular, up to 17 cm in length. Szpunar catalogues forty axes of this type as well as a number of related types which may also belong to the TRB culture (ibid., 11–18). A Bytyń-type axe was found with later TRB material at the settlement of Kornice in Silesia and there are a number of hoards ascribed to the TRB culture.

The best-known is the Bytyń hoard, discovered in 1873 (Pieczyński 1985). Apart from six flat axes it also contained two copper figures of oxen, which were apparently joined together by a yoke. One of the axes is now lost and it is only known from drawings and descriptions made in the 1870s by Virchow. Four of the axes (inclusive of the lost example) are hexagonal in cross-section and were cast in bivalve moulds, while the remaining two are less well made and appear to have been cast in an open mould (ibid., 4); they were all made of arsenical copper (between 0.4 and 1 per cent), as indeed were the two oxen (2.3 per cent and 4 per cent of arsenic; ibid., 6). The oxen were most probably cast using the *cire perdu* method and the yoke in fact appears to have served as a pouring funnel. This hoard should probably be assigned to the TRB culture, but the oxen at least must have been made in a metallurgically more advanced region to the south or south-east.

Only small quantities of copper objects have been found on the TRB settlements in Poland, mostly in the South-eastern group. From Gródek Nadbużny we may note three needles, an awl, a fragment of a an axe, spirals and a copper ring. At Zimne, on the Wolhynian Plateau, there were found three cast and hammered native copper axes (Jastrzębski, pers. comm.); a strongly arsenical copper awl (2.5 per cent) was found at Niedźwiedź, and small quantities of copper were also noted at Bronocice (Hensel and Milisauskas 1985).

Crucibles as well as copper slag from the settlements at Gródek Nadbużny and Ćmielów suggest that some copper working, however experimental, was taking place, and burnt clay tubes from Janówek in Silesia have been interpreted as fragments of bellows (Wiślański 1979, 237). On the basis of

C-14 dates from Ćmielów (see Appendix) it is reasonable to assume that the smelting of copper should be associated with the Classic phase of the TRB in this area, taking place from 5000 BP (3800 BC) onwards. Similar evidence for early metal working in the southern regions of the TRB culture has come to light at the settlement of Makotřasy in Bohemia (Pleslová-Štiková 1977). Here too crucibles and copper slag have been found; spectral analysis of the latter shows that arsenical copper was used and it has been suggested that its source may have lain in the east Alpine region. Similarities in the material culture and the use of Swabian silex, suggest that the Bohemian TRB may have had connections with the Altheim group.

The south Scandinavian flat copper axes are very similar to the Bytyń type and they very probably share a common source of origin. They occur in a few hoards, but by and large are found singly as stray finds. Occasionally they are accompanied by other copper objects, for example at Bygholm near Horsens, where four axes, three spiral rings and a copper dagger were deposited in a clay vessel (Brøndsted 1957, 188, Fig.). Randsborg (1978, 306) divided the so-called Bygholm-type flat axe into two variants: one, known from Bygholm itself, has a sharply defined butt and edge (ibid., Fig. 1: top left), and the other is a more rounded form with arched broad sides (ibid., Fig. 1: top right). The former is mostly found in western Denmark, while the latter appears east of the Great Belt. Another variant, less numerous, is the so-called tongue-shaped axe which is less well made and so far has been found mainly in the central part of Denmark (ibid., Fig. 3).

On the basis of the size and especially the weight of the copper axes, Randsborg argues that the axe distribution reveals a pattern wholly compatible with their suggested function as a means of exchange from the 'primary' areas (that is east central Jutland, Scania and the island of Fyn) to the peripheral zones, where lighter axes are more common and from where commodities such as flint and amber could have been obtained (ibid.). We do not known whether this was the sole function of the copper axes; they may also have served as tools, perhaps reserved for special tasks. If, as Randsborg suggests, the weight of the copper axes was a significant factor in determining their distribution, then a contrast emerges with regard to the nature of the distribution of the flint axes in the region. As discussed earlier in this chapter, Olausson's (1983) study of the flint axe hoards showed that there was no relation between the length (and thus by implication also weight) of the axe and its distance from the precurement source. In other words, long and short (heavy and light) axes were being exchanged without discrimination. Although the distribution pattern of copper axes in relation to weight is not as clearcut as Randsborg suggests, lighter axes do tend to be more dominant in the peripheral areas. One may therefore ask why there should be such a difference between the distribution of copper and flint axes.

Randsborg has attempted to interpret this pattern in terms of the function of copper axes as an exchange medium; but saying that the pattern 'can not be taken to imply a local axe production' (1978, 306) does not explain why such a pattern should emerge. We cannot estimate the actual number of copper axes that reached southern Scandinavia during the TRB, but judging by the overall presence of copper in northern and central Europe at that time, the numbers could not have been very high. Thus, if we accept that copper axes were a rare and yet desirable commodity and were used as an exotic means of exchange, then it is reasonable to suggest that, through the economical use of the material, for example by recasting into smaller and therefore lighter implements, more axes would have been available for exchange. Is it therefore not possible that at least some of the 'imported' axes were recast? Here may lie the explanation both for the presence of more lighter axes in the periphery and for the existence of the less shapely tongue-axes. Indeed, Randsborg comments upon the relatively poor quality of the northern axes, saying they were 'almost like bars' (ibid., 306); surely we are talking here about ingot axes. The Bytyń hoard from Poland with its combination of bivalve and smaller open-cast axes may be an example of local recasting.

So far no archaeological evidence from southern Scandinavia has come to light to support the idea that axes were recast locally. Indeed, Randsborg argued that because of the dangers involved in working with arsenical copper the 'arsenical copper province is consequently both a proof of the nonexistence of metallurgy in Denmark in the Early Neolithic and of the status of the copper axes as a medium of exchange, rather than as tools of practical use' (ibid., 306). This is a reasoning with which one may take issue. The arsenic copper axes found in southern Scandinavia prove one thing only: that in the absence of local raw material, axes of arsenic composition found their way into this region; they neither prove nor disprove anything else.

Even more obvious is the fact that these arsenical axes were produced by someone, somewhere, and the accruing evidence from central Europe for metallurgy based on the use of arsenical copper shows clearly that it was a highly skilled and accomplished activity. In her study of the early copper technology in the Alpine zone, which was based to a large extent upon the use of arsenical copper, Ottaway (1982, 196) was able to conclude: 'However small the quantities of metal used . . . they are not the results of stumbling efforts of people who did not really know what they were doing'. If we therefore accept that early metalsmiths were accomplished craftsmen who were able to work with arsenical coppers, there is no reason to believe that such skill and knowledge could not have been passed together with the traded objects. We do not as yet know which source and which area provided the TRB communities in Poland and southern Scandinavia with copper objects and copper technology although, in the context of arsenical copper, an east Alpine source is perhaps more probable than other, more remote regions.

Moreover, is it not simplistic to assume that the Early Neolithic communities of northern Europe would be desirous of metal objects without having any interest in the properties of the raw material from which they were made? Indeed, the evidence for metalworking in the southern regions of the TRB from about 5000 BP (3800 BC) onwards, and an even earlier, recently documented metal-melting in the Kujavian Lengyel culture, suggest that such knowledge was present in northern Europe as well, although in view of the lack of locally available raw material, the practice need not have been on a large scale, but rather as and when required.

The suggestion that southern Scandinavian TRB communities may occasionally have become involved in metalworking activities naturally remains to be verified. It is offered here as a less improbable alternative to Randsborg's interpretation of the way copper axes appear to be distributed in that area. Moreover, if at all, such evidence is not very likely to derive from funerary or other ritual monuments and yet, in spite of appearances, settlement archaeology in Denmark still needs to match the same degree of enthusiasm as that which is afforded to other categories of archaeological site.

In general discussions on the subject of early copper objects in central and northern Europe, one of the primary themes has always been the so-called European copper horizon (Lomborg 1962, 5–15; Schrickel 1966, 297–313; Preuss 1966, 181–90; Randsborg, 1970, 181–90; Jażdżewski 1973b). This took on a particular significance in the synchronisation of culturally different contexts on the basis of the presence or absence of specific types, the ultimate aim being an identification of the initial source. Particularly prominent in such discussions are the copper trinkets and especially the coper discs of Jażdżewski's (1936 and 1973b) Stollhof-Brześć Kujawski type, which are sparsely but widely distributed throughout Europe and regularly invoke comparisons with the gold discs of south-eastern Europe.

It is not our purpose to pursue here these geographically wide-ranging parallels; all such studies so far have failed to provide a satisfactory answer beyond the notion of a common copper horizon and some distant, as yet not clearly defined, source. For the present it seems of more importance to concentrate on establishing a local chronology for the presence of copper in northern Europe. Only when we know during which periods different communities were becoming familiar with copper items will it be possible to tackle the wider issues of contacts and influences.

Thus, the most significant result of the revised north European chronology is the fact that the 'copper horizon' appears to be splitting into serveral independent horizons, at least as far as the placement of copper trinkets within the funerary context is concerned. This break-up was already hinted at by Bakker (1979, 127), who aptly wrote that 'the conception of one metal horizon right across Europe, and stemming from one export area, has outlived its usefulness'. It is further supported by the different composition of metal in the various areas where copper trinkets are found. Thus, the ornaments from the Danish TRB contexts are made exclusively of arsenical copper (Ottaway's C-3 group), while trinkets from the megalithic chambers in the Western TRB and a few finds from the central German contexts (for example Preußlitz; Preuss 1966, 137–41) are of mixed but non-arsenical copper groups – the pure (B), native (A) and high silver content (C-1) coppers of Ottaway's classification. A good example of the mixed character of such finds are the two spiral cylinders from the chamber at Buinen in the Netherlands which, while archaeologically contemporary, have been shown to belong to two different metal groups (Bakker 1979, 1929). Similarly, the metal analysis of the copper trinkets used by the Lengyel Brześć Kujawski group shows that native (A), pure (B) and copper with antimony (C-2; Ottaway 1973, Fig. 9) were all used. Ottaway suggested that the native copper at Brześć Kujawski may derive from the Carpathian *Siebenbürgen* area, but the C-2 copper could have been of Slovakian origin (ibid., 308–9).

Since the trinkets from Brześć Kujawski have always served as a 'barometer' for nothern Europe, it is perhaps worth commenting briefly on the chronology of the copper objects in that group. The copper trinkets appear in graves during phase III of the post-LBK in Kujavia (Czerniak 1980, 95). One grave containing copper objects at the settlement of Krusza Zamkowa is dated to 5330 ± 65 BP (Bln-1811, 4194 ± 96 BC). The end of phase III is dated by a C-14 determination from Broniewice of 5060 ± 60 BP (Bln-1312, 3867 ± 80 BC). From the settlement at Brześć Kujawski itself there is now evidence of not only the use but also the working of copper. One of the pits associated with house No. 41 (site 3) has yielded a fragment of a crucible and copper slag with a melted piece of metal (Grygiel 1986, 247). The house is dated to 5370 ± 180 BP (Lod-165, 4216 ± 200 BC). The dates for the second phase of the occupation at Brześć Kujawski (which corresponds to Czerniak's phase III in Kujavia) range between 5370 ± 180 BP (Lod-165, 4216 ± 200 BC) and 5130 ± 160 BP (Lod-163, 3946 ± 169 BC). It therefore appears that copper was used by the communities of the Brześć Kujawski group during the period 4250–3850/3800 BC, although towards the end of this period the supply appears to have diminished and the trinkets in the late phase III graves are of a lesser quality and often made by reshaping and re-using broken pieces (Czerniak 1980, 96–7; Grygiel 1986, 188).

In view of this dating of the use of copper among the Brześć Kujawski communities, it is perhaps not surprising that traces of copper were found at Sarnowo and Leśniczówka (Sarnowo and Pikutkowo phases repectively), although one can hardly talk about copper using in the early Kujavian

TRB. On present evidence it appears that the early TRB groups in this area either did not care much for copper trinkets or, as is more likely, did not have wide-ranging contacts which would furnish them with such a commodity.

An interesting question which arises in this context is that of why the copper supply to the Brześć Kujawski was interrupted. One of the possible interpretations may be related precisely to the developing interest in metal-working among the south-eastern TRB communities. Although the amount of copper objects in that area is small, there is evidence from a number of sites that copper was being worked there from about 5000 BP (3800 BC) onwards, and contemporary evidence from Bohemia (Makotřasy) suggests that on the southern fringes of the TRB culture incipient metal technology was practised. The sources of the raw material used by the South-eastern TRB communities are not known. Some of the copper objects are made of arsenical copper (of the type also used in Bohemia), but native copper from south-eastern Europe may also have been available via the Tripolye culture contacts. It is therefore possible that at least some copper which previously found its way to Kujavia was now directed towards southern Poland.

There may also have been shifts in contacts, and new networks were clearly being established at this time. The assumed prominence of the Oder river basin in the traffic of copper axes to southern Scandinavia is of particular relevance, especially when east Alpine sources are taken into consideration. The large amber hoard from near Wrocław could plausibly support this link.

The dating of the Danish trinkets can now be synchronised with the earliest TRB horizon in this area, that is the Volling/Svaleklint/Oxie horizon which is dated to 5100–4800/4700 BP (4000–3600/3500 BC). The Barkær date of 5150 ± 80 BP (*c.* 3960 BC) would provide the earliest dating of copper, although the precise background to this site remains to be clarified. The copper disc from Konens Høj has been dated to 4850 ± 100 BP (K-919, *c.* 3650 BC) and the dates from the Rude long barrow suggest a similar period betwen 4900 and 4800 BP (K-3124 and K-3125, 3700–3600 BC). The C-14 dates obtained from the human bones in association with the disc from Rude gave a later date (about 700 radiocarbon years younger; T. Madsen 1980, 88), but this was a dating carried out on bones which had been stored for over half a century and thus cannot be considered reliable. Moreover, on archaeological grounds Madsen has argued that the grave containing the copper disc was primary in the barrow and that accordingly the disc itself should be dated to the early TRB, although he also advocated a revision of the extremely narrow copper horizon.

Copper objects are also known from a number of earthen long barrows, for example the copper disc at Salten and spiral cylinders at Skive. Imitations of such discs in amber have already been mentioned (Sjørup and Skibshøj). In addition, three of the above graves also contained type IV flint axes which are regarded as diagnostic of the Volling group. The Bygholm hoard, by virtue of the vessel containing the copper axes, should be assigned to the Volling group and presumably the Aarupgård hoard should also be considered contemporary. Furthermore, one is struck by the geographical concentration of the copper finds in east central Jutland (on Djursland and around the modern town of Horsens), while amber imitations are found further to the north-west (West of Viborg) where copper may not have been so easily procured or, at least, was not squandered in burial rituals.

The evidence outlined above does suggest that copper is introduced to southern Scandinavia early in the TRB and that it is placed equally early in graves and, by analogy, in hoards. The precise dating is still difficult, but it seems that the main contenders for the copper were the Volling group communities and an average date of 5000/4900 BP (3800/3700 BC) is most likely. It is not possible to say whether all the copper that reached Denmark was swifly disposed off in rituals. Some copper artefacts quite probably remained in use for longer – the amber imitations of copper axes (Fig. 88) found in some of the Danish passage graves suggest that familiarity with such artefacts persisted longer into the TRB and the copper axes may well have been used in a range of activities (ceremonial or otherwise) long after they were first introduced into the area. Clearly, more contexted and dated evidence is necessary to clarify the somewhat blurred picture with regard to the longevity of use of copper in the Northern TRB culture, but the time of introduction of copper into southern Scandinavia by about 3800 BC seems relatively well documented.

The appearance of copper objects within the Western TRB group, however, is not yet clear. Using comparisons with the Northern TRB, Schlicht (1973) dated the north-west German and Dutch trinkets to the EN-C period, but the revised dating no longer allows such a synchronisation. First of all, the different metal compositions of the copper objects (with a notable lack of arsenical copper) suggest a different source from that which supplied the Northern group. Secondly, in the context of accessible, stone-built chambers, it is not always possible to ascertain the relationship between the copper trinkets and the burials they are supposedly accompanying.

Bakker (1979, 130) pointed out that the earliest pottery, which is found in the chambers with copper trinkets, belongs to his Drouwen C phase and that the majority of vessels belong to the D and E phases. The C and D-1 pottery can currently be ascribed only to a very general horizon dating to after 4700/4600 BP (3500/3400 BC) or Brindley's Horizon 3 (Chapter 5.4), while the E pottery is later still. It is therefore difficult to escape the conclusion that the custom of placing copper trinkets in the graves of the Western TRB cannot be earlier than 4700/4600 BP (3500/3400 BC) and thus does not relate directly to the custom observed in southern Scandinavia. It is of course possible that copper ornaments may have been present in the west earlier and their deposition in the funerary context only occurs after a certain period of use; there is currently no evidence either to support or to refute such an idea. The fact that the Western TRB copper objects are made of different metal adds weight to the arguments that the Western and Northern TRB copper horizons are chronologically separate phenomena, a feature entirely in keeping with differences in other funerary customs in the two areas.

The above-suggested chronology of the copper objects in the TRB culture naturally needs to be verified through future research and new, better-contexted and dated finds. But it does demonstrate that the use of specific types in order to arrive at synchronisations may be very misleading. Certain copper types, such as beads or spiral rings, are so ubiquitous as to be devoid of chronological significance. Other types such as copper discs may, by virtue of their rarity, have their chronological significance over-emphasised. The Stollhof-Brześć Kujawski discs are different from those found in southern Scandinavia and they can now also be dated differently. The northern copper discs may, however, have been valued for their antiquity. Whichever is the case, their significance in the Northern TRB relates less to when and where they were made, and more to when and how they were used by the local population; the latter issues at least appear to be clear.

If the dating suggested above is principally correct, then it is not even possible to think in terms of a uniform copper horizon within the TRB culture, let alone a common European horizon. The copper appears in different areas at different times and seems to be put to varied uses. It also arrives from various, not yet clearly defined sources, which complicates the picture further. In the European context there is a clear need to revise our approach to the study of the chronological and cultural significance of copper metalworking and the dissemination of objects. Their study in just one cultural context – that of the TRB – shows the real complexity of the issue.

7

The settlement patterns of the TRB culture

Human occupation impresses itself upon any particular area in many different ways. Not only does it induce a change in the natural environment, but more visibly it leaves a record of its presence in a combination of features: permanently occupied settlements, sites temporarily used and visited in connection with a wide range of economic and industrial activities, places of burial and sites of non-domestic activities and, last but not least, stray objects, all of which, taken together, form a settlement pattern created by a particular group of people. Such a pattern does not arise randomly, but is the result of a complex relationship between environmental, economic, cultural, social and political factors which condition the choices available to that group of people.

It is self-evident that these factors operated no less in prehistory than they do today, and ideally a study of a prehistoric settlement pattern would take all these elements into account. But our recognition of the significance which each factor had in a prehistoric context is obscured by the nature and the shortcomings of archaeological evidence. In reality, prehistoric settlement studies are by and large limited to search for the basic features of a settlement system among the economic factors; other aspects are usually left out of any consideration.

Such a limited approach unfortunately still dominates the study of the settlement pattern of the TRB culture. Where such studies are undertaken at all, they are by and large synonymous with the study of a site location in a landscape, the identification of the economic potential of the site's closest environment and, less frequently, with establishing the relationship between the permanent and seasonally occupied sites.

Although some sort of settlement study is available for most areas of the TRB culture distribution, these are widely divergent in approach and the amount of available information. Since landscape studies form the most commonly investigated aspect of settlement, these will be considered first, after which an attempt will be made to consider the relationship between sites which can be shown to have had a specific function in the overall system; arrangements on sites and TRB architecture will also be considered. Finally, there follows a brief discussion of a relatively recently discovered type of site, the enclosed variety.

7.1 TRB sites in the natural landscape

The earlier consideration of the natural environment of the North European Plain revealed that, while there are certain general features typical of the area as a whole, there are also strong variations in the geographical, topographical and vegetational character of individual regions. These very local elements would have had the most direct influence upon the way in which individual landscapes were settled. Thus, in order to identify the general principles which guided settlement across the North European Plain, it is necessary first of all to discuss some of the settlement studies carried out in different regions.

The early TRB sites in south-west Scania are found within three landscapes, each characterised by a somewhat different vegetational cover (Larsson 1985). The two early groups, Oxie and Svenstorp, are found predominantly on dry, sandy elevations covered with a mixed-oak forest in which oak and lime were dominant and the rich undergrowth included large amounts of hazel (for example along the Sege river). The people were also attracted to a hilly landscape interspersed with bogs, marshes and stretches of open water, where the mixed-oak forest consisted chiefly of oak and lime with a high proportion of elm and ash (for example the Sturup area). Both regions were also varied topographically. The third type of landscape, of morainic, clayey soil with a large coverage of elm, appears to have been exploited mainly at a somewhat later stage, by the communities of the Bellevuegards group.

The site catchment analysis within a 1 km radius of several Scanian settlements has revealed a close relationship between the presence of sandy/gravel soils and wet boggy environments, suggesting that the presence of a variety of habitats within a short distance from the site was of fundamental importance. Larsson further argues that this variety indicates that many sites may have been located at the edge of a forest, where a combination of forest, meadow and arable land created ideal settlement conditions.

Settlement studies from Denmark show remarkable conformity with observations made in other regions. Analysis of the settlement pattern in east central Jutland (T. Madsen 1982, 215–17) indicates that there was a higher than average association of sites with sandy soils, which is particularly important when we note that the eastern half of the Jutland peninsula is composed predominantly of morainic clays. Moreover, the settlements as well as graves appear to have been located in areas where different soil types were easily available in the immediate vicinity of the site. The importance of both the dry, higher ground and the low-lying wetter landscape (sea, lake and water courses) underlines further the phenomenon of topographical and ecological variety which characterises TRB settlement in most of its distribution area.

Distribution maps of the three-phase settlement in east central Jutland (ibid., Fig. 3) perhaps put undue emphasis upon the coastal location of sites. While many of the TRB sites were located along the coast and often upon the earlier Ertebølle sites (for example Norsminde), it is now becoming appparent that the seemingly empty inland areas also supported a TRB population right from the very beginning. The recent reappraisal of the Danish TRB chronology (Chapter 5.3.2), coupled with the reinterpretation of early graves (Chapter 9.1) and the constantly increasing number of the Volling group long barrows (Thorvildsen 1941; T. Madsen 1979 and 1987, 234), shows very clearly that not only coastal but also inland territories were settled by the TRB population. That the inland settlement continued and even expanded during the Middle phase is supported by the distribution of tombs with stone-built chambers which, in addition to coastal locations, are found further inland along the major river courses (T. Madsen 1982, Fig. 11).

Despite the fact that most of the Danish islands are composed of morainic clay, the preference for location on sandy or, at least, the presence of sandy soil in the vicinity of the settlement, is also evident. Thus, although sand is rare on Langeland, about one-third of the early TRB sites were located on this type of soil and the same pattern can be discerned throughout the later TRB (Skaarup 1985, 349).

In the area of south-west Fyn the TRB settlement, corresponding to the Middle phase in east central Jutland, is also found to be associated with the sandy soils, although the conditions are reminiscent of those on Langeland. It is unfortunate that N. Andersen's (1981, 75–82, Figs 16–20) analysis does not indicate the relative availability of sand and clay, since only then could one determine whether the sandy soils are being sought out deliberately. Andersen's analysis does nevertheless show that at least 25 per cent of land within a 2 km radius of the known Fuchsberg phase sites consists of sandy soil, and the ceremonial site of Sarup has 59 per cent sandy soil in its vicinity. The three settlements known to date from the Late phase (characterised by MN V ceramics) show greater diversity. Sarup, which by now has a purely domestic status, is associated mainly with sandy soil, Sønderby exclusively with clay and Brunshuse's 2 km radius involves little land altogether. Of the tombs on south-west Fyn 75 per cent are located on clay while the rest are found on sand. Topographical factors suggest that proximity to the coastline in the location of tombs (71 per cent of tombs are within 1 km of the present-day coastline) may have been of greater importance than the choice of soil. That the fertile clays may also have been under early cultivation is seen from the ard marks preserved under the Snave dolmen.

The earliest settlement of the Eastern TRB group (Sarnowo phase)

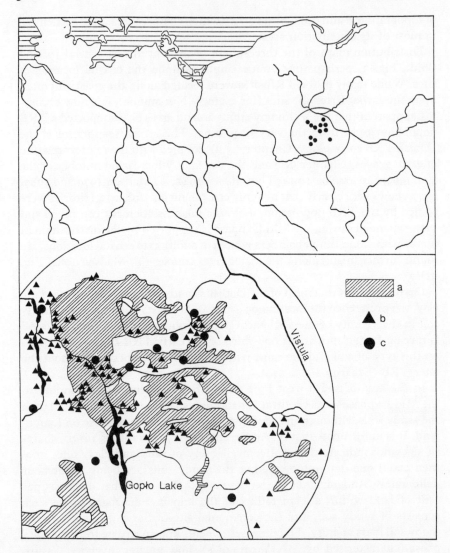

Figure 89 Distribution of LBK, post-LBK and TRB sites in the region of Kujavia:
a-the extent of black earth, b-LBK and post-LBK sites, c-TRB sites (source Kośko
1980).

remains little known, with only sporadic finds in Kujavia and Greater
Poland (Wiślański 1969, 72, Map 4; 1979, 198–200). The sites are found in
relatively close proximity to those of the older LBK or the partly contemporary Lengyel groups, but they occupy a different environment. In contrast to the rich-soil-loving LBK, who often chose low-lying river terraces
for their settlements, the TRB groups settled mainly upon sandy elevations

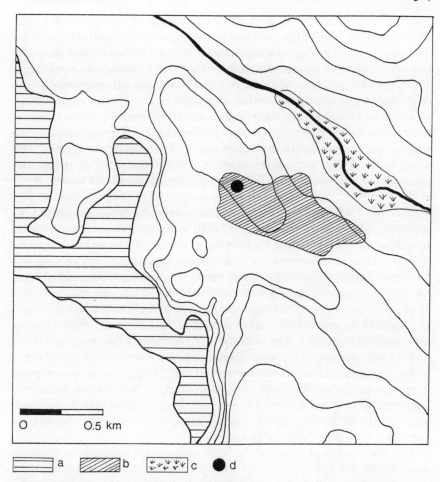

a b c d

Figure 90 Location of the TRB camp site at Łącko, Kujavia: a-Mielno lake, b-podzolic sandy soils, c-marshy valley, d-TRB site (Source: Domańska and Kośko 1983).

where sandy or light loam podzolic soils predominated (Fig. 89). This type of landscape, which covers a large area of lowland Poland, supported a mixed-oak temperate forest; it was not settled by the LBK, but by the lowland hunting-gathering populations.

Specific locations indicate that, as elsewhere in the TRB culture area, the sites were placed at the edge of such an environment in close proximity to the more fertile brown soils as well as the much poorer marshy and boggy soils usually present in the stream valleys and by lakes. The small camp-site at Łącko (Domańska and Kośko 1983, 4: Fig. 90), for example, was located at the edge of a natural elevation which formed an island of podzolic sandy soil in a predominantly brown earth environment. The site was less than 500 m from the edge of the lake, and in the opposite direction was the same distance from the boggy, marshy valley of a small stream. A similar situation was evident at a somewhat later Sarnowo site (Sadłowska 1971). The landscape around Sarnowo is the result of heavy glaciation (Poznań phase of the Baltic glaciation) and consists mainly of relatively flat morainic clays in which all elevations are composed of sands and gravels. The settlement site and the adjacent barrow cemetery are located on a narrow sandy terrace which stands 4–5 m above the boggy valley of the Zgłowiączka river. The importance of the wet environment is evident not only in the spatial proximity to the site, but also in the use of riverine deposits in burial rituals at the cemetery (Midgley 1985, 238).

Once the TRB culture of this region becomes established, the settlement expands. The area of the Eastern TRB's distribution becomes larger, involving the area of Polish lowland between the Vistula and Oder rivers. Three major environmental zones become important, underlying the variety of occupied landscapes. The sandy environment continues to form the dominant zone of the TRB settlement (about 80 per cent of sites derive from sandy locations). The internal expansion of the TRB means, however, that some of the areas previously occupied by the LBK and Lengyel groups also begin to be settled. The third type of zone where the developed TRB culture sites are found is the landscape of poor-quality sands and gravels, which was covered with a drier forest containing a large proportion of pine. Throughout, the settlement clearly avoids large areas which are uniform in character. Where topography allowed, sites were located high in the landscape, at the edge of the interfluves (60 per cent) or along the higher river terraces (Wiślański 1969; 1979, 200–7).

The South-eastern group of the TRB culture developed in an environment which differed substantially from the natural conditions encountered throughout most of the European lowland. The large loess upland settlements, such as Niedźwiedź, Ćmielów and Gródek Nadbużny, were for a long time the dominant element in the archaeological record and thus gave the impression of a different settlement process from that which was observed in the lowland zone. However, it is now evident that such upland sites belong to the TRB culture in its fully developed form and do not represent its early stages. It is therefore particularly interesting to note that the 'dichotonous regularities' in the South-eastern TRB settlement pattern (the settling of rich as well as poor environments) discussed by Kruk (1980, 49–50) reflect to a large degree the process which we saw further north, for example in Kujavia.

There are indications that the South-eastern TRB culture begins outwith the loess zone, and that its proliferation on the loess uplands is a result of internal expansion combined with the decrease or transformation of the Lengyel communities. Traces of the TRB settlements have been identified in the sandy and light loam areas which surround and dissect the southern uplands. Originally such areas would have supported pine or, under favourable conditions, deciduous forest, thus approximating to the natural conditions prevalent in the lowland zone. These regions did not attract the LBK and Lengyel settlement but supported late Mesolithic communities, which may have come under some influence from their farming neighbours. Indeed, the strongly Mesolithic element witnessed in the lowland TRB development makes such a hypothesis highly acceptable.

Thus, a number of sites investigated along the Kamienna river (at the northern boundary of the Sandomierz upland) were found in a sandy environment (Kruk 1980, 97). They reveal traces of short-lived occupation in the form of pottery scatters, a few pits and post-holes, which are in full agreement with the evidence of early TRB settlement noted in the Polish lowland. Similar observations were made along the upper Bug and Dniestr where 'lowland' environments as well as the loess uplands appear to have been occupied by the TRB groups (Jastrzębski, pers. comm.). Moreover, pollen spectra from the Sandomierz area contain evidence of anthropogenic activities (forest fires) which date to the second half of the Atlantic, thus preceding the phase of the classic TRB upland settlement. This region was of no interest to the earlier LBK and Lengyel groups, and the TRB is the earliest Neolithic culture represented here. It is therefore possible that the anthropogenic activities documented in the pollen record could be related to activities of the oldest TRB phase in the south-east, which took place outside the loess zone.

We noted earlier that the developed TRB culture in Kujavia took over at least some of the areas which previously supported the LBK and Lengyel communities. Exactly the same process is seen in the South-eastern group; the relative scarcity of the 'lowland'-character environment suggests that this process may have been stronger than in the north. Kruk's (1980, Maps 2 and 3) investigations of the Neolithic cultures in south-east Poland revealed that the main areas of the LBK and Lengyel settlement (the Miechów and Sandomierz uplands) also became the main centres of the TRB culture. Evidence from the Miechów upland shows that altogether 94 per cent of the TRB sites were located on the loess, although there was a preference for the black earth (75.8 per cent) rather than the brown earth (18.2 per cent; Kruk 1973, 78, Table 14). This contrasts with the Lengyel culture, which clearly preferred the brown earth (58.3 per cent; ibid., Table 13), and may help to explain the partial co-exstence of these two groups.

In terms of topography, the classic phase sites tended to be located in the upland zone (62.2 per cent), although they are found mostly along the upland's edge (48.5 per cent). The valley sites (29.3 per cent) were also associated with elevated terraces, always above the flood plain. There was a strong tendency to place the large upland settlements such as Bronocice or Ćmielów in exposed positions which were naturally defensive in character.

The area of Mecklenburg is clearly the least researched. The available evidence is relatively poor in comparison with the neighbouring regions, but it suggests that here, as elsewhere along the North European Plain, the morainic landscape of sands and sandy clays was of particular importance, while the heavier, pure clay soils were less sought after. The finds diagnostic of the early period are few and far between. However, a comparison of the distribution maps of the early megaliths (Schuldt 1972a, Map 3), bog finds (Nilius 1971a, Map VIII) and ceramic finds (Preuss 1966, Map 1; see also Gramsch 1971a, Fig. 3) suggests that the central lake belt was of primary importance. This region of numerous lakes, streams, rivers and strongly differentiated soils offered a wide variety of natural environments. It was fairly well settled towards the end of the Mesolithic (Gramsch 1973) and clearly played a major role in the development of the TRB culture. The coastal settlement is more difficult to interpret; the importance of the area around the Wismar Bay and of Rügen is evidenced not only in the presence of the earliest megaliths and votive deposits, but also in numerous thin-butted axes (Bastian 1954, Map 1), although the stretch of coast from Rostock as far east as Rügen is largely devoid of finds.

The later TRB is found over the whole of Mecklenburg, largely it seems, as a result of internal expansion and thus infilling of the area between the central lakes and the coast; there is even some expansion onto the heavier, clayey soils of the Überkmark region. The only area which appears to be unpopulated by the TRB communities is the relatively poor sandy landscape of south-western Mecklenburg (Nilius 1971a, Maps 2, 4, 6–8, 10), although the presence of the long barrows with timber-built chambers in the northern part of this region suggests that the 'emptiness' may be largely illusory.

Turning now to the remainder of the north German area we note similar difficulties in the interpretation of the early settlement, since such studies as are available concern the later fully developed period characterised by *Tiefstich* pottery. There is clearly an urgent need to study the settlement pattern of the early phase, not only in order to understand the way the settling of different landscapes changed over time, but also to enhance our understanding of the change from a hunting-gathering to a farming economy over this area.

Indeed, few though they still are, the early sites known along the German lowland indicate precisely the environment in which hunter-gatherer and farming activities were not mutually exclusive but complementary. Coastal regions were of importance. The sites of Rosenhof and Siggeneben-Süd in east Holstein reveal a settlement location which allowed the exploration of marine and inland environments (Meurers-Balke 1983, Fig. 2). Reconstruction of the contemporary landscape around Siggeneben-Süd suggests that the site was located in a relatively sheltered bay with a hinterland of gently reliefed boulder clay hills. These were covered by a mixed-oak forest in which lime and oak were dominant species. Closer to the bay, a meadow-land interspersed with ash, alder and hazel stands offered good grazing terrain (ibid., 36–7).

Wet, marshy landscapes, which along the entire North European Plain supported the earlier hunting-fishing groups, appear to have been equally attractive to the early TRB communities. The site of Boberg was situated on a sandy dune within the flat marshes of the Elbe estuary (Schindler 1953, Plate II) and moorland edge locations are documented in numerous TRB sites along the Satrup and Brennen Moors (Schwabedissen 1958a and b). The recently excavated site at Bistoft (Johansson 1979 and 1981) was located on an island in a landscape of numerous lakes and streams in the Neolithic period. The most emphatic expression of the importance of such an environment is the location of the Hüde I site (Deichmüller 1963, 1965 and 1969; Kampffmeyer 1983). Irrespective of the difficulties in the inter-pretation of the cultural sequence recovered from Hüde, the location of this site, in the peaty basin of the Dümmer lake surrounded by sandy heath and morainic hills, replicates that of numerous Mesolithic camps. Indeed, the current interpretation of the Hüde site as a hunting/fishing station associ-ated with a permanent TRB site in the Dammer upland, suggests the importance of hunting and fishing in the early, precariously balanced economy.

Bakker (1982, 96) has argued that one reason why the German TRB was interested in the peaty areas and the Dutch was not, could be related to different habitat potential. It is equally feasible to suggest that, by the time the TRB people settled on the Drenthe plateau and in the Veluwe, they were confident and well-established farmers. The lack of peaty bog settle-ment in the Netherlands would then reflect a different economic strategy from that of the earlier period.

Bakker's study of the two major centres of TRB settlement in the Netherlands, the Drenthe plateau and the Veluwe area, confirms the general principles of preference for soils that were sandy but close to others, allowing a variety of natural habitats. Two landscapes were of particular importance on the Veluwe: the foothills of the very high and dry boulder clay ridges with settlements located on the coversands, and the marginal moist valleys, where the sites were placed on the higher, dry ground (ibid., 108–11, Fig. 6). Similar circumstances were noted along the Drenthe plateau where, in addition, the landscape of low sand-covered ridges to the north and west was also settled (ibid., 107). Most of the settlements, as well as the Drenthe *hunebedden*, were placed on dry ground, but the importance of wetter environments is indicated by votive peat deposits of pottery and flint axes (ibid., 88).

The pollen spectra from the Veluwe region indicate the existence of an open woodland with oak, hazel, lime and birch. Pollen analysis from beneath the Drenthe *hunebedden* shows that the mixed oak forest was

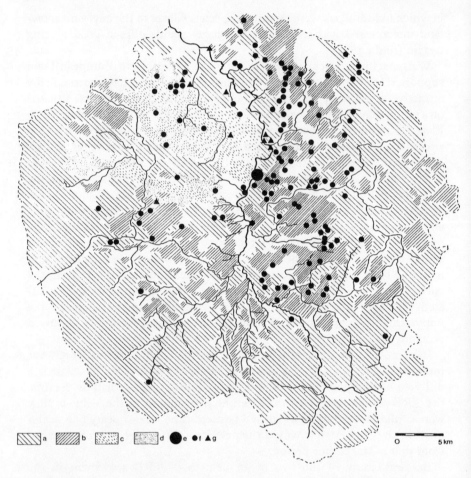

Figure 91 Distribution of TRB finds in the vicinity of Uelzen, Lower Saxony: a-coversands, b-glacial sands, c-loess, d-loess-developed brown earth, e-enclosures, f-graves and settlements, g-stray finds (Source: Schirnig 1979a).

already partly thinned out and that, in some cases, regeneration took place prior to the construction of the barrow (see Chapter 8.1).

It is interesting to compare the settlement pattern of the later TRB in the areas of Uelzen (Fig. 91), Osnabrück (Fig. 92) and Magdeburg (Fig. 93), three regions for which more detailed information is available. The rolling, morainic landscape with glacial coversands and a fair proportion of loamy sands dominates the Osnabrück and Uelzen regions, although in both areas there are substantial stretches of marshy lowlands with predominantly sandy soils broken up by light loams along the river valleys. Small areas of loess-developed brown earth are found to the north-west of Uelzen and east of Osnabrück between the Teutoburger Wald and Wiehengebirge (Schirnig

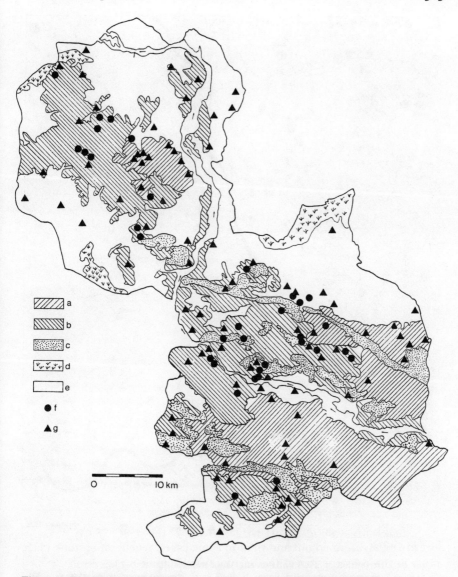

Figure 92 Distribution of TRB finds near Osnabrück, Lower Saxony: a-loess-derived brown earth, b-dry to medium-dry sands, c-heavily weathered brown earths, d-marshes, e-clays and sandy clays, f-tombs, g-stone/flint implements (Source: Schirnig 1979b).

1979a, Fig. 1; Schlüter 1979, Map 2). The morainic landscape around Magdeburg, which borders on the middle German black earth region, is found north of the river Ohre and east of the Elbe valley, where clayey soils, inland dunes and valley sands are commonest. The famous Magdeburger

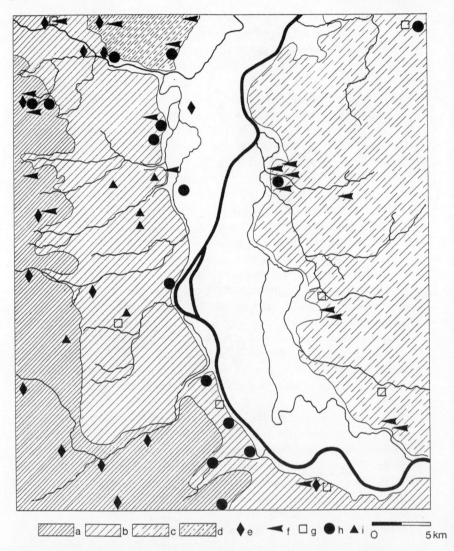

Figure 93 Distribution of TRB finds on the Magdeburger Börder: a-black earth
covered upland (50 m above valley floor), b-black earth covered upper valley slopes
(below 50 m), c-sand dunes and sandy clays, d-morainic clays, e-Baalberge finds, f-
Altmark *Tiefstich* finds, g-Walternienburg finds, h-Bernburg finds, i-
Walternienburg and Bernburg finds (Source: Lies 1974).

Börde, west of the Elbe, is an area of black earth upland and richly developed topography along the edge of the interfluve (Lies 1974, 59–60).

In all three regions there is a clear correspondence between the morainic
landscape and the distribution of megaliths. Near Osnabrück (Fig. 92) the
tombs are confined exclusively to the morainic zone, where they are found

clustering on the dry to medium-dry coversands, and where they show a particular preference for the narrow river valleys which dissect the morainic uplands. Near the Uelzen (Fig. 91), the tombs are found mainly in a broad zone of glacial sands to the east of the Ilmenau river and in smaller numbers to the west, occupying a similar landscape. Palynological investigations from one of the Lüneburger Heide tombs at Oldendorf, along the broad valley of the river Luhe, give some idea of the natural environment in this area. Groenman-van Waateringe (1979a, 72) envisages 'primarily alder growing along the banks of the river with some willow and birch, merging via a zone with elm, ash and hazel into the woodland with oak, lime and ash, in which the funerary monuments were constructed'.

Although hardly any tombs survive around Magdeburg today, they were noted towards the end of the nineteenth century. They are known to have followed the sandy river valleys deep into the boulder plateau, in contrast to settlements which remain at the plateau's edge (Preuss 1980, Fig. 19). Apart from sandy and clayey soils, black earth soils are found in all three regions. Apparently, no megaliths are found on the loess near Osnabrück, and Schlüter (1979, 232) points out that the one grave found in the loess landscape south of the Wiehengebirge is in fact on an isolated pocket of sand. On the other hand, the distributions of settlement sites, pottery scatters and stone tools show that TRB settlement extended well beyond the morainic landscape into the marshy lowland and even onto the loess region. Schlüter therefore argued for the existence of a 'non-megalithic TRB group which settled in the lowlands and partly also on the loess' (ibid., 233).

This constrasts somewhat with the evidence from around Uelzen, where apparently up to one-eighth of the tombs are found on the loess, and Magdeburg, where megaliths are found on the black earth west of the Elbe. It has been argued that because they contain Walternienburg-Bernburg material, they are later than *Tiefstich*, but Lies (1974, 72) mentions an unexplored long mound high on the upland whose size suggests it may contain a TRB *Tiefstich* chamber.

In his discussion of the Baalberge settlement, Preuss (1966, 48–54) argued that this group is found almost totally in the area of the loess-derived black earth of central Germany and hardly ever enters other soils, not even the degraded black earth which was commonly settled by the earlier LBK and Rössen communities. He suggested that it was either because the Baalberge was contemporary with some older culture which precluded its occupation of certain areas, or because temporary forestation restricted settlement during the period in question. The latter seems extremely unlikely, not only from a purely ecological point of view but in the light of the subsequent TRB settlement in this region, which is not confined to the black soils.

Preuss' statement about Baalberge settlement has now been repeated many times in the literature, but little attempt has been made to explain such a settlement pattern, or indeed to review the situation in the light of new evidence and different theories on settlement processes. On the one hand it is hardly surprising that a population settling in a predominantly black earth environment should focus their settlement strategy upon such soils; on the other hand it is of interest to note that while many of the Baalberge findspots derive from the black earth, there are also a number of finds outwith the black earth, especially along the River Ohre, the middle reaches of the Bode, and along the Elster and Helme. This fact, plainly evident from Preuss' distribution map (ibid., Map 3), is generally not commented upon. One wonders, however, whether this reflects a circumstance which we have already discussed in connection with the South-eastern group, namely that the settlement on the loess is the result of a strong internal expansion of the Baalberge which initially settled the moist and wooded river valleys that approximated to the conditions prevailing in the lowland zone. This premise is in complete contrast to the generally accepted view that the Baalberge originated on the loess, and via Brandenburg gave rise to the TRB culture as we know it in Mecklenburg (Preuss 1980, 11). Very little can be said about the settlement pattern of the succeeding TRB phases in this area. Preuss' map of the Salzmünde finds (ibid., Map 4) shows a very limited distribution and Salzmünde's independent status is doubtful; the situation is similar with regard to the Walternienburg-Bernburg groups, and the claims for a complex settlement pattern based on defensive or upland sites (Starling 1988) remain to be investigated further.

7.1.1 Summary

The above discussion of the TRB settlement pattern demonstrates that the location of individual settlements was clearly bound up with the environmental conditions prevalent in each of the studied regions. There are none the less certain common factors which suggest that, in spite of the great diversity of locally available environments, it is possible to discern some general characteristics of settlement which are relevant to the TRB as a whole.

Thus, the TRB culture shows a remarkable preference for the lighter sandy soils, this preference being particularly clear in such areas as the Jutland peninsula and the Danish islands, where sandy soils are not the main feature of the edaphic landscape. However, while it was obviously important to locate the settlements upon dry sandy elevations, another conspicuous feature of the TRB settlement (which moreover contrasts greatly with the earlier LBK and post-LBK patterns) is the topographical and ecological diversity of the immediate surroundings. Where site catchment analysis has been undertaken, the results reveal that a variety of natural habitats – forest, pastoral, arable – were within easy access of settlement; this suggests that from the start of the TRB culture was involved in the exploitation of a whole range of economic resources.

In areas of strong topographical differentiation, especially in Little Poland, Kujavia and central Germany, the settlement reveals a vertical as well as a horizontal expansion. In contrast to the earlier pattern of the LBK and post-LBK, which concentrated within a relatively restricted zone of valley settlement, the TRB culture expands onto the edge of the upland where most of the permanent settlements are concentrated. However, contact with the valley is not severed as many of the smaller, satellite sites are still found in the lower parts of the landscape.

Sherratt (1981) argued that the expansion into the upland zone was directly related to technological innovations in farming, especially the introduction of the plough (see Chapter 8.4.2). While improvements in farming technology undoubtedly had an impact upon settlement, the expansion into a wider landscape must have been part of a more complex economic change in which a diversification between the arable and pastoral elements played an equally important role. Moreover, the regular location of the upland settlements in what could be defined as defensive positions may also suggest a degree of social tension which need not be directly related to economic expansion.

7.2 The nature of the TRB settlements

A further aspect that has recently found expression in the TRB settlement studies is the recognition of a complex spatial and functional relationship between sites. While most of the research in this field has, once again, been carried out in southern Scandinavia, the broad categories identified here – permanent settlements, seasonally occupied sites and ceremonial places – find a wider application within the TRB culture as a whole.

7.2.1 Permanent residential sites

The first category of sites to be discussed here are the residential sites which form the basis of the settlement pattern throughout the entire area of the TRB culture distribution. The permanent nature of such sites during the later, developed phase of the TRB can reasonably be determined from a set of recurrent features such as the presence of rich cultural material, traces of domestic activities involving food preparation, various crafts and industries, storage facilities, domestic architecture and, occasionally, constructions of defensive character.

It is much more difficult to determine the nature of the early residential sites since the information from the early TRB is scanty and at best fragmentary. A number of scholars have suggested that the early TRB settlements were short-lived, fitting the model of shifting settlement (T. Madsen 1982; Bogucki 1988). Early TRB sites, such as Oxie, Mosegården, Siggeneben-Süd, Sarnowo or Łącko, show that from the onset the settlement pattern was not homogeneous. Evidence from Jutland suggests that many sites were small, not exceeding 500–700 m² (Madsen 1982, 205), but other Danish sites, to judge from the quantity of recovered material (cf. Havnelev with over 4,500 potsherds and over 800 flint tools; Mathiassen 1940), may well have been larger.

From south-west Scania there is evidence of small sites, such as Svenstorp (1600 m²), but also of larger sites such as Oxie where cultural material was found over an area of 10,000 m², although Larsson (1985, 80) stressed the difficulty of delineating the boundaries of early sites.

From the Eastern TRB group we may point to a relatively small site at Łącko (less than 200 m², although how much of the site was damaged through sand quarrying cannot be estimated; Domańska and Kośko 1983), but also to a much larger settlement complex at Sarnowo where traces were recovered beneath the entire cemetery of 50,000 m² (Wiklak 1986).

Permanent residential sites are the main feature of the developed TRB and these are documented throughout the entire area of the TRB culture. Some of the sites (for example Bronocice or Ćmielów) appear to have been occupied over a long period of time, as evidenced by the presence of stylistically different ceramics and, less frequently, by the horizontal displacement of settlement features.

The size of settlements is often hard to gauge because, as in the earlier period, excavation is usually very limited; for example, only 1.5 per cent of the estimated surface area of the Bronocice settlement was subject to excavation (Hensel and Milisauskas 1985, 56) and often it is even less, although surface investigations can offer reasonable indications of the spread of cultural material. On the whole the settlements in the lowland area of the TRB tend to be smaller than those known from the southern upland regions, but this could be the result of more intensive settlement studies in the South-eastern group.

Settlement studies from the Northern TRB group show, however, that in comparison with the early TRB, settlements became progressively larger; in Jutland they range betwen 0.4 and 3 ha in size (T. Madsen 1982, 207). The famous Troldebjerg site on Langeland covered about 2.5 ha. It comprised twenty-five houses and the excavations yielded rich archaeological material including over 50,000 pottery sherds and a faunal assemblage in excess of 24,000 bone pieces (Winther 1935 and 1938; Skaarup 1985, 47–9). Recent investigations on the island of Bornholm have also indicated the presence of large permanent settlements; at Grødbygård so far 3 ha have been excavated, revealing foundations of large houses. The richness and spread of cultural material around Grødbygård suggests that originally the settlement may have extended over 10 ha in size (Kempfner-Jørgensen and Watt 1985).

While the presence of solid houses on a number of lowland TRB sites (see below) is perhaps the strongest argument in favour of permanent settlements, there is relatively little information about settlements throughout this area, as most finds are either accidental (for example Wittenwater) or, more often than not, derive from small-scale excavations.

In his studies of the settlement pattern of the Eastern TRB group, Wiślański (1969) suggested that an average village size in this region would not exceed about 1,500 m² since surface settlement traces are usually confined to such areas. However, surface estimates can hardly provide a basis for estimating the size of settlements. On the one hand excavations in central Pomerania, at Łupawa, revealed four partly contemporary settlement complexes over an area of about 12 ha (Jankowska 1980). Evidence from excavations in Silesia, however, suggests that most sites were between 3 and 4 ha in size and very occasionally sites up to 14 ha in size are also known (Wojnowice; Wiślański 1979, 204).

The specific topographical conditions prevalent in the areas of the Southern and South-eastern TRB groups led to the development of upland settlement; the available data suggest that upland sites played a key role in the overall settlement pattern. Such sites as Ćmielów, Gródek Nadbużny and Wallendorf represent typical upland settlements, with habitation traces found in each case over a roughly similar area of around 10 ha.

At Ćmielów (Podkowińska 1950 and 1952), the excavations were unfortunately limited to a 20 m wide trench running transversely to the main axis of the elevation. While three separate concentrations of features were noted, little can be judged about the size of the settlement during the different stages of occupation. At least two settlement phases were identified at Gródek Nadbużny (Wiślański 1979, 211; Jastrzębski, pers. comm.), but apparently large areas of the site were not built up but were left free and surrounded by pits and other settlement features; the free areas may have been of importance in herd-keeping, serving as places in which livestock could be kept safely during the night. Traces of defences – a ditch and, at a different place, a palisade – were noted and the evidence of destruction by fire at the end of the occupation does suggest that the settlement was abandoned in the wake of an attack.

That some of the upland settlements remained small, while others became larger and may therefore represent crucial settlement foci, is documented by two recent excavations in the area of Little Poland, at Niedźwiedź and at Bronocice. At Niedźwiedź the TRB traces did not extend beyond an area of about 2 ha, but the presence of two solidly built timber houses leaves little doubt as to the permanent nature of the settlement (Burchard 1981; Hensel and Milisauskas 1985, 78–84).

At Bronocice (Kruk and Milisauskas 1977, 1981a, 1981b, 1983 and 1985; Hensel and Milisauskas 1985, 52–78) the initial TRB settlement was of size similar to that at Niedźwiedź (*c.* 2 ha, Bronocice phase I). Subsequently the settlement was moved eastwards along the elevation and expanded to about 18 ha during the second and third occupation phases. It is also possible that at some stage during phase II part of the elevation was settled by people of a different cultural group, the Lublin-Wolhynian culture, and it was their settlement that appears to have been protected by an extensive ditch system (Kruk and Milisauskas 1985, 41–51).

At Wallendorf (Behrens 1973, 198–9; Fig. 94), which is assumed to belong to the Salzmünde phase, traces of up to thirty houses were recognised, some of them clustered in groups, others forming linear patterns. The course of an interrupted ditch east of the houses may also represent a fragment of an enclosing system, and post-holes clustering around the ditch ends could represent the remains of a gateway.

The question of the defences of TRB settlements is still problematic. The evidence from the Southern and South-eastern groups suggests that sites were often located in a naturally defensive landscape. Kruk's (1973, 102) research in the area of Niecka Nidziańska revealed that about two-thirds of upland sites were placed in such positions, but there is still relatively little consistent evidence of defences, although ditches and palisades often feature in reports from older excavations (Jażdżewski 1936, 293). The naturally defensive Dölauer Heide elevation was additionally surrounded by a complex of ramparts, ditches and palisades which altogther enclosed an area in excess of 20 ha (Behrens and Schröter 1980, 13–17). However, in spite of excavations, the precise function of this 'stronghold' during the early TRB is still uncertain; unequivocal settlement traces belong to the later, Bernburg phase and these are confined mainly to the area of the northern spur.

7.2.2 Sites of a temporary nature

The next category is represented by a somewhat heterogeneous group of sites which appear to have been used on an irregular basis for a variety of economic and industrial activities. The importance of such sites should not be underestimated, as they indicate the establishment of a complex settlement network which enabled the regular exploitation of a variety of sources indispensable to the overall balance of the TRB economy.

First and foremost, we should distinguish the so-called hunting stations or catching sites. Their presence was initially identified by Skaarup (1973), who reviewed south Scandinavian evidence from a number of sites in coastal locations. He was able to demonstrate that, while a number of sites were established during the Ertebølle, they were repeatedly used by the TRB populations, often right up to the end of the TRB culture.

Most of the sites revealed evidence of fishing and hunting and some attested to a degree of specialisation. Thus, the small island of Hesselø, north of Zealand, appears to have been very popular with seal hunters and to have been visited during the winter months (ibid., 13–58). The Sølager site, by Roskilde Fjord, while it provided evidence of a wide range of wild fauna, was used particularly in order to catch winter migrating birds and it

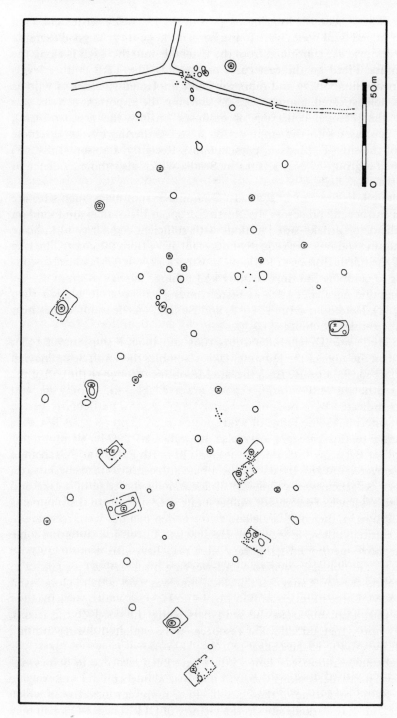

Figure 94 TRB settlement at Wallendorf revealing house structures and hearths (H) (Source: Behrens 1973).

may well have been the hunting outpost of the Havnelev settlement 3 km further inland (seal bones were found here; ibid., 59–117). A good example of a site whose use continued from the Ertebølle into the TRB is along the Norsminde Fjord on the east coast of Jutland. The TRB culture levels contained some pottery and numerous flint implements; bones of wild as well as domesticated animals were present, but the important activity was clearly the seasonal collection of molluscs (mainly the *Herzmuscheln*), which contrasts with the emphasis on oyster-gathering by the Ertebølle users of the site (T. Madsen, pers. comm.). Recently, Larsson (1985, 78) identified a group of coastal sites in Scania which also show evidence of brief, seasonal visits.

Although, in contrast to southern Scandinavia, not many such sites are known further inland across the North European Plain, they are found on lake islands or in lake-side locations with sufficient regularity to indicate that hunting stations were equally important away from the coast. The lake belt of the north European lowland, in particular, offered favourable conditions to combine hunting, fowling and fishing. By way of examples we may mention here sites such as Bistoft, near Flensburg (Johansson 1979 and 1981), Heidmoor (Hingst 1958) and Boberg, on the sandy dunes near the Elbe estuary (Schindler 1953).

The Hüde site (Deichmüller 1963, 1965 and 1969; Kampffmeyer 1983; Fig. 5), on the edge of the Dümmer lake, resembles the south Scandinavian sites in its continuous use from the late Mesolithic through to the end of the TRB. Although only interim reports are available, the variety of wild species indicated by a preliminary analysis suggests a particularly varied habitat offering a wide range of wild species (see Chapter 8.4). A few sites belonging to this category may also be indicated in Mecklenburg, for example at Basedow (Schuldt 1974a), and in north Poland at Szlachcin, a site discovered towards the end of the nineteenth century (Jażdżewski 1936, 112–15). Szlachcin was originally situated along the edge of a lake and revealed evidence of a series of timber-built jetties; at one of them remains of an upturned, dug-out canoe and two wooden paddles were recovered.

Interestingly, the evidence from Hesselø and Bistoft indicates that some of the above-mentioned temporary sites may have had a multi-purpose function, additionally serving as flint-working places. A large quantity of flint debris at Bistoft suggests that local flint was worked here (Johansson 1981, 108). Large numbers of flint blanks on Hesselø, which were made of flint locally available from the sand flats along the coast of the island, equally imply that suitable flint resources were exploited during hunting expeditions to the island (Skaarup 1973, 18–19).

A substantial number of flint scatters have been recorded in Schleswig-Holstein, particularly along the coast and coastal inlets on the western side of the Baltic, and some of these are likely to represent localities in which surface flint was worked; sites in the vicinity of Oldenburger-Dannau may also belong to this category (Hoika 1987, 127 and 189–91). Although no research on this subject has been conducted with regard to the Eastern TRB group, surface finds consisting chiefly of flint scatters are known from the area of western Pomerania and some of these finds may well represent locations at which on-the-spot production took place. Surface flint is found abundantly throughout this area.

At the opposite end of this industrial spectrum are of course the flint mines (Chapter 6.2), which were probably also operated on a temporary basis. Here a variety of industrial practices can be observed. At some flint mines, for instance at Kvarnby, southern Sweden (Olausson *et al.* 1980), flint workshops were established alongside the mines; the whole sequence of the industrial process can be identified, from the extraction of raw material to the production of finished tools. Elsewhere, for example at Świeciechów or Krzemionki Opatowskie (Balcer 1983), the raw material was inspected and prepared in the form of blanks. This was then transported to the not too distant settlements, where the craftsmen undertook the mass production of semi-products and completed tools, which were then supplied to other sites over a larger territory.

With reference to functionally differentiated sites, yet another category emerges. Settlement pattern investigations in the Eastern and South-eastern groups reveal small sites with relatively insignificant settlement traces represented by scatters of flint tools, small amounts of pottery, two or three pits and, very occasionally, traces of flimsy structures (Wiślański 1969, 102–5; Kruk 1973, 99–106).

In the upland settlement of the Little Poland area the settlements, whose permanent nature has been documented through excavation, are distributed quite far apart along the upland's edge. These small scatters of finds are regularly encountered in the vicinity of the large sites as well as in the area between the clear settlement concentrations, often entering deeper into the interfluves. Kruk has argued that the TRB settlement pattern on the loessic upland was clearly related to economic differentiation in which the large, permanent settlements played a key role. In this context, he interprets the small scatters as traces of brief, periodic settlement episodes related to a whole range of economic activities within the wider landscape around the permanent sites.

On the other hand, taking into consideration the location within the landscape and the ephemeral nature of such sites, Wiślański argued that they played a major role within the partly mobile pastoral branch of the TRB economy. They are interpreted as periodically visited sites, representing a network of overnight or short-stay camps in the seasonal movement of herds in the upland pastures (Wiślański 1969, 160–1), at which it was also possible to conduct a whole range of other activities: hunting, fishing, and using many resources that were available in the vicinity.

7.3 Domestic architecture of the TRB culture

Considering the number of settlements that are known or have been investigated, the domestic architecture and organisation of settlements still
remain among the more elusive aspects of the TRB culture. While the
houses are known, they are few and far between and structures interpreted
as such are often doubtful to say the least. Many settlements are known
simply from surface collections of flint and pottery. Houses, however,
unlike for example stone-built tombs, do not leave traces on the surface and
are thus very difficult to recognise. Moreover, post-TRB podsolisation of
the sandy soils which supported a substantial proportion of the TRB
settlement has obliterated ground traces of pits and post-holes.
This process has been further aided by more or less continuous agricultural activities, both in prehistory and in modern times. Thus even
the most expertly conducted excavation often fails to register traces of
houses.

This difficulty is best exemplified by the recent investigations of the TRB
settlement at Bronocice in southern Poland (Kruk and Milisauskas 1977,
1981a, 1981b, 1983 and 1985; Hensel and Milisauskas 1985). Three
chronologically different cultural complexes – the Lublin-Wolhynian,
TRB and Baden groups – occupied intensively an area of about 50 ha on an
upland shelf above the Nidzica valley. Although over $7,000\,m^2$ of the
settlement were investigated, no house structures belonging to any of the
cultural groups were identified. Judging by the quality and quantity of
evidence recovered, the excavation standards were high and we can assume
that house traces would have been recoveed had they survived. In the case
of areas of particularly intensive TRB occupation, the excavators noted
patches of burnt clay which they interpreted as remains of collapsed house
walls. Occasionally, pieces of daub would reveal imprints of posts up to
12 cm in diameter; pits containing evidence of flint-working, in conjunction
with domestic rubbish, hearths and ovens, were clustered around clay
areas, indicating the type and range of domestic activities. Yet no actual
house plans were recovered, although clearly the size and the permanent
nature of the settlement imply that houses must have been built there.

Apart from the difficulties of finding and recognising TRB houses, there
is an additional problem caused by the debate in southern Scandinavia over
the interpretation of structures which, in the light of more recent findings,
can no longer be accepted as houses. The discovery in Denmark of numerous earthen long barrows and the recognition of causewayed enclosures
have created a climate of reinterpretation of some of the TRB houses. The
classic example of this trend are the structures from Barkær and Stengade
which for a long time were accepted as houses but have now been placed
in the category of earthen long barrows (T. Madsen 1979; Midgley 1985).
The interpretation of Barkær, for years a model of what a TRB house
should be, has been debunked by the original excavator, P.V. Glob (1949

and 1975). Indeed, many of Barkær's principals conform without any doubt to elements typical of earthen long barrows, but it remains unique in the way in which various architectural and ritual features were combined and elaborated (Midgley 1985, 144–5).

The Stengade structures (Skaarup 1975, Plans 1–4, Figs 13 and 45) consisted chiefly of two parallel rows of stone layers containing rich cultural deposits. Initially, they were interpreted as 36 m × 4.5 m and 33 m × 2–3 m houses, built upon a framework of timber posts resting on stone foundations. The wattle-and-daub walls offered partial support to a gable roof whose rafters rested on the ground some way beyond the side walls. The excavator still believes them to be houses (Skaarup 1985, 39), but a number of scholars regard them as examples of timber and stone-built barrows, the latter interpretation having been elegantly and convincingly argued by Liversage (1981 and 1983; see also T. Madsen 1979; Midgley 1985).

The assignment of the Barkær and Stengade structures to the earthen long barrow category does not, however, solve all the problems presented by these sites. In both instances the monuments were placed upon earlier TRB settlements and some of the features, such as the interior post-holes at Barkær and some of the post-holes at Stengade, may well form elements of earlier structures and should be investigated further.

Other Danish TRB houses have been reinterpreted as features typical of causewayed enclosures. Recently, Eriksen and Madsen (1984) have argued that structures such as the three early TRB houses from Knardrup Galgebakke or the later TRB longhouses from Äs Vig and Sigersted should be placed in this category. The three structures at Knardrup Galgebakke (Larsen 1958), which were associated with Virum-style pottery, appeared upon excavation to be rather diffuse sets of stone foundations with a few post-holes in between; the arrangements measured 6–7.5 m × 3.5–5 m. In one structure only, house B (ibid., Fig. 4), did the post-holes outline a rectangular shape. There does not seem to be any particularly good reason why Eriksen and Madsen argue against these remains being houses. They criticise the standard of the excavation and cite the site's location on a very pronounced promontory, which is typical of causewayed enclosures (Eriksen and Madsen 1984, 80). The first criticism could apply to an infinite number of sites, in Denmark and elsewhere, and constitutes an argument for re-excavation rather than re-interpretation of poorly acquired evidence. With regard to their second point, it should be noted that causewayed enclosures often acquired a domestic character, even during the TRB, so the location alone need not be a crucial argument. Stating that their interpretation as ditches is 'just as likely as their interpretation as houses' does not contribute much to the debate.

The two later structures, at Sigersted and Äs Vig, were claimed by Davidsen (1978, 22–28, 58–62 and 151–5) to represent long houses. In the case of Sigersted, one has to agree with the criticism that the features represent not houses but two rows of closely spaced post-holes: fifty-three post-holes make up the 25.5 m long eastern row and twenty-five post-holes make up the 15 m long western row; a few post-holes are found still further west (ibid., Fig. 6). There is nothing in the available plan or description to support the interpretation as a house. Moreover, nearly all the post-holes contained in their fill lithic and ceramic materials of the Store Valby style; this suggests that the post-hole arrangements, whatever their function, were later – dug into the settlement material rather than contemporary with it. The re-interpretation of the As Vig reconstruction – also severely criticised as 'all too abnormal from almost any point of view' (Eriksen and Madsen 1984, 78), is justified in so far as, since only the last 2 m of this 38 m long structure were seen by professional archaeologists while the rest was destroyed in grave digging and was poorly recorded, this site can only be interpreted as a series of features whose function and form can no longer be elucidated. Once more, there seems to be no good grounds for re-interpretation in favour of a causewayed enclosure.

One more site which came under suspicion in this context is the settlement of Troldebjerg on Langeland, where Winther (1935, 13–19, Figs 8–26) excavated a whole series of features which he interpreted as a long house. The main elements involved a continuous bedding trench up to 0.5 m wide, 0.3 m deep and 71 m long. At a distance of 1–2 m from this trench there was a row of stone-packed post-holes, although the latter did not run in a straight line but rather formed three or four segments; a massive cultural layer accompanied these features. Winther's interpretation envisaged a long dwelling whose roof rested on an elaborate facade of posts and wattle-and-daub and sloped away from the lake shore to rest against the higher ground 4–5 m away from the bedding trench.

In 1977 the Forhistorisk Museum of Moesgård carried out an exploration of the long house area to investigate whether these features could be interpreted as the ditch and palisade system of a possible causewayed enclosure. However, the excavation established that no ditch system ever existed there (Skaarup 1985, 47–9). Eriksen and Madsen (1984, 78) argue that the features at Troldebjerg presumably represent some sort of fence, a palisade with a row of posts beyond. Unfortunately, this interpretation does not explain the presence of a rich cultural layer right up against it; indeed one cannot help thinking that the question of the form and function of Winther's long house was not the main objective of these investigations.

One wholly sympathises with Eriksen and Madsen's sentiment that scholars should not be willing to accept inadequate evidence purely on the grounds that the TRB population, whose architectural and constructional skills are evident in their burial and ritual monuments, had to build and live in large houses. Moreover, it is clear that the presence in central Europe of a well-established domestic architecture of the LBK and related cultures

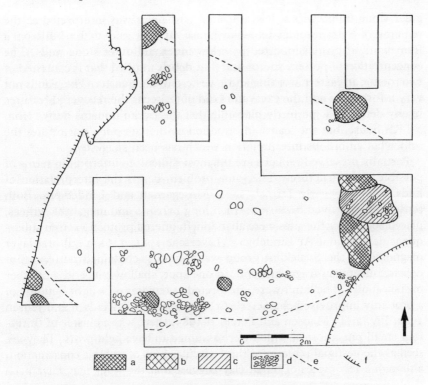

Figure 95 Plan of the structure at Łącko: a–c-pits with a differential mixture of
burnt soil (strong to weak), d-stone frame, e-limit of stone frame, f-limit of modern
damage (Source: Domańska and Kośko 1983).

has had a profound influence upon scholars tackling problems of northern
regions and may have led them to expect what was really never there. On
the other hand, one firmly believes that re-interpretation should be undertaken only when there are good reasons for doing so. The current debate
in southern Scandinavia shows clearly that desperate attempts to fit the
poor and, by present-day standards, wholly inadequate evidence into a new
mould, do not clarify but often obscure the issue.

After this cautionary tale let us now review some of the evidence for the
TRB houses. As previously noted, the structures are still rare and widely
dispersed throughout the culture's distribution area, and they do not easily
fit into a pattern which could reveal either chronological or regional trends.
Examples of the early TRB houses are known from Poland, north Germany
and Denmark, where they are relatively small and mostly, but not invariably, rectangular in form.

At Łącko (Domańska and Kośko 1983; Fig. 95), which is one of the
earliest sites within the eastern TRB group, a partially preserved quadran-

gular stone frame with a few asociated post-holes was interpreted as the remains of a trapezoidal tent-like house. It was said to be built on a framework of posts supported by a low inner and outer stone walls. The concentration of pottery sherds and flint debris implied that it consisted of two rooms: an eastern working and a western living quarter. The plan is not very informative and the excavators did not discuss the recovered features in any detail. It is perfectly plausible that the Łącko remains derive from a TRB house, but the scanty information neither supports nor refutes the somewhat ambitious interpretation which has been suggested.

Partially preserved remains are the most difficult to interpret in terms of possible superstructures. The same problem besets the interpretation of finds from two early Danish sites, Mosegården and Lindebjerg. Both settlements survived because earthen long barrows and megalithic graves, placed soon after the sites were abandoned, offered protection from subsequent destruction. At Lindebjerg (Liversage 1981, 116), a cultural layer diagnostic of the Svaleklint group was found; it contained pottery, flint debris, burnt clay fragments and, in one spot, shallow pits and a number of stake-holes. The latter were interpreted as remains of 'a light building of a probably improvised character'. At Mosegården (T. Madsen and Jensen 1982, Fig. 2; T. Madsen and Petersen 1985) there was a cluster of thirty-four small pits, most of which were assumed to have held posts. They are seen as the vestigial remains of three circular huts of unclear construction, although a few pieces of burnt clay suggest that the walls may have been daubed.

The Mosegården huts were associated with traces of various domestic activities: there was a fireplace to the east and a considerable scatter of pottery sherds and flint debris in the area between the hearth and the huts; some unworked flint tools were also found in the rubbish area further east. Mosegården is interpreted as a small base camp of the Volling group (500–600 m²) in which a group of about fifteen people lived for a relatively short period. Moreover, on the basis of general observations, Madsen has argued that we should abandon the idea of large villages (which we have mistakenly carried over from the central European context) and accept that small camps, such as Mosegården, were typical of the early farming groups in Denmark. Presumably by implication this pattern should be expected in other TRB regions.

To expect a repeat of a central European scenario in a different environment and against a dissimilar cultural background is unwarranted and the original interpretations of Barkær and Stengade were obvious examples of such misconceptions. It is reasonable to assume that communities entering a new cultural and economic context will initially operate on a small scale. However, the size of early sites is of importance and the prime question which needs to be answered is: how do we reliably determine the size of such an early unit? The Mosegården site was preserved under a long barrow and here the size of the monument was clearly responsible for the size of the settlement preserved beneath. How much of the settlement may have been destroyed during the building of the barrow, and indeed how much of it remained uncovered and became obliterated by later activities, cannot be estimated. Madsen and Jensen (1982, 64–5) argued that most of the site had been preserved and that it was never originally larger, but the fact that two of the huts were clearly destroyed by the barrow-building is self evident when the plans are considered in detail (ibid., Plans 2–4).

This point is of greater importance than it may initially appear; a good example in this context is offered by the Sarnowo settlement in the Eastern TRB group (Gabałówna 1968 and 1969a; Niesiołowska-Średniowska 1982; Wiklak 1986). The settlement belongs to the early phase of the TRB in Kujavia and while in absolute terms it is older than Mosegården, in relative terms the two are wholly comparable. Mosegården was found beneath one barrow, whereas settlement traces at Sarnowo are known from at least three barrows. Moreover cultural debris was incorporated in all nine mounds, suggesting that other settlement traces may have been missed during the early explorations of the cemetery. The area of the cemetery covers roughly 50,000 m²; additionally, part of the settlement (area 1A) which was never covered by burial mounds, and of which 850 m² was excavated, was found 50 m north-west of the cemetery complex. The cultural material of the pre-barrow period at Sarnowo is homogeneous and archaeologically contemporary.

While hearths, pits containing charcoal and cultural material were found during the early investigations of the cemetery (Chmielewski 1952, 53–73), only the meticulous excavation of barrow 8 by Gabałówna revealed traces of a building (Wiklak 1982; Midgley 1985, Fig. 26a). It survived as a rectangular spread of daub 6 m × 10 m in size. The excavation report also mentions eighteen post-holes (0.15–0.3 m in diameter and 0.2–0.4 m deep) along the edge of the daub spread; these post-holes presumably represent the remains of the walls of the building, although we have no other information on the superstructure. The daub pieces were mostly flat on one side and many appear to have been 'painted' white, an interesting detail suggesting that the houses may have been whitewashed.

Foundation trenches of two more houses were found in area 1A (Fig. 96). These appeared as charcoal-stained areas of grey sand bordered by post-holes. The plan shows that both were roughly rectangular structures of the N–S orientation. They measured 3 m × 4.1 m and 5 m × 6 m and were similarly planned, with a small ante-chamber to the south and a larger room beyond which contained a hearth. While no evidence survived to aid the above-ground reconstruction, the dove-tailing technique (observed in the burnt ritual building from the Gaj long barrow; Chmielewski 1952, 89) may have been used at Sarnowo as well.

Thus this early site of the TRB in Kujavia appears to have been of

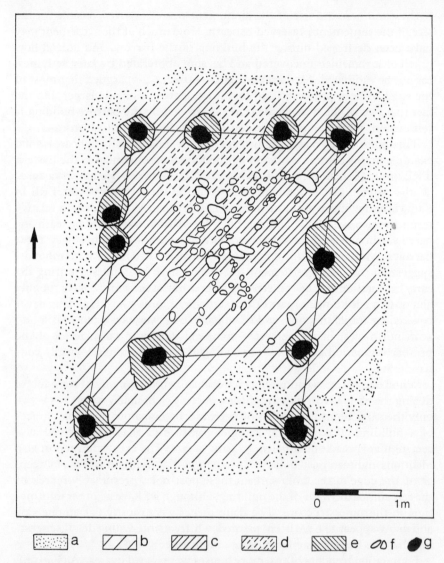

Figure 96 Plan of house no. 1 at Sarnowo, site 1A: a-yellow sand, b-grey sand, c-grey sand with charcoal, d-burnt sand, e-grey-brown sand, f-stones, g-post-holes (Source: Wiklak 1986).

considerable size. In real terms there were probably a number of separate household clusters, although it is equally possible that the settlement shifted horizontally over a certain period of time. However, we still have an area which, potentially at least, represents a complex of a fundamentally different size from those recovered at the Mosegården and Lindebjerg barrows. The circumstances at Sarnowo remind us of the need for caution when we not only pronounce upon the size of the settlement but also subsequently proceed to make inferences about its population, land-use pattern and relation to other sites in the vicinity.

Evidence of other houses dating from the early TRB is not very satisfactory. A small dwelling is quoted from Muldbjerg, where an E–W oriented hut was discovered during the excavation in the Aamose bog on Zealand (Troels-Smith 1960a, 597). The hut was 6–7 m long and 3 m wide; some hazel stakes were found along the sides and Troels-Smith suggested that reeds may have been used in the construction of the walls. Flint debris and a large quantity of charcoal were found in the interior; evidence of domestic activities outside the hut was confined to the southern, lake-facing side.

It is rather disappointing that no definite houses of the early period have so far been found in northern Germany. Traces of a timber structure placed against the original beach at Siggeneben-Süd (Meurers-Balke 1983, Plate 19) can hardly be interpreted in terms of an inhabited house, but are probably the remains of a landing platform for boats. Vague remains of a burnt structure, at least 8.5 m × 8.5 m in size and dated to about 5100 BP (3900 BC), came to light at Schönermark in Mecklenburg (Geisler 1965), but nothing is known of its construction. Traces of a later TRB structure are known from Ralswiek on Rügen, where an irregularly shaped feature containing hearth and cultural material has been interpreted as the remains of a small house (Nilius and Warnke 1984).

The only other relevant site is the Hunte 1 settlement on the Dümmer lake, where Reinerth's (1939) excavations during the 1930s uncovered timber floors made of split logs. Although altogether thirteen houses were found, a later critique by Dürr (1960) implied that only four of them were associated with the TRB, and even then they probably date to the late phase. The structures are all relatively small, on average 4 × 4 m in size, with an ante-chamber and a larger room beyond. Posts and wattle were used for the construction of the walls, and these apparently supported a gable roof (Schirnig 1979c, Fig. 7).

A few structures from middle Germany have also been claimed as belonging to the early TRB (Baalberge). Of the three houses from Diebzig, only one is known in plan (Preuss 1966, 141–3; Fig. 97: 3). A bedding trench with post-holes up to 25 cm thick outlined an area measuring 5 m × 4.25 m which was open to the south-east. Two large hearths in pits were apparently found in the interior as well as a number of broken amphorae of Baalberge type. One more plausible Baalberge house comes from Drosa (ibid., 143–4). It was roughly rectangular, 10.7 m × 8.7 m in size and had rounded corners, although a Baalberge burial crouched in the eastern part of this structure could imply that this was a grave chamber rather than a house.

An identical pattern of settlement comprising small houses can be observed on other sites of the Southern TRB group. At Wallendorf (Behrens

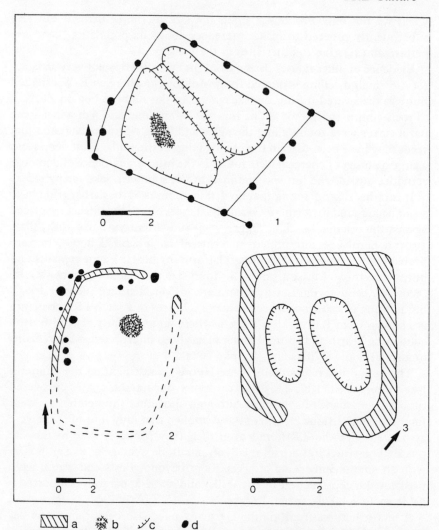

Figure 97 House plans from Dohnsen [1], Wallendorf [2] and Diebzig [3]: a-trenches, b-hearths, c-limit of interior pits, d-post-holes (Source: Preuss 1966; Schirnig 1979d).

1973, 198–9; Figs 94 and 97: 2), which is generally assumed to be a Salzmünde settlement of about 10 ha in size, nine or ten house plans were uncovered and an additional twenty-one or twenty-two were assumed on the basis of the presence of hearths. The houses were on average between 4 m and 7 m wide and between 5.5 m and 8 m long. The construction is mostly based on individually placed posts. One partially preserved house revealed a bedding trench with rounded corners and post-holes to the

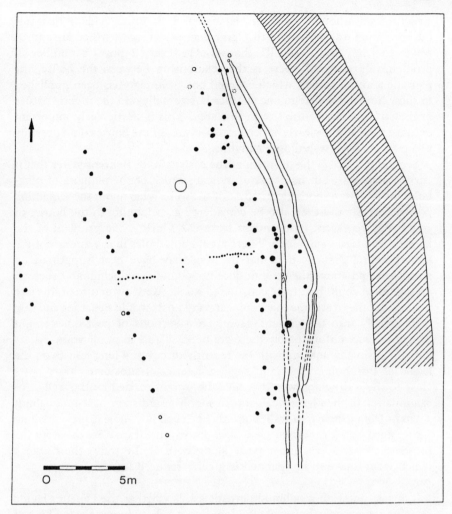

Figure 98 Plan of the structure from Dölauer Heide (Source: Behrens 1973).

inside as well as the outside (Fig. 97: 2). The plan of the settlement shows some of the houses in clusters, while others form linear patterns. The course of an interrupted ditch to the east of the houses may represent the remains of an enclosing system round the settlement.

In stark contrast to the above is the assumed long house from Dölauer Heide (Behrens and Schröter 1980, 21–3; Fig. 98), which is so far the only structure of this type from this area. Behrens' interpretation of the ground traces is of a somewhat trapezoidal building, 21 m × 6.5–8 m in size. It consisted of two rooms separated by two short rows of smaller posts, which retained a 3 m gap between them. A row of post-holes to the west of the structure was thought of as an extension. It is quite evident that this interpretation was influenced to a large degree by models which are appropriate to LBK and post-LBK houses. However, it poses a number of problems. First of all, there is the relationship between the house, the palisade and the barrow which covered both. No plan has been published to show how they relate to one another horizontally and the precise nature of the stratigraphy of the site in this area. This is particularly important because some of the clearly superfluous features of the house could possibly relate to the barrow-building activities.

Secondly, there is the problem of the eastern wall. Behrens states that it curved outwards, but he does not indicate which of the plethora of post-holes outline the hypothetical course of the wall. What about the remaining post-holes? Should they also be considered as belonging to the house, or could they represent independent features? Thirdly, the problem of the house's roof is not explained. There are no post-holes in the interior of the house; Behrens' suggestion that the roof may have been supported on stands erected above the ground does not sound convincing, and such an arrangement could hardly be considered stable. With a stucture of this size it is reasonable to assume that roof-carrying posts would be larger and dug more deeply into the ground. Here, cross-sections of post-holes might provide a clue; unfortunately these are not available in publication. Alternatively, using an analogy with the recently discovered long houses on the island of Bornholm, one could suggest a series of subsidiary inner posts close to the wall which would reduce the weight carried by the walls. An examination of the plan reveals three roughly equidistant post-holes about 1.5 m in from the eastern wall, but only one such post-hole is present along the western wall (others may have been destroyed). If we were to accept the presence of subsidiary inner posts along both of the walls, the distance which would have to be spanned is greatly reduced from 6.5–8 m to 3.5–5 m.

The last question we should perhaps ask is whether the Dölauer Heide remains represents a house at all. One cannot help being reminded here of the comment Eriksen and Madsen (1984) made with reference to the Sigersted structure – that is represented merely two rows of post-holes. This could equally apply to the Dölauer Heide, especially when we consider the proximity of the said house to the palisade and, in the light of discoveries elsewhere, the function of the entire enclosure system (see below, Chapter 7.4).

It is possible that a horse-shoe shaped dwelling may have been a regular feature of the domestic architecture of the Northern TRB. About twenty-five structures of this type were excavated by Winther at Troldebjerg (1935, 6–13, Figs 2–7; 1938, 5–6, Figs 1–6). The houses, in rows of about a dozen, were found on both sides of a low hill about 10–20 m from the lake shore. They were between 5 and 7 m in diameter, constructed on a framework of posts, with the straight wall of wattle-and-daub and the curved side walls lower and stacked with turves, against which the roof sloped away from the lake.

An example of another horse-shoe shaped hut, very similar in plan to the Troldebjerg dwellings, has recently come to light at the contemporary site of Hanstedgård on Jutland (Eriksen and Madsen 1984, Fig. 7). The curved wall was seen partly in a double row of stake-holes and in a bedding trench surrounded by post-holes. The straight wall was delineated by just four post-holes and two of them were aligned with post-holes in the middle of the structure, which were assumed to provide roof supports. The original appearance of this house was reconstructed as a low, wattle-and-daub curved wall and a taller, more solid straight wall which may have been of similar construction.

Rectangular house forms, however, are also present in the Northern TRB architecture. The interim reports from excavations in the south of Bornholm not only confirm their presence, but may also show the evolution of this house form (Kempfner-Jørgensen and Watt 1985). The earliest house is the rectangular structure from Runegård (ibid., 95, Fig. 13) which, on the basis of ceramics, has been associated with the MN I style. It appears as a setting of individual post-holes delineating an area of 9.5 m × 6 m, with two centrally placed interior posts. A second pair of central post-holes (close to the first set) were thought by the excavators to be evidence of repair, but it is equally possible tht both were part of a contemporary roof-supporting arrangement. Chronologically later and somewhat more elaborate are the houses from a nearby location at Grødbygård (ibid., 87–8, Figs 2–3) and another Bornholm site, Limensgård (F.O. Nielsen and P.O. Nielsen 1985, Figs 15–17). Here the outline of the houses was defined by a foundation trench which contained small post-holes, the size ranging from 10 m to 18 m in length and from 6.2 m to 7 m in width. Central post-holes in each house were roughly equidistant from one another (three at Grødbygård and five at Limensgård), and at both sites there were post-holes about 1 m inside the walls, twice as closely spaced as the central posts and alternating *vis-à-vis* one another. All these houses are dated to the final TRB period. Because of the interim nature of the report, there is no information pertaining to the type of wall and roof construction, although the regular layout does correspond to the types of house known from other European contexts.

Rectangular houses do in fact appear in other areas of the TRB culture, although the known house plans display a wide range of variations. The best-documented examples derive from Lower Saxony and central Poland. A house roughly comparable in size to the Danish examples is known from Flögeln, near Cuxhaven (Zimmermann 1979, Fig. 99: A). Shallow trenches delimited an area of 12.8 m × 4.8 m. Three pairs of post-holes along the central axis carried the roof and the interior was divided into four sections,

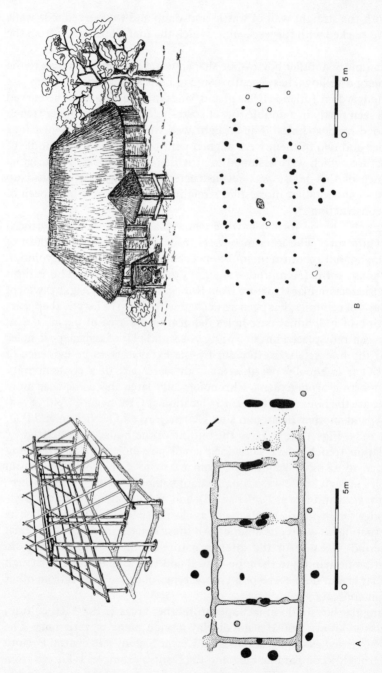

Figure 99 Ground plans and reconstruction of houses at Flögeln [A] and Wittenwater [B] (Source: Schirnig 1979c; Zimmermann 1979).

the divisions running across central posts. In contrast to the Danish examples, the subsidiary roof-supporting posts were located outside the walls; a reconstruction suggests a heavy timber framework with rafters supported by a central ridge and additional, horizontal beams resting outside the walls.

Another example of a house comes from a long-known site at Wittenwater, near Uelzen, which survived under a later Bronze Age mound (Voss 1965; Schirnig 1979d; Fig. 99: B). A pattern of individual post-holes (spaced between 1 m and 1.3 m apart) shows the outline of a rectangle with rounded corners 15.6 m × 6 m in size. Post-holes preserved in the interior may have been chiefly roof supports, but they also divide the inner space into three rooms of roughly equal size. The middle room contained a centrally placed hearth; a heavy concentration of flint tools and debris in the north-east corner suggests that tool-making may have taken place indoors. Food preparation, on the other hand, appears to have been an outdoor activity: a quern stone was found outside two post-holes which were interpreted as providing the support for a roof over a working area. Other post-holes to the south of the house were interpreted as a storage structure.

Contemporary with the Wittenwater building are two small rectangular structures from Dohnsen, near Celle (Schirnig 1979d; Fig. 97: 1). The post-holes, which delineated areas of 4.9 × 4 m and 5–5.8 m × 4.1 m, were set between 1 m and 1.5 m apart. The interiors of these structures were dug deep into the ground (up to 1.4 m), however leaving a shelf of walls around the edge and creating large pits in the interior, which in both instances contained hearths. In view of the depth involved, it is perhaps more likely that, as similar finds from Poland suggest, the Dohnsen structures represent roofed workshops rather than regular houses.

Although many large, upland settlements are known in the South-eastern TRB group, they tend to the the result of prolonged, and sometimes even multi-cultural occupation of suitably located elevations. Accepting the inevitable changes which occurred during the occupation of such sites, investigations can nevertheless throw light upon the settlement organisation.

Thus, like Bronocice, the Ćmielów settlement was also located on an isolated elevation about 500 m long and varying between 170 m and 200 m in width (Podkowińska 1950 and 1952). No house plans were recovered here, but three major complexes were noted, clearly separated by empty spaces. Within all three there was the usual assortment of small and large pits, although most were concentrated in the middle complex which was presumably the main living area. An interesting arrangment is revealed when we consider the evidence of specialised activities. We discussed earlier (Chapter 6.3.2) the regional importance of the Ćmielów settlement in the production of axes and other flint tools; thus it is not surprising to find that a large complex of flint workshops was located towards the

northern edge of the settlement. Pottery-making and other activities were
also carried out towards the outer limits of the sites; their traces were not
observed in the central area, where copper-smelting and pitching activities
took place. A similar arrangement of various workshops concentrated
towards the outer limits of the settlement was also noted at another upland
site in this region, Gródek Nadbużny.

Only two sites from the South-eastern group offer reliable evidence of
houses, and the arrangements on these sites differ from those just described. Two structures were found at the upland site of Niedźwiedź
(Burchard 1981; Hensel and Milisauskas 1985, 78–84, Fig. 37). The irregular layout of individual post-holes identified one house which was
4.5 m wide and survived to just under 10 m in length. The other building
was also rectangular; it measured 23 m long and 7.5 m wide (Fig. 100).
Individual post-holes varied between 0.45 m and 0.75 m in diameter, and
there were three central post-holes along the building's main axis. Additional post-holes at the eastern end may indicate an entrance.

Apart from the preserved house plans, the site at Dobroń, near Sieradz,
also offers some insight into the domestic arrangements present on the
settlement. Here two contemporary complexes, each comprising two
houses and a range of associated pits, were found about 30 m apart (Pelisiak
1985, Figs 3 and 11). On the basis of the pattern of preserved post-holes,
the buildings appear as somewhat irregular rectangles, ranging from 5.3 m
to 10 m in length and up to 5.5 m in width. The wall posts must have
been substantial since some of the post-holes were up to 0.4 m in diameter
and up to 0.65 m deep; in view of the absence of central posts, they
must have carried the weight of the roof. Daub pieces with branch imprints
indicate the covering of walls. The suggested reconstruction of the best-
preserved building (Fig. 101) is, however, somewhat conjectural;
it is evident from the plan that many post-holes, especially in the south-
eastern corner, indicate secondary rebuilding rather than original
construction.

A number of further post-holes found to the north of one compound
were interpreted as possibly representing a fence which surrounded the
houses. In the yard between the two houses and the fence there were several
pits and a large hearth which was also surrounded by post-holes. The
excavator suggested that, judging by the content of the hearth, pottery may
have been fired there and thus he postulated that the area was roofed over
(Pelisiak 1985, 25); a store of clay found close by strengthens this interpretation. Post-holes were also associated with a 3.6 m × 1.6 m pit in the
other complex. In conjunction with the content of the pit – animal bones,
acorns etc. – this suggests that the pit may have been a roofed storehouse.

Such an interpretation is particularly interesting in view of the fact that
many sites reveal similar features. The usual interpretations tend to centre
around semi-subterranean dwellings, but they never appear convincing; to

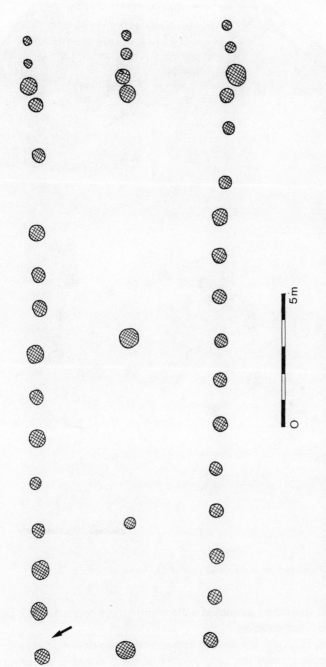

Figure 100 Plan of the larger house at Niedźwiedź (Source: by kind permission of B. Burchard).

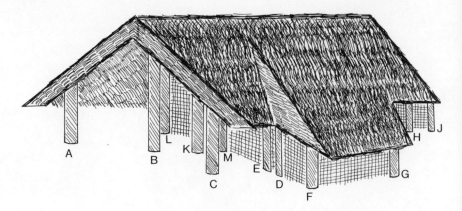

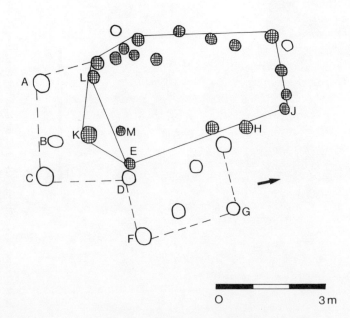

Figure 101 Reconstruction and ground plan of the house at Dobroń (Source: Pelisiak 1985).

regard such structures as roofed cellars and stores seems to be a far more appropriate interpretation.

Surprisingly, relatively little is known about the domestic arrangements and architecture from the later phases of the Eastern TRB group. The regularly quoted rectangular house of the Wiórek phase from Zarębowo has never been published in full (Wiślański 1979, 203). It is said to have measured 12 m × 7.5 m and it apparently replaced an earlier building; it had clay-daubed walls and was divided into two rooms, one of which contained the remains of an oven. Traces of small, rectangular buildings, 5.8 m × 5.5 m in size, were uncovered on a late TRB site in Tarkowo in Kujavia (Kośko 1981, Fig. 29).

7.4 Enclosed sites of the TRB

The enclosed sites within the TRB culture represent a new category of site for this area. At present the evidence is limited by and large to the Northern TRB group, although undoubtedly these sites represent a much more widespread phenomenon. It has been decided to discuss these sites briefly and separately from the other evidence for settlements and ritual sites of the TRB because their limited distribution does not yet allow their incorporation into the overall pattern of the cultural landscape in the TRB.

The discovery of the enclosed sites, some of which reveal a remarkable similarity to the British causewayed enclosures, within the Northern TRB began with the excavations at Büdelsdorf in Schleswig-Holstein, although initially the palisade/ditch system was interpreted as being the remains of settlement defences (Hingst 1970, 1971a, 1971b). The first causewayed enclosure to be excavated in Denmark was at Sarup on the island of Fyn (N. Andersen 1974a, 1974b, 1975, 1977, 1981, 1988a, 1988b) and subsequent investigation on a number of sites in east central Jutland (Toftum, Bjerggård, Lønt, Hevringholm; T. Madsen 1978a, 1978b, 1988; B. Madsen and Fiedel 1987) confirmed the presence of this type of monument. This recognition, moreover, has resulted in reinterpretations and new investigations at previously known TRB settlement sites (Bundsø, Troldebjerg, Trelleborg, etc.) and today at least fifteen sites from southern Scandinavia can be placed in this category. Doubtless more examples will be recognised in due course.

Evidence from other areas of the TRB culture unfortunately still remains ambiguous. A number of 'enclosed settlements' have been known for a long time in central Germany and southern Poland (Jażdżewski 1936; Grimm 1958), but these have always been considered to represent defensive sites of one sort or another, and without new excavations any correlation of central European and northern evidence is still difficult. On the other hand, the recognition of enclosure sites throughout Neolithic Europe opens up a new dimension for the future interpretation of this clearly pan-European phenomenon (Burgess *et al.* 1988).

Since the currently available evidence from the Northern TRB has recently been assessed in some detail (T. Madsen 1988; N. Andersen 1988a and 1988b), the following discussion will only outline briefly the most important features of the sites in question.

The evidence from the Danish enclosures suggests that there are a number of features which, while displaying individuality on specific sites,

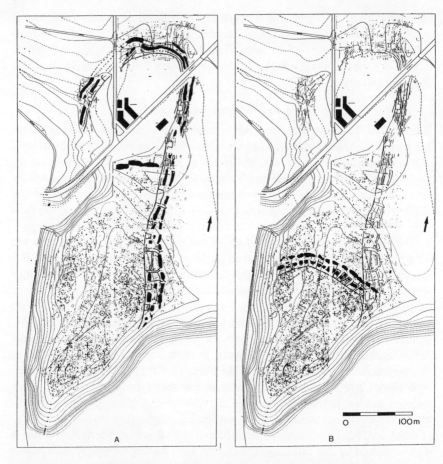

Figure 102 Two TRB enclosures at Sarup: A-enclosure during the Fuchsberg
phase, B-enclosure during the later MNI phase (Source. N. Andersen 1988a).

nevertheless reveal a strong degree of common tradition. The most obvious
is the presence of ditch segments separated by causeways which either cut
off a promontory (Fig. 102) or outline the perimeter of the site (Fig. 103).
Such ditches form either single (Bjerggård, Stävie) or double rows (Sarup,
Toftum); at least four rows have been identified at Büdelsdorf, although
neither their sequence nor the precise course can be fully determined (Fig.
103). Sometimes the individual ditch segments appear to have been fenced
or surrounded by arrangements of posts (Büdelsdorf, Sarup).

At a number of sites the ditches are accompanied by timber palisades,
which may be either set into a bedding trench (Büdelsdorf, Sarup, Hevringholm) or free-standing (later phase at Sarup); both forms may also be
present on one site (Büdelsdorf). Most of the sites appear to have been
relatively simply laid out, although this is not the case with the almost

completely excavated site of Sarup. The very complex arrangements identified here and the similar complexity hinted at in Büdelsdorf warn us
against too simple an interpretation, especially when only partial excavation
has been undertaken.

Thus at Sarup (N. Andersen 1988a) two chronologically distinct enclosure systems have been identified: the earlier, larger complex cutting off
a promontory of about 8.5 ha in area was constructed during the Fuchsberg
phase, while the later complex, reduced in size to about 3 ha, belongs to the
later part of MN I period. The two sites are 120 radiocarbon years apart
(see Appendix).

The older enclosure consists of a 572 m long trench which curves and
doubles back at the north end of the promontory (Fig. 102: A). This trench
held within it a sturdy palisade of split oak timbers about 0.5 m thick and
assumed to have been between 2 m and 3 m in height. Only one formal
entrance across this palisade has been noted and it appears to have been
concealed from outside by an independent stretch of fence.

Adjacent to the outside of this palisade and running nearly all the way
along it was a series of roughly rectangular enclosures fenced by smaller
timber posts (only 1–1.5 m in height). Some of the enclosures were accessible from the inside of the palisade area, but to most of them access was
gained from the outside, sometimes guided by additional stretches of fence
(N. Andersen 1988a, Fig. 18: 3–5). Within and between this enclosure
system there ran two rows of ditch segments: the inner row was more
irregular on account of the differently sized enclosures, while the outer row
was more regular with longer ditch segments running roughly parallel to
the palisade. On the northern curve, where the small enclosures were not
detected, the ditch segments were longer (82 m and 101 m) in contrast to the
shorter stretches elsewhere (4.7–24.1 m).

The younger phase complex enclosed a considerably smaller area and
differed in construction. The inner palisade was simply hammered into
the ground over a distance of 159 m and is estimated to have contained
about 900 posts placed three deep. Outside this palisade ran a row of small
ditches surrounded by settings of posts forming parallelograms; further to
the outside the second row of longer ditches was more regularly arranged
with very narrow causeways in between (Fig. 102: B). In both phases the
interior of the enclosure was also used, as is indicated by the presence of
numerous post-holes and offering pits.

While Sarup reveals the most sophisticated design among all the south
Scandinavian causewayed enclosures, individual features noted here are
also encountered elsewhere. Ditch segments surounded by fences or rows
of free-standing posts were observed at Büdelsdorf, for example, but they
were further away from the palisade than at Sarup and the timber settings
around them were laid out on the plan of a rectangle (Fig. 103). Not many
interiors of causewayed enclosures have been investigated, but the presence

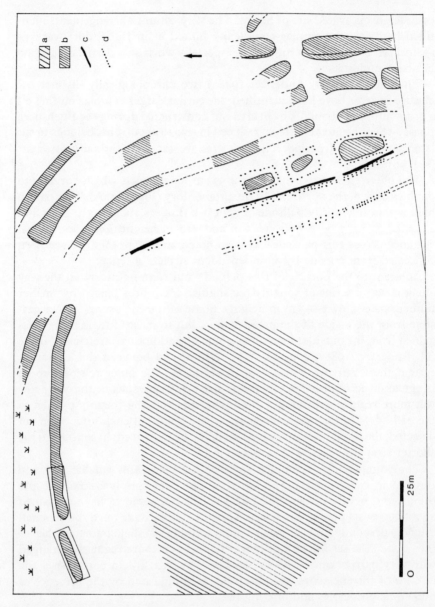

Figure 103 TRB enclosure at Büdelsdorf: a-interior with traces of activity, b-ditches, c-palisade, d-rows of posts (Source: Hingst 1971b).

of offering pits has been noted at Årupgård, Lønt and at Stävie (T. Madsen 1988, 309, 315 and 319).

All the investigated sites offer evidence for a wide range of activities, most of which are seemingly of a non-domestic nature. The digging of ditches appears to have been particularly important in itself, as is very clearly shown in the complicated layout at Sarup, and so must the almost immediate backfilling since on many sites evidence of natural silting-up of ditches is lacking. Subsequent recutting of ditches seems to have been equally important on some sites, for example at Toftum and Bjerggård (ibid., 320), but less so at Sarup; where it is observed, the initial pattern of immediate backfilling follows.

In many instances deposits were made in connection with activities which took place at the bottom of ditches or in recuts. These include various combinations of organic materials such as animal bones or oyster shells, pottery and heaps of flint implements; more rarely, specific deposits such as dogs skulls (Bjerggård) or human jaws (Sarup) were placed in ditches. Frequently these activities were asociated with the lighting of fires.

An interesting depositional pattern was recorded at Sarup. During the Fuchsberg period the palisade appears to have been more of a focus of deposition than were the ditches: 2261 artefacts were recovered from the 81 m long excavated stretch of the palisade trench, while 140 m of excavated ditch segments yielded 1343 artefacts of which 1158 came from the northern ditches (N. Andersen 1988a, 348–50). During the later phase the ditches received only a few deposits (altogether 130 finds) and the whole focus seems to have shifted towards the interior where twenty-three contemporary pits contained offerings of pottery, flint axes and a very fine battle axe (ibid., 360; N. Andersen 1988b, 151, Fig.).

Thus the depositional pattern offers some indication of the importance of various segments of the enclosure and there is a clear change of focus in the placement of goods from near the facade to the enclosed interior. It is perhaps too early to make generalisations about other sites, but it is possible that where timber facades were constructed these were the focus of the offerings, while in the absence of the facades (as at Toftum and Bjerggård) this function was fulfilled by ditches. It is on the latter sites, moreover, that ditch recutting also appears to have been more frequent than elsewhere.

Evidence of pottery manufacture noted at a few causewayed enclosures offers an important dimension to the possible function of these sites as centres of ritual pottery production. Recent investigations at the enclosure at Hevringholm on the Djursland peninsula revealed a pit which was used for the firing of Fuchsberg-style pottery (B. Madsen and Fiedel 1987). Similar evidence has come from the enclosures at Büdelsdorf and Stävie. At

Büdelsdorf several baking ovens were found in the central part of the enclosure. They were either kilns covered with a clay dome or pits covered by a conical-shaped setting of stones (Bjørn and Hingst 1973). Similar types were noted at Stävie, although the ceramic material from this site on the whole belongs to the final phase of the TRB culture (Larsson 1982). Moreover, the firing of pottery appears to have taken place in the immediate post-enclosure phase at Sarup. A pit containing sherds from at least forty-four vessels characteristic of the Blandebjerg style was interpreted by N. Andersen as residue from an unsuccessful firing (1977, 31).

While there is a relatively clear general structural and functional affinity among the south Scandinavian enclosures, their relation to the few sites from other areas of the TRB culture is still difficult to assess. The central German sites are known under the term *Höhensiedlungen*, but this name covers a wide variety of types whose common characteristic is a location high in the landscape in a prominent position. Indeed, a number of South-eastern TRB settlement sites described earlier in this chapter are located precisely thus. Moreover, a general lack of landscape surveys, especially from the air, makes it difficult to determine the range involved. The presence of banks, ditches and palisades in association with cultural material has traditionally been interpreted as evidence for some sort of defensive system.

Starling (1988, 419) recently used the German site category of *Höhensiedlung* synonymously with enclosed site. Yet even his brief survey reveals that not all upland sites were enclosed, that due to the paucity of research it is simply not known whether some of the lowland sites may also have been enclosed, and that for the majority of enclosed sites there is no evidence to suggest that traces of occupation and the enclosing system were contemporary. The upland location of a site does not in itself imply that it has a different status from a lowland site. Kruk's (1973) research in southern Poland has shown that upland settlement often simply made good economic sense in terms of exploitation of a wide range of resources. Moreover, the distribution pattern of the central German *Höhensiedlungen* is very puzzling since, with a few exceptions along the Saale river, they tend to concentrate along the western periphery of the Elbe-Saale TRB settlement area (Starling 1988, Fig. 21: 2–4). Three possibilities immediately spring to mind: this unusual distribution is a result of research bias, there was a need for an upland location as a precaution against the intrusion of different peoples from the west or, most likely of all, we should not be surprised to see a substantial upland settlement in what is effectively the Harz foreland.

It is not the intention here to suggest that all *Höhensiedlungen* were simply settlements, but it would be equally incorrect, in view of the ambivalence of the German evidence, to place every upland site in the same category as Dölauer Heide or Quenstedt. There is little virtue in interpreting the function of sites whose features remain mostly unknown.

At Dölauer Heide near Halle, the enclosing ditch system on the natural elevation above the Saale river, which in places incorporates up to six ditches, embraces an area of about 25 ha and consists of two enclosures: a larger enclosure to the south and a smaller on the northern spur of the elevation (Fig. 104; Behrens and Schröter 1980). The ditches and banks were apparently quite substantial, in places exceeding 3 m in depth. That some measure of protection of the interior was involved is suggested by the fact that the stretches with the highest number of ditches correpond precisely with the naturally least defensive aspects of the site.

Traces of a burnt palisade were registered at a sufficient number of places within the perimeter to suggest that it probably ran all the way round the inside. An estimated 20,000 trees would have been used in its construction (Behrens and Schröter 1980, 15). Although the ditches at Dölauer Heide do not appear to have been segmented, the presence of a palisade (possibly even a double palisade) inside the ditched area accords well with the circumstances observed in the southern Scandinavian enclosures. Moreover, the palisade trench appears to have contained a substantial amount of older TRB pottery (Baalberge and Salzmünde), charcoal, ash, burnt flint and burnt bones. While there is no indication of the possible pattern of such deposits, their presence at the palisade contrasts strongly with the apparent lack of cultural material from the interior of the site and recalls the concentration of activities against palisades at sites such as Sarup and possibly at Troldebjerg (T. Madsen 1988, 318). In this context, the interpretation of post-hole arrangements preserved beneath barrow No. 6, usually regarded as the foundations of a TRB house, may take on a different meaning. The arrangements may well represent a surviving segment of free-standing enclosure or shorter palisades set against the inner side of the enclosure. The considerable presence of what is described as domestic debris within the area could, in fact, reflect concentrated depositional activity.

The use of at least part of the site – the northern spur – for later Bernburg settlement is again in accordance with circumstances in the north where the ceremonial function of the site is being replaced by one of a more domestic nature, although such settlements may on occasions have performed the additional function of guardianship of an earlier, time-honoured ritual place.

Among the other central German sites we should recall the presence of enclosing features at Wallendorf (Fig. 94), where a stretch of a ditch and an entrance may represent a fence round a settlement but could also reflect an earlier (or later), functionally different structure. Similarly, traces of enclosing ditches are known from Derenburg (with only late TRB material) and the site of Salzmünde, where cultural material and burials date to the

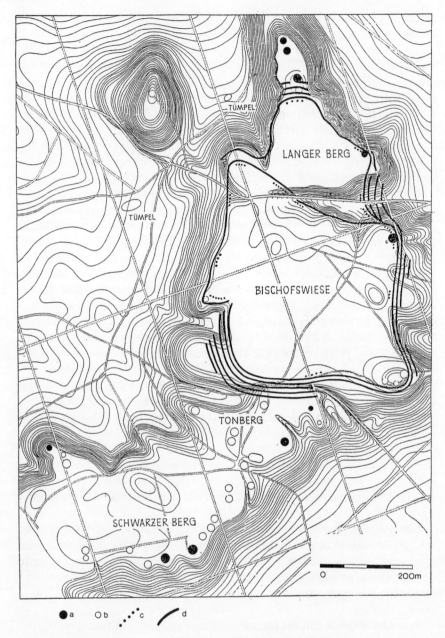

Figure 104 TRB enclosure at Dölauer Heide: a-excavated burial mounds, b-unexplored burial mounds, c-timber palisade, d-ditches (Source: Behrens and Schröter 1980).

Salzmünde phase itself, but the paucity of information makes it impossible to offer any interpretation (Starling 1988).

One more site from central Germany, at Quenstedt, remains to be mentioned. The main features recovered here have been described by Behrens (1981d): five concentric circles of post-holes (varying from 35–40 m to 90–100 m in diameter), four entrances, Baalberge-phase burials in the free interior, and the ubiquitous Bernburg settlement, represent the main elements of the site. The original attribution of this complex structure – interpreted as a free-standing arrangement of posts of a general ritual nature – to the early TRB (Baalberge phase) has recently been questioned by Behrens (1984). A new radiocarbon date for charcoal from Quenstedt of 5660 ± 65 BP (KN-2864, *c*. 4500 BC), as well as the presence of stray sherds of *Stichbandkeramik* and Rössen, opens up the possibility that the timber structure may belong to an earlier cultural context, which would place it together with the Lengyel horizon enclosures in Czechoslovakia (Whittle 1988).

With reference to the eastern periphery of the South-eastern TRB group, enclosed sites have long been thought to represent upland 'fortified' settlements. As early as the 1930s Jażdżewski (1936, 293) quoted a number of TRB sites from the Wolhynian plateau which showed traces of earthen banks and ditches, and whose location in the landscape closely approximates to that of the central German *Höhensiedlungen*. However, at some of these sites, for example at Winniki and Grzybowice Małe, the fortifications are thought to belong to a much later, mediaeval period while at others, for example at Zimne and Gródek Nadbużny, new excavations have shown that such ditches belong not to the TRB but to the late Lengyel local group known as the Lublin-Wolhynian culture (Peleščišin 1971; Jastrzębski, pers. comm.).

It is not improbable that some of the upland settlements were indeed in need of defensive structures. This may have been particularly important in the regions where a number of contemporary but culturally separate communities lived in close proximity. Precisely such circumstances appear to have existed at Bronocice, where the TRB and Lublin-Wolhynian groups were sharing the same elevation above the Nidzica valley (Kruk and Milisauskas 1985). Of the three ditches recovered here none can be assigned directly to the TRB culture. The earliest ditch, accompanied by a timber palisade, was associated with the Lublin-Wolhynian settlement located in the western part of the elevation. This settlement post-dates a brief TRB episode on the same spot and was either contemporary with or preceded the main TRB occupation of the eastern part of the elevation (Kruk and Milisauskas 1981b, 104–5). In this context it is interesting to note that at Zimne and Gródek Nadbużny the Lublin-Wolhynian settlement with the 'defensive system' also preceded the main occupation of these sites by the TRB culture.

The second ditch, partly overlying the earlier complex, post-dates the TRB settlement but its dimensions (only 1 m deep and up to 4 m wide) hardly make it a defensive structure, and it has been suggested that its function was similar to that of a cattle kraal. The third ditch, which also post-dates TRB occupation, cuts off the eastern part of the elevation but only halfway. The excavators assumed that it continued across the promontory since 'a defence ditch on only one side makes no sense' (Hensel and Milisauskas 1985, 76). Yet it is precisely this segment that contained large quantities of ash, charcoal and artefacts and one cannot but form the impression that its function was other than defensive. Thus at Bronocice there may have been three ditches reflecting three different functions: a defensive system around the settlement, a stock-keeping enclosure and possibly a ditch with a strongly ritual aspect. Only the final publication, however, will allow a proper assessment of their roles.

7.4.1 Discussion

The recognition of enclosed sites within the TRB culture reflects a process which, to a greater or lesser extent, is taking place in many other regions of Europe. Intensified research over the last two decades has revealed quite dramatically that Neolithic enclosures represent a widespread European phenomenon confined neither to a particular geographical region, nor to a specific cultural setting, nor to a clearly defined chronological horizon. Indeed, a survey of recent literature shows that, just as we have begun to come to grips with the problems posed by the European megalithic tradition, we are now facing the new challenge of understanding and interpreting the equally varied and bewildering evidence of Neolithic enclosures, with all the familiar questions as to the origin and function of a related and yet clearly differentiated class of site (Burgess *et al.* 1988 and bibliography therein). Perhaps one of the lessons that can be carried over from the study of megaliths is the recognition that formal similarities between sites from distant areas, no matter how attractive they appear, are of lesser importance than the context of sites within their own cultural setting. It is the local character of enclosed sites that bears most profoundly upon their significance.

The problems asociated with the interpretation of the European Neolithic enclosures, the nature of the activities evidenced and the more general questions as to the social significance of public monuments in the context of dispersed Neolithic settlement, have recently received a good airing from a practical as well as theoretical point of view. In the light of present knowledge of the TRB sites, there is little point in reiterating general comments which have been well expressed elsewhere (ibid.). However, there are a number of issues which are worth emphasising in the specific context of the TRB culture itself.

It is obvious that a serious attempt at the interpretation of the function of enclosures in the TRB is premature. The enclosures are a relatively recent discovery and have yet to be recognised in the vast area which separates southern Scandinavia from central Germany and southern Poland. Given the record of the last two decades it is reasonable to assume that this gap is more illusory than real and that soon enclosed sites will come to light in this area as well. They may provide the badly needed link between the apparently disparate evidence available today; not until this gap has been filled or proved to be real will it be possible to assess fully the evidence from the TRB enclosures.

Moreover, it must be remembered that the majority of sites have been investigated on a very small scale: for example, the interior of the main enclosure at Dölauer Heide still remains untouched, and other central German sites are even more fragmentarily known. Sarup, being the only satisfactorily excavated site in Denmark, warns against interpretation based on insufficient knowledge. Would we ever have known the complexity of its layout and the sophistication of activities if only a few sections had been cut across a couple of ditches? Yet, by and large, this is the case with the remainder of the Danish sites.

Furthermore, even the relatively incomplete record of TRB enclosures reveals their enormous diversity of form and use. The fifteen or so enclosures from the Northern TRB provide ample evidence for varied, multiphase construction and a wide range of activities of different significance and emphasis on individual sites.

One of the issues most difficult to resolve is the apparent difference between the defensive and non-defensive character of sites. On present evidence the TRB enclosures which display a greater emphasis on defence appear to be slightly earlier (cf. the dating of Dölauer Heide, Chapter 5.5). They emerge in those regions of the TRB which were already supporting farming populations (the Elbe-Saale region) and where, as is documented in southern Poland, several cultural groups coexisted and may well have been in competition with one another for prime farming and grazing land and other resources. In such circumstances the demarcation of space for public use may have required a strong physical manifestation. This differs considerably from the situation in the north of the TRB area where there is no contemporary evidence of competition between culturally separate people and where the defensive aspect on enclosed sites is apparently lacking. However, quite a number of the sites seem to have been located on low-lying promontories, often surrounded by boggy, marshy terrain, making direct access to the site difficult and emphasising, at least symbolically, the desire for seclusion. This impression is strengthened by the presence on some sites of palisades and enclosing fences. It will be interesting to see whether future discoveries of enclosed sites in other areas of the TRB will conform to this pattern.

It is generally argued that places with an important role within a social hierarchy of sites will reveal a greater investment of labour in construction and maintenance. While the construction of such sites as Dölauer Heide, Büdelsdorf and Sarup would have made considerably greater demands on manpower than appears to have been the case elsewhere, their relationship to other sites is still unclear. It has been suggested that Büdelsdorf was close to a major communication route (Bakker 1976, 83) and such a vital position may have necessitated the construction of an exceptionally impressive site. On the other hand, some sites may have been used by a larger group of people than others, with the relative labour investment reflecting the size of population and area rather than a greater social importance.

Another aspect which is regularly discussed and is inextricably linked with the interpretation of enclosed sites is the range and type of activities performed there. Although there is now a general awareness that between the two diametrically opposed interpretations of 'ritual' and 'domestic' there is a whole range of combinations involving varying degrees of emphasis from one to another, there is still a strong tendency towards polarisation in our thinking.

A more profitable line of enquiry may perhaps consider under what circumstances a 'domestic' activity acquires 'ritual' symbolism and vice versa. One example pertinent to the TRB culture will suffice. Pottery represents one of the commonest examples of domestic residue, and pottery-making is generally considered a clearly domestic activity, most probably performed by individual households as and when required. However, evidence from a number of southern Scandinavian enclosures suggests that on particular occasions this activity was carried out in enclosures, for example at Hevringholm or Büdelsdorf, and also in the third phase at Sarup where both 'ritual' and 'domestic' elements were emphasised. Pottery-making therefore appears to have acquired a symbolic dimension and was performed as an important communal activity. Some of the vessels may well have been disposed of immediately in a ceremony at the enclosure – placed against the facade or thrown into the ditches – while other vessels may have been taken away to be treated similarly in front of the local ancestral tomb. It is not inconceivable that a proportion of such pottery was simply used on settlement sites for the cooking and storing of produce.

The idea of periodic communal pottery-making is particularly attractive in the context of the Danish TRB and may well hold a key to the interpretation of northern ceramic styles. The occasions may have provided excellent opportunities for the exchange of ideas about style and decoration, as well as their meaning, and this accords well with the rapid dispersion of ideas (and styles) throughout the Northern group. Moreover, the close correspondence between deposits at enclosures and in front of tombs strengthens the connection between these two types of site within the wider ritual landscape and may further illustrate the changing pattern of emphasis from ceremonies at public places towards those at local sites.

On a much less dramatic scale such a pattern can also be observed elsewhere. The quantity of debris, especially pottery, in the burnt palisade slots at Dölauer Heide is curiously reminiscent of the situation in the north. The apparent lack of traces of activity in the centre of the enclosure also argues in favour of the ceremonial activity being concentrated in the vicinity of the palisade. Deliberate destruction of clay drums in the course of burial rituals (Starling 1988, 434), and their normally fragmented condition when found on settlements, may express a less tenuous connection than is apparent at first sight.

There is very clearly a wide scope for investigation of other evidence: the presence of exotic goods, the disposal of stone and flint implements and food residue, and the deposition of cereal grain in a condition which excludes storage, are just a few of the more obvious signs of activities whose function may have fluctuated depending on the context.

The relationship between enclosures and other types of monument present within the cultural landscape is another theme worth pursuing. Locational studies from Denmark are beginning to indicate a very definite spatial relation between enclosures and tombs (a circumstance by no means limited to the TRB; cf. the situation in the Neolithic of southern England). The distribution of enclosures and tombs in east central Jutland (T. Madsen 1988, Fig. 17: 10) suggests a ritual/ceremonial landscape where an individual enclosure was surrounded by a group of tomb clusters whose construction began at the time of use of the enclosure. The same pattern discussed in greater detail in Chapter 9.4, has been identified near Sarup on south-west Fyn. Moreover, while the evidence is still lacking, it is very tempting to suggest that the tomb clusters further south in the North European Plain, especially in Mecklenburg and west of the Elbe, also imply the existence of public ceremonial centres in their vicinity. There are good grounds for recognising in these patterns the emergence of territories appropriate to specific social groups, although there is no reason to suggest that the use of enclosures did not involve several social groups, with meetings and ceremonies possibly alternating between individual sites (this would perhaps explain in the simplest way the practice of recutting previously dug ditches).

The distribution of enclosed sites and burial monuments in the south of the TRB culture area is more difficult to interpret. In southern Poland the evidence of burial is still relatively poor and on the whole limited to flat cemeteries, and the overall pattern is difficult to assess. The peripheral distribution of enclosures in central Germany also reveals little relationship with burial monuments, but a close relationship is clearly in evidence at Dölauer Heide. Not only do we find there numerous contemporary burials within and outwith the enclosed area, but also many of the Baalberge/Salzmünde graves, which were seemingly inconspicuous and unmarked, became incorporated later in substantial burial mounds, with Dölauer Heide remaining a focus for burial activity throughout the TRB and thereafter. Indeed, the construction within the enclosed perimeter of a trapezoidal mound (relatively rare in this area) above what clearly must be interpreted as the remains of a smaller ritual structure and not a house, emphasises even further the connection with ceremonial activities.

The TRB enclosures are beginning to emerge as an important feature in our understanding of cultural development in the north European Neolithic. There are still too few of them and their currently known distribution covers a mere fraction of the area concerned. Yet there can be little doubt that, in a manner similar to the megalithic tombs, they belong to a common European tradition which, at different times and in different areas, assumes a significant role in the maintaining and regulating of social intercourse between different groups.

The range of basic features characterising the enclosure phenomenon is in itself immensely wide and becomes further selected and augmented according to the requirements of individual groups and as a direct response to local conditions. As already noted earlier, the causewayed enclosures need to be understood through the prism of their local cultural context. Only when we have a fuller appreciation of their role in individual areas will we be able to offer a meaningful interpretation of this phenomenon in its European dimension.

8

The economy of the TRB culture

There is still considerable debate over the introduction of a farming economy into the north European lowlands. This debate is on a number of different levels: some are relevant to a general discussion of Neolithic economies, while others are of greater local significance, relating to the specific environmental and social conditions prevailing across the North European Plain. In the former we may include not only the general problems relating to farming (the nature of floral and faunal assemblages, the distinction between wild and domesticated species, introduction from outside or development from within), but also the interpretation of the complex relationship between plants, animals, man and environment. In this area the gap still looms large between environmental and social determinism, and Dennell has rightly drawn attention to the need to consider the physical as well as social environments if we are to create a framework within which to interpret changes in prehistoric economies (Dennell 1985). The simplistic division between hunter-gatherers and farmers has long been shown to obscure a multitude of economic practices and has failed to offer any explanation as to why societies move from one form of exploiting their environment to another, or as to how these changes come about.

These latter themes are also of specific relevance to the North European Plain. In certain areas of Europe, where evidence for late hunting-gathering communities is poor, there is little challenge to the theory of Neolithic colonisation (Vencl 1986). But the North European Plain, as we saw earlier, provides unequivocal evidence for the presence of Mesolithic groups which adapted in various ways to the advantages and shortcomings of the north European environment. Not only is it impossible to sweep them aside to make way for Neolithic farmers, but we must also face the fact that both were in contact with, or at least aware of, each other for a considerable period before the growing of crops and keeping of livestock became the mainstay of the economy in the north. This opens up an area of discussion of the ways in which different economic, and therefore social, systems co-existed in relative proximity and influenced one another. Moreover, the transition into farming in this region was not synchronous and this further complicates the interpretation of how and why some areas were less susceptible than others. To date there have been a number of attempts to explain the introduction and subsequent development of farming in the North European Plain, and we shall review some of these in the general discussion of the TRB economy. First, however, we should examine some of the archaeological data which are available for the interpretation of the TRB farming economy.

8.1 Pollen analytical evidence

Reliance upon pollen analysis as a source of information about the natural environment is now well established in the reconstruction of prehistoric economies. This method is also regularly employed, albeit with variable frequency and effect, in research on the TRB culture. Only in certain areas, notably southern Scandinavia and the Netherlands and to a lesser degree in Poland and north-west Germany, have the results of pollen analyses been incorporated into the overall interpretation of economic issues.

From a purely historical perspective, it is hardly surprising that pollen records play such a fundamental role within south Scandinavia, since it was a Danish palaeobotanist, J. Iversen, who first recognised the possibility of interpreting man's influence on the natural environment through the study of pollen records (Iversen 1941). However, the application of pollen analyses in archaeology inevitably presents a whole range of problems which revolve round two major themes. One concerns the causal interpretation of changes within the vegetational sequence – whether these were of an ecological or anthropogenic nature and, in the case of the latter, the identification of processes which can best account for such changes. Since pollen is best preserved in damp, boggy and marshy environments which usually represent landscapes of less direct economic interest, the second major concern is the correlation between pollen and archaeological evidence.

Pollen samples from various localities in northern Europe reveal, in segments corresponding to the Atlantic/Sub-Boreal climatic transition, clear traces (albeit variable in intensity) of floral change, which are generally regarded as indications of anthropogenic activities. These comprise a complex set of related phenomena among which there is regular evidence of burning of the virgin forest cover, a decrease in the frequency of tree pollen associated with an increase in grasses and, not infrequently, the presence of cereal pollen.

The initial interpretation of this phenomenon, which is known as *landnam* (from a Danish phrase for land occupation) was advanced by Iversen (1941, 25). Iversen recognised a three-phase sequence, beginning with a recession of tree pollen and an increase in various herbs and grasses; the frequent occurrence at this stage of charcoal led him to regard this as the actual phase of land clearance. This was followed by the farming phase, characterised by the presence in the pollen spectra of *Plantago lanceolata* ('the "trail" of the Neolithic farmer', ibid., 27). Thirdly, the subsequent recovery in tree pollen, coupled with the recession of birch and hazel, which initially took advantage of the clearance, was thought to represent the regeneration of the original forest: the settlers evidently moved away to a different location.

Thus Iversen created an explanatory model of shifting cultivation, whereby the settlement would move to a new location every fifty to one hundred years. He assumed that *landnam* was a diachronic phenomenon and that the pastoral rather than the cereal-growing activities were the main force behind it (see comments by Smith 1981, 155–6). Although Iversen's *landnam* interpretation was based upon an interconnected series of observations from various pollen spectra, he was also aware of the fact that in many of the Danish pollen diagrams the decline of elm, which he placed precisely at the Atlantic/Sub-Boreal transition, preceded the actual *landnam* phenomenon.

At Draved Mose, near Copenhagen, this was accompanied by a layer of charcoal and the appearance of *Plantago lanceolata*. The elm decline here was dated to about 5000 BP (K-738, 4980 ± 100 BP) and the episode appeared relatively short-lived, ending about 4900 BP. Such a phenomenon was also noted at Korup Sø on Djursland, in the vicinity of the famous Barkær site. The elm decline (sample 7) is accompanied by a coresponding fall in ivy and the presence of a small amount of *Plantago lanceolata*. The *landnam* phase begins higher up in the diagram (sample 11) with 'a sudden and violent increase in the frequency of herb pollen' (Iversen 1941, 27, Plates II and III) and then an increase in *Betula* and an even more dramatic increase in *Corylus*.

A more recent study by Troels-Smith in the vicinity of Barkær revealed a similar sequence, with the elm decline and the appearance of *Plantago lanceolata* apparently dated to about 5150 BP (Troels-Smith 1982, 44, n. 15). In the pollen samples from the Aamose bog on Zealand, Troels-Smith also pointed to the early elm decline preceding the classic *landnam* phase. The drop in elm pollen goes hand in hand with the appearance of cereals, *Plantago lanceolata* and such plants as wild garlic (*Allium ursinum*), vine (*Vitis sp.*) and elder (*Sambucus nigra*) (Troels-Smith 1953, 53; 1982, 40). This horizon is now dated on the revised Muldbjerg dates to about 4750 BP; a classic *landnam* phenomenon is seen higher up in the diagram.

Similar patterns have been registered in south-east Scania, where the elm decline begins about 4950 BP and the *landnam* phase, with cereals and *Plantago lanceolata*, is registered from about 4650/4550 BP (Larsson 1985, 58). The cumulative pollen diagram from Östergötland shows that here the elm decline begins at 5100/5200 BP (dated at Mabo Mosse to 5130 ± 65 BP; Göransson 1982a, Fig. 5), but the apparent regeneration of the primaeval forest is accompanied by the presence of cereals, grasses and light-loving plants.

The detailed story is clearly seen in the diagram from Mabo Mosse. Immediately following the decline not only of elm but also of lime and ash, there is an unprecedented rise in the curve of charcoal particles which are present until 4750 BP. At the same time the presence of bracken (*Pteridium*) increases; cereals also make their appearance during this period. Very similar patterns are observed at Striern, Kyrkviken and Alvastra. In all areas light-loving species (aspen, bracken) flourish. At the time when the original forest seems to have 'regenerated', cereal pollen continues to be present. A similar phenomenon of cereal presence after the forest recovery is also seen in some of the Danish diagrams, for example at Ordrup Mose (Iversen 1941, 60–61, Plate I) and *Plantago* is present during this stage at Korup Sø (ibid., 63, Plates II and III). The increase of bracken immediately after the elm decline is seen clearly in the pollen spectra from Aamose and Dyrholmen.

A number of pollen analyses are known from the distribution areas of the Eastern and South-eastern TRB (Wiślański 1969; Kruk 1980). Yet the interpretation of this evidence is very difficult because on the whole the analyses are not related to specific cultural complexes. Indeed the fact that in many crucial regions (Kujavia, Greater Poland and Little Poland) the early TRB groups often settled in the vicinity of the older Neolithic settlements of Lengyel and Lengyel-Polgar groups, makes it virtually impossible to determine which, if any, should be credited with the vegetational changes seen in the pollen spectra. Only in very exceptional circumstances can the pollen data be related with reasonable certainty to the TRB culture; this appears to be the case on the Biłgoraj Upland in south-east Poland and in the vicinity of the Budzyńskie Lake in Greater Poland.

The TRB culture represents the oldest Neolithic settlement of the Biłgoraj Upland. Since the region is outwith the south-east Polish loessic landscape, and was of no concern to the various LBK and Lengyel-Polgar communities, it is reasonable to correlate the pollen evidence with the TRB populations. In the profile from Imielty Ług, in the segements belonging to the second half of the Atlantic, the decline in pollen of elm and ash and the general recession of oak are associated with the persistent presence of charcoal. This is followed by an increase in the pollen of grasses and plants belonging to the *Polypodiaceae* family. At the same time a slight increase in hazel and birch pollen can be observed. Kruk states very clearly that not just one but a whole sequence of fires was noted in the Atlantic/Sub-Boreal transition, and later in the diagram pollen of cereals is also registered (Kruk 1980, 152).

Another pollen diagram from which the late Atlantic/early Sub-Boreal segment can be related to the TRB culture derives from the sediments of the Budzyńskie Lake in Greater Poland (Wiślański 1969, Fig. 28). Although some LBK and Lengyel occupation is known here, it was relatively dispersed and insignificant, whereas intensive TRB settlement around the boggy lake is well documented (ibid., 195). In the relevant segements of the pollen diagram we note that elm and lime decline more or less at the same time. This is accompanied by a general recession of other tree species, clearly seen in the curve for oak and hazel. A corresponding increase is observed in *Artemisia, Rumex, Plantago lanceolata* and *major*, all somewhat delayed in relation to the elm/lime decline, with high values in the early Sub-Boreal. Cereals are also present sporadically in the late Atlantic and much more pronounced in the early Sub-Boreal, during which *Secale* appears to form a continuous curve although its status as a grown crop is still disputable.

Pollen analysis of pre-barrow surfaces is another important branch of pollen analytical research. Although the information derived from such a context reveals only the conditions present in a given locality immediately prior to the construction of the barrow, a whole series of such analyses – especially when they cover monuments from a succession of cultural groups in a particular area – enables us to build up a picture of vegetational change which is as detailed and informative as that derived from master diagrams, and has the additional advantage of association with clear archaeological contexts. The only region within the TRB where such research has been undertaken on a large scale is the Netherlands. There are isolated examples from other regions, however, and before we move on to consider the Dutch evidence an example from the Eastern TRB group should be mentioned, where an extraordinarily lucky circumstance provides evidence of the environment from underneath one of the Sarnowo barrows and from an archaeologically contemporary settlement, the two localities being less than 100 m apart (Dąbrowski 1971).

The four settlement samples show that relatively little clearance took place, with the tree pollen accounting for about 60 per cent. Cereals were common but no weeds of cultivation were encountered; the presence of *Thalictrum*, which belongs to the open shrub landscape, is of note. The pollen analyses from the cultivated field underneath the barrow revealed a totally different picture: the area was mostly open (20 per cent of tree pollen) and grasses and herbaceous plants were well represented: *Artemisia* (25 per cent), *Compositae* (14 per cent), and weeds of cultivation: *Centaurea* (3 per cent), *Rumex* (0.4 per cent) and varieties of *Plantago* (0.8 per cent). The very high average for cereals (4.6 per cent) suggests that the field was cultivated immediately prior to the construction that took place there. All four main cereals were present, wheat, barley, millet and especially rye, although that latter two are thought to represent weeds rather than cultigens. The presence of wheat and barley on what was clearly one field argues against a monoculture, and the presence of charcoal in the plough furrows suggests that the area was burned to release nutrients or, possibly, that ashes were deliberately scattered before cultivation and incorporated into the soil during ploughing.

The variations in the two sets of Sarnowo samples should be explained not only by the different contexts (settlement and a field) but also on the basis of the different tree-pollen representations. It is unlikely that a mainly cleared and a mainly forested landscape could be registered only 100 m apart, so there is clearly a chronological difference involved, although the precise timescale is unknown. The settlement samples, indicating only a modest clearance with some cultivation, could relate to the intial settling of the TRB group at Sarnowo at about 5500 BP, while the pollen spectra from the barrow may indicate that a relatively rapid clearance process followed. Unfortunately the stratigraphy at Sarnowo is very complex, but the overall evidence indicates that the time difference between the settlement on the slight hill and the cultivation of the field down below is very small. It is highly regrettable that no master diagram is so far available from the vicinity for comparison purposes, especially since the circumstances at Sarnowo would allow us to relate the specific changes to the general floral history of the neighbourhood.

Such correlations between the master diagrams and pollen spectra from surfaces preserved below prehistoric barrows are possible in the context of the Dutch TRB, however, since good evidence is now available from the Drenthe area (Waterbolk 1958; Van Zeist 1959; Groenman-van Waateringe 1978; Casparie and Groenman-van Waateringe 1980). The master diagrams from Emmen and Bargeroosterveld (south-east part of the Drenthe plateau) show that the TRB people were interested primarily in the elm- and lime-rich forests which were present especially on the weathered boulder clay ridges, on whose loamy moist sands fields may have been cultivated (Bakker 1982, 103). The scale of forest clearance can be seen from about 4950 BP in the decrease of elm pollen from 15 per cent to 5 per cent at Emmen I, 20 per cent to 8 per cent at Emmen V, and also of lime from 20 per cent to 10 per cent at Bargeroosterveld and from 18 per cent to 8 per cent at Nieuw-Dordrecht (Van Zeist 1959). There are difficulties in showing that the TRB was directly responsible for this clearance, however, since on present evidence the TRB cannot be dated to much before 4650 BP. Indeed Bakker wondered whether a sort of agrarian Swifterbant should not be considered in the context of the pre-TRB occupation of the Drenthe plateau (1982, 116).

The pollen from beneath the barrows shows that the activities of the TRB people on the Drenthe had not degraded the elm/lime forest totally (*Tilia* values are much higher than for the subsequent PFB and BB barrows; Groenman-van Waateringe 1978, 142). From the presence of various types of plants, the TRB barrows appear to have been placed either on abandoned fields (high values of *Cerealia*, *Gramineae* and *Rumex*) which in some instances were already turning into heath (high *Calluna*), on pastures (high *Gramineae* and *Rumex*) or on abandoned fields which had also been grazed (*Gramineae* and *Cerealia*).

Traditional explanations of the early post-elm decline phase (4950–4450 BP at Emmen and Bargeroosterveld) in the Netherlands have involved mainly arable activities (Van Zeist 1959), based to a degree on the Troels-Smith model. Casparie and Groenman-van Waateringe (1980) argue, however, that the elm/lime forest clearances were on a scale much greater than could be explained by Troels-Smith's model involving the cutting of foliage to provide fodder for livestock. On the basis of many pollen spectra from beneath the Drenthe and Veluwe barrows, they argue that the presence or absence of certain plant species (especially *Plantago lanceolata*, which is invariably linked with pastoral activities) is dependent more on the type of cleared forest and the conditions of the soil than on the type of economy practised by a particular cultural group. They suggest that the very low values of *Plantago lanceolata* from beneath the TRB barrows on the Drenthe are due to the combination of the specific hydrogaphic conditions (the impervious nature of the boulder clay) and the moist loamy sands which became readily compacted and did not offer conditions suitable for the expansion of *Plantago lanceolata*. However, in areas of different soil and forest cover, *Plantago lanceolata* is present, for example beneath the Emmen D43 barrow which is located outwith the lime/elm environment (ibid., 15). This can also be seen in the master diagram from Nieuw-Dordrecht, where at *c.* 4350 BP *Plantago lanceolata* shows high values, while in the chronologically corresponding horizons at Emmen and Bargeroosterveld these values remain low.

Casparie and Groenman-van Waateringe's research on the pre-barrow spectra has very important implications for the future interpretation of pollen evidence. The results of their work show that the whole range of natural conditions must be taken into account and not just the pollen spectrum itself. In their own words 'the pollen picture is determined primarily by the type of soil present and consequently the way in which vegetation regenerates, rather than by the culturally linked or economic use of the soil' (ibid., 60).

The more or less synchronous decline of elm seen in pollen diagrams over a large area of Europe which marks the transition from the Atlantic to the Sub-Boreal, is a matter of continued polemic among scholars. The explanations range from physical to anthropogenic factors and any combination of these. A climatic change at the Atlantic/Sub-Boreal transition, which can be seen in increased humidity and peat humification in certain areas, and which undoubtedly also involved a decrease in average temperatures, has been thought to have caused the elm decline (Nilsson 1961; Iversen 1973). On the other hand some palaeobotanists (Iversen also adopted this view at one point) have argued that, while a degree of climatic deterioration did indeed occur at the time in question, it was not so dramatic as to be the only cause of the elm decline. In certain areas the elm decline is not accompanied by the recession of species which would have suffered equally under bad climatic conditions (Van Zeiss 1959).

The most consistent arguements for anthropogenic causes of the elm decline have ben advanced by Troels-Smith, although these became entangled in the controversy over which population – the Ertebølle or the TRB – was responsible for this phenomenon. In contrast to many Scandinavian scholars, Troels-Smith firmly associates the elm decline and the subsequent evidence of agricultural activities with the late Ertebølle. It is the classic *landnam* which marks the arrival of the TRB groups, whom he credits with the establishment of pastures (Troels-Smith 1953 and 1982).

The small amount of cereal pollen following upon the elm decline indicated the cultivation of small plots, while the presence of certain plants, for example *Hypericum, Allium ursinum* or *Fragaria*, has led Troels-Smith to believe that cattle were not allowed to graze freely, since such plants would not have thrived in areas regularly trampled by livestock. Consequently, the animals must have been stalled and provided with fodder (branches of elm, ivy and mistletoe), the intensive gathering of which led to the elm decline.

This view has been criticised on many occasions. Even Iversen, who eventually accepted Troels-Smith's ideas, felt that lopping alone could not explain the elm decline and that the effort involved in the collection of fodder would have demanded too much investment of time and effort. He suggested that the girdling of trees would in any case have been a much more efficient method. Moreover, many scholars hold the view that the climatic conditions of the late Atlantic/early Sub-Boreal would have enabled the livestock to graze outside for most of the year (Iversen 1941, 56; Jankuhn 1969, 39–40).

Recently, Rowley-Conwy has also argued against Troels-Smith's ideas, pointing to the extraordinary scale of the operations which would have been required and the size of the herds that would have been needed to consume such a quantity of fodder (Rowley-Conwy 1982, 205).

The view adopted here as the cause of elm decline is one which many scholars are now beginning to accept, that of a combination of climatic factors and human interference (Mitchell 1956; Smith 1981; Göransson 1984). Far from being a compromise, such a view recognises that the causes and effects of an ecological change would not have gone unnoticed and that they would subsequently have been acted upon in a way which was advantageous. Recently, Göransson has once again brought into general discussion the concept of a rational prehistoric man be he a hunter-gatherer or a farmer, who was well acquainted with and who utilised rather than overexploited his environment.

Göransson drew attention to the fact that climatic change can activate the beetle responsible for Dutch elm disease and that this initially may have started the elm decline. He also commented upon the fact that a recently destroyed elm forest in southern Sweden is now in the process of regeneration because dying elms seeded profusely, although in contrast to girdled trees they did not sprout from the roots. The young seedlings, however, grow in conditions of improved light and improved soil nutrition (Göransson 1984). If we take Göransson's reasoning a step further, is it inconceivable that this rebirth of the elm (and other tree species) would have been recognised and acted upon? The re-enactment of the natural process through the girdling of elm and other trees (ash and lime) would have a dual effect: the trees would not only seed profusely, but would also sprout from the roots. With the nutritiously enriched soil, this would have created circumstances conducive to the practice of a farming economy.

Göransson's interpretation of the pollen record from the Atlantic and Sub-Boreal offers an exciting if controversial model for the development of farming. He reminds us once again that evidence for clearances is recorded in some areas of Europe (for example Ireland, England, Sweden) prior to the elm decline; sporadic finds of cereals and varieties of *Plantago* are present in some diagrams prior to 5150 BP (Göransson 1984; see also Smith 1981 and references therein). Göransson therefore poses two important questions: when did farming begin, and should the evidence from pollen diagrams from the elm decline onwards be seen (in some areas at least) not as the beginning of farming, but rather as its expansion?

Like Iversen, Göransson also distinguishes three phases of land use, but in contrast to earlier Danish interpretations, he regards the elm decline as the beginning of a whole sequence of related events which span the early and middle phases of the TRB. The first phase (5150–5100 BP) involves the girdling of trees, not only elm but also lime and ash, which encourages sprouting from the roots. This is followed immediately by a phase of repeated burning to improve grazing. The phase spans the period 5100–4650 BP. The regular and persistent presence of charcoal particles in the Östergötland pollen diagrams is seen as an amalgam of repeated burning episodes which eventually lead to the formation of scrub woodland. It is during this phase that the light-loving species such as aspen (*Populus tremula*) and bracken (*Pteridium*) reach high values. The third phase, beginning about 4650 BP, which according to Iversen represented the regeneration of primaeval woodland, is seen by Göransson as the development of scrub into coppice woods which are used for grazing and cereal-growing. He explains that 'the light, open coppice wood produces much pollen. The pollen rain from the coppice wood thus gives false picture of the primeval forest coming back to areas used extensively during the Early Neolithic' (Göransson 1982a, 214). The coppice wood is thus a much more effective way of using land and allows permanent cultivation by the methodical use of a number of small coppice groves.

Irrespective of whether Göransson's 'working hypothesis' will find additional support in palaeobotanical and archaeological evidence and become widely accepted by scholars, it has profound implications for our understanding of the relationship between prehistoric man and his environment. It would be very surprising if it did not reopen some long-overdue debates.

We shall have to reconsider the extent to which Atlantic hunter-gatherers modified and improved their environment, as well as the question of when they realised the potential of the transformed forest to become not merely an exploited, but a rationally utilised landscape. What was their contribution to and participation in the introduction of (or indeed the extension of) farming, not only in northern Europe, but beyond? All these issues are of fundamental importance to the study of the development of the TRB culture.

With regard to the established farming economy, the model incorporates the previously somewhat isolated phenomenon of the elm decline within a complete framework for the interpretation of post-Atlantic vegetational phenomena. It also obviates the need to interpret the elm decline and the later *landnam* as essentially unrelated. Moreover, it will help to explain the clearly spurious dichotomy between the pastoral and agricultural activities of early north European farmers. Such a model does not deny that in certain regions or at particular times there may have been an emphasis upon one or the other, but it allows us to dispense with explanations which are neither common sense nor supported by archaeological evidence (for example an all-year-round stabled cattle economy). It will also allow us to dispense with the wholly unsuitable model of slash-and-burn agriculture, replacing it with the 'rational' use of the transformed forest landscape. Repeated burning where necessary of forest scrub for improvement of grazing, and the utilisation of a number of coppice woods, are not the same as shifting settlement round the landscape in the never-ending search for fertile land. Indeed, archaeological evidence speaks firmly against such a view.

8.2 Plants in the TRB

The cultivation of crops and the collection of a variety of wild plants clearly formed an important element in the TRB economy, complementing animal husbandry. Yet our knowledge in this field is relatively limited. Plant foods decay very easily and their consumption leaves little or no residue; they will survive only in very exceptional circumstances, for example in waterlogged conditions or when subject to accidental or intentional burning. The pollen analysis already discussed provides some information on the type of crops grown. Since cereals are not native to northern Europe, their presence in pollen spectra enables us to assume that at least common varieties were cultivated. It is more difficult to determine which of the wild plants were used, and direct evidence is necessary. This comes primarily in the form of impressions of cereal grains (rarely other plants) on pottery and pieces of daub found on settlements. Plant foods occasionally survive in storage pits

as charred seeds or dried-out fragments. Trees useful to the economy can
be identified from surviving lumps of charcoal, and in a less direct way
agricultural and plant-processing tools can also contribute useful information.

All the basic cereals appear to have been present in the TRB (wheat,
barley, millet and oats), although some of the wheat varieties as well as
millet and oats may, initially at least, have been present as weeds of cultivation rather than deliberately sown crops. Wheat and barley, on the other
hand, appear so regularly in the form of grain impressions and in actual
finds of seeds that their cultivation is beyond doubt.

Among the wheats, emmer (*Triticum dicoccum*) and einkorn (*Triticum
monococcum*) represent the main varieties and are found throughout the
whole area of the TRB. Other wheats such as bread wheat (*Triticum
aestivum*) or club wheat (*Triticum compactum*) are less common and, if
deliberately sown, were certainly of lesser importance. The preliminary
identification of seeds and grain impressions from Bronocice suggests that
bread wheat was predominant (Hensel and Milisauskas 1985, 63, Table 15),
but this is not so far attested elsewhere.

Emmer is by far the most commonly encountered wheat and may well
represent the main cultivated variety. It appears in the Eastern and South-
eastern groups in the form of impressions and it also constitutes the main
cereal in finds from settlement grain stores (for example at Ćmielów and
Zarębowo). The monocultural growing of emmer has been suggested more
than once (Wiślański 1969, 189; 1979, 213; Kruk 1980, 205). In the Northern group emmer impressions are more numerous than those of other
wheats. A recent presentation of cereal impressions from the main Danish
sites shows that emmer accounts for 55 per cent of all cereals (and this figure
would rise to over 80 per cent if the Sarup find was added), while einkorn
and barley impressions are roughly equal at 18 per cent and 17.4 per cent
respectively. Bread wheat accounts for only 9.6 per cent (G. Jørgensen
1977, Table 5). In southern Sweden emmer is on the whole more common
than einkorn and barley. The recent suggestion by Larsson (1985) regarding the possible preference for wheat- and barley-growing in different
regions of South-east Scania is based on so few impressions that for the
time being it must remain unverified.

Evidence from the central German region is also mostly based on grain
impressions. Emmer features prominently among the impressions on early
ceramics (Baalberge and Salzmünde) and was common in the later
Walternienburg-Bernburg settlement at Schalkenburg (Behrens and
Schröter 1980, 99). On the other hand, in the large find from Lietfeld
einkorn was twice as numerous (Murray 1970). Emmer and einkorn are
known from the sporadic impressions on the pottery from the Dutch
hunebedden (Van Zeist 1959; 1968, 155 and 158) and einkorn is said to have

been the main wheat found at Hunte 1 on the Dümmer (Willerding 1970, 332).

The other main cereal in the TRB was barley. It was present in two varieties: six-row barley (*Hordeum vulgare*) and two-row barley (*Hordeum distichum*), the former being by far the more popular (Wiślański 1969, 192–3; Kruk 1980, 209). Barley is well suited to cultivation on the mixed lowland soils and it is more resistant to cold than wheat. These were the most likely reasons for its increased popularity during the later TRB. Barley appears to be the commonest cereal in the Western group: in the chamber at Dötlingen, distr. Oldenburg, it accounted for 60 per cent of all cereal impressions (Hopf 1961, 406). Similarly, the later TRB sites in the Eastern group also indicate the increased importance of this cereal. At the Mrowino settlement 572 grain impressions were found on potsherds and daub. Over 52 per cent were identified as barley and only 7 per cent were wheats (mostly unidentified; Tetzlaff 1981, 179). Barley was also dominant in the late TRB Mątwy group in Kujavia, where among 299 grain impressions only eight belonged to other cereals (Kośko 1981, 137). The large cereal find from Dannau, east Holstein, consisted of 70 per cent barley and only 24 per cent emmer (Kroll 1981). It is also possible to observe a slight increase in barley towards the later TRB in Denmark (Rowley-Conwy 1979), but it is not until the Bronze Age that it becomes more important than wheat.

Claims that cereals in the TRB were grown monoculturally are regularly advanced (Wiślański 1969, 189; 1979, 213; Kruk 1980, 205), but the evidence is very scanty. Seed impressions on pottery and pieces of daub found on settlements are neither a reliable nor an appropriate source of information; large quantities of cereal grain are necessary to identify such a practice. Such finds are not numerous in the TRB; the relative proportions of various cereals from a few substantial grain hauls are presented in Figure 105.

The finds from Radziejów and Sarup are both exceptionally pure, consisting of 99.5 per cent and 94 per cent emmer respectively. They contained a negligible amount of other cereals and a few weeds. At Radziejów the wheat, mixed with large lumps of charcoal, was dumped into a pit and a fine richly decorated and deliberately broken amphora (Fig. 14) was placed on top (Gabałówna 1970c). At Sarup the wheat (together with some burnt bones) was contained in two funnel-necked beakers which, together with a typical Fuchsberg lugged beaker, were deposited in a pit within a causewayed enclosure. In both instances the cereal grain was subject to burning prior to the deposition; the Radziejów wheat was burned beyond consumption.

Both of these finds derive from clearly non-domestic contexts and therefore the purity of cereals need not necessarily imply that they were grown monoculturally. If the burning of wheat and its subsequent deposi-

	Lietfeld	Ćmielów	Zarębowo	Radziejów	Sarup	Dannau
Einkorn *Triticum monococcum*	33.5%	✓	20.0%	0.44%	0.46%	0.1%
Emmer *Triticum dicoccum*	63.3%	50.0%(?)	70.0%	99.5%	93.97%	23.9%
Flax *Linum usitatissimum*	0.8%	✓				
Peas *Pisum sativum*		50 seeds				
Barley *Hordeum vulgare*	2.4%					
Wild Apple *Malus silvestris*			✓			

Figure 105 Major cereal finds from TRB sites.

tion were part of a ceremony (perhaps a thanksgiving after a harvest), then the wheat may have been deliberately cleaned and selected. This is currently the preferred explanation, especially since other finds, which come from settlements, do not show such purity.

While emmer was the most common cereal everywhere except at Dannau, the presence of other cereals indicates that these were gathered and stored together. This is particularly clear at Książnice Wielkie, where only half of the stored grain was emmer and four other wheats made up the rest. Einkorn was also found at Zarębowo (20 per cent) and Lietfeld (33.5 per cent). The cereal find from Dannau also implies that cereals were mixed, since it is unlikely that crops would have been grown separately only to become mixed up in storage. Each of the ten analysed samples from Dannau contained a mixture of barley and emmer, as well as a fair amount of weeds.

Another argument against the monocultural growing of cereals is offered by the evidence from Sarnowo, where the pollen of four cereals (wheat, millet, barley and rye) were noted. The circumstances at Sarnowo suggest that this represents not an accumulation over several years during which time the crops may have been rotated, but more probably the last crop grown in the field. Only the find from the Ćmielów storage pit could be used in the argument for monocultural growing: the combination of emmer grain and peas suggests that the grains were selected in readiness for future sowing.

Leguminous plants such as peas (*Pisum sativum*), lentils (*Lens culinaris*) or beans (*Vicia faba*) are known to have accompanied the cereal crops from the very beginning of agriculture (Dimbleby 1967) and their regular, albeit not numerous, appearance in TRB contexts suggests that they played an important role in the overall diet. Peas are easily stored, have many uses and can be grown on most soils; large finds are infrequent, but a collection of about fifty seeds from a grain store at Ćmielów is noteworthy (Klichowska 1975). Lentils were recently found among the charred plant remains at Schalkenburg (Behrens and Schröter 1980, 99), where another pit also contained broad beans.

Flax may have been grown not only for the oil in the seeds but also for its fibre. At Ćmielów 18 cm³ of flax seeds were found and the use of flax for the extraction of oil is documented in oil deposits in a collared flask found at Dötlingen (Hopf 1961, 407). Impressions of flax are also apparently present on pottery sherds from a Drouwen tomb (Buurman and Pals 1974, 10, Table 1).

It is reasonable to assume that a great variety of wild plants would have been gathered throughout the seasons to provide nourishment and medicines and to add variety to the diet, yet our knowledge in this respect is limited. It is very unlikely, for instance, that edible forest fungi will have been preserved yet they were undoubtedly gathered – as they are to this day

– in the forests across the North European Plain. Nuts and wild fruits (apples, raspberries, cherries, plums and elder berries) are occasionally discovered; all have been identified on settlements of the South-eastern group (Kruk 1980, 272–3, List II).

Certain plants, such as sorrel (*Rumex*) and wild garlic (*Allium ursinum*), may already have been grown as vegetables, while others, such as *Polygonum aviculare L, Berberis vulgaris, Matricaria chamomilla L or Hypericum*, were collected for medicinal or magical purposes (Wiślański 1969, Table LIV; Kruk 1980, 272–3). Timber would have been of fundamental importance for construction purposes and fuel. Among the more commonly identified species are pine, oak, yew, birch, alder, beech, elm and maple. In spite of only sporadic evidence, we can assume that gathering was an all-year-round activity and did not necessarily contribute any less than contemporary agriculture to the overall balance of the TRB plant economy.

8.3 Animal husbandry in the TRB

Before we embark upon a consideration of the contribution of animals to the TRB economy, the nature of the available evidence must be appreciated. We need hardly reiterate that a faunal assemblage is the final result of a sophisticated process in which multiple factors of deposition, preservation and recovery combine to create a fragmentary and unbalanced record. These very obvious and general limitations are reinforced in relation to the TRB culture by the scarcity of bone assemblages and their very uneven distribution throughout the culture's area. The only relatively good data belong to the later TRB and come from Denmark and southern Poland, while a few well-studied assemblages come from central Germany. The remaining regions are underrepresented to such a degree that comparative discussion and identification of regional or long-term trends in animal husbandry are virtually impossible.

The size of assemblages varies enormously, from as many as 24,000 identifiable fragments at Troldebjerg to as few as twenty-eight pieces at Gristow (Nilius 1973, 266; Nyegaard 1985, 454), and are clearly biased towards the lower end of the scale. Comparison is made difficult by the divergence of contexts and by the mostly superficial level of analysis which rarely goes beyond identification of the main species in terms of bone percentages. There is little information on the age and sex of animal groups, and on the whole the interpretation of TRB faunal assemblages is confined to general rather than specific issues. Nevertheless, the evidence collected to date does reveal certain consistencies and regularities and provides at least an initial basis for the discussion of the role of animals in the TRB.

Figure 106 illustrates the relationship between wild and domestic species in the major assemblages. Since nearly all of them contain an element of wild fauna, we may assume that hunting did play a role within the overall economy, although it varied through time and from area to area. On the

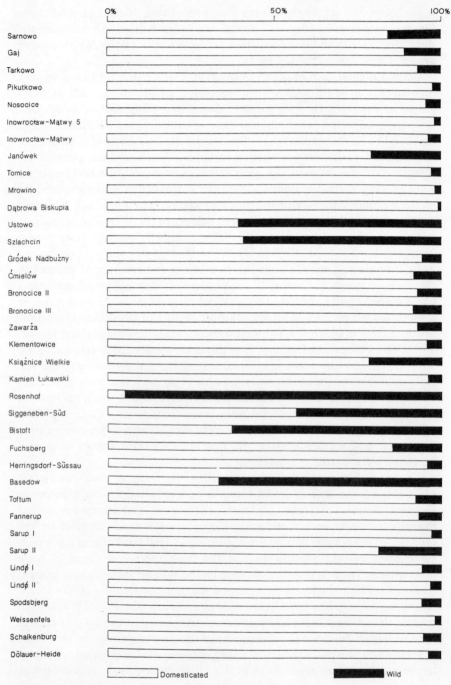

Figure 106 Ratio of domesticated to wild species in major bone assemblages from TRB sites (based on bone percentages).

whole, the assemblages from the Southern and South-eastern groups display a smaller proportion of game than those further north. Different environmental conditions in the largely loessic landscape in the south, and possibly even a different cultural background against which the economy developed in the south, may be significant factors. On the other hand wild species may be overrepresented on some of the northern TRB sites designated as hunting stations. Only the useful parts of caught animals may have been taken away for consumption and other uses, the rest being left behind; the bones of domestic animals on such sites are likely to represent mostly the provisions brought there by the hunters from elsewhere. For the same reasons precisely, bones of wild animals from permanent settlements may appear less numerous and may mislead us as to the real exploitation of wild faunal resources.

To what extent the apparently chronologically significant decrease in hunting, seen quite dramatically on the north German sites from 95.2 per cent at Rosenhof to 4.3 per cent at Süssau, reflects the real situation is difficult to determine, since the number of assemblages is small and it is precisely in this area that hunting sites are known. Such a decrease is not found in Denmark. Comparative early material is not known and the amount of wild animal bones on the later sites varies greatly, suggesting that other factors (the use of hunting sites, differences due to coastal/inland locations) may have been of significance. That wild fauna contributed to the Danish TRB economy throughout is also seen from other sources (See Chapter 7.2.2).

Bistoft, Basedow and Szlachcin stand out clearly in having a larger proportion of wild than of domestic species, but this is not surprising since they are examples of the now-numerous hunting stations. Ustowo may also belong to this category, but the status of Rosenhof is still open to question and we shall discuss the evidence from this site later.

There are remarkable correpondences between the Bistoft and Basedow sites. Both were hunting camps located on lake islands and were used during the early and middle stages of the TRB. Although the proportion of identifiable mammalian bones from the total assemblage at Bistoft exceed that at Basedow (55 per cent and 18 per cent), the relative proportions are astonishingly similar. The wild species account for 63 per cent and 67.3 per cent respectively and the proportion of red deer (just over 54 per cent) is identical on both sites, although there is a greater variety of fauna at Bistoft where numerous fish remains were also found (Gehl 1974; Johansson 1981, 102–4).

The sample from Szlachcin is much smaller (only 213 bone fragments) but there are close similarities: wild animals account for 59.6 per cent and red deer for 59 per cent of the wild animals, but wild horse and tortoise also feature within the assemblage.

The Ustowo site may not represent a typical hunting station, but wild animals (39.9 per cent of the total sample) clearly contribute to the overall diet. Again deer bones are the most frequent (48.9 per cent) but beaver, horse and auroch are also found in significant numbers. At the north German site of Siggeneben-Süd, wild animals account for 43.7 per cent of the total bone assemblage. The cultural material and the pattern of find dispersal on the site suggest, however, that this was a permanent settlement. The relatively large proportion of wild animals may reflect its advantageous location, which allowed the inhabitants to explore marine, lake-side and inland environments. Yet again the proportion of red deer bones approximates that from other sites (57.1 per cent); this extraordinary correspondence may in fact reflect underlying trends in the exploitation of this species throughout the forested landscapes of the north European lowlands. Seal and wild cat were also significant at Siggeneben-Süd (11.4 per cent and 14.3 per cent); wild cattle and pig were not very common (only 5.7 per cent), while their domestic counterparts obviously were (44.9 per cent and 34.7 per cent; Meurers-Balke 1983, 115–18).

Let us now review the evidence for domestic animals from TRB contexts. Figure 107 shows the relative proportions of the main species within major individual assemblages. Unfortunately these have been subject to different forms of analysis, and the figures are mostly expressed as percentages of the total number of animal bones. Nevertheless certain regularities can be shown to apply to the TRB culture as a whole.

Cattle are clearly the most important domesticate in all areas and throughout the period. Pigs most often follow in second place and sheep/goats only rarely move from the third position. On the whole cattle make up at least half of the bone assemblages in the Eastern group, and although the series studied are very small, the same seems to be the case on permanent sites as well as on hunting stations (66 per cent and 50 per cent at Szlachcin and Ustowo). Cattle dominance is shown in all the studied assemblages from the upland settlements of the South-eastern group (up to 70 per cent) and the same is the case in the Elbe/Saale area (up to 80 per cent at Wissenfels). From north German sites the importance of cattle is not only notable in individual assemblages, but it also appears to increase in the long term. The Danish assemblages are more difficult to interpret. Madsen's (1982) arguments for the importance of the pig in the early TRB can be neither confirmed nor refuted since hardly any data for this early period are available at present. It is interesting to note, however, that all the main domesticates (cattle, pig, sheep and goat) appear on early sites, albeit in very small quantities. The assemblages from the Fuchsberg phase onwards show unequivocally that cattle is the most common species, followed by pigs; sheep and goats are much less frequent.

The only two sites where pig bones outnumber those of catle are Toftum (66 per cent) and Troldebjerg (47 per cent). The first assemblage is not only small (105 identifiable bones), but also comes not from a domestic site but

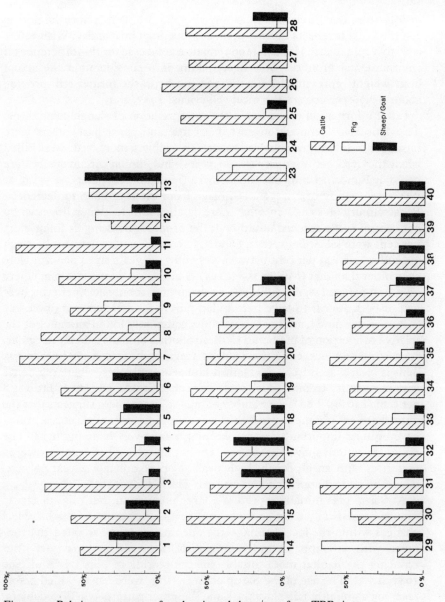

Figure 107 Relative percentages of cattle, pig and sheep/goat from TRB sites:
Eastern group 1-Sarnowo, 2-Gaj, 3-Tarkowo, 4-Pikutkowo, 5-Nosocice,
6-Inowrocław-Mątwy, 5,7-Inowrocław-Mątwy (early), 8-Inowrocław-Mątwy (late),
9-Janówek, 10-Tomice, 11-Inowrocław 55, 12-Mrowino, 13-Dąbrowa Biskupia;
Southern group 14-Gródek Nadbużny, 15-Ćmielów, 16-Bronocice II, 17-Bronocice
III, 18-Zawarża, 19-Niedźwiedź, 20-Klementowice, 21-Książnice Wielkie,
22-Kamień Łukawski; north and south Germany 23-Siggeneben-Süd,
24-Fuchsberg, 25-Heringsdorf-Süssau, 26-Weissenfels, 27-Derenburg,
28-Schalkenburg; Northern group 29-Toftum, 30-Troldebjerg, 31-Lyø,
32-Fannerup, 33-Blandebjerg, 34-Sarup I, 35-Sarup II, 36-Bundsø, 37-Lindø I,
38-Lindø II, 39-Lidsø, 40-Spodsbjerg.

mainly from one ditch of a causewayed enclosure; it therefore cannot be assumed that it reflects normal practices in animal husbandry. With reference to Troldebjerg, Higham (1969) made a good case for this difference on environmental grounds. Moreover, taking into consideration the actual meat weight represented by cattle and pig here, the former still provide about 65–76 per cent of the meat (Nyegaard 1985, 454).

Little information exists to aid the interpretation of slaughter patterns. The data from Denmark suggest that cattle and particularly steers were raised for meat. Higham showed that at Troldebjerg most cattle were killed when they reached maturity (3.5–4 years) and similar circumstances are noted at Bundsø, Lindø and Spodsbjerg (Higham 1969, 204).

A recent study of a large assemblage from the Bernburg settlement at Schalkenburg gives us somewhat more detailed information. Altogether 70 per cent of cattle reached adulthood, the proportions being as follows: 23 per cent were killed between 2.5 and 3.5 years of age, 27 per cent between 3.5 and 5 years, 23 per cent between 5–7 and 7–10 years and 4 per cent were even older than that (Müller 1985, 185). This was in contrast to pig, where only 39.9 per cent were adults, and to sheep/goat at only 49.7 per cent; over half of both appear to have been killed purely for meat consumption.

Pigs, as we noted, are the second most commonly found animal, but the relative proportion of pig bones to those of other animals is fairly irregular, suggesting that local conditions played a significant role in pig husbandry. This is clearly seen from the Danish faunal assemblages, where pig bones vary in quantity from as mush as 47 per cent (Troldebjerg) to as little as 8 per cent (Lidsø). The large number of pigs at Troldebjerg suggests that the immediate environment (probably large areas of deciduous forest) must have been an important factor in keeping a relatively large pig herd. The slaughter pattern shows that 90 per cent of pigs were killed before reaching maturity, with an especially high peak at approximately 2 years of age, when the animal approaches adult body size (Higham 1969, 204).

At Sarup pigs initially represent a large population, but this appears to reduce dramatically from 43.6 per cent to 14.4 per cent and might reflect changes within the local habitat – the opening up of the wooded environment, with an emphasis on the storage of cattle fodder for winter, thus reducing the habitat most suitable for the rearing of pigs (N. Andersen 1981, 91–3). The age of the Sarup animals (they were mostly killed before reaching 27 months) displays the same slaughter pattern as at Troldebjerg, with meat supply as a primary objective; data from other Danish sites, such as Fannerup (Rowley-Conwy 1985a) and Bundsø (Degerbøl 1939), on the whole present the same picture.

Assemblages from the South-eastern TRB reveal that generally pigs are second in importance to cattle, on the whole not exceeding 25 per cent of the total bone assemblages. There are, however, a number of interesting exceptions. At Książnice Wielkie, a late TRB site, there is a clear relationship between an increase of pig and a corresponding decrease in cattle bones. Kruk has argued that this change reflects a real increase in the consumption of pork and a diversion within cattle husbandry from meat consumption to a greater reliance on dairying and other produce, indicating a more multi-functional role for cattle herds towards the later period of the TRB (Kruk 1980, 303).

The two chronologically successive assemblages from Bronocice (II and III) show, however, that pigs were less important here than cattle and sheep/goats. This situation is also noted at Schalkenburg, where pigs are also in third place as regards the number of bones, this position being retained when the minimum number of individuals is taken into account. The kill-off pattern resembles that of the Northern group, with only 39.9 per cent of animals reaching maturity and 32.4 per cent being killed in their first year (Müller 1985, Table 7).

With the exception of the last two sites, the presence of sheep and goats within the TRB appears to be relatively insignificant. Danish evidence implies that the small numbers kept were reared mainly for consumption. This is seen in the high mortality rate of young animals at Troldebjerg (79 per cent were killed before their second year), Bundsø (61 per cent) and Lindø (68 per cent; Higham 1969, 205). The relative increase in the number of small ruminants towards the end of the TRB has been argued to indicate a more open landscape with good grazing ground. Higham suggested that natural salt marshes offered a good habitat for grazing sheep and goats, and that this is shown by their relative importance on all the coastal sites. That sheep and goats were important for products other than meat is indicated by the Schalkenburg assemblage, where 49.3 per cent of animals reached maturity. Müller argued that milk and wool produce were of considerable importance.

8.4 Interpretation of the TRB economy

Generally speaking, we may describe the economy of the TRB culture as based on mixed farming, that is cereal growing and animal husbandry, supplemented by hunting and gathering. The evidence outlined above shows that each of these elements played a role, yet their exact contributions are difficult to ascertain since they will have varied not only through time but also according to the potential of the settled areas and the adaptability of individual human groups. Moreover, factors such as bad harvests, decimation of livestock through disease, and conflicts between neighbouring communities could all, periodically, have induced dramatic changes which may not be revealed in the archaeological record. The differential survival of animal and plant remains and the bias towards the study of domestic varieties, based on the assumption that farming represents economic progress, all impose constraints upon the reconstruction of the overall economy.

These constraints are particularly evident when we attempt to interpret the faunal assemblages described above. There is an underlying assumption that the relative proportions of animal bones reflect the corresponding relationship in livestock and indicate the importance of individual species. Similarly, the presence or absence of wild animal bones is usually taken at its face value to express directly the contribution of hunting. Yet it is self-evident that patterns observed in faunal assemblages from settlements relate chiefly to meat consumption and need not reflect the number of live animals which made up herds and flocks. Moreover, assemblages derived from other contexts, such as causewayed enclosures, votive or burial deposits, display biases in their contextual settings and may camouflage rather than reveal the normal state of economic affairs.

The direct evidence discussed earlier shows clearly that, while the importance of hunting within the TRB should not be exaggerated in terms of its overall contribution to the economy, it nevertheless played a substantial role. While it probably decreased through time, hunting features prominently in the north European lowlands and is a significant reminder of the strength of earlier traditions in this area. This contrast with the much greater farming emphasis of the TRB groups settled on the loessic landscape to the south, where hunting of wild game appears to have been carried out on a greatly reduced scale and where no sites devoted specifically to this pursuit have so far come to light. The lowland and upland patterns of wild fauna appear to confirm not only the general environmental differences between north and south, but also the heterogeneous nature of the TRB economy, with its reliance upon and continuity of previously existing local traditions.

The role of hunting in the European lowlands is evident not only in the variety and proportion of wild species in the faunal assemblages, but also in the presence of hunting stations, some of which continued in use over a long period of time. The Hüde and Hunte 1 sites along the Dümmer lake in Lower Saxony are good examples of such repeatedly used locations. The archaeological evidence for the use of Hüde spans the period from 6150 BP to 4650 BP and involves the Ertebølle-Ellerbek as well as TRB groups. The popularity of such locations was doubtless related to the variety of surrounding habitats, which in turn is reflected in a wide range of available game: beaver, fox, wolf, bear, wild horse, badger, otter, pine marten, not to mention the numerous wild fowl and fish (Kampffmeyer 1983).

While on some sites particular species were caught (hunters visiting the island of Hesselø specialised in catching seal), others reveal a mixture of marine and terrestrial fauna (Skaarup 1973). Fish remains are well represented on many of these coastal sites and large number of fish bones from Bistoft (carp, pike, eel), Hüde and Oldesloe-Wolkenwehe attest to the importance of fishing further inland. Fish were undoubtedly an invaluable additional source of food in the lake districts of Mecklenburg and

Pomerania. The collection of molluscs did not cease during the TRB and many sources previously exploited by the Ertebølle-Ellerbek communities continue to be used for the same purpose; at Sølager, Norsminde or Verup Mose a great variety of molluscs were collected although the most common variety seems to have been cockles (Skaarup 1973). Mussels are known on north German sites, for example at Neukirchen-Sütel and Süssau, and riverine mussels (especially *Unio*) are also regularly found in Kujavia Wiślański 1969, 169; Hoika 1987, 115).

That the overall contribution of hunting to the provision of protein decreased towards the later TRB can be judged from the assemblages in north Germany and Denmark (Fig. 106), where the proportions of wild to domestic species clearly change in favour of the latter. This is doubtless an indication of the transformation within the economy, the increased experience of and improvement in farming methods leading towards a greater reliance upon this sector of the economy. On the other hand, sites such as Ustowo, which belongs to the late TRB phase, where nearly 40 per cent of the animal bones belong to wild species, may indicate that some groups continued to hunt on a substantial scale, perhaps responding to a demand and filling a gap within the complex network of economic exchanges.

Indeed, we should perhaps pose the question as to whether hunting was of purely economic significance or whether it also fulfilled a social need. The constant, even if small, proportion of wild animals within the later TRB assemblages would tend to suggest that hunting may well have played a role in fulfilling the common human need for varied experience, excitement and even danger. The social significance of hunting can in fact be inferred from other, somewhat circumstantial evidence. Teeth of wild animals, boars' tusks, fish vertebrae etc. continue to provide (as they did during the Mesolithic period) inspiration in the sphere of personal adornment. This is seen in numerous finds of personal ornaments throughout the TRB area and is perhaps most emphatically documented in the profusion of such ornaments buried with the dead at the Ostorf cemetery (Bastian 1961; Schuldt 1961).

Although we can demonstrate that hunting did make a valid contribution, domestic animals provided a firm basis for the TRB economy. The full range of domesticates (catle, pigs, sheep and goats) is found even in the early assemblages (Sarnowo, Sigersted, Havnelev, Barkær), but there are no clear indications as to the relative importance of particular species since these assemblages are either very small or have not been sufficiently analysed. The somewhat later material, however, leaves us in no doubt that cattle must have been the chief meat supplier, and there are indications that cattle herds in the north were managed differently from those further south.

The north German data are not very specific, but Danish evidence suggests that cattle were kept mainly with a view to consumption. On the basis of bone analysis from Troldebjerg, Higham and Message (1969) were able to show that herd management was geared to meat production: steers were raised to an age of 3–4 years, by which time they would have attained about 90 per cent of their potential maximum weight. At Troldebjerg 60 per cent of cattle were killed just after their third winter; of the older animals about 80 per cent were females, which suggests that mature cows were kept for stock replenishment and secondary produce. A similar meat-oriented attitude emerges from other TRB settlements: at Spodsbjerg on Langeland about 80 per cent of cattle were slaughtered by the time they were 3.5–4 years old (Nyegaard 1985, 433), and the Troldebjerg-type pattern is also seen at Fannerup (Rowley-Conwy 1985a).

Evidence from the Eastern TRB group is simply not sufficiently detailed to indicate trends in livestock management, but the presence of base-perforated clay vessels has been interpreted as an indication of an at least partly dairying economy (Kośko 1981, 141). The Southern and South-eastern groups, however, offer more specific information, which suggests a herd management strategy substantially different from that in the north. Among the major differences is the greater contribution to meat consumption by other species, although this varies from site to site. This trend is particularly noticeable towards the later period; at Klementowice and Książnice Wielkie the decrease in cattle bones is accompanied by a corresponding increase in pig bones, while at Schalkenburg sheep/goats make a substantial contribution.

It is not merely the relative animal proportions which are revealing. Although cattle were important on many sites, the bones of young animals are on the whole less numerous. Kruk has already argued that general meat consumption trends indicate a fundamental change in the overall economy – not so much a reduction of cattle as livestock, but more a change to multi-functional role involving dairying and providing draught power (Kruk 1980, 313). Excellent support for this trend derives from the assemblages at the Bernburg settlement of Schalkenburg. The analysis of cattle bones from this site identified not only a large proportion of older animals (50 per cent were 5 or more years old), but also a relatively high proportion of castrated animals which showed a degree of pathological change in their hip joints; all the evidence suggests that at least some cattle were employed in pulling heavy loads, either for farming purposes or for transport (Müller 1985, 211).

Although a discussion of the origin of wheeled vehicles is outwith the scope of our work, we may digress momentarily and note that the earliest evidence of wheeled transport in this part of Europe, present in the form of decoration on pottery, is associated with the TRB culture. The vehicle motifs appear in realistic representations as well as more schematic versions, whose interpretation is open to question.

The best representation of a four-wheeled vehicle is on the well-known vessel from the TRB settlement at Bronocice. The pot derives from a secure

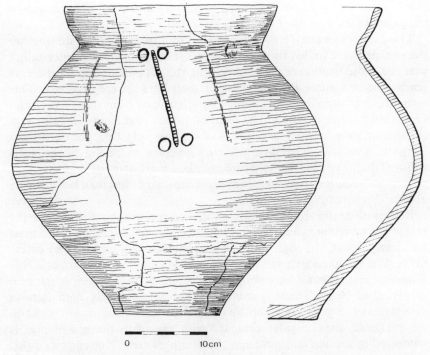

0   10cm

Figure 108 Schematic representation of a four-wheeled vehicle on a vessel from Ostrowiec Świętokrzyski (Source: Uzarowiczowa 1975).

TRB context and is dated to *c.* 4700–4500 BP (Milisauskas and Kruk 1977, 217–19; Piggott 1983, 41–2). A different version is seen on a TRB vessel which was found in 1942 at Ostrowiec Świętokrzyski. Two identical motifs carried out in stab-and-drag technique are placed opposite each other on the vessel's shoulder. Each motif consists of a 15—16 cm long line accompanied at either end by two perfectly drawn circles (Fig. 108). On the basis of stylistic comparison with pottery from the Ćmielów and Niedźwiedź settlements, this vessel may be placed in a horizon dating to 4800–4500 BP (Uzarowiczowa 1975), which corresponds well with the date of the Bronocice pot. Although the two motifs vary in style and form, there is little doubt as to what they represent.

A number of other, more schematic decorations on TRB vessels may also represent vehicles. A repeated motif of four circles on a pot from Kujavia has been interpreted as a pictoral representation of a four-wheeled vehicle (Fig. 13: 8?); a few other TRB vessels carry designs which, with a degree of imagination, may be interpreted along similar lines.

We may also mention in passing the controversy over the decorated slab in a Hessian gallery grave at Züschen, which falls roughly into the same chronological horizon. The very schematic drawing is said to represent a pair of oxen pulling a cart (see Piggott 1983 for a detailed presentation of the arguments).

The pictures on the TRB vessels do not unfortunately indicate whether the vehicles were pulled by oxen or horses, but in view of the uncertainty over the domestication of the horse during the 5th millennium BP, it seems reasonable to assume that oxen rather than horses were involved. This assumption is supported to a degree by other finds from the TRB group, for instance a pot handle in the form of yoked oxen from Krężnica Jara (Wiślański 1979, 242). The position of the two yoked copper oxen from Bytyń is less clear. They are generally assumed to belong to the TRB culture (ibid, 237), but the *cire perdu* method used suggests that they may be imports acquired from further to the south-east rather than locally made objects (Piggott 1983, 42).

Returning to the subject of animal husbandry, we should consider the role of the remaining animals. On the whole pig bones are the second most frequently found, although on a few sites they are outnumbered by ovicaprids. The slaughter patterns from assemblages where details are available show that most animals were slaughtered young: at Troldebjerg 90 per cent of pigs died before reaching maturity, with an especially high ratio at approximately 2 years (Higham 1969), and the same patterns are noted on other Danish sites. Similar evidence with regard to the age of pigs is witnessed in the assemblages from the South-eastern (Kubasiewicz 1984, 61) and Southern groups. At Schalkenburg 32.4 per cent died by the age of 12 months and only 40 per cent reached maturity (Müller 1985).

With reference to pig husbandry there is an interesting contrast between what is revealed in the assemblages and what is theoretically assumed to have occurred, at least during the early stages of the culture. A number of Scandinavian scholars have suggested that initially pigs were more important in the economy than cattle. T. Madsen argued that the early TRB sites were located in a relatively heavily forested environment which would limit the size of cattle and sheep/goat herds but was favourable towards the raising of pigs, and that large herds could have been kept with a minimum of effort. Only the progressive clearance of the landscape for cultivation created circumstances which led to a greater importance of cattle from the Fuchsberg phase onwards (T. Madsen 1982, 230). This theme has been taken up by Larsson, who suggested that similar circumstances may have prevailed during the corresponding period in south-west Scania (Larsson 1985, 92).

Theoretically this model is extremely well suited to the interpretation of the economic potential of the environment across the entire expanse of the European lowland. Unfortunately, there are no reliable faunal assemblages from southern Scandinavia dating to this early phase. Madsen's argument is based upon the location of sites in relation to soil types, the high percentage of pig bones at Toftum, and their gradual decrease in later assemblages

(1982, Fig. 17). However, recent re-evaluation of Danish data shows that the number of pigs on later TRB sites is immensely variable and does not reveal a chronologically significant decrease, but rather fluctuates according to the location and environment of individual sites (Fig. 107).

Moreover, the data from Toftum, which clearly form the only factual basis for Madsen's argument, are used inappropriately. We already noted that the bones derive from a causewayed enclosure ditch. They may represent the remains of a ceremonial meal or a ritual deposition not related specifically to the consumption of meat; indeed other ditches from Toftum may in future reveal different species compositions. Furthermore, there are no comparable materials from other south Scandinavian causewayed enclosures or contemporary settlements and we are not in a position to judge how far the ceremonial use of animals approximates to their domestic use.

In the context of analogous finds from Britain, Legge (1981) has argued that assemblages from causewayed enclosures reveal different 'consumption' patterns from those observed on settlements, and that they represent the use of available surplus from the economies. It is at present not possible to say whether the Toftum pigs represent such a surplus, and even if they do, this still does not support the contention that they were economically more important than cattle, although they may have had ceremonial significance. Indeed the whole problem of the importance of pigs and cattle in south Scandinavia needs to await new and well-analysed evidence.

Information derived from the faunal assemblages from north Germany and Kujavia does not in any way support the suggestion that pigs contributed in a more substantial way than cattle at any stage of the TRB culture, and the same picture emerges from the Southern and South-eastern groups.

An interesting supposition can be made, however, from the two assemblages at the Sarup settlement, which post-date the use of the site for ceremonial purposes. The assemblages, which on C-14 dates are separated by about sixty years, show a dramatic decrease in the number of pig bones from 43.7 per cent to 14.4 per cent, and a corresponding though less startling increase in the number of cattle bones as well as a greater proportion of wild animals. Andersen suggested that the clearance of the landscape in the vicinity of Sarup reduced the environmental potential for pig husbandry in favour of cattle (N. Andersen 1981, 93). Assuming that there is little point in keeping a large pig herd when the animals are not contributing to the meat supply, the relative changes in the proportions of species at Sarup may indeed reflect an actual reduction in the number of pigs kept. If this is correct and if, furthermore, we assume that the changing environment was the chief cause, then the magnitude of such an environmental change over a relatively short period of time would be quite staggering. On the other hand, the earlier presence of a dense settlement in the area, seen in the actual settlements as well as in the profusion of megalithic tombs whose construction pre-dates the events discussed, would suggest that the neighbourhood of Sarup was fairly well cleared and well established economically. Thus, such dramatic changes in the faunal assemblages at Sarup may require explanations other than environmental.

The role of small ruminants (sheep and goats) is perhaps most difficult to assess. The animals require a relatively open grazing landscape which was not present in the North European Plain during the second half of the 6th millennium BP. Yet sheep and goats appear, albeit in small numbers, among the earliest assemblages. The relatively high proportion of sheep/goats on the sites of the Eastern group may be somewhat misleading. The bone samples are in fact very small; they derive from the mounds of long barrows and thus incorporate earlier settlement material scraped up from extensive surfaces. The landscape at Sarnowo may have offered some advantageous grazing conditions on the slopes of surrounding hills. On the other hand, the black earth Kujavian uplands supported a contemporary Lengyel settlement and the possibility of exchanges involving livestock should not be dismissed.

Sheep and goats are found in the early TRB in the Northern group. Their presence is acknowledged on sites such as Havnelev (Mathiassen 1940), Sigersted (P.O. Nielsen 1985), Barkær (Glob 1949) and Sølager (Skaarup 1973), but on the whole they are represented by a few bones only. There is a steady increase in the relative frequency of these animals during the later TRB period, however, and this consistency can perhaps serve (more assuredly than the fluctuating frequency of pig) as a measure of the opening up of a forested landscape. The presence of sheep and goats may have been particularly significant on the coastal sites where, in contrast to inland locations, salt marshes provided a superior as well as a longer grazing season (Higham 1969, 206). The slaughter pattern from the Danish sites is on the whole consistent and implies that sheep and goats were reared mainly for consumption: most animals at Troldebjerg, Bundsø and Lindø were killed before or during their second year, the proportions quoted by Higham being 79 per cent, 68 per cent and 61 per cent respectively (ibid., 205).

The more sophisticated exploitation of sheep and goats is suggested by the evidence from the late TRB settlement at Spodsbjerg on Langeland. Here, half of the identified individuals (fifteen of twenty-eight) were over 3 years old and most of these died after their sixth year. This contrasts with the meat-oriented pattern identified by Higham on the other Danish sites and may suggest that secondary produce (milk and wool) become a more valuable commodity towards the end of the TRB (Nyegaard 1985, 433–5).

From a largely theoretical perspective Wiślański argued that during the later TRB, the ecologically different demands of domestic species led to a diversification of animal husbandry which ultimately may have resulted in local specialisation. For the purpose of grazing, the livestock was divided into two groups: one involved mainly pigs while the other combined cattle, sheep and goats. The valley forests would have provided ideal feeding grounds for pigs since they are not inhibited by thick undergrowth and, with the exception of young animals, are less in danger from predators than other domestic species. The seasonal stay of pig herds in the forest would likewise encourage cross-breeding with wild pigs, thus ensuring a healthy livestock. Ethnographic evidence from Poland indicates that such summer forest-feeding of pig herds was still a widespread practice during the nineteenth century (Wiślański 1969, 161–2).

Cattle and sheep, on the other hand, would be taken to the seasonally available pastures along the edges of upland landscapes. Here the boundary betwen forest and meadow would offer ideal grazing for both species, with the cattle exploring the edge of the forest and the sheep grazing on the meadows and forest glades. This habitat boundary is also frequented by wild game and thus pastoral and hunting activities could be easily combined. The preponderance of camp sites along the upland's edge supports this general model, and more direct evidence now available from Kujavia suggests a degree of specialisation directly related to the ecological conditions of a settled landscape.

We noted previously that from the Wiórek phase onwards, the internal expansion of the TRB in Kujavia involved the extension of settlement outwith the mainly sandy lowland onto the black earth uplands, the latter being more akin in ecological conditions to the southern loess uplands. On the one hand, this extension of the settlement indicates a mature and competent economy which is sufficiently flexible to flourish in greatly varied environments. On the other hand, expansion onto an already cleared landscape (Kujavian black earth areas were previously settled by the LBK and Lengyel communities) allows the diversification of an economy, a fact which is particularly well exemplified in the faunal assemblages of the late TRB settlements which existed in these two environments.

The sites located in the upland, open landscape reveal the predominance of cattle and sheep (sheep constituting 50 per cent of the total bone assemblage at Dąbrowa Biskupia) and are likely to reflect the growth in the importance of the latter domesticate in open environments. The lowland sites on the other hand reveal no presence of sheep, but only cattle and pigs (Kośko 1981, 139). It is not unreasonable to recognise in this pattern a degree of local specialisation in animal husbandry, based on the exploitation of domestic species best suited to a particular settled environment.

Indeed, a similar interpretation can be suggested in relation to evidence from the South-eastern group. The Bronocice settlement with its greater emphasis on sheep and goats (Milisauskas and Kruk 1977, 217), contrasts with the neighbouring Zawarża where a strongly cattle-oriented strategy appears to have been in operation. Such differences can be argued to show that livestock management at individual sites may have been part of a regional economic strategy, and that a degree of specialisation fulfilled the economic needs with trading and exchange as integral elements.

That the animal contribution to the economy was not limited to the provision of meat and fat is self-evident. Wild animals would have provided furs and pelts, and the use of antler, particularly for flint-working tools, is well attested throughout the TRB. Bone was used for making a wide range of tools, and leather-working was undoubtedly also common. Moreover, it is precisely here, outwith the meat market, that animals which do not feature prominently in bone assemblages (such as sheep and goats) could make a substantial contribution. Evidence that spinning and weaving were among the common domestic activities comes in the form of spindle whorls, shuttles and loom weights. Sheep's wool and goat's hair could have provided raw materials for the manufacture of garments and pieces of cloth (possibly blankets?); such objects may have featured prominently in trade and exchange. The data from Schalkenburg show that some sheep and goats were kept beyond 4 years of age (about 20 per cent); Higham (1969) states that sheep will supply wool until 7–8 years old and that rams provide more wool than wethers and ewes.

In this context it is particularly interesting to recall that one of the distinguishing characteristics of the South-eastern group is the zoomorphic decoration of ceramic vessels, and that the animal which features most prominently in such decoration is the ram. These representations not only occur in contexts which may imply ritual significance, but also decorate large jars used for storage of grain (Ćmielów). While a consideration of the symbolic content of ram representations on pottery would have to take into account the broader theme of figural motifs throughout the Neolithic and cannot be attempted here, some of this significance may have arisen from its economic importance. We should perhaps observe that, interestingly, ram-decorated vessels were not found at Bronocice, but an amphora with a stylised ram's head is known from an isolated Baalberge context (Behrens 1973, Fig. 29: f).

8.4.1. Interpretation of pollen evidence

Evidence pertaining to the interpretation of arable methods and land use in the TRB culture is difficult to evaluate. This is best seen in the fact that often the same evidence is used to support diametrically opposed models such as slash-and-burn and permanent cultivation.

As we have already noted, the initial interpretation of the *landnam* phenomenon supported the idea that early farmers in Denmark cleared areas of forest, often with the use of fire, and subsequently grew cereals and used the land for pasture. The regeneration phase noted in many pollen diagrams suggested that, following the exhaustion of the soil, the particular plot was abandoned, the farmers moved to another locality and the forest was able to regenerate (Iversen 1941).

This model of slash-and-burn was adopted by many archaeologists and became dominant in the interpretation of Neolithic farming, not only in the north but throughout most of Europe. Additional support for the slash-and-burn cultivation theory was derived from studies of present-day swidden agriculturalists (Boserup 1965; Tabaczyński 1970); the interpretation of archaeological evidence (Soudský 1966), demographic studies and radiocarbon data (Ammerman and Cavalli-Sforza 1971, 1973, 1984; Clark 1975) all contributed to the maintenance of this view. It is only in recent years that the study of early European economies has begun to challenge the view that Neolithic farming was based on slash-and-burn cultivation.

Let us first consider how the pollen record from the TRB culture fits the model of slash-and-burn cultivation. Implicit in Iversen's interpretation of the *landnam* phenomenon was that it was not synchronous. However, the now vastly increased C-14 data suggest, to the contrary, that the *landnam* phenomenon is roughly coeval (*c*. 4650/4550 BP) over a large area of northern Europe (Göransson 1984).

Another series of problems lies in the interpretation of the pollen record. In recent years a number of palynologists have re-emphasised the fact that pollen diagrams do not faithfully represent vegetational change: they may have been distorted by a combination of biological, chemical and geographical factors which are difficult to determine. Distinguishing between a single event and a whole series of events which become amalgamated is an additional interpretative problem. Rowley-Conwy drew attention to the fact that if the *landnam* phenomenon was to represent an amalgam of clearances, as suggested by Troels-Smith (1953), then the stages of clearance, cultivation and regeneration would give a blurred picture of vegetational change and not a clear illustration of the sequence. Jarman and Bailey pointed out that the classic *landnam* phase, such as that identified at Ordrup Mose, does not support slash-and-burn cultivation but rather represents an agricultural episode of unknown duration, with the fire having been used in the initial clearance of the landscape (Jarman *et al.* 1982, 136).

While there is no *a priori* reason why fire should not be used to clear vegetation, not only is there a discrepancy in the interpretation of fire traces from pollen diagrams, but also the pollen record itself is variable: some pollen diagrams reveal a strong presence of charcoal while others do not. How should this be explained and what relevance does it have in the context of the slash-and-burn model?

In some areas of NW Europe (Ireland, central Sweden and England) traces of fire have been shown to pre-date not only the *landnam* phenomenon, but also the elm decline (Göransson 1984). This is generally interpreted as evidence that hunter-gatherers manipulated the natural environment in order to improve grazing conditions for herbivorous animals and to exercise some sort of control over game; there are no suggestions that they practised slash-and-burn cultivation. Should all traces of fire in pollen contexts which can be related to the presence of farming communities within a particular region therefore immediatley be interpreted as indicating slash-and-burn cultivation?

Iversen himself argued that initial fire clearances may have been related to the pastoral aspect of the TRB economy, creating improved grazing conditions in a forested environment, and that only a small proportion of such a landscape would have been used for cereal cultivation (Iversen 1941, 29–30). In this context the pollen evidence from Östergötland is as fascinating as it is difficult to interpret. Pollen diagrams from this area, analysed by Göransson, reveal a substantial presence of charcoal particles in the segments dated to about 5050–4550 BP. This is interpreted as evidence that regular forest-burning to improve the extensive forest-grazing took place in this region of Sweden; some cereal cultivation was taking place alongside.

While the unbroken presence of charcoal particles in the pollen spectra does attest burning, it does not offer any information either on the number of burning episodes or on their frequency: were the forests burned every five years or every fifty years? Was it only in one locality that this activity was taking place, or should we perhaps assume that a process similar to the later 'coppice wood' management was taking place, with a number of different areas being involved on a rotational basis?

Although Göransson states that the subsequent coppice wood phase, in contrast to the fire-grazing phase, represents a permanent type of cultivation, there is no evidence to suggest that the 'fire-grazing phase' was any more impermanent than the use of twenty-five or thirty coppice woods. Apart from indicating that burning was taking place, the pollen evidence on its own does not answer the question of shifting or stable activities.

Analysis of pollen samples from under the Sarnowo long barrows provides evidence for the presence of charcoal particles in the context of a cultivated field. Dąbrowski (1971) argued that the presence of four main cereals (wheat, barley, millet and rye) implies that the field was cultivated over a number of years and that crop rotation was a most likely practice. Groenman-van Waateringe (1979a, 70) believes, however, that pollen spectra from under barrows do not incorporate more than the pollen rain from a couple of years. The presence of four cereals at Sarnowo could mean that they were grown together or that some were accompanying weeds (especially *Secale cereale*). The presence of charcoal has been interpreted as evidence for slash-and-burn cultivation, although in view of the relatively open landscape, forest-burning is less likely. Kruk (1980, 191) suggested as an alternative that ashes may have been deliberately spread out over the field; the burning of the previous year's stubble is another possibility.

While the evidence from Sarnowo could be used in support of slash-and-burn cultivation, it represents one specific episode. The lack of a master diagram for this area makes generalisation difficult; it should be noticed that pollen samples from the area of the settlement do not reveal traces of charcoal, even though the degree of forestation of the surrounding area appears to have been three times higher and some clearance may reasonably have been expected.

While some of the pollen evidence from the TRB culture does suggest the use of fire, other pollen diagrams show no indication of fire as a clearance agent. Indeed in some instances there is little indication of the classic *landnam* phase. This evidence was initially registered by Iversen, who felt that, in some instances, unless slow sedimentation affected the pollen record, 'the relatively slight density of forest and its wealth of grass made a clearance fire unnecessary' (1941, 52–3).

This problem has been discussed at length by Groenman-van-Waateringe who, using her knowledge of vegetation change in the Veluwe area of the Netherlands, argued that *Plantago lanceolata* will not develop in the extensively grazed open woodland, where it becomes replaced by *Succissa*. She suggested that some of the Danish pollen records which puzzled Iversen may represent a rather slow opening of woodland by grazing which, in contrast to Iversen's model, did not require any substantial clearance by man (Groenman-van-Waateringe 1978, 143). Rowley-Conwy (1982) also drew attention to the fact that progressive grazing of the forest may lead to the establishment of grassy areas, and the girdling of trees noted about 400 years before the true *landnam* could be part of this relatively slow process, which does not make a dramatic impact on the pollen record.

Perhaps the most significant factors which emerge from the above, as well as our earlier discussions of the pollen evidence, are the inconsistency of the pollen record and the difficulties inherent in the interpretation of the whole sequence of events from the elm decline through to *landnam*. The Danish pollen record on the whole offers no support for the slash-and-burn cultivation model (although it does attest to the occasional use of fire in clearances) but, equally, it offers little in the way of an explanation for the elm decline and *landnam*. On the other hand, the interpretation of the Östergötland material has put the elm decline and *landnam* into new perspective by seeing the two phenomena as part of a long-term vegetational sequence, and has provided renewed discussion of slash-and-burn cultivation in the TRB context, a theme for which clearly some support could also be sought in the pollen record from the Eastern and South-eastern groups. The pollen evidence as it stands at present is confusing and therefore other evidence for TRB land use needs to be examined.

8.4.2 Direct cultivation evidence

The primary source of evidence for the existence of cultivated fields in the TRB culture comes from a fortuitous preservation of scratch-marks on ancient surfaces protected beneath TRB burial mounds. Examples are known from the Eastern group, where two sites have been identified at Sarnowo and Łupawa, and from the Western group, where a Neolithic field was found beneath peat near Bornwird in Friesland possibly dating to the end of the TRB culture (Fokkens 1982). By far the largest number derives from Denmark, where over twenty examples are known, found beneath monuments dating from the Fuchsberg phase onwards (Thrane 1982).

By and large the traces are preserved in small patches. In the Northern group they are often confined to the interiors of stone-built chambers, and at present they do not offer sufficient evidence for us to comment upon the possible size of the fields. Indeed, initially such discoveries were interpreted as 'ritual ploughing' connected with ceremonies during the construction of burial mounds (Ørsnes 1956; Pätzold 1960). While it is possible that ritual ploughing may have been performed occasionally (at Lundehøj the furrows appear to have been scratched onto the surface of the artificially laid floor), it is more probable that its confinement to the chamber results from limited investigation or, possibly, because of the chamber floor suffered least disturbance during the construction.

In many instances, however, it is clear that such traces run beneath the chamber walls (for example at Fuglebæksbanke; Ebbesen and Brinch Petersen 1974) or are so abruptly terminated by them (for instance at Himmelev; Skaarup 1982a) as to confirm that they are only partially preserved. Moreover, excavation of entire mounds shows clearly that such traces can survive over large areas: at Skibshøj, for instance, they were noted beneath the mound to the east of the dolmen chamber. At Steneng they covered an area of 230 m² and at Snave nearly the entire area of 45 m long mound revealed criss-cross patterns (Thrane 1982, Fig. 3). So far, only the marks from underneath the Sarnowo barrow have been subject to pollen analysis; the results indicated beyond doubt that cereal cultivation took place there. At Bornwird grains of *Hordeum vulgare* were found in the soil above the ancient field (Fokkens 1982, 99), but there need not be any direct connection between these two finds.

Such scratch-marks are normally interpreted as ard-marks or traces left over from the use of a simple plough such as a crook-ard (Sherratt 1981, 268; Rowley-Conwy 1981, 94; 1987). Experiments with a variety of plough types have shown, however, that a simple standard plough such as a crook-ard was more suitable for creating a seed drill (such is the interpretation of the Bornwird marks) and was not likely to leave pronounced traces. The ard-marks found in a variety of Neolithic contexts appear to correspond more to traces left by a rip-ard, an implement particularly suitable for creating grassland from woodland and bringing into arable new ground or old fallow (Reynolds 1981, 103).

Although it is reasonable to assume that repeated cultivation of a particular field would result in the self-obliteration of ard-marks, there are multi-directional and criss-crossing patterns preserved which imply that such activity took place more than once. Thus at Sarnowo, some of the SE–NW-running furrows appear to duplicate and overlap one another, allowing us to infer at least two episodes in the cultivation of the field. Four separate directions were noted at Bornwird (Fokkens 1982, Fig. 5) and similar observations can be made with regard to Snave (Thrane 1982, Fig. 3). Only one general plan has been published so far, but the ard-mark pattern appears to be very complex, showing a number of overlaps and multitudinous directions again implying a series of activities.

Reynolds (1981, 104) has warned against counting the number of directions of ard-marks and transferring these to the number of cultivations. He suggested that multi-directional ploughing could reflect regular periods of fallow. With reference to the criss-cross pattern he suggested that this could imply an area was taken into arable once or twice only. However, the criss-cross pattern is encountered with such amazing regularity, not only within the TRB and Neolithic, but also in later contexts, as to suggest that criss-cross ploughing (or at least criss-cross 'rip-arding') may have been a standard practice, especially upon fields which were reclaimed after fallow. This method, in the absence of a mouldboard, would have the additional advantage of loosening the soil and helping to extract unwanted roots. The possibility that criss-cross ploughing may have offered an effective way of combating the weeds should also be considered (Groenman-van Waateringe 1979b).

It is by no means clear whether all the identified ard-marks are the result of a draught-pulled plough. The question of distance is important here, since it has been argued that in the case of the crook-ard a distance of 30–40 cm between the furrows is necessary to prevent the ard from slipping back (Rees 1979). Many of the ard-marks from TRB contexts are closely spaced: at Sarnowo the average distance was 13 cm, and for some of the Danish examples as little as 10 cm are quoted (Wiklak 1982, 40; Thrane 1982, 21). One wonders, therefore, whether some of the ard-marks may in fact have been made using hoes rather than with a plough pulled by oxen. On the other hand, in the use of rip-ard, which pulls rather than pushes at the soil, the distance may have been less important and the closeness of the furrows may also indicate a need to sow closely, possibly suggesting that the fields in these instances were quite small.

Although the earliest dated ploughs in northern Europe belong to the fourth millennium BP, the evidence from many regions of Europe makes it plain that the implement was in use long before then. Discussing the introduction of a simple crook-ard into northern Europe, Sherratt (1981, 270–1) suggested that, considered together with the evidence for the use of a cart, the period of 4550–4450 BP indicated a relevant horizon during which this innovation was generally adopted. With reference to Sarnowo, Sherratt concluded that a date of 4625 ± 40 BP (from the later settlement of Zarębowo) was of more relevance than the earlier date from Sarnowo itself. The Sarnowo stratigraphy is somewhat complex, but essentially the plough-marks survived beneath a layer of daub which is believed to represent the remains of a domestic structure from a later habitation layer which, in turn, preceded the construction of the barrow. Such a sequence of cultivated field, followed by habitation, followed by a burial monument, is not unique (cf. Himmelev: Skaarup 1982, 21; a settlement is known to move onto abandoned fields at Łupawa: Jankowska 1980). Thus, if the stratigraphy at Sarnowo has been correctly interpreted, the date of 5570 ± 60 BP; which relates to the habitation layer, is not a *terminus post quem* but in fact a *terminus ante quem* for the ard-marks. Allowing even the Groningen correction of approximately 200 radiocarbon years, the ploughing at Sarnowo is still very early. Upon overall considerations of the evidence it cannot be later than 5150 BP. Accepting, of course, that the traces recovered here are the result of animal-drawn implements, the introduction of the plough would be earlier than suggested by Sherratt.

We should also note that, from the Northern TRB group there are now fourteen examples of ard-marks, preserved beneath monuments which date to the Fuchsberg/MN I (*c*. 4650 BP) stage. These can hardly date the introduction of the plough to this region; rather they attest to its widespread use, which by then was clearly part of standard agricultural practice.

Little circumstantial evidence from the TRB culture can be brought into the discussion regarding the introduction of the plough. The presence of castrated oxen and evidence for their use as draught animals is, as we saw earlier, well documented in the later TRB context, but osteological information from the crucial early period is still inadequate. The expansion of the TRB settlement, once it becomes established in individual regions, onto heavier soils which are generally regarded as more difficult to cultivate, has already been discussed (Chapter 7.1). Although this process is not synchronous throughout the area, the technological ability to cope with a wider and more demanding environment is obviously relevant in this context.

While the suggestion may appear somewhat controversial, there is no *a priori* reason why the appearance of the plough on the North European Plain should not be dated to sometime soon after the middle of the 6th millenium BP. While direct evidence is lacking and the prospect of ard-marks ever appearing in the late Lengyel context is remote, connections with the south are nevertheless very evident in the presence of copper objects, ornaments and axes among the Brześć Kujawski Lengyel groups. On present evidence these offer a relatively well-defined, if narrow, horizon of about 5350–5150 BP, and it is perhaps this horizon which should be considered to account for the introduction of novel elements to the southern fringes of the North European Plain.

The direct evidence of the TRB culture arable fields is not conclusive in documenting either the presence or absence of slash-and-burn cultivation, but the drastic reductions in soil fertility, the resultant poor yields and the building-up of weeds are the argonomic arguments commonly suggested in support of this practice. However, evidence for slash-and-burn agriculture

derived from ethnographic and historical sources pertains to areas of marginal agricultural potential. The very specific climatic and edaphic conditions
prevalent in such regions diverge considerably from those of temperate
Europe.

Lüning pointed out that arguments for rapid soil exhaustion under
Neolithic cultivation have no sound basis and that a long fallow period is
not the best way of restoring the fertility of soil. Using results from the
long-term experimental farming stations at Rothampsted and Göttinger, he
argued that good crop yields can be maintained using the same plot over a
long period of time and that these will improve if manuring and crop
rotation are practised (Lüning 1980; see also Rowley-Conwy 1981).

Although it is difficult to prove that manuring was practised deliberately
during the TRB, the presence of domestic animals from the very beginning
indicates that manuring may initially have occurred accidentally, when
animals grazed in harvested fields. There is no reason whatsoever to
presume that early farmers would fail to make the connection between
manuring and good harvests. Moreover, the main crops grown in the TRB
(and other Neolithic cultures) were emmer and einkorn; these varieties are
said to make fewer demands on the soil and to reduce its fertility less than
other wheats (Jarman *et al.* 1982, 140). The fertilising qualities of leguminous plants must have been realised long before cultivation reached northern Europe, as their regular presence among the Neolithic plants
suggests. They are well documented in TRB contexts and were likely to
have been used in crop rotation. Finds such as Ćmielów suggest that cereals
and pulses may even have been grown together.

Discussing the prehistoric weeds Groenman-van Waateringe stated that
while the initial eradication of weeds from a freshly ploughed woodland soil
would not have been a problem, after two or three years of cultivation
'weeds were rampant since ard ploughing leaves large strips of land un-
loosened' (1979b, 363). The criss-cross ploughing regularly noted beneath
barrows with preserved ard-marks may indicate that this type of ploughing
may have helped not only in the initial breaking up of the soil, but also to
keep the weeds down. Groenman-van Waateringe argued that clearance of
a new plot would have been simpler than trying to eradicate the weeds. It
takes a long time for a specific weed and crop association to develop, and
the reason why Neolithic crops have such a small weed admixture is related
precisely to the nature of shiting cultivation. This idea finds favour with
archaeologists who believe that TRB crop purity was due not to cereal
selection but to shifting cultivation (T. Madsen 1982, 225).

Knörzer, on the other hand, argued that the harvesting method, reaping
only ears and not stems, reduced the quantity of collected weeds as only the
tall species were gathered. His studies of cereals from the LBK and Rössen
sites in the Rhineland prove the point well (Knörzer 1971). Some of the
TRB cereal finds are very free of weeds indeed; this is quoted as an

additional argument for the practice of slash-and-burn cultivation. The question of the presence or absence of weeds in this context is very interesting and a number of explanations are possible. Firstly, as already noted, the weed-free cereals from Denmark and Poland derive on two occasions from ritual contexts; a particular selection of grain may have been involved there. Five types of weed, albeit in a very small quantity, were identified at Radziejów (Wiślański 1979, 213). Six types were associated with the Sarup wheat, again in a small quantity (G. Jørgensen 1977, 58, Table 1). The clean grain from Ćmielów came from a storage pit and a possible selection in the preparation for sowing has already been suggested. The samples from Dannau, however, all contained an admixture of weeds, especially small grasses, and Kroll argued that the cleared soils had been quickly overgrown (Kroll 1981, 87).

We should perhaps ask whether cereal finds are the best indication of the presence or absence of weeds. When we consider the pollen samples from the Sarnowo field, the presence of weeds is quite high (Dąbrowski 1971, Table 1) and the same can be said about the fields from beneath the Dutch barrows which were abandoned only shortly prior to the building of the monuments (Waterbolk 1958; Casparie and Groenman-van Waateringe 1980). The evidence from the fields thus suggests a considerable presence of weeds; this points to the pure cereal finds in the TRB being due more to the nature of harvesting and careful seed selection than to shifting cultivation. Moreover, the burning of field cover documented at Sarnowo may, like criss-cross ploughing, represent one of the many ways in which the weeds were kept under control.

Groenman-van Waateringe proposed another model of Neolithic land use which could be of relevance to the TRB. She suggested that the presence of certain wild plants in pollen diagrams represented 'outskirts' vegetation, particularly likely to grow along the edge of cleared habitats, and that it might indicate the existence of hedges. This would have the advantage of separating the arable and grazing fields, containing and protecting livestock; they would also encourage the growth of other plants such as blackberries, raspberries, cherry and apple, all of which are known to have been collected in the TRB and which constitute a valuable source of food.

The tendency to argue against slash-and-burn and in favour of more permanent cultivation in the TRB seen in the recent literature (e.g. Rowley-Conwy 1981), reflects a more general trend in the study of prehistoric economies which results from the re-appraisal not only of archaeological evidence, but also of the theoretical models applied in its interpretation. It is becoming increasingly clear that the impact of the early farmers upon their environment was conditioned not merely by the cultural factors but also, and primarily, by the nature of the environment itself. Pollen evidence shows that, in some regions, the clearance process was relatively slow with a progressive opening up of the landscape through grazing, while elsewhere the natural conditions evidently demanded a more dramatic intervention through the agency of forest fires. While the overall evidence does not support slash-and-burn cultivation as a primary force behind the TRB economy, evidence from areas such as Östergötland suggests that, in some localities, regular buring of vegetational cover was an integral part of the economic strategy.

Although the fleeting character of early TRB settlement is regarded by some scholars as evidence for shifting cultivation, this phenomenon need not be interpreted in terms of slash-and-burn agriculture but should rather be seen as reflecting a balance between the farming and foraging aspects, the latter being an important feature of the early TRB economy. On the other hand there is sufficient evidence to argue for some movement within the arable landscape throughout the TRB, which should however be interpreted more as a long-term than a short-term solution. From the location of burial monuments in all regions it is clear that some of the cultivated fields were given over to non-agricultural purposes. Other fields are shown to have been transformed into pasture lands, and the adjustment of the balance between the arable and pastoral aspects of the economy must have been an important solution in the overall economic strategy for the entire duration of the culture.

It would be futile to interpret the nature and development of the TRB economy from a perspective of one particular viewpoint and to search for one specific economic model. This is suggested not only by the evidence reviewed in the preceding pages but, first and foremost, by the varied environment of the vast area in which the TRB culture established itself. The variety of natural landscapes of the North European Plain, offering different ecological conditions, had a profound influence upon the choice and subsequent development of economic strategies. Clearly, the zone of high arable potential in the loessic landscape along the southern fringes of the Plain offered possibilites which were fundamentally different from those encountered along the littoral; each major landscape was further divided into local ecological habitats which presented different possibilities and constraints.

The appreciation of the economic potential inherent within each landscape and the ability of the TRB populations to adapt to different conditions are clearly manifest in the evidence discussed above. Other evidence, such as material culture, the organisation of crafts and industries, and social complexity, show that these people were innovative, adaptable and, above all, flexible in their aproach to various challenges. It is therefore hardly surprising that the same qualities should reveal themselves in the approaches that the TRB farmers displayed in establishing and developing a successful economy.

8.5 Introduction of farming across the North European Plain

While the reader may choose to disagree with most or even all of the interpretations presented in the preceding pages of this chapter, the discussion must surely leave him or her in no doubt that the various TRB communities were successfully engaged in a farming economy. But the process which led to the adoption of cultivated cereals and the keeping of livestock is neither easily perceived nor to be explained in terms of a uniform model. Thus, while it may appear unorthodox to discuss the economy before discussing its inception, the belief that the knowledge of basic facts has to precede their interpretation has guided the order of discussion. It is only now, having acquired some degree of familiarity with the salient features of the TRB economy, that we can apply ourselves to the difficult question of what processes were involved in the introduction and spread of farming throughout the North European Plain.

In the opening paragraphs of this chapter we noted that there has been considerable discussion about the introduction of farming in northern Europe. It is extremely important, however, to note that the current polemic on this subject, so vivid in the recent archaeological literature, is in fact concerned with southern Scandinavia, which forms but one of many regions in the vast area occupied by the TRB culture. Thus, while some of the concerns expressed in the above-mentioned works are of general nature and bear upon the universal problem of the transition from hunting-gathering to farming, many arguments are of local importance only and are not relevant in the broader context of the North European Plain. As an example we may quote the arguments about the demise of marine resources put forward by Rowley–Conwy (1983) in his discussion of the transition from foraging to farming in Denmark. While the depletion of this particular resource is indeed of relevance to those groups of people who lived along the Danish coast, most of the hunter-gatherers of the North European Plain did not live on the coast and did not subsist on oysters; their demise would thus have been of no consequence to the greatest part of the late Mesolithic population of the area under study.

Secondly, overall consideration of the evidence shows that the emergence of the TRB culture in southern Scandinavia was accomplished at a later time and by somewhat different processes than those which operated across the rest of the North European Plain.

Eschewing temporarily the arguments advanced for the adoption of a farming economy in southern Scandinavia we should note that for the time being there is no basis for discussing the introduction of farming along the North European Plain from an economic perspective. In order to interpret the reasons behind a transition from one form of subsistence to another, in this instance from foraging to farming, some knowledge and understanding of *both* is required. This, however, is not possible in our case.

While by now we have become reasonably familiar with the Bandkeramik phenomenon and have developed some degree of understanding regarding the economic activities pursued both on and off the loess landscape, we have very little knowledge and perception of the socio-economic conditions prevailing in most regions of the North European Plain. D. Clarke wrote that

> in the European temperate forest zone, the subsistence basis was *probably* focused on various root/foliage/fruits and nut combinations epxloited in techniques which *perhaps* in some sense already approximated to simple forest horticulture. . . . An abundant mammal fauna *probably* provided ample meat supplies with less need for advanced husbandry techniques, except in winter.
>
> (D.L. Clarke 1978, 33; my italics)

More than a decade later this quotation, as well as any, reflects the state of knowledge of the late Mesolithic period over most of the North European Plain.

Although research into the socio-economic aspects of foragers here is hampered by the paucity of evidence, the main stumbling block appears to be the incessant preoccupation by the majority of scholars with typo-chronological analyses of lithic assemblages. Looking through some major syntheses on the subject one forms the distinct impression that lowland European Mesolithic people were concerned with little else but knapping flint. Even the more ambitious attempts at discussion of the socio-economic issues of the lowland Mesolithic do not move beyond the construction of predative human adaptations which derive from 'Hypothetical models based on ethnographic, ecological and theoretical considerations' (Price 1980, 225).

Neither has this deficiency in the Mesolithic record been challenged by those concerned with the emergence of the TRB culture, since most of the discussions on the subject were conducted through the prism of material culture as scholars pursued ceramic connections between distant regions or investigated the 'Mesolithic' or 'Bandkeramik' traits within lithic industries. However, people may learn to make pots or use different tools, but they usually do not have to, and often did not, change the way in which they acquire food.

We have already noted that the LBK and its congeners settled along the southern fringes of the North European Plain in environments which, ecologically, were most suitable for sustaining farming activities. To what extent this has affected and created displacement in hunter-gatherer settlement patterns is difficult to determine, although by and large these areas appear to have been of marginal, if any, interest to the Mesolithic hunters. This seems to have been the case in Kujavia, where the upland zone was not explored by the hunter-gatherers but became one of the formative centres of the whole LBK cycle. A similar situation is noted in Upper Silesia, where the LBK and late Mesolithic finds distribution underlines the ecological exclusiveness of the area, and recent research in Little Poland also suggests that environments approximating to lowland conditions may have supported non-Bandkeramik populations (Kruk 1983, 272). The two cultural complexes appear to have been exclusive in their distribution in Mecklenburg, with the LBK essentially confined to the fertile Uckermark region where Mesolithic finds are totally lacking (Gramsch 1971a, 128–30, Fig. 1). The LBK does not reach Lower Saxony and only small enclaves of Rössen have been identified (Schwabedissen 1979c, Fig. 4). The situation in the Netherlands reflects the already-clear pattern of little geographical overlap between the early LBK and the local Mesolithic, although a more complex situation emerges with the appearance of the advanced LBK (Louwe Kooijmans 1976a).

The ecological exclusiveness of the late Mesolithic and LBK, and the visible groupings within these two complexes, do not however, imply that human populations during the later 7th and early 6th millennium BP lived in isolation. Irrespective of differences which may have existed in the socio-economic conditions of different north European foragers, there are clear indications that they had their own well-established exchange networks and channels of communication. We need only remind ourselves of the distribution of certain raw materials such as Rügen or chocolate flint, to realise the extent of contacts with people outside the immediate local territories. These may often have cut across the areas already settled by the farmers (cf. Mesolithic chocolate flint distribution networks; Schild 1987).

It is inconceivable that the long period of co-existence and territorial proximity of the lowland hunter-gatherers and early farmers would have gone unnoticed by both, and that the two populations would not have established some contacts with one another, although these would have varied in form and intensity and need not always have been of a peaceful nature. Indeed, long-term contact between foragers and farmers is the necessary prerequisite of the availability model recently suggested by Zvelebil and Rowley-Conwy (1984) as an explanation for the transition from hunter-gatherer to farmer. Although they imply that this model should be understood in terms of the entire zone in which foragers and farmers came into contact, the applications so far have been limited to peripheral areas of this zone rather than its whole extent, and in the TRB context to Denmark. Yet any attempt to understand the appearance of a farming economy in the latter area must of necessity take into account what happens across the whole North European Plain which stands between the Danish hunter-gatherers and the central European farmers. But it is precisely in this area, for reasons already explained, that the greatest difficulty exists.

In a recent attempt to interpret the relationship between foragers and farmers along the North European Plain, Bogucki (1987) postulated possible scenarios (drawn chiefly from general ethnographic models) of such contacts in terms of economically advantageous exchanges, especially of protein and carbohydrates. He suggested that one form of exchange may have involved the acquisition of game from hunter-gatherers in return for cereals. While this is not a new concept, and while such exchanges most probably took place in some areas at least, they are very difficult to demonstrate archaeologically. The presence of wild animals in bone assemblages and wild plants on farmers' settlements may be interpreted in two ways: either they were acquired from hunter-gatherers, or they may represent subsidiary pursuits of the farmers themselves. The mere presence of wild species in a farming context does not explain the process of acquisition. On the other hand Bogucki's idea of exchange does not square with his interpretation of the Lengyel culture's economic strategy: 'seasonal and animal shortfalls in domestic plant and animal production had to be buffered by the exploitation of wild resources in order to support the large Lengyel communities' (1987, 7). 'Consumption' of wild species does not equal 'exploitation of wild resources'; moreover, if Lengyel communities could not produce enough food to provide for themselves, they were hardly likely to have had surplus food for trading and exchange. Either the Lengyel economy was badly managed or, as seems more likely, the exchanges with hunter-gatherers were on a much more complex level.

Although Bogucki (1987) concerns himself greatly with the possibilities of exchange between the farmers and indigenous lowland communities, he makes only a passing comment on two of the best archaeological sources documenting such contacts: pottery and stone axes. The presence of one or two isolated objects in a foreign milieu does not automatically attest to contacts and exchanges. This is not the case with ceramic technology, however, or indeed with the highly typical implements such as *hohle durchlochte Schuhleistenkeile* and *Breitkeile*, whose initial cultural provenance is not in doubt.

Pottery-making among some of the late Mesolithic communities represents one aspect of contact between the hunter-gatherers and farming communities of the North European Plain. As we have already seen, pottery has been found on many Ertebølle-Ellerbek sites as well as in related groups across the North European Plain, and recently a number of Mesolithic inland assemblages containing pottery have also been commented upon in northern and central Poland (Cyrek *et al.* 1983; Bagniewski 1979 and 1980).

How do we reagard the appearance of pottery vessels in these obviously Mesolithic contexts? It is reasonable to assume that containers of some kind had been used prior to the manufacture of clay pots, especially for the purpose of gathering food plants. They were likely to have been made from organic materials such as leather, wood or reeds, although they were not likely to have been used for cooking. Indeed, examples of wooden vessels

are known from Christiansholm (Becker 1947); typologically they correspond to the Ertebølle pottery and they are an excellent example of a
container made of organic material which may have been commonly used
by Mesolithic groups. It is possible that the form and shape of the Ertebølle
pottery could have been inspired by the local, organic material prototypes,
but it is more likely that the idea itself arrived from outwith the Ertebølle.

As a technique, pottery-making was probably relatively easy to assimilate
and it certainly did not require the long-term accumulation of knowledge
which is essential for the successful growing of cereals and animal husbandry. The study by Hulthén of ceramic technology from Denmark and
Sweden concludes that the Ertebølle culture was technically less accomplished and that the actual technique was undoubtedly acquired through
contacts with pottery-making farming groups. The influence of the LBK
culture pottery is supported by the apparent knowledge of *chamotte* and
plant-tempering, which are typical of LBK technology (Hulthén 1977, 49).
Hulthén also suggests that the Mesolithic groups learned to select and
prepare clays, but the actual technique required longer experience and it
was not until the subsequent TRB culture that this technology was fully
developed (ibid., 51).

The pottery which is associated with assemblages which are otherwise
Mesolithic in character from the Polish finds represents ceramics similar to
the so-called Pit-Comb wares. It is difficult to determine whether these
should be regarded as westerly extensions of the Pit-Comb culture or as
ceramics locally made by the late Mesolithic groups.

The presence of stone tools *hohle durchlochte Schuhleistenkeile* and *Breitkeile* – in the North European Plain offers another example of contacts
between Mesolithic and Neolithic communities. Not only is there a large
number of such axes known from well north of the LBK and Rössen/Leng-
yel settlement boundaries, but they are also found in clear late Mesolithic
contexts. A fragment of a *Breitkeil* was found with the Ertebølle-Ellerbek
material at Förstermoor, and a number of other axes are known from
various localities in the area of Satrup Moor (Schwabedissen 1967, Fig. 1).
A fragment of a perforated *Breitkeil* comes from the Ertebølle settlement at
Ralswiek-Augustenhof on Rügen, where a decorated bone plate of the
Brześć Kujawski type was also found (stroke-decorated STBK sherds are
also known from the neighbouring Lietzow-Buddelin settlement; Gramsch
1971, 131). Shaft-hole stone axes have also been encountered in Denmark,
especially on the Danish islands, in equally clear Ertebølle contexts (Store
Åmose, Vester Ulslev or Brændegård; A. Fischer 1982, 7–12).

Comparison of Mesolithic and Neolithic flint industries has not on the
whole been very successful; it leads mostly to divergent opinions which
tend to reflect the personal views and prejudices of individual researchers
and adds little to the understanding of possible relationships between
industries. Vencl has argued that 'the origin of neolithic cultures cannot be

inferred on the basis of the lithic industries alone' (Vencl 1986, 48). While this point is not disputed, there is most clearly a difference between immigrant famers who, in certain areas of Europe, arrived with a complete cultural package, and areas where 'neolithic culture' appeared as a result of a more complex process involving the integration of indigenous peoples. Our previous discussion of the TRB lithic materials shows clearly that its flint industry, while not identical to the earlier industrial tradition, is directly related to it; differences to be seen are due not so much to the 'immigrant Neolithic' as to the different functions of tools, the use of varied raw materials and the overall development of the industry through time.

Indeed a number of scholars have also argued that Mesolithic flint technology influenced certain aspects of the flint industries of the LBK and late LBK communities in their various enclaves on the North European Plain. Newell has argued for a very close correspondence between the Dutch Mesolithic and LBK flint industries; this has been disputed by Louwe Kooijmans who, nevertheless, conceded a degree of similarity (Newell 1972; Louwe Kooijmans 1976b). A number of LBK and late LBK assemblages in Poland have been shown to contain typical Mesolithic microliths (trapezes), although it is not certain to what extent these should be regarded as intrusive or merely as 'rare' elements of Neolithic industries.

With regard to stone tools, the presence of *Walzenbeile* in areas of Neolithic settlement is usually thought to reflect Mesolithic exchanges (Gramsch 1971a; Czerniak 1980) and Czerniak has argued that the tendency of the Kujavian shoe-last celts to become more symmetrical is also a direct result of Mesolithic influences.

Another interesting possibility of a Mesolithic contribution to Neolithic industries has arisen in connection with the recent publication of the so-called household cluster associated with the Brześć Kujawski settlement (Grygiel 1986). The manufacture of antler axes at Brześć Kujawski was carried out by one household; it involved a considerable degree of secrecy and Grygiel argued, on the basis of a whole range of ritual and other associations, that it was probably done by a craftsman who '. . . came from "outside" the community at Brześć Kujawski, from the realm of the Funnel Beaker culture which is increasingly seen as descending from late Maglemosian traditions (ibid., 261).

No research has so far been carried out in connection with antler axes of the LBK and late LBK complexes, although they apparently became gradually more common in post-LBK contexts. Kulczycka-Leciejewic-zowa (1979) suggested that this increase related to an improvement in manufacturing techniques, although it could equally well represent a dissemination of techniques acquired from outside. The manufacture of antler axes has a long and well-established tradition in the north European Mesolithic and this field opens up the possibility of investigating an important area of the Mesolithic contribution.

The conditions across the North European Plain clearly cannot be viewed in the same light as those further south. The LBK and late LBK settlement areas are smaller and more dispersed, and there is little dynamism of the sort seen in their southern counterparts. It is generally assumed that the environmental conditions of the European lowland prevented the expansion of early farming. While these conditions were most certainly an arresting factor, one wonders how much this may have been due to the strong presence of indigenous populations. The contacts between the two groups, which clearly are only partly represented in the archaeological record, are stronger than those observed anywhere else and indicate that while both complexes were clearly different in their socio-economic structures, they nevertheless were viable partners. The exchange of objects does not take place in a social vacuum and the examples outlined above lead one to suggest that social rather than economic considerations may, at least initially, have played a leading role in the exchanges.

It is hard to imagine that the *hohle durchlochte Schuhleistenkeile* and *Breitkeile*, clearly technically inferior to the excellent sharp-edged Mesolithic flint axes, would have much value as working tools. On the other hand, it is not inconceivable that they should be regarded as exotic luxury objects, helping to enhance the personal status of the individuals who acquired them (this may be the meaning of shaft-hole axes in the Vester Ulslev graves). Very much the same could apply to the Brześć Kujawski type ornaments.

Although pottery is generally thought of as primarily utilitarian, its presence within the Mesolithic context may have been as much symbolic as practical; ample ethnographic evidence draws our attention to the fact that the two functions are not mutually exclusive.

Although the actual process of transition from foraging to farming is obscured by the lack of evidence and by differing research perspectives, certain aspects are beginning to emerge. Firstly, the transition from forager to farmer in the North European Plain, as indeed elsewhere, must be considered from both sides of this artificial divide, a point stressed emphatically in many recent hunter-gatherer studies (Bailey 1983; Zvelebil 1986). All too frequently in the past scholars have become mesmerised by the few cereal grains or bones of domesticates and hailed what was still essentially a foraging economy as 'Neolithic'; attention must be paid to the overall circumstances and not just to selected details.

Secondly, it is now clear, although it may be difficult to demonstrate archaeologically, that the process of transition must have begun immediately after the early farmers made forays into the North Europen Plain (cf. Podgaj 32; Chapter 4.2); yet the ultimate emergence of the predominantly farming groups must be seen as the result of a cumulative process of integration between foragers and farmers in which both were active participants. The involvement of indigenous communities rather than the mere expansion of the southern farmers is documented in the distinctly different make-up of the TRB population, which comprises indigenous as well as external anthropomorphic elements (Schwidetzky 1978).

The formative areas, many of which are characterised by their closeness to the initial farming enclaves, are found throughout the entire plain (Łącko, Sarnowo, Berlin-Britz, Engern-Brinkhof, Boberg, Rosenhof, Dümmer, Swifterbant or Hazendonk), and although the pace, intensity and ultimate development may be different, the process follows broadly similar lines. The involvement of people over a large area is particularly important because it explains why the developed TRB was such a dynamic and successful phenomenon in the whole of northern Europe. It also fits well with the model proposed by Zvelebil and Rowley-Conwy (1984) for the availability phase.

To what extent southern Scandinavia participated in this process is still a matter of polemic, and many pages have recently been filled discussing the transition from foraging to farming in this region (Rowley-Conwy 1983 and 1985b; Zvelebil and Rowley-Conwy 1984; Jennbert 1984 and 1988; T. Madsen 1987). Scandinavia's geographically remote position implies that direct contacts with the early farmers would have been less likely, or at least would have occurred less frequently, than further south in the lowland. The pottery manufacture among the Ertebølle groups, as well as the presence of shaft-hole axes, shows that contacts did exist, although their routes are not clear.

Zvelebil and Rowley-Conwy propose a three-stage model of transition from hunting-gathering to farming. The stages theoretically involve the availability phase, during which farming is known to the hunter-gatherers but they do not take it up, the substitution phase characterised by the adoption of farming with hunting-gathering continuing alongside, and the consolidation phase during which farming becomes the dominant element of the overall economic strategy in a said community (Zvelebil and Rowley-Conwy 1984, 105–6). Rowley-Conwy maintains that after the long availability phase (spanning the Ertebølle culture), farming became the only viable alternative which would support the sedentary coastal communities. These communities, which during the Ertebølle period acquired an extraordinary degree of affluence, faced an economic crisis due to increased population pressure in the face of diminishing marine resources, among which the decrease in the oyster population was particularly significant. In practical terms the changeover from foraging to farming is seen as dramatic and complete because of the incompatibility of the two economic strategies (Rowley-Conwy 1983).

The view put forward by Jennbert (1984 and 1988) differs fundamentally from the above, since she argues principally for a slow and progressive integration of farming elements into an essentially hunting-gathering economy. This incorporation is not determined by economic pressure and necessity, but rather arises from the social needs and requirements of the Ertebølle communities. The farming elements – ceramics, cereals and domesticates – appear initially as exclusive gifts which have no decisive influence upon the overall character of the community. The nature of the transition is gradual and novelties become easily absorbed into an already socially complex culture. Rowley-Conwy (1986, 80) recently suggested that there is little difficulty in combining the two theories; while Jennbert's proposition outlines the mechanisms of the change, his explains the moment at which this transition took place.

These two explanations cannot, however, be reconciled so simply, for they stem from different theoretical perspectives, economic necessity and social desirability, and they envisage a fundamentally different pace and scale of transformation.

On the subject of economic necessity, doubts have been expressed as to the need for such a drastic measure as total economic transformation to counteract a clearly minor environmental setback (T. Madsen 1987, 235). While a shortage of oysters and a general deterioration of coastal resources may have affected those living around the coast, it could not have had the same effect inland. A movement away from the coast and a concentration on inland resources, such as a manipulation of climax forest to reduce reliance on the coast, may have provided an immediately available and less drastic option. Such a process has indeed been postulated by Paludan-Müller, who argued moreover that only when indland resources were efficiently explored would we expect a gradual introduction of domesticates and then of cultivated plants (Paludan-Müller 1978, 154).

Coastal versus inland settlement patterns and the resulting different economic adaptations feature prominently in interpretations of the Danish data, both Ertebølle and TRB, yet it can be argued that this dichotomy has always been overemphasised. Indeed it is now clear that such a dramatic division was not a feature of the TRB and neither should it be applied so strictly to the Ertebølle. However, even if we assume that such a division existed, the coastal communities, while sedentary, would be considerably less experienced in the manipulation of natural resources than their inland neighbours. Coastal resources simply do not lend themselves so easily to human interference and management. Yet it is the crisis among the coastal communities which is said to have been responsible for the adoption of an economic strategy of which they might have had knowledge, but otherwise little preconditioning and experience.

As we have seen, the lack of evidence pertaining to the economy of the early TRB culture and the relatively good database for the developed TRB are partly responsible for the apparent contrast between the Ertebølle and TRB economic strategies. Yet it may be precisely because the early Danish TRB was not totally dependent upon farming that we appear to have a 'shortage of evidence' for this early period. Other considerations suggest that in accordance with Paludan-Müller's model, it is the inland population, especially the Jutland Volling group, which takes on a leading and dominant role at the onset of the Neolithic in Denmark. The apparently later emergence of the Oxie and Svaleklint groups (note their markedly more coastal distribution) may still fit Rowley-Conwy's model of a need for economic adjustments along the coast, but if this is the case, the coastal communities are not the instigators of the change, but benefit from what already appears to have taken place further inland. Whichever way we perceive the Danish evidence, the environmental changes along the Danish coast cannot be regarded as a primary cause for the introduction of farming.

Zvelebil and Rowley-Conwy (1984) proposed four factors which, in their view, support the idea of a rapid change to a predominantly farming economy: 1) continued use of coastal hunting sites coupled with the abandonment of permanent Ertebølle settlements; 2) presence of cereals and domesticated animals in the earliest Neolithic; 3) appearance of causewayed enclosures which in their view implies a complex economy; 4) analysis of C-13 showing an abrupt change from marine to terrestrial diet. The Danish evidence offers very little information on the relative importance of hunting-gathering during the period from 5150/5050 BP to 4600 BP. The first reasonably informative assemblage from a domestic context derives, as we have seen, from Troldebjerg. Is it merely a question of poor preservation of material from the early TRB period? If so, each of the four above factors can be interpreted in a way different from that proposed by Zvelebil and Rowley-Conwy.

It is difficult to see how the continued use of hunting stations along the coast (some of which were visited throughout the duration of the TRB) can be used to argue for a rapid change to farming. On the contrary, it indicates that marine resources continued to play a role in the overall economy and, moreover, were not depleted as drastically as suggested. The abandonment of permanent coastal Ertebølle camps can be explained as well by the movement away from the coast to explore inland resources as by the establishment of farming settlements elsewhere; we have already noted the importance of inland development in the early TRB.

While cereals and domesticates appear to be present in the early TRB, their overall contribution to the economy is not known. There are very few animal bone assemblages from the period in question, and only a few cereal impressions have been identified (and these may have been imported). The earliest cereal grain in Denmark is dated to 4580 BP (K-2978) and does not derive from a domestic context. The appearance of ceremonial centres cannot be explained merely in economic terms (Chapter 7.4) and in any case it was at least 550 radiocarbon years after farming was introduced to Denmark before large ceremonial centres were being constructed and used.

The C-13 analysis of Danish Mesolithic and Neolithic skeletons does indeed indicate a difference in the diet, with the coastal Mesolithic people living predominantly on seafood and the Neolithic people subsisting mainly on terrestrial foods. There are also indications that inland Mesolithic communities did not subsist on seafood (Tauber 1981, 232). But the difference in C-13, while indicating predominantly one or another form of food, still does not answer the question of how much food came from either source. We may further argue that one would not expect a farmer, even if he lives close to the sea, to feed himself predominantly on seafood. However, if a large, chronologically valid body of C-13 measurements were to become available, it might be possible to determine changing trends; at present we can only distinguish coarse rather than subtle differences which cannot be used to argue for either a long or a short transition period.

With reference to southern Scandinavia, Rowley-Conwy (1985b, 188) argues for a very long availability phase, from about 6450 BP to 5150 BP (5400–3950 BC), about 1300 radiocarbon years. While we will probably never know precisely when Danish hunter-gatherers became aware of the farmers' presence, it probably did not happen much before 5500 BP (4400 BC) when pottery first appeared in the Danish Ertebølle culture. Thus the availability phase appears to have been of a considerably shorter duration, about 450 years in real terms (if we assume that the TRB did not appear in Denmark before 4000 BC). Moreover, it is interesting to note that it is synchronous with the time when the first traces of farming are perceived in Schleswig-Holstein.

Pursuing this argument further, the substitution phase (5150/5050–4650/4600 BP, 3950/3850–3400/3300 BC) takes on a different significance and presents the entire transition model in a different perspective: the substitution phase becomes even longer than the availability phase, about 550/650 years. Such a relationship between the two phases is not only more acceptable theoretically, but also makes good sense in terms of the available evidence.

The direct source of the Danish farming economy is said to have been the area of north Germany. Yet Rowley-Conwy denies the presence of farming here prior to about 5150 BP (3950 BC), arguing that the evidence from the north German sites is not sufficient to confirm the operation of a farming economy. However, should we dismiss the presence of cereal pollen in diagrams from Rosenhof and various localities in Satrup Moor corresponding to the Ertebølle horizon (Schütrumpf 1972) just because the quantity is small? Precisely the same phenomenon is now being observed in Sweden in the form of small amounts of cereal pollen in levels pre-dating 5150 BP (3950 BC; Göransson 1984). While it is possible to argue that grain impressions on pottery in an Ertebølle context may have arrived as imports from further south, cereal pollens will generally not travel that far.

Similar criticism has been applied to the presence of a few domesticates in Ertebølle contexts (at Rosenhof and Bregentwedt-Förstermoor). These are argued to have come as prestigious imports from the south or to have been escaped animals caught by Mesolithic hunters. Rowley-Conwy (1985b, 190) argues that 'it does not seem very likely that cattle should be kept if they were only to provide such a minor part of the food intake'.

Would we really expect vast quantities of cereals and large herds of cattle in a community which is only beginning to experiment with growing cereals and keeping farm animals? Quite to the contrary, to document the incipient stages of a farming economy in the European lowland we would hope to discover precisely the circumstances evidenced at Rosenhof and other Schleswig-Holstein sites: small amounts of cereals and a few domesticates being assimilated within a predominantly hunting-gathering context.

While the north German evidence is patchy, and fuller publication of material from this area is essential, it is precisely here that we see hunters in transition! This is the essence of Jennbert's (1984 and 1988) theory – a gradual incorporation of farming elements into a hunter-gatherer milieu – and it is clearly demonstrated in the north German assemblages.

It has not been the purpose of this discussion to demolish the forager-farmer transition model proposed by Zvelebil and Rowley-Conwy. But it is an advantage, as well as a disadvantage, of a theoretical model that, in view of the incomplete database, it can be moulded to reflect a particular opinion. Rowley-Conwy uses the model to argue that the transition to farming in Denmark was rapid. Using the same set of data it is possible to argue to the contrary. The model itself remains highly appropriate to circumstances witnessed across the North European Plain; it is in the application and the interpretation of this model that one chooses to differ.

9

Funerary traditions in the TRB culture

Megaliths in northern Europe represent the most tangible remains of the various TRB populations. It is hardly surprising that they should have attracted early antiquarian interest and, indeed, continue to command scholarly attention to the present day. The history of research into the megaliths need not be narrated here; the interested reader is referred to a number of publications which deal with this theme in some detail (Nordman 1935; Sprockhoff 1938; Daniel 1958; Jacob-Friesen 1959; Schuldt 1972a; Bakker 1979). There are, however, a number of stages in the long research into the subject which are of fundamental importance and these will be briefly reviewed.

The study of megaliths has always played a prominent role in Scandinavian research. The original classification of the northern megaliths proposed by the nineteenth-century Danish scholar J.J. Worsaae, a classification which survives in general terminology to this day, distinguished between the *Stendysse* (dolmen) and the *Jættestue* (passage grave). Respecting the old Danish folklore tradition, the former was further subdivided into the *Langdysse* (dolmen in a long barrow) and *Runddysse* (dolmen in a round barrow). This classification underwent further elaboration through the studies of the Swedish archaeologist Oscar Montelius (1905), who distinguished as many as nine different types of tomb, although only the main types, the dolmen, the passage grave and the stone cist, were used as diagnostic elements for the typo-chronological division of the Scandinavian Stone Age. This basic division was used by A.P. Madsen in his superbly illustrated survey of the Danish chambered tombs (1896 and 1990) and, in fact, survived until the mid-1940s when the old typo-chronological scheme was replaced by the new terminology of Becker (1947).

Investigations of earth graves and dolmens were published by Johansen (1917) and Thorvildsen (1941), and passage grave excavations were published by Nordman (1917a and 1917b) and Rosenberg (1929). Nordman (1935), moreover, in a series of Rhind lectures given in Edinburgh in 1932, offered a general survey of Scandinavian tombs. While accepting, in principle, the scheme of Montelius, he suggested a number of modifications. Thus he recognised that tomb types were not suitable chronological indicators because 'old forms of sepulture . . . remain in use for a long time, even though new types are introduced side by side with them' (ibid., 16). Furthermore, he refuted the idea of the north European origin of Scandinavian megaliths, believing that it was not possible to 'imagine an internal northern "development" without contact with the surrounding world' (ibid., 15–16), and although he accepted that the Scandinavian dolmens acquired their specific form in the north, he believed that they were nevertheless modelled on the Breton monuments. In fact, he argued that from that source 'the impulses leading to the building of stone tombs attacked the Dutch-German-Danish megalithic areas on a broad front, from Holland to the northern point of Jutland' (ibid., 86). Similar sentiments, using a British source for the expansion of religious ideas, were later also expressed by Brøndsted (1957, 192–3).

For the north German plain the most important contribution to the study of megaliths was the work of Sprockhoff; his life-long devotion to the subject provides us with a complete catalogue of the German tombs: *Atlas der Megalithgräber Deutschlands* (1966, 1967 and 1975). In his early research Sprockhoff also subscribed to the then-current view that the megalithic culture of southern Scandinavia had direct connections with western Europe, especially the British Isles. The oldest chambered tombs in Scandinavia were distributed like beads along the coasts of Jutland, the Danish islands and Sweden, indicating the importance of maritime connections. Sprockhoff (1938, 15) even referred to the Limfjord as the *'prähistorische Nordostseekanal'*. Irrespective of the initial connections with western Europe he argued that, once established, the megalithic culture (as the TRB was called by him) developed along its own lines. He was under such a strong influence from current Danish research that, in spite of obvious differences, the Danish typology was superimposed directly onto the German material. The north German dolmens, the *Urdolmen* and the extended dolmen, were derived from Holstein, where they were said to have developed under direct influence from Jutland and the Danish islands, a sentiment echoed many years later in the studies of Aner (1963). After the initial period, when the early megalithic tradition was establishing itself on both sides of the Elbe, Sprockhoff distinguished two separate north German traditions: to the east (in Mecklenburg, on Rügen and along the western fringes of Pomerania) the strong dolmen influence from the north stimulated the development of the great dolmen; in contrast, to the west of the Elbe, the small passage grave, or the so-called Holstein chamber, gave rise to a whole series of passage graves. Additional stimuli from the south (the area of the French and Westphalian stone cists) led to the development of the very long chambers in Emsland.

This appreciation of the different megalithic provinces throughout the north German plain as essentially separate but contemporary developments, was probably the most significant element of Sprockhoff's research.

It is of interest to note that these provinces were retained in Sprockhoff's Atlas, with each of the provinces (Schleswig-Holstein, Mecklenburg and Lower Saxony) accorded a separate volume (Sprockhoff 1966, 1967 and 1975).

Among the more recent work on the north German TRB tombs we should note a series of publications dealing with the graves on the Lüneburger Heide (Laux 1971, 1979 and 1984; Körner and Laux 1971 and 1980), in Emsland (Schlicht 1968, 1972 and 1979; Knöll 1983) and in the Sachsenwald (Sprockhoff 1952a, 1952b and 1954). Flat graves have been excavated mainly in the Stade district (Wegewitz 1955; Tempel 1972) and in Schleswig-Holstein (Hingst 1974); a large cemetery complex has recently come to light at Heek, distr. Borken (Finke 1984). A general survey of the German megaliths, as well as a number of specific topics on the theme of burial ritual, appeared in the proceedings of a symposium devoted entirely to the region of Lower Saxony (Schirnig 1979f).

In Mecklenburg, between 1964 and 1973 Schuldt was involved in a massive investigation of chambered tombs, in the course of which over 100 chambers were excavated. A series of interim reports were published annually in the *Jahrbuch für Bodendenkmalpflege in Mecklenburg* (1965–73) as well as in regionally arranged pamphlets of the *Museum für Ur- und Frühgeschichte Schwerin* (Schuldt 1966a, 1966b, 1967, 1968, 1970, 1971, 1979). In addition, Schuldt (1972a) published a major synthesis which was concerned mainly with the architectural development of the Mecklenburg dolmens and passage graves.

For the region of central Germany we still rely chiefly on U. Fischer's (1956) study of Neolithic burial ritual which included chapters on the Baalberge group and its congeners and on the megaliths of the Altmark region. In 1966 Preuss published a monograph on the middle German Baalberge group which contained an up-to-date catalogue of graves, and subsequently he discussed the Altmark tombs (Preuss 1973 and 1980). Behrens' (1957 and 1958; Behrens and Schröter 1980) studies included a number of investigations of burial and related monuments around Halle. Recently, the Walternienburg-Bernburg graves were also discussed in a short monograph (Beier 1984).

With reference to the Eastern and South-eastern TRB groups, the investigations of earthen long barrows in Kujavia and western Pomerania, and some large, flat-grave cemeteries in the area of the Lublin upland are of significance (see Midgley 1985 for references).

We still lack a modern general synthesis on the subject of the Scandinavian megaliths, although a number of general issues have been discussed by Kaelas (1956, 1967 and 1983), Kjærum (1967a) and recently P.O. Nielsen (1984). This gap is filled, however, partly by the wealth of publications on specific types of monument and partly by a number of exciting new discoveries.

Modern research into Danish TRB burial practices began with Becker's (1960 and 1967a) work on the middle TRB stone-packing graves, which were then further investigated in Jutland by T. Madsen (1976) and E. Jørgensen (1977). A similar type of grave was also recognised by Hansen (1972) to have existed on the Danish islands. TRB cult houses were investigated by Kjærum (1955 and 1967b), Becker (1969), Marseen (1960) and Faber (1977). Kjærum carried out excavations of Jutland's passage graves (1957 and 1969) and more information was published by E. Jørgensen (1971 and 1977) and Skaarup (1982a and 1985). Ebbesen's (1975 and 1978) work on the Danish pottery includes discussions of passage graves and dolmens and he has published a monograph on the great dolmen at Vedsted (Ebbesen 1979a). Additional investigations of dolmens have been reported by Thorvildsen (1941), Berg (1956), Skov (1973), Kock and Gebauer (1976), Thorsen (1981) and Christensen *et al.* (1979) among others. A more recent publication by Skaarup (1985) contains a complete inventory of all the known burial monuments on the south Danish islands.

However, by far the most fascinating research of the last decade involves the early TRB burial monuments. The attention afforded to the investigation of monuments comprising timber constructions has led to the recognition of various types of grave (Stürüp 1966; T. Madsen 1972 and 1975; Kjærum 1977) and of early elaborate funerary and ritual monuments (Skaarup 1975 and 1985; Glob 1975; Faber 1976; C. Fischer 1976; Rønne 1979; T. Madsen 1980; Liversage 1981, 1982 and 1983). The results of these numerous investigations as well as the general discussion concerning the structural complexity of the early TRB monuments, foreshadowing subsequent stone-using architecture, were discussed by T. Madsen (1979) and formed the basis of the present author's earlier work (Midgley 1985). It is no exaggeration to suggest that Danish research has overturned many suppositions about the simplicity of TRB burial customs and that it provides the main stimulus for the reappraisal presented in this chapter.

9.1 Non-megalithic grave forms of the TRB

We may still have reasons for believing that at least some members of TRB communities were buried in simple pit graves. However, new evidence, which forces us to reinterpret many previously held ideas, makes it more difficult to uphold the view that what looks like a simple pit grave today was indeed just that in its original form. Occasionally human remains are found within settlement rubbish pits (for instance a skull and a child's skeleton at Niedźwiedź; Hensel and Milisauskas 1985, 81), but it is hard to determine to what extent such finds represent an accepted and regular form of burial.

In the Eastern TRB group, a concentration of eight pits containing burials was found in the southern part of the Sarnowo settlement (Wiklak 1986; Kapica 1986, Fig. 1). The graves were arranged in rows running N–S, across a slight elevation. The grave pits were rectangular, with slightly rounded corners, and measured up to 2.4 m in length, 1 m in width and 1.4 m in depth. The brief excavation report does not mention any structural elements, although a concentration of charcoal had been noted in one grave. Some of the graves contained one body placed in an extended position, but at least three graves contained the remains of several individuals. The anthropological analysis of skeletal remains revealed that some of the bodies were charred before or during the ceremony, and strongly cremated bones of at least five individuals were also identified in the multiple graves. The specialist report (Kapica 1986) suggested that partial burning (more akin to smoking) may have been carried out over some of the graves. It must be noted that the soil conditions on many of the Kujavian sites (be it settlements or long barrows) are not sympathetic to the preservation of organic materials (see Midgley 1985, 162) and only secondary features, such as pit outlines, offer clues as to the possible use of coffins or timber structures.

A number of so-called flat-grave cemeteries are known from the central lake belt in Mecklenburg around the Schwerin, Plau and Müritz lakes. The best known is the Ostorf cemetery, located on the small island of Tannenwerde on the Ostorf lake, near Schwerin. It was investigated by antiquarians such as Friedrich Lisch (from 1877 to 1879) and Robert Beltz (1904) and was excavated by Schuldt in 1961. The graves were concentrated in the western part of the island; altogether about forty were investigated. Save for a shift in orientation, little change appears to have taken place in the course of the long use of the site. Only a few grave pits were clearly identified and these appeared oval in shape, with a somewhat stepped profile, filled with reddish sand or gravel. No features indicative of grave construction came to light, although some of the skeletons appear to have been weighed down with large limestone boulders (Bastian 1961; Schuldt 1961). Most of the skeletons recovered in 1961 were well preserved and supported the picture gained during the earlier investigations. The dead were buried in an extended position; during the early use of the cemetery they were oriented E–W, but later this orientation was reversed (Bastian 1961, 71–2). The bodies were accompanied by generous grave goods, amongst which the most common was elaborate jewellery made of the bones and teeth of wild animals. Transverse arrowheads were also found, two graves containing twenty-two examples each, and most graves were additionally furnished with freshly made flint blades and flakes, the making of which apparently formed a part of the burial ceremony.

On the basis of the finds, and especially the proliferation of what the excavator regarded as "hunters' trophies", the cemetery was interpreted as belonging to an economically and culturally backward group who, while in contact with the neighbouring farmers, were themselves essentially hunter-gatherers. We shall return to this subject later, but for the moment we should merely observe that the most informative aspect of this cemetery is its continuous use throughout the TRB, demonstrated in the associated pottery finds which span all the ceramic styles, with plain, two-handled amphorae representing the earliest stage (ibid., Fig. 57: a, b) and hanging vessels as well as other forms indicating the late TRB ceramic wares (ibid., Fig. 58).

Although the Danish version of the flat grave, the so-called earth grave (*jordgrav*), has been known since the nineteenth century (Müller 1898), the type was formally defined by Johansen (1917) and further studied by Thorvildsen (1941). Even such early research showed that the term 'earth grave' covered a variety of forms. Thorvildsen (1940, 43; 1941, 64–9) pointed out that earth graves identifiable on the basis of different earth-fill and not displaying stone features (for example at Volling, Langkastrup or Skærbæk) were few and far between. Other forms were identified by stone edging (for instance at Forum or Sædding), while others appeared under stone piles and some additionally had paving along the bottom; the latter appeared especially popular in Vendsyssel. A number of graves revealed features which strongly suggested the use of timber, for instance the trough shape of the stone setting around the Sønderhede grave, or indeed the trough-shaped pit of the famous Volling grave, which also contained traces of charred timber at the bottom.

Thus, as early as 1941, Thorvildsen was suggesting a variety of grave forms, involving trunk cists and stone supports. Moreover, he pointed out that over half of the earth graves were covered with a low earth mound, bringing the earth graves firmly into a closer relationship with simple dolmens. On the basis of associated finds Thorvildsen argued for at least partial contemporaneity of the earth graves and early dolmens. Later research by Becker (1960) showed that this form continued in construction well into the TRB and may indeed have developed into the more elaborate version present in the tradition of the stone-packing graves which became an important feature of the later TRB.

In the last two decades Danish research in this field has made remarkable progress with the excavation of sites such as Konens Høj (Stürüp 1966) and Troelstrup (Kjærum 1977). The most significant results of this research were a recognition of the structural complexity present in the fragmentary remains of the earth graves (a phrase whose continued use in the Danish literature is sanctioned by tradition rather than by the concepts it originally conveyed) and an appreciation of the variety of grave forms which existed side by side from the very begininning of the TRB culture.

The excavation of Konens Høj identified a grave form which most probably had a tent-like appearance (Fig. 109): two heavy timber posts, one at each end of a paved floor, supported a horizontal ridge against which the chamber walls rested. Additional supports in the form of low stone walls were provided at ground level. T. Madsen (1972) identified a number of Konens Høj type graves in Jutland and pointed out that the self-supporting

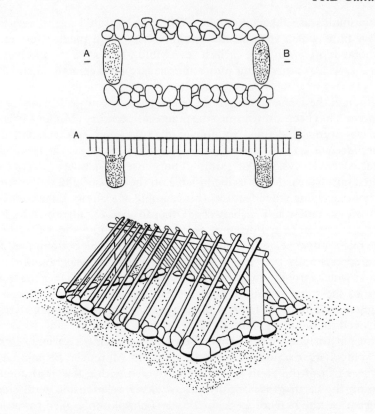

Figure 109 Konens Høj grave: plan and reconstruction (Source: Liversage 1983).

nature of this structure makes the use of stone supports generally superfluous and that many graves may ultimately give the appearance of simple
inhumation graves.

Another type of grave was recognised at the Troelstrup barrow, where
two identical chambers were excavated (Kjærum 1977). This type consists
of a rectangular box-like chamber built in timber and set within a corresponding stone setting. The chamber could be entered through a small
passage. Depending on the relative proportions of stone and timber used in
the construction, two further variants of this type were identified by
T. Madsen (1979, 309): the Skibshøj variant, where the chamber walls are
constructed in stone and covered with a timber roof, and the Lindebjerg
variant, where a timber-built chamber is set in a horse-shoe shaped bedding
trench. Wooden coffins also appear to have been used regularly, for
example at Bygholm Nørremark. It is possible that a similar interpretation
can be given to some of the earth graves which do not reveal any stone
elements such as Skærbæk, Lomborg or the Volling grave, where a

charcoal layer was found towards the bottom of the grave pit (Thorvildsen 1941, 66).

We should not be led to believe that the above-mentioned grave forms cover all the earth graves. The structures revealed beneath a long mound at Tolstrup (grave 2; T. Madsen 1975), Skivum (a pit with a pair of deep post-holes at each end) and Rimsø (a grave pit with a central post-hole; Madsen and Nielsen 1977, Figs. 2 and 7) do not conform to any of the above types but represent further variants of the earth grave form. Nor should we assume that the long-known graves can be easily classified in terms of the new types: good examples are the Årslev and Lindebjerg chambers, which were originally interpreted as being of the Konens Høj type, but are now thought to represent the Troelstrup type and its variants (T. Madsen 1979, 309).

We should note further that in Denmark, as elsewhere in the TRB culture province, the earth graves do not represent a short-lived tradition which terminates with the emergence of stone-built chambers. On the contrary, excavations at Stålmosegård on Zealand revealed a regular cemetery of such graves which, on the basis of associated pottery, were built during the time when MN I–III ceramic styles were in vogue. The cemetery was therefore contemporary with the construction and use of megaliths, especially the passage graves. The Stålmosegård structures display a wide range of forms from stone-paved and timber-decked pits, through graves set in a rectangular stone setting, to larger constructions reminiscent of stone cists or mini-megaliths (Hansen 1973).

While such earth graves were being used during the later TRB on the Danish islands, a different grave type, the so-called stone-packing grave, made its appearance during the MN II period in Jutland. Having first been identified at Østerbølle (Vestergaard Nielsen 1952) and then defined by Becker (1960), the stone-packing graves now number well over 400. The best-known and most thoroughly researched are the examples at Herrup (Becker 1969), Thorsted (Becker 1967a), Nørre Onsild (Becker 1960) and Vroue Hede (E. Jørgensen 1977); their strong concentration within northern and western Jutland has led to the suggestion that the stone-packing graves represent a regional burial ritual (ibid., 186). On present evidence this appears to be largely the case, but this conclusion may also result from a specific research policy directed at a region where such graves are well known. Becker (1960, 66) did in fact refer to a number of sites south of the Danish border (particularly the cemetery at Flensburg) where similar finds have been made.

The graves, which appear as 'human length' pits packed with small to medium-sized stones, are usually placed in pairs forming long rows which are divided into smaller units (Fig. 110). The rows can be very long indeed: at least 600 m Herrup, about 1200 m at Torsted and up to 1700 m at Vroue Hede (Becker 1967a, 27; E. Jørgensen 1977, Fig. 2). A typical version is a unit consisting of a pair of E–W oriented graves with a small timber structure, the so-called mortuary house, directly west of the graves. Grave goods, mostly but not exclusively flint axes, are placed in the graves as well as in the mortuary house. At some stage the house was dismantled and the whole unit covered by a common mantle of stones. Apart from this classic arrangement a number of variations are found (Fig. 110: B). These may involve a greater number of graves per house (from three to eight), a different positioning of the graves (east and west of the mortuary house) or solitary graves.

Becker (1960, 64–5) argued that stone-packing graves, which span the period of MN III–V ceramics, represent a direct evolution from earth graves and continue the earlier tradition. E. Jørgensen (1977, 186), on the other hand, argued that the consistent lack of a mortuary structure in association with earth graves suggests a different tradition and that the stone-packing graves cannot be derived from the former. This no longer appears to be the case. We may now point to chronologically earlier arrangements which foreshadow not only the mortuary house of the stone-packing graves, but also the cult houses, sometimes found in association with a group of megalithic chambers. The recently published find from Strynø (Skaarup 1985, 337–9, Figs 390–2) included an earth grave and the remains of a small (2.1 × 1.3 m) timber structure which was open to the north-west and contained a small flint axe. On the island of Sejerø, off the north-west coast of Zealand (Liversage 1982, Figs 1–6) there is a similar ritual complex. It comprised a timber-built grave and a flimsy timber building in which two funnel-necked beakers decorated in the Svaleklint style were deposited. The Strynø structure had been compared with the western feature at Rustrup in Jutland (C. Fischer 1976), which is generally thought of as a grave but could equally well represent the remains of a small, open-ended building west of the original grave.

Thus we may point to the continuity from the early to the later TRB as seen in the ceremonial buildings associated with actual graves. That the above forms represent only one of many types of cult construction is further supported by the find from Fakkemose on Langeland (Skaarup 1985, 206–8, Fig. 220–1), where a double grave was found next to a small, circular enclosure. The stone-packing graves clearly continue from the early TRB the idea of the close relationship between graves and cult houses.

The examples we have just discussed reveal beyond any doubt that not only was there a great variety of structures within the earth grave category, but that the graves were architecturally more complex than originally assumed. Bearing in mind the residual form of this structural complexity, it is possible to review the interpretation of the so-called flat graves which are regularly encountered in other regions of the TRB culture.

Figure 110 Danish stone-packing graves: A-Herrup, B variations in the placement of graves and mortuary house, C-Bondesgård and Torsted (Source: Becker 1967a).

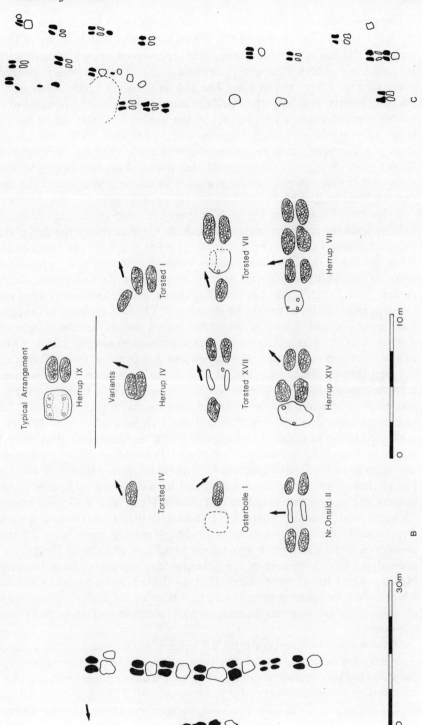

The classic example must surely be the grave from Kläden, distr. Lübz in Mecklenburg (Just 1963, 68–75, Figs 45, 46, 49), which is one of the earliest TRB graves in Mecklenburg and is preserved beneath a much later Bronze Age tumulus. The grave survived as a rectangular, multi-layered stone setting, 2.8 × 2 m in size. The through-shaped cavity, with stone packing heavily sunk into the middle, clearly represents the remains of a timber-built chamber which was set within a stone wall; the lack of stones at the eastern end is strongly suggestive of an entrance. Other flat graves from Mecklenburg, such as the three graves from Venz on the island of Rügen with their stone packing and clay floors, doubtless belong to the stone and timber category of flat graves. One of the graves contained the famous Venz lugged beaker (Nilius 1971a, 24; Fig. 27: 1).

A number of corresponding finds of stone-enclosed graves have come to light beneath the round mounds of the middle German Baalberge group. At Polleben, distr. Eisleben (Preuss 1966, 159–60), a 2.8 × 2 m rectangular stone setting with stone-free interior contained the partially preserved bones of one skeleton, accompanied by two vessels. At Kalbsrieth, distr. Artern (ibid., 171), a slab-built rectangular structure had stones piled on top in pyramid fashion (a tent-like chamber?). The best evidence of timber-built graves comes from the Preußlitz round barrow in the Bernburg district (ibid., 137–41). Grave no. 2 was a rectangular setting, 1.2 × 0.8 m in size, with ten 0.4 m tall oolite stones and a slab-paved floor. Traces of decayed timber planks were found to line the interior of this structure; moulded planks, apparently with bark still preserved, were lying irregularly on top of the skeleton, and the chamber itself was half filled with earth. The remaining eight graves did not contain stone elements, but most of them contained traces of decayed or moulded wood; the dead were thus buried either in timber-built chambers or placed in wooden coffins. Although the majority of the Baalberge graves are found beneath round mounds, the use of timber was by no means confined to such mounds. Recent excavations at the neolithic complex of Dölauer Heide and at Schalkenburg (Behrens and Schröter 1980) have indicated that free-standing graves were equally complex structures. At Schalkenburg, post-holes in the corners of rectangular grave pits represent all that remains of the graves' superstructures. A number of the Salzmünde group graves from Dölauer Heide mound no. 6 were interpreted as timber and clay lined graves which, at a later stage, were enclosed by a trapezoidal ditch (subsequently covered with an earthen mound), which incorporated them into one monument.

At the western periphery of the TRB culture, in Drenthe province, there is comparable evidence. At the Ekelberg cemetery some of the flat graves had stone packing round the edge, and similar structures were found under the tumulus at Zeijen (Bakker 1979, 187 and 197). The stone-built cist in the Diever barrow (ibid., 185–7) is likely to have been covered with a timber roof. The bottom of this cist was lined with a layer of crushed, burnt granite gravel, and if the notion that the skeletal remains therein were cremated is correct, it is possible that the timber elements were set on fire. Upon their collapse the stones covering the cist fell into the interior.

There is no lack of comparable evidence from the north German area of the Western TRB group. Investigations of the recently discovered TRB cemetery at Heek, distr. Borken (Finke 1984, 27–32), revealed fifteen graves which contained from one to seven vessels per grave. The interim report describes each grave as a rectangular pit, 2 × 1 m in size and between 1.5 and 2 m deep. There were posts set in the corners of the pits and the walls were lined with timber planks; in one instance the bottom of the grave had been lined with some organic substance prior to the place-ment of the body there.

At Himmelpforten, distr. Stade (Tempel 1979, 111–12), six graves belonging to the early *Tiefstich* phase were excavated in 1933. One of the graves (no. I) appeared in the form of a massive 3 × 4.5 m stone packing with rough stones along both sides. The packing was 0.75 m below the original ground level. Charcoal pieces found amongst the stones suggest that the timber elements in this grave were destroyed by fire. Grave no. III was a long, oval pit with partially preserved stone packing carefully arranged in two layers. A stone pavement of 0.9 × 0.75 m was found at the bottom of another pit (grave no. IV). Grave no. V appeared as a rectangular stain, which in cross-section was between 12 and 14 cm thick and 55 cm wide. It has been interpreted as the rotted remains of a wooden coffin; an upturned shoulder cup at the north-east end is thought to have stood on top of the coffin and fallen inwards from the collapse of the coffin's lid.

A similar arrangement of grave goods was identified as Issendorf, distr. Stade (Tempel 1972, Fig. 3). Here, seven vessels appear to have been placed on the roof of a timber grave. They would have fallen into the cavity upon the grave's decay but before it silted up with sand.

Although neither the Himmelpforten nor the Issendorf graves were covered with barrows or were incorporated within heavy stone settings, similarly constructed graves are known from precisely such contexts. We may mention here the long barrows at Oldendorf (Laux 1971) and Tosterglope (Dehnke 1940), and the round mound of Horneburg, where timber-built and stone-built chambers were found side by side. Sometimes such timber chambers are simply found in the neighbourhood of megaliths, as at Gudendorf, distr. Cuxhaven (Tempel 1979, 114, fig. 2), where a classic example of a stone-framed timber-built chamber is known to have stood next to the now destroyed megalithic chamber.

We could continue with many more descriptions of flat grave construc-tions, but this is unnecessary since the examples outlined so far indicate the variety of forms involved. We shall discuss the wider implications of this phenomenon in the later part of this chapter, but before we move on to the megalithic graves, it must be stressed once more that the TRB flat graves are far from being simple structures. Instead, they must be interpreted as elaborate constructions in which timber, and often stone, were used to create a multitude of architectural forms within one common tradition.

9.2 Megalithic graves of the TRB

The various typological studies of the north European megaliths distinguish two basic forms: dolmens and passage graves. Although this time-honoured division is retained here for descriptive purposes, it will be perfectly clear that this strict typology, which has all too frequently assumed a chronological status, can no longer fulfil the needs of the study and interpretation of these monuments. The following discussion will therefore attempt to suggest some of the changes which need to be made in our approach to the interpretation of the 'megalithic phenomenon'. But it will be equally clear that, unless the form of the monuments and the ways in which different types were used are fully understood, attempts at an interpretation of functional, social and other aspects will remain unsatisfactory.

Figure 111 shows the extent of the dolmen province within the TRB culture. The densest concentration of dolmens is in Denmark, from where between 5,000 and 6,000 monuments are usually quoted, although less than one-third are still preserved in a recognisable form (Glob 1971). Next in density are Schleswig-Holstein and Mecklenburg, where dolmens are equally well represented (Sprockhoff 1966; Schuldt 1972a). The river Elbe appears to form an effective western boundary of the TRB's dolmen province. In contrast to neighbouring Schleswig-Holstein and Mecklenburg, dolmens are only sporadically encountered in Lower Saxony and appear to be completely absent from the Netherlands. *Urdolmen* are apparently not found west of the Weser, and only one, Barskamp, is quoted as an example of this form from northern Lower Saxony (Laux 1979, 63, Fig. 7: 1). A few extended dolmens are known north of Hanover in the Elbe-Weser triangle and on the Lüneburger Heide (ibid., Fig. 2). A dolmen is known from one of the Haaßel long barrows (ibid., Fig. 7: 2), although today it would probably be classed as an open *Urdolmen* with a complex entrance rather than as an extended dolmen. A good example of the latter with a short passage is to be noted quite far to the west at Werploch, distr. Emsland (Schlicht 1979, 44). There are further examples of dolmens in a group of barrows at Bliedersdorf, distr. Stade, where entrance constructions such as thresholds, closing stones and short passages can be identified among the remains (Sprockhoff 1975).

Figure 111 Distribution of dolmens in the TRB culture (Source: Aner 1963; Sprockhoff 1966, 1967, 1975; Schuldt 1972a; Laux 1979).

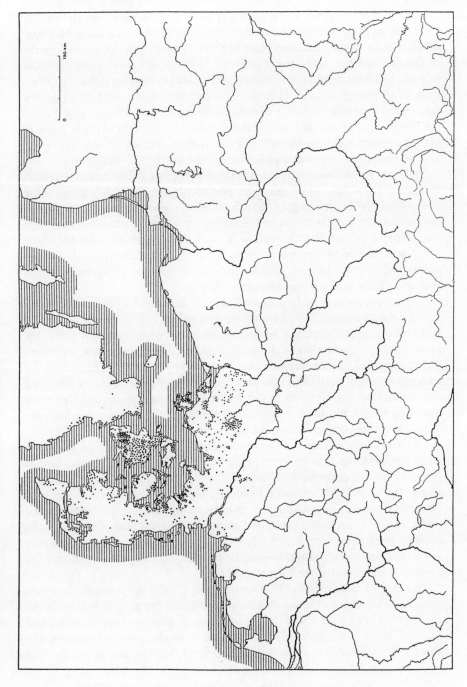

Large dolmens appear to be absent from Lower Saxony, but the search for this form in the literature is made difficult by the fact that many German scholars refer to the chambers built of three or more pairs of stones simply as *Großsteingräber* (large stone graves). It is possible that some of these ruined chambers would prove, upon excavation, to be large dolmens rather than small passage graves. However, even if additional numbers of graves turn out to represent a variety of dolmen forms, Lower Saxony, and indeed the entire area of the Western TRB culture, is predominantly a passage grave province, not only by virtue of the quantity present in the region but also by the sheer size and sophistication of some of the chambers.

The only major systematic investigation of the north European megaliths in recent years has taken place in Mecklenburg (Schuldt 1972a). The monuments from this region therefore offer a good starting point for a discussion of the main forms and chief constructional features of the TRB megaliths. Through the excavation of over 100 chambers, Schuldt identified and redefined the major chamber forms of dolmens and passage graves. Moreover, he was able to indicate a number of variants which appear to have regional significance.

The simple dolmen or *Urdolmen* (Fig. 112) is defined by Schuldt (1972a, 19) as a small rectangular chamber no more than 2 m in length, 1 m wide and 1 m in height. Between four and six boulders, placed on their sides, are used for the construction of the walls and one, rarely two, large boulders form a capstone. According to Schuldt, the closed *Urdolmen*, where all the wall stones are of equal height and access to the interior could be obtained only by moving the capstone, is the prototype for the open-ended *Urdolmen* found in Mecklenburg; the latter are present in three variants which are thought to represent a sequential development.

The arrangement may involve an entrance end-stone that does not reach up to the capstone, leaving a 0.6 m gap which is blocked with small stones (for example Barendorf, ibid., Plates 6: b and 33), or a half-height threshold and a closing slab (for example Frauenmark; ibid., Plate 2: a), or a pair of boulders protruding beyond the chamber end creating a short passage which may also include a threshold stone (Barendorf; ibid., Plate 2: b). In Mecklenburg these *Urdolmen* variants are found roughly in equal numbers in rectangular or trapezoidal mounds, but the majority (about thirty) are covered with round stone cairns (ibid., 22).

The extended dolmen or *erweiterte Dolmen* (Fig. 114) purports to represent the next stage in the development of dolmen form. It differs from the *Urdolmen* in two major respects: it is always accessible from outside, and the wall stones are placed upright resulting in the greater height of the chamber's interior. The chamber is rectangular in plan, and generally does

Figure 112 Closed *Urdolmen* from Mankmoos in Mecklenburg (Source: Schuldt 1972a).

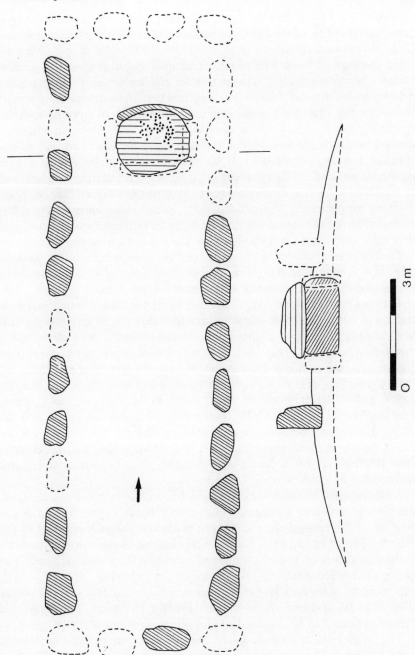

not exceed 2.5 m in length, 1.5 m in width and 1.5 m in height. It is constructed of five or six boulders with two transversely placed capstones (Schuldt 1972a, 22).

On the basis of twenty excavated structures, Schuldt identified several variants according to the arrangement of the entrance: 1) an extended dolmen with a threshold and a door block, where the entrance is narrowed to half of the chamber's width by the presence of an upright and the remaining gap is closed with a door stone (Fig. 114: A); 2) an extended dolmen to which access is gained through a gap between two wall stones (Schuldt 1972a, 22–3, Plate 11: b, c); 30 an extended dolmen with a short passage at one end (ibid., 23–4; Fig. 114: B). All three variants are believed to represent a further development of the *Urdolmen* form. The extended dolmens are generally surrounded by a round stone cairn; only a few examples have been found within a rectangular or trapezoidal mound, and they have then been set transversely to the mound's long axis.

The difference between the extended and the great dolmen or *Großdolmen* (Fig. 115) is related to size. If more than three pairs of stones are used in the construction, the chamber falls into the great dolmen category. The chambers of great dolmens are between 2.5 and 8 m long, about 2.5 m wide and 1.5 m tall inside. The entrance arrangements are more elaborate and five variants have been identified: 1) with half-width door stone and a threshold (Schuldt 1972a, 24–5, Fig. 9); 2) with entry gap between two end-stones (ibid., 25, Fig. 10, Plate 13: b); 3) with short passage (ibid., 26, Plate 13: a; Fig. 115: A, C); 4) with passage and ante-chamber (Schuldt 1972a, 26–7, Plates 15: d and 16); 5) with porch entrance (ibid., 27–8, Fig. 11, Plate 18: a; Fig. 115: B). Variant no. 5 is known on Rügen and the adjacent mainland. Schuldt stated (1972a, 29) that the first three types are found mostly in rectangular barrows; the ante-chamber and porch-type great dolmens are often found in trapezoidal mounds, but most are still surrounded by round or oval mounds.

A fundamental feature which distinguished a dolmen with a passage from the passage grave or *Ganggrab* (Fig. 116; Schuldt 1972a, 29–31) is the position of the passage. In a dolmen it is always placed at one end of the chamber (Figs 114 and 115), but when it is leading towards one of the sides of the chamber (Fig. 116) the structure is classified as a passage grave. The passage may lead either to the middle of the side (Fig. 116: A) – such chambers are sometims known as Lower Saxon chambers – or off centre (Fig. 116: B), forming the so-called Holstein chambers (originally this variant appeared to be confined to Holstein).

The Mecklenburg passage grave chambers are on average 10 m long, 2.6 m wide and 1.8 m tall and have trapezoidal, rectangular or oval ground plans. Between five and six pairs of boulders form the sides, and from three to five capstones span the top. The floor is laid with red sandstone slabs and lined with clay and/or crushed flint. Frequently the whole interior is

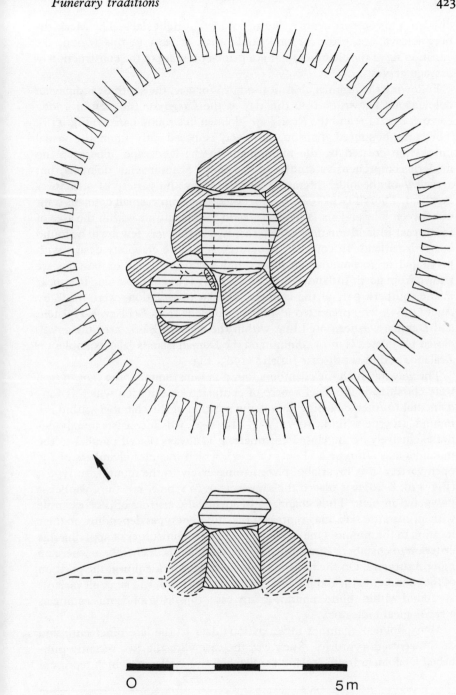

Figure 113 *Urdolmen* with a short passage from Mechelsdorf in Mecklenburg
(Source: Schuldt 1972a).

divided into compartments by means of low, upright slabs. The Mecklenburg excavations prove beyond doubt that, at least in this region, the partitioning of the chamber floor is a primary feature of the construction of passage graves.

Following the original classification of Worsaae, the south Scandinavian dolmens are known even to this day as the *Langdysse* (dolmen in a long barrow; Fig. 117) and the *Runddysse* (dolmen in a round barrow; Fig. 118). This time-honoured division, however, is based only upon the visual impression created by the monuments in the landscape. There are no modern comprehensive studies of the south Scandinavian dolmens, but a review of the older literature shows clearly the variety of structures involved. Thorvildsen (1941, 69–70) noted that simple, small dolmens built of between four and six large stones tend to concentrate within the area of south-east Jutland and the Danish islands, and that very few are to be found in north Jutland. In contrast, structures of a more elaborate design with polygonal or rectangular chambers and a threshold and/or passage are known from north Jutland, while considerably fewer of these tend to appear in the southern part of the country. Similar observations were made by Aner (1963), who presented a study of dolmens from Schleswig-Holstein and Denmark. Aner noted that within the western Baltic area the small, closed Urdolmen is most common on the Danish islands (280 examples on Zealand) and in south-east Jutland (1963, Fig. 3).

The way in which the chambers found in long mounds (the *Langdysser*) were classified is the chief source of confusion. A criterion which is fundamental to Aner's classification is the position of the chamber within the mound. In type 1 (ibid., 10–12; Fig. 119: 1–3), which consists mainly but not exclusively of the closed chambers, it is always placed parallel to the mound's axis. In type 2 (Fig. 119: 4–7), which includes chambers of the open variety, it is invariably placed transversely to the mound. In type 3 (Fig. 119: 8–10) it is placed the same way as in type 2, but the chamber is polygonal in plan. Thus chambers of identical construction, for example with an entrance slab, may represent two different types depending on their location in the mound. One can only imagine the difficulties of applying this criterion to chambers surrounded by round mounds or chambers where no mound survives. On the basis of evidence from Mecklenburg, the position of the chamber in the mound is not related to its form, and since all variants are found within round mounds in any case, this criterion is misleading as a typological indicator.

Many dolmen chamber investigations date to the late nineteenth and early twentieth centuries. Such was the case with the two recently published Urdolmen from Zealand at Ølstykke and Kellerød, which represent

---

Figure 114 Extended dolmens from Mecklenburg: A-Everstorfer Forst, B-Gnewitz (Source: Schuldt 1972a).

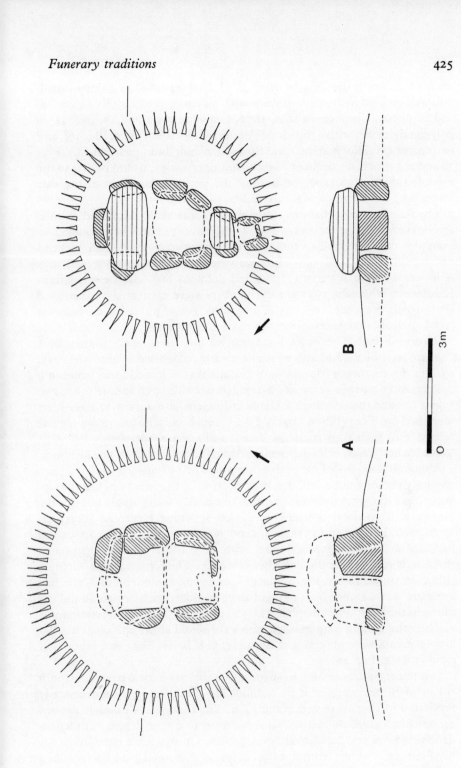

small chambers of the closed variety (P. O. Nielsen 1984). A group of small dolmens on Lyø includes *Urdolmen* with an entrance stone (Kong Lavses and Boyeshøj; Christensen *et al.* 1979, catalogue nos 1 and 13, Fig. 41), a polygonal dolmen with a threshold (Vesterrødhøj; ibid., no. 5, Fig. 39), and two chambers (Klokkestenen and Store Stenshøj; ibid., nos 3 and 10, Figs 38 and 40) which, according to Mecklenburg typology, would belong to the extended dolmen category because of the upright placement of the side stones and the presence of a threshold.

The Klokkestenen chamber, together with a recently published dolmen at Klokkehøj (Thorsen 1981, Fig. 1, 2), have recently been quoted as examples of a particular version of the extended dolmen with inclined end-stones. These are very commonly found around Faborg and may represent a regional variant. Extended dolmens may also be cited from Langeland, where in 1951 three chambers were excavated at Pæregård (Berg 1956). A recent inventory of megalithic graves published by Skaarup (1985) reveals a considerable range of such chambers.

Returning briefly to older literature we note that, apart from simple dolmens, complex structures were also clearly recognised. Nordman (1935, 13, Fig. 6), following Montelius, mentions that 'a mixed form between a dolmen and a passage grave . . . always has one side open and there are two stones outside the opening'. Extended dolmens also appear to have been identified by Thorvildsen (1941, 65–6), and both scholars make regular reference to such constructional details as passages, thresholds and even 'stone frames' which echo the elements described earlier from Mecklenburg.

Although dolmens of other than simple closed or open form have been regularly commented upon, it is only because of the Mecklenburg publications that the great dolmens are now frequently being singled out in the literature. Two great dolmens excavated at Vroue Hede (E. Jørgensen 1977, 38–9, Fig. 34, and 135–7, Fig. 200) were set within long mounds and had chambers of trapezoidal plan with very short passages and small thresholds just before the chamber entrance. The Vedsted great dolmen (Ebbesen 1979a, 16–25, Fig. 6, Plate I), set within a round mound, also had a trapezoidal chamber built of eight large boulders with dry-stone walling filling in the gaps. The chamber was 3.75 m × 1.25–1.75 m in size and was reached along a 3 m long passage with a threshold at the entrance. Similar arrangements were observed at Brejninggård, Barrit Skov and other sites (ibid., 38–41, Fig. 46).

It is not the purpose here to suggest that the typological development of the dolmen form suggested by Schuldt for Mecklenburg was necessarily replicated further north within the TRB. The existence of a clearly defined group of polygonal dolmens (Fig. 120) attests to a large degree of independent structural and functional development. On the other hand, even the brief survey of south Scandinavian dolmens presented here shows that a sufficient number of key elements identified in Mecklenburg appear regu-

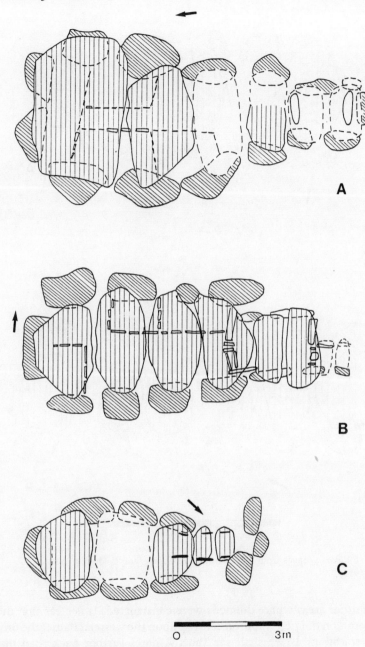

Figure 115 Great dolmens from Mecklenburg: A-Gaarzerhof, B-Kruckow, C-Dwasieden (Source: Schuldt 1972a).

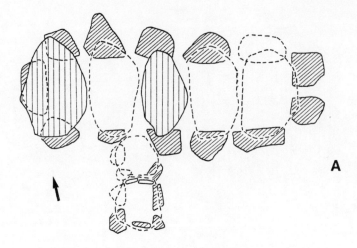

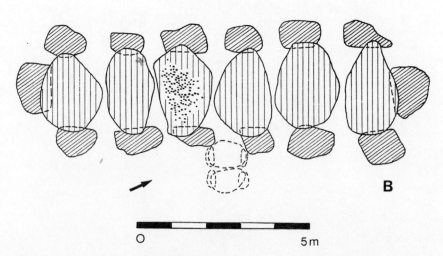

Figure 116 Passage graves from Mecklenburg: A-Gaarzerhof, B-Qualitz (Source: Schuldt 1972a).

larly in other areas where dolmens were constructed. It is clear that there was a common dolmen tradition centred upon the western Baltic; the origin of this tradition, as we shall see shortly, dates further back than many scholars in the past have been willing to admit.

A comparison of the distribution of passage graves with that of dolmens (Figs 111 and 121) shows the considerable shift of the 'megalithic zone', particularly towards the west and south. The entire Western TRB group is

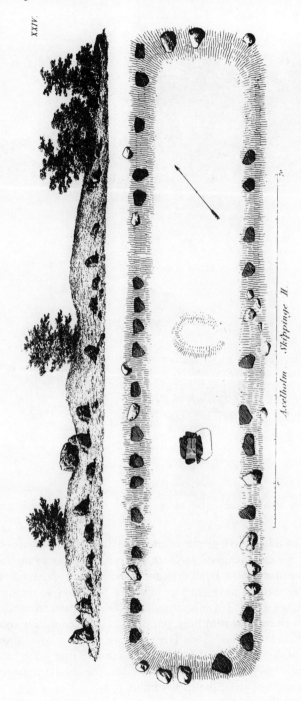

Figure 117 A Danish *Langdysse* at Axelholm on Zealand (Source: A.P. Madsen 1896).

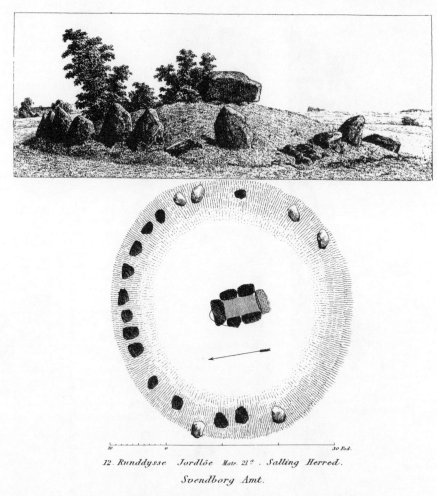

12. *Runddysse   Jordlöe   Matr. 21ª.   Salling Herred.*
Svendborg Amt.

Figure 118 A Danish *Runddysse* at Jordlöe on Fyn (Source: A.P. Madsen 1900).

included in the passage grave province and here this phenomenon is clearly associated with the expansion of *Tiefstich* pottery, reaching as far south as the northern boundary of the Baalberge complex. In the opposite direction, the Oder river appears to have been an effective boundary to the development of the passage grave. It is also important to note that, in areas where dolmens were built in large numbers, passage graves account for considerably fewer monuments. Thus from Denmark we only know of about 600 passage graves (Glob 1971) and Schuldt's catalogue lists only fifty-four examples (1972a, 116–39). On present knowledge, the reverse appears to be true of the area west of the Elbe (Sprockhoff 1975).

The megalithic area of the western part of the North European Plain,

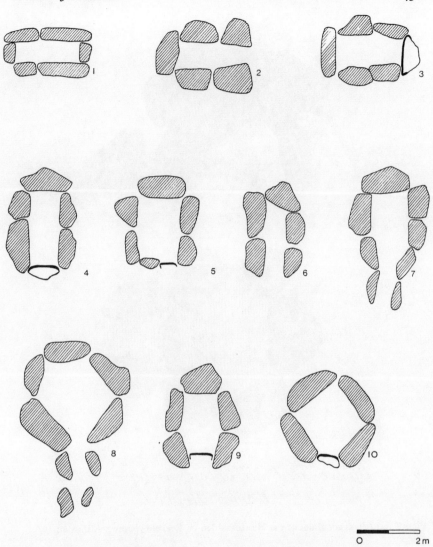

Figure 119 Aner's classification of dolmens in long mounds (Source: Aner 1963).

where the passage grave is the predominant type of tomb, is sometimes called the 'Saxon zone' (U. Fischer 1979, 36). It covers the morainic lowland between the Ijsselmeer and the western Baltic and comprises the present-day areas of Drenthe, Lower Saxony, Holstein and Altmark with a noticeable protrusion into the *Mittelgebirge*. Megaliths are not distributed evenly through this region, but as elsewhere along the North European Plain form discrete concentrations, with the intervening landscape being free of tombs. Several such groups can be distinguished following, at a

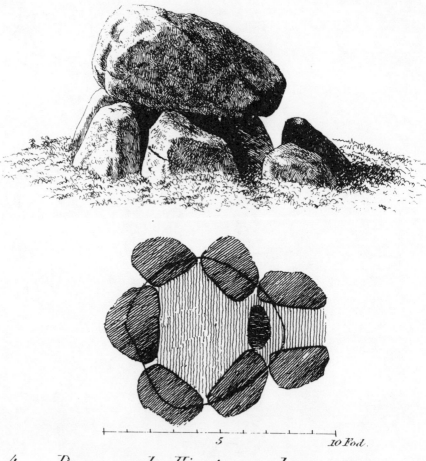

4.   *Dysse ved Hjortegaardene. Matr 8.*
              Horns Herred.

Figure 120 A polygonal dolmen at Hjortegaarden on Zealand (Source: A.P. Madsen 1896).

distance, the course of the Elbe from Bremerhaven to Magdeburg: in the Elbe–Weser triangle, on the Lüneburger Heide, around Salzwedel, Stendal and in the Haldenslebener Forst. Moving further west, megaliths are found in large groups along the middle Hunte and the Hümmling (especially along the northern tributaries of the Hase) and on the Drenthe plateau (Fig. 121).

Figure 121 Distribution of passage graves in the TRB culture (Source: Brøndsted 1957; Sprockhoff 1966, 1967 and 1975; Schuldt 1972a; Bakker 1979; Laux 1979; Schlicht 1979).

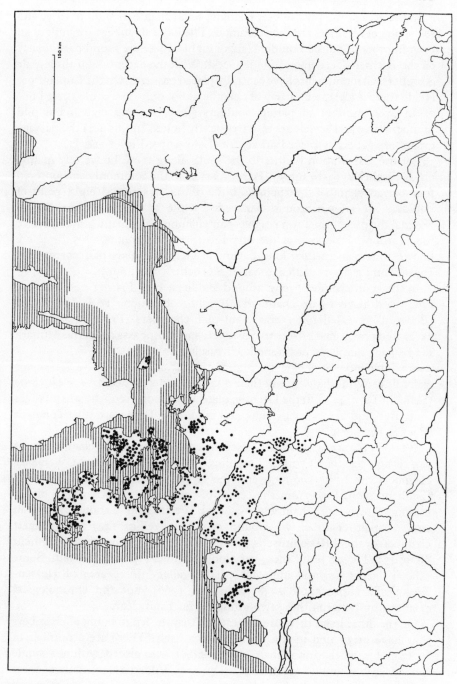

In the area of the Elbe-Weser triangle, small chambers built of three and four pairs of boulders are very common. The large chambers are built of an even number of paired boulders (six or eight); these are found particularly on the Bremen-Uerden and Stade Geest. With the exception of three-pair chambers, all monuments have centrally placed passages. On the Lüneburger Heide there is a greater variety of chambers: not only do we find these built of an even number of paired boulders (four, six and eight), but odd numbers (five and seven) are also frequently noted. In this area the passage graves are generally placed off centre (Laux 1979, Figs 2 and 3).

For the distribution further to the south along the Elbe we rely mainly on U. Fischer's (1956) survey. Here, apart from the commonly encountered four-paired chambers, structures built of six, seven and eight pairs of boulders are known around Salzwedel, while in the neighbourhood of Stendal the prevailing form is a five-pair chamber. Not many graves survive today around Jerichow; of the fifty recorded monuments, only three are known today: an earthen long barrow at Gehrden, a six-pair chamber at Lütnitz and a destroyed chamber at Körbelitz (ibid., 69).

In the southernmost group around Haldensleben, Fischer noted eight-, nine- and twelve-pair chambers. Recent excavations at Haldensleben (Bebertal) revealed nine- and eight-pair chambers (Preuss 1973). The excavated graves had off-centre passages, and most passages in the Altmark tombs were similarly positioned (U. Fischer 1956, 76).

Small chambers are likewise common in the area west of the Weser, for example at Wildeshausen, but their number gradually decreases westwards (Schlicht 1979, 44). On the Drenthe plateau the most frequent size involves four, five and six pairs; seven- and nine-pair forms are also common (Bakker 1979, Fig. 77).

While in the area east of the Weser the enlargement of the chamber stops at a certain size (eight pairs), it seemingly continued in the west. Ten-pair chambers are quite common and the largest appear on the Hümmling (Schlicht 1979, Fig. 7), in the centre of the Western TRB group distribution; fifteen-pair chambers occur at Werlte and Lähden, while an eighteen-pair chamber was found at Thuine (Fig. 122). The largest chamber in the TRB culture is that of Werlte: 29.5 m in length (Schlicht 1979, 45). The origin of these very long chambers is still uncertain. Some scholars argue for the influence of the gallery grave area of Hessen-Westphalia (Sprockhoff 1938; Schrickel 1966), but the chronological relationship between these two groups is far from clear.

On the other hand there are indications that the lengthening of chambers may have originated in the Emsland area itself. There are a number of monuments where more than one chamber was placed within a single mound. A long mound at Kleinenkneten, near Wildeshausen, contains three chambers placed in a line (Schlicht 1979, 45, Fig. 5) and at Großenkneten

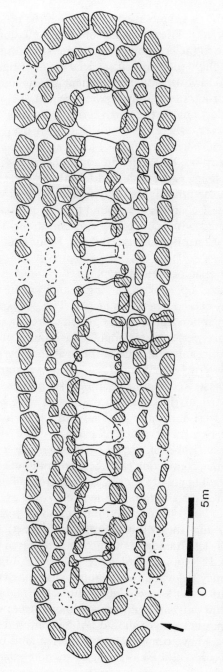

Figure 122 Passage grave in a double stone setting at Thuine in Emsland (Source: Schlicht 1979).

5m

there are two closely set chambers, one with five, the other with ten pairs of side stones (ibid., 45). The placement of several medium-size chambers may have given rise to the erection of one larger structure instead of a few smaller ones. Although there is still a need to investigate the problem through adequate fieldwork, local development appears more likely than an external influence from a culturally separate region.

The greatest variety among the north European passage graves is found in Denmark, however, where we may distinguish oval, rectangular, bi-chamber and double chamber types. The oval chamber passage graves (Brøndsted 1957, 227–37; P.O. Nielsen 1972, 16–26; Fig. 123) are usually no more than 3 m long, 1.5 m wide and less than a person's height. The passage here, as in the other types, is long and narrow, varying in length from 4 to 10 m. These chambers are found in Jutland, mainly in Himmerland and Djursland, with noticeable concentrations in northern and western Zealand, eastern Fyn, Langeland and Møn (Brøndsted 1957, 234, Map).

The rectangular chambers (ibid, 277, map 279 and 285; Fig. 124) are usually larger in size, up to 10 m in length and 3 m in width, and their internal height may exceed a person's height. The passages usually lead to the centre of the chamber, but some are placed more towards one end. Not all the chambers are perfectly rectangular in ground plan. Their distribution contrasts noticeably with that of the oval chambers; there is merely a scatter in the north of Jutland and a few isolated examples can be noted down the eastern coast. Rectangular chambers are numerous on the islands, however, where particularly large concentrations have been recorded on north Fyn, north, west and south Zealand and all the lesser islands.

Apart from the two major types of passage grave we must note the bi-chamber version (Ebbesen 1978, 59, Fig. 45; Fig. 125). Two, or sometimes even three, connecting chambers are built one behind the other, with the passage leading only to the chamber in front. This type of passage grave has a restricted distribution; of the twenty-five examples quoted by Ebbesen (1978, 149), all but four are found in north Jutland (particularly around Limfjord) and they clearly represent a north Jutland variant. Another, somewhat less homogeneous group is represented by the double passage graves (ibid., 159, n. 45; Skaarup 1985, 372; Fig. 126). Here two chambers, which may be oval or rectangular, share one end wall, but each is approached by its own passage. This group is typical of Zealand and the adjacent islands, and only six examples are known from other parts of the country. Double passage graves should not be confused with monuments where two chambers have been covered by one mound but are essentially two separate structures. Ebbesen (1978, 60–1) notes that there are about thirty examples of such passage graves and they are seen to concentrate along the Hjerbæk fjord in north Jutland and Roskilde in north-east Zealand.

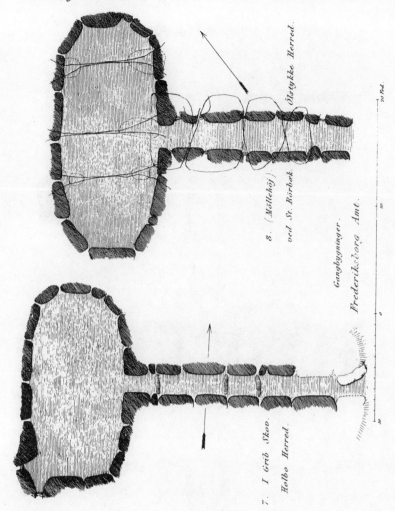

Figure 123 Oval chamber passage graves from Zealand (Source: A.P. Madsen 1896).

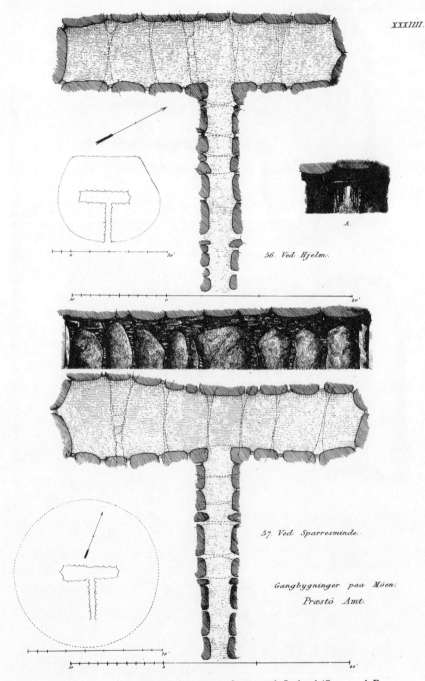

Figure 124 Rectangular chamber passage graves from north Jutland (Source: A.P. Madsen 1900).

2.Bind. XIV.

24. Gangbygning. Suldrup. Matr 7ª. Hornum Herred.
Aalborg Amt.

Figure 125 Bi-chambered passage grave at Suldrup in north Jutland (Source: A.P. Madsen 1900).

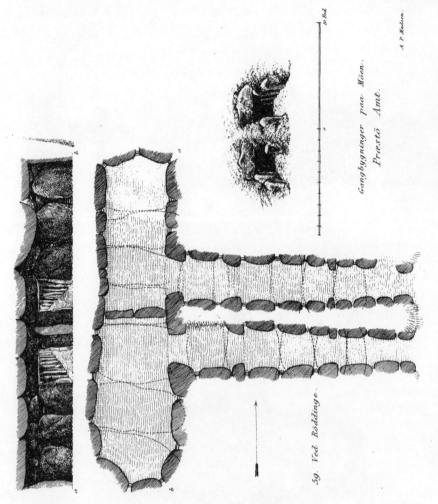

Figure 126 Double chamber passage grave at Röddinge on Zealand (Source: A.P. Madsen 1896).

Additionally, Skaarup (1985, 372–3) pointed recently to another group of passage graves on the southern Danish islands whose trapezoidal chambers associate them with similar forms in north Germany. This may indicate a western Baltic group, a connection strengthened by the fact that many passage graves on the south Danish islands, in contrast to those in the rest of the country, are surrounded by rectangular mounds and therefore have relatively short passages, precisely in the manner noted in Mecklenburg.

Closely associated with the Danish burial monuments is a group of curious structures first identified at Tustrup (Kjærum 1955). These are the so-called cult houses, a number of which have come to light in Jutland during the last two decades (Kjærum 1967a and 1967b; Becker 1969; Faber 1977; Fig. 127). Two of the houses, Tustrup and Ferslev, clearly form part of a larger ceremonial setting, each standing in a group of megalithic graves. No such association can be seen in the case of Herrup (Becker 1969), Foulum (Becker 1973b) or Engedal (Faber 1977), where instead stone-packing graves of the later TRB have been found to overlay the ruined houses. On present evidence such cult houses appear to have been built and used during the time when MN I (Herrup) to MN III (Ferslev) styles of pottery were in use.

The buildings reveal a general similarity of ground plan, although they differ in constructional detail. Tustrup and Ferslev appear to represent one variant, that of a single-roomed, open-ended building, while the others consist of a rectangular inner room with an open, half-sized forecourt in front. The construction involves sides built of vertical timbers set in bedding trenches, although sometimes the back wall is shown to have been made of horizontal planks slotted into vertical posts. The heavy outer stone supports are conspicuous at Tustrup; they may result from the better preservation of the structure or indicate a combined timber and stone architecture of the kind we have already discussed in connection with grave structures.

The non-domestic character of these buildings is evident from their close association with the graves as well as from the nature of the deposits found. All the cult houses contained substantial deposits of pottery, which on the whole is stylistically homogeneous and suggests use of the structure during a specific ceramic phase (two such phases being identified at Tustrup). The pots were placed in groups in the middle or, more commonly, against the wall, with particular importance being attached to bowls and pedestalled bowls. Some of the buildings were destroyed by fire.

The interpretation of their function varies from a house built over a grave (as may have been the case at Ferslev where a structure strongly reminiscent of a Konens Høj type grave was encountered in the middle) to a ceremonial place connected with offerings, or even small temples (Becker 1973b, 75), although all Danish scholars agree that these structures do not represent normal dwelling houses.

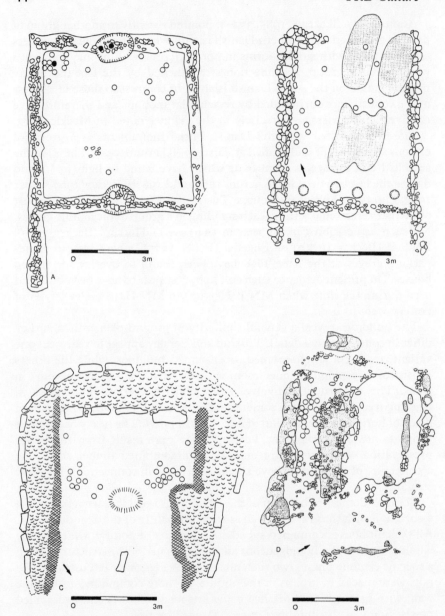

Figure 127 TRB cult houses from Denmark: A-Herrup, B-Engedal, C-Tustrup D-Ferslev (Source: Kjærum 1955 and 1967a; Becker 1969; Faber 1977).

While the precise determination of the function of the cult houses may be a matter for discussion, they do not represent a new element within the ritual of the TRB culture. Ceremonial timber houses with strong burial associations are known from the earthen long barrows. Their occurrence is by no means limited to Denmark, since examples of timber houses are also known from the areas of Mecklenburg and Kujavia (Midgley 1985, 148–61). Although there are clear regional variations reflected in the architecture of such structures, the common elements – most notably the spatial association with graves and the ultimate destruction by fire – allow such structures to be placed within a common conceptual framework of burial-related ritual.

Thus the continuity between the early and later TRB in ceremonial structures has been demonstrated. Indeed, it may be argued that the so-called mortuary houses accompanying the stone-packing graves continue the idea of cult houses, from the early TRB structures of Sejerø (Liversage 1982) or Rustrup (C. Fischer 1976), through Tustrup and Ferslev to the late TRB cult houses of Herrup and Vroue Hede (Becker 1973b; E. Jørgensen 1977).

9.3 Burial ritual of the TRB culture

The many types of burial-related monuments discussed above go hand in hand with the bewildering variety of burial activities practised by the TRB people. Evidence available today reveals not only this variety, but also the changing customs which developed within the broader framework of the TRB culture ritual.

The TRB culture burials which conform to the custom of extended inhumation are so numerous and so widespread that without doubt we should regard it as a predominant burial rite which, in some areas at least, continued throughout the entire duration of this culture. Sources of the origin of this custom have been discussed by the writer elsewhere (Midgley 1985, 197–8) and it will suffice to say that, in common with many other elements of the TRB culture, it is deeply rooted in the customs and traditions of the preceding north European hunting and gathering communities. The Mesolithic traditions are very strongly reflected in some of the early TRB burials; for instance, the Dragsholm burial (Brinch Petersen 1974) can be distinguished from the numerous Danish Mesolithic burials merely through its different grave goods. Indeed, the 'Mesolithic manner' of burials at Ostorf and at a number of similar cemeteries in Mecklenburg was the prime reason why such sites were thought to belong to small, economically backward groups of Mesolithic survivors (Bastian 1961; Schuldt 1961).

Generally the TRB graves contain single inhumations. This appears to be the case irrespective of whether the graves are found individually (such as Dragsholm) or forming cemeteries in or near settlements (such as

Sarnowo, Bronocice, Zauschwitz), or whether they were incorporated into earthen long barrows (Sarnowo, Gaj, Perdöhl or Bygholm Nørremark). There are also a number of graves where skeletal remains have not survived but an individual burial can reasonably be inferred from the size of the grave itself.

Apart from the individual burials we have sufficient evidence to suggest that double, or even larger, burials were perhaps more common than originally thought. As examples we may quote here the double graves from Lohals and Fakkemose (Skaarup 1985, 206–8 and 324–5), at least two multiple burials from the Sarnowo settlement (Kapica 1986), and a burial of four male individuals at Bygholm Nørremark where, as already mentioned, a single grave was also encountered (Rønne 1979). Single as well as multiple burials are also known from many of the South-eastern TRB group cemeteries, although the specific chronological position of these is not clear.

Fire appears to have played an important role in the burial ritual of the entire TRB culture, although we cannot always be certain whether it constituted the final element within the ritual. In a number of early TRB contexts, particularly earthen long barrows, we have unequivocal evidence that burial structures were set on fire. This may have involved the actual grave (as at Skibshøj or Konens Høj), a timber structure which was associated with the grave (Leśniczówka), or other constructional elements such as the facade (Rude; see Midgley 1985, 148–61).

That this activity was not uncommon can be judged further from the regular association of charcoal with graves which need not have been incorporated into barrows. Some of the graves at the settlement of Sarnowo have yielded skeletal remains whose burnt ('smoked') condition may have resulted precisely from such grave–firing activity (Kapica 1986, 102, n. 23). Comparable evidence can be quoted from Denmark where a number of the previously discussed earth graves yielded charcoal, or from the Netherlands where the 'cremated' remains in a cist at Diever may indicate similar activity (Bakker 1979, 186).

From the Southern group of the TRB we need only mention the collective burial houses of the Walternienburg-Bernburg group (such as Derenburg, Niederbösa and Schönstedt; Beier 1984), many of which were set on fire after a long period of use. Other evidence suggests that fire regularly featured in rituals relating to the use of stone-built chambers: the almost universal appearance of layers of burnt flint lining the floors, traces of fire in front of passage graves, and occasionally burnt or scorched human bones within the chambers themselves.

Turning now to the evidence derived from the megalithic chambers, let us begin our survey in Mecklenburg. The most startling discovery of Schuldt's (1982a, 71–5) researches is the fact that, among the excavated chambers of Mecklenburg, there is no evidence of extended (or crouched) inhumations. Within all the chambers where primary and occasionally secondary TRB burials were found, the human remains consisted exclusively of selections of bones from individuals who had previously been either buried or exposed elsewhere. Such deposits are not confined merely to the chambers of passage graves, but are also found as primary deposits in all types of dolmen, including the *Urdolmen*. These practices not only contradict the admittedly scanty evidence available from the Danish dolmens, but also raise once more the question of the appropriateness of a functionally singular interpretation of thse monuments.

Two *Urdolmen*, both from the Everstorfer Forst group of chambers, contained primary TRB burials. In the Barendorf chamber the deposit, which was accompanied by a collared flask, consisted of a pile of bones placed in one corner; this included a fragmented skull, some ribs, vertebrae and long bones (ibid., 71). At Naschendorf (ibid., Fig. 43) one skull, lacking its lower jaw, was placed in a corner, while another was in a small pit. Two lower jaws were lying in the middle of the chamber and a few fragmentary bones were scattered in the middle of the floor intermixed with eight transverse arrowheads. Both of the chambers were sealed after the depositions, and the grave goods place both deposits early in the TRB.

The discovery of this type of deposit within the *Urdolmen* is significant in a number of respects. First of all, it documents the early beginning of a custom involving the deposition of selected human bones brought into the chamber from elsewhere. It therefore offers a possible interpretation for the use of the very small dolmen chambers many of which are concentrated on Zealand (Aner 1963, Fig. 3). These chambers do not exceed 0.8 m in width and 1.4 m in length and could barely have contained fully extended inhumations. The usual explanation involves crouched burials, but this practice is confined to the Baalberge group and its congeners and is not encountered anywhere else within the TRB.

Moreover, the sealed condition of these and many other deposits from Mecklenburg throws new light upon the nature of the 'chaos' among the bones reported regularly in the megalithic chambers from the nineteenth century onwards. It shows tht such 'chaos' was not necessarily the result of regular and periodic clearings to make room for new interments, but that it could reflect the original manner of depositions within the chamber.

Evidence recovered by Schuldt from the chambers of extended and great dolmens, as well as from the passage graves, shows that the custom of selective bone deposition continued while these monuments were under construction and use. From the moment when passage graves come into use, or possibly even earlier, we observe a further refinement and elaboration of this custom, which reflects broader changes taking place among the TRB populations throughout the megalithic area. We have already commented upon the significance of the numerical difference and distribution of the passage graves and great dolmens and this change can now be illustrated further through burial customs.

One of the important features of this process is the division of chambers into compartments by means of rows of low red sandstone slabs (Schuldt 1972a, 60–3). With the exception of the *Urdolmen*, this feature appears in all other types of chamber: as an apparently secondary feature in some of the dolmens, and as a primary element in the passage graves (Fig. 128). The extended dolmens have either one or two compartments constructed at the end of the chamber and along one of the side walls. Among the great dolmens there are generally three or four compartments, although as many as six were noted at Lancken Granitz (Schuldt 1972a, Figs 37 and 39). At Liepen (ibid., Fig. 27) there was one compartment built transversely to the end and one against each of the side walls, with a narrow passage between them. In the relatively large end compartment there was a deposit of bones belonging to three individuals, including three incomplete skulls but only two jaw bones and some other bones which displayed old breakages. Similar finds came from the two side compartments: the southern had parts of a shattered skull, whilst in the northern there were two deposits each with a skull. A very small pile of human bones was placed at the beginning of the inner narrow passage. Most of the bones had been compressed by the weight of the earth that filled the chamber.

The number of compartments increases with the passage graves: four or five compartments are most commonly encountered, although in one chamber at Neu-Gaarz (ibid., Fig. 40) there were as many as nine. The same picture of incomplete bone deposits emerges here, although not all the compartments were necessarily used. Occasionally, as at Liepen, the bones within a compartment may be further divided into separate piles, each accompanied by a fragmentary skull or skulls. In some cases there were also deliberate bone deposits within the short inner passage between the segments.

Schuldt argued that the custom of chamber segmentation arrived with the passage graves and that the appearance of this feature in the dolmens reflected a secondary TRB use of such chambers. However, there are two aspects of this feature worthy of consideration: its function and its possible origin. Although Schuldt suggested that the compartment divided the chamber for individual bone deposition, such a function cannot be clearly demonstrated. There are instances where the compartments are empty; elsewhere, bones were placed in the undivided part of the chamber, although we cannot always determine whether these represent primary or secondary deposits.

Recent analysis of human remains from the two Swedish passage graves

Figure 128 Passage grave from Gnewitz in Mecklenburg showing the division of the chamber into compartments (Source: Schuldt 1972a).

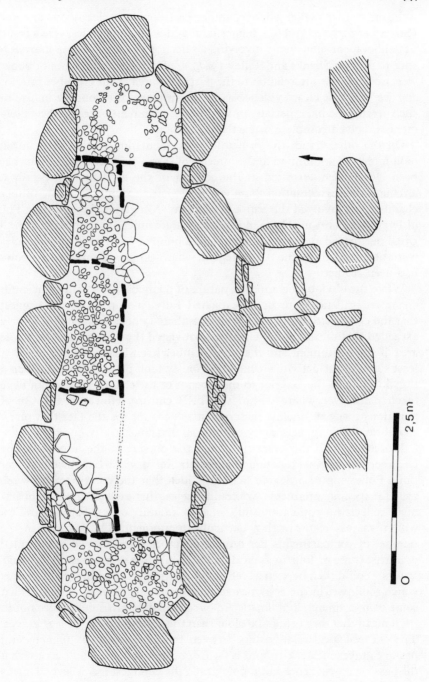

2,5 m

– the only other region where chamber partitioning is clearly documented (Strömberg 1971, 251–66) – suggested that discrete bone piles were a result of deliberate arrangements involving a selection of certain bones in preference to others (Shanks and Tilley 1982). Unfortunately the types of bones were not discussed in relation to the particular area of the chamber interior and we still lack clear evidence as to the primary or secondary nature of such arrangements, especially in view of the argument over whether interments involved complete or partial depositions.

On the other hand, the principle of segmentation of the TRB burial monuments is not limited to the interior of stone-built chambers. This has been clearly demonstrated in the context of the earthen long barrows, although the segmentation there was not related specifically to the timber chamber but involved the entire monument (Midgley 1985, 128–48). The different segments may have indicated separate functions within the overall ritual performed at the monument, and a number of striking consistencies were observed throughout the region where timber-chambered barrows had been studied.

While the obviously composite nature of many barrows with stone-built chambers still needs to be investigated fully, it is plausible to suggest that the construction of stone-built chambers (whose accessibility clearly exceeded that of the timber chambers) obviated the need to use the whole area of the monument and that the chamber itself became the focus of at least some of the activities which previously took place outside it. Such a transition, from the exterior to the interior of the chamber, need not have taken place everywhere within the TRB culture. However, the use of partitions made of organic materials may account for the fact that many chambers today appear empty of internal divisions.

Moreover, with this transition from the outside to the interior of the chamber, the original function of segmentation may also have changed over time. Following to a degree Schuldt's idea that the compartments were used for specific interments, we could suggest that each chamber compartment reflected a population unit, such as a family or a group of families, which was associated with a particular monument. The increase in the number of compartments per type of chamber – one or two in extended dolmens, three or four in great dolmens, four, five or more in the passage graves – could then be seen as reflecting the progressive number of groups which took part in the activities at a common ritual centre. The fact that some compartments in dolmens are of secondary construction does not in itself mean that they cannot be older than the appearance of passage graves. The chronological relationship between the more complex dolmens and passage graves in Mecklenburg is far from clear, and even if we accept that the passage graves represent typologically the youngest form, several forms may have been built and used contemporaneously. The coming together of groups of families may have begun relatively early within the TRB, and the primary segmentation of passage graves may simply be a reflection of an already established ritual and social order.

Evidence of burial from chambers in other areas is very poor. U. Fischer (1956, 79) comments on an almost complete absence of TRB skeletal material from the Altmark chambers. At the Wötz dolmen near the entrance were found a skull and jaw bone together with a few ribs and long bones, and traces of long bones were also noted in another chamber in the same locality. Most of the human remains from the Altmark area, however, belong to the secondary use of the chambers by the Corded Ware culture.

The situation is equally uninformative when we consider Lower Saxony. Human bone does not survive in the chambers and examples of depositions are known only from Oldendorf and Fallingbostel. At Oldendorf, Sprockhoff (1952b, 79) found the remains of two individuals in the south-eastern corner of the chamber: long bones belonging to an individual over 23 years of age, and a shoulder blade and teeth from an individual aged about 30 years. Another grave at Oldendorf apparently also contained the remains of at least three individuals (Laux 1971).

The deposit from Fallingbostel (Tempel 1979, 137–9, Figs 4 and 4), however, is of the same nature as those from Mecklenburg. Three large heaps of bones were found on the chamber's floor: at the east end there were fragments of fifteen skulls and other bones, while the middle deposit contained mostly long bones. An assortment of various bones was placed at the west end of the chamber.

None of the chambers from Lower Saxony or Drenthe revealed evidence for partitioning of the interior, but it should be noted that the chambers in this TRB group became progressively longer, a fact whose chronological significance in the area of the Lüneburger Heide appears to have some support in the ceramic deposits found in the chambers of varying length (Laux 1979). There is no reason to suppose that similar processes of communal consolidation should not have been taking place in the area west of the Elbe. The chronologically valid increase in the size of the chambers may represent a different expression of a number of communities coming together, and the size of the chamber may be directly related to the size of the group which used that particular monument. The very large chambers of Emsland, which are further aggrandised by excessively elaborate stone settings, may in this context represent particularly large communities.

The burial evidence from Denmark is not only poor in relation to the thousands of megaliths known from that country, but it is also very confusing. Danish scholars firmly believe that dolmens were intended for single inhumations, and the available evidence supports the view that at least some of the dolmen chambers were used for this purpose. Thus the dolmens from Ølstykke and Kellerød on Zealand each appear to have contained one burial, placed in an extended position and accompanied by grave goods of pottery and flint/bone artefacts. The Kellerød individual was placed in the middle of the chamber, which was subsequently filled with earth. At Ølstykke, the dead person was laid towards one of the sides of the chamber (P.O. Nielsen 1984, 337–8, Figs 256 and 257). At the extended dolmen of Klokkehøj on south-west Fyn, the primary burial (which dates to the Fuchsberg period) involved an extended inhumation of a male of about 20–35 years of age. This was accompanied by the skull of a 5-year-old child and a small collection of shoulder and arm bones (not in anatomical order) from another adult. Secondary burials at Klokkehøj were inserted into the chamber towards the end of the TRB culture. These were placed in two piles and represent the fragmentary remains of at least twenty-two people – thirteen adults and nine children (Thorsen 1981, 117–20, Figs 6 and 7, 126–31, Figs 11 and 12).

These three dolmen finds are the only reliable examples of extended inhumations connected with Danish dolmens and even here in one instance, at Klokkehøj, the primary inhumation was associated with what appears to be a selective choice of bones. Additional but not very clear evidence comes from a number of other dolmen chambers. At Brunemose (Thorvildsen 1941, catalogue no. 131), a skull was found in a corner of a rectangular chamber and remains of long bones were in the middle; at Skjerngård in Jutland, the remains of two individuals were found (ibid., no. 60), and from Store Stenshøj on Lyø there are reports of disintegrated human bones (Christensen *et al.* 1979, catalogue no. 3). The rectangular mound at Frellesvig on Langeland contained two extended dolmen chambers (Skaarup 1985, 114–21). The mid-nineteenth century investigations recovered human remains in both: each apparently contained the bodies of a man and a woman, who were laid in opposite directions to one another. However, recent analysis of skeletal material remains from one of the chambers identified fragments of two skulls without jaw bones, two thigh bones and two pelvic bones: one pelvic bone was identified as belonging to a man and one skull to a woman. Such scanty remains can be interpreted either way: as very poorly preserved extended inhumations, or as two depositions of selected bones belonging to two or more individuals.

Indeed, we have precisely such deposits from the Oldenbjergård dolmen on Langeland, which was investigated by Winther (Skaarup 1985, 132–3, Figs 103 and 104). One of the chambers apparently contained two E–W oriented extended inhumations, while in the other Winther encountered, upon the flint cobbled floor, five discrete piles of bones (mostly limbs), each with a skull on top. Some doubt has been expressed due to the presence of a Corded Ware type flint dagger, but the nature of these deposits is very much in character with the TRB custom common in Mecklenburg.

Any discussion of the TRB burial ritual associated with the Danish passage graves is hampered at the outset by the fact that many of the investigations took place years ago, and there has been no attempt to collate the various pieces of evidence. Moreover, apart from their prolonged use by the TRB populations, many of the chambers were also used by later cultural groups, most notably those of the Corded Ware. Their activities are regularly attested by the presence of grave goods and votive depositions within and around the chambers.

Some of the Danish passage graves contain a large number of skeletal remains. These are known from the islands rather than from Jutland, but at present it is not possible to tell whether this is a reflection of a real difference between the two regions or simply a factor of preservation and recovery. Thus from the chambers on the islands we have various estimates ranging from the remains of nine persons at Nørregård, Lolland (Nordman 1917b, 59) to over eighty at Uggerslev on Fyn (A.P. Madsen 1900, 8). A recent skeletal analysis of remains from Hulbjerg on Langeland suggests the presence of about fifty people (Bennike 1985, 471). In many instances, however, such remains include not only primary TRB burials, but also subsequent interments. It is generally assumed that the burials found in the upper layers of the chamber filling or in the passage are secondary additions, with the dead lying in an extended position (for example at Splittorfs Høj; Ebbesen 1975, Fig. 219), or, very rarely, crouched (Ebbesen quotes four examples from the islands; ibid., 324, n. 31). The real problem arises when we attempt to identify burials of the TRB cultures: should we distinguish between the primary TRB burials (those placed immediately after the chamber construction) and secondary TRB burials? Are the latter intrusive, or do they continue an established custom?

What of the actual burial rite? The fragmentary skeletal material which can be identified as belonging to the TRB is regularly found in a poor state of preservation. Descriptions in older literature regularly refer to the 'chaotic' arrangement of the bones in the chambers (Nordman 1917a, 241; Rosenberg 1929, 214), with the bones usually placed in greater or lesser piles. From the chambers described by A.P. Madsen we may select a few examples. Thus, in the double passage grave at Snæbum, Jutland (A.P. Madsen 1900, 16–17; Ebbesen 1978, 22–7; Fig. 129) the north chamber had a stone pavement which stopped short of the sides. In this stone-free space round the inner edge of the chamber there were various mixed-up piles of long bones, ribs and skulls. There were two extended skeletons in the passage leading to the southern chamber, two more were lying in the middle of the chamber, and various piles of skulls and bones were found along the walls. At Bistrup (A.P. Madsen 1896, 26–8, Plates XXVII and XXVIII) there were traces of a fierce fire on the chamber floor and the earliest deposit, placed against the west wall, consisted of burnt stones, charcoal and singed and charred human bones. At Uggerslev (A.P. Madsen 1900, 7–9; Fig. 130), which appears to have been one of the most profusely used chambers, four separate groupings were identified. At the west end of the chamber there were the skeletal remains of three persons, each in a little pile

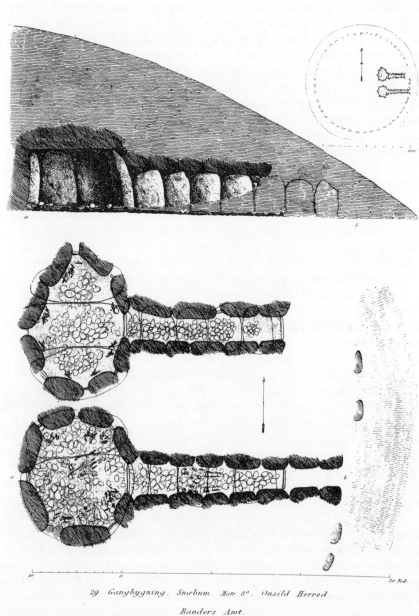

2 Bind XIX.

29. Gangbygning. Snæbum Matr. 8ᵃ. Onsild Herred.

Randers Amt.

Figure 129 Complex burial deposits in two passage graves at Snæbum in north Jutland (Source: A.P. Madsen 1900).

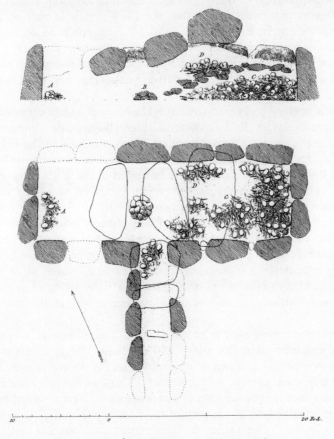

Gangbygning. Ullerslev. Matr. 14. Skam Herred.
Odense Amt.

Figure 130 Passage grave at Uggerslev on Fyn revealing elaborate arrangements of human remains (Source: A.P. Madsen 1900).

with a skull on top. At the opposite end there was an enormous pile of bones reaching halfway up the chamber: skulls had been placed side by side and on top of one another, and surrounded in all directions by thigh, arm and other bones. Not one of the skulls was face up and the whole deposit was covered with a layer of stones. In the chamber at Kyndeløse (Ebbesen 1975, 325, n. 31), twenty skulls were found together in one corner, and at Rævehøj (Nordman 1917b, 80–7) a pile of nine skulls had been placed against the wall.

The arrangements in the chambers described above could hardly be thought of as 'chaotic', although the skeletons were disarticulated. The bones appear to have been placed carefully according to a more or less uniform pattern, with a skull or group of skulls and close together. A different interpretation of burial practices has recently been suggested by Skaarup (1985, 372), who argued that the TRB burials in passage graves were complete interments. The 'chaos' so frequently encountered in the chambers was merely the result of disturbances through regular additions of bodies over a long period of time. This argument is based on skeletal material recovered in 1960–1 from the passage grave at Hulbjerg, Langeland.

The TRB pottery recovered from the Hulbjerg chamber represents all the MN ceramic styles (ibid., 197–200). Interestingly, this contrasts with pottery found outside the passage, which belongs mostly to the MN I/II styles (ibid., 200–2). Four separate funerary layers were distinguished, of which the lower two were said to have belonged to the TRB culture. The upper layers represented secondary use of the chamber, mostly by Corded Ware populations. The second layer (upper TRB) was sealed with stones but, judging by the degree of filtration of later cultural material right to the chamber floor, this was hardly an effective sealing. A large quantity of fatty organic material, noted particularly in the lower part of the chamber, was thought to have derived from slowly decaying bodies placed there by the TRB people. Many of the bones were at least partially articulated; this was especially noticeable in the case of the vertebrae, as well as the hands and feet.

The chamber contained the remains of at least thirty-six adults and seventeen children (Bennike 1985, 470–2, Table 4). It is surprising, however, in view of the claimed stratigraphy, that the skeletal material from these four layers was not analysed separately. Thus, we have no information about the sex, age or even number of interments which represented each of the cultures involved, let alone each of the funerary layers. This is wholly unsatisfactory, particularly since the bone report mentions that most of the women and children were found just below the stones which apparently sealed off the TRB deposits from the later additions. One cannot escape the impression that either the bone specialist did not share the excavator's faith in the chamber's stratigraphy, or the bones simply became mixed up after the excavation. The only conclusion that can be drawn about the Hulbjerg burials is that they represent a Danish Neolithic population; they neither prove nor disprove the manner in which the TRB people buried their dead.

Apart from the ceramic grave goods accompanying the burials, layers of broken pottery, flint and amber objects are regularly encountered either side of the entrance to the south Scandinavian tombs. Occasionally, ceramic deposits may involve thousands of sherds which constitute hundreds of vessels (Bagge and Kaelas 1950), but generally the numbers are smaller (between thirty-five and forty vessels). Initially, some scholars were inclined to regard such finds as grave goods which were periodically cleared out of the chambers (Rosenberg 1929, 246), while others suggested that such deposits represented votive offerings placed in front of the tomb in association with a burial or some other ceremony (Nordman 1917a, 305; Thorvildsen 1946, 87).

Kjærum's (1969, 26–8) excavations at the Jordhøj passage grave by the Mariager Fjord provided stratigraphic evidence which enabled him to distinguish unequivocally between the votive offerings and the far less numerous ceramic material, which had been thrown out of the chamber. This and the subsequent investigations at a number of other tombs have shown that vessels were placed along the top of the kerb on a shelf-like arrangement of slabs which stretched for several metres either side of the entrance. The dispersion of the sherds on the ground indicated that either vessels were deliberately smashed on the spot or they tumbled down in the course of time to the foot of the kerb.

This custom was by no means limited to the passage graves. Indeed, a review of the evidence for ceremonial activities within the south Scandinavian TRB shows that the custom of ceramic offerings in front of the tomb's facade has an ancestry which, like many of the phenomena already discussed, dates to the very beginning of the TRB culture. Votive deposits of pottery, albeit in much smaller numbers, have been identified at some of the enclosures surrounding timber-built chambers. Thus the Svaleklint-style ceramics were found in association with the timber facades at Lindebjerg (Liversage 1981, 97) and Rude (T. Madsen 1980, 94), and a number of other sites offer indications that the custom was much more widespread.

Likewise, deposits recovered from the Jutland cult houses of Ferslev (thirty-six vessels), Tustrup (twenty-six vessels) and Engedal (twenty-eight vessels), or indeed finds from mortuary houses accompanying the stone-packing graves, may be shown to have originated as early as offerings found at Rustrup, Strynø and Sejerø.

Returning to offerings in front of chambered tombs we may note that there are few publications describing ceramic offerings in front of the early TRB dolmens. Finds of polished thin-butted axes have been found in such contexts on a few occasions, for example at the Bøgo and Møn dolmens

(P.O. Nielsen 1977, 103–4). However, Skaarup's (1985) survey of tombs from the south Danish islands contains a number of dolmens where early TRB pottery (of the Virum and Fuchsberg styles) was deposited in front of some chambers.

By far the largest offerings of pottery involved the early MN styles, although generally not more than two or three stylistically separate groups can be identified in deposits from in front of the great dolmens and passage graves. Pottery representing each style is usually so homogeneous as to suggest that all such vessels were placed in front of the tomb during one specific ceremony. Vessels chosen for such offerings are richly decorated and appear to have been selected specifically for this purpose; the commonest forms include funnel-necked beakers, pedestalled bowls accompanied by clay ladles, and the so-called Troldebjerg and other shouldered bowls (Figs 41 and 43).

Troldebjerg-style pottery is found in front of Jutland's great dolmens, for example at Vedsted, Præsthøj and Borre (Ebbesen 1879a, 71). Comparable materials are known from in front of the north Jutland passage graves, for example at Hagebrogård (E. Jørgensen 1977, 14–15, Figs 14–16 and 20). Both types of monuments were clearly used contemporaneously.

On the Danish islands offerings found in similar circumstances generally only include vessels of the Klintebakke and Blandebjerg styles, as seen for example at the extended dolmens of Pæregård (only 1 km from the Klintebakke settlement; Berg 1956, 118–19), the great dolmens of Grønhøj and Brejninggård and numerous passage graves (Ebbesen 1979a, 39).

Although on the Danish islands the pottery continues to be placed in the chambers until the end of the TRB, after the Blandebjerg style goes out of fashion the kerb offerings cease and only very rarely do we find later pottery in such contexts (Ebbesen 1975, 168). Ebbesen (1978, 118–22) pointed to a somewhat greater duration of such offerings in Jutland, where pottery beside the chambers as well as in cult houses spans the MN I–III styles. As on the islands, so in Jutland the later styles are rarely encountered, and although in both regions the tradition of offerings in front of the monuments continues, the content of the offerings changes: pottery is replaced by deposits of burnt and unburnt flint tools, mostly axes and chisels.

The change in the type of offering placed outside the tombs is reflected, to a degree, in the grave goods which accompany the later TRB use of the chambers; the amount of pottery in Jutland and on the islands gradually diminishes and flint tools assume a relatively more significant role. They not only appear in association with stone-built chambers, but are also quite important in the burials in stone-packing graves.

Concerning the content of the offerings in front of as well as within the chambered tombs, we should note that the change in emphasis from pottery to flint tools is reflected by changes elsewhere. Thus, the decrease in the quantity of pottery which makes its way into funerary contexts goes hand in hand with a dramatic reduction in ceramic variety: from MN III onwards there are fewer types of pot being made and the forms become less distinct; the decoration becomes simpler in design and fewer decorative techniques are used. The strong regional variation in pottery, which was contemporary with the intensive monument-building programme, gives way to more homogeneous ceramic styles over most of Denmark. This change in turn corresponds with the re-use of the already existing ritual centres, possibly reflecting more stable social conditions in which ceremonial aspects acquire a different significance.

The greater emphasis on the placement of flint tools in later TRB funerary contexts may reflect not only the decreasing importance of pottery, but also the changing significance of axes and other tools in the overall ritual. Thus Skaarup (1985, 376–7) has pointed out that a comparable change can be observed in votive offerings placed in wet environments. Where it can be demonstrated that specific locations were used over a long period of time, pottery appears to be replaced by thick-butted axes, chisels and stone battle axes. Conversely, the number of axe hoards dramatically declined: only sixteen thick-butted TRB axe hoards were quoted by P.O. Nielsen (1979, 32–9) in contrast to 246 thin-butted examples (P.O. Nielsen 1984, 382). Even if we accept the different duration of the periods during which the respective types were deposited, the overall pattern argues very strongly for changing ritual significance between the early and late TRB axes.

Comparison with other regions of the TRB culture suggests that this custom of offerings in front of the chambered tombs was practised uniquely in southern Scandinavia and represents a specific aspect of ritual not evidenced elsewhere. Bakker (1979, 152) has pointed out that the absence of offerings outside the entrance and the profusion of ceramic and flint deposits within the chamber in the Western TRB group constitute two fundamental differences between the megaliths of the Northern and Western groups.

In other regions where chambered tombs were in use, pottery and flint tools are occasionally found within and immediately outside the entrance to the tomb. Sherds were discovered towards the outer end of the passage at one of the tombs in Haldenslebener Forst (Bebertal 14), and in another (Bebertal 13) sherds were found beneath the passage's paving stones. Preuss (1980, 79) was undecided as to whether these represented goods removed from the chamber or depositions placed in accordance with the custom we observed in Scandinavia. Similar circumstances were noted at a number of tombs in Mecklenburg, where pottery and flint implements came to light in the ante-chambers of some of the great dolmens (such as Sassen; Schuldt 1970, Fig. 7) and in the passage of passage graves. In the case of the passage grave at Naschendorf (Schuldt 1968, 16, Fig. 36), a

substantial find immediately outside the passage consisted of richly decorated sherds of funnel-necked beakers, conical and shouldered vessels, and
a pedestalled bowl as well as a few flint implements. However, sherds
belonging to the same vessels were also found on the floor of the chamber,
and in view of the secondary activities of the Globular Amphora people, it
is reasonable to interpret the material from outside the chamber as the
result of clearance.

On the other hand the profusion of grave goods, especially pottery, in a
number of the Western TRB chambered tombs is quite staggering. Thus
the Havelte D53 tomb contained 649 pots (Bakker 1979, 13), at Wechte 2
there were over 450 pots (Knöll 1983), and at Emmeln 2, 1,200 vessels and
573 transverse arrowheads were found (Schlicht 1969). Even when long use
of the chambers is taken into consideration, the sheer quantity of the
material deposited within them makes one wonder whether some of the
depositions were made on occasions other than burials and could reflect a
related tradition of offerings, differing only in the choice of the interior
rather than the exterior of the tomb.

One is also brought to wonder about the status of some finds associated
with the timber-built chambers. The circumstances encountered at Issendorf
and Himmelpforten suggest that sometimes vessels were placed outside, on
top of the timber graves, and found their way into the grave only upon the
collapse of the roof. The homogeneous nature and quantity of finds indicate
not a prolonged deposition, but rather a placement on one particular
occasion, perhaps reflecting, on a smaller scale, the Scandinavian tradition.

9.4 Interpretation of TRB burial ritual

The idea of an independent development of megaliths in different regions
of north-west Europe does not represent a new concept (Renfrew 1973 and
1980), and today most scholars accept this view as a working hypothesis.
However, while the distinctive character of the fully developed megalithic
tradition in different regions can usually be effectively determined, and
while typological similarities between distant monuments are no longer
regarded as more significant than their cultural context, the emergence of
these local traditions is more difficult to identify. Thus, one of the most
significant results of research into the TRB culture is the accumulation of
evidence which now allows us to view the north European funerary tradition, both typologically and contextually, as essentially a local
phenomenon. This identification of the local character of the monuments
which we have just discussed does not imply an isolation of the TRB
culture province from the rest of Europe, but instead offers an opportunity
to perceive it in the same broad perspective that has recently been argued
by Bradley (1984) for contemporary Britain.

The difficulties in interpreting the origin of the TRB culture megaliths
stem primarily from the persistent assumption that stone-built chambers

are fundamentally different from other forms of contemporary graves. Thus, while Schuldt (1972a, 93–4) argued that we could no longer doubt that the *Urdolmen* was the prototype for the entire typological sequence of megaliths around the western Baltic, he was unable to account for the emergence of the *Urdolmen* itself.

Yet the existence of a well-established early TRB timber mortuary architecture offers us a new background against which to interpret the appearance of the megaliths. We have already argued that once and for all we can dispense with the idea that the so-called earth or flat graves were, in contrast to megaliths, simple structures. The types of graves identifiable in the north european archaeological record show convincingly that the earth graves were varied and elaborate structures, displaying a degree of architectural sophistication not in any sense inferior to that of stone-built chambers. While clearly the timber forms display regional differences based upon local custom and preference, the TRB culture is, from the very beginning, characterised by a rich architectural tradition which allows us to place the 'earth graves' on the level of constructional competence commonly credited to megaliths.

In this context the north european *Urdolmen* should be seen as a stone version of an already established and popular grave form, the most important difference between the two types of grave lying in the choice of building materials. Indeed, the more or less chronologically imperceptible difference between the *Urdolmen* and extended dolmen may suggest that even the more elaborate dolmen form already existed in a timber version. The traditionally emphasised dichotomy between the earth grave and the dolmen becomes even less pronounced when we realise that many of the timber-built graves contained relatively large stones (for example Troelstrup and Preußlitz), and that, conversely, timber was used in the construction of stone-built chambers (for example Tannenhausen: Gabriel 1966; and Tinaarlo: Bakker 1979, 15–16). Furthermore, evidence outlined previously shows that the onset of the megalithic tradition, whose synchronous appearance over a geographically large area could never be satisfactorily explained, does not bring about the demise of timber architecture. The latter continues uninterrupted throughout the duration of the TRB culture.

The above interpretation of the emergence of megaliths out of the locally present architectural forms carries a number of important implications. The close correspondence between the dolmens and timber-built graves suggests a dramatic change neither in the burial ritual nor in the social organisation of the TRB community. The timber chambers and early dolmens represent by and large individual graves and should be interpreted as representing burial on a local level, and as forming ritual centres of local significance. Indeed, by the time dolmens are being built, the ritual landscape within the TRB culture appears to be well established. The idea of a communal chamber appears to develop as a result of the accessibility of stone-built chambers. In some regions, it may well represent a cumulative effect of the prolonged use of chambers, although the evidence from Mecklenburg may suggest that varied rituals were practised in different areas of the culture.

The typological evolution of dolmens demonstrated by Schuldt in Mecklenburg clearly indicates the general principles of such a development. In terms of megalithic technology the one crucial transformation is from the *Urdolmen* to the extended dolmen: the increase in the height of the chamber and the change in the direction of the capstones. Once the principle of the extended dolmen is established and the technological expertise has been developed, the construction of the great dolmen is merely a logical extension and is of dubious chronological significance. The difference is merely of size, and theoretically at least, there is no limit to the length of the chamber; indeed some of the extended dolmens are in fact larger than the great dolmens.

We have already noted that the lack of modern research on the south Scandinavian dolmens makes a comparison with other TRB regions difficult, and Aner's (1963) typological study added confusion to an already obscure picture. A few recent publications (E. Jørgensen 1977; Ebbesen 1979a; Skaarup 1985) suggest that although the south Scandinavian dolmen tradition developed along somewhat different lines from that in Mecklenburg, the same principles of evolution from simple to complex forms applied. The great dolmens in north Jutland were certainly constructed towards the later period of the Volling group (Vroue Hede; E. Jørgensen 1977), but they also continued to be built contemporaneously with the passage graves (Ebbsen 1979a, 38–41).

One problem concerning the south Scandinavian dolmens was always caused by the polygonal form (Fig. 120), which has a very dense distribution on Djursland and the opposite coast of north-west Zealand (*c*. 80 per cent; Kaelas 1983, Fig. 5), with the rest more scattered in Jutland and along the west coast of Sweden. Almost all scholars were agreed that a polygonal dolmen could not have developed from a rectangular form, and argued for a western European origin (Kaelas 1956, 10–14; Aner 1963, 28). This theory was further firmly supported by a scatter along the Limfjord and Mariager Fjord which was the suggested route of arrival. Given the fact that a west European source for the polygonal dolmen cannot be indicated easily, the evidence within Denmark itself, coupled with our better understanding of megalithic development, strongly suggests that the polygonal dolmen is a result of local, southern Scandinavian development. Quite a number of the Danish extended dolmens display anything but a rectangular ground plan (for example A.P. Madsen 1896, Plate VII: 16; 1900, Plates IV: 4 and XI: 18); such ground plans could easily have led to a polygonal form that became favoured in certain regions of southern Scandinavia.

Moreover, the chronological relationship between the polygonal and the great dolmen is far from clear, and the great dolmens with their pear-shaped chambers may also have played a role. Such elements as the passage, threshold and closing slab are clearly present in all types of dolmen, and in any case do not appear to be related to the shape of the chamber.

Just as traditional typological studies tend to separate the simple and complex dolmens, so the differences between these and the passage graves also appear to have been exaggerated. This is particularly evident when we consider that the burial ritual and the nature of associated activities reveal a striking continuity in use of such typologically differentiated chambers. Indeed, one wonders to what extent the traditional typology, which has been stretched to its limits by the researches of Schuldt, can still be employed in the context of a functional discussion of megaliths.

It is quite extraordinary that in Mecklenburg Schuldt (1972a) did not perceive any connection between the development sequences of dolmens and passage graves. He argued that the Mecklenburg passage grave was the result of a strong influence either directly from the Danish islands or by way of Schleswig-Holstein. While it is not suggested here that the development of the megalithic tradition within the various TRB culture regions should be regarded in isolation since evidence of contacts within the whole distribution area argues emphatically not only for short- but also for long-range connections, local development must not be undervalued. Thus in Mecklenburg, apart from the different positioning of the passage, little difference can be shown between the extended and great dolmens on the one hand, and the passage graves on the other. There was certainly no major technological change involved in the erection of the passage graves, and there is no difference in the use of the typologically different graves. The primary positioning of compartments within the passage graves and their apparently secondary construction within the dolmen chambers have no significance in terms of overall architectural design. Nor is the position of the chamber within the mound immediately relevant; it may relate to the provision of easy access, or it may even reflect a chronologically independent event.

Evidence from Denmark is equally suggestive of local, internal evolution of the passage grave form, and indeed Ebbesen (1978, 58–61) has argued that the entire megalithic tradition is of a distinctly local origin. Although we still lack evidence for chronological differentiation within the Danish passage graves, it is generally assumed that the relatively small oval chambers stand at the head of the sequence. A comparison between these and the Danish great dolmens shows exceptional similarity, so much so that it is not always possible to distinguish typologically between the two. There can be little doubt that both chamber forms are in a very close typological and chronological relationship; in addition, some of the passage grave chambers are so small that a link with polygonal dolmen chambers may also be relevant. The distribution of the small oval chambers, which do not move south beyond the River Eider, argues for their origin within the distribution area.

The more sophisticated passage graves, the bi-chambered graves from north Jutland and the true double passage graves from Zealand, represent examples of regionally developed versions. Skaarup (1985, 372-3) added another small group of graves with trapeze–shaped chambers and short passages which are common on the south Danish islands and in south Jutland. These show close similarities with the north German types, and thus emphasise contacts within the western Baltic region.

The Western TRB is predominantly the province of passage graves, which display their own peculiarities, chiefly their exceptional chamber length. In older research the view that passage graves reached west of the Elbe from southern Schleswig-Holstein tended to predominate (Sprock-hoff 1938; Aner 1963) and a less clearly defined influence from the Atlantic zone was also suggested (Nordman 1935). The difficulty in interpreting the development of the megaliths in the area west of the Elbe stems from the apparently late emergence of the TRB culture here. This is clearly at odds with the early finds from the Dümmer in the Ems area, and certainly as far as Lower Saxony is concerned, the TRB culture is witnessed in the Fuchsberg ceramics and in contemporary timber–built chambers on the Lüneburger Heide. While not numerous, dolmens are found throughout the area from the Bremen Geest to the Elbe, and extended dolmens are also known from the Ems area (Laux 1979, Fig. 2; Schlicht 1979, 44). Although this evidence is sporadic, there is no reason to assume that at least some parts of the Western TRB area did not participate in the general process witnessed to the east and north of the Elbe. Indeed, the profusion of very small passage graves (three pairs of stones with an offset passage) in north-eastern Lower Saxony may suggest that this form developed here rather than in southern Schleswig. At any rate, from the Fuchsberg phase onwards, this region was closely in touch with the Northern TRB group and influences must have crossed the Elbe in both directions. That the Western TRB passage grave developed along independent lines is clearly visible in the exceptionally long chambers which are present throughout the area from Drenthe to Magdeburg but not apparently to the east of the Elbe.

Recent archaeological discussion of Neolithic communities has consis-tently singled out the megaliths as the key factor in the interpretation of the social development of the people under consideration. It invested megaliths with functions which range from their being markers of boundaries between groups, to mechanisms capable of controlling social stress (Renfrew 1973 and 1976; Chapman 1981); all this without sufficient con-sideration of the whole ritual landscape in which they constitute but one element.

And yet our study of the TRB culture indicates that hand in hand with the richness and complexity of the pre-megalithic architecture go the aggrandisement of the immediate burial area as well as the creation of ritual centres which can be perceived on both local and regional levels. The emergence of the megaliths merely continues this process. Indeed, by the time the megaliths are built the ritual landscape in northern Europe is well established, and the changes within that landscape observable in the TRB are not related simply to the emergence of megaliths; rather, the megaliths are only one of the most accessible elements through which this process may be observed. The interpretation of this phenomenon is clearly of significance well beyond the boundaries of the TRB culture.

On the level of the individual monument, the most obvious elaboration of burial is expressed in the placement of the grave in an area enclosed by a disproportionately large timber and/or stone setting, which subsequently becomes covered by an earthen mound. This practice is evidenced in the TRB culture from the very beginning and attested over a wide area from Jutland to the Elbe–Saale region and from Kujavia to Lower Saxony, since many of the so-called earth or flat graves were originally enclosed by earthen mounds.

For a long time now we have distinguished the so-called earthen long barrows (mounds covering timber-built chambers) as a separate category of TRB monuments (Midgley 1985). It is becoming more difficult to maintain this distinction, however, since the practice clearly continues in association with the stone-built chambers. Indeed, it is not unusual to find both types of chamber within the confines of a single barrow (for example Barkær, Troelstrup and Tosterglope).

On the other hand, barrows covering timber chambers have regularly revealed traces of other structures: timber mortuary houses, internal partitioning etc. On the whole such features are not known to us from the mounds containing stone-built chambers, but one suspects that investigations confined mostly to the immediate vicinity of the chamber are at least partly responsible for the poor state of knowledge the interior of mounds.

Even among the earliest barrows there is a considerable variety of size and form. The size appears to bear no relation to the type of chamber, and the principle behind the choice of shape is equally unclear. In general, triangular mounds are found in the eastern part of the TRB province (Kujavia, western Pomerania) and rectangular forms are common in the west (Lower Saxony), with the trapezoidal mound overlapping both zones (Midgley 1985, 75–84). The circular mound is especially characteristic of the southern TRB area (the region of the Baalberge group), but its association with the dolmen chambers in Mecklenburg, (where it is half as common as the long mound) and in southern Scandinavia cannot be explained by influence from the south.

In a detailed study of the barrows containing timber-built chambers the author argued for maintaining the original Childean suggestion that long barrows had prototypes in the continental long houses, and that it was possible to demonstrate the validity of this concept with reference to the Eastern TRB group monuments. The unique circumstances in Kujavia showed not only the contemporaneity and geographical proximity of long house villages and long barrow cemeteries, but also the strikingly close resemblance in dimensions, ground plan and spatial arrangement of individual structures within the groups (Midgley 1985, 207–19). Similar sentiments have been voiced by Hodder (1984), who argued that many elements of similarity between the continental long house and the long barrow are not coincidental but imply a significant relationship within the change from domestic to ritual symbolism.

Yet this relationship requires further investigation, particularly since many of the mounds appear to have been altered, not merely through the passage of time, but evidently as part of an overall ritual. Timber-built enclosures have on occasion been replaced by larger stone versions (for example at Bygholm Nørremark), and many barrows acquired their final shape in a series of extensions (such as at Barkær, Østergård or Troelstrup) or by superimposition of a differnt shape (cf. Gaarzerhof; Schuldt 1972a, Plate 12), or by destruction which need not have been a result of different cultural activity. These phenomena are by no means restricted to northern Europe, since evidence from elsewhere attests to regular alteration, reshaping and incorporation of a sequence of constructions whose ultimate version often bears little resemblance to the initial form (see for example Kinnes 1981; Masters 1983).

The prolonged maintenance of monuments, the attention paid to the alteration and reconstruction of mounds and enclosures surrounding the burial chamber, and the clear communal involvement and participation, allow the supposition that these monuments represent something more than merely places for the disposal of the community's dead. The idea that in fact they formed local ceremonial centres has been voiced on a number of occasions and is substantiated by evidence of the whole range of activities associated with the funerary context.

Thus the use of fire is regularly observed in association with burial monuments. The clearest and most consistent evidence for this practice comes from Denmark, where the majority of timber graves were ultimately destroyed by fire, but there is sufficient, if patchy, evidence of this practice being widespread. In the Eastern TRB group the burning appears to have been associated not so much with the grave, but rather with the accompanying mortuary house, and indicates a somewhat different facet of the same phenomenon. Ceremonial burning of select cereals, sometimes in association with burial (Grygiel 1980), may represent yet another dimension of the same process. Unlike the timber chamber, the stone-built grave is not destroyed by fire; yet there is consistent evidence that fires were lit inside the stone chambers.

On a local level, ritual centres are formed in many ways and although most commonly the graves are found within barrows, this is by no means a hard and fast rule. In some instances a solitary barrow was a focus of prolonged activities. Elsewhere barrows are placed together in groups which most commonly display clustered or linear arrangements. The clusters of monuments in Kujavia, for instance, are arranged in accordance with strict rules guiding the spatial arrangement of the monuments within the landscape in a pattern which quite clearly replicats the settlement of a differnt cultural complex (Midgley 1985, 313–16). From other regions we may quote clustered arrangements of usually between three and ten monuments. On Djursland a ritual centre at Tustrup comprised a mortuary house, two dolmens and a passage grave (Kjærum 1958). In the Sachsenwald, barrows originally containing timber-built chambers are clustered in groups separated by 2–4 km intervals (Sprockhoff 1954, Fig. 8). That such clusters can sometimes be quite large is shown by the megaliths in the Haldenslebener Forst area, where about 130 chambered tombs were originally built in an area of 20 km² (Preuss 1973, Fig. 1).

Clustered concentrations may be contrasted with linear arrangements, sometimes stretching over several kilometres. Thus, from the nineteenth-century studies of von Estorff, we have a record of two lines of megaliths (34 in total) in the vicinity of Altenmedingen on the Lüneburger Heide (Sprockhoff 1974, 58–61) and shorter rows can still be seen surviving in Mecklenburg, as is the case with the monuments in the Everstorfer Forst near Wismar (Schuldt 1968, Fig. 2; 1972a, Fig. 1).

The regional significance of such arrangements will be examined shortly, but for the present we should note that once a locality has been chosen, it appears to have been used over a long period of time. This is evident from the accumulation of monument types. In the Everstorfer Forst (Fig. 131), one group of barrows comprises eight *Urdolmen* and two extended dolmens, while the other group includes one *Urdolmen*, one extended and one great dolmen as well as two passage graves.

Laux (1979, 68) observed that in Lower Saxony specific locations were used consistently, and the chambers within each cluster were small and medium, medium and large or all three together, but never only small and large. If the typological development from small to large chambers is accepted, then the continuity of use of the ritual centre can reasonably be confirmed. From Denmark the classic example is present at Vroue Hede, where the unbroken use of the ritual centre spans the entire TRB culture in this area (E. Jørgensen 1977).

Moreover, a specific location outside the settled area may have been chosen. This is most emphatically documented by the cemetery on the Tannenwerde island on the Ostorf lake in Mecklenburg (Bastian 1961; Schuldt 1961). The island today is only 115 m long and 50 m wide and there is no evidence that it was ever settled, especially in view of the fact that

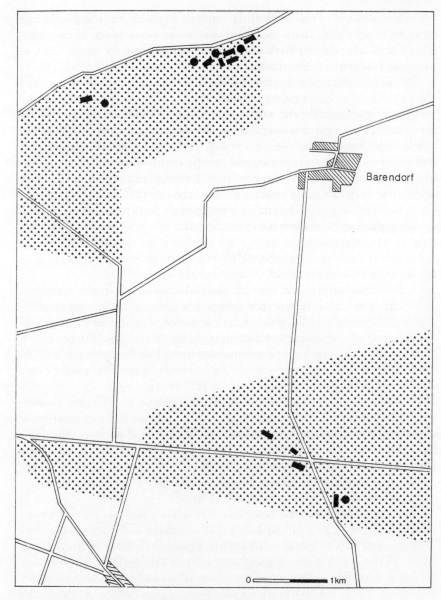

Figure 131 Linear arrangement of chambered tombs in the two cemeteries at
Everstorfer Forst in Mecklenburg (Source: Schuldt 1968).

the cemetery is located at the highest point of the island. And yet it
was repeatedly used for burials whose ritual aspects remained unchanged
over centuries and displayed a characteristic degree of conservatism in
the choice of accompanying goods, in the position of the dead and in

the activities which accompanied the burial ceremony. Many similar sites have been discovered in the lake belt of Mecklenburg, albeit not necessarily on the lake islands, indicating that this practice was not uncommon.

The choice of islands or off-shore islands as ritual centres, which may have served larger populations, is particularly apt in the Danish context and is a problem which merits future scholarly attention. The location of the famous Barkær monuments on Djursland represents just such a circumstance, since the site was originally an island in Korup Sø, which formed an inlet of the Kolind Sund. That this island formed a ritual focus within the surrounding landscape, and that it retained such a character over a long period of time, is revealed emphatically in the very complex sequential construction of the two monuments including the presence of timber-and stone-built chambers, mortuary houses and the votive character of the numerous associated deposits (Glob 1949; Midgley 1985).

The ritual complexes recently investigated on the islands of Sejerø, 11 km north-west of Zealand (Liversage 1982) and Strynø, off Langeland (Skaarup 1985, 337–9) confirm such a pattern. The Sejerø island is sufficiently large to have supported its own population, but its isolation may equally well have been of ceremonial importance for Zealand. A small settlement dated to MN I–II appears to have existed on the island of Lyø (Christensen *et al.* 1979), but evidence of earlier TRB is lacking. Yet the presence of a varied group of megaliths (sixteen dolmens and two passage graves) suggests that the island attracted the interest of the coastal communities of south-western Fyn. Such a relationship, of course, remains to be established, but Lyø's isolated yet sufficiently close location south-west of Fyn may have been a factor which made it suitable for regular use as an off-shore ritual centre during a certain stage within the TRB.

The supreme example of the choice of an island as a ritual centre is Rügen (Fig. 132). Although only fifty-four megaliths survive there today, 236 chambered tombs were recorded on the island early in the nineteenth century (Schuldt 1972a, 10), concentrating along the eastern and southern coasts with the western, mainland-facing coast seemingly devoid of monuments. Schuldt's catalogue (1972, 119–24) records more than 250 tombs, of which 230 are classed as great dolmens. The survey of the existing monuments shows that, apart from two *Urdolmen* and one extended dolmen, the rest represent one particular type, the great dolmen with porch entrance, which with one or two exceptions is not encountered in other parts of Mecklenburg.

This extraordinary concentration of megaliths is in stark contrast to the virtual absence of monuments on the adjacent part of the mainland (Schuldt 1972a, Map 9), yet other finds clearly indicate a TRB presence here. Even if we allow for substantial destruction of megaliths, one can hardly escape the conclusion that Rügen served as a major ritual centre for

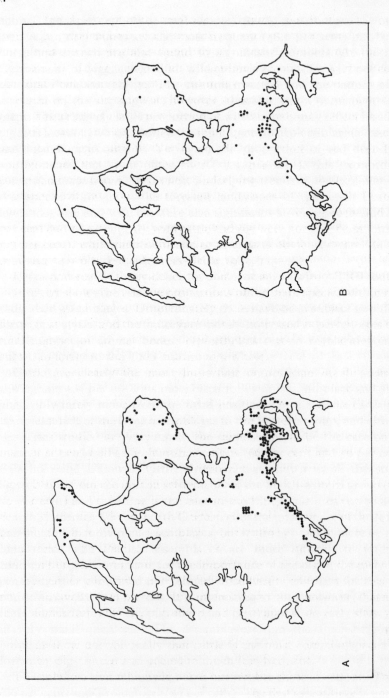

Figure 132 Comparison of nineteenth-century [A] and present-day [B] distribution of tombs on the island of Rügen (Source: Schlette 1985).

the population of north-east Mecklenburg. This is further supported by the architectural unity and exclusivity of the Rügen tombs, suggesting either a relatively short but intensive, or prolonged but conservative period of construction. This location of a ritual centre on Rügen takes on a particular significance when we remind ourselves that the island was the source of a valuable commodity: the coastal cliffs provided the so-called Rügen flint (Chapter 6.1) for the manufacture of axes and other tools. While the Mecklenburg axes have yet to be studied in terms of raw materials, Bastian's TRB axe distribution (1954, maps 1–3) indicates that Rügen was one of the main sources of this commodity. Thus the creation of a ritual centre on this island gives some credence to the frequently discussed but rarely demonstrable link between a community, its ancestors and an important resource.

Indeed, it is further of interest to note that the Rügen dolmen concentration fits well into the overall pattern of distribution of megaliths in Mecklenburg (Fig. 111). The earliest stone-built chambers, the *Urdolmen*, are recorded throughout most of the area, displaying a somewhat diffuse but wide distribution. It is again particularly informative to note a degree of correspondence between these and the early TRB thin-butted axes (expecially around the Wismar Bay; Bastian 1954, Map 1), both distributions showing a homogeneous settlement of the TRB culture at this stage. The barrows with timber-built chambers present in the south-west of Mecklenburg are in a chronologically ambivalent relationship to the *Urdolmen*. Their concentration here may be related to the geological conditions, south-west Mecklenburg clearly being outside the morainic landscape of large erratic boulders (Schuldt 1972a, Map 15).

The distribution of the remaining megaliths, extended dolmens, great dolmens and passage graves, is in stark contrast to that of the *Urdolmen*, and reveals unmistakable spatial and typological exclusiveness. Thus, the extended dolmens are concentrated chiefly in the central lake belt, with particularly strong conglomerations around the Krakow, Plau and Müritz lakes; a small outlying group is found along the middle stretches of the Recknitz river. The great dolmens have an even more dramatic distribution, We have already noted the porch entrance variant on Rügen, and dolmens with ante-chambers concentrate between the Peene and Schwinge rivers. A few great dolmens are scattered throughout Mecklenburg – aptly named the general Mecklenburg variant by Schuldt. The passage graves are seen to be encircling the extended dolmen area to the north and west; they do not enter the regions where the great dolmens are concentrated. The largest groups are on the middle Recknitz and middle Warnow rivers, with two smaller concentrations, one on the Elbe and the other along the Baltic coast by Rerik.

The distribution pattern created by the various burial monuments in Denmark is difficult to interpret. This is partly due to the large number of monuments, their unclear chronological relationship and a neglect of regional studies which are only now beginning to play a role in Danish research. In general the simple dolmens and Jutland's early earth graves reveal a dense but not concentrated distribution, suggesting that their chief significance was at a local rather than a regional level. Clear concentrations appear to be associated with the more elaborate dolmen forms: the polygonal dolmens identify two groups facing each other across the Samsø Belt (Kaelas 1983, Fig. 5) and conglomerations of great dolmens begin to emerge in central and south-west Jutland (Gebauer 1978, Fig. 1; Ebbesen 1979a, Fig. 2a). While the oval ground plan passage graves tend to be found predominantly in Jutland, the rectangular forms are more common on the islands. We have already noted the regional variants which identify specific groups: bi-chambered in north Jutland, double passage graves on Zealand and mounds containing two separate chambers in north Jutland and northeast Zealand. Stone-packing graves have been recorded in the north of Jutland, but reservations on their distribution have already been expressed.

To the west of the Elbe there are clearly defined concentrations of tombs, although the small number of dolmens and the profusion of passage grave chambers indicate that the Western TRB group was following a somewhat different course with regard to megalithic architecture. On the basis of a small number of ceramic associations, Laux (1979, 78) attempted to define a typological sequence of tomb development from timber-built and *Urdolmen* chambers, through progressively larger chambers to passage graves with six and seven pairs of stones. This sequence does not appear to have support outside the Lüneburger Heide, and even here timber-built chambers, extended dolmens (of which there are only few) and three- and four-pair passage graves are all contemporary – they all contain early *Tiefstich* (Laux's B-type) pottery.

Indeed, while the actual development from a small to a large chamber may be typologically valid, the whole series appears to have developed with extraordinary speed. This is particularly well documented by evidence from the Drenthe and the Emsland tombs, where large quantities of pottery have been found in some of the chambers, apparently reflecting a ceremonial which did not involve the clearance of chambers. While many tombs contain pottery of different styles, there is an important lesson to be learnt from the fact that chambers with between two and ten pairs of side stones all appear to have been built during the time when Drouwen B pottery was in fashion (Bakker 1979, Fig. 78). Similarly, large chambers in Altmark correspond with this evidence and suggest that if the progressive elongation of the chamber has typological validity, then Laux's entire passage grave sequence could have developed within one ceramic phase!

The tomb distribution within the TRB culture, be it in megalithic or other versions, does not present a simple picture. It is a cumulative effect of lengthy processes which involve monuments on individual, local and regional levels that cannot always be clearly distinguished. A comparison of the distribution of tombs with those of other TRB diagnostic features leads us to interpret the former as representing the ritual landscape which reflects only some aspects of the TRB culture, identifiable by means of 'tombless' and 'tomb-filled' zones, additionally aided by regionally diagnostic architecture and ritual elements.

The pattern of a ceremonial landscape is less evident during the early stages of the TRB culture (involving mainly timber–built chambers and simple dolmens), where the emphasis is clearly upon the individual sites and, at most, locally significant groups of monuments. It is possible to identify the emergence of a local centre in continuous use and the maintenance of an individual monument (for example Sarnowo, Barkær) or a group of monuments, where the chronologically earliest structures form a focus for the development of the whole complex, which often remains in use throughout the duration of the TRB (for example Tustrup and Everstorfer Forst).

One of the most fascinating aspects of the distribution of monuments, which bridges the gap between local and regional levels, is the regularly encountered linear arrangement of megaliths in the landscape, as rows either of single or of grouped monuments. This pattern was noted by prehistorians a long time ago; research by Danish, German and Dutch scholars identified a number of the so-called barrow roads, which often correspond to the known mediaeval routes and along which the oldest identifiable monuments are indisputably TRB megaliths.

We have already mentioned Bakker's (1976) paper bringing together the main concepts and ideas behind the discovery of the TRB routes in Scandinavia and the western part of the North European Plain. Since his discussion no substantial new research on the subject has been published, although E. Jørgensen's (1977, 203–8) work in the north of Jutland at Vroue Hede augments the available evidence. At Vroue Hede the TRB megaliths identify a stretch of prehistoric 'road' which clearly forms a section of a major route network identified in north Jutland. An important feature, which occurs regularly in other areas where such stretches have been suggested, is the apparently unbroken continuity of use of such a route. The line of the Vroue Hede monuments, which run parallel to, but at a distance from, the edge of the glacial end moraine, was established early in the TRB (the C-14 dates of the earth graves and great dolmens date it to the Volling group), and was subsequently 'filled in' during the later TRB. The most conspicuous monuments were doubtless the great dolmens and passage graves, but the discovery of long rows of stone-packing graves following the course of the route is even more significant, especially as they may be seen as cognate with the similar, east-west-running Herrup group of graves only 8 km to the north–west. Not only does the construction of stone-packing graves along the route attest to the continuity of both settlement and route use, but it also adds a further dimension to the importance of burial structures. It is clear that the positioning of monuments along the barrow route was not limited to megaliths. The early TRB earth graves and the stone-packing graves are given the same locational importance as the megaliths, a fact which puts the various categories of monuments on the same level and further underlines the *unity* of megalithic and non-megalithic structures.

While we cannot at present enter into detailed discussion of the possible route networks connecting the TRB groups, it is of interest to note that the evidence from regions of the TRB other than those discussed by Bakker offers enormous potential for investigation of this theme, although such studies have not so far been carried out. A few examples will illustrate the point.

The early nineteenth-century surveys of barrows in western Pomerania carried out by von Plön provide valuable evidence on the arrangement of now completely destroyed monuments around the present-day town of Pyrzyce (Midgley 1985, 23–4, Fig. 3). Some of the stretches reveal linear arrangements of barrows and many of the western Pomeranian monuments display a strongly linear distribution, following at a distance rivers and streams and mapping out local networks along the edge of the upland. The region of Mecklenburg offers ample opportunity for pursuing such a theme. Many of the barrow complexes investigated by Schuldt reveal a linear arrangement of monuments, for example the two barrow groups at the Everstorfer Forst, at Barendorf and Naschendorf, where continuity of settlement is witnessed clearly in the development of monuments in both groups (Fig. 131). An 1825 map of the region around Loitz on the Schwinge (Schuldt 1970, Fig. 2) displays several barrow lines which may reflect a local network of communication routes still perceptible, albeit less clearly, from the distribution of existing monuments.

Bakker (1979, 81) suggested that the crossing of the Elbe, which was of particular importance for connections between Mecklenburg and Lower Saxony, was via Lauenburg-Artlenburg (a route suggested by the distribution of thick-butted late TRB and Corded Ware culture axes) following Lüneburg-Celle-Hanover. Should we choose to follow the argument of barrows constructed along principal communication networks, the existence of such a route is suggested by the earthen long barrows of the Hagenow district, which also connect with the west and the Sachsenwald barrow concentrations. It is interesting that the only area west of the Elbe where earthen long barrows are known with certainty is precisely the Lüneburger Heide, that is, on the other side of the Lauenburg crossing of the Elbe.

A different but comparable opportunity for the investigation of the TRB routes is of course offered by the distribution of the TRB flint in the areas east of the Elbe. Investigations of the distribution of Rügen flint would doubtless reveal interesting patterns. The study of routes connecting the central Polish and Wolhynian flint sources could also identify important trading networks, some of which may indicate regularly used routes.

Let us now return to the discussion of the TRB culture's ritual landscape. It is particularly difficult to observe the emergence of ritual zones on a regional level, and yet this is precisely the pattern that suggests itself from the overall distribution of tombs and associated monuments. The discrete groupings of tombs identify communities which are brought together through ritual ceremonial and manifest their identity not only through the spatial arrangement of monuments within the landscape, but also through a degree of preference for architectural and ritual detail.

Thus, in Mecklenburg the emergence of regional centres manifests itself after the architectural transition from the *Urdolmen* to more complex forms, and results in several separate zones (Schuldt 1972, Map 9). Even if we allow for a certain time-lag related to the typological development of monuments, this period was not of particularly long duration. The emergence of regional communities is clearly perceived in the distribution of tomb types and their architectural exclusiveness.

The horizon which indicates the crystallisation of distinct ritual zones within the TRB is closely related to the appearance of large 'public monuments' of the causewayed enclosure type (Chapter 7.4). As noted earlier this type of site was identified in the TRB only recently, and although at present the evidence is limited, it undoubtedly represents a much more widespread phenomenon.

Let us examine in detail one example of such a regional complex, that on south-west Fyn (N. Andersen 1981), whose beginnings date to the Fuchsberg phase (3500/3400 BC). The causewayed enclosure at Sarup is found in association with chambered tombs of which 108 are dolmens. Andersen's regional analysis identified sixteen localities, roughly 6 km² in size, each represented by a cluster of dolmens (ibid., Fig. 12). While it is clear that not all the dolmens were constructed at the same time, their distribution in clusters suggests that, once a particular locality was chosen, the area retained its ceremonial significance and new dolmens were erected in the vicinity of the existing ones, with each monument seemingly being used in only one ceremony (for example Klokkehøj). The dolmen clusters may thus be seen as monuments of local importance, with each cluster representing a small population, while the causewayed enclosure represents a contemporary ritual centre which involved most or all of the identified groups in a larger communal activity.

Thus the ritual landscape documented on south-west Fyn during the Fuchsberg phase illustrates two opposing forces which seem to characterise the TRB community. We shall discuss this issue again at greater length in the Chapter 10. For the moment we should note that the ritual landscape on south-west Fyn, which is repeated in one form or another throughout the TRB, reveals the divisive function of the tomb clusters, dividing the population into small local groups, while the causewayed enclosure, in contrast, functions on an integrative level, acting as a focus for individual groups to come together in communal activities and celebrations.

In the later stage, at about 3150 BC, the ritual landscape around Sarup appears to have altered. The enclosure itself is smaller, only one-third of its original size, and only twelve passage graves appear to have been built during this period (ibid., Fig. 14). The initial impression is that of ritual impoverishment. Yet it is perhaps important to remember that the earlier tombs disappear only from the contemporary distribution map and not from the landscape itself. The decrease in the building of tombs (passage graves) may simply mean that older tombs continue in use; deposits of contemporary pottery at a number of south-west Fyn dolmens show that this was indeed the case. The previously established ritual landscape may have served the needs of a new population to a large extent and only some modification, exemplified in the construction of the few passage graves, may have been necessary. On the other hand, there may have been a population shift and an economic change (some indication of this can be inferred from the different relation of monuments to soil type), which could have substantially affected the significance of ritual activities. This problem naturally needs to be investigated further, especially in view of the fact that the decrease in the number of tombs built is not reflected in other spheres of material culture, with ceramic styles being at their most flamboyant and extravagant precisely at this time.

One more aspect needs to be touched upon here. In recent interpretative frameworks the emergence of the so-called formal disposal areas – cemeteries, clusters of tombs and other monuments – has been strongly linked with social stress, exploitation of critical resources and social re-structuring of communities (Chapman 1981). To what extent can the complex ritual landscape observed in the TRB be assumed to represent a complex system of social relations between different population groups? Does the segmentation of the TRB population implied in the tomb distribution reflect the segmentation of the community on a social level? It is generally argued that human groups will express their distinctiveness in times of stress. What is of interest is the fact that, precisely at the time when regional ritual landscapes become manifest, we observe many 'identity' elements: there is a profusion of ceramic styles with rich decoration for ceremonial use, local effort is directed towards the construction and maintenance of tombs, and communal effort is employed in the creation of large public monuments. These elements are usually interpreted as symbols of stress. And yet, not only do we lack evidence of economic stress but also, to the contrary, we must assume a great surplus of the resources which allow the creation of such elaborate phenomena, unless, of course, we assume that such symbols indicate a very prosperous society which finds its egalitarian philosophy stretched to the limits. We shall return to this theme in due course.

10

The social dimensions of the TRB culture

Viewed from an archaeological perspective, prehistoric social systems are usually defined in static terms although it is obvious that in reality they are dynamic states, constantly adjusting in response to various challenges. The pressures placed upon the social system may be ecological, technological, demographic or political in nature; they may be internal or operating from outside, but they will always provoke social response. Furthermore, a society which is in a stage of transition, and which therefore effectively draws upon the social experience of two different systems, the old and the new, will inevitably develop its own social arrangements. These will not merely borrow, but will modify, transform or even deliberately obscure the familiar social institutions in order to meet new circumstances and satisfy new requirements.

These observations are particularly pertinent in the context of the TRB culture. First of all, although the archaeological record of the TRB is in many ways inadequate, the changes evident in its settlement pattern, economic and technological adaptations and ritual tradition leave us without any doubt as to the dynamic nature of this culture. Secondly, if we accept the premise that the emergence of the TRB was the result of a fusion of the hunter–gatherer and early farming communities, then it follows that within its social system we should encounter features characteristic of both types of society; neither would necessarily need to be present in its pristine form.

The aim of this chapter is to discuss the salient features of the social system characteristic of the TRB. However, these cannot be interpreted meaningfully without some perception of the social arrangements operating among the north European hunter-gatherers and the central European farmers, who provide models on which the TRB communities drew for their own social institutions.

10.1 The north European hunter-gatherers

While we remain relatively poorly informed about the social organisation of the late Mesolithic communities of the North European Plain, there is sufficient evidence to suggest that social contacts were frequent and took place over a fairly substantial area. The so-called 'social territories', which are identified by the stylistic similarity of their material culture, are around 100 and 200 km in diameter (Gramsch 1973; Arora 1973; Price 1980) across the North European Plain but somewhat smaller along the Baltic littoral. On ethnographic analogy this range is argued to reveal the maximum band and to represent the highest level of interaction between individual groups.

The manner of such interactions is difficult to ascertain in archaeological evidence, and discussions of prehistoric hunter–gatherer societies regularly stress that the social and ideological aspects of these communities can seldom be perceived. The nature of social institutions which, on ethnographic analogy, are applicable in the hunter-gatherer context, centre around the ritual and ceremonial. Among the largely dispersed populations, ceremonies and rituals provide fundamental mechanisms through which alliances can be maintained with neighbouring groups. Apart from promoting solidarity by integrating individual groups into a wider communal network, they also provide opportunities for arranging marriages and exchanging information and commodities; they allow the display of individual status to a wider audience and, importantly, serve as devices for the solution of disputes and the maintenance of peace.

The specific form of late Mesolithic rituals is not known, but rare discoveries of Mesolithic burials suggest that funerary ceremonies may have provided a focus for ritual activities. The known Mesolithic burials offer only brief glimpses of burial customs and associated rituals, indicating principles of social distinction based on age and sex. Similarities in Mesolithic burial to the west (Brittany: Barrière 1956; Rozoy 1971) and east of the North European Plain (Zvejnieki: Zagorskis 1973; Olenij Ostrow: Kozłowski and Kozłowski 1975) imply that comparable conditions may have prevailed over a substantial area of Europe. This uniformity is a vital clue for our understanding of why, in spite of the considerable geographical distances involved, the subsequent cultural and social changes in northern and western Europe reveal a number of striking similarities.

10.2 *The central European farmers*

The cultural landscape of the central European farmers was dominated by a homestead and/or village of substantial timber houses and an associated range of fields and pastures in close proximity, with the main economic activities limited largely to an ecologically restricted loessic zone. Long-term settlement continuity is documented over most of the area, the settlements being occupied over many generations and houses repaired or rebuilt many times over.

The social organisation of the central European farmers is believed to have been based upon lineages, with a household representing a minimal and a *Siedlungskammer* corresponding to a maximal lineage, although there are differences of opinion as to whether or not such lineages were arranged hierarchically (Hodder 1984; Thomas 1987; Bogucki 1988). The scale of the different economic activities suggests that some may have been organised by individual households (garden horticulture, craft specialisation), while others were the communal responsibility of the entire lineage (maintenance of animal herds). The latter now finds support in the appearance in the archaeological record of enclosure systems, which may have fulfilled both economic and other communal needs.

Many scholars today accept the view that the 'domestic' scene was the important social context among the early farmers and that it constituted a suitable forum for the symbolic expression of the relationship between the basic socio-economic units. The symbolic elaboration of the domestic scene is indicated in the interior arrangement within the houses and in the spatial and functional relation between the households within a village, as well as in the very specific ways in which material culture (particularly pottery) is displayed within and outside the houses (Hodder 1984; Grygiel 1986). When combined, these elements are taken to express symbolically the relationships between various lineages and individual members (men: women, young: old) engaged in competition for the control of major resources, the most prominent being labour and reproduction.

10.3 The TRB culture

Although the degree to which both hunter-gatherers and early farmers contributed to the evolution of the social system within the TRB is difficult to infer directly from the archaeological record, one way of exploring this theme is through an investigation of the ways in which the cultural and ritual landscapes were imposed upon the North European Plain.

Our discussion of the settlement pattern of the TRB (Chapter 7.1) showed that, especially during the formative early period, it differed from that which characterised the central European farming groups. The TRB settlements were more dispersed and located in topographically and ecologically more varied landscapes. The general impression of the TRB settlement is of a continuation of a pattern characteristic of the late Mesolithic groups. Moreover, in the initial stages at least, the sites appear to have been occupied for only relatively short periods of time. The remains of flimsy huts and small houses give little impression of permanence, again being more akin to the late Mesolithic structures than to the solid long houses known from further south. Only when the TRB culture becomes fully established, during the period between 3600/3500 BC and 3200 BC, do we witness the presence of larger sites and permanent structures, although the architecture does not appear to have been influenced by the southern models. It is worthy of note, however, that the establishment of larger sites in the southern distribution of the TRB (Southern and South-eastern groups) may have been accomplished earlier than further north. The closer presence and greater influence of the Lengyel farming communities and different ecological conditions were doubtless important factors in this development.

The available evidence does not, however, indicate the importance of the LBK/Lengyel-style nuclear households. The significant socio–economic unit appears to have been a larger group of several related families evolving from a minimal late Mesolithic band. It is nevertheless highly appropriate to regard the TRB society as based upon lineages, among which ancestral lineal descent was of fundamental importance.

The considerable continuity from the late Mesolithic into the TRB patterns is further highlighted by the wide range of occupied habitats, which correspond with the varied and flexible subsistence basis. In chapter 8.3, it was demonstrated that the reliance upon and exploitation of the various natural resources present across the North European Plain did not cease with the adoption of farming; hunting and gathering accompanied the agricultural and pastoral pursuits. The continued use of previously esta-blished hunting stations is documented in many coastal regions, and similar circumstances probably prevailed along the entire length of the north European lake belt. Temporary camp sites were regularly established in conjunction with various subsistence and craft activities.

This use of the environment on a broad basis demands different social arrangements from those which focus on a network of fields and pastures close to home. It is precisely within the context of these wide-ranging economic pursuits that the knowledge of the ecological as well as the social environment, which the late Mesolithic hunter-gatherers commanded, may have been put to significant use. Knowledge of and access to seasonally exploitable resources, and the extensive information networks within and between the late Mesolithic communities of the North European Plain, would have provided a framework into which a novel economy could successfully be incorporated.

Thus the diffuse nature of the TRB settlement pattern and the at least partially mobile economic basis can be viewed as extensions of the late Mesolithic system. If, given the numerous ethnographic analogies, we accept that ritual and ceremonial institutions – while not strongly manifest in the archaeological record – were also of significance among the dispersed populations of the north European hunter-gatherers, then the initial source of the ritual and ceremonial phenomena of the TRB culture is not difficult to identify. However, the ritual landscape imposed by the TRB populations is of a richness, variety and magnitude not previously encountered in the North European Plain, and its significance can be understood only if interpreted within the social context of the TRB culture itself.

The most dramatic aspect of the TRB's ritual landscape manifests itself in the presence of burial monuments whose architectural variety, burial customs and associated rituals were described in detail in Chapter 9. The monumental burial is complemented by the presence in a number of areas of large 'public ceremonial centres' of an enclosure variety, and less tangibly by the deposition within the landscape of votive pottery offerings as well as flint axes and other hoards (chapters 4.7 and 6.4.3). Although these various phenomena have been described separately, they must now be considered as integral features, combined together in the complex ritual system of the TRB society.

While death is not an everyday occurrence, every society, past and present, has to come to terms with and find a way of dealing with it. There is overwhelming evidence, from the earliest prehistory to modern times, of a variety of human responses ranging from simple, immediate abandonment to elaborate funeral rituals which may span a period of several years (Huntington and Metcalf 1979; Chapman *et al.* 1981). While we cannot pronounce upon the individual human feelings evoked by death and burial within the TRB culture, our discussion should concern the social reasons which, in contrast to other contemporary communities, led to burial ritual assuming such a dominant role across the north European lowland.

Social relations between dispersed populations which are engaged in economic pursuits that involve a constant contradiction between the need for mobility and a permanent presence over a large area, demand social arrangements different from those operating either within communities which focus upon a network of permanent fields and pastures close to home, or within groups that are entirely mobile. Social relations in the TRB culture could not have been regulated on a daily basis when different economic activities separated the community even further. They had to be regulated on occasions when there was the widest and most intensive social contact. It is perhaps not surprising that at least some such occasions would have arisen during burial ceremonies that required the presence of not just the nearest but the furthest of kin. Such occasions, as well as other ceremonies, may already have been a feature of the late Mesolithic hunter-gatherers, and given the initial similarity in the actual burial ritual, may equally represent an extension of an already established custom.

However, the incorporation of an agrarian economy created both problems of competition in exploiting natural resources, and problems of maintaining the right to use land, secure crops and protect animal herds. This is where the social significance of ancestors within simple agrarian communities becomes manifest. The tangible presence of ancestors through formal burial allows the communities to legitimise their claim to specific land as well as the right to use the particular resources of the area. However, in a dispersed settlement system, ancestors' graves must take on some degree of physical prominence and be permanently visible, irrespective of whether or not any given area is currently occupied; in other words, they must become monuments.

Recently, Chapman (1988) has discussed the manner in which a 'space' in the landscape becomes transformed into a 'place' through the regular

performance of activities, and how familiarity with a 'place' may ultimately
lead to an identity with it. 'Space' and 'place', however, are not merely
physical concepts, but also feature within a framework of social relations:
social space offers a dimension within which a range of social activities can
be established and a 'place' may acquire particular social significance. The
evidence presented in Chapter 9 leaves one in little doubt that TRB burial
monuments were an important feature, marking out social space and defining key social places within the landscape. Indeed, a social identity with the
ancestors' tombs which, in contrast to contemporary settlement sites did
not shift within the landscape, offered a focus around which social activities
could centre on a permanent basis.

In simple agrarian societies, moreover, ancestors are perceived as media-
tors between the living and the intangible spirit world. Having a direct
influence upon the daily affairs of the community, the ancestors (and their
tombs) become a suitable forum for the symbolic expression of concepts
significant for many aspects of community life. The symbolic elaboration
of the TRB burial monuments took on a very specific form and it is
important to consider the source of this symbolism.

The idea that the European monumental burial mounds, despite their
extraordinary architectural variety, owe their origin to the central European long houses is nowadays generally accepted. Hodder (1984) outlined
a range of features among the north-west European megaliths which repli-
cate the arrangements characteristic of long houses; detailed arguments for
the derivation of long barrows from long houses have been presented by the
writer in the context of the Kujavian monuments (Midgley 1985, 206–19)
and others have, at various times, expressed similar views (Sprockhoff
1938, Childe 1949b; Glob 1949; Ashbee 1966; 1970; Piggott 1967, Reed
1974, Kinnes 1975, 1981; Marshall 1981). And yet these explanations have
always retained a degree of ambiguity, the link between the houses and the
burial mounds being visible in form but less clearly perceived in social
terms.

Because of the specific settlement pattern and economic structure, there
was little incentive within the TRB to elaborate the domestic sphere which
played such an important role among the farmers living to the south of the
North European Plain. The central European farmers possessed an impressive and powerful symbol in the form of a village of solidly built long
houses. The long houses not only conveyed the more obvious concepts of
permanence and lineage solidarity which could be perceived equally well by
those within as well as outside the system, but also provided a focus for the
symbolic expression of social relations between individuals and lineages
(Hodder 1984).

There should be nothing surprising in the fact that this symbol was
borrowed and transformed from a domestic to a ritual sphere. Copying
from one context to another can express competition between different

communities, or it may enhance the new concepts that are to be symbolised and expressed. That the borrowing was not accidental has been argued by the writer on the basis of the comparable spatial arrangements between the Lengyel villages and the TRB barrow cemeteries in Kujavia, where the two phenomena overlap chronologically (Midgley 1985, 206–19). Indeed, the puzzling exaggerated form of the barrows in this area may be precisely a reflection of such a contextual transference. Once the principle and the symbolic meaning become established, the form may take on a less specific character; this could explain why the more northerly and westerly versions of the TRB burial mound display a somewhat different form. In addition, different local tastes and preferences may also have played a role. Moreover, initially there may even have been a degree of parody or caricature, not only in the exaggeration of the borrowed form, but also in the contrast between the number of individuals who occupied a long house and the number who were placed within the confines of a burial monument.

That the connection between the central European long houses and the TRB burial mounds is not merely coincidental, is illustrated by additional features. Firstly, many of the early TRB mounds were erected upon abandoned TRB settlements (ibid., 49), thus strengthening the symbolic value of the borrowed model and emphasising the link between the place of the living and the place of the dead. Secondly, the material culture of the central European farming communities (especially pottery) played a significant role within the domestic sphere, where it was used symbolically to express the competition between and within lineages in negotiations for power between men and women (Hodder 1984). The symbolic function of material culture is equally strongly manifest in the TRB, where it was employed in a bewildering variety of ways in different rituals. Its symbolism, like that of the houses, was simply borrowed from one context, the domestic, and used in a more appropriate form and in a more suitable context, the ritual.

An additional dimension within the TRB can be perceived in the relationship between monumental burial and material culture, that of consumption. Bradley (1985) has argued that the consumption of labour in the construction of monuments and the consumption of commodities by their withdrawal from circulation, are widespread phenomena of social change. The disposal of vast quantities of flint axes or amber beads in hoards, the phenomenon of votive deposits of pottery in bogs, and at the height of ritualisation the disposal of pottery during ceremonies at tombs or enclosures, all underline the involvement of lineages and individual members in a complex web of social relations.

Once the basic ritual landscape within the TRB is established and its social context confirmed, we observe an intensification of the social function of burial monuments. The increase in social activities takes place against the background of improving technology, greater investment of labour in the economy, clear economic surplus, demographic pressure and an increase in competition within and between groups.

The resultant social change is seen at all levels of the TRB community. The increased disposal of richly decorated pottery in bogs and of axe hoards in similar wet environments, albeit varying in intensity from one area to another, indicates not only the social significance of economically marginal land, but also increased competition for status among individuals. In a pattern of still relatively short-lived settlement, a degree of social stability and lineage solidarity at the local level is achieved by the maintenance of existing monuments and by the extension of local individual ritual centres. The building of new tombs in previously chosen localities, however, also indicates the competition for status with other lineages and is particularly well documented in the architectural development of the tombs. In some areas, such as the Western TRB group, the competition is reflected in the erection of ever longer chambers, while the architectural elaboration of and subsequent change from a 'dolmen' to a 'passage grave' characteristic of the Northern group may express an equally competitive social climate. Indeed, the increased social tension and competition between lineages perhaps offers the best explanation for why the elaborate architectural development of the north European megaliths appears to have been accomplished within an extraordinarily short period of time.

Additionally, we observe a symbolic elaboration through more varied burial rituals and the deposition of vast quantities of exquisitely decorated pottery within and outside the tombs. In the Western TRB this takes the form of the periodic placement of 'service sets' within the chamber (Schlicht 1972; Brindley 1986a), and pottery is sometimes found deliberately smashed on the floor of chambers in central Germany (U. Fischer 1956; Preuss 1973 and 1980) and in Mecklenburg (Schuldt 1972a). In southern Scandinavia this custom is particularly striking, with communal burials inside the chamber and the seemingly deliberate destruction of pottery in designated areas either side of the entrance to the tomb.

While there are still many gaps and inconsistencies within the actual burial record of the TRB, the shift from individual to communal burial observed throughout most of the TRB region (often manifest in the deposition of selected skeletal fragments) may also have been intended to strengthen the lineage solidarity and to mask the increasing status differences between individuals, the communal burial rite being a symbolic denial of reality. The communal burial rite and the associated elaborate rituals, moreover, argue strongly in favour of the importance of ancestral descent and the social significance of the community elders. The latter's access to specific ritual knowledge and contact with ancestors may have provided an important mechanism for social control and for maintaining their position of authority.

On a regional level the social forces are directed towards the construction of large 'public monuments', whose segmentary features have on occasion been interpreted as reflecting the segmentary nature of TRB society. Although the 'public monuments' are a relatively new discovery within the TRB and their currently known distribution is limited (Chapter 7.4), their function in alleviating social tension derived from competition would have been in the collective involvement in construction and the massive consumption of both labour and other commodities. This is evident as much in Scandinavia as in central Germany. The importance of larger regional units in the social relations of the TRB is further emphasised not only in the regional architectural styles of burial monuments, but also in the distribution of ceramic styles throughout the area.

The highly decorated character of the TRB pottery of this period has already been discussed in some detail (Chapter 4.4.3) and a number of reasons have been suggested for a swift and widespread acceptance of certain forms and motifs. Gebauer's (1984) stylistic study of the Danish TRB pottery demonstrated that, even when stylistic differentiation is at its height, the style groups cover substantial geographical areas which cannot be correlated with local groupings (such as may be represented by individual local centres). Similar conclusions of a significant function in social intergration, cross-cutting the residential units, have been reached in J. Voss' (1982) study of pottery from the Western TRB group.

Thus we may point to the multi-level significance and symbolism of the TRB pottery. On a local level it is incorporated into a tomb-oriented ritual where, similarly to the LBK, it may have been employed in context of male/female opposition. However, its use as a medium for exchange of social information on a regional level and its stylistic similarity over large areas emphasise the essentially contradictory need for social affiliation and social integration on a level above that of the local lineage.

In regions where evidence for burial monuments is incomplete (the Eastern and South-eastern TRB) or where for geological reasons the construction of stone-built chambers was largely augmented by the erection of other forms (Southern TRB), there are nevertheless some indications of competition and social stress. A number of south-eastern TRB settlements appear to have been abandoned as a result of attack (Chapter 7.2) and others may yet prove to have been surrounded by defensive structures. From the same area there are a number of large flat grave cemeteries where unusual ritual involved the deliberate mutilation of bodies and where groups of individual graves were brought together under a common mantle of stones or a low mound. Moreover, on a number of sites in the Eastern, South-eastern and Southern TRB settlement, elaborate vessels were being used in rituals which sometimes involved the 'consumption' of agricultural produce, or in which they were apparently being deliberately destroyed. While the precise interpretation of this somewhat disparate evidence is still difficult, such activities may reflect social conditions similar to those of the more northerly regions of the TRB.

As the economic demands and other pressures increased beyond the point where they could be controlled ritually, we see a different social response. The settlement pattern becomes more nucleated with larger, permanently occupied sites. The domestic architecture of the late TRB is still imperfectly known, but in some areas at least there appears to be a trend towards larger and more solidly built houses. It is perhaps not inappropriate to suggest that these settlements were occupied by the lineages which, through skilful negotiation in rituals, emerged successful from the previously competitive period. Moreover, just as during the early TRB many burial mounds were erected upon abandoned settlements, so now the situation is reversed: many late TRB settlements are consciously located on or in the vicinity of previous ritual sites. The settlement pattern of the TRB culture appears to have come full circle.

While in some areas of the TRB the previously built tombs continue to be used for burial, they are no longer constructed. Elsewhere less ambitious versions are being built and most of the burial-associated ritual loses its importance. Throughout the whole area of the TRB the pottery loses most of its distinctive character, regional styles by and large disappear and vessels are no longer very important in rituals. Similarly axes are no longer disposed of in hoards. Both axes and a small quantity of pottery are used as grave goods, but axes now replace pottery in placements in front of tombs, although the overall frequency of such deposits decreases dramatically. The removal of pottery from rituals suggests that in the fundamental social context of reproduction, the role of women may have diminished; land has become a far more important commodity than labour.

Material culture is now found in large quantities on settlements and it is evident that few goods are deliberately taken out of circulation. The symbolism of material culture does continue to some extent, although it now appears within the domestic context and unusual vessels (hanging vessels, drums, ram-handle pots) are known from late TRB sites.

The discussion of the social dimensions within the TRB culture has deliberately focused on the general appearance of the society. Many aspects of social behaviour and specific social strategies remain ambivalent, but the overall picture is relatively clear. While the precise contribution of each remains a matter of debate, the emergence of the TRB culture social system represents a fusion of two fundamentally different systems: the north European hunter-gatherers and the central European farmers. Moreover, it represents the development, out of familiar social experiences, of a new set of behavioural rules and strategies which, through time, deviated even further from the original models.

TRB society can be described as tribal in the sense that it was composed of individual local groups of ancestral descent (lineages) in which the principal authority appears to have rested with the elders. However, the lineages' independence was typically limited by the need for integration on a larger, regional scale through economic exchange and social affiliation. All these major characteristics become clearly visible in the investigation of the links between the economy, settlement, ritual practices and the use of material culture. The temporal dimension of these links, spanning a period of one and a half millennia, demonstrates moreover that the TRB social system, far from being static, possessed an inner dynamic which manifested itself in the initial establishment of a set of rules and social strategies, their intensification and their subsequent demise, all within a single cultural context.

All too often a prehistoric social system is described in static terms and it is the emergence of a new cultural complex that is taken to indicate social change. In the case of the TRB it has been argued on a number of occasions that the emergence of the Corded Ware culture was of considerable significance in the social transformations of northern Europe. But when the evidence for the social arrangements in TRB society is examined against the changing economic and cultural background, the transient nature of its social system is more than apparent.

The subsequent appearance in northern Europe of the large complex known as Corded Ware was preceded by the relatively brief and geographically less extensive Globular Amphora culture. The emergence of the latter, precisely in the area which is regarded as the 'cradle' of the TRB culture, implies that much of the 'new' social character was already present in the final stages of the TRB and was merely developed along new trajectories leading, ultimately, to the vastly increased social network characteristic of the Corded Ware culture. Among the more significant patterns we may perhaps include a shift towards the recognition of the individual through an increased presence of small single graves, even if initially these form cemeteries (cf. the Herrup stone-packing graves; Chapter 9.1). While the late TRB ceramics lose the vitality and flamboyance of the earlier styles, their geographical extent is considerably larger, suggesting an increased scale of regional and inter-regional contacts. It is these patterns that provide the social foundations for the emergence of new systems across the north European lowland. For too long the crucial difference between social change and cultural change has been obscured by a specific 'cultural' label. The transient nature of TRB society bears witness to the independent dynamics of prehistoric social systems.

11

Conclusions and summary

The available radiocarbon dates from various TRB cultural contexts throughout the area of its distribution offer us a reasonable basis upon which to order its internal chronology and to date its beginning as well as its end (see Chapter 5 and Appendix). We can now say with some confidence that in the areas between the lower Elbe and the middle Vistula rivers the TRB culture emerges soon after 4500 BC. In the same area it comes to an end at around 2900 BC, although small local enclaves may have continued until 2750 BC. Moreover in the western and northern distribution areas the TRB appears to have been present until 2850/2650 BC.

However, neither the beginning nor the end of this cultural complex can be defined in simple terms. The various themes discussed in this work demonstrate that the emergence of the TRB culture was the consequence of a complex relationship between the lowland hunter-gatherers and the neighbouring southerly farmers. This relationship cannot as yet be defined clearly in all its aspects, but ultimately it led to the development of a novel set of social and economic phenomena which shaped the cultural scene of northern Europe for a period of one and a half millennia. The demise of the TRB culture presents us with an equally difficult process which is even less clearly perceived in the archaeological record and whose interpretation remains largely intuitive. The problem of the TRB's end is further obscured by the presence of several cultural groups: not only the Corded Ware culture, which was the successor of the TRB, but also the Globular Amphora culture in the central area of the TRB's distribution, and in the southerly regions the northward influences of the Baden (Radial Ware) culture, although the latter appears to have had a minimal effect on the TRB culture as a whole.

These few concluding pages do not offer an opportunity to become involved in a detailed discussion of the relationship between the TRB and the Globular Amphora and Corded Ware cultures, nor in a review of the polemical discussion concerning the interpretation of these new complexes. The European Corded Ware culture forms the subject of the author's current research, the results of which will be presented in due course. Thus, rather than becoming embroiled in the minute comparisons of similarities and differences, we shall consider this transition through the broad perspective of cultural change that was taking place in the late Neolithic.

The *Globular Amphora culture* (3200/3100–2700 BC) is known in the archaeological record primarily from its material culture and characteristic rituals; generally less is known about the various aspects of its settlement and economy. Among the leading pottery forms there are various bowls and amphorae; the eponymous form is the most common. Flint axes and chisels are commonly found on settlements and in burials, although apparently battle axes were not fashionable and only their miniature amber imitations seem to have been employed in rituals. For funerary purposes the dead were either placed in stone cists sometimes covered by low mounds, or in areas where they were present, secondary use was made of stone-built megalithic chambers. In many areas where the Globular Amphora culture is found, there is also evidence of animal burials, especially cattle. The economy appears to have been based on cereal growing and animal husbandry; the animal burials suggest that cattle may have been of particular significance, although there is no evidence to imply a pastoral economy.

In the initial stage of its development the Globular Amphora culture is found in the areas of Mecklenburg, Brandenburg, Pomerania, Greater Poland and Kujavia although ultimately its distribution extended considerably further south and east (Wiślański 1966; 1979, 261–99). A small presence of the Globular Amphora culture can be noted in Schleswig-Holstein (Hoika 1987, 99–101) and Lower Saxony (Nelson 1988, 125–7), but it played no significant role in the areas of the Northern and Western TRB groups. The few vessels characteristic of this culture in Denmark (Ebbesen 1975, 226–40) must be seen purely as the results of exchange and contacts between neighbouring populations, just as the apparent influence of the Globular Amphora wares on the late TRB ceramics in the Western group has been interpreted by Bakker (1979, 134–5) as evidence for sporadic contacts rather than close cultural relationships.

The very complex socio-cultural conditions which must have prevailed over much of the north European lowland do not exclude the possibility that in the shadow of the developing TRB there remained local populations which did not belong to it formally. Such groups may have shared some of its cultural elements, such as pottery or basic tools, yet at the same time retained many aspects of the traditional hunter-gatherer way of life. Evidence discussed in Chapters 2.1 and 8.5 suggests that some hunter-gatherers may have co-existed alongside the northern farming populations. It is among these rather shadowy figures, perhaps in conjunction with the final and by now largely displaced post-LBK populations, that we should look for the origins of the Globular Amphora culture. Interestingly, while there is little evidence of the Globular Amphora culture in southern Scandinavia, the presence of the Pitted Ware culture may well represent a related phenomenon.

However, we should not regard the Globular Amphora culture as a successor to the TRB, but rather as a cultural complex that arose alongside, under the direct stimulus and influence of the TRB populations. In many ways it imitates the TRB, but it is also sufficiently independent to have developed individual customs and traditions. The evidence from the TRB itself indicates that after a period of dynamic development in the socio-cultural sphere, when without any doubt it was a leading cultural force on the North European Plain, it acquired a tendency towards disunity and began to break up into smaller groups of purely local significance. However, while the emergence of the Globular Amphora culture may have accelerated this disintegration process, and doubtless substantially curtailed the TRB's activities in the area between the lower Elbe and middle Vistula, the underlying reasons for the TRB's demise lay not in the presence of another cultural group, but in the course upon which the TRB populations themselves had embarked.

It is at this point that we may turn to the *Corded Ware culture* (3000/ 2800–2300 BC) which represents one of the most studied but also one of the least understood complexes of the late European Neolithic. In Denmark it is usually referred to as the Single Grave culture (*Enkeltgravskultur*), and in Sweden as the Battle Axe culture (*Stridsyxekultur*). The term Protruding Foot Beaker culture (*Standvoetbeker cultuur*) is regularly used in Holland, while in the remaining area of its vast distribution either it is known as the Corded Ware culture, or occasionally a local name (such as the Złota culture or the Rzucewo culture) is applied.

The distribution of the Corded Ware culture varies in accordance with the classificatory procedures adopted by individual scholars, although its manifestation in one form or another can be perceived over a large area between the North Sea, southern Scandinavia, the Russian Plain and most of central Europe as far south as the Alps (Krzak 1980). While there is considerable differentiation between the local Corded Ware groups, the principal features which tend to be prominent throughout this vast area include cord decorated vessels (especially beakers), asymmetrical battle axes, individual inhumations under small round barrows, a dispersed settlement pattern and the importance of livestock in the overall economy.

One of the problems facing scholars of the Corded Ware culture is the origin of this complex, although the more fanciful notions of horse-mounted Eastern warriors have now been abandoned and an autochthonous evolution within a local context is regarded now as a more appropriate working concept. Other problems include the interpretation of the so-called pan-European horizon (identified on the basis of a beaker, A-type amphora and A-type battle axe), the central European horizon (identified by the common herringbone decorative pattern and multi-facetted battle axe) and the more or less contemporary emergence of numerous local groups (Machnik 1979; Van der Waals 1985).

One notion which explicitly or implicitly emerges in many discussions of the Corded Ware culture is the idea of discontinuity with the preceding period and the appearance in much of northern and central Europe of a new set of cultural patterns. However, the discontinuity in the archaeological record apparent in northern Europe at the beginning of the TRB culture can be interpreted as a result of developments which involved locally available patterns that became fundamentally altered in the face of the new socio-economic problems and challenges presenting themselves to the varied north European populations. Such an interpretation offers an alternative explanation for the apparent discontinuity by emphasising that its source may lie within the local traditions rather than being an external factor.

It is thus possible to offer a similar interpretation of the emergence of the late Neolithic cultural pattern in Europe. With regard to the basic material culture neither the beaker, nor the amphora, nor battle axes nor the use of cord in decoration can be regarded as new elements, although clearly they acquire a different significance. Moreover, the changes which take place in the material culture, and in the way it appears to be used symbolically during the late TRB, herald the developments which become so manifest in the Corded Ware culture. Many of these changes have been noted in discussing the various themes throughout this work; the most important will be reiterated here.

Thus we observe the blurring of regional boundaries, previously sharply defined through numerous contemporary ceramic styles, which in the late TRB were replaced by less distinctive pottery. We may further recall the withdrawal of pottery from ceremonial use and its replacement by tools and weapons, a feature especially prominent in the context of the northern stone-packing graves but also noted in the late deposits at megaliths.

Turning now to the economy, the opening up of the landscape by the TRB populations created opportunities for the exploitation of a much wider environment than was available to the early Neolithic farmers in central Europe. Moreover, the TRB populations also incorporated into their economy many agricultural innovations. As we have already seen, the use of the plough and animal traction led to more intensive cereal-growing, while the exploitation of such secondary products as milk or wool changed the overall role of animals in the economy. These developments also required an increase in the size of herds, which in turn led to the demand for larger expanses of grazing land. It is these innovations, so successfully applied by the TRB and their contemporaries throughout much of northern and central Europe, that led to the ultimate development of the subsistence patterns characteristic of many Corded Ware groups.

We have already dwelled at some length on the social change perceivable within the late TRB (Chapter 10). We noted, among other things, a decreasing emphasis on the 'communal' (the abandonment of megalith construction and use of ceremonial places) and the steadily growing emphasis on the 'individual'. Again, the northern stone-packing graves are a good example of this transition where both elements are in fact given expression: they are individual graves but still within a communal setting. There is similar evidence for a slow shift towards single inhumation burials throughout the late TRB, for example the graves in the late TRB cemetery at Heek (Finke 1984) or the very late burials from the Radziejów group in the Eastern TRB; the latter, incidentally, were accompanied by sacrificial animal burials (Kośko 1988, 95). There can be little doubt that it is within the late TRB that we should look for the causes of the wide-ranging changes that occurred over much of northern and central Europe during the early 3rd millennium BC.

Naturally, the response of specific populations would have varied from region to region; such regional differentiation is evident as much in the TRB culture as it is characteristic of the Corded Ware groups. Nor was this response necessarily synchronous. The available C-14 dates (see Appendix) show that this transition takes place from about 3000 to 2800 BC, although many areas, such as northern Germany and Poland, lack a sufficient series of radiocarbon determinations to enable us to define this transition more clearly. The pattern of gradual change from the TRB to the Corded Ware is well supported by the dating of these two complexes in the Netherlands, where one can point to an overlap of about 150 years.

The situation in southern Scandinavia is generally interpreted as reflecting a complete substitution of the TRB by the Corded Ware with no co-existence between the two; only a very slight overlap between the Store Valby period and the Underground Grave period is accepted by some scholars (Malmros and Tauber 1977; Davidsen 1982; Ebbesen 1984). A few comments are therefore necessary here. As already noted in Chapter 5 there is in fact an overlap of dates from 2850 BC (K-2501, which is the earliest Corded Ware date from Denmark) to about 2650 BC (K-1843), although the remainder of the Danish Corded Ware dates are younger. This overlap is moreover very significant in the context of our interpretation of the way in which the process of change began in the late TRB. Unless we revive the now-abandoned concept of a 'migration' of Corded Ware into Denmark, we must expect some sort of overlap since a new cultural complex does not emerge overnight. It is also significant that our review of the late TRB chronology has shown that settlement dates consistently provide younger values than those from burials. In a recent review of the Neolithic on the southern Danish islands, Skaarup (1985, 379–86) has argued that there is no dramatic change between the TRB and Corded Ware in this area, but rather that one can point to a continuity of settlement and even of the basic material (such as flint assemblages) and that some change in the economy (for example from wheat to barley) is already visible in the TRB. He also noted that of the forty-five Corded Ware burials only seven are not associated with megaliths and that the custom of grave goods including axes and chisels, characteristic of the late TRB and early Corded Ware, makes it very difficult to distinguish which secondary burial in a chambered tomb belongs to which culture. When we remind ourselves of the vast evidence for the secondary use of megalithic chambers throughout Denmark, it is possible to suggest that we have simply failed to recognise, or else wholly misinterpreted, the emergence of the Corded Ware culture in southern Scandinavia, by taking its manifestation in the developed form (the Undergrave period) for its beginning.

This discussion of the transition from the TRB to Corded Ware returns us to a problem which is of regular concern to all archaeologists: the question of culture change. This is neither a new problem nor one for which a universal model has yet been arrived at, with the interpretative frameworks ranging from the earlier theories of outside influence such as migration and diffusion, to the more recent emphasis upon change from within, expressed by the wide range of ecological, social and ideological paradigms.

However, in any attempt to determine what causes cultural change it is necessary to examine the entire culture and not just some of its components. Such an investigation discourages monocausal explanations (a pertinent example in the context of the TRB culture is the premise that a decline in oyster resources along the Danish coast triggered the introduction of a farming economy into this region; Rowley-Conwy 1984 and 1985) and stimulates an enquiry into the dynamics of the entire cultural system. It scrutinises the relationship between the individual components – material culture, crafts and industries, economy, settlement and ritual practices – within a specific context which was significant to the prehistoric people involved, and it permits us to observe the process in which these individual components influenced one another.

The recognition of the cultural dynamics of the TRB culture is perhaps the most significant observation emerging from the investigation of the TRB culture offered in the preceding chapters. The case for a constantly evolving character of this complex is in fact so strong that one feels compelled to risk suggesting a concept of changing culture, rather than cultural change, as a more appropriate interpretative model.

This process of change involves all the cultural elements discussed, and each of the four suggested chronological phases in the TRB is characterised by its own configuration of relationships between material culture, settlement patterns, the economy and ritual manifestations; development from one phase to the next is a direct result of mutual influences operating within the entire system.

The reader may well enquire as to the purpose of following through in such detail the study of one particular complex, and wonder about the implications of a study such as this for current concerns of archaeological interpretation. As a reaction against the limited and rather specific purpose of processual archaeology there has been, among European archaeologists, a renewed interest in the contribution which archaeology should be making towards a broader historical debate. The last few years have witnessed the reintroduction of historical analysis to archaeology, with the writings of Childe (1925; 1936; 1949a; 1951), Collingwood (1946) and Braudel (1973) providing some of the interpretative frameworks. While on the one hand this clearly represents a return to some of the paradigms which were widely held by European scholars prior to the impact of New Archaeology, the latter, while now itself overtaken by new theoretical developments, has contributed very considerably to the broader archaeological discussions of today by tackling fields of enquiry previously regarded as outwith the scope of archaeology.

However, if archaeologists are to make a contribution to long-term history, then one of our first tasks must be to refamiliarise ourselves with the overall body of archaeological data and not confine outselves to one or two currently fashionable themes, be it the economy, social structure or any other. Unlike previous approaches, we must go beyond the passive record-ing and description of overall data and become involved in actively knowing and understanding the past, looking with interpretative insight into the past events as they reveal themselves through the archaeological record. It is within this framework of enquiry that the study of one entire cultural complex assumes a new significance.

Drawing upon the work of Braudel (1973), Ian Hodder (1987) em-phasised a number of concepts of particular relevance to archaeology's contribution to history. Thus, he referred to the long-term continuum, to structural/social history, and to the individual and the specific event as three fundamental scales of historical analysis particularly relevant to archaeology. Within the context of our investigation of the TRB culture these three levels of inquiry are particularly well documented and it is the pursuit of these themes that will serve as the conclusion to this study.

Understanding the role of the natural environment and its formative contribution to the trajectories of cultural development of past, as well as present, societies is now recognised as a fundamental factor in the study of human development. Thus, it is worth re-emphasising the significance of the geographical background against which the TRB culture emerges. The distribution of the TRB encompasses two environmentally different zones, with the Northern, Eastern and Western groups occupying the diverse habitats of the North European Plain, and the Southern and South-eastern groups settling the less differentiated and already partially open environ-ments of the central European loess belt. These environmental differences had a profound influence on the way in which the settlement patterns and economy of the TRB developed. The geographical distinction between the southern 'upland' and the northern 'lowland' TRB is therefore directly related to the natural landscape which influenced the distinctly different trends underlying the socio-economic development of the TRB in these two zones.

Indeed, this is a pattern that can be traced further back. It reveals itself in the distinctive pattern of hunting and gathering groups across the North European Plain and their more elusive presence further south, where instead a strong element of the LBK and post-LBK offered a differential input into the social and economic structures discussed previously. One could also point to the communication routes as another long-term influence, with the major rivers of the North European Plain fulfilling the dual role of north–south contact routes and east–west oriented boundaries. These patterns transcend any specific chronological span.

In the context of the socio-structural level of analysis, the most significant observation relates once more to the cultural dynamics of the TRB. This dynamic character has already been observed, but it should be noted that it is precisely the merging together of different cultural components that refutes the statics of archaeological evidence and confirms the changing character of the culture.

To illustrate this point we may first of all recall the relationship between the various cultural components of the early TRB phase (4000/3900–3600 BC). The fleeting settlement pattern of this period enhances our understanding of the economic development as well as of the emerging social structure of the TRB. Conversely, the manner in which elements of the farming economy were incorporated into the traditional hunter-gatherer pursuits across the North European Plain could not be appreciated fully without an understanding of the settlement pattern. The significance of the settlement pattern at this stage is moreover enhanced by our observation of the contemporary ritual landscape, whose permanence counterbalances the fleeting character of settlement sites. Both demonstrate the contribution from hunter-gatherers and farmers to the emerging social structure of the TRB.

One further important consequence of the holistic investigation of the TRB culture in a long-term perspective is the recognition of the subtle interplay between the economic and ritual (social) landscapes and the way in which new meanings were demonstrably imposed upon the existing patterns. The social and economic landscapes are interlocked in an intricate web of relationships offering scope for the interpretation of the ways in which individuals, by coming together or moving apart, shaped their destinies.

The concept of a landscape being perceived as a place (or collection of places) whose significance alters in harmony with changes in technology and social structure has already been mentioned. To illustrate this point we need only recall that, during the earlier period of the TRB, tombs were located on briefly occupied and then abandoned settlements, a phenomenon seen as clearly in Kujavia as in Jutland; the regular placement of the Dutch *hunebedden* on old pastures may well be one of many permutations of this process. This pattern is seemingly reversed during the later TRB, when large ceremonial centres, such as Sarup or Dölauer Heide, appear to be abandoned in their ceremonial role and, instead, assume domestic functions. These, however, are not random or accidental occurrences; the domestic/ritual ritual/domestic dichotomy, which integrates the entire landscape through the process of votive and hoard deposits, demonstrates a structural pattern in which continuity is masked by apparent change. The use of the landscape, however, is not broken; it does not become 'abandoned' but its various parts take on a new, different meaning. It is through the change in the function of sites, and thus the change in their meaning, that individuals express their participation in and reaction to the social and economic changes within the community.

We could hardly assess the function of the material culture of the TRB by pursuing only the stylistic analysis of pottery or the typological development of flint axes. At various times individuals, singly or in groups, bestow meaning on the material culture by integrating it with the ritual sphere, thereby investing it with a social significance that is understood by the entire community. At other times, this same material culture is returned to its domestic sphere with its associated, somewhat mundane functions. It is through these changes that we are able to interpret the multi-functional role of the material culture in the TRB. The hoards and votive offerings, present most distinctly in times marked by little communal activity, underline the individual involvement in and reaction to the constraints and opportunities of this particular socio-economic system.

It is in this spirit of integration of individual occurrences and their temporally and spatially cumulative effects that this study of the TRB culture has been presented. It is hoped that the study of this common totality of events, actions and their tangible symbols, which constituted the cultural unity of northern Europe of that time, will stimulate new thoughts and encourage further debate, thereby contributing to the historical interpretation of past societies.

Appendix: TRB culture radiocarbon dates

The dates are expressed in radiocarbon years BP and have been calibrated to dendro-years using the calibration Algorithm of Robinson (1984). To account for the effects of isotopic fractionation the relevant C-14 dates of marine shells have been adjusted by eighty years and this is indicated by *.

Eastern TRB group dates

Sarnowo phase

1	Sarnowo	GrN-5035	5570 ± 60	BP	4417 ± 60	BC

Pikutkowo phase

2	Nowy Młyn	Lod-20	4950 ± 20	BP	3752 ± 95	BC
3	Pikutkowo	GrN-13354	4950 ± 60	BP	3752 ± 66	BC
4	Wietrzychowice	Lod-60	5170 ± 180	BP	3991 ± 203	BC

Wiórek phase

5	Dąbrowa Biskupia	?	4870 ± 80	BP	3670 ± 91	BC
6	Inowrocław Mątwy	Bln-1314	4580 ± 50	BP	3329 ± 79	BC
7	Opatowice 7	Gd-2765	4840 ± 80	BP	3637 ± 96	BC
8	Radziejów	M-1846	4860 ± 200	BP	3647 ± 231	BC
9	Radziejów	GrN-5045	4710 ± 40	BP	3747 ± 84	BC
10	Radziejów	Lod-1	4670 ± 380	BP	3397 ± 467	BC
11	Radziejów	M-1845	4590 ± 190	BP	3314 ± 255	BC
12	Zarębowo	GrN-5044	4625 ± 40	BP	3380 ± 50	BC
13	Zberzyn	Lod-159	4720 ± 110	BP	3490 ± 141	BC

Luboń phase

14	Mrowino	GrN-14017	4480 ± 35	BP	3165 ± 90	BC
15	Opatowice	Gd-2764	4460 ± 80	BP	3133 ± 142	BC
16	Opatowice	Lod-20	4320 ± 180	BP	2953 ± 239	BC
17	Ustowo	Bln-1807	4510 ± 80	BP	3214 ± 140	BC

Miscellaneous TRB dates (Western Pomerania and Mecklenburg)

18	Gnewitz	Bln-472	4250 ± 100	BP	2900 ± 125	BC
19	Łupawa	Gd-1905	5170 ± 50	BP	3982 ± 62	BC
20	Łupawa	Bln-1870	4510 ± 60	BP	3218 ± 119	BC
21	Łupawa	Bln-1495	4295 ± 70	BP	2911 ± 80	BC
22	Łupawa	Bln-1313	4025 ± 60	BP	2568 ± 98	BC
23	Schönermark	KN-?	5100 ± 70	BP	3913 ± 86	BC

Northern I TRB group dates (Schleswig-Holstein)

Rosenhof phase

24	Rosenhof	KN-?	5410	± 80	BP	4274 ± 90	BC
25	Rosenhof	KN-?	5390	± 80	BP	4253 ± 96	BC
26	Rosenhof	KN-I.500	5380	± 40	BP	4248 ± 58	BC
27	Rosenhof	KN-2135	5370	± 50	BP	4235 ± 70	BC
28	Rosenhof	KN-2334	5340	± 55	BP	4196 ± 82	BC
29	Rosenhof	KN-?	5230	± 80	BP	4053 ± 107	BC
30	Rosenhof	KN-?	5200	± 80	BP	4018 ± 102	BC

Siggeneben-Süd phase

31	Bistoft	KI 1285	5180	± 60	BP	3993 ± 76	BC
32	Siggeneben-Süd	KN-2273	5690	± 60	BP	4552 ± 82	BC
33	Siggeneben-Süd	KN-2425	5280	± 55	BP	4155 ± 91	BC
34	Siggeneben-Süd	KN-2267	5180	± 65	BP	3990 ± 82	BC
35	Siggeneben-Süd	KN-2271	5170	± 70	BP	3983 ± 87	BC
36	Siggeneben-Süd	KN-2111	5150	± 60	BP	3961 ± 76	BC
37	Siggeneben-Süd	KN-2268	5070	± 80	BP	3876 ± 94	BC
38	Siggeneben-Süd	KN-2269	5060	± 65	BP	3865 ± 81	BC
39	Siggeneben-Süd	KN-2272	4990	± 75	BP	3793 ± 84	BC
40	Siggeneben-Süd	KN-2405	4910	± 60	BP	3713 ± 65	BC

Satrup phase

41	Bistoft	KI 921.01	4700	± 65	BP	3466 ± 96	BC
42	Bistoft	KI 1231	4680	± 60	BP	3441 ± 88	BC
43	Heidmoor	H491?46	5140	± 115	BP	3954 ± 134	BC
44	Heidmoor	H30145	5020	± 105	BP	3825 ± 114	BC
45	Heidmoor	Y-443b	4530	± 170	BP	3235 ± 237	BC
46	Heidmoor	Y-443h	4210	± 80	BP	2818 ± 106	BC
47	Südensee Damm	Y-472	4960	± 50	BP	3762 ± 58	BC
48	Südensee Damm	KN-667	4830	± 70	BP	3627 ± 86	BC
49	Südensee Damm	GrN-6589	4815	± 65	BP	3611 ± 84	BC
50	Südensee Damm	GrN-6592	4800	± 85	BP	3590 ± 108	BC
51	Südensee Damm	KN-138	4740	± 75	BP	3517 ± 107	BC
52	Südensee Damm	GrN-6591	4710	± 85	BP	3480 ± 116	BC
53	Südensee Damm	KN-666	4610	± 60	BP	3361 ± 82	BC

Fuchsberg phase

54	Fuchsberg	KN-?	4860	± 80	BP	3659 ± 92	BC

Later TRB in Schleswig-Holstein

55	Bistoft	KI 1231	4610	± 120	BP	3350 ± 169	BC
56	Neukirchen Sütel	H-922	4490	± 60	BP	3184 ± 122	BC
57	Oldenburg Dannau	KN I.506	4400	± 40	BP	3022 ± 74	BC
58	Heringsdorf Süssau	KN I.494	4410	± 40	BP	3037 ± 79	BC
59	Heringsdorf Süssau	KN I.512	4400	± 40	BP	3022 ± 74	BC
60	Heringsdorf Süssau	KN I.508	4390	± 40	BP	3007 ± 68	BC
61	Heringsdorf Süssau	KN I.507	4370	± 45	BP	2984 ± 65	BC
62	Heringsdorf Süssau	KN I.458	3960	± 45	BP	2487 ± 48	BC
63	Heringsdorf Süssau	KN I.491	3950	± 40	BP	2478 ± 42	BC
64	Heringsdorf Süssau	KN I.425	3770	± 80	BP	2210 ± 129	BC

Northern II TRB group dates (southern Scandinavia)

Oxie group

65 Dragsholm	K-2291	4840 ± 100 BP	3634 ± 117 BC
66 Muldbjerg	K-129	4940 ± 160 BP	3740 ± 176 BC
67 Muldbjerg	K-128	4910 ± 160 BP	3706 ± 178 BC
68 Muldbjerg	K-126	4880 ± 170 BP	3672 ± 193 BC
69 Muldbjerg	K-127	4850 ± 120 BP	3643 ± 138 BC
70 Muldbjerg	K-125	4840 ± 170 BP	3627 ± 197 BC
71 Muldbjerg	K-132	4660 ± 150 BP	3412 ± 199 BC
72 Muldbjerg	K-131	4610 ± 150 BP	3346 ± 206 BC
73 Muldbjerg	K-124	4600 ± 170 BP	3330 ± 231 BC
74 Värby V22	KN-103	4900 ± 120 BP	3698 ± 133 BC

Svaleklint group

75 Jordløse Mose XV	K-3776	4980 ± 65 BP	3783 ± 74 BC
76 Lindebjerg	K-1695	5010 ± 100 BP	3814 ± 109 BC
77 Øgårde	K-4333	5060 ± 65 BP	3865 ± 81 BC
78 Præstelyngen	K-1473	5010 ± 100 BP	3814 ± 109 BC
79 Præstelyngen	K-2057	4950 ± 100 BP	3752 ± 108 BC
80 Præstelyngen	K-1656	4890 ± 110 BP	3689 ± 123 BC
81 Præstelyngen	K-2056	4830 ± 100 BP	3623 ± 119 BC
82 Præstelyngen	K-2058	4790 ± 100 BP	3577 ± 125 BC
83 Rude	K-3124	4910 ± 90 BP	3711 ± 99 BC
84 Rude	K-3125	4810 ± 70 BP	3604 ± 91 BC
85 Sølager	K-1724	4650 ± 100 BP	3405 ± 136 BC
86 Thimsens Torveskaer	K-3775	4950 ± 65 BP	3753 ± 72 BC
87 Ulkestrup Lyng	K-3778	4860 ± 135 BP	3653 ± 154 BC

Volling group

88 Barkær	K-?	5150 ± 80 BP	3961 ± 97 BC
89 Konens Høj	K-919	4850 ± 100 BP	3645 ± 116 BC
90 Mosegården	K-3463	5080 ± 90 BP	3887 ± 103 BC
91 Mosegården	K-3464	4890 ± 90 BP	3690 ± 100 BC
92 Norsminde	K-2192	4960 ± 100 BP	3763 ± 108 BC
93 Norsminde	K-2190	4750 ± 80 BP	3530 ± 110 BC
94 Norsminde	K-2191	4740 ± 80 BP	3518 ± 111 BC
95 Norsminde	K-2189	4710 ± 80 BP	3480 ± 110 BC
96 Rustrup	K-2254	4970 ± 100 BP	3773 ± 108 BC
97 Rustrup	K-2255	4920 ± 100 BP	3721 ± 109 BC
98 Rustrup	K-2253	4910 ± 100 BP	3710 ± 110 BC
99 Vroue Hede	K-2428	4740 ± 100 BP	3517 ± 129 BC
100 Vroue Hede	K-2424	4660 ± 100 BP	3418 ± 135 BC

Virum group

101 Bygholm Nørremark	K-3473	4740 ± 90 BP	3517 ± 119 BC
102 Lohals	K-2277	4620 ± 100 BP	3367 ± 140 BC
103 Maglelyng	K-3779	4700 ± 65 BP	3466 ± 96 BC
104 Ølstykke	K-2356	4710 ± 100 BP	3480 ± 131 BC

Fuchsberg group

105 Kellerød	K-3515	4490 ± 65 BP	3183 ± 127 BC
106 Klokkehøj	K-2954	4550 ± 65 BP	3281 ± 112 BC
107 Sarup	K-2632	4760 ± 90 BP	3542 ± 118 BC
108 Sarup	K-2629	4690 ± 90 BP	3456 ± 120 BC
109 Sarup	K-2631	4620 ± 90 BP	3368 ± 126 BC

110	Sarup	K-2630	4600 ± 90	BP	3342 ± 130 BC
111	Sarup	K-2628	4580 ± 70	BP	3321 ± 107 BC
112	Sarupgård	K-3491	4390 ± 80	BP	3025 ± 122 BC
113	Toftum	K-2981	4770 ± 70*	BP	3556 ± 99 BC
114	Toftum	K-2988	4730 ± 90	BP	3505 ± 120 BC
115	Toftum	K-2986	4690 ± 90	BP	3456 ± 120 BC
116	Toftum	K-2987	4680 ± 90	BP	3443 ± 121 BC
117	Toftum	K-2983	4670 ± 90*	BP	3431 ± 121 BC
118	Toftum	K-2982	4630 ± 90*	BP	3382 ± 124 BC
119	Toftum	K-2979	4620 ± 70	BP	3371 ± 96 BC
120	Toftum	K-2984	4610 ± 85*	BP	3357 ± 120 BC
121	Toftum	K-2980	4600 ± 85*	BP	3344 ± 122 BC
122	Toftum	K-2978	4580 ± 85	BP	3317 ± 127 BC
123	Toftum	K-2985	4500 ± 85	BP	1197 ± 147 BC

MN I

124	Foulum	K-1601	4540 ± 110	BP	3254 ± 169 BC
125	Foulum	K-1602	4530 ± 100	BP	3241 ± 159 BC
126	Hanstedgård	K-4215	4670 ± 80	BP	3431 ± 109 BC
127	Hanstedgård	K-4216	4580 ± 80	BP	3319 ± 121 BC
128	Hanstedgård	K-4214	4560 ± 80	BP	3291 ± 127 BC
129	Herrup (Ib)	K-1766	4650 ± 100	BP	3405 ± 136 BC
130	Herrup (Ib)	K-1768	4530 ± 100	BP	3241 ± 159 BC
131	Herrup (Ib)	K-1769	4530 ± 100	BP	3241 ± 159 BC
132	Herrup (Ib)	K-1767	4510 ± 100	BP	3211 ± 161 BC
133	Jörlanda (Ib)	St-1838	4500 ± 170	BP	3194 ± 238 BC
134	Karbjerg (Ib)	K-978	4490 ± 120	BP	3180 ± 183 BC
135	Lånum (I–II)	K-1771	4510 ± 100	BP	3211 ± 161 BC
136	Norsminde	K-2665	4480 ± 85	BP	3165 ± 148 BC
137	Norsminde	K-2188	4400 ± 100	BP	3046 ± 150 BC
138	Sarup (Ib)	K-2767	4480 ± 90	BP	3165 ± 153 BC
139	Vroue Hede (Ia)	K-1566	4570 ± 100	BP	3299 ± 150 BC
140	Vroue Hede (Ib)	K-1568	4560 ± 100	BP	3285 ± 153 BC
141	Vroue Hede (Ib)	K-1567	4430 ± 100	BP	3089 ± 157 BC

MN II

142	Fannerup I	K-4050	4420 ± 95	BP	3073 ± 150 BC
143	Fannerup I	K-4049	4390 ± 70	BP	3021 ± 109 BC
144	Fannerup II (II/III)	K-4051	4350 ± 65	BP	2968 ± 84 BC
145	Ferslev	K-717	4430 ± 120	BP	3093 ± 179 BC
146	Tustrup	K-727	4440 ± 120	BP	3108 ± 180 BC
147	Tustrup	K-718	4390 ± 120	BP	3037 ± 171 BC
148	Vindinge C	K-2127	4460 ± 100	BP	3135 ± 162 BC
149	Vindinge I	K-2128	4390 ± 100	BP	3032 ± 147 BC

MN III

150	Sarup	K-2911	4400 ± 65	BP	3033 ± 107 BC
151	Sarup	K-2766	4340 ± 90	BP	2968 ± 139 BC

MN V

152	Dorthealund pit C	K-2275	4200 ± 100	BP	2803 ± 131 BC
153	Dorthealund pit C	K-2273	4110 ± 100	BP	2689 ± 145 BC
154	Dorthealund pit E	K-2429	4220 ± 100	BP	2827 ± 127 BC
155	Dorthealund pit N	K-2432	4550 ± 100	BP	3271 ± 155 BC

156	Dorthealund pit N	K-2430	4540 ± 100 BP	3256 ± 157 BC
157	Klokkehøj	K-3012	4250 ± 80 BP	2863 ± 97 BC
158	Klokkehøj	K-3013	4200 ± 80 BP	2807 ± 109 BC
159	Klokkehøj	K-3014	4140 ± 80 BP	2732 ± 123 BC
160	Kornerup	K-2115	4090 ± 100 BP	2662 ± 146 BC
161	Lidsø	K-2270	4390 ± 100 BP	3032 ± 147 BC
162	Lidsø	K-2272	4300 ± 100 BP	2919 ± 124 BC
163	Lidsø	K-2269	4260 ± 100 BP	2873 ± 123 BC
164	Lidsø	K-2271	4210 ± 100 BP	2815 ± 129 BC
165	Øster Ristofte	K-1789	4310 ± 100 BP	2930 ± 125 BC
166	Vester Årup	K-1931	4430 ± 100 BP	3089 ± 157 BC
167	Vester Årup	K-1930	4370 ± 100* BP	3005 ± 140 BC
168	Vecter Årup	K-1983	4160 ± 100 BP	2754 ± 138 BC
169	Vester Årup	K-1932	4100 ± 100 BP	2676 ± 146 BC
170	Vroue Hede	K-1571	4300 ± 100 BP	2919 ± 124 BC
171	Vroue Hede	K-1573	4270 ± 100 BP	2884 ± 122 BC
172	Vroue Hede	K-1572	4230 ± 100 BP	2838 ± 126 BC
173	Vroue Hede	K-2426	4220 ± 100 BP	2827 ± 127 BC
174	Vroue Hede	K-1574	4210 ± 100 BP	2815 ± 129 BC
175	Vroue Hede	K-2425	4180 ± 100 BP	2778 ± 134 BC
176	Vroue Hede	K-2427	4110 ± 100 BP	2689 ± 145 BC

South-eastern TRB group dates

Early phase

177	Bronocice I	DIC-719	5060 ± 110 BP	3867 ± 122 BC
178	Gródek Nadbużny	KN-243	5050 ± 110 BP	3857 ± 121 BC
179	Gródek Nadbużny	Gd-2163	5030 ± 90 BP	3835 ± 101 BC
180	Gródek Nadbużny	Gd-2160	5010 ± 110 BP	3815 ± 120 BC

Classic phase

181	Bronocice II	DIC-362	4940 ± 125 BP	3741 ± 136 BC
182	Bronocice II	DIC-542	4800 ± 70 BP	3592 ± 93 BC
183	Bronocice II	DIC-718	4690 ± 70 BP	3455 ± 100 BC
184	Ćmielów	GrN-5087	4775 ± 40 BP	3568 ± 68 BC
185	Ćmielów	GrN-5090	4700 ± 40 BP	3462 ± 85 BC
186	Ćmielów	H-566	4675 ± 110 BP	3436 ± 146 BC
187	Ćmielów	GrN-5036	4650 ± 40 BP	3403 ± 58 BC
188	Ćmielów	GrN-5088	4615 ± 40 BP	3370 ± 50 BC
189	Gródek Nadbużny	Gd-2441	4830 ± 90 BP	3623 ± 98 BC
190	Niedźwiedź	Bln-927	4715 ± 100 BP	3486 ± 131 BC
191	Niedźwiedź	M-2323	4640 ± 190 BP	3380 ± 249 BC
192	Niedźwiedź	M-2322	4600 ± 191 BP	3327 ± 254 BC
193	Niedźwiedź	M-2321	4470 ± 190 BP	3154 ± 260 BC

Late phase

194	Bronocice III	DIC-716	4610 ± 120 BP	3350 ± 169 BC
195	Bronocice III	DIC-360	4600 ± 120 BP	3337 ± 171 BC
196	Bronocice III	DIC-363	4520 ± 60 BP	3236 ± 116 BC
197	Stryczowice	Lod-63	4360 ± 210 BP	3007 ± 280 BC
198	Stryczowice	Lod-62	4250 ± 180 BP	2862 ± 235 BC

Other

199	Krzemionki	Lod-211	5230 ± 170 BP	4059 ± 195 BC

Southern TRB group dates

Baalberge phase

200	Bernburg	Bln-2041	4735 ± 50	BP	3511 ± 90 BC
201	Brežno	GrN-8803	5090 ± 45	BP	3895 ± 70 BC
202	Makotřasy	GrN-7102	4870 ± 60	BP	3672 ± 68 BC
203	Makotřasy	KN-2506	4790 ± 160	BP	3570 ± 191 BC
204	Makotřasy	GrN-6929	4715 ± 60	BP	3484 ± 95 BC
205	Makotřasy	GrN-7101	4660 ± 55	BP	3416 ± 78 BC
206	Makotřasy	GrN-6928	4550 ± 110	BP	3269 ± 167 BC
207	Postoloprty	Bln-482	4925 ± 80	BP	3727 ± 87 BC
208	Prag (?)	KN-2505	4680 ± 60	BP	3441 ± 88 BC
209	Quenstedt	Bln-2005	4630 ± 40	BP	3384 ± 51 BC
210	Steinabrunn	KN-2477	4960 ± 55	BP	3762 ± 63 BC
211	Weissenfels	Bln-1353	4635 ± 60	BP	3389 ± 80 BC

Salzmünde phase

212	Dölauer Heide	H209/579	4970 ± 90	BP	3773 ± 98 BC
213	Dölauer Heide	Bln-64	4780 ± 100	BP	3565 ± 126 BC
214	Dölauer Heide	Bln-53	4630 ± 100	BP	3380 ± 138 BC
215	Schönstedt	GrN-8255	4475 ± 45	BP	3158 ± 105 BC
216	Wallendorf (?)	KN-2376	5040 ± 60	BP	3845 ± 76 BC

Bernburg phase

217	Aspenstedt	H210/271	4560 ± 100	BP	3285 ± 153 BC
218	Burgerroth	FRA-86	4040 ± 100	BP	2595 ± 145 BC
219	Dölauer Heide	H253/208	4520 ± 110	BP	3225 ± 171 BC
220	Dölauer Heide	Bln-1856	4390 ± 85	BP	3027 ± 128 BC
221	Dölauer Heide	Bln-838a	4380 ± 100	BP	3019 ± 144 BC
222	Dölauer Heide	Bln-912	4340 ± 100	BP	2967 ± 132 BC
223	Dölauer Heide	Bln-838	4105 ± 100	BP	2683 ± 146 BC
224	Niederbösa	GrN-9148	4460 ± 40	BP	3131 ± 100 BC
225	Nordhausen	GrN-9150	4520 ± 35	BP	3238 ± 91 BC
226	Pevestorf (Corded?)	Hv-582	4380 ± 100	BP	3019 ± 144 BC
227	Pevestorf (Corded?)	KN-2461	4330 ± 55	BP	2944 ± 62 BC
228	Pevestorf (Corded?)	KN-2459	4270 ± 55	BP	2887 ± 65 BC
229	Pevestorf (Corded?)	KN-2460	4130 ± 55	BP	2724 ± 102 BC
230	Quenstedt	KN-2418A	4420 ± 45	BP	3056 ± 91 BC
231	Quenstedt	KN-2420	4380 ± 55	BP	3001 ± 84 BC
232	Quenstedt	KN-2417	4310 ± 50	BP	2924 ± 52 BC
233	Quenstedt	KN-2419	4280 ± 50	BP	2897 ± 56 BC
234	Wandersleben	Bln-2371	4220 ± 70	BP	2831 ± 93 BC

Western TRB group dates

Early TRB

235	Denekamp	GrN-4092	4930 ± 120	BP	3730 ± 131 BC
236	Hüde	Hv-327	4895 ± 85	BP	3696 ± 94 BC
237	Hüde	Hv-373	4840 ± 130	BP	3631 ± 150 BC
238	Hüde	Hv-1221	4800 ± 85	BP	3590 ± 108 BC
239	Hüde	Hv-813	4740 ± 70	BP	3517 ± 102 BC
240	Hüde	Hv-349	4710 ± 90	BP	3481 ± 90 BC

Bakker phases B, C, D1

241 Flögeln	Hv-8452	4795 ± 60	BP	3588 ± 83	BC
241 Flögeln	Hv-8454	4730 ± 85	BP	3505 ± 115	BC
242 Flögeln	Hv-8450	4500 ± 65	BP	3200 ± 126	BC
243 Flögeln	Hv-8453	4400 ± 65	BP	3033 ± 107	BC
244 Odoorn D32c	GrN-13184	4630 ± 60	BP	3394 ± 80	BC
245 Odoorn	GrN-2226	4590 ± 80	BP	3332 ± 118	BC
246 Odoorn D32a	GrN-12609	4550 ± 40	BP	3290 ± 86	BC
247 Oldendorf	GrN-6503	4625 ± 60	BP	3379 ± 80	BC
248 Oldendorf	GrN-6777	4355 ± 55	BP	2970 ± 72	BC
249 Oldendorf	GrN-6276	4300 ± 60	BP	2916 ± 66	BC

Bakker phase E

250 Anlo	GrN-1824C	4410 ± 60	BP	3046 ± 106	BC
251 Gittrupf 707	GrN-12263	4490 ± 60	BP	3184 ± 122	BC
252 Harderwijk	GrN-7746	4520 ± 70	BP	3233 ± 127	BC
253 Heek	GrN-11762	5030 ± 70	BP	3835 ± 83	BC
254 Heek	GrN-11763	4980 ± 60	BP	3783 ± 70	BC
255 Heek	GrN-11765	4890 ± 80	BP	3691 ± 90	BC
256 Heek	GrN-9202	4520 ± 35	BP	3238 ± 90	BC
257 Heek	GrN-1176b	4480 ± 60	BP	3166 ± 120	BC
258 Heek	GrN-11764	4400 ± 60	BP	3032 ± 101	BC

Bakker phases F, G

259 Angelslo	GrN-4200	4415 ± 65	BP	3956 ± 110	BC
260 Angelslo	GrN-4201	4380 ± 75	BP	3009 ± 111	BC
261 Angelslo	GrN-5103	4355 ± 45	BP	2970 ± 60	BC
262 Angelslo	GrN-5767	4315 ± 50	BP	2929 ± 66	BC
263 Angelslo	GrN-2370	4145 ± 100	BP	2735 ± 141	BC
264 Angelslo	GrN-5070	4100 ± 30	BP	2693 ± 95	BC
265 Glimmer	GrN-6156	4380 ± 40	BP	2994 ± 63	BC
266 Nottuln	GrN-12414	4240 ± 60	BP	2855 ± 79	BC

Miscellaneous dates

Late Mesolithic

267 Bergumermeer	GrN-6845	7940 ± 75	BP	6842 ± 152	BC
268 Ellerbek	Y-440	6060 ± 200	BP	4995 ± 230	BC
269 Ertebølle	K-1525	5110 ± 100	BP	3920 ± 115	BC
270 Flynderhage	K-1450	5230 ± 80	BP	4053 ± 107	BC
271 Lietzow-Buddelin	Bln-560	5190 ± 120	BP	4011 ± 144	BC
272 Lietzow-Buddelin	Bln-561	5815 ± 100	BP	4708 ± 118	BC
273 Ralswiek	Bln-562	5455 ± 100	BP	4315 ± 101	BC
274 Osa	?	5730 ± 50	BP	4607 ± 75	BC
275 Vedbæk Boldbaner	K-1303	6510 ± 110	BP	5425 ± 146	BC

Lengyel dates

276 Broniewice	Bln-1313	5060 ± 60	BP	3867 ± 80	BC
277 Krusza Zamkowa	Bln-1811	5330 ± 65	BP	4194 ± 96	BC
278 Brześć Kujawski	Lod-165	5370 ± 180	BP	4216 ± 200	BC
279 Brześć Kujawski	Lod-163	5130 ± 160	BP	3946 ± 169	BC

Bibliography

Åberg, N. (1918) *Das nordische Kulturgebiet in Mitteleuropa während der jüngeren Steinzeit*, vols I & II, Uppsala and Leipzig.

Albert, W. (1985) 'Merkmalanalyse neolithischer Steinartefakte', *Jahresschrift für Mitteldeutsche Vorgeschichte* 68, 93–120.

Albrethsen, E.E. and Brinch Petersen, E. (1975) *Gravene på Bøgebakken Vedbæk*, Søllerød.

—— (1976) 'Excavation of a Mesolithic cemetery at Vedbæk, Denmark', *Acta Archaeologica* 47, 1–28.

Ammerman, A.J. and Cavalli-Sforza, L.L. (1971) 'Measuring the rate of spread of early farming in Europe', *Man* 6, 674–88.

—— (1973) 'A population model for the diffusion of early farming in Europe', in C. Renfrew (ed.), *The Explanation of Culture Change*, Duckworth, London, 343–57.

—— (1984) *The Neolithic Transition and the Genetics of Populations in Europe*, Princeton University Press, Princeton.

Andersen, N.H. (1970) 'Rævebakken. Et bopladskompleks fra sten- og bronzealder på Nordvestfyn', *Fynske Minder* 101–10.

—— (1974a) 'En befæstet, yngre stenalderboplads i Sarup', *Fynske Minder* 71–88.

—— (1974b) 'Sarup: Et befæstet neolitisk anlæg på Sydvestfyn', *Kuml* 1973/1974, 109–20.

—— (1975) 'Die neolithische Befestigungsanlage in Sarup auf Fünen (Dänmark)', *Archäologisches Korrespondenzblatt* 5, 11–14.

—— (1977) 'Sarup. Keramikgruber fra to bebyggelsesfaser', *Kuml* 1976, 11–46.

—— (1981) 'Sarup. Befæstede neolitiske anlæg og deres baggrund', *Kuml* 1980, 63–103.

—— (1982) 'A Neolithic Causewayed Camp at Trelleborg near Slagelse, West Zealand', *Journal of Danish Archaeology* 1, 31–3.

—— (1988a) 'The Neolithic causewayed enclosure at Sarup, on South-West Funen, Denmark', in C. Burgess, P. Topping, C. Mordant and M. Maddison (eds), *Enclosures and Defences in the Neolithic of Western Europe*, British Archaeological Reports International Series 403, Oxford, 337–62.

—— (1988b) *Sarup: Befæstede kultpladser fra bondestenalderen*, Jysk arkæologisk Selskab, Århus.

Andersen, N.H. and Madsen, T. (1978) 'Skåle og bægre med storvinkelbånd fra yngre stenalder', *Kuml* 1977, 131–60.

Andersen, S.H. (1975) 'Ringkloster, en jysk indlandsplads med Ertebøllekultur', *Kuml* 1973/1974, 11–108.
—— (1982) *Jægerfolket i stenalderen*, Lademanns Danmarkshistorie Stenalderen 1, København.
Andersen, S.H. and Nielsen, P.O. (1982) *Jæger og bonde i stenalderen*, Lademanns Danmarkshistorie Stenalderen 2, København.
Aner, E. (1963) 'Die Stellung der Dolmen Schleswig-Holsteins in der nordischen Megalithkultur', *Offa* 20, 9–38.
—— (1968) 'Die Groß-Steingräber Schleswig-Holsteins', *Führer zu vor- und frühgeschichtlichen Denkmälern* 9, 46–69.
Arora, S.K. (1973) 'Mittelsteinzeitliche Formengruppen zwischen Rhein und Weser', in S.K. Kozłowski (ed.), *The Mesolithic in Europe*, University of Warsaw Press, Warsaw, 9–21.
Ashbee, P. (1966) 'The Fussell's Lodge Long Barrow', *Archaeologia* 100, 1–80.
—— (1970) *The Earthen Long Barrow in Britain*, Dent, London.
Bąbel, J. (1980a) 'Kult topora w neolicie ziem polskich', *Wiadomości Archeologiczne* 45, 3–44.
—— (1980b) 'PL6 Krzemionki', in G. Weisgerber (ed.), *5000 Jahre Feuersteinbergbau*, Deutsches Bergbau-Museum, Bochum, 586–95.
—— (1986) 'The problems of the investigations of the flint mine at Krzemionki near Ostrowiec Świętokrzyski, Kielce and Tarnobrzeg Voivodeship', *International Conference on Prehistoric Flint Mining and Lithic Raw Material Identification in the Carpathian Basin*, Budapest and Sümeg, 27–42.
Bagge, A. and Kaelas, L. (1950/1952) *Die Funde aus Dolmen und Ganggräbern in Schonen, Schweden*, vols I (1950) and II (1952), Wahlström and Wildstrand, Stockholm.
Bagniewski, Z. (1979) 'Problem związków ludności mezolitycznej i neolitycznej na terenie Polski południowo-zachodniej', in W. Wojciechowski (ed.), *Początki Neolityzacji Polski Południowo-Zachodniej*, Polska Akademia Nauk, Wrocław, 21–35.
—— (1980) 'Das Problem der Koexistenz mesolithischer und neolithischer Gesellschaften im Südteil des mitteleuropäischen Flachlandes', in B. Gramsch (ed.), *Mesolithikum in Europa*, Veröffentlichungen des Museums für Ur- und Frühgeschichte Potsdam Band 14/15, 113–19.
Bailey, G.N. (ed.) (1983) *Hunter-gatherer Economy in Prehistory*, Cambridge University Press, Cambridge.
Bakker, J.A. (1976) 'On the possibility of reconstructing roads from the TRB period', *Berichten van de Rijksdienst voor het Oudheidkundig Bodemonderzoek* 26, 63–91.
—— (1979) *The TRB West Group. Studies in the Chronology and Geography of the Makers of Hunebeds and Tiefstich Pottery*, Amsterdam.
—— (1982) 'TRB Settlement Patterns on the Dutch Sandy Soils', *Analecta Praehistorica Leidensia* 15, 87–124.
Bakker, J.A., Vogel, J.C. and Wiślański, T. (1969) 'TRB and other C14 dates from Poland', *Helinium* 9, 3–27 and 209–38.
Balcer, B. (1975) *Krzemień Świeciechowski w Kulturze Pucharów Lejkowatych. Eksploatacja, obróbka i rozprzestrzenienie*, Ossolineum, Wrocław.

—— (1976) 'Position and stratigraphy of flint deposits, development of exploitation and importance of the Świeciechów flint in prehistory', *Acta Archaeologia Carpathica* 16, 179–99.

—— (1977) 'Z badań nad krzemieniarstwem neolitycznym w dorzeczu górnej Odry', *Przegląd Archeologiczny* 25, 5–51.

—— (1980) 'A study of socio-economic aspects of Neolithic flint working on the example of the Funnel Beaker culture (FBC)', in R. Schild (ed.), *Unconventional Archaeology. New Approaches and Goals in Polish Archaeology*, Ossolineum, Wrocław, 87–107.

—— (1981a) 'Wyniki badań nad krzemieniarstwem kultury pucharów lejkowatych na ziemiach Polski', in T. Wiślański (ed.), *Kultura Pucharów Lejkowatych w Polsce*, Polska Akademia Nauk, Poznań, 59–79.

—— (1981b) 'Związki między kulturą pucharów lejkowatych (KPL) a kulturą trypolską (KT) na podstawie materiałów krzemiennych', in T. Wiślański (ed.), *Kultura Pucharów Lejkowatych w Polsce*, Polska Akademia Nauk, Poznań, 81–91.

—— (1983) *Wytwórczość Narzędzi Krzemiennych w Neolicie Ziem Polskich*. Polska Akademia Nauk, Wrocław.

Balcer, B. and Kowalski, K. (1978) 'Z badań nad krzemieniem pasiastym w pradziejach', *Wiadomości Archeologiczne* 43, 127–43.

Barrière, C. (1956) *Les civilisations tardenoisiennes en Europe Occidentale*, Bière, Paris.

Bastian, W. (1954) 'Das dünnackige Flintbeil in Mecklenburg und seine Bedeutung für die Entstehung der Megalith- und der östlichen Einzelgrabkultur', *Jahrbuch für Bodendenkmalpflege in Mecklenburg* 1954, 37–60.

—— (1961) 'Das jungsteinzeitliche Flachgräberfeld von Ostorf, Kreis Schwerin', *Jahrbuch für Bodendenkmalpflege in Mecklenburg* 1961, 7–130.

Becker, C.J. (1939) 'En stenalderboplads paa Ordrup Næs in Nordvestjælland', *Aarbøger* 1939, 199–280.

—— (1947) 'Mosefunde lerkar fra yngre stenalder', *Aarbøger* 1947, 1–318.

—— (1949) 'Hafted Neolithic celts II. With observations on a new Funnel–Beaker type from Zealand', *Acta Archaeologica* 20, 231–48.

—— (1952a) 'Ørnekul paa Nesklø. En Sjællandsk stenalderboplads med hustomter', *Aarbøger* 1952, 60–102.

—— (1952b) 'Die nordschwedischen Flintdepots. Ein Beitrag zur Geschichte des neolithischen Fernhandels in Skandinavien', *Acta Archaeologica* 23, 31–79.

—— (1954a) 'Die mittel-neolithischen Kulturen in Südskandinavien', *Acta Archaeologica* 25, 49–150.

—— (1954b) 'Stenalderbebyggelsen ved Store Valby i Vestjælland. Problemer omkring tragtbægerkulturens ældste og yngste fase', *Aarbøger* 1954, 127–97.

—— (1956) 'The date of the Neolithic settlement at Trelleborg', *Acta Archaeologica* 27, 91–108.

—— (1957) 'Den tyknakkede flintøkse. Studier over tragtbægerkulturens svære retøkser i mellem-neolitisk tid', *Aarbøger* 1957, 1–37.

—— (1960) 'Stendyngegrave fra mellem-neolitisk tid', *Aarbøger* 1959, 1–90.

—— (1966) 'Vor ældste industri', *Skalk* 1966, 3–7.

—— (1967a) 'Gådefulde jyske stenaldergrave', *Nationalmuseets Arbejdsmark*, 19–30.

—— (1967b) 'The inter-relationship of the TRB and Battle-Axe cultures in Denmark', *Palaeohistoria* 12, 33–41.

—— (1969) 'Grav eller tempel? En kult-bygning fra yngre tenalder ved Herrup, Vestjylland', *Nationalmuseets Arbejdsmark*, 17–28.

—— (1973a) 'Studien zu neolithischen Flintbeilen', *Acta Archaeologica* 44, 125–86.

—— (1973b) 'Problems of the Megalithic "Mortuary Houses" in Denmark', in G. Daniel and P. Kjærum (eds), *Megalithic Graves and Rituals*, Papers Presented at the Third Atlantic Colloquium, Moesgård 1969, København, 75–9.

—— (1980) 'DK Dänemark: Hov-Bjerre-Aalborg-Hillerslev-Fornaes-Stevns Klint', in G. Weisgerber (ed.), *5000 Jahre Feuersteinbergbau*, Deutsches Bergbau-Museum, Bohum, 456–73.

—— (1982) 'Om grubekeramisk kultur i Danmark. Korte bidrag tilen lang diskussion (1950–1980)', *Aarbøger* 1980, 13–33.

Bednarczyk, J., Czerniak, L. and Kośko, A. (1980) 'Z badań nad zespołem osadniczym ludności z kręgu kultur ceramiki wstęgowej w Kruszy Zamkowej, stan. 3, woj. Bydgoszcz (część sepulkralna)', *Sprawozdania Archeologiczne* 32, 55–83.

Bednarczyk, J. and Kośko, A. (1974) 'Relacje chronologiczne między kulturami cyklu wstęgowego a kulturą pucharów lejkowatych na terenie Polski północno-zachodniej', *Pomorania Antiqua* 5, 9–26.

Behre, K.E. (1979) 'Die natürliche Umwelt der Trichterbecherkultur', in H. Schirnig (ed.), *Großsteingräber in Niedersachsen*, Hildesheim, 199–202.

Behre, K.E., Menke, B. and Streif, H. (1979) 'The Quaternary geological development of the German part of the North Sea', in E. Oele, R.T.E. Schüttenhelm and A.J. Wiggers, (eds), *The Quatenary History of the North Sea*, Acta Universitatis Upsaliensis 2, Uppsala, 85–113.

Behrens, H. (1953) 'Ein Siedlung- und Begräbnisplatz der Trichterbecherkultur bei Weißenfels an der Saale', *Jahresschrift für Mitteldeutsche Vorgeschichte* 37, 67–108.

—— (1957) 'Trapezförmige Grabenanlage unter jungsteinzeitlichem Grabhügel bei Halle (Saale)', *Ausgrabungen und Funde* 3, 225–8.

—— (1958) 'Ein jungsteinzeitlicher Grabhügel von mehrschichtigem Aufbau in der Dölauer Heide bei Halle (Saale)', *Jahresschrift für Mitteldeutsche Vorgeschichte* 41/42, 213–42.

—— (1959) 'Die Rössener Kultur und die frühneolithische südskandinavische Trichterbecherkultur', *Acta Arachaeologica* 30, 167–84.

—— (1960) 'Diskussionsbemerkungen zu einigen neueren tschechischen Auffassungen über der Ursprung der Trichterbecherkultur', *Archeologické rozhledy* 12, 579–87.

—— (1973) *Die Jungsteinzeit im Mittelelbe-Saale-Gebiet*, VEB Deutscher Verlag der Wissenschaften, Berlin.

—— (1981a) 'Der Walternienburger und der Bernburger Keramikstil und die Walternienburg-Bernburger Kultur', *Jahresschrift für Mitteldeutsche Vorgeschichte* 63, 11–16.

—— (1981b) 'Radiocarbon-Daten für das Neolithikum des Mittelelbe-Saale-Gebietes', *Jahresschrift für Mitteldeutsche Vorgeschichte* 63, 189–93.

—— (1981c) 'Die Schnurkeramik – nur ein Problem der Klassifikation?', *Jahresschrift für Mitteldeutsche Vorgeschichte* 64, 9–14.

—— (1981d) 'The first 'Woodhenge' in middle Europe', *Antiquity* 55, 172–8.

—— (1984) 'Ein hohes Radiocarbondatum für ein mitteldeutsches neolithisches Woodhenge', *Archäologisches Korrespondenzblatt* 14, 259–62.

Behrens, H. and Schröter, E. (1980) *Siedlungen und Gräber der Trichterbecherkultur und Schnurkeramik*, Veröffentlichungen des Landesmuseums für Vorgeschichte in Halle Band 34, Berlin.

Beier, H.J. (1984) *Die Grab- und Bestattungssitten der Walternienburger und der Bernburger Kultur*, Neolithische Studien III, Martin-Luther Universität Halle-Wittenberg, Halle.

Beltz, R. (1910) *Die vorgeschichtlichen Altertümer des Großherzogtums Mecklenburg*, Schwerin.

Bennike, P. (1985) 'Stenalderbefolkningen på øerne syd for Fyn, in J. Skaarup *Yngre Stenalder på øerne syd for Fyn*, Meddelelser fra Langelands Museum, Rudkøbing, 467–91.

Berg, H. (1951) *Klintebakken. En boplads fra yngre stenalder på Langeland. Tre langelandske megalitgrave*, Meddelelser fra Langelands Museum, Rudkøbing.

—— (1956) 'Langdolmen bei Pæregaard, Langeland', *Acta Archaeologica* 27, 108–27.

Binford, L.R. (1980) 'Willow smoke and dogs' tails: hunter-gatherer settlement systems and archaeological site formation', *American Antiquity* 45, 4–20.

Bjørn, A. and Hingst, H. (1973) 'Back- und Töpferöfen der jüngeren Steinzeit aus Schleswig-Holstein', *Die Heimat* 80, 107–10.

Bogucki, P. (1979) 'Tactical and strategic settlements in the early Neolithic of lowland Poland', *Journal of Anthropological Research* 35, 238–46.

—— (1982) *Early Neolithic Subsistence and Settlement in the Polish Lowlands*, British Archeological Reports International Series 150, Oxford.

—— (1984) 'Linear Pottery ceramic sieves and their economic implications', *Oxford Journal of Archaeology* 3, 15–30.

—— (1987) 'The establishment of agrarian communities on the North European Plain', *Current Anthropology* 28, 1–24.

—— (1988) *Forest Farmers and Stockherders. Early Agriculture and its Consequences in North-Central Europe*, Cambridge University Press, Cambridge.

Bogucki, P. and Grygiel, R. (1981) 'The household cluster at Brześć Kujawski 3: small-site methodology in the Polish Lowlands', *World Archaeology* 13, 59–72.

Bokelmann, K. and Paulsen, H. (1973) 'Die Steinzeit in Schleswig-Holstein. 1.Teil: Flintbearbeitungstechnik', *Die Heimat* 80, 110–16.

Boserup, E. (1965) *The Conditions of Agricultural Growth. The Economics of Agrarian Change Under Population Pressure*, Allen & Unwin, London.

Bradley, R. (1984) *The social foundations of prehistoric Britain: themes and variations in the archaeology of power*, Longman, London and New York.

—— (1985) *Consumption, change and the archaeological record. The archaeology of monuments and the archaeology of deliberate deposits*, University of Edinburgh Department of Archaeology Occasional Paper 13, Edinburgh.

Brandt, K.H. (1961) 'Die steinerne Streitaxt von Boberg 15', *Hammaburg* 13, 31–8.

—— (1967) *Studien über steinerne Äxte und Beile der jüngeren Steinzeit und der Stein-Kupferzeit Nordwestdeutschlands*, Hildesheim.

—— (1971) 'Eine neue kulturell bestimmbare Hammeraxt', *Jahresschrift für Mitteldeutsche Vorgeschichte* 55, 65–78.

Braudel, F. (1973) *The Mediterranean and the Mediterranean world in the Age of Philip II*, Collins, London.

Brinch Petersen, E. (1973) 'A survey of the Late Palaeolithic and the Mesolithic of Denmark', in S.K. Kozłowski (ed.), *The Mesolithic in Europe*, University of Warsaw Press, Warsaw, 77–127.

—— (1974) 'Gravene ved Dragsholm. Fra jægere til bønder for 6000 år siden', *Nationalmuseets Arbejdsmark*, 112–20.

Brindley, A.L. (1986a) 'Hunebed G2: excavation and finds', *Palaeohistoria* 28, 27–92.

—— (1986b) 'The typochronology of TRB West Group pottery', *Palaeohistoria* 28, 93–132.

Broadbent, N.D., Johansen, O.S., Moe, D., Becker, C.J., Zvelebil, M. and Rowley-Conwy, P. (1985) 'Comments on transition to farming in Northern Europe', *Norwegian Archaeological Review* 18, 115–30.

Brøndsted, J. (1957) *Danmarks Oldtid. I, Stenalderen*. Glydendal, København.

Bukowska-Gedigowa, J. (1975) 'Kultura pucharów lejkowatych w dorzeczu górnej Odry', *Przegląd Archeologiczny* 23, 83–186.

Burchard, B. (1973) 'Z badań neolitycznej budowli trapezowatej w Niedźwiedziu, pow. Miechów (Stan. 1)', *Sprawozdania Archeologiczne* 29, 59–81.

—— (1981) 'Kultura pucharów lejkowatych w Małopolsce Zachodniej', in T. Wiślański (ed.), *Kultura Pucharów Lejkowatych w Polsce*, Polska Akademia Nauk, Poznań, 221–38.

Burenhult, G. (1984) *The Archaeology of Carrowmore*. Theses and Papers in North-European Archaeology 14, Stockholm.

Burgess, C., Topping, P., Mordant, C. and Maddison, M. (eds) (1988) *Enclosures and Defences in the Neolithic of Western Europe*, vols I and II, British Archaeological Reports International Series 403, Oxford.

Buurman, J. and Pals, J.P. (1974) 'Some remarks on prehistoric flax in the Netherlands', *Berichten van de Rijksdienst voor het Oudheidkundig Bodemonderzoek* 24, 107–11.

Casparie, W.A. and Groenman-van Waateringe, W. (1980) 'Palynological analysis of Dutch barrows', *Palaeohistoria* 22, 7–65.

Chapman, J. (1988) 'From "space" to "place": a model of dispersed settlement and Neolithic society', in C. Burgess, P. Topping,

C. Mordant and M. Maddison (eds), *Enclosures and Defences in the Neolithic of Western Europe*, British Archaeological Reports International Series 403, Oxford, 21–46.

Chapman, R. (1981) 'The emergence of formal disposal areas and the 'problem' of megalithic tombs in prehistoric Europe', in R. Chapman, I. Kinnes and K. Randsborg (eds), *The Archaeology of Death*, Cambridge University Press, Cambridge, 71–81.

Chapman, R., Kinnes, I. and Randsborg, K. (eds) (1981) *The Archaeology of Death*, Cambridge University Press, Cambridge.

Childe, V.G. (1925) *The Dawn of European Civilisation*, London.

—— (1936) *Man Makes Himself*, London.

—— (1949a) *Social Worlds of Knowledge*, London.

—— (1949b) 'The origin of Neolithic culture in Northern Europe', *Antiquity* 23, 129–35.

Chmielewski, W. (1952) *Zagadnienie grobowców kujawskich w świetle ostatnich badań*, Łódź.

Christensen, C. (1982) 'Stenalderfjorden og Vedbækbopladserne. Havspejlets svingninger 5500–2500 f. Kv', *Nationalmuseets Arbejdsmark*, 169–78.

Christensen, T., Ebbesen, K., Frederiksen, F., Hansen, T., Nyberg, J. and Pedersen, E. (1979) 'En neolitisk boplads på Lyø', *Aarbøger* 1978, 74–131.

Clark, J.G.D. (1952) *Prehistoric Europe. The Economic Basis*, Methuen, London.

—— (1965) 'Traffic in stone axes and adze blades', *The Economic History Review* 2nd series 18, 1–28.

—— (1975) *The Earlier Stone Age Settlement of Scandinavia*, Cambridge University Press, Cambridge.

Clarke, D.L. (1978) *Mesolithic Europe: The Economic Basis*, Duckworth (Reprint), London.

Cofta-Broniewska, A. and A. Kośko (1982) *Historia Pierwotna Społeczeństw Kujaw*, Państwowe Wydawnictwo Naukowe, Warszawa.

Cyrek, K., Grygiel, R. and Nowak, K. (1983) 'Podstawy wydzielenia mezolitu ceramicznego na niżu polskim', in T. Malinowski (ed.), *Problemy Epoki Kamienia na Pomorzu*, Słupsk, 85–110.

Czarnecki, M. (1980) 'The Mesolithic in the Szczecin Lowland', in B. Gramsch (ed.), *Mesolithikum in Europa*, Veröffentlichungen des Museums für Ur- und Frühgeschichte Potsdam Band 14/15, 345–55.

Czerniak, L. (1979) 'Z badań nad problematyką równoleżnikowych kontaktów kulturowych społeczeństw dorzeczy Odry i Wisły w młodszej epoce kamiennej (Zagadnienie tzw. wpływów kultury rösseńskiej), *Wiadomości Archeologiczne* 46, 123–30.

—— (1980) *Rozwój społeczeństw Kultury Późnej Ceramiki Wstęgowej na Kujawach*, Adam Mickiewicz University of Poznań Archaeological Series 16, Poznań.

Czerniak, L. and Kośko, A. (1980a) 'Zagadnienie efektywności poznawczej analizy chronologicznej ceramiki na podstawie cech technologicznych', *Archeologia Polski* 25, 247–80.

—— (1980b) 'Badania sondażowe w Inowrocławiu – Mątwach, stan. 5, woj. Bydgoszcz', *Sprawozdania Archeologiczne* 32, 29–54.

Czerniak, L. and Piontek, J. (1980) 'Próba modelowego opisu form organizacji społecznej i gospodarczej ludności kultur wstęgowych na

podstawie analizy zespołów osadniczych typu Brześć Kujawski',
Archeologia Polski 24, 335–58.

Dąbrowski, M.J. (1971) 'Analiza pyłkowa warstw kulturowych z
Sarnowa, pow. Włocławek', *Prace i Materiały Muzeum
Archeologicznego i Etnograficznego w Łodzi* 18, 147–63.

Daniel, G. (1958) *The Megalith Builders of Western Europe*, London.

Davidsen, K. (1975) 'Tragtbægerkulturens slutfase. Nye C 14
dateringer', *Kuml* 1973/1974, 165–78.

—— (1976) 'Neolitiske lerskiver belyst af danske fund', *Aarbøger* 1973,
5–72.

—— (1977) 'Relativ kronologi i mellemneolitisk tid. En diskussion af
C.J. Beckers kronologisystem på baggrund af nye og gamle
stratifgrafiske fund', *Aarbøger* 1975, 42–77.

—— (1978) *The Final TRB Culture in Denmark. a Settlement Study*,
Arkaeologisker Studier V, Akademisk Forlag, København.

—— (1982) 'Undergravstid på de danske øer', *Aarbøger* 1980, 38–51.

Dębowska, J. (1980) 'Dąbki, gm. Darłowo, woj. koszalińskie,
stanowisko 9', *Informator Archeologiczny. Badania 1979*, 25–6.

Degerbøl, M. (1939) 'Dyreknogler. (Bundsø. En yngre stenalders
boplads paa als)'. *Aarbøger* 1939, 85–198.

Dehnke, R. (1940 *Die Tiefstichtonware der Jungsteinzeit in Osthannover*,
Hildesheim and Leipzig.

Deichmüller, J. (1963) 'Neue Ausgrabungen am Dümmer', *Nachrichten
aus Niedersachsens Urgeschichte* 32, 84–7.

—— (1965) 'Eine Rössener Stilvariante am Dümmer', *Germania* 43,
334–43.

—— (1969) 'Die neolithische Moorsiedlung Hüde I am Dümmer,
Kreis Grafschaft Diepholz. Vorläufiger Abschlußbericht', *Neue
Ausgrabungen und Forschungen in Niedersachsen* 4, 28–36.

Dennell, R. (1985) *European Economic Prehistory. A New Approach*,
Academic Press, London.

Dimbleby, G. (1967) *Plants and Archaeology*, John Baker Publishers
Ltd, London.

Domańska, L. (1989) 'Elements of a food-producing economy in the
Late Mesolithic of the Polish lowland', in C. Bonsall (ed.), *The
Mesolithic in Europe*, Papers presented at the Third International
Symposium, Edinburgh 1985, John Donald Publishers Ltd,
Edinburgh, 447–55.

Domańska, L. and Kośko, A. (1974) 'Z badań nad charakterem więzi
kulturowej stref pojezierno-nadmorskiej i wielkodolinnej niżu
międzyrzecza Odry i Wisły w dobie początków procesu neolityzacji',
Studia Archaeologica Pomeranica, 23–52.

—— (1983) 'Łącko, woj. Bydgoszcz, stanowisko 6 – obozowisko z fazy
I ("AB") kultury pucharów lejkowatych', *Acta Universitatis
Lodziensis, Folia Archaeologica* 4, 3–55.

Dorka, G. (1939) *Urgeschichte des Weizacker-Kreises Pyritz*, Szczecin.

—— (1961) 'Eine Grube mit Trichterbechern aus Berlin-Britz',
Berliner Blätter für Vor- und Frühgeschichte 9, 35–46.

Driehaus, J. (1960) *Die Altheimer Gruppe und das Jungneolithikum in
Mitteleuropa*, Mainz and Bonn.

Dürr, H.W.A. (1960) *Zur Ausgrabung an der Hunte bei Dümmerlohausen
1938/39*, Bad Cannstatt.

Ebbesen, K. (1975) *Die jüngere Trichterbecherkultur auf den dänischen Inseln*, Arkæologiske Studier II, Akademisk Forlag, Copenhagen.
—— (1978) *Tragtbægerkultur i Nordjylland. Studier over jættestuetiden*, Nordiske Fortidsminder Serie B Bind 5, København.
—— (1979a) *Stordyssen i Vedsted. Studier over tragtbægerkulturen i Sønderjylland*, Arkæologiske Studier VI, Akademisk Forlag, København.
—— (1979b) 'Stenalderlerkar med ansight', *Kuml* 1978, 99–115.
—— (1982) 'Yngre stenalders depotfund som bebyggelseshistorisk kildemateriale', in H. Thrane (ed.), *Om Yngre Stenalders Bebyggelseshistorie*, Odense, 60–79.
—— (1984) 'Yngreolitiske tap-stridsøkser. Nyt lys på enkeltgravstiden', *Kuml* 1982–1983, 121–37.
—— (1985) 'Tragtbægerkulturens grønstensøkser', *Kuml* 1984, 113–53.
Ebbesen, K. and Brinch Petersen, E. (1974) 'Fuglebæksbanken', *Aarbøger* 1973, 73–106.
Ebbesen, K. and Larsen, C. (1980) 'Askeby-fundet. Tragtbægerkulturens forrådskar', *Aarbøger* 1978, 45–73.
Ebbesen, K. and Mahler, D. (1980) 'Virum. Et tidligneolitisk bopladsfund', *Aarbøger* 1979, 11–61.
Embleton, C. (1984) *Geomorphology of Europe*, Macmillan, London.
Eriksen, P. (1982) 'Det mellemneolitiske bopladskompleks ved Fannerup på Djursland – en foreløbig orientering', in H. Thrane (ed.) *Om Yngre Stenalders Bebyggelseshistorie*, Odense, 80–7.
—— (1985) 'Det neolitiske bopladskompleks ved Fannerup', *Kuml* 1984, 9–76.
Eriksen, P. and Madsen, T. (1984) 'Hanstedgård. A settlement site from the Funnel Beaker culture', *Journal of Danish Archaeology* 3, 63–82.
Faber, O. (1976) 'Hus eller grav? Et anlæg fra yngre stenalder ved Varde', *Mark og Montre*, 5–11.
—— (1977) 'Endnu et kulthus. Et stenaldertempel ved Engedal i Midtjylland', *Antikvariske Studier*, 35–45.
Feustel, R. (1972) 'Die Walternienburg/Bernburger Totenhütte von Schönstedt im Thüringer Becken', *Alt-Thüringen* 12, 31–58.
Feustel, R. and Ullrich, H. (1965) 'Totenhütten der neolithischen Walternienburger Gruppe', *Alt-Thüringen* 7, 105–202.
Finke, W. (1984) 'Ein Flachgräberfeld der Trichterbecherkultur bei Heek, Kreis Borken', *Ausgrabungen und Funde in Westfalen-Lippe* 1 (1983), 27–32.
Firbas, F. (1954) Die Synchronisierung der mitteleuropäischen Pollendiagramme', *Danmarks Geologiske Undersøgelse* II, Række Nr 80, 12–21.
Fischer, A. (1982) 'Trade in Danubian shaft-hole axes and the introduction of Neolithic economy in Denmark', *Journal of Danish Archaeology* 1, 7–12.
—— (1983) 'Handel med skolæstøkser og landbrugets indførelse i Danmark', *Aarbøger* 1981, 5–16.
Fischer, C. (1976) 'Tidlig-neolitiske anlæg ved Rustrup', *Kuml* 1975, 29–72.
Fischer, U. (1951) 'Zu den mitteldeutschen Trommeln', *Archaeologia Geographica* 2, 98–105.

—— (1953) 'Über Nachbestattungen im Neolithikum von Sachsen-Thüringen', *Festschrift des Römisch-Germanischen Zentralmuseums in Mainz* 3 (1952), 161–81.

—— (1956) *Die Gräber der Steinzeit im Saalegebiet*, Berlin.

—— (1958) 'Neolithische Siedlung in Anhalt', *Archaeologia Geographica* 7, 1–7.

—— (1961) 'Zum Problem der spätneolithischen Gruppenbildung an Saale und mittlere Elbe', in J. Böhm and s. de Laet (eds), *L'Europe à la fin de l'âge de la pierre*, Actes du Symposium consacré aux problèmes du Néolithique européen, Praha, 415–29.

—— (1976) 'Ein Chronologiesystem im Neolithikum', *Germania* 54, 182–4.

—— (1979) 'Europäische Verbindungen der niedersächsischen Großsteingräber', in H. Schirnig (ed.), *Großsteingräber in Niedersachsen*, Hildesheim, 27–42.

Fokkens, H. (1982) 'Late Neolithic occupation near Bornwird (Province of Friesland)', *Palaeohistoria* 24, 91–113.

Forssander, J.E. (1936) 'Skånsk megalitkeramik och kontinentaleuropeisk stenålder', *Meddelanden från Lunds Universitets Historiska Museum* 1936, 13–77.

Furthmann, F.W. (1979) 'Zwei neolithische Horte von Rügen', *Jahrbuch für Bodendenkmalpflege in Mecklenburg* 1978, 31–6.

Gabałówna, L. (1960) 'Sprawozdanie z prac wykopaliskowych w osadach kultury pucharów lejkowatych w Radziejowie Kujawskim i Opatowicach, pow. Radziejów Kujawski, w roku 1958', *Sprawozdania Archeologiczne* 11, 21–35.

—— (1961) 'Archaeological investigations at Radziejów Kujawski', *Archaeologia Polona* 4, 121–36.

—— (1964) 'Uwagi o kulturze pucharów lejkowatych w fazie wióreckiej na Kujawach, *Prace i Materiały Muzeum Archeologicznego i Etnograficznego w Łodzi* 11, 29–42.

—— (1966) 'Ze studiów nad grupą brzesko-kujawską kultury lendzielskiej. Brześć Kujawski – stanowisko 4', *Acta Archaeologica Lodziensia* 14, 1–183.

—— (1968) 'Sprawozdanie z prac wykopaliskowych w Sarnowie, pow. Włocławek, przeprowadzonych w 1967r. na stan.1 i 1A', *Prace i Materiały Muzeum Archeologicznego i Etnograficznego w Łodzi* 15, 135–47.

—— (1969a) 'Sprawozdanie z badań archeologicznych w Sarnowie, pow. Włocławek, przeprowadzonych w r.1968 na stanowiskach 1 i 1A, *Prace i Materiały Muzeum Archeologicznego i Etnograficznego w Łodzi* 16, 51–7.

—— (1969b) 'Badania nad kulturą pucharów lejkowatych w Sarnowie, pow. Włocławek i w jego najbliższej okolicy', *Sprawozdania Archeologiczne* 20, 43–52.

—— (1970a) 'Wyniki analizy C-14 węgli drewnych z cmentarzyska kultury pucharów lejkowatych na stanowisku w Sarnowie – z grobowca 8 i niektóre problemy z nimi związane', *Prace i Materiały Muzeum Archeologicznego i Etnograficznego w Łodzi* 17, 77–91.

—— (1970b) 'Cmentarzysko płaskie kultury pucharów lejkowatych ze stanowiska 2A w Czamaninku, pow. Radziejów Kujawski', *Prace i*

Materiały Muzeum Archeologicznego i Etnograficznego w Łodzi 17,
93–108.

—— (1970c) 'Jama "A" ze spalonym zbożem z osady kultury pucharów
lejkowatych na stanowisku 1 w Radziejowie Kujawskim', *Prace i
Materiały Muzeum Archeologicznego i Etnograficznego w Łodzi* 17,
157–63.

—— (1971) 'Z nowszej problematyki neolitu kujawskiego', *Prace i
Materiały Muzeum Archeologicznego i Etnograficznego w Łodzi* 18,
247–52.

Gabriel, I. (1966) 'Das Megalithgrab zu Tannenhausen, Kr. Aurich',
Neue Ausgrabungen und Forschungen in Niedersachsen 3, 82–101.

Gebauer, B. (1978) 'Mellemneolitisk tragtbægerkultur i Sydvestjylland.
En analyse af keramikken', *Kuml* 1977, 117–57.

—— (1984) 'The meaning of material culture', *Kontaktstencil* 1983/84.

Gehl, O. (1974) 'Die Jagd- und Haustiere der steinzeitlichen Siedler
von Basedow', *Jahrbuch für Bodendenkmalpflege in Mecklenburg* 1973,
67–87.

—— (1980) 'Nutzung von Haus- und Wildtieren nach dem
Knochenfundgut der neolithischen Siedlung bei Glasow an der
Randow, Kreis Pasewalk', *Jahrbuch für Bodendenkmalpflege in
Mecklenburg* 1979, 39–48.

Geisler, H. (1965) 'Die Ausgrabungen auf dem Eichberg bei
Schönermark, Kr. Angermünde, 1963 und 1964', *Ausgrabungen und
Funde* 10, 121–3.

Gendel, P.A. (1984) *Mesolithic Social Territories in Northwestern Europe.*
British Archaeological Reports International Series 218, Oxford.

Glob, P.V. (1945) 'Studier over den jyske enkeltgravskultur', *Aarbøger*
1944, 1–282.

—— (1949) 'Barkær. Danmarks ældste landsby', *Nationalmuseets
Arbejdsmark*, 1–12.

—— (1952) *Danske Oldsager: II Yngre Stenalder*, København.

—— (1971) *Danish Prehistoric Monuments*, Thames & Hudson,
London.

—— (1975) 'De dødes lange huse', *Skalk* 6, 10–14.

Godłowska, M. (1981) 'Zarys problematyki wzajemnych oddziaływań
kultur ceramiki promienistej i pucharów lejkowtych w Małopolsce',
in T. Wiślański (ed.), *Kultura Pucharów Lejkowatych w Polsce*,
Poznań, 239–57.

Göransson, H. (1980) 'Pollen analytical investigations in Cloverhill
Lough, Carrowmore, Co. Sligo, Ireland', in G. Burenhult (ed.), *The
Carrowmore Excavations. Excavation Season 1980*, Stockholm
Archaeological Report 7, Stockholm, 125–38.

—— (1982a) 'The utilisation of the forests in North-West Europe
during Early and Middle Neolithic', *Pact* 7 part II (Journal of the
European Study Group on Physical, Chemical and Mathematical
Techniques Applied to Archaeology), Strasbourg, 207–21.

—— (1982b) 'Neolitikums begynnelse i Östergötland, Sverige, enligt
pollenanalytiska data', in T. Sjøvold (ed.), *Introduksjonen av jordbruk
i Norden*, Foredrag holdt ved fellesnordisk symposium i Oslo april
1980, Universitetsforlaget, Oslo–Bergen-Tromsø, 99–123.

—— (1984) 'Pollen analytical investigations in the Sligo area', in G.

Burenhult (ed.), *The Archaeology of Carrowmore*, Theses and Papers in North-European Archaeology 14, Stockholm, 154–93.

Gorczyca, K. (1981) 'Grobowiec kujawski w Zberzynie, woj. Konin', *Fontes Archaeologici Posnanienses* 30 (1979), 1–20.

Gramsch, B. (1966) 'Neue Ausgrabungen auf dem spätmesolithischen Siedlungsplatz "Buddelin" bei Lietzow, Kr. Rügen', *Ausgrabungen und Funde* 11, 179–83.

—— (1971a) 'Zum Problem des Übergangs vom Mesolithikum zum Neolithikum im Flachland zwischen Elbe und Oder', in F. Schlette (ed.), *Evolution und Revolution im Alten Orient und in Europa*, Berlin, 127–44.

—— (1971b) 'Sondierung auf dem steinzeitlichen Siedlungsplatz in der Augustenhofer Niederung bei Ralswiek, Kr. Rügen', *Jahrbuch für Bodendenkmalpflege in Mecklenburg* 1970, 7–120.

—— (1973) *Das Mesolithikum im Flachland zwischen Elbe und Oder*, Deutscher Verlag der Wissenschaften, Berlin.

—— (1978) 'Die Lietzow-Kultur Rügens und ihre Beziehungen zur Ostseegeschichte', *Petermanns Geographische Mitteilungen* 3, 155–64.

Gregg, A.S. (1988) *Foragers and Farmers. Population Interaction and Agricultural Expansion in Prehistoric Europe*, University of Chicago Press, Chicago and London.

Grimm, P. (1958) *Die vor- und frühgeschichtlichen Burgwälle der Bezirke Halle und Magdeburg*, Berlin.

Gringmuth-Dallmer, E. and Altermann, M. (1985) 'Zum Boden als Standortfaktor ur- und frühgeschichtlicher Siedlung', *Jahresschrift für Mitteldeutsche Vorgeschichte* 68, 339–55.

Groenman-van Waateringe, W. (1971) 'Hecken im westeuropäischen Frühneolithikum', *Berichten van de Rijksdienst voor het Oudheidkundig Bodemonderzoek* 20–1, 295–9.

—— (1978) 'The impact of Neolithic man on the landscape in the Netherlands', in S. Limbrey and J.G. Evans (eds), *The Effect of Man on the Landscape: the Lowland Zone*, CBA Research Report No. 21, London, 135–46.

—— (1979a) 'Palynological investigations of five German burial mounds', *Archaeo-Physika* 8, 69–84.

—— (1979b) 'Weeds', in M. Ryan (ed.), *The Origins of Metallurgy in Atlantic Europe*, Proceedings of the Fifth Atlantic Colloquium, Dublin, 363–8.

Grygiel, R. (1980) 'Jama ze spaloną pszenicą kultury pucharów lejkowatych z Opatowic, woj. włocławskie', *Prace i Materiały Muzeum Archeologicznego i Etnograficznego w Łodzi* 26, 41–55.

—— (1986) 'The household cluster as a fundamental social unit of the Lengyel Culture in the Polish Lowlands', *Prace i Materiały Muzeum Archeologicznego i Etnograficznego w Łodzi* 31, 43–270.

Gummel, H. (1913) 'Fund von Viervitz auf Rügen', *Mannus* 5, 300.

Hansen, P.V. and Madsen, B. (1983) 'Flint axe manufacture in the Neolithic. An experimental investigation of a flint axe manufacture site at Hastrup Vægnet, East Zealand', *Journal of Danish Archaeology* 2, 43–59.

Hansen, U.L. (1972) 'Mellem-neolitiske jordgrave fra Vindinge på Sjæland', *Aarbøger* 1971, 5–70.

—— (1973) 'Stålmosegård – en mellem-neolitisk sjællandsk gravplads', *Nationalmuseets Arbejdsmark*, 73–84.

Harck, O. (1980) 'Landschaftgeschichte und Archäologie an der Westküste der jütischen Halbinsel', in G. Kossack (ed.), *Archsum auf Sylt*, Römisch-Germanische Forschungen 39, Mainz, 32–63.

Härke, H. (1989) 'The Unkel Symposia: the beginnings of a debate in West German archaeology', *Current Anthropology* 30, 406–10.

Helbæk, H. (1954) 'Prehistoric food plants and weeds in Denmark', *Danmarks Geologiske Undersøgelse* II, Række Nr 80, 250–61.

Hensel, W. and Milisauskas, S. (1985) *Excavations of Neolithic and Early Bronze Age Sites in South-Eastern Poland*, Ossolineum, Wrocław.

Herfert, P. (1962) 'Die Steinäxte der Trichterbecherkultur im Elb-Saale-Gebiet', *Wissenschaftliche Zeitschrift der Martin-Luther-Universität Halle-Wittenberg* 11, 1097–140.

Herms, A. (1928) 'Die Megalithgräber des Kreises Jerichow I', *Festschrift des Magdeburger Museums für Natur- und Heimatkunde zur 10. Tagung für Vorgeschichte*, 243–62.

Higham, C.F.W. (1969) 'The economic basis of the Danish Funnel-Necked Beaker (TRB) culture', *Acta Archaeologica* 40, 200–9.

Higham, C.F.W. and Message, M. (1969) 'An assessment of a prehistoric technique of bovine husbandry', in D. Brothwell and E. Higgs (eds), *Science in Archaeology*, Thames & Hudson, London, 315–30.

Hingst, H. (1958) 'Die Trichterbecherkultur', in H. Hingst (ed.), *Vorgeschichte des Kreises Stormarn*, Neumünster, 24–7.

—— (1970) 'Eine jungsteinzeitliche Siedlung in Büdelsdorf', *Heimatkundliches Jahrbuch für den Kreis Rendsburg* 20, 55–69.

—— (1971a) 'Ein befestigtes Dorf aus der Jungsteinzeit in Büdelsdorf (Holstein)', *Archäologisches Korrespondenzblatt* 1, 191–4.

—— (1971b) 'Eine befestigte jungsteinzeitliche Siedlung in Büdelsdorf, Kr. Rendsburg-Eckernförde', *Offa* 28, 90–3.

—— (1974) 'Flachgräber der Stein- und Bronzezeit aus Schleswig-Holstein', *Offa* 31, 19–67.

—— (1985) 'Großsteingräber in Schleswig-Holstein', *Offa* 42, 57–112.

Hjelmqvist, H. (1982) 'Economic plants from a Middle Neolithic site in Scania', *Meddelanden från Lunds Universitets Historiska Museum* 1981–1982, 108–13.

Hodder, I. (1982a) *Symbols in Action*, Cambridge University Press, Cambridge.

—— (1982b) 'Sequences of structural change in the Dutch Neolithic', in I. Hodder (ed), *Symbolic and Structural Archaeology*, Cambridge University Press, Cambridge, 162–77.

—— (1984) 'Burials, houses, women and men in the European neolithic', in D. Miller and C. Tilley (eds), *Ideology, Power and Prehistory*, Cambridge University Press, Cambridge, 51–68.

—— (1986) *Reading the Past. Current Approaches to Interpretation in Archaeology*, Cambridge University Press, Cambridge.

Hoika, J. (1971) 'Mittelneolithische Trichterbecherkultur in Nordostholstein', *Offa* 28, 27–46.

—— (1973) 'Keramik vom Übergang zwischen Früh- und

Mittelneolithikum aus Holstein', *Archäologisches Korrespondenzblatt* 4, 405–7.

—— (1979) 'Funde aus einem Megalithgrab in Kampen/Sylt', *Kölner Jahrbuch für Vor- und Frühgeschichte* 16, 40–53.

—— (1981) 'Jungsteinzeitliche Siedlungsreste aus Oldenburg-Dannau, Kreis Ostholstein', *Offa* 38, 53–72.

—— (1983) 'Neolithikum', *Kreis Herzogtum Lauenburg* I (Führer zu archäologischen Denkmälern in Deutschland), Stuttgart, 56–70.

—— (1986) 'Die Bedeutung des Oldenburger Grabens für Besiedlung und Verkehr im Neolithikum', *Offa* 43, 185–208.

—— (1987) *Das Mittelneolithikum zur Zeit der Trichterbecherkultur in Nordostholstein*, Offa-Bücher 61, Neumünster.

Hopf, M. (1957) 'Botanik und Vorgeschichte. 1. Allgemeines. 2. Die Bernburger Getreidefunde vom Lietfeld bei Burgdorf, Kr. Goslar', *Jahrbuch des Römisch-Germanischen Zentralmuseums Mainz* 4, 1–22.

—— (1961) 'Bearbeitung und Auswertung vorgeschichtlicher pflanzlicher Funde', *Berichte des 5. internationalen Kongresses der Vor- und Frühgeschichte*, Hamburg 1958, 404–7.

Hulthén, N. (1977) *On Ceramic Technology during the Scanian Neolithic and Bronze Age*. Thesis and Papers in North-European Archaeology 6, Stockholm.

Huntington, R. and Metcalf, P. (1979) *Celebrations of Death*, Cambridge University Press, Cambridge.

Ilkiewicz, Z. (1989) 'From studies on cultures of the 4th millennium BC in the central part of the Polish coastal area', *Przegląd Archeologiczny* 36, 17–55.

Iversen, J. (1941) 'Landnam i Danmarks stenalder', *Danmarks Geologiske Undersøgelse* II, Række Nr. 66.

—— (1960) 'Problems of the early post-glacial forest development in Denmark', *Danmarks Geologiske Undersøgelse* IV, Række Bd. 4. Nr. 3, 5–32.

—— (1973) 'The development of Denmark's nature since the last Glacial', *Danmarks Geologiske Undersøgelse* Ser. No. 7-C, 1–126.

Jacob-Friesen, K.H. (1959) *Einführung in Niedersachsens Urgeschichte*. I, *Steinzeit*, Hildesheim.

Jadczykowa, I. (1970) 'Sprawozdanie z badań prowadzonych w latach 1967 i 1968 na stanowisku 1 w Wietrzychowicach, pow. Koło', *Prace i Materiały Muzeum Archeologicznego i Etnograficznego w Łodzi* 17, 125–43.

Jankowska, D. (1980) *Kultura pucharów lejkowatych na Pomorzu Środkowym*, Wydawnictwo Naukowe Uniwersytetu Im. Adama Mickiewicza, Poznań.

—— (1983) 'Kultury pucharów lejkowatych i amfor kulistych na Pomorzu', in T. Malinowski (ed), *Problemy Epoki Kamienia na Pomorzu*, Słupsk, 147–66.

Jankowska, D., Kośko, A., Siuchniński, K., Quitta, H. and Kohl, G. (1979) 'Untersuchungen zur Chronologie der neolithischen Kulturen im polnishen Tiefland', *Zeitschrift für Archäologie* 13, 219–40.

Jankuhn, H. (1969) *Vor- und Frühgeschichte von Neolithikum bis zur Völkerwanderungszeit*, Deutsche Agrargeschichte 1, Stuttgart.

Jarman, M.R., Bailey, G.N. and Jarman, H.N. (1982) *Early European*

Agriculture: its Foundations and Development, Papers in Economic
Prehistory 3, Cambridge University Press, Cambridge.

Jastrzębski, S. (1985) 'Imports of the Tripolye culture pottery in the
south-eastern group of the Funnel Beaker culture', *Memoires
Archeologiques*, 71–92.

Jażdżewski, K. (1932) 'Zusammenfassender Überblick über die
Trichterbecherkultur', *Praehistorische Zeitschrift* 23, 77–110.

—— (1936) *Kultura Pucharów Lejkowatych w Polsce Zachodniej i
Środkowej*, Polskie Towarzystwo Prehistoryczne, Poznań.

—— (1938) 'Cmentarzyska kultury ceramiki wstęgowej i związane z
nimi ślady osadnictwa w Brześciu Kujawskim', *Wiadomości
Archeologiczne* 15, 1–105.

—— (1961) 'Kultura pucharów lejkowatych, rozważania na temat jej
genezy i systematyki', *Prace i Materiały Muzeum Archeologicznego i
Etnograficznego w Łodzi* 6, 73–100.

—— (1965) 'Młodsza epoka kamienia', in J. Kostrzewski,
W. Chmielewski, and K. Jażdżewski (eds), *Pradzieje Polski*,
Wrocław, 55–118.

—— (1970) 'Wzajemny stosunek do siebie elementów północnych,
południowych i zachodnich w obrębie kultury pucharów
lejkowatych', *Prace i Materiały Muzeum Archeologicznego i
Etnograficznego w Łodzi* 17, 49–76.

—— (1973a) 'The relations between Kujavian barrows in Poland and
megalithic tombs in northern Germany, Denmark and Western
European countries', in G. Daniel and P. Kjærum (eds), *Megalithic
Graves and Ritual*, Papers presented at the Third Atlantic
Colloquium, Moesgård 1969, København, 63–74.

—— (1973b) 'Zagadnienie najwcześniejszego poziomu występowania
miedzi w Europie środkowej', *Prace i Materiały Muzeum
Archeologicznego i Etnograficznego w Łodzi* 20, 5–13.

—— (1981) *Pradzieje Europy Środkowej*, Zakład Narodowy im.
Ossolińskich, Wrocław.

Jennbert, K. (1984) *Den produktiva gåvan. Tradition och innovation i
Sydskandinavien för omkring 5300 år sedan*, Acta Archaeologica
Lundensia, Ser. prima in 4°, 16, Lund.

—— (1985) 'Neolithisation – a Scanian perspective', *Journal of Danish
Archaeology* 4, 196–7.

—— (1988) 'Der Neolithisierungsprozeß in Südskandinavien',
Praehistorische Zeitschrift 63, 1–22.

Jennsen, J. (1982) *The Prehistory of Denmark*, Methuen, London and
New York.

Jeppesen, J. (1984) 'Funktionsbestemmelse af flintredskaber.
Slidsporsanalyse af skrabere fra Sarup', *Kuml* 1982–1983, 31–60.

Jessen, K. (1939) 'Kornfund. Bundsø. En yngre stenalders boplads paa
Als', *Aabøger* 1939, 65–84.

Jochim, M.A. (1976) *Hunter-Gatherer Subsistence and Settlement. A
Predictive Model*, Academic Press, New York.

Johansen, K.F. (1917) 'Jordgrave fra Dyssetid', *Aarbøger* 1917, 131–47.

Johansson, L. (1979) *Socio-ekonomiska strukturer i tidigt neolitikum och
deres förutsättningar*, Göteborg.

—— (1981) 'Bistoft LA 11. Siedlungs- und Wirtschaftsformen im frühen Neolithikum Norddeutschlands und Südskandinaviens', *Offa* 38, 91–129.

Jørgensen, E. (1971) 'Hagebrogård – jættestuen', *Nationalmuseets Arbejdsmark*, 77–92.

—— (1977) *Hagebrogård – Vroue – Koldkur. Neolithische Gräberfelder aus Nordwest Jütland*, Arkaeologiske Studier IV, København.

Jørgensen, G. (1977) 'Et kornfund fra Sarup. Bidrag til belysning af tragtbægerkulturens agerbrug', *Kuml* 1976, 47–64.

Just, F. (1963) 'Frühneolithische Funde und bronzezeitliche Hügelgräber "auf dem Kampen" im Forst von Kläden, Kreis Lübz, *Jahrbuch für Bodendenkmalpflege in Mecklenburg* 1963, 31–83.

Kaelas, L. (1955) 'Wann sind die erste Megalithgräber in Holland entstanden? Ein Datierungsversuch', *Palaeohistoria* 4, 47–79.

—— (1956) 'Dolmen und Ganggräber in Schweden', *Offfa* 15, 5–24.

—— (1967) 'The megalithic tombs in South Scandinavia – migration or cultural influence', *Palaeohistoria* 12, 287–321.

—— (1983) 'Megaliths of the Funnel Beaker culture in Germany and Scandinavia', in C. Renfrew (ed.), *The Megalithic Monuments of Western Europe*, Thames & Hudson, London, 77–91.

Kampffmeyer, U. (1983) 'Der neolithische Siedlungsplatz Hüde I am Dümmer', in G. Wegner (ed.), *Frühe Bauernkulturen in Niedersachsen*, Staatliches Museum für Naturkunde und Vorgeschichte, Oldenburg, 119–34.

Kapica, Z. (1986) 'Identyfikacja antropologiczna pochówków z osady kultury pucharów lejkowatych (KPL) w Sarnowie (stan. 1A), woj. Włocławek', *Sprawozdania Archeologiczne* 38, 91–107.

Kempfner-Jørgensen, L. and Watt, M. (1985) 'Settlement sites with Middle Neolithic houses at Grødby, Bornholm', *Journal of Danish Archaeology* 4, 87–100.

Kinnes, I. (1975) 'Monumental function in British Neolithic burial practice', *World Archaeology* 7, 16–29.

—— (1981) 'Dialogues with death', in R. Chapman, I. Kinnes and K. Randsborg (eds), *The Archaeology of Death*, Cambridge University Press, Cambridge, 83–91.

Kirkowski, R. (1987) 'Kultury cyklu wstęgowego na ziemi chełmińskiej', in T. Wiślański (ed.), *Neolit i Początki Epoki Brązu na Ziemi Chełmińskiej*, Toruń, 55–74.

Kirsch, E. (1981) 'Die Havelländische Kultur und ihre kulturellen Beziehungen', *Jahresschrift für Mitteldeutsche Vorgeschichte* 63, 99–111.

Kjærum, P. (1955) 'Tempelhus fra stenalder', *Kuml*, 1955, 7–35.

—— (1957) 'Storsensgrave ved Tustrup', *Kuml* 1957, 9–23.

—— (1967a) 'The chronology of the passage-graves in Jutland', *Palaeohistoria* 12, 323–33.

—— (1967b) 'Mortuary houses and funerary rites in Denmark', *Antiquity* 41, 190–1.

—— (1969) 'Jættestuen Jordhøj', *Kuml* 1969, 9–66.

—— (1977) 'En langhøjs tilblivelse', *Antikvariske Studier* (tilegnet Knud Thorvildsen), 19–26.

Klichowska, M. (1975) 'Najstarsze zboża z wykopalisk polskich', *Archeologia Polski* 20, 83–104.

Kliewe, H. (1979) 'The quaternary history of the Baltic: the German

Democratic Republic', in V. Gudelis and L.K. Königsson (eds), *The Quaternary History of the Baltic*, Acta Universitatis Upsaliensis 1, Uppsala, 185–93.

Knöll, H. (1952) 'Wanderungen, Handel, Ideenausbreitung und Töpferwerkstätten bei der norddeutschen Tiefstichkeramik', *Archaeologia Geographica* 2, 35–40.

—— (1953) 'Zum Frühneolithikum des Nordens', *Festschrift des Römisch-Germanischen Zentralmuseums in Mainz* 3, 29–56.

—— (1959) *Die nordwestdeutsche Tiefstichkeramik und ihre Stellung im nord- und mitteleuropäischen Neolithikum*, Münster.

—— (1976) 'Frühneolithische Flaschengefässe des Nordens', *Bericht der Römisch-Germanischen Kommission* 57, 1–47.

—— (1978) 'Reichverzierte Becher des Frühneolithikums aus Jütland', *Germania* 56, 395–405.

—— (1980) 'Nordhessische Kragenflaschen', *Fundberichte aus Hessen* 19/20, 177–81.

—— (1981) *Kragenflaschen. Ihre Verbreitung und ihre Zeitstellung im europäischen Neolithikum*, Offa-Bücher 41, Neumünster.

—— (1983) *Die Megalithgräber von Langerich-Wechte (Kreis Steinfurt)*, Bodenaltertümer Westfalens 21, Münster.

Knörzer, K.H. (1971) 'Urgeschichtliche Unkräuter im Rheinland, ein Beitrag zur Entstehungsgeschichte der Segetalgesellschaften', *Vegetatio* 23, 89–111.

Koch Nielsen, E. (n.d.) *Typeopdeling og datering af tidligneolitiske tragtbægre*, Unpublished manuscript.

Kock, J. and Gebauer, B. (1976) 'En dysse fra Aal sogn – om anlægget og dets keramik', *Mark og Montre*, 12–24.

Körner, G. and Laux, F. (1971) *Vorgeschichte im Landkreis Lüneburg*, Museumsverein für das Fürstentum Lüneburg, Lüneburg.

—— (1980) *Ein Königreich an der Luhe*, Museumsverein für das Fürstentum Lüneburg, Lüneburg.

Kośko, A. (1980) 'The position of Funnel Beaker culture in the lowland model of neolithization', in J.K. Kozłowski and J. Machnik (eds), *Problèmes de la néolithisation dans certaines régions de l'Europe*, Ossolineum, Wrocław, 123–38.

—— (1981) *Udział południowo-wschodnioeuropejskich wzorców kulturowych w rozwoju niżowych społeczeństw kultury pucharów lejkowatych*, Adam Mickiewicz University of Poznań Archaeological Series 19, Poznań.

—— (1982a) 'Epoka Kamienia', in A. Cofta-Broniewska and A. Kośko (eds), *Historia Pierwotna Społeczeństw Kujaw*, Państwowe Wydawnictwo Naukowe, Warszawa, 11–120.

—— (1982b) 'Z badań nad problematyką równoleżnikowych kontaktów kulturowych społeczeństw dorzeczy Odry i Wisły w młodszej epoce kamienia. Zagadnienie tzw. wpływów kultury michelsberskiej', *Wiadomości Archeologiczne* 47, 161–7.

—— (1982c) 'Infiltracje osadnicze najstarszych rolników, in A. Cofta-Broniewska and A. Kośko (eds), *W Poszukiwaniu Rodowodu Społeczeństwa Kujaw*, Urząd Miejski w Inowrocławiu, Inowrocław, 13–23.

—— (1983) 'Łojewo, gm. Inowrocław, woj. Bydgoszcz, stan. 4, osada z

fazy późnolubońskiej (V) kultury pucharów lejkowatych',
Sprawozdania Archeologiczne 35, 23–50.

—— (1985) 'On the research of the beginnings of the parallel
developmental ties of the cultural systems of the boundary of the
Eastern and Western Europe', *Mémoires Archéologiques*, 37–49.

—— (1988) *Osady Kultury Pucharów Lejkowatych w Inowrocławiu-
Mątwach woj. Bydgoszcz, Stanowisko 1*, Adam Mickiewicz University
of Poznań, Inowrocław.

Maśko, A. and Prinke, A. (1977) 'Sierakowo, woj. Bydgoszcz, stan. 8 –
osada a fazy II (wczesnowióreckiej) kultury pucharów lejkowatych',
Fontes Archaeologici Posnanienses 26, 1042.

Kossinna, G. (1909) 'Der Ursprung der Urfinnen und der
Urindogermanen und ihre Ausbreitung nach dem Osten', *Mannus* 1,
17–52.

—— (1910) 'Der Ursprung der Urfinnen und der Urindogermanen und
ihre Ausbreitung nach Osten', *Mannus* 2, 59–91.

—— (1921) 'Entwicklung und Verbreitung der steinzeitlichen
Trichterbecher, Kragenfläschchen und Kugelflaschen', *Mannus* 13,
13–40 and 143–65.

Kowalczyk, J. (1956) 'Osada kultury pucharów lejkowatych w miejsc.
Gródek Nadbużny w świetle badań 1954 roku', *Wiadomości
Archeologiczne* 23, 23–48.

—— (1957) 'Badania osady kultury pucharów lejkowatych w Gródku
Nadbużnym, pow. Hrubieszów, przeprowadzone w r. 1955',
Wiadomości Archeologiczne 24, 37–52.

—— (1958) 'Prace badawcze w 1957 r. osady kultury pucharów
lejkowatych w Gródku Nadbużnym, pow. Hrubieszów', *Wiadomości
Archeologiczne* 25, 314–31.

Kozłowski, J.K. and Kozłowski, S.K. (1975) *Pradzieje Europy od XL
do IV tysiąclecia p.n.e.*, Państwowe Wydawnictwo Naukowe,
Warszawa.

—— (1986) 'Foragers of Central Europe and their acculturation', in M.
Zvelebil (ed.), *Hunters in Transition*, Cambridge University Press,
Cambridge, 95–108.

Kozłowski, S.K. (1975) *Cultural Differentiation of Europe from 10th to
5th Millennium* BC, University of Warsaw Press, Warsaw.

—— (1976a) 'Studies on the European Mesolithic K points',
Archaeologia Polona 17, 7–25.

—— (1976b) 'Studies on the European Mesolithic. II. Rectangles,
rhomboids and trapezoids in northwestern Europe', *Helinium* 16,
43–54.

Kristiansen, K. (1982) 'The Formation of tribal systems in later
European prehistory: northern Europe, 4000–500 BC', in C. Renfrew,
M.J. Rowlands and B.S. Segraves (eds), *Theory and Explanation in
Archaeology*, Academic Press, New York, 241–80.

—— (1984) 'Ideology and material culture: an archaeological
perspective', in M. Spriggs (ed.), *Marxist Perspectives in Archaeology*,
Cambridge University Press, Cambridge, 72–100.

Krog, H. (1979) 'The quaternary history of the Baltic', in V. Gudelis
and L.K. Königsson (eds), *The Quaternary History of the Baltic*,
Acta Universitatis Upsaliensis 1, Uppsala, 207–17.

Kroll, H. (1981) 'Mittelneolithisches Getreide aus Dannau', *Offa* 38, 85–90.

Kruk, J. (1973) *Studia osadnicze nad neolitem wyżyn lessowych*, Ossolineum, Wrocław.

—— (1980) *Gospodarka w Polsce południowo-wschodniej w V–III tysiącleciu p.n.e.*, Ossolineum, Wrocław.

—— (1983) 'Zarys rozwoju rolnictwa neolitycznego w środowisku dorzecza górnej Wisły', in J.K. Kozłowski and S.K. Kozłowski (eds), *Człowiek i środowisko w pradziejach*, Państwowe Wydawnictwo Naukowe, Warszawa, 267–75.

Kruk, J. and Milisauskas, S. (1977) 'Radiocarbon-Datierung aus Bronocice und ihre Bedeutung für die Zeitbestimmung der Trichterbecherkultur in Südost Polen', *Archäologisches Korrespondenzblatt* 7, 249–56.

—— (1979) 'Befestigungen der späten Polgár-Kultur bei Bronocice (Polen)', *Archäologisches Korrespondenzblatt* 9, 9–13.

—— (1981a) 'Chronology of Funnel Beaker, Baden-like and Lublin–Wolhynian settlements at Bronocice, Poland', *Germania* 59, 1–19.

—— (1981b) 'Wyżynne osiedle neolityczne w Bronocicach, woj. kieleckie', *Archeologia Polski* 26, 65–113.

—— (1982) 'Die Wagendarstellung auf einem Trichterbecher aus Bronocice in Polen', *Archäologisches Korrespondenzblatt* 12, 141–44.

—— (1983) 'Chronologia absolutna osadnictwa neolitycznego z Bronocic, woj. kieleckie', *Archeologia Polski* 28, 257–320.

—— (1985) *Bronocice. Osiedle obronne ludności kultury lubelsko – wołyńskiej (2800–2700 lat pne)*, Ossolineum, Wrocław.

Krzak, Z. (1980) *Geneza i Chronologia Kultury Ceramiki Sznurowej w Europie*, Ossolineum, Wrocław.

Kubasiewicz, M. (1984) 'Die Haustiere im Neolithikum Polens', in H. Schwabedissen (ed.), *Die Anfänge des Neolithikums vom Orient bis Nordeuropa*, Teil IX, Bönau Verlag, Köln and Wien, 44–72.

Kulczycka-Leciejewiczowa, A. (1979) 'Pierwsze społeczeństwa rolnicze na ziemiach polskich kultury kręgu naddunajskiego', in W. Hensel and T. Wiślański (eds), *Prahistoria Ziem Polskich*, II *Neolit*, Polska Akademia Nauk, Wrocław, 19–164.

Kupka, P.L.B. (1924) 'Die mitteldeutschen Ganggräber und die Tonware ihrer Zeit', *Beiträge zur Geschichte, Landes- und Volkskunde der Altmark* 4, 429–43.

—— (1927) 'Die steinzeitliche Besiedlung Mitteldeutschlands. Chronologisches und Typologisches', *Beiträge zur Geschichte, Landes- und Volkskunde der Altmark* 5 (3), 109–53.

—— (1928) 'Alter, Wesen und Verbreitung der mitteldeutschen Steinzeitkulturen', *Beiträge zur Geschichte, Landes- und Volkskunde der Altmark* 5 (4), 201–62.

—— (1938) 'Neues über Langdolmenkeramik, über Rössener und über Schönfelder Tonware', *Beiträge zur Geschichte, Landes- und Volkskunde der Altmark* 7 (1), 1–24.

Langenheim, K. (1935) *Die Tonware der Riesensteingräber in Schleswig–Holstein*, Neumünster.

Lanting, J.N. and Mook, W.G. (1977) *The Pre- and Protohistory of the Netherlands in Terms of Radiocarbon Dates*, Groningen.

Larsen, K. (1958) 'Stenalderhuse på Knardrup Galgebakke', *Kuml* 1957, 24–43.

Larsson, L. (1982) 'A causewayed enclosure and a site with Valby Pottery at Stävie, western Scania', *Meddelanden från Lunds Universitets Historiska Museum* 1981–1982, 65–107.

—— (1985) *The Early Neolithic Funnel Beaker Culture in south-west Scania, Sweden*, British Archaeological Reports International Series 264, Oxford.

Laux, F. (1971) 'Ein Steingrab bei Oldendorf im Landkreis Lüneburg', *Archäologisches Korrespondenzblatt* 1, 195–8.

—— (1979) 'Die Großsteingräber im nordöstlichen Niedersachsen', in H. Schirnig (ed.), *Großsteingräber in Niedersachsen*, Hildesheim, 59–82.

—— (1984) 'Bemerkungen zu jungsteinzeitlichen Grabanlagen im Aller-Tal', *Die Kunde* N.F. 34/35 (1983/84), 37–76.

Lech, J. (1981a) *Górnictwo krzemienia społeczności wczesnorolniczych na Wyżynie Krakowskiej*, Ossolineum, Wrocław.

—— (1981b) 'Flint mining among the early farming communities of central Europe', *Przegląd Archeologiczny* 28, 5–55.

Lech, J. and Młynarczyk H. (1981) 'Uwagi o krzemieniarstwie społeczności wstęgowych i wspólnot kultury pucharów lejkowatych. Próba konfrontacji', in T. Wiślański (ed.), *Kultura Pucharów Lejkowatych w Polsce,*. Poznań, 11–36.

Legge, A.J. (1981) 'Aspects of cattle husbandry', in R, Mercer (ed.), *Farming Practice in British Prehistory*, Edinburgh University Press, Edinburgh, 169–81.

Lichardus, J. (1976) *Rössen–Gatersleben–Baalberge. Ein Beitrag zur Chronologie des mitteldeutschen Neolithikums und zur Entstehung der Trichterbecherkultur*, Bonn.

Lies, H. 91974) 'Zur neolithischen Siedlungsintensität im Magdeburger Raum', *Jahresschrift für Mitteldeutsche Vorgeschichte* 58, 57–111.

Liversage, D. (1981) 'Neolithic monuments at Lindebjerg, northwest Zealand', *Acta Archaeologica* 51, 85–152.

—— (1982) 'An Early neolithic ritual structure on Sejerø', *Journal of Danish Archaeology* 1, 13–18.

—— (1983) 'Træbyggede grave fra den ældste bondestenalder', *Nationalmuseets Arbejdsmark*, 5–16.

Liversage, D. and Singh, P.K. (1985) 'A comparison of two Neolithic flint industries', *Journal of Danish Archaeology* 4, 70–8.

Lomborg, E. (1962) 'Zur Frage der bandkeramischen Einflüsse in Südskandinavien', *Acta Archaeologica* 33, 1–38.

—— (1977) 'Klokkebæger- og senere Beaker-indflydelser i Danmark', *Aarbøger* 1975, 20–41.

Louwe Kooijmans, L.P. (1971) 'Mesolithic bone and antler implements from the North Sea and from the Netherlands:, *Berichten van de Rijksdienst voor het Oudheidkundig Bodemonderzoek* 20/21 (1970–1971), 27–73.

—— (1974) 'The Rhine/Meuse delta, four studies on its prehistoric occupation and holocene geology', *Analecta Praehistorica Leidensia* 7.

—— (1976a) 'The Neolithic at the Lower Rhine. Its structure in chronological and geographical respects', in S.J. De Laet

Acculturation and Continuity in Atlantic Europe, Proceedings of the Fourth Atlantic Colloquium, Ghent 1975, Brugge, 150–73.

—— (1976b) 'Local developments in a borderland. A survey of the Neolithic at the Lower Rhine', *Oudheidkundige Mededelingen uit het Rijksmuseum van Oudheden te Leiden* 57, 227–97.

—— (1980a) 'De Midden-Neolithische Vondstgroep van het Vormer bij Wijchen en het Cultuurpatroon rond de Zuidelijke Noordzee', *Oudhedigkundige Mededelingen uit het Rijksmuseum van Oudheden te Leiden* 61, 113–208.

—— (1980b) 'Archaeology and coastal change in the Netherlands', in F.H. Thompson (ed.), *Archaeology and Coastal Change*, The Society of Antiquaries of London Occasional Paper (New Series) I, London, 106–33.

Lüning, J. (1967) 'Die Michelsberger Kultur. Ihre Funde in zeitlicher und räumlicher Gliederung', *Berichte der Römisch-Germanischen Kommission* 48, 1–350.

—— (1980) 'Getreideanbau ohne Düngung', *Archäologisches Korrespondenzblatt* 10, 117–22.

Machnik, J. (1979) 'Krąg kulturowy ceramiki sznurowej', in W. Hensel and T. Wiślański (eds), *Prahistoria Ziem Polski*. Tom 2: *Neolit*, Ossolineum, Wrocław, 337–411.

Madsen, A.P. (1896) *Gravhøje og Gravfund fra Stenalderen i Danmark*. I, *Det østlige Danmark*, Kjøbenhavn.

—— (1900) *Gravhøje og Gravfund fra Stenalderen i Danmark*. II, *Fyen og Jylland*, Kjøbenhavn.

Madsen, B. (1984) 'Flint axe manufacture in the Neolithic: experiments with grinding and polishing of thin-butted flint axes', *Journal of Danish Archaeology* 3, 47–62.

Madsen, B. and Fiedel, R. (1987) 'Pottery manufacture at a Neolithic causewayed enclosure near Hevringholm, E. Jutland', *Journal of Danish Archaeology* 6, 78–86.

Madsen, B. and Nielsen, P.O. (1977) 'To tidlig-neolitiske jordgrave', *Antikvariske Studier* (tilegnet Knud Thorvildsen), 27–34.

Madsen, C. and Thrane, H. (1983) 'Sydvestfynske dysser og yngre stenalders bebyggelse', *Fynske Minder* 1982, 17–42.

Madsen, T. (1972) 'Grave med teltformet overbygning fra tidligneolitisk tid', *Kuml* 1971, 127–49.

—— (1975) 'Tidlig neolitiske anlæg ved Tolstrup', *Kuml* 1973–1974, 121–54.

—— (1976) 'Stendyngegrave ved Fjelsø', *Kuml* 1975, 73–82.

—— (1977) 'Jættestuen Hørret Skov I. Et nyt fund af fodskåle med massiv midtdel', *Kuml* 1976, 65–94.

—— (1978a) 'Toftum ved Horsens. Et "befæstet" anlæg tilhørende tragtbægerkulture', *Kuml* 1977, 161–84.

—— (1978b) 'Toftum – ein neues neolithisches Erdwerk bei Horsens, Ostjütland (Dänemark)', *Archäologisches Korrespondenzblatt* 8, 1–7.

—— (1979) 'Earthen long barrows and timber structures: aspects of the Early Neolithic mortuary practice in Denmark', *Proceedings of the Prehistoric Society* 45, 301–20.

—— (1980) 'En tidligneolitisk Langhøj ved Rude i Østjylland', *Kuml* 1979, 79–108.

—— (1982) 'Settlement systems of early agricultural societies in east

Jutland, Denmark: a regional study of change', *Journal of Anthropological Archaeology* 1, 197–236.

—— (1987) 'Where did all the hunters go? An assessment of an epoch-making episode in Danish prehistory', *Journal of Danish Archaeology* 6, 229–39.

—— (1988) 'Causewayed enclosures in south Scandinavia', in C. Burgess, P. Topping, C. Mordant and M. Maddison (eds), *Enclosures and Defences in the Neolithic of Western Europe*, British Archaeological Reports International Series 403, Oxford, 301–36.

Madsen, T. and Jensen, H.J. (1982) 'Settlement and land use in early neolithic Denmark', *Analecta Praehistorica Leidensia* 15, 63–86.

Madsen, T. and Petersen, J.E. (1985) 'Tidligneolitiske anlæg ved Mosegården. Regionale og kronologiske forskelle i tidligneolitikum', *Kuml* 1982–1983, 61–120.

Magny, M. 91982) 'Atlantic and Sub-Boreal: dampness and dryness?', in A. Harding (ed.), *Climatic Change in Later Prehistory*, Edinburgh University Press, Edinburgh, 33–43.

Mahler, D. (1981) 'Hunter's storage – farmer's birth', *Kontaktstencil* 1981, 51–62.

Malmer, M.P. (1962) *Jungneolithische Studien*, Bonn and Lund.

Malmros, C. (1980) 'Den tidlige enkeltgravskultur og stridsøksekultur', *Aarbøger* 1979, 62–8.

Malmros, C. and Tauber, H. (1977) 'Kulstof-14 dateringer af dansk enkeltgravskultur', *Aarbøger* 1975, 78–95.

Mania, D. (1973) 'Eiszeitliche Landschaftsentwicklung im Kartenbild dargestellt am Beispiel des mittleren Elbe-Saale Gebietes', *Jahresschrift für Mitteldeutsche Vorgeschichte* 57, 17–47.

Mania, D. and Preuss, J. (1975) 'Zu Methoden und Problemen ökologischer Untersuchungen in der Ur- und Frühgeschichte', *Symbolae Praehistoricae*, 9–59.

Marseen, O. (1960) 'Ferslev-huset. En kultbygning fra jættestuetid', *Kuml* 1960, 36–55.

Marshall, A. (1981) 'Environmental adaptation and structural design in axially-pitched long houses from Neolithic Europe', *World Archaeology* 13, 101–21.

Maruszczak, H. (1983) 'Procesy rzeźbotwórcze na obszarze Polski w okresie ostatniego zlodowacenia i w holocenie', in J.K. Kozłowski and S.K. Kozłowski (eds), *Człowiek i środowisko w pradziejach*, Państwowe Wydawnictwo Naukowe, Warszawa, 32–42.

Masters, L. (1983) 'Chambered tombs and non-megalithic barrows in Britain', in C. Renfrew (ed.), *The Megalithic Monuments of Western Europe*, Thames & Hudson, London, 97–112.

Mathiasen, T. (1939) 'Bundsø, en yngre stenalders boplads på Als', *Aarbøger* 1939, 1–55.

—— (1940) 'Havnelev – Strandegaard', *Aarbøger* 1940, 1–55.

—— (1943) 'Stenalderbopladser i Aamosen', *Nordiske Fortidsminder* 3, 2–146.

—— (1944) 'The Stone Age settlement at Trelleborg', *Acta Archaeologica* 15, 77–98.

Meurers-Balke, J. (1983) *Siggeneben-Süd. Ein Fundplatz der frühen Trichterbecherkultur an der holsteinischen Ostseeküste*, Offa-Bücher 50, Neumünster.

Midgley, M.S. (1985) *The Origin and Function of the Earthen Long Barrows of Northern Europe*, British Archaeological Reports International Series 259, Oxford.

Mildenberger, G. (1953) *Studien zum mitteldeutschen Neolithikum*, Leipzig.

Milisauskas, S. (1978) *European Prehistory*, Academic Press, New York.

Milisauskas, S. and Kruk, J. (1977) 'Archaeological excavations at the Funnel Beaker (TRB) site of Bronocice', *Archaeologia Polona* 18, 205–28.

Miller, D. and Tilley, C. (1984) 'Ideology, power and prehistory: an introduction', in D. Miller and C. Tilley (eds), *Ideology, Power and Prehistory*, Cambridge University Press, Cambridge, 1–15.

Mitchell, G.F. (1956) 'Post-boreal pollen diagrams from Irish raised bogs', *Proceedings of the Royal Irish Academy* 57B, 185–251.

Młynarczyk, H. 1976 'Materiały krzemienne z grobowców kujawskich w Sarnowie, Gaju, Leśniczówce i Wietrzychowicach', *Światowit* 35, 55–90.

Modderman, P.J.R. (1971) 'Bandkeramiker und Wandernbauerntum', *Archäologisches Korrespondenzblatt* 1, 7–9.

Montelius, O. (1875) 'De svenske flintyxornas olika typor', *Tidskrift för Antropologi* 1.

—— (1894–1905) *Orienten och Europa* (Antiqvarisk Tidskrift för Sverige), Stockholm.

Müller, H.H. (1985) 'Tierreste aus Siedlungsgruben der Bernburger Kultur von der Schalkenburg bei Quenstedt, Kr. Hettstedt', *Jahresschrift für Mitteldeutsche Vorgeschichte* 68, 179–220.

Müller, S. (1888) *Ordning af Danmarks Oldsager* I, København.

—— (1898) 'De jydske enkeltgrave fra stenalderen', *Aarbøger* 1898, 157–289.

—— (1913) 'Sønderjyllands stenalder', *Aarbøger* 1913, 168–322.

—— (1918) *Oldtidens Kunst i Danmark. I, Stenalderen*, København.

Murray, J. (1970) *The First European Agriculture*, Edinburgh University Press, Edinburgh.

Nagel, E. (1980) 'Ein Siedlungsplatz der Trichterbecherkultur in Glasgow, Kreis Pasewalk', *Jahrbuch für Bodendenkmalpflege in Mecklenburg* 1979, 7–38.

—— (1986) 'Neolithische Siedlungsfunde der Trichterbecherkultur aus Lindenbeck, Kreis Lübz', *Jahrbuch für Bodendenkmalpflege in Mecklenburg* 1985, 87–98.

Nelson, H. (1988) *Zur inneren Gliederung und Verbreitung neolithischen Gruppen im südlichen Niederelbegebiet*, British Archaeological Reports International Series 459, Oxford.

Newell, R.R. (1972) 'The Mesolithic affinities and typological relations of the Dutch Bandkeramik flint industry', *Alba Regia* 12, 9–37.

—— (1973) 'The post-glacial adaptations of the indigenous population of the Northwest European Plain', in S.K. Kozłowski (ed.), *The Mesolithic in Europe*, University of Warsaw Press, Warsaw, 399–440.

—— (1980) 'Mesolithic dwelling structures: fact and fantasy', in B. Gramsch (ed.), *Mesolithikum in Europa*, Veröffentlichungen des Museums für Ur- und Frühgeschichte Potsdam Band 14/15, 235–84.

Neustupný, E. (1968) 'Absolute chronology of the Neolithic and

Aeneolithic periods in Central and South-Eastern Europe', *Slovenská Archeologia* 16, 19–60.

Nielsen, F.O. and Nielsen, P.O. (1985) 'Middle and Late Neolithic houses at Limensgård, Bornholm', *Journal of Danish Archaeology* 4, 101–14.

Nielsen, H. (1987) 'An early Neolithic pottery deposition at Ellerødgård I, southern Zealand', *Journal of Danish Archaeology* 6, 63–77.

Nielsen, P.O. (1977) 'Die Flintbeile der frühen Trichterbecherkultur in Dänemark', *Acta Archaeologica* 48, 61–138.

—— (1979) 'De tyknakkede flintøkser kronologi', *Aarbøger* 1977, 5–71.

—— (1982) *Dysser og dolke i stenalderen*, Lademanns Danmarkshistorie Stenalderen 3, København.

—— (1984) 'Flint axes and megaliths – the time and context of the early dolmens in Denmark', in G. Burenhult (ed.), *The Archaeology of Carrowmore*, Theses and Papers in North-European Archaeology 14, Stockholm, 376–87.

—— (1985) 'De første bønder. Nye fund fra den tidligste Tragtbægerkultur ved Sigersted', *Aarbøger* 1984, 96–126.

Niesiołowska, E. (1967) 'Materiały neolityczne ze stanowiska 6 w Pikutkowie, pow. Włocławek', *Prace i Materiały Muzeum Archeologicznego i Etnograficznego w Łodzi* 14, 79–129.

Niesiołowska-Średniowska, E. (1973) 'The problem of Mesolithic tradition in the Neolithic cultures of Poland', in S.K. Kozłowski (ed.), *The Mesolithic in Europe*, University of Warsaw Press, Warsaw, 441–53.

—— (1981) 'Niektóre problemy związane z materiałami krzemiennymi kultury pucharów lejkowatych z fazy AB, pochodzącymi z grobowca 8 w Sarnowie, woj. włocławskie', in T. Wiślański (ed.), *Kultura Pucharów Lejkowatych w Polsce*, Poznań, 37–57.

—— (1982) 'Materiały krzemienne z fazy AB kultury pucharów lejkowatych z grobowca 8 w Sarnowie w woj. włocławskim', *Prace i Materiały Muzeum Archeologicznego i Etnograficznego w Łodzi* 27, 85–155.

Niklasson, N.H. (1925) *Studien über die Walternienburg-Bernburger Kultur. (Jahresschrift für die Vorgeschichte der sächsischthüringischen Länder* 13, 1–183.)

Nilius, I. (1971a) *Das Neolithikum in Mecklenburg*, Schwerin.

—— (1971b) 'Beziehungen des mecklenburgischen Neolithikums zu Skandinavien', in F. Schlette (ed.), *Evolution und Revolution im Alten Orient und in Europa*, Berlin 120–6.

—— (1973) 'Die Siedlung der Trichterbecherkultur bei Gristow, Kr. Greifswald', *Zeitschrift für Archäologie* 7, 239–70.

—— (1975) 'Bemerkungen zu einigen auffälligen Keramikfunden in der Trichterbechersiedlung von Gristow, Kreis Greifswald', *Symbolae Praehistoricae*, 123–32.

Nilius, I. and Warnke, D. (1984) 'Ein eingetiefter Gebäudegrundriß der mittelneolithischen Trichterbecherkultur von Ralswiek, Kreis Rügen', *Jahrbuch für Bodendenkmalpflege in Mecklenburg* 1983, 83–101.

Nilsson, T. (1961) 'Ein neues Standardpollendiagramm aus

Bjärsjöholmsjön in Schonen', *Lunds Universitets Arsskrift* N.F. 2
(56), 2–36.

Nitzschke, W. (1986) 'Ein verzierte Trommel der Salzmünder Kultur
von Gerstewitz, Ortsteil von Zorbau, Kr. Hohenmölsen',
Ausgrabungen und Funde 31, 149–51.

Nobis, G. (1962) 'Die Tierreste prähistorischer Siedlungen aus dem
Satrupholmer Moor (Schleswig-Holstein)', *Zeitschrift für
Tierzüchtung und Züchtungsbiologie* 77, 16–30.

——— (1975) 'Zur Fauna des ellerbekzeitlichen Wohnplatzes Rosenhof in
Ostholstein I (Grabung 1968–73)', *Schriften des
Naturwissenschaftlichen Vereins für Schleswig-Holstein* 45, 5–30.

Nordman, C.A. (1917a) 'Studier öfver gånggriftkulturen i Danmark',
Aarbøger 1917, 269–332.

——— (1917b) 'Jættestuer i Danmark, Nya fynd', *Nordiske Fortidsminder*
2, 55–118.

——— (1935) *The Megalithic Culture of Northern Europe.* (Finska
Fornminnesföreningens Tidskrift 39, 1–137.)

Nyegaard, G. (1985) 'Faunalevn fra yngre stenalder på øerne syd for
Fyn', in J. Skaarup *Yngre Stenalder på øerne syd for Fyn*,
Meddelelser fra Langelands Museum, Rudkøbing, 426–57.

Okulicz, Ł. (1976) *Osadnictwo strefy wschodniobałtyckiej w I tysiącleciu
przed naszą erą*, Ossolineum, Wrocław.

Olausson, D.S. (1983) *Lithic Technological Analysis of the Thin-Butted
Axe. Experiments to Investigate the Effects of Heat Treatment on
Use-wear on Flint Tools*, University of Lund, Lund.

Olausson, D.S., Rudebeck, E. and Säfvestad, U. (1980) 'Die
südschwedischen Feuresteingruben – Ergebnisse und Probleme', in
G. Weisgerber (ed.), *5000 Jahre Feuersteinbergbau*, Deutsches
Bergbau-Museum, Bochum, 183–204.

Ørsnes, M. (1956) 'Om jættestues konstruktion og brug', *Aarbøger*
1956, 221–32.

Ottaway, B. (1973) 'Earliest copper ornaments in northern Europe',
Proceedings of the Prehistoric Society 39, 294–331.

——— (1982) *Earliest Copper Artifacts of the Northalpine Region: Their
Analysis and Evaluation*, Schriften des Seminars für Urgeschichte der
Universität Bern, Bern.

Paludan-Müller, C. (1978) 'High Atlantic food gathering in northwest
Zealand, ecological conditions and spatial representation', in
K. Kristiansen and C. Paludan-Müller (eds), *Studies in Scandinavian
Prehistory and Early History*. The National Museum of Denmark,
120–57.

Pape, W. (1979) 'Histogramme neolithischer 14-C Daten', *Germania*
57, 1–51.

Pätzold, J. (1960) 'Rituelles Pflügen beim vorgeschichtlichen Totenkult
– ein alter indogermanischer Bestattungsbrauch?' *Praehistorische
Zeitschrift* 38, 189–239.

Peleščišin, M.A. (1971) 'Kul'tura lijčastogo posudu', *Archeologija
URSR* 1, 231–40.

Pelisiak, A. (1985) 'Sprawozdanie z badań wykopaliskowych
przeprowadzonych na osadzie kultury pucharów lejkowatych na stan.
1 w Dobroniu, woj. sieradzkie, w latach 1982–1983', *Sprawozdania
Archeologiczne* 37, 9–27.

Petersen, K.S. (1985) 'Det sydfynske arkipelag. Det geologiske udvikling med særlig hensyntagen til havniveauændringer og den marine molluskfauna', in S. Skaarup *Yngre Stenalder på øerne syd for Fyn*, Meddelelser fra Langelands Museum, Rudkøbing, 15–27.

Pieczyński, Z. (1985) 'Uwagi o skarbie miedzianym z Bytynia, woj. poznańskie', *Fontes Archaeologici Posnanienses* 34 (1982–5), 1–7.

Piggott, S. (1967) '"Unchambered" long barrows in Neolithic Britain', *Palaeohistoria* 12 (1966), 381–93.

—— (1983) *The Earliest Wheeled Transport from the Atlantic Coast to the Caspian Sea*, Thames & Hudson, London.

Pleslová-Štiková, E. (1977) 'Die Entstehung der Metallurgie auf dem Balkan, im Karpatenbecken und in Mitteleuropa, unter besonderer Berücksichtungung der Kupferproduktion im ostalpenländischen Zentrum', *Památky Archeologické*, 68, 56–73.

Podkowińska, Z. (1950) 'Osada neolityczna na górze Gawroniec w Ćmielowie, pow. Opatów', *Wiadomości Archeologiczne* 17, 95–146.

—— (1952) 'Prace wykopaliskowe na stanowisku "Gawroniec-Pałyga" w Ćmielowie, w pow. opatowskim 1950r', *Wiadomości Archeologiczne* 18, 201–42.

—— (1961) 'Spichrze ziemne w osadzie kultury pucharów lejkowatych na Gawrońcu-Pałydze w Ćmielowie, pow, Opatów, *Archeologia Polski* 6, 21–63.

Preuss, J. (1958) 'Ein Gräbhugel der Baalberge Gruppe von Preußlitz, Kr. Bernburg', *Jahresschrift für Mitteldeutsche Vorgeschichte* 42, 197.

—— (1966) *Die Baalberger Gruppe in Mitteldeutschland*, Berlin.

—— (1973) 'Megalithgräber mit Alttiefstichkeramik im Haldensleben Forst', Neolithische Studien II, Martin-Luther Universität Halle-Wittenberg, Halle, 127–207.

—— (1980) *Die altmärkische Gruppe der Tiefstichkeramik*, Berlin.

Price, T.D. (1973) 'A proposed model for the procurement systems in the Mesolithic in northwestern Europe', in S.K. Kozłowski (ed.), *The Mesolithic in Europe*, University of Warsaw Press, Warsaw, 455–76.

—— (1980) 'Regional approaches to human adapation in the Mesolithic of the North European Plain', in B. Gramsch (ed.), *Mesolithikum in Europa*, Veröffentlichungen des Museums für Ur- und Frühgeschichte Potsdam Band 14/15, 217–34.

Prinke, A. and Skoczylas, J. (1980) *Neolityczne Surowce Kamienne Polski środkowo-zachodniej*, Państwowe Wydawnictwo Naukowe, Warszaw.

Prinke, D. and Weber, A. (1983) 'Konary, Gm. Dąbrowa Biskupia, woj. Bydgoszcz, stan. 6A–6B', *Sprawozdania Archeologiczne* 34, 25–51.

Raddatz, K. (1952) 'Frühneolithische Keramik aus der Uckermark', *Germania* 30, 6–13.

—— (1956) 'Ein Gefäß der Rössener Kultur aus der Uckermark', *Offa* 15, 25–30.

—— (1979) 'Zur Funktion der Großsteingräber', in H. Schirnig (ed.), *Großsteingräber in Niedersachsen*, Hildesheim, 127–41.

Raetzel-Fabian, D. (1986) *Phasenkartierung des mitteleuropäischen Neolithikums. Chronologie und Chorologie*, British Archaeological Reports International Series 316, Oxford.

Randsborg, K. (1970) 'Eine kupferne Schmuckscheibe aus einem Dolmen in Jütland', *Acta Archaeologica* 41, 181–90.
—— (1975) 'Social dimensions of Early Neolithic Denmark', *Proceedings of the Prehistoric Society* 41, 105–18.
—— (1978) 'Resource distribution and the function of copper in Early Neolithic Denmark', in M. Ryan (ed.), *The Origins of Metallurgy in Atlantic Europe*, Proceedings of the Fifth Atlantic Colloquium, Dublin, 303–18.
Rech, M. (1971) 'Einige tiefstichverzierte "Prachtbecher" und ihre historische Aussagekraft', *Die Kunde* N.F. 22, 27–43.
—— (1979) *Studien zu Depotfunden der Trichterbecher- und Einzelgrabkultur des Nordens*, Offa-Bücher 39, Neumünster.
—— (1980) 'Die Silexbeildeponierung in Norddeutschland', in G. Weisgerber (ed.), *5000 Jahre Feuersteinbergbau*, Deutsches Bergbau-Museum, Bochum, 294–8.
Reed, R.C. (1974) 'Earthen long barrows: a new perspective', *The Antiquaries Journal* 131, 33–57.
Rees, S. (1979) *Agricultural Implements in Prehistoric and Roman Britain*, British Archaeological Reports British Series 69, Oxford.
—— (1981) 'Agricultural tools: function and use', in R.J.M. Mercer (ed.), *Farming Practice in British Prehistory*, Edinburgh University Press, Edinburgh, 66–84.
Reinerth, H. (1939) 'Ein Dorf der Großsteingräberleute', *Germanen-Erbe* 4 (8), 226–42.
Renfrew, C. (1973) *Before Civilisation: The Radiocarbon Revolution and Prehistoric Europe*, Jonathan Cape, London.
—— (1976) 'Megaliths, territories and populations', in S.J. De Laet (ed.), *Acculturation and Continuity in Atlantic Europe*, Brugge, 198–220.
(—— (1980) 'Towards a definition of context; the north German megaliths', *Nachrichten aus Niedersachsens Urgeschichte* 49, 3–20.
Reynolds, P. (1981) 'Deadstock and livestock', in R.J.M. Mercer (ed.), *Farming Practice in British Prehistory*, Edinburgh University Press, Edinburgh, 97–122.
Robinson, S.W. (1984) *Calibration Algorithm*. (Calibration from radiocarbon time-scale to dendroyears.)
Rønne, P. (1979) 'Høj over høj', *Skalk* 5, 3–8.
Rosenberg, G. (1929) 'Nye jættestuefund', *Aarbøger* 1929, 189–262.
—— (1933) 'To jættestuer', *Nationalmuseets Arbejdsmark*, 5–14.
Rowley-Conwy, P. (1979) 'Forkullet korn fra Lindebjerg. En boplads fra ældre bronzealder', *Kuml* 1978, 159–71.
—— (1981) 'Slash and burn in the temperate European Neolithic', in R.J.M. Mercer (ed.), *Farming Practice in British Prehistory*, Edinburgh University Press, Edinburgh, 85–96.
—— (1982) 'Forest grazing and clearance in temperate Europe with special reference to Denmark: an archaeological view', in M. Bell and S. Limbrey (eds), *Archaeological Aspects of Woodland Ecology*, British Archaeological Reports International Series 146, Oxford, 199–215.
—— (1983) 'Sedentary hunters: the Ertebølle example', in G.N. Bailey (ed.) *Hunter-Gatherer Economy in Prehistory*, Cambridge University Press, Cambridge, 111–26.
—— (1984) 'The laziness of the short-distance hunter: the origins of

agriculture in western Denmark', *Journal of Anthropological Archaeology* 3, 300–24.

—— (1985a) 'Mellemneolitisk økonomi i Danmark og Sydengland. Knoglefundene fra Fannerup', *Kuml* 1984, 77–111.

—— (1985b) 'The origins of agriculture in Denmark: a review of some theories', *Journal of Danish Archaeology* 4, 188–95.

—— (1986) 'Between cave painters and crop planters: aspects of the temperate European Mesolithic', in M. Zvelebil (ed.), *Hunters in Transition*, Cambridge University Press, Cambridge, 17–32.

—— (1987) 'The interpretation of ard marks', *Antiquity*, 61, 263–6.

Rozoy, J.G. (1971) 'Tardenoisien et Sauveterrien', *Bulletin de la Societè Prèhistorique Française* 68, 345–74.

Rudebeck, E. (1987) 'Flintmining in Sweden during the Neolithic period: new evidence from the Kvarnby-S. Sallerup area', in G. de G. Sieveking and M.H. Newcomer (eds), *The Human Uses of Flint and Chert*, Cambridge University Press, Cambridge, 151–7.

Sadłowska, A. (1971), 'Sytuacja morfologiczna okolicy cmentarzyska kultury pucharów lejkowatych na stanowisku 1 w Sarnowie, powiat Włocławek', *Prace i Materiały Muzeum Archeologicznego i Etnograficznego w Łodzi* 18, 105–12.

Salomonsson, B. (1963) 'An early neolithic settlement site from SW Scania', *Meddelanden från Lunds Universitets Historiska Museum* 1962–1963, 65–122.

—— (1970) 'Die Värby funde. Ein Beitrag zur Kenntnis der ältesten Trichterbecherkultur in Schonen', *Acta Archaeologica* 41, 55–95.

Samsonowicz, J. (1923) 'O złożach krzemieni w utworach jurajskich północno-wschodniego zbocza Gór Świętokrzyskich', *Wiadomości Archeologiczne* 8, 17–24.

—— (1925) 'Odkrycie pierwotnych złóż krzemienia szarego białonakrapianego', *Wiadomości Archeologiczne* 9, 99–101.

Schild, R. (1987) 'The exploitation of chocolate flint in central Poland', in G. de G. Sieveking and M.H. Newcomer (eds), *The Human Uses of Flint and Chert*, Cambridge University Press, Cambridge, 137–49.

Schild, R., Królik, H. and Marczak, M. (1985) *Kopalnia Krzemienia Czekoladowego w Tomaszowie*, Ossolineum, Wrocław.

Schindler, R. (1953) 'Die Entdeckung zweier jungsteinzeitlicher Wohnplätze unter dem Marschenschlick im Vorgelände der Boberger Dünen und ihre Bedeutung für die Steinzeitforschung Nordwestdeutschlands', *Hammaburg* 4, 1–17.

—— (1961) 'Rössener Elemente im Frühneolithikum von Boberg', *Hammaburg* 13, 9–29.

Schirnig, H. (1979a) 'Siedlungsräume der Trichterbecherkultur am Beispiel des Landkreises Uelzen', in H. Schirnig (ed.), *Großsteingräber in Niedersachsen*, Hildesheim, 223–7.

—— (1979b) 'Das "Huntedorf" bei Lembruch am Dümmer', in H. Schirnig (ed.), *Großsteingräber in Niedersachsen*, Hildesheim, 235–8.

—— (1979c) 'Die Siedlung Hüde I am Dümmer', in H. Schirnig (ed.), *Großsteingräber in Niedersachsen*, Hildesheim, 239–40.

—— (1979d) 'Die Siedlung auf dem Lührsberg bei Dohnsen, Kreis Celle', in H. Schirnig (ed.), *Großsteingräber in Niedersachsen*, Hildesheim, 241–3.

—— (1979e) 'Die Siedlung auf dem Schwarzen Berg bei Wittenwater,

Kr. Uelzen', in H. Schirnig (ed.), *Großsteingräber in Niedersachsen*, Hildesheim, 244–6.

—— (ed.) (1979f) *Großsteingräber in Niedersachsen*, Hildesheim.

Schlicht, E. (1965) 'Die Funde aus dem Steingrab 2 von Emmeln, Kr. Meppen', *Germania* 43, 351–4.

—— (1968) *Die Funde aus dem Megalithgrab 2 von Emmeln, Kr. Meppen*, Göttinger Schriften zur Vor- und Frühgeschichte 9, Neumünster.

—— (1971) 'Töpferwerkstätten in Niedersachsen vor 4500 Jahren', *Die Kunde* N.F. 22, 14–26.

—— (1972) *Das Megalithgrab 7 von Gross Berssen, Kreis Meppen*, Göttinger Schriften zur Vor- und Frühgeschichte 12, Neumünster.

—— (1973) 'Kupferschmuck aus Megalithgräbern Nordwestdeutschlands', *Nachrichten aus Niedersachsens Urgeschichte* 42, 13–52.

—— (1979) 'Die Großsteingräber im nordwestlichen Niedersachsen', in H. Schirnig (ed.), *Großsteingräber in Niedersachsen*, Hildesheim, 43–58.

Schlüter, W. (1979) 'Die Siedlungsgebiete der Trichterbecherkultur im Osnabrücker Raum', in H. Schirnig (ed.), *Großsteingräber in Niedersachsen*, Hildesheim, 228–34.

Schrickel, W. (1957) *Westeuropäische Elemente im Neolithikum und in der frühen Bronzezeit Mitteldeutschlands* I and II, Leipzig.

—— (1966) *Westeuropäische Elemente im neolithischen Grabbau Mitteldeutschlands und die Galeriegräber Westdeutschlands und ihre Inventare* I and II, Bonn.

Schuldt, E. (1961) 'Abschliessende Ausgrabungen auf dem jungsteinzeitlichen Flachgräberfeld von Ostrof 1961', *Jahrbuch für Bodendenkmalpflege in Mecklenburg* 1961, 131–78.

—— (1965) 'Ein kammerloses Hünenbett von Stralendorf, Kreis Schwerin', *Jahrbuch für Bodendenkmalpflege in Mecklenburg* 1965, 9–29.

—— (1966a) *Dolmen und Gangräber an der Recknitz*, Schwerin.

—— (1966b) 'Die Großsteingräber an der mittleren Recknitz', *Jahrbuch für Bodendenkmalpflege in Mecklenburg* 1966, 7–20.

—— (1966c) 'Das kammerlose Hünenbett von Gnewitz, Kreis Rostock', *Jahrbuch für Bodendenkmalpflege in Mecklenburg* 1966, 20–5.

—— (1967) *Riesensteingräber an der Warnow*, Schwerin.

—— (1968) *4000jährige Gräber im Everstorfer Forst*, Schwerin.

—— (1970) *Dolmenlandschaft an der Schwinge*, Schwerin.

—— (1971) *Steinzeitliche Grabmonumente der Insel Rügen*, Schwerin.

—— (1972a) *Die mecklenburgischen Megalithgräber. Untersuchungen zu ihrer Architektur und Funktion*, Berlin.

—— (1972b) *Steinzeitliche Keramik aus Mecklenburg*, Schwerin.

—— (1974a) 'Die steinzeitliche Inselsiedlung im Malchiner See bei Basedow, Kreis Malchin', *Jahrbuch für Bodendenkmalpflege in Mecklenburg* 1973, 7–65.

—— (1974b) 'Der Bernstein im Neolithikum Mecklenburgs', *Jahrbuch für Bodendenkmalpflege in Mecklenburg* 1973, 99–120.

—— (1979) *Ur- und frühgeschichtliche Denkmäler beiderseits großer Straßen*, Schwerin.

Schulze-Motel, J. (1972) 'Kulturpflanzenabdrücke aus der Baalberger Gruppe', *Jahresschrift für Mitteldeutsche Vorgeschichte* 56, 59–60.

Schütrumpf, R. (1972) 'Stratigraphie und pollenanalytische Ergebnisse der Ausgrabung des Ellerbekzeitlichen Wohnplatzes Rosenhof (Ostholstein)', *Archäologisches Korrespondenzblatt* 2, 9–16.

Schwabedissen, H. (1944) *Die mittlere Steinzeit im westlichen Norddeutschland*, Offa-Bücher 7, Neumünster.

—— (1953a) 'Moorsiedlung Oldesloe-Wolkenwehe, Kr. Stormarn', *Germania* 31, 230–1.

—— (1953b) 'Fruchtschalen aus Schleswig-Holstein und ihre Zeit', *Offa* 12, 14–66.

—— (1955a) 'Siedlung Heidmoor, gem. Berlin, Kr. Segeberg', *Germania* 33, 256–8.

—— (1955b) 'Siedlung Sachsenwaldau, Kr. Stormarn', *Germania* 33, 258.

—— (1958a) 'Untersuchungen mesolithisch-neolithischer Moorsiedlungen in Schleswig-Holstein', *Neue Ausgrabungen in Deutschland*, 26–42.

—— (1958b) 'Die Ausgrabungen im Satruper Moor', *Offa* 16, 5–28.

—— (1958c) 'Die jungsteinzeitlichen Wohnplätze der Trichterbecherkultur aus Sachsenwaldau und Wolkenwehe', in H. Hingst (ed.), *Vorgeschichte des Kreises Stormarn*, Neumünster, 24–7.

—— (1962) 'Die Haustierhaltung in Schleswig-Holstein im Lichte der Archäologie', *Zeitschrift für Tierzüchtung und Züchtungsbiologie* 77, 255–76.

—— (1963) 'Der neolithische Fundplatz Fuchsberg im Satruper Moor', *Praehistorische Zeitschrift* 41, 202–4.

—— (1967) 'Ein horizontierter "Breitkeil" aus Satrup und die mannigfachen Kulturverbindungen des beginnenden Neolithikums im Norden und Nordwesten', *Palaeohistoria* 12, 409–68.

—— (1968) 'Der Übergang vom Mesolithikum zum Neolithikum in Schleswig-Holstein', *Führer vor- und frühgeschichtlichen Denkmälern* 9, 9–26.

—— (1970) 'Ausgrabungen auf dem neolithischen Wohnplatz Sachsenwaldau, Kreis Stormarn (Schleswig-Holstein)', *Praehistorische Zeitschrift* 45, 220–5.

—— (1972) 'Rosenhof (Ostholstein), ein Ellerbek-Wohnplatz am einstigen Ostseeufer', *Archäologisches Korrespondenzblatt* 2, 1–8.

—— (1979a) 'Die "Rosenhof Gruppe". Ein neuer Fundkomplex des Frühneolithikums in Schleswig-Holstein', *Archäologisches Korrespondenzblatt* 9, 167–72.

—— (1979b) 'Zum Alter der Großsteingräber in Norddeutschland', in H. Schirnig (ed.), *Großsteingräber in Niedersachsen*, Hildesheim, 143–60.

—— (1979c) 'Der Beginn des Neolithikums im nordwestlichen Deutschland', in H. Schirnig (ed.), *Großsteingräber in Niedersachsen*, Hildesheim, 203–22.

—— (1980) 'Ertebølle/Ellerbek – Mesolithikum oder Neolithikum?' in B. Gramsch (ed.), *Mesolithikum in Europa*, Veröffentlichungen des Museums für Ur- und Frühgeschichte Potsdam Band 14/15, 129–42.

—— (1981) 'Zwei frühneolithische Gefäße von Klenzau, Kreis

Ostholstein, und deren Beziehung zur "Rosenhof Gruppe"', *Offa* 38, 41–51.

Schwantes, G. (1939) *Die Vorgeschichte Schleswig-Holsteins (Stein- und Bronzezeit)*, Neumünster.

—— (1958) *Geschichte Schleswig-Holsteins* 1, *Die Urgeschichte*, Neumünster.

Schwarz-Mackensen, G. (1982) 'Die Linienbandkeramik, in Norddeutschland – Umwelt, Wirtschaft und Kultur der frühen Ackerbauern, *Bericht der naturhistorischen Gesellschaft zu Hannover* 125, 161–81.

Schwidetzky, I. (1978) 'Stand und Aufgaben der prähistorischen Anthropologie unter besonderer Berücksichtung des Neolithikums', in H. Schwabedissen (ed.), *Die Anfänge des Neolithikums vom Orient bis Nordeuropa* Böhlau Verlag, Köln and Wien, 317–40.

Shackleton, M.R. (1958) *Europe. A Regional Geography*, 6th edn, Cambridge.

Shanks, M. and Tilley, C. (1982) 'Ideology, symbolic power and ritual communication: a reinterpretation of Neolithic mortuary practices', in I. Hodder (ed.), *Symbolic and Structural Archaeology*, Cambridge University Press, Cambridge, 129–54.

—— (1987) *Re-Constructing Archaeology*, Cambridge University Press, Cambridge.

Sherratt, A. (1981) 'Plough and pastoralism: aspects of the secondary products revolution', in I. Hodder, G. Isaac and N. Hammond (eds), *Pattern of the Past*, Cambridge University Press, Cambridge, 261–305.

Siuchniński, K. (1969) *Klasyfikacja czasowo-przestrzenna kultur neolitycznych na Pomorzu Zachodnim*. Część 1: Katalog zródeł archeologicznych, Szczecin.

—— (1972) *Klasyfikacja czasowo-przestrzenna kultur neolitycznych na Pomorzu Zachodnim*. Część 2: Opracowanie analityczne, Szczecin.

—— (1981) 'Zagadnienie grupy ustowskiej (britzko-ustowskiej) kultury pucharów lejkowatych', in T. Wiślański (ed.), *Kultura Pucharów Lejkowatych w Polsce*, Poznań, 137–60.

Skaarup, J. (1973) *Hesselø–Sølager. Jagdstationen der südskandinavischen Trichterbecherkultur*, Arkæologiske Studier 1, København.

—— (1975) *Stengade. Ein langeländischer Wohnplatz mit Hausresten aus der frühneolithischen Zeit*, Rudkøbing.

—— (1982a) 'The excavation of a passage grave site at Himmelev, central Zealand', *Journal of Danish Archaeology* 1, 19–30.

—— (1982b) 'Siedlungs- uns Wirtschaftsstrukturen der Trichterbecherkultur in Dänemark', *Offa* 39, 39–52.

—— (1985) *Yngre Stenalder på øerne syd for Fyn*, Meddelelser fra Langelands Museum, Rudkøbing.

Sklenář, K. (1983) *Archaeology in Central Europe: the First 500 Years*, Leicester University Press, New York.

Skov, T. (1973) 'Fire megalitanlæg fra NV-Jylland'. *Holstebro Museum Årsskrift* 1972–1973, 16–50.

Smith, A.G. (1981) 'The Neolithic', in I. Simmons and M. Tooley (eds), *The Environment in British Prehistory*, Duckworth, London, 125–209.

Smolla, G. (1980) 'Das Kossinna-Syndrom', *Fundberichte aus Hessen* 19/20, 1–9.

Soudský, B. (1966) *Bylany. Osada nejstaršich zemědělců z mladši doby kamenné*, Československá Akademie, Praha.

Sprockhoff, E. (1926) *Die Kulturen der jüngeren Steinzeit in der Mark Brandenburg*, Berlin.

—— (1938) *Die nordische Megalithkultur*, Berlin.

—— (1952a) 'Zwei Megalithgräber, aus Schleswig und Holstein', *Offa* 10, 15–28.

—— (1952b) 'Ein Grabfund der nordischen Megalithkultur von Oldendorf', Kr. Lüneburg', *Germania* 30, 164–74.

—— (1954) 'Kammerlose Hünenbetten im Sachsenwald', *Offa* 13, 1–16.

—— (1966) *Atlas der Megalithgräber Deutschlands*. Teil 1: *Schleswig-Holstein*, Textband und Atlasband, Bonn.

—— (1967) *Atlas der megalithgräber Deutschlands*. Teil 2: *Mecklenburg, Brandenburg*, Textband und Atlasband, Bonn.

—— (1975) *Atlas der Megalithgräber Deutschlands*. Teil 3: Niedersachsen-Westfalen, Textband und Atlasband, Bonn.

Srejović, D. (1969) *Lepenski Vir. Nova praistorijska Kultura u Podunalju*, Srpska književna zadrug, Belgrade.

Stankowski, W. (1981) *Rozwój Środowiska Fizyczno-Geograficznego Polski*, Państwowe Wydawnictwo Naukowe, Warszawa.

Starkel, L. (1983) 'Palaeografia i klimat późnego plejstocenu i holocenu', in J.K. Kozłowski and S.K. Kozłowski (eds), *Człowiek i środowisko w pradziejach*, Państwowe Wydawnictwo Naukowe, Warszawa, 14–31.

Starling, N.J. (1988) 'The Neolithic *Höhensiedlungen* of central Germany', in C. Burgess, P. Topping, C. Mordant and M. Maddison (eds), *Enclosures and Defences in the Neolithic of Western Europe*, British Archaeological Reports International Series 403, Oxford, 419–45.

Steinmetz, W.D. (1982) 'Anmerkungen zum nordischen Frühneolithikum', *Neue Ausgrabungen und Forschungen in Niedersachsen* 15, 13–52.

Strömberg, M. (1968) *Der Dolmen Trollasten*, Acta Archaeologica Lundensia Series 8, No. 7, Bonn and Lund.

—— (1971) *Die Megalithgräber von Hagestad*, Acta Archaeologica Lundensia Series 8, No. 9, Bonn and Lund.

Stuiver, M. and Pearson, G. (1986) 'High-precision calibration of the radiocarbon timescale, AD 1950–500 BC', *Radiocarbon* 28, 805–38.

Stürüp, B. (1966) 'En ny jordgrav fra tidlig-neolitisk tid', *Kuml* 1965, 13–22.

Sulimirski, T. (1960) 'Remarks concerning the distribution of some varieties of flint in Poland', *Światowit* 23, 281–307.

—— (1968) *Corded Ware and Globular Amphorae North-East of the Carpathians*, London.

Szczurek, T. (1981) 'Osada fazy młodszej kultury pucharów lejkowatych w Gorzowie (stanowisko 10)', in T. Wiślański (ed.) *Kultura Pucharów Lejkowatych w Polsce*, Poznań, 161–70.

Szpunar, A. (1987) *Die Beile in Polen I (Flachbeile, Randleistenbeile, Randleistenmeißel)*, Prähistorische Bronzefunde 9: 16, München.

Tabaczyński, S. (1970) *Neolit Środkowoeuropejski. Podstawy Gospodarcze*, Ossolineum, Wrocław.

Tauber, H. (1972) 'Radiocarbon chronology of the Danish Mesolithic and Neolithic', *Antiquity* 46, 106–10.

—— (1981) '13C evidence for dietary habits of prehistoric man in Denmark', *Nature* 292 No. 5821, 332–3.

Tempel, W.D. (1972) 'Erdgräber der Trichterbecherkultur in der Gemarkung Issendorf, Kreis Stade', *Neue Ausgrabungen und Forschungen in Niedersachsen* 7, 46–59.

—— (1979) 'Flachgräber der Trichterbecherkultur', in H. Schirnig (ed.), *Großsteingräber in Niedersachsen*, Hildesheim, 111–16.

Testart, A. (1982) 'The significance of food storage among hunter-gatherers: residence patterns, population densities, and social inequalities', *Current Anthropology* 23, 523–30.

Tetzlaff, W. (1981) 'Osada kultury pucharów lejkowatych w Mrowinie, woj. poznańskie', in T. Wiślański (ed.), *Kultura Pucharów Lejkowatych w Polsce*, Poznań, 171–90.

Thomas, J. (1987) 'Relations of production and social change in the neolithic of north-west Europe', *Man* 22, 405–30.

Thomsen, N. (1971) 'Tragtbægerkultur i Sydvestjylland – Jerne sogn', *Mark og Montre*, 5–12.

—— (1977) 'Tragtbægerkultur i Sydvestjylland 3', *Mark og Montre*, 5–17.

Thorsen, S. (1981) '"Klokkehøj" ved Bøjden. Et sydvestfynsk dyssekammer med bevaret primærgrav', *Kuml* 1980, 105–46.

Thorvildsen, K. (1940) 'Jordgraven fra Volling', *Fra Danmarks Ungtid*, Arkæologiske Studier tilegnet Johannes Brøndsted, København, 42–55.

—— (1941) 'Dyssetidens Gravfund i Danmark', *Aarbøger* 1941, 22–87.

—— (1946) 'Grønhøj ved Horsens. En Jættestue med Offerplads', *Aarbøger* 1946, 73–94.

Thrane, H. (1982) 'Dyrkningsspor fra yngre stenalder i Danmark', in H. Thrane (ed.), *Om Yngre Stenalders Bebyggelseshistorie*, Odense, 20–8.

Tilley, C. (1984) 'Ideology and the legitimation of power in the middle neolithic of southern Sweden', in D. Miller and C. Tilley (eds), *Ideology, Power and Prehistory*, Cambridge University Press, Cambridge, 111–46.

Troels-Smith, J. (1953) 'Ertebøllekultur-Bondekultur', *Aarbøger* 1953, 5–62.

—— (1960a) 'The Muldbjerg dwelling place: an early neolithic archaeological site in the Aamosen bog, West-Zealand, Denmark', *The Smithsonian Institute Report for 1959*, 577–601.

—— (1960b) 'Ivy, mistletoe and elm: climate indicators – fodder plants: a contribution to the interpretation of the pollen zone border VII–VIII', *Danmarks Geologiske Undersøgelse* IV, Række 4, 4–32.

—— (1967) 'The Ertebølle culture and its background', *Palaeohistoria* 12, 505–28.

—— (1982) 'Vegetationshistoriske vidnesbyrd om skovrydninger, planteavl og husdyrhold i Europa, specielt Skandinavien', in T. Sjøvold (ed.) *Introduksjonen av jordbruk i Norden*, Foredrag holdt ved

fellesnordisk symposium i Oslo april 1980, Universitetsforlaget,
Oslo-Bergen-Tromsø, 39–62.

Umbreit, C. (1937) *Neue Forschungen zur ostdeutschen Steinzeit und
frühen Bronzezeit*, Leipzig.

Uzarowiczowa, A. (1975) 'Ornament na naczyniu kultury pucharów
lejkowatych z Ostrowca Świętokrzyskiego', *Wiadomości
Archeologiczne* 40, 3–12.

Uzarowiczowa-Chmielewska, A. (1979) 'Jamy neolityczne datowane
radiowęglem z osady w Stryczowicach, woj. kieleckie', *Wiadomości
Archeologiczne* 44, 131–42.

Van Giffen, A.E. (1925) *De hunebedden in Nederland I*, Utrecht.

—— (1927) *De hunebedden in Nederland II*, Utrecht.

Van der Waals, J.D. (1977) 'Excavations at the natural levée sites S2,
S3–5 and S4', *Helinium* 17, 3–27.

—— (1985) 'Discontinuity, cultural evolution and the historic event',
Proceedings of the Society of Antiquaries of Scotland 114, 1–14.

Van Zeist, W. (1959) 'Studies on the post-Boreal vegetational history of
the south-eastern Drenthe (Netherlands)', *Acta Botanica Neerlandica*
8, 156–85.

—— (1968) 'Prehistoric and early historic food plants in the
Netherlands', *Palaeohistoria* 14, 41–173.

Vang Petersen, P. (1984) 'Chronological and regional variation in the
late Mesolithic of eastern Denmark', *Journal of Danish Archaeology* 3,
7–18.

Vencl, S. (1986) 'The role of hunting-gathering populations in the
transition to farming: a central European perspective', in M. Zvelebil
(ed.), *Hunters in Transition*, Cambridge University Press, Cambridge,
43–51.

Voss, J.A. (1982) 'A study of western TRB social organisation',
Berichten van de Rijksdienst voor het Oudheidkundig Bodemonderzoek
32, 9–102.

Voss, K.L. (1965) 'Stratigrafische Notizen zu einem Langhaus der
Trichterbecherkultur bei Wittenwater, Kr. Uelzen', *Germania* 43,
343–51.

Voytek, B.A. and Tringham, R. (1989) 'Rethinking the Mesolithic: the
case of South-East Europe', in C. Bonsall (ed.), *The Mesolithic in
Europe*, Papers Presented at the Third International Symposium,
Edinburgh 1985, John Donald Publishers Ltd, Edinburgh, 492–9.

Waterbolk, H.T. (1958) 'Pollen spectra from neolithic grave
monuments in the northern Netherlands', *Palaeohistoria* 5, 39–51.

Weber, A. (1983) *Studia nad obrządkiem pogrzebowym grupy Łupawskiej
kultury pucharów lejkowatych*, Uniwersytet im. Adama Mickiewicza w
Poznaniu, Seria Archaeologiczna 21, Poznań.

Weber, T. (1979) 'Vergleichende Studien zur Ertebølle Kultur',
Zeitschrift für Archäologie 13, 163–217.

—— (1980) 'Flintinventare der Ertebølle- und der
Trichterbecherkultur im südwestlichen Ostseeraum', in B. Gramsch
(ed.), *Mesolithikum in Europa*, Veröffentlichungen des Museums für
Ur- und Frühgeschichte Potsdam Band 14/15, 143–50.

Wegewitz, W. (1955) 'Drei neue Groß steingräber im Kreise Harburg',
Jahrbuch des Römisch-Germanischen Zentralmuseums Mainz 2, 27–54.

Whittle, A. (1988) 'Contexts, activities, events – aspects of Neolithic and Copper Age enclosures in central and western Europe', in C. Burgess, P. Topping, C. Mordant and M. Maddison (eds), *Enclosures and Defences in the Neolithic of Western Europe*, British Archaeological Reports International Series 403, Oxford, 1–19.

Więckowska, H. (1973) 'Outline of the division of cultures of the Polish Mesolithic', in S.K. Kozłowski (ed.), *The Mesolithic in Europe*, University of Warsaw Press, Warsaw, 595–612.

—— (1975) 'Społeczności łowiecko-rybackie wczesnego holocenu' in W. Chmielewski (ed.), *Paleolit i Mezolit*, Ossolineum, Wrocław, 339–434.

Wiklak, H. (1982) 'Wyniki badań wykopaliskowych w obrębie grobowca 8 w Sarnowie w woj. włocławskim', *Prace i Materiały Muzeum Archeologicznego i Etnograficznego w Łodzi* 27, 33–83.

—— (1986) 'Osada i cmentarzysko fazy sarnowskiej kultury pucharów lejkowatych na stan. 1A w Sarnowie, woj. Włocławek', *Sprawozdania Archeologiczne* 38, 77–89.

Willerding, U. (1970) 'Vor- und frühgeschichtliche Kulturpflanzenfunde in Mitteleuropa', *Neue Ausgrabungen und Forschungen in Niedersachsen* 5, 287–375.

Winther, J. (1926) *Lindø* I, Rudkøbing.

—— (1928) *Lindø* II, Rudkøbing.

—— (1935) *Troldebjerg*, Rudkøbing.

—— (1938) *Troldebjerg*, Tillæg, Rudkøbing.

—— (1943) *Blandebjerg*, Rudkøbing.

Wiślański, T. (1966) *Kultura amfor kulistych w Polsce północno-zachodniej*, Ossolineum, Wrocław.

—— (1969) *Podstawy gospodarcze plemion neolitycznych w Polsce północno-zachodniej*, Ossolineum, Wrocław.

—— (1973) Ze studiów nad genezą kultury pucharów lejkowatych', *Archeologia Polski* 18, 91–126.

—— (1979) 'Kształtowanie się miejscowych kultur rolniczo-hodowlanych. Plemiona kultury pucharów lejkowatych', in W. Hensel and T. Wiślański (eds), *Prahistoria Ziem Polski* Tom 2: *Neolit*, Ossolineum, Wrocław, 165–260.

Wiślański, T. and Czarnecki, M. (1970) 'Osada kultury pucharów lejkowatych w Kosinie, pow. Pyrzyce (stan.6)', *Materiały Zachodniopomorskie* 16, 73–105.

Wojciechowski, W. (1970) *Zagadnienie chronologii relatywnej kultur młodszej epoki kamienia na Dolnym Śląsku na tle środkowoeuropejskiej systematyki neolitu*, Ossolineum, Wrocław.

—— (1973) *Osada ludności kultury pucharów lejkowatych w Janówku, powiat Dzierżoniów*, Acta Universitatis Wratislaviensis No. 183, Wrocław.

—— (1981) 'Z zagadnień kultury pucharów lejkowatych na Dolnym Śląsku', in T. Wiślański (ed.), *Kultura Pucharów Lejkowatych w Polsce*, Poznań, 207–20.

Zagorskis, F. (1973) 'Das Spätmesolithikum in Lettland', in S.K. Kozłowski (ed.), *The Mesolithic in Europe*, University of Warsaw Press, Warsaw, 651–69.

Zimmermann, W.H. (1979) 'Ein Hausgrundriß der Trichterbecherkultur von Flögen – Im Örtjen, Kreis Cuxhaven', in

H. Schirnig (ed.), *Großsteingräber in Niedersachsen*, Hildesheim, 247–53.

Żurowski, T. (1962) 'Krzemionki Opatowskie, pomnik starożytnego górnictwa', *Rocznik Świętokrzyski* 1, 17–96.

Zvelebil, M. (1986) 'Mesolithic prelude and neolithic revolution', in M. Zvelebil (ed.), *Hunters in Transition*, Cambridge University Press, Cambridge, 5–15.

Zvelebil, M. and Rowley-Conwy, P. (1984) 'Transition to farming in northern Europe: a hunter-gatherer perspective', *Norwegian Archaeological Review* 17, 104–28.

Index